THE
MARTIAL ARTS
SOURCEBOOK

OTHER BOOKS BY JOHN CORCORAN

THE COMPLETE MARTIAL ARTS CATALOGUE

THE OVERLOOK MARTIAL ARTS DICTIONARY

THE ORIGINAL MARTIAL ARTS ENCYCLOPEDIA

THE MARTIAL ARTS COMPANION

THE
MARTIAL ARTS
SOURCEBOOK

JOHN CORCORAN

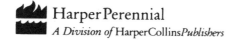 HarperPerennial
A Division of HarperCollins*Publishers*

FOR JOE LEWIS,

A SUPERB MENTOR AND

FRIEND TO THE END.

On the cover: Performing a tae kwon do form on the beach at sunset, Largo, Florida's Jim Graden captures the aesthetic and spiritual essence of the martial arts. Courtesy of Jim Graden; photo by Dave Levine.

HarperCollins books may be purchased for educational, business or sales promotional use. For information, please write: Special Markets Department, HarperCollins Publishers, Inc., 10 East 53rd Street, New York, NY 10022.

FIRST EDITION

Designed by Helene Wald Berinsky

Library of Congress Cataloging-in-Publication Data
Corcoran, John, 1948–
    The martial arts sourcebook / by John Corcoran.
      p.   cm.
    ISBN 0-06-273259-5
    1. Martial arts.   I. Title.
  GV1101.C66 1994
  796.8—dc20   93-46842

94 95 96 97 98 PS/CW 10 9 8 7 6 5 4 3 2 1

CONTENTS

ACKNOWLEDGMENTS

As a professional martial arts magazine editor for some twenty years, I have collected a remarkable amount of reference material throughout my career. Approximately 75 percent of this book was written from these personal resources. However, about 25 percent of the contents was collectively contributed by knowledgeable—and generous—martial arts experts around the world.

I call them "generous" because, in many, many cases, they submitted information for this book which held no particular personal benefit. For example, Geneva, Switzerland's Olivier Muller, one of Europe's foremost kickboxing administrators, sent me a copy of a Spanish-language martial arts magazine. Likewise, New York's Curtis Sliwa, founder of the Guardian Angels, fulfilled my request for supplying British martial arts magazines. These people helped me put together valuable pieces of a global puzzle that resulted in this massive reference book.

The following 143 people and organizations did the following things—and, what's more, helped me put together valuable pieces of a global puzzle that have resulted in this landmark reference work. It is their book as much as mine.

CONSULTANTS

European Martial Arts: Michael Deubner, martial arts journalist and promoter, Bensheim, Germany (World Association of Kickboxing Organizations World and European Championship results).

Japanese Karate-do: Randall Hassell, karate-do writer and historian, St. Louis, Missouri (traditional martial arts; Japan Karate Championships winners lists).

Jujutsu: Dr. L. Bruce Holbrook, administrator, Charleston, West Virginia (jujutsu championship results and jujutsu organizational mailing lists).

Kickboxing: Paul Maslak, kickboxing ratings pioneer, Los Angeles, California (kickboxing/sport karate consultation and a massive amount of kickboxing results from 1980 to 1988).

Korean Martial Arts: Rod Speidel, editor, *Taekwondo Times*, Bettendorf, Iowa (miscellaneous World Taekwondo Federation winners' lists; *Taekwondo Times* Hall of Fame recipients).

Martial Arts Films: Gary Daniels, actor and black belt, Irvine, California (foreign martial arts films; photographs).

Okinawan Karate: Sid Campbell, karate pioneer and author, Oakland, California (Okinawan karate, Kobayashi-ryu karate forms, and traditional karate consultation).

MAJOR CONTRIBUTORS

Joe Corley, karate/kickboxing pioneer and promoter, Atlanta, Georgia (PKA kickboxing results; photographs).

John Graden, retired karate champion and instructor, St. Petersburg, Florida (research material; Walt Bone Memorial recipients; photograph).

Mike McCoy, NASKA Ratings editor, Gainesville, Florida (NASKA-sanctioned karate tournament results).

Mike Sawyer, International Sport Karate Association co-chairman (ISKA world championship data, 1986–92; photograph).

John Sells, karate historian and writer, Lompoc, California (numerous Japanese and Okinawan karate kata; photograph).

Jay T. Will, kickboxing referee, Atlanta, Georgia (data on various halls of fame; Top Ten rating lists; PKA world championship kickboxing results; photographs).

Douglas Wong, kung-fu master, Los Angeles, California (research material; photograph).

World Taekwon-do Federation: Dr. Un Yong Kim, Colonel Bok Sik Kim and Chong Woo Lee, Seoul, Korea (various results from the WTF World Taekwon-do Championships, European Taekwon-do Championships, and U.S. Taekwon-do Championships; photograph).

CONTRIBUTORS—ASIA

Jackie Chan, film star, Kowloon, Hong Kong (photographs).

Kenzo Nakasone, martial arts product supplier, Naha, Okinawa, Japan (Okinawan karate masters' birth and death dates).

CONTRIBUTORS—AUSTRALIA
J.R. Barnes, New South Wales, Australia (photograph).

Peter Wright, administrator, Budokan Karate, Sydney, Australia (official Budokan karate forms).

CONTRIBUTORS—EUROPE
Ennio Falsoni, president, World Association of Kickboxing Organizations, Milan, Italy (World Association of Kickboxing Organizations world championship results).

Gerard Finot, Muay Thai pioneer and instructor, Euclid, Ohio, and Paris, France (European martial arts magazine information).

Guardian Angels, British Branch, London, England (British martial arts magazine information).

Benny Hedlund, publisher, *The Swedish Fighter*, Malmo, Sweden (European martial arts supply company mailing lists).

Olivier Muller, co-chairman, International Sport Karate Association, Geneva, Switzerland (European martial arts magazine information).

CONTRIBUTORS—UNITED STATES
Sam Allred, karate pioneer, Albuquerque, New Mexico (National Karate Black Belt Grand Championship results).

Paul Arel, karate pioneer, South Windsor, Connecticut (Kokondo kata and organizational affiliates).

Frank Babcock, Karate International Council of Kickboxing president, St. Louis, Missouri (KICK world championships results).

Christine Bannon-Rodrigues, world karate champion, Warwick, Rhode Island (personal championship history; PKL Top 10 results).

Richard Baptista, karate promoter, Boston, Massachusetts (New England Open Nationals results; sport karate photographs).

David Baumgartner, executive assistant, Florida Karate Center, Gainesville, Florida (ISKA world championship data).

Terry Bell, Japanese consulate, Atlanta, Georgia (samurai film data).

Mitchell Bobrow, president, Otomix, Santa Monica, California (rare photographs; research data).

Jeff Bolt, kung-fu pioneer and promoter, Houston, Texas (U.S. National Chinese Martial Arts Competitions results).

Art Camacho, martial arts film choreographer, Los Angeles, California (photograph).

Larry Carnahan, president, North American Sport Karate Association, Minneapolis, Minnesota (Diamond Nationals results).

Dave Cater, editor, *Inside Kung Fu*, Los Angeles, California (1st World Wushu Championship results).

Nick Cerio, karate pioneer, Warwick, Rhode Island (miscellaneous kenpo information).

John Chung, retired forms champion, Mineola, New York (International Taekwon-do Federation's hyung).

Tony Cogliandro, karate instructor, Saugus, Massachusetts (kenpo forms; Boston International Karate Championship results; photograph).

Milo Dailey, administrator, Rapid City, South Dakota (American Taekwon-do Association's forms; photograph).

Fumio Demura, karate master, Santa Ana, California (photographs).

George Dillman, karate pioneer, Reading, Pennsylvania (photograph).

Rocky DiRico, karate champion, Franklin, Massachusetts (photograph).

Troy Dorsey, world kickboxing champion, Dallas, Texas (photograph).

James Dussault, Korean martial arts instructor, Venice, Florida (miscellaneous Korean martial arts data; photographs).

David Dye, aikido instructor, Costa Mesa, California (Yoshinkai aikido information).

Emil Farkas, karate pioneer, Los Angeles, California (Japanese martial arts magazine information).

George Foon, publisher, Know Now Publications, Los Angeles, California (photographs).

Gary Forbach, kung-fu forms champion, San Clemente, California (photograph).

Chuck Francis, karate black belt, Los Angeles, California (research data).

Neva Friedenn, film producer, Los Angeles, California (Jackie Chan film information).

Bob Gilroy, tang soo do black belt, Los Angeles, California (*Variety's* all-time box-office champions).

Jerry Gould, karate pioneer and historian, Renton, Washington (Shobayashi-ryu karate forms).

Reylson Gracie, jujutsu master, Corona del Mar, California (photograph).

Nick Gracenin, wushu administrator, Sharon, Pennsylvania (wushu championship results; organizational addresses; photographs).

Jim Graden, retired kickboxing champion and instructor, Largo, Florida (research material).

Mark Greenblatt, computer consultant, Los Angeles, California (computer consultation).

Jim Harrison, karate pioneer, Missoula, Montana (research information).

C. Bruce Heilman, Reading, Pennsylvania (Okinawan karate forms).

Cheryl Henson, staff photographer, *Sport Karate News*, Chico, Texas (photographs).

Master Morio Higaonna, karate master, San Marcos, California (Okinawan karate information).

Alanna Higaonna, karate administrator, San Marcos, California (Japanese translations).

Tokey Hill, karate champion, New Hyde Park, New York (photographs).

Hong Kong Trade Development Council, Miami Office (kung-fu associations).

John Huppuch, administrator, World Hwa Rang Do Association, Downey, California (official hwa rang do forms; photograph).

Joe Hyams, author and black belt, West Los Angeles, California (photographs).

Ed Ikuta, staff photographer, C.F.W. Enterprises, Burbank, California (photographs).

Skipper Ingham, karate pioneer, Hamilton, Bermuda (photograph).

Master Soo Kim, Cha Yon Ryu founder, Houston, Texas (photograph).

Roy Kurban, retired karate champion and promoter, Arlington, Texas (Fort Worth National Pro-Am results).

Jim Lantrip, kickboxing administrator, Madisonville, Kentucky (WAKO U.S. Championship results).

Lori Lantrip-Stanley, karate champion, Evansville, Indiana (photograph).

James Lew, actor and retired national forms champion, Los Angeles, California (photographs).

Joe Lewis, retired world kickboxing champion, Wilmington, North Carolina (photographs; Top Ten data).

Andre Alex Lima, martial arts journalist, Venice, California (Brazilian martial arts magazines).

Greg Lindquist, instructor, Overland Park, Kansas (Okinawan kempo forms; Okinawan karate information).

Ronald Lindsay, instructor, Bastrop, Texas (Matsumura orthodox karate forms).

Lewis Lizotte, karate pioneer and promoter, Enfield, Connecticut (North American Championship winners list).

Domingo Llanos, karate champion, West Haverstraw, New York (photograph).

Terry Maccarrone, karate historian, Patchogue, New York (Matsubayashi-ryu karate forms).

Rick Mandris, pro boxing and kickboxing trainer, Hollywood, Florida (foreign martial arts magazines).

Kathy Marlor, karate instructor and champion, St. Petersburg, Florida (research material).

Jim Mather, administrator, San Jose, California (official Gosoku-ryu kata; WUKO championship results).

Ric Martin, instructor, Largo, Florida (Uechi-ryu karate forms).

Chuck Merriman, karate pioneer, Niantic, Connecticut (Japanese Goju-ryu karate forms; photograph).

Jenice Miller, promoter, Los Angeles, California (Mardi Gras Nationals results).

Ken Min, tae kwon do pioneer and promoter, Berkeley, California (miscellaneous World Taekwon-do Federation World Championship results; AAU National Taekwon-do Championship results).

Anthony Mirakian, karate-do pioneer, Watertown, Massachusetts (Okinawan karate forms data; rare photographs).

Hidetaka Nishiyama, karate-do pioneer, Los Angeles, California (Japanese karate-do information).

Hidy Ochiai, karate master and champion, Vestal, New York (photographs).

Ed Parker, karate pioneer and promoter, deceased (miscellaneous International Karate Championships results).

Alan Paul, executive editor, *Official Karate*, New York City (*Official Karate's* Legion of Honor recipients).

Mrs. Shikuko K. Pinto, St. Petersburg, Florida (Japanese language translation).

Grandmaster Jhoon Rhee, tae kwon do pioneer, Washington, D.C. (miscellaneous historical data and photographs).

Kang Rhee, tae kwon do master, Memphis, Tennessee (photograph).

Phillip Rhee, actor & producer, Beverly Hills, California (photographs).

Scott Rhodes, journalist, Hoboken, New Jersey (martial arts movie stills).

T.J. Roberts, film star, Los Angeles, California (photograph).

Don Rodrigues, coach, John Paul Mitchell National Karate Team, Warwick, Rhode Island (photographs; John Paul Mitchell Team data).

Bob Rosenbaum, karate instructor, El Toro, California (research material).

Cynthia Rothrock, film star, Los Angeles, California (photograph).

Mark Russo, ninjutsu instructor, Tampa, Florida (miscellaneous ninjutsu data).

Mike Schuhmann, karate black belt, Clearwater, Florida (photographs).

Scott Shaw, hapkido instructor, Hermosa Beach, California (dynasty data).

Alex and Annellen Simpkins, journalists, San Diego, California (Duk Sung Son photograph).

Curtis Sliwa, Guardian Angels founder, New York, New York (British martial arts magazine information and Guardian Angels mailing list).

Stuart Sobel, martial arts businessman, Los Angeles, California (martial arts films; Benny Urquidez kickboxing data and photographs).

John Soet, editor, *Inside Karate*, Los Angeles, California (*Inside Karate* Hall of Fame recipients; film research information).

Allen Steen, karate pioneer and promoter, Dallas, Texas (miscellaneous U.S. Karate Championships results).

Mary Townsley, photographer, Palatine, Illinois (photograph).

Robert Trias, karate pioneer and promoter, deceased (USKA Grand Nationals results).

Benny Urquidez, world kickboxing champion, Van Nuys, California (photographs).

Jean-Claude Van Damme, film star, Chatsworth, California (photograph).

Mark Van Schuyver, author/journalist, Broken Arrow, Oklahoma (photograph).

George Waite, karate black belt, Los Angeles, California (photograph).

Don Wilson, film star & world kickboxing champion, Los Angeles, California (miscellaneous kickboxing data and photographs).

Curtis Wong, publisher, C.F.W. Enterprises, Burbank, California (martial arts supply company mailing list; photograph).

Keith Yates, author/journalist, Garland, Texas (rare photographs).

PHOTO CONTRIBUTORS—MOTION PICTURES AND TELEVISION

American International Pictures; Billy Jack Enterprises; Cannon Films (Karen Raiman); Capital Cities/ABC-TV; Columbia Pictures; Creative Film Concepts (Phillip Rhee); Famous Films; Golden Harvest Studios (Hong Kong); Shelley Jeffrey Public Relations; Landmark Films; Miramax Films; The Movie Group; New Line Cinema; Paramount Pictures; PM Entertainment Group (E. J. Levine); Shaw Bros. Studios (Hong Kong); the Showtime (cable) Channel; TriStar Pictures (Hollace Davids); 20th Century-Fox (Jasmine Madatian); United Artists; Universal Pictures (Jeffrey Sakson); Viacom; Warner Bros. Pictures; Warner Bros. Television.

INTRODUCTION

This book was inspired by my twenty-plus years of work as a martial arts magazine editor. *The Martial Arts Sourcebook* came about because I spent a great amount of time throughout my career answering the questions of and providing information for readers from all over the world. Most of these questions, I realized, fell into precise categories. Everyone wanted a certain type of information, but couldn't find it in any single source, book or magazine.

The vast majority of readers were seeking information about a particular art or style, instructor or organization, winner or loser of a martial arts contest, or martial arts films or stars. I finally decided to write the definitive book offering the types of information everyone was seeking but couldn't find without investing a lot of time, effort and money.

As I compiled this book, it began taking on bigger and bigger dimensions requiring more and more research. Finally, I realized that, to complete it properly, I had to appeal to everyone: white belt beginners to veteran experts, every practitioner of every art and style, strict traditionalists to sports enthusiasts. I have consequently ended up with, I believe, a book that offers something for everybody.

Although I have made every human attempt to be as complete as possible, gaps do exist in this book. I'm sure there are obscure styles, weapons and organizations not yet included here, as well as black belt winners lists from some major U.S. tournaments that eluded my best efforts to uncover them. Further, the deadline to turn in the material for this book abruptly ended research that probably could have gone on infinitely. So I sincerely apologize for any omissions.

Last, martial arts literature, from which much of my material was culled, is susceptible to typographical errors. Hence, an earlier mistake in print could have been carried over during the research for this book.

Readers are invited to fill in any valid voids with contributions and the new information will appear in future reprints of this book. I'll also acknowledge each new contributor. Send your information to: John Corcoran, 2901 South Sepulveda Blvd., Suite 101, West Los Angeles, CA 90064, U.S.A.

STYLES AND PRACTICES OF THE MARTIAL ARTS

This section comprises information of particular interest to traditional martial artists. The following chapters list literally several thousand arts and styles, forms and weapons, most of them falling into the category of classical martial arts practices. In addition there is a guide to the dynasties of China, Japan and Korea.

CHAPTER 1

MARTIAL ARTS AND STYLES OF THE WORLD

The following is the most comprehensive list of global martial arts and styles ever published in one book, a total of 1,158. No attempt was made to provide literal translations, definitions or other types of support information since this is to some extent available in other published sources. The arts and styles appearing here can serve as a checklist for correct spellings and countries of origin. It's also a quick reference source for historians and researchers.

This list includes traditional, nontraditional and contemporary eclectic systems. The author makes no claims, even by mere inclusion, of an art or style's legitimacy. What appears here is simply a list of what once existed and what exists today.

CHINA

Given its two-thousand-year martial heritage, there is understandably a mind-boggling number of Chinese kung-fu styles. According to eminent martial scholars Donn F. Draeger and Robert W. Smith, there were over four hundred types of Chinese boxing extant in China's history. However, by 1969, when their masterwork, *Asian Fighting Arts*, was published, the authors pointed out that 1) some of those systems "had died out due to obsessive secrecy; 2) some were derivative; and 3) some contemporary styles had duplicated the names of earlier ones."

Further, since 1969 untold masters have created their own styles while other systems have faded into obscurity. Even current experts are unsure of the exact number. In a 1992 magazine article, Sifu Adam Hsu wrote, "The number of kung-fu styles we have in China can go as high as four hundred or as low as two hundred. Thus it may be safe to place the total at about three hundred."

All of which makes it impossible to know at any given time precisely how many kung-fu styles exist in the world. The same, in fact, could be said about all the other martial arts as well. What appears in this chapter is a large sampling of past and present systems, the most, to my knowledge, ever published in one book.

Several other factors add to the difficulty of tracing all the old and new systems. For one, Chinese martial arts were practiced in secrecy for many centuries and, to some extent, still are today. Only recently, particularly in the excellent publication *Inside Kung Fu*, has a vast amount of information been made public. As a result, more and better data are coming to the forefront of martial arts literature. We're also learning that the names of Chinese arts and styles have often been misspelled in the past.

Then there's the serious problem of the Chinese language and its numerous methods of translation. Many styles carry two names, one in Cantonese and another in Mandarin. There are also different systems of what's called "romanization" (Wade-Giles, Yale, Meyer-Wempe) for translating both, each of which allows the Western reader to convert the Chinese language to something familiar.

However, by the 1980s, China had developed its own system of romanization known as *Hanyu pinyan*. This is the system that, for example, changed "Peking" into "Beijing." This new method also combines words that earlier would have appeared separately, i.e., "t'ai-chi ch'uan" becomes "taijiquan." To simplify an extremely complex situation, I have included any and all versions of art and style names. This assures that nothing is omitted. In a further simplification, I have omitted all use of apostrophes, which tended to complicate spellings and translations. Thus, "t'ai-chi ch'uan" becomes simply "tai-chi chuan."

Literal translations appear for only the most popular systems, usually when the style is better known in the Western world by its English translation. This will allow neophytes to identify the style about which they might have read or heard and immediately make the connection to its authentic Chinese name.

JAPAN

The hundreds of Japanese martial arts and styles fall into two categories, the ancient Bujutsu and its twentieth-century counterpart, the Budo. Styles deriving from these two classifications are distinguished, in literary terms, by the suffixes *jutsu* and *do*, respectively.

A virtual explosion of arts and styles occurred during Japan's feudal era, when warriorship and militarism was at an all-time zenith. More emphasis was placed on the sword at that time than on any other means of combat. Consequently, kenjutsu developed far more *ryu* (schools) than any other art.

Notably, some feudal martial systems, like the Katori Shinto-ryu, for one example, were of a composite nature and taught the techniques of more than one armed and/or unarmed method. Consequently, as you pore over the Japanese systems in this chapter you will occasionally find a single style listed under several arts. It is possible, too, that kenjutsu and iaijutsu grew simultaneously and perhaps enhanced each other's development, which explains why some kenjutsu ryu share the same name as iaijutsu ryu.

According to martial scholars Draeger and Smith, "During the height of the Japanese feudal era some 725 jujutsu systems were officially documented in Japan, as were 1,700 schools of kenjutsu, 412 iaijutsu schools, and 460 yarijutsu ryu." Most have not survived the march of time and have fallen into oblivion. By 1867, in fact, kenjutsu decreased to just over two hundred active styles, with only a few of them extant today; and iaijutsu presently has but a handful of sects.

But according to two other martial scholars, Oscar Ratti and Adele Westbrook, there were far more. In their comprehensive *Secrets of the Samurai*, the authors claim "at least 10,000 ryu existed when Emperor Meiji came to power." They, too, emphasize that that number dwindled magnificently to the present day.

By 1960, according to Draeger and Smith, there were an estimated "75 karate-do and 30 karate-jutsu styles, 14 sects of aikido, and pure yarijutsu was virtually nonexistent." In a February 1987 *Black Belt* magazine article, one aikido expert claimed there were over 40 styles of aikido alone; if accurate, this means more than 26 new styles of aikido were created between 1960 and 1986! This example, in itself, demonstrates the enormous difficulty I encountered in compiling this chapter alone.

OKINAWA

Almost all of the major Okinawan karate styles were founded between 1915 and 1940. This includes many of the earliest Japanese karate-do systems founded in Japan by transplanted Okinawan masters and their Japanese disciples. The relatively small number of these systems, together with their subsequent thorough documentation by Western karate students and historians, leaves very little question about Okinawan karate's twentieth-century origins and development.

At this October 25, 1936, conference of Okinawan karate masters in Naha City it was agreed that the Okinawan martial arts known as "Tode" ("Chinese hands") be called "karate" ("empty hands"). Back row standing, left to right: Shuri-te Master Shinp an Gusukuma, Naha-te Master Choryo Maeshiro, Shuri-te Master Choshin Chibana, and Tomari-te Master Genwa Nakasone. Front row seated, left to right: Shuri-te Master Chotoku Kyan, Shuri-te Master Kentsu Yabu, Shuri-te Master Chomo Hanashiro, and Naha-te Master and founder of Goju-ryu karate Chojun Miyagi. Courtesy of karate Master Anthony Mirakian

PHILIPPINES

As with Japan's samurai and China's kung-fu, Arnis or Escrima was originally used to protect one's family, property and/or *barangay* (barrio or rural district within a town). According to an article written by Grandmaster Nes Fernandez for *Kung Fu* magazine, "It appears that many barangays, and there are thousands in the Philippines, have ownership of specific fighting styles. This leads one to hypothesize that, like kung-fu, Arnis has more styles than have currently been identified. Like the Chinese art of kung-fu, many of the differences are subtle, but some are vast and break from the traditional teachings of Arnis."

My research has led to a list of 52 such styles that appear here. Remarkably, a whopping 43 of them were identified in Dan Inosanto's excellent book, *The Filipino Martial Arts.*

UNITED STATES

Kajukenbo and Kenpo (Kara-ho) originated in Hawaii before the islands became an official part of the United States. These two styles are listed under both headings.

Note, too, the number of awkward and even corny style names composed in American karate and kung-fu. Some mixed-style experts, in naming their own new system, combined parts of the Chinese, Korean, English and/or Japanese languages. Once again, I make no representations whatsoever concerning the validity of any martial art or style appearing in this chapter, or, for that matter, in this entire section.

FORMAT

Listings are in alphabetical order by country of origin; styles appear under the art from which they derive. To make this distinction visible, entries appearing in bold letters are martial *arts*; those that appear indented under an art and in regular type are *styles*. Almost every country had or has a native form of wrestling, not all of which are cited here. Listings include armed and unarmed practices.

ARGENTINA

KARATE
Shutokan

AUSTRALIA

AIKIDO
Tenshin Sho Kai

KARATE
Aishin-Kai
Freestyle
Geido-Kai
Gokan-ryu
Goshin-ryu
Gosu-Kai
Jushin-ryu
Kenkokan
Kime
San Chi Kai
Shin Bu Kai
Shishido
Tae Ki Yon
Te Whanau Tahi
Zen Do Kai

KUNG-FU
Chi Ryu
Chow Wing Kune Do
Hung Kuen
Jeet So Do
Lung Chi
Mae Palm Tao
Nam Wah Pai
Tai Ki Kuen
Tun Chi Do

TAE KWON DO
Yau Hawk Tao

BRAZIL

CAPOEIRA

GRACIE JUJUTSU; BRAZILIAN JUJUTSU

BURMA

BAMA LETWHAY

BANDO

BANSHAY; BANSHEI (WEAPONS)

BURMESE BOXING

LETHWEI (BOXING)

MYANMA LETWHEI (KICKBOXING)

NABAN (WRESTLING)

THAING

CANADA

JUJUTSU
Can-ryu
Kindai-Ha Shinto-ryu

KARATE
Chu Fen Do
Kindai-Ha Shito-ryu
Seikido

CHINA

CHIAO-TI; CHIH YU-HSI; SHUAI-CHIAO (WRESTLING)
Pai-Chang
Shang Pu
Shuai-Go

CHIH YU-HSI

CHUAN-FA; KEN FAT; KEMPO; CHINESE KEMPO
Chugoku

GO-TI; SHUAI-CHIAO (WRESTLING)
Bao Din; Kuai Chiao (fast wrestling)

JOU FA

KUNG-FU; WU SHU; GUNG-FU; CHINESE BOXING
Ax Hand

Bai-Ma-Sya-Shan: See Ti-Tang

Ba-Ji

Bak-Sing

Bak-Sing Choy-Li-Fut

Black Tiger: See Sil Lum (Northern)

Bok Fu Pai ("White Tiger")

Bok Mei Pai; Pat Mei Pai ("White Eyebrow")

Cannon Fist

Cha Chuan

Chang Chuan; Changquan ("Long Fist")

Chang Chuan Pi-Kua

Chia Chia Chuan

Chi-Chi-San

Chien Yuen

Chi Hsing

Chi Hsuan Men

Chi Hsuan Sho

Chi Jiao

Ching-Nien Chuan

Chin-Na; Feng-Chiu Shu; Tso-Ku Shu; Ti-Sha Shou

Cho Chiao

Choi Li Fo Chia Chuan

Choy

Choy-Gar; Choy-Ga; Tsai

Choy-Li-Fut; Choy-Lay-Fut Hung-Hsing

Choy Mok

Chuan Chu Shing Ie

Chung Chuan

Chung Tao Chuan

Crane: See Hok

Dachenquan

Dim Mak

Di-Tang

Don Bei

Drunken Style: See Tsui Pak Hsien

Drunken Monkey: See Tai-Sing Pek-Kwar

Du

Eagle Claw: See Xing-Chiao

Eighteen Daoist Palms

Eight Drunken Fairies: See Ti-Tang

Eight Immortals

Eight Trigrams: See Pa-Kua

Emei

Er-Liang-Men; Erh-Lang-Men

Fan-Tzu; Fan-Tzu-Men; Ba-Fan

Feng-Chiu Shu: See Chin-Na

Five Animals: See Wu Hsing Chuan

Five Elders

Five Families

Fong Ngan

Fu-Jow Pai; Fu-Chiao Pai ("Tiger Claw")

Fu Hu Chuan

Fukien

Fut

Fut-Gar; Fut-Ga; Fu-Jya ("Buddha Palm")

Grand Earth

Hakka Chuan

Hao Chuan: See Pak-Hoc

Hap Ka

Ho-Chi

Hok; Hork Yang ("Crane")

Honan

Hop-Gar; Ho-Jya; Ho-Chia; Lama

Hou Chuan; Ta-Cheng Chuan; Ta Sheng

Hsia Chia Chuan

Hsien Lie He Chuan; Hsin I Liu He Chuan ("Six Harmonies")

Hsing-I; Hsing-Yi; Hsing-I Lu-Ho Chuan; I-Chuan; Xingyiquan
   Five Element Xing-I
   Six Harmonies Xing-I

Hua Chien

Hua Chuan

Hua Mountain

Hung-Chia

Hung Chuan

Hung-Fat

Hung-Ga

Hung-Gar; Hung-Kuen; Hung Chuan; Hung Kune

I-Chuan; Yi-Quan; (originally, Ta-Cheng Chuan)

Jow-Ga

Kang-Fa

Ke-Chia

King-Li

Kuei Ting

Kuen Hue Hok Pai ("Tiger Crane")

Kung Chia

Kung-Ki Chuan

Kung Li

Kun Lun Pai

Kuen Hue Hokpai

Kuo Chuan

Kwantung

Kwong Sai Look Leum

Lan Shou

Lau-Gar; Lau-Ga

Law Horn

Lay-Gar

Le-Fa

Liang-I ("Two Instruments")

Lien Wan

Li-Gar; Li-Chia

Liu-Chia Chuan

Liu-Gar; Li-Ga; Liu-Jya

Liu-He

Liu-Ho Chuan

Liu-Ho Pa-Fa

Lo-Han Chuan

Long Fist: See Chang Chuan

Loong Fu Pai

Loong Kuen Chuan

Loong Ying Mor Kiu ("Southern Dragon"; "Dragon Style Magical Arms")

Lor Horn Mon

Lost Monkey: See Tai-Sing Pek-Kwar

Lost Track: See Mi-Chung

Luk Hop Kuen

Lung-Hsing ("Dragon"); Lung-Hsing Pa-Kua Chang ("Dragon Style Eight Trigrams Palm")

Ma-Chung Lama-Pei

Mi-Chung; Mi-Chung-I ("Lost Track")

Mian Chuan

Mien Chuan

Mi-Tsung-I; Yen Ching Chuan

Mo-Chia; Mo-Jia-Quan

Mo Chuan

Mok-Gar; Mok-Ga; Mo-Jya

Monkey: See Tai-Sing Pek-Kwar

My-Jong-Law-Horn

Nam Wah Pai

Nan Chuan

Natural System

Ng Ga Kin ("Five-Formed Fist")

Northern Dragon

Northern Long Fist

O-Mei Shan

Pa-Chi Chuan; Pajiquan

Pa Chuan

Pa-Fa Chuan

Pak-Hoc; Pai-Ho Chuan ("White Crane"); Hao Chuan; Ta Sheng ("Crane Boxing")
   Bai-Ho
   Chang Er Gau Fukien White Crane
   Tibetan Crane
   Wu Mei White Crane

Pak-Pai

Pa-Kua; Paqua Chang; Baguazhang ("Eight Trigrams")

Chiang Jung Chiao
Chiu Loong Paqua Chang
Combined
Honan
Hopei
Pa-Kua Leung Yee
Shansi
Tzu Jan Te
Wu-Tang; Wutang Chuan; Wu-Tang-Shan
Pa Ming Chuan
Pangai-Noon
Pao ("Leopard")
Pao Chui
Pat Mei Pai: See Bok Mei Pai
Pa Shih Chuan
Pa Tuan Chin
Pei-Pai Fo-Chia Chuan
Phoenix Eye Fist: See Fong Ngan Chuan
Pi-Kua Chuan; Pi-Qua
Plum Flower Fist
Plum Flower Praying Mantis: See Tang-Lang
Po Kwa Zen
Praying Mantis: See Tang-Lang
Pu Don
Que Moi Shantung
Ru He Chuan
Sam Sow Chi
San-Hwang Pao-Chui; Hsing-Kung Chuan
San Soo
Seven Stars Praying Mantis: See Tang-Lang
Shaolin: See Sil Lum
Shau-Wan Chuan
Sil-Lum; Siu-Lum; Sil-Lum Pai ("Shaolin")
　　Long Fist (Northern)

Northern
Fukien Sil-Lum
Honan Five Animals
　Shantung
　Shantung Black Tiger
　Shensi Sil-Lum
　Wu Hsing Chuan ("Five Animals"; "Five Animals Pattern Fist") [The Five Animals are: Tiger (Fu), Leopard (Bao), Snake (Sare), Crane (Hok), Dragon (Loong)]

Southern
Choy-Gar
Hung-Gar
Lau-Gar
Li-Gar
Mok-Gar
Phoenix Eye Fist
Six Harmonies: See Hsien Lie He Chuan
Six Harmonies Praying Mantis: See Tang-Lang
Six Methods Praying Mantis: See Tang-Lang
Snake and Hawk
Southern Dragon: See Loong Ying Mor Kiu
Southern Praying Mantis: See Tang-Lang
Stone Monkey: See Tai-Sing Pek-Kwar
Sum-Yee
Sun Ping Chuan
Syin-Yee Liu Ha Pa Fa Chuan
Ta-Cheng Chuan ("Great Achievement Boxing"): See I-Chuan
Ta-Hung Men
Tai-Chi Chuan; Taijiquan ("Grand Ultimate Fist")
　Chang
　Chen
　Cheng
　Fu
　Hao
　Hsu
　Hu Lei Jia ("Thunder")
　Lee (modified)
　Li
　Lui
　Sun
　Tsuen
　Wu Jianquan
　Wu Yuxiang
　Yang
Tai-I Chuan ("Great Mind Boxing")
Tai-Sing Pek-Kwar; Ta-Sheng Pek-Kwar; Ta-Sheng-Men; Taodo Hou Quan ("Monkey")
　Lost Monkey
　Mi Hou Quan ("Crafty Monkey")
　Southern Monkey
　Stone Monkey
　Tall Monkey

Tieh Hou Quan ("Iron Monkey")
Wood Monkey
Ying Chiao Fan Tzu; Zui Hou Quan ("Drunken Monkey")
Tai-Tsu Chuan; Tai-Tsu-Chang Chuan ("Emperor's Long Fist")
Tall Monkey: See Tai-Sing Pek-Kwar
Ta-Mo
Tam Tui; Tan-Tui
Tang-Lang; Tang-Lang Chuan ("Praying Mantis")
　BaBo Tang Lang
　Ba Pu Tang Lang ("Eight Steps Praying Mantis")
　Bare Mantis
　　Chi-Hsing Tang-Lang ("Seven Stars Praying Mantis"); Tang-Lang Gou-Dz (Praying Mantis Hook)
　　Chu Gar Praying Mantis
　　Jook Lum
　　Kawan-Pai Tang-Lang; Liu-Hor Tang-Lang ("Six Harmonies Praying Mantis")
　　Kwong Sai Jook Lum; Tsu-Chia Tang-Lang ("Southern Praying Mantis")
　　　Chow Gar; Zhou Gar
　　　Chuka Shaolin ("Phoenix Eye Fist")
　　Liu-He Tang-Lang ("Six Methods Praying Mantis")
　　Mei-Hwa Tang-Lang; Mei-Hua Tang Lang ("Plum Flower Praying Mantis")
　　Qi Xing ("Seven Star Praying Mantis")
　　Shwei-Shou Tang-Lang
　　Tai Mantis; Tai-Chi Mantis
　　Wah Lum Tam Tui Praying Mantis
Tang Shou Tao
Tao-Chia Chuan
Tao-Ga
Tao-Te-Ching
Tao Yin
Ta Sheng: See Pak-Hoc
Tieh-Hsien Chuan
Tien-Hsueh
Tien-Shan-Pai
Tiger Claw: See Fu-Jow Pai

Tiger Crane: See Kuen Hue Hok
  Pai
Ti Kung Chuan
Ti-Sha Shou: See Chin-Na
Ti-Tang; Ti-Kung; Bai-Ma-Sya-Shan
    Tsui Pa Hsien ("Eight Drunken
    Fairies")
Tongbei
Tsai-Chia Chuan
Tsai-Li-Fu
Tsien Tao
Tso-Ku Shu: See Chin-Na
Tsui Chuan Lo Han Tao
Tsui Pak Hsien ("Drunken")
    Lok Hop Tsui Pak Hsien
      ("Drunken Six Harmonies")
Tuan Chuan
Tung-Hai Chuan
Tung Pi; Tungpi Chuan
Two Element Boxing
Two Instruments: See Liang-I
Tzujan Men; Tsu-Jan Men
Tzu Men Chuan
Ving-Tsun: See Wing Chun
Wah Kuen
Wah-Lum; Wa-Lum
Wah Lum Tam Tui
Wei-To Men
Wenjin
White Crane: See Pak-Hoc
White Eyebrow: See Bok Mei Pai
White Lotus
Wing Chun; Wing-Tsun; Ving-Tsun;
  Yung Chun
    Futshan Pai
    Jiu Wan
Wood Monkey: See Tai-Sing Pek-
  Kwar
Wu Chuan
Wudang
Wu Kung
Wu Shong Tuo Kao
Wu-Tang: See Pa-Kua
Wu Wei
Xing-Chiao ("Eagle Claw")
    Eagle Claw Fan-Tzu
    Ying Jow Pai ("Northern Eagle
    Fist")
Xingyiquan: See Hsing-I
Xin-Yi
Yee Chuan
Yen Ching Chuan: See Mi-Tsung-I
Ying Jow Pai: See Xing-Chiao
Ying Yee Chuan
Yi-Quan: See I-Chuan

Yu Chia
Yueh-Fei Chuan
Yueh-Lien Chuan
Yueh San-Shou
Yung-Chun Chuan
Zhao
Zuijiuquan ("Drunkard's Boxing")

SANSHOU (AN ART AND A SPORT)

SHUAI CHIAO: SEE CHIAO-TI

TAMO CHIEN

TI-SHA SHOU

TSO-KU SHU

WU SHU; WUSHU: SEE KUNG-FU

COMMONWEALTH OF INDEPENDENT STATES (FORMERLY USSR)

SAMBO; SOMBO; CAMBO

SAMO-ABORONA BEZ ORUZHIA; ROKUP ASHNI-BOI

EGYPT

SEBEKKHA ("CROCODILE SPIRIT")

ENGLAND

JUJUTSU
Kempo Jujitsu

KARATE
Ashanti
Bushido-ryu
Smizen-ryu
Ty-Ga
Washindo-ryu

KUNG-FU
Hap Kune Do

TAEKWON-DO
Sulkido

WESTERN BOXING

WRESTLING
Cornish; Corno-Breton

FRANCE

AIKI-TAIDO

BOXE AMERICAINE (A.K.A. AMERICAN FULL-CONTACT KARATE OR KICKBOXING)

CHAUSSON

HANDICAP ZERO

KARATE
Kick-Jutsu

KUNG-FU
Wou Kuen Do

KUSHINRYU

LA BOXE FRANCAISE; FRENCH BOXING (SPORT)

LA CANNE

QWAN KI DO

SAVATE (AN ART AND A SPORT)

SEI-NO-IKI

WA-JUTSU

GREECE

GREEK BOXING (AN ART AND A SPORT)

PANKRATION; PANCRATION; PANCRATIUM (AN ART AND A SPORT)

HAWAII

HAKOKO (WRESTLING)

LUA
E-Lua Lima
Kaala

KAKALAAU (STICK FIGHTING)

KOSHO-RYU KEMPO
Kajukenbo
Kenpo (Kara-Ho)

KUIA-LUA (A JUDO-LIKE SPORT)

KULAKULAI

MOKOMOKO (BOXING)

MUSHI-JUTSU

ICELAND

WRESTLING
Glimae (sport)

INDIA

BAHIMSENEE

BANDESH

BINOT

CHEENA ADI

FARI GATKA; FARI-GADKA

HUNUMANTEE

KALARI PAYAT
Northern
Southern

KHUTU VARASAI

LATHI

MARMA ADI (NERVE CENTER STRIKES)
Northern Marman
Southern Varmam; Varmaniyam

**MALLA-KRIDA; MALLA-YUDDHA;
NIYUDDHA-KRIDE**

MUSHTI-YUDDHA; MUKI BOXING

NATA

SILAMBAM
Durakana
Kalabathu
Kuravangi
Nagam Patheraru
Paneari

**VAJRAMUSTI; VAJRAMUSTI GUSTI
(WRESTLING)**

INDONESIA

BERSILAT
Chekak

GATKA; GADKA

GULAT
Banjang

KALARI PAYAT

MAIN TINDJU; BAJAWAH BOX

PENTJAK-SILAT; PENCAK SILAT
Bagalombang Dua-Blas Silat
Bahkti Negara
Bangau Putih
Baru Silat
Bhakti Negara
Budoja Indonesia Matarm
Champaka Putih
Delima
Eka Sentosa Setiti
Ende
Harimau Silat
Jokuk
Karena Matjang
Kebudajaan Ilmu Silat Indonesia
Kendang Silat
Kendari Silat
Kerojok
Kumango Silat

Langka-Tiga Silat
Lintow
Mustika Kwitang
Pamur Silat
Paraiman Silat
Patai Silat
Pauh Silat
Pera Taki Sendo
Perisai Diri
Perisai Sahkti
Persatrian Hati
Petjut Silat
Porbikawa
Putimandi Silat
Samull Petjut Silat
Sandang Silat
Serak
Set Hati
Setia Hati Terate; Sedulur Tunggal
   Ketjer
Sikwitang Silat
Silat Menangkabau; Silat Padang
Silat Putra
Sisemba; Semba; Sempak (an art
   and a sport)
Strelak Silat
Sulat
Sundra Silat; Bundung Silat
Tapak Suji
Tapu Silat
Tjampur
Tjatji; Tjatjing; Main Tjatji
Tridharma
Tjinkrik
Tunggal Hati
Undukayam Silat

PUKULAN; POEKOELAN
Klipap
Kuntao
Mina Kabauw
Petjut
Si Matjan
Suchi Hati
Tjemantik
Tji Minjie
Tiji Monjet

RANDAI

SILAT

SUNDRA SILAT
Tji-Andur
Tji-Bedujut
Tji-Jingkrik
Tji-Kabon

Tji-Kalong
Tji-Kampek
Tji-Karet
Tji-Krik
Tji-Malaja
Tji-Mande
Tji-Matjan
Tji-Petir
Tji-Uler
Tji-Waringin

TJAKALELE

JAPAN

AIKIDO
(Appearing beside some styles is
the name of its founder)
Aiki-kendo (sport)
Kobu-jutsu (Tetsuomi Hoshi)
Korindo (Minoru Harai)
Nihon Goshin
Otsuki-ryu (Yutaka Otsuki)
Shindo Iten-ryu
Shindo Rokugo-ryu
Shin Riaku Heiho
Shinshintoitsu; Shishin Toitsu
   (Koichi Tohei)
Shinwa Taido (Yoichiro Inoue)
Takemusu Kai
Teko
Tenshin Sho Kai
Tomiki-ryu; Goshin-Jutsu-Kata
   (Kenji Tomiki)
Ueshiba; Uyeshiba (Morihei
   Ueshiba)
Yae-ryu
Yobukai
Yoseikan (Minoru Mochizuki)
Yoshin; Yoshinkan (Gozo Shioda)
Yoshokai

AIKI-JUTSU; AIKI-JUJUTSU
Daito-ryu; Goten-jutsu
Mugen-ryu
Shidare Yanagi-ryu
Takeda-ryu
Yamate-ryu

AIKIKENDO (AN ART AND A SPORT)
Aiki-Kenpo

ATEMI

BATTO-JUTSU
Toyama-ryu

BIKEN-JUTSU

BOJUTSU
Kashima-ryu
Kukishin-ryu
Shindo-Muso-ryu
Tenshin Shoden Katori Shinto-ryu;
  Katori Shinto-ryu; Katori-ryu

CHIGIRIKI-JUTSU

CHIKARA KURABE; KUMIUCHI

CHIKUJO-JUTSU

CHUKOSHIKA

COREUM

FUKI-BARI

GEKIGAN-JUTSU

GENKATSU

HAKUDA

HAYAGAKE-JUTSU

HOBAKU

HOJO-JUTSU; HOBAKU-JUTSU

HOJUTSU

IAIDO
Hasegawa-ryu
Hokushin-Itto ryu
Hokushin Shinoh-ryu
Kamashita Shinto-ryu
Katori-Shinto-ryu
Mukai-ryu
Muso Jikiden Eishen-ryu
Omori-ryu
Shinkendo
Toyama-ryu; Gunto Soho
Yagyu-ryu

IAIJUTSU
Eishin-ryu
Hasegawako-ryu
Katori-ryu; Katori Shinto-ryu
Muso-ryu; Shin Muso
  Hayashizaki-ryu
Omori-ryu
Tamiya-ryu; Tamiya Shinken-ryu
Toyama-ryu
Yagyu Shingan-ryu Heiho

IKAKU-RYU

JOBAJUTSU; BAJUTSU

JODO
Shindo-Muso-ryu Jodo

JOJUTSU
Shindo-Muso-ryu
Shin-Tai-Kan

JUDO; KODOKAN JUDO

JUJUTSU; JIU-JITSU
Araki Kempi-ryu
Arata-ryu
Asayami Ichiden-ryu
Budoshin
Daito-ryu
Danzan-ryu; Kodenkan Danzan-
  ryu
Date-ryu
Goshin-jutsu
Hakko-ryu
Hakutsu-ryu
Hideyoshi-ryu
Hontai Yoshin-ryu
Iwaga-ryu
Jikishinkage-ryu
Juki-ryu
Jukishin-ryu
Kage-ryu
Kango-ryu
Kashima Shinto-ryu
Katori Shinto-ryu
Kiraku-ryu
Kito-ryu
Kogusoku
Kosogabu-ryu
Kyushin-ryu
Maniwa Nen-ryu
Miura-ryu
Nihon-ryu
Ryoishinto-ryu
Sawa-Dochi-ryu
Sekiguchi-ryu; Seikiguchi-ryu
Shibukawa-ryu
Shimmei Sakkatsu-ryu
Shindo Muso-ryu
Shindo-Yoshin-ryu
Shin-No-Shindo-ryu
Shinowara-kan
Shinshinto-ryu
Shinto-Yoshi-ryu
Sosuishitsu-ryu; Sosuishi-ryu
Takagi-ryu
Takeuchi-ryu; Takenuchi-ryu
Tanshin-ryu
Tenjin-Shinyo-ryu
Toshu Kakuto
Tsutsumi-ryu
Yagyu-Shingan-ryu
Yoshin-ryu; Hontai Yoshin-ryu
Yoshioka-ryu

JUKEN-DO

JUKEN-JUTSU

JUTTE-JUTSU

KAKUSHI BUKI-JUTSU

**KARATE (AN ART AND A SPORT);
KARATE-DO; KARATE-JUTSU**
Ashihara
Ashi-hari
Aishin-kai
Chito-ryu
Doshinkan
Geido-kai
Gensei-ryu
Genshin-ryu
Gima Ha Shoto-ryu
Goju-ryu
Gosoku-ryu
Hayashi-ha
Joshin Mon; Jyoshin Mon
Kamishin-ryu; Shorinji-Tetsu-
  Kempo
Kanbukan: See Renbukai
Kenkojuku
Kenkokan; Shorinji-ryu Kenkokan
Kenseikan
Kenshikan; Kenshikan Kenpo
Kenyu-ryu
Kobukan
Koei-kan
Koshiki (sport)
Kosho-ryu Kempo
Kushin-ryu
Kyokushinkai; Oyama-ryu
Nippon Kempo
Nippon Shorinji Kempo; Shorinji
  Kempo
Renbukai; Renbukan; Kanbukan
Rengokai
Renshinkai
Ryobukan; Shindo-Jinen-ryu
Saibukan
Sankukai; Nanbudo; Sankudo
Seido; Seidokan
Seiki-dojo
Sendai
Shinbu-kai
Shinden-ryu
Shindojinen-ryu
Shinto-ryu
Shito-ryu
    Hayashi-Ha
    Itosukai
    Kenyukai
    Kiyatake-Ha
    Ryu-E-Ryu
      Seikikai
        Seishinkai; Motobu-Ha
        Seishinkai

Shiroma-kai
Shitokai
Shukokai; Tani-Ha Shito-
ryu
Shito Kempokai
Tani-Ha Shukokai
Shobu-kai
Shorinji Kempo: See Nippon
Shorinji Kempo
Shorinji-ryu
Shorinji-ryu Kenkokan
Shorinji-ryu Renshinkan
Shotokai
Shotokan
Shudokan
So-ryu
Soyoujyuku
Taido
Tai-Jutsu
Take-Nami-do
Toon-ryu
Wado-ryu
Washin-ryu
Yamato-ryu
Yin Shinkai
Yoseikan
Yoshukai

KARUMI-JUTSU

KEIBO SOHO

KEMPO

KENDO
Jikishin-Kage-ryu
Shoden Mutto-ryu

KENJUTSU; GEKKEN
Abe-ryu; Abe-Tate-ryu
Aizu-Kage-ryu
Anazawa-ryu
Araki-ryu
Bokuden-ryu
Chujo-ryu
Gan-ryu
Hasegawa-ryu
Hikida-ryu; Hikida-Kage-ryu
Hoki-ryu
Hokushin-Itto-ryu
Hozan-ryu
Itto-ryu
Itto Shoden Muto
Jigen-ryu
Jikishin-Kage-ryu
Kashima Shinto-ryu
Katori-Shinto-ryu
Kosho-ryu

Koto-Eiri-ryu
Maniwa Nen-ryu
Mijin-ryu
Muji-Shin-Jen-ryu
Mujushin-Ken-ryu
Muso-Jukiden-Eishin-ryu
Nen-ryu
Niten Ichi-ryu; Nito-ryu
Omori-ryu
Ono-Ha Itto-ryu
Shindo Muso-ryu
Shingen-ryu
Shinkage-ryu
Shinshinto-ryu
Shinto-ryu
Takeuchi-ryu
Tamiya-ryu
Tensinmegen-ryu
Tenshin Shoden Katori Shinto-ryu;
Katori Shinto-ryu; Katori-ryu
Yagyu Shinkage-ryu

KIAI-JUTSU

KICKBOXING (SPORT)

KOBUDO

KOGUSOKU

KOPPO; KOSHIKI KOPPO

KOSHI MAWARI; KOSHI NO MAWARI

KUMIUCHI: SEE CHIKARA KURABE

KUSARIGAMA-JUTSU; GUSARI
Araki-ryu
Chigiriki-Jutsu
Hikida-ryu
Hoen-ryu
Ichin-ryu
Isshin-ryu
Kyoshin-Meichi-ryu
Masaki-ryu
Shindo-ryu
Shuchin-ryu
Toda-ryu

KYUDO
Ogasawara-ryu

KYUJUTSU
Hioki-ryu
Kajima-ryu
Nichioku-ryu
Nihon-ryu
Ogasawara-ryu
Soken-ryu

MASAKI-RYU

NAGINATA-DO (AN ART AND A SPORT)
Jikinshinkage-ryu

NAGINATA-JUTSU
Jikishin-Kage-ryu
Katori Shinto-ryu; Katori-ryu;
Tenshin Shoden Katori Shinto-ryu;
Sanwa-ryu
Seikan-ryu
Seni-ryu

NINJUTSU
Fuma-ryu
Koga-ryu
Togakure-ryu

NIPPON KEMPO

NOROSHI-JUTSU

SASUMATA-JUTSU

SENBAN NAGE-JUTSU

SENJO-JUTSU

SHINOBI-JUTSU

SHIN-TAIDO

SHOOTBOXING (SPORT)

SHUBAKU

SHURIKEN-JUTSU

SODEGARAMI-JUTSU

SOJUTSU

SUIEI-JUTSU

SUIJOHOKO-JUTSU

SUMO; SUMAI (SPORT)

TACHI-UCHI SHIAI

TAIHO-JUTSU

TAI-JUTSU
Dakentaijutsu
Jutaijutsu

TAIKI-KEN (KUNG-FU)

TANTO-JUTSU

TEGOI

TESSEN-JUTSU

TETSUBO-JUTSU

TORITE

TOSHU KAKUTO; TOSHU-KAKUTO-KYOHAN-TAIKEI

TO-SO-JUTSU

UCHI-NE

WA-JUTSU

YARI-JUTSU
Doki-ryu
Hozo-In-ryu; Hozoin-ryu
Shinkage-ryu
Tendo-ryu
Tenshin Shoden Katori Shinto-ryu

YAWARA
Goshindo Miura-ryu

YOSHIN-RYU

YUBI-JUTSU

KOREA

BANG SOO DO

BOOL MOO DO

CHUNG SIM DO

CIREUM; SIREUM (SPORT)
Tong-Cireum

HAPKIDO; BI SOOL; HO SHIN SOOL; YU KWON SOOL; YU-SOOL; YUSUL

HWARANG-DO

KEMPO (JUJUTSU)

KEUPSO CHIRIGI

KONG SOO DO

KUK SOOL WON
Buldo My Sool
Koong Joong My Sool
Sado Mu Soo

KUM-DO; KE-AK BONG; BONG HEE (AN ART AND A SPORT)

KUN GEK DO (AN ART AND A SPORT)

KUNG-FU
Sib Pal Gee

KUNG-SOOL

KWONBOP; KWONPUP
Neikya (Sorim)
Weikya (Songkae)

MA-SOOL

PACHIGI; PAKCHIGI

SUBAK; SOO BAHK GI

SUI SA DO

TAE KWON; TAE KWONPUP

TAE KWON DO (AN ART AND A SPORT)*
Chang-Hon Yu
Chang Moo Kwan; Chang Mu
   Kwan

Chi Do Kwan
Chung Do Kwan
Chung Yung Kwan
Gedo Kwan; Ge Do Kwan
Han Mu Kwan; Han Moo Kwan
Hwa Rang Kwan
Ji Do Kwan; Jee Do Kwan
Jung Do Kwan
Kang Duk Kwan
Kook Moo Kwan
Moo Duk Kwan
Moon Mu Kwan
Oh Do Kwan; O Do Kwan
Song Moo Kwan; Sang Moo Kwan
Yun Moo Kwan

TAE KYON; CHABI

TAE SOO DO

TANG SOO DO-MOO DUK KWAN; TANG SOO DO (ORIGINALLY SOO BAHK DO)

TANG-SU

YUDO (JUDO)

MALAYSIA

BERSILAT
Bayan Silat
Chekak
Kelantan
Lintan
Medan
Peninjuan
Silat Buah
Silat Puah
Terelak

POC KHEK

SILAT GAYUNG

OKINAWA

KARATE; KARATE-JUTSU; OKINAWA-TE; TE; TO-DE; TO-TE
Gensei-ryu
Goju-ryu
Hakutsuru-te; Hakutsuru-ken
Honshin-ryu
Ishimine-ryu
Issin-ryu
Itato-ryu
Itokazukei
Jodo

Kingairyu
Kojo-ryu
Kushin-ryu
Motobu-ryu
Naha-te
Okinawan Kempo
   Ryukyu Kempo
   Shudokan
Okinawa-Te
Ryuei-ryu; Ryu-Ei-ryu
Ryukyu-ken
Seidokan
Shorei-ryu
Shorinji-ryu
Shorin-ryu
   Chubushorin-ryu
   Kenshinkan
   Kobayashi-ryu
   Matsubayashi-ryu
   Matsumura Kenpo
   Matsumura Orthodox;
      Matsumura Seito
      Matsumura Shorin-ryu
   Nanbushorin-ryu
   Seibukan
   Seidokan
   Shobayashi-ryu
   Shorin Kempo
   Sukunaihayashi
Shuri-te
Tomari-te
Oyadomari
Toon-ryu
Toyama-ryu
Tozan-ryu
Uechi-ryu

KOBUDO; TE-GUA

KOBU-JUTSU; RYUKYUKOBU-JUTSU

KYUSHO-JUTSU

TEGUMI (WRESTLING)

TOIDE (JUJUTSU)

TUITE

UFUCHIKU KOBU-JUTSU

PHILIPPINES

ARNIS; ARNIS DE MANO; ESCRIMA; ESTOCADA; ESTOGUE; FRAILE; KALI; SINAWALI
Abanico
Abecedario

---

*Not all of the kwans appearing under tae kwon do consolidated to form this art. If, however, tae kwon do can be compared to the art of karate (and it *can* because both share considerable similarities), then each kwan can be considered a style.

Abierta
Bergonia
Bohol
Cabisedario
Cebuano
Derobio
Disalon
Doce Pares
Dos Manos
Doublecado
Etalonio
Fondo Puerta
Herada Bantanqueno
Illonga
Ilocano
Kabaroan
Kalirongan
Kiliradman
Largada Pesada
Largo Mano
Lastico
Literada
Magalaya
Moro
Mountain (northern type)
Numerado
Pagaradman
Pagkalikali
Pampango
Panandata
Pangasinan
Pekiti Tirsia
PMAS Combat Escrima
Precia Punialada
Redondo
Repeticion
Reterida
Rompipan Cempiapa Etalonia
Samar
Serrada; Serada
Sinawali
Sumbrada
Sumkeate
Tagalog
Taosug; Sulu
Toledo
Toledo-Collado
Trisello; Crosses
Villabrille
Waray

BUNO

DITSO

DUMOG

KUNTAO; KUNTAU; KUNTAW; KUNTOW

PANAN-TUKAN (BOXING)

SIKARAN; SIKIRAN

TAPADO

YAW YAN

SCOTLAND
KARATE
Kafdo

TUKIDO

SINGAPORE
KUNG-FU
Xian-Jia-Po Tao-Quan

SILAT MELAYU

SUMATRA
KARATE
Tanghan Kosong; TAKO

THAILAND
MUAY THAI; THAI BOXING (AN ART AND A SPORT)

KRABI-KRABONG

TAIWAN
KUOSHU
Eight-Steps Praying Mantis
Ta Hao ("Invincible White Crane")

SUAI JOW (JUDO)

TIBET
KUNG-FU
Lama Pai
Lion's Roar
    Baahk Hok Kyuhn ("White Crane")
    Haap Ga Kyuhn ("Haap Family")
    Maht Jung Lama Pai ("Esoteric Principle Lama Style")

UNITED STATES
AIKIDO
Koga method (law-enforcement self-defense)

AMERICAN KARATE (AN ART AND A SPORT)
Bushidokan
Chinese Goju
Chuan Chi Do
Chun Kuk Do (Chuck Norris, founder)
Combat Karate
Combato
Dan-Te
Enshin
Goju-Kai USA
Goju-Shorin
Goshin-do
Isshin Kempo
Ja Shin Do
Kali-Kan
Kang-Chuan Do
Kanzen Goju
Keedok-Kyo
Keichu-do
Keishan-kan
Kenpo: See Kosho-Ryu Kempo
Ketsuga-ryu
Ketsuka
Kojasho
Kokusai
Kosho-Ryu Kempo (James Mitose)
    Kenpo (Kara-ho—Prof. William K.S. Chow)
        Kajukenbo (Adriano Emperado)
        Kajukenbo (John Leone)
            Kenpo Karate (Bill Ryusaki)
            Go-Shin Jutsu (S. Gascon)
            Ukidokan Karate (Benny Urquidez)
        Kenkabo (Sid Asuncion)
            Won Hop Keun Do (Al Dacascos)
    Kenpo (Cha-3)
    Kenpo (Nick Cerio's)
        American Shaolin Kempo (Fred Vallari)
        DiRico's Kenpo (Rocky DiRico)
        Oki-ryu Kenpo (Don Rodriguez)
        Tenchi-Kenpo (Norm Armstrong)
    Kenpo (Ed Parker)
        Kenpo (Black Karate Federation)

Kenpo (Sam-Pai)
Kenpo (Shaolin)
Kenpo (Al Tracy)
Lima Lama (Tino
    Tuilosega)
Tai Karate (David
    German)
Te-Ken Jutsu Kai
    (M. Oshiro)
Kwan Yin Do
Musashi Kindai-ryu
Mu Tau
Nisei Goju
Pai-Lum Kempo
Seido
Sendo-ryu
Shingo-Ju-ryu
Shin-Toshi
Shorei-Goju
Shorin Do Kenpo
Shoto-Shinkai
Tai Shin Doh
Tai-Zen
Tetsu-Ken-ryu
USA Goju
Wadokikai
Wu Ming Ta

Wu Ying Tao
Yoshukai
Zendo-ryu

AMERICAN KICKBOXING (SPORT)
Kickboxing Katsugo

BONG SOOL (AN ART AND A SPORT)

JEET KUNE DO

JUJUTSU
Juko-ryu
Ketsugo
Miyama-ryu
Niseido
Oikiru-ryu
Small Circle
Vee-Jutsu

KUNG-FU
Chi Tao
Gung-Mau
Hong Chun
Hung Jung Soo
Jun Fan
Kung Shio Tao
Lee San Pai
Pai Lum
Tao Kune Do

Tien Long Pai
Tum-Pai
Wei Kuen Do
White Lotus

KYUK-KI-DO (SPORT)

TAEKWON-DO
Cha-Yon-ryu
Choi Kwang Do
Choson Do
Chung Sim Do
Nam Seo Kwan
Pasaryu
Song Ahm

VIETNAM
CO-VO-DAO (WEAPONS)

CUONG NHU

NHU DAO (JUDO)

QWAN KI DO

THANH LONG

VIET VO DAO

VOVINAM

YIN YANG TAO

CHAPTER 2

ASIAN DYNASTIES

As a researcher, I have often encountered history books written about traditional martial arts that use a confusing number of historical eras, or dynasties. I was never sure where I was at any given time and realized not one of these books carried a guide to historical Asian dynasties. This is the first martial arts book to do so. They appear in chronological order.

The dynasties, or ruling governments, of the three most prevalent Asian nations—China, Japan and Korea—have bounded between glorious eras when arts and philosophies flourished to long periods of corruption and war, when their people suffered greatly. At no time in recorded history did these three geographic locations, which came to be separate sovereign countries, ever not have at least a cultural, if not political, influence upon one another.

As you view their respective dynasties and the periods of time within which they existed, you can see how governments and ideologies came and went. In the interim there were often wars of transformation.

These three countries are culturally vast and, in the case of China, geographically spacious; their ultimate intertwined destinies are still being shaped.

CHINA

Name	Period
Chou Dynasty	1122–769 B.C. (Eastern) Dynasty
Tung (Eastern) Dynasty	770–476 B.C.
Tung (Eastern) Dynasty	475–221 B.C. (Warring State Period)
Ch'in Dynasty	221–206 B.C.
Han Dynasty	206 B.C.–A.D. 220
Six Dynasty Period	220–589

(This period is the interim between the Han and Chin dynasties, so named because of the rapidly successive dynasties having their capital at Nanking.)

Chin Dynasty	265–420
Nan-Ch'ao (Southern Dynasties)	420–589
Sui Dynasty	589–618
Tang Dynasty	618–907
Five Dynasties & Ten Kingdom Period	907–960

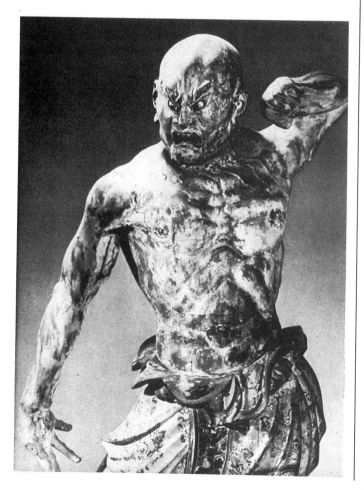

A Japanese Nio Bodhisattva guardian deity glares fiercely and threatens evil trespassers with a karate fist. This type of giant, foreboding sculpture is found guarding the gate entrances of Buddhist temples. The karate-like poses represent some of the earliest documented evidence of the ancient existence of martial arts. Courtesy of the John Corcoran Archives

DYNASTIES
1) Hou Liang
2) Hou T'ang
3) Hou Chin
4) Hou Han
5) Hou Chou

(This period encompassed these kingdoms: Wu, Nan T'ang, Nan P'ing, Ch'u, Ch'ien, Hou Shu, Min, Pei Han, Nan Han and Wu Yueh.)

Name	Period
Sung Dynasty	960–1279
Chin or Juchen Dynasty	1115–1234
Yuan or Mongol Dynasty	1206–1368
Ming Dynasty	1368–1644
Ch'ing or Manchu Dynasty	1644–1911
Japanese Governmental Control	1912–1945

JAPAN

Name	Period
Liu Sung Dynasty	420–502
Liang Dynasty	502–557
Sui Dynasty	581–618

Name	Period
Nara Period (beginning of the Japanese Imperial State)	710–784
Heian Period	794–1185
Kamakura Bakufu (establishment of military government)	1192–1333
Muromachi or Ashikaja Shogunate	1338–1573
Oda Regime	1550–1560
Hideyoshi Regime	1582–1598
Edo Bakufu or Tokugawa Shogunate (the strongest period of samurai influence)	1603–1867
Meiji Restoration	1868–1945

KOREA

Name	Period
Kokuryo Dynasty	37 B.C.–A.D. 668
Silla Dynasty	668–935
Ko Ryo Dynasty	935–1392
Yi Dynasty	1392–1909
Japanese Occupation of Korea	1909–1945
Korean Independence	1945–

CHAPTER 3

OFFICIAL FORMS OF
KARATE AND TAE KWON DO

To lend a simple explanation to what some people make very complex, forms are to the Eastern martial arts what shadow boxing is to Western boxing. Call them a prearranged series of movements designed against multiple imaginary opponents. They can be performed solo or in a group, armed or unarmed. Forms are given such importance in the martial arts that very few styles do *not* practice them.

The practice of forms is one of the most widespread and important aspects of the martial arts. In almost every art and style, forms are a mandatory requirement for promotion up through the ranks.

Forms are the textbook of a system because every *principle* of the style, and not just its techniques, is located somewhere within one or more of the patterns, or is a combination of two or more concepts from the forms. Some styles emphasize a large number of forms, others a deep understanding of just a few. Many practice the same or very similar forms, sometimes with different names, sometimes in different order. Two schools of the same style often show minor differences in the same form.

Some forms having the same name conversely bear no resemblance to each other. Last, stylists to this day continue to debate origins and developments of forms down to the finest nuance. All of which makes this section an indispensable guide about who does what.

CONTENT

This chapter contains a thorough list of the official kata ("formal exercises"), or, as they are collectively called, the "forms" of many popular styles of karate and karate-do, as well as the poomse, hyung or patterns of tae kwon do. This was no easy task even for the limited number of styles addressed here.

For one, there are literally hundreds of styles of karate. With the constant and widespread division and proliferation of martial systems all over the world, it is altogether impossible to list *every* style's forms. The official forms of these styles—and even of the most popular styles—have rarely been published. So research alone could not provide an answer. It required extensive contact with knowledgeable sources to compile and depict those that appear here as accurately as possible.

Grandmaster Chojun Miyagi, founder of Goju-ryu karate, one of the world's most popular martial arts styles. Courtesy of karate Master Anthony Mirakian

In most cases the data was supplied by prominent or veteran martial experts and masters of that particular style. Contributors were chosen for their expert specialty and were asked to depict their style's forms as accurately as possible according to the practices of the style's original or current grandmaster. Nevertheless, as my contributors openly admitted, there were sometimes slight variations even among practitioners of the *same* style.

KARATE

Most karate kata originated in Okinawa and were named after Chinese kung-fu experts who taught the Okinawans. Perhaps the largest number of karate kata were created in and stem from the three main branches of Okinawa's shorin-ryu system of karate: Kobayashi-ryu, Matsubayashi-ryu and Shobayashi-ryu. Of the forms used today, most appear to have been devised sometime between 1750 and 1950. Reputedly, the oldest kata still in use today is Seisan.

Of particular interest, too, are the kata of Shotokan karate-do. Shotokan's founder, Master Gichin Funakoshi, the acknowledged "father of modern karate," was an Okinawan Shuri-te (one of the three original schools of Okinawan karate) stylist who later changed the names of the Okinawan kata and modernized them in order to firmly establish karate in Japan among the Japanese.

This was a major transition in that Shotokan was subjected to subsequent spin-offs of many derivative styles and, as they all spread across the world, they brought with them versions of the original Okinawan kata. Consequently, many diverse variations of the so-called "pure" kata are still practiced today. Further, the order of the forms may vary from school to school, at the discretion of the instructor, even though they are the same forms practiced by the same stylists.

This comparative chart shows the names of the kata of the current Japanese styles, in alphabetical order, and their earlier Okinawan counterparts:

Japanese	Okinawan
Bassai Dai	Passai Sho
Bassai Sho	Passai Dai
Chinte	Chinte
Enpi	Wansu
Gankaku	Chinto
Gojushiho	Useshi; Gojushiho
Hangetsu	Seisan
Heian Godan	Pinan Godan
Heian Nidan	Pinan Shodan
Heian Sandan	Pinan Sandan
Heian Shodan	Pinan Nidan
Heian Yondan	Pinan Yondan
Jiin	Jiin
Jion	Jion
Jitte	Jitte
Kanku Dai	Kusanku Dai
Kanku Sho	Kusanku Sho
Meikyo	Rohai
Nijushiho	Niseshi
Sochin	Sochin
Tekki Shodan	Naihanchi Shodan
Tekki Nidan	Naihanchi Nidan
Tekki Sandan	Naihanchi Sandan
Unsu	Unsu
Wankan	Wankan

TAE KWON DO

Tae kwon do, officially founded in April 1955, is said to be derived from earlier Korean forms of combat and the kata of the Okinawan karate schools of Shuri-te and Naha-te. From 1945 to 1965, some seventeen *kwans*, or "schools," of Korean martial arts were founded. Prior to the establishment of tae kwon do, there were originally nine *kwans*, all of which merged to form tae kwon do.

To eliminate confusion and attempt to elevate tae kwon do as a universal sport, the nine kwans were officially abolished and given numerical designations upon the formation of the Korea Taekwon-do Association on September 14, 1961. For the record, those kwans and serial numbers are as follows: Song Moo Kwan, 1st kwan; Han Moo Kwan, 2nd kwan; Chang Moo Kwan, 3rd kwan; Moo Duk Kwan, 4th kwan; Oh Do Kwan; 5th kwan; Kang Duk Kwan, 6th kwan; Jung Do Kwan, 7th kwan; Ji Do Kwan, 8th kwan; and Chung Do Kwan, 9th kwan.

Today there is one official set of tae kwon do forms, called "poomse," recognized by the South Korean government and the members of the vast World Taekwon-do Federation based in Seoul. Another set of forms, called "hyung," are recognized by General Hong Hi Choi's maverick International Taekwon-do Federation. Both sets of forms are represented here.

KUNG-FU

Chinese kung-fu "sets," as they are called, were for the most part created much earlier than those of karate. Many of them stem from the important Shaolin (or Sil Lum) system, whose five basic forms were the Dragon, Snake, Crane, Tiger and Leopard. Because of the massive number of kung-fu systems, and the secrecy still surrounding many systems, kung-fu's stylistic sets proved impossible to collect and disseminate here.

For one, numerous translations exist for a single word. Second, kung-fu masters even today do not readily divulge all the information about their systems and many sets thus go unnamed and uncategorized; consequently, these systems' sets could be incomplete even if they made their way to print. Third, those that I was able to find contained names susceptible to numerous translations. Fourth, one kung-fu system alone could embrace literally hundreds of armed and unarmed sets.

For these sound reasons, I have omitted kung-fu sets in this chapter. Perhaps in future editions, if and when this book is updated, kung-fu sets can be logically collected and added.

FORMAT

In most examples, the forms appear in the order in which they are taught; when that is unknown they simply appear in alphabetical order. When possible, the forms were divided into armed and unarmed.

When a name or names appear under the title of each style, the first name represents that style's founder and the second, if any, the current grandmaster. Last, to eliminate redundancy, roman numerals were used to designate a series of the same kata. In other words, instead of listing Kusanku Dai, Kusanku Sho, etc., they appear on one line as Kusanku I & II.

AMERICAN KARATE FORMS

CERIO'S KENPO (NICK CERIO SYSTEM)

Unarmed

Blocking I–V
Pinan I–III
Cat I–V
Circle of the Tiger
Circle of the Leopard
Circle of the Crane
Circle of the Panther
Eye of the Hurricane
Lin Wan Kune
Bassai Dai
Empi
Kanku Sho & Dai

Armed

Shushi No Kon Sho
Combat Bo I–III
Kanegawa Ni Cho Game
Matsuhiga No Kama
Matsuhiga No Sai
Hamahiga No Sai
Japanese sword (iaido)
Nunchaku
Chinese Twin Sticks
Kwando

KAJUKENBO

Basic
Pinians I–VII
Intermediate
Pinians VIII–XIV

KOKONDO (PAUL AREL SYSTEM)

White Belt

Taikyoku I & II

Yellow Belt

Taikyoku III
Pinan I

Green Belt

Pinan II
Henka I
Pinan III

Red Belt

Konsho
Henka II

Brown Belt

Pinan IV & V
Uke
Konni
Bo Ichi Ban
Sai Ichi Ban
Konsan
Geri
Saifa
Bo Ni Ban
Sai Ni Ban

1st-Degree Black Belt

Basai
Bo San Ban
Sai San Ban

2nd-Degree Black Belt

Kanku
Go Jushiho
Henka III
Tonfa Ichi Ban
Seienchin (optional)

3rd-Degree Black Belt

Seienchin
Henka IV
Sushiho

Advanced Black Belt Forms

Empi
Jion
Unsu
Rohai
Niaha
Jutte
Naihanchi
Gankaku
Hangetsu
Henka V & VI
Kokonso
Kokonyo

NAM SEO KWAN TAE KWON DO (KEITH YATES SYSTEM)

Unarmed

Chunji
Tan Gun
Toe San
Won Hyo
Yul Gook
Chung Guen

Ti Gye
Hwa Rang
Chug Mu
Chul Gi
Kwang Gye
Basai
Po Un
Sip Soo
Kae Bek
Choi Young
Nam Seo

Armed

Happo Jo Aiki
Kengi Ichi
Sai Kime

PARKER'S KENPO (ED PARKER SYSTEM)

Yellow Belt

Star Block (Blocking Set 1)
Short Form 1

Orange Belt

Kicking Set 1
Long Form 1

Purple Belt

Stance Set 1
Coordination Set 1
Short Form 2

Blue Belt

Striking Set 1
Finger Set 1
Long Form 2

Green Belt

Coordination Set 2
Short Form 3

3rd-Degree Brown Belt

Stance Set 2
Blocking Set 2
Long Form 3

2nd-Degree Brown Belt

Kicking Set 2
Staff Form 1

1st-Degree Brown Belt

Striking Set 2
Long Form 4

1st-Degree Black Belt

Finger Set 2
Nunchaku Set 1
Two-Man Form

2nd-Degree Black Belt

Long Form 5

3rd-Degree Black Belt

Long Form 6

4th-Degree Black Belt

Long Form 7

5th-Degree Black Belt

Long Form 8

AUSTRALIAN KARATE FORMS

BUDOKAN KARATE (UNARMED)

Beginner

Taikyoku I
Heian I
Heian II

Intermediate

Heian III
Heian IV
Heian V
Tekki I
Basai-Dai
Kanku-Dai
Jion

1st-Degree Black Belt

Jitte
Empi
Hangetsu
Tekki Nidan

2nd-Degree Black Belt

Basai-Sho
Kanku-Sho
Chinte
Tekki Sandan

3rd-Degree Black Belt

Nijushiho
Sochin

JAPANESE KARATE FORMS

CHITO-RYU; YOSHUKAI (DR. TSUYOSHI CHITOSE, FOUNDER; MAMORU YAMAMOTO)

Kata Ichi
Shihohai
Pinan I–V
Naifanchi I–III
Seisan
Oyadomari-Bassai
Chinto
Rochin
Tenshin
Niseishi-Sho
Sanseiru
Ryusan

GOJU-RYU (JAPANESE) (CHOJUN MIYAGI SYSTEM)

Beginner

Gekisai I & II

Kihon Gata (Basic Kata)

Sanchin
Tensho

Kaishu Gata (Intermediate Kata)

Saifa
Seiunchin
Sanseru

Advanced Kata

Shisochin
Seisan
Seipai
Kururunfa
Suparinpei

GOSOKU-RYU (TAKAYUKI KUBOTA SYSTEM)

Unarmed

Heian I–V
Tekki I
Bassai Dai
Kanku Dai
Kanku Sho
Hangetsu
Gojushiho Sho
Unsu
Ichi No Kata
Uke No Kata
Ni No Kata
Gosoku
Gosoku Yodan
Denkogetsu
Sanchin
Tamashii
Rikyu
Gosoku Godan
Raiden

Armed

Kubota Jitsu
Taigo Hoku Jitsu
T-Hold Jitsu
Sankaku Kiri
Atemi No Kata
Toshin Ryu
Kenshin Ryu
Jiyuji Uke Kata
Washi No Kata
Shindo Tsue Jitsu
Taiho Jitsu / Keibo Jitsu
Kubotai Jitsu
Kubokido No Kata

JUDO (JIGORO KANO SYSTEM)

Nage-No-Kata
Katame-No-Kata
Go-No-Sen-No-Kata
Kime-No-Kata
Ju-No-Kata
Koshiki-No-Kata
Kodokan-Goshin-Jutsu
Seiyoku-Zenyo Kokumin-Taiiku-
   No-Kata
Fujoshi-Yo Goshin-No-Kata
Ippan-Yo Goshin-No-Kata

KUSHIN-RYU (KENFEI KINJO & SANOSUKE UESHIMA)

Unarmed

Gekisai
Sanchin
Seisan
Seiunchin
Suparinpei
Passai Sho
Passai Dai
Chinto
Kusanku

KYOKUSHINKAI (MASUTATSU OYAMA SYSTEM)

Taikyoku I–V
Pinan I–V
Naihanchi I–III
Sanchin
Tensho
Salfa
Bassai
Kwanku
Jion
Jutte
Hangetsu
Enpi

Gankaku
Yantsu

RENBUKAI; RENBUKAN (CO-OP SYSTEM)

Kihon I–IV
Shihokebanashi
Pinan
Naihanchi I–III
Bassai Sho
Bassai Dai
Kusanku Sho
Kusanku Dai
Jiin
Jion
Empi
Seisan
Jitte
Rohai
Sochin
Nijushiho
Unsu
Gojushiho
Gojushiho Dai

SHITO-RYU (KENWA MABUNI SYSTEM)

Unarmed

Pinan I–V
Naifanchi I–III
Juroku
Jitte
Jion
Jiin
Shinpa
Aoyagi
Chinte
Chinto
Bassai Dai
Bassai Sho
Rohai
Wankan
Wanshu
Kosokun Dai
Kosokun Sho
Shihokosokun
Unsu
Sochin
Niseishi
Sanchin
Saifa
Sanseiru
Shisochin
Seisan
Gojushiho
Seipai

Kururunfa
Suparinpei
Nipaipo
Hakucho; Hakakusho
Paipuren

KOREAN FORMS

HWA RANG DO (DR. JOO BANG LEE)

Unarmed Hyung

Hwa Rang In
Hwa Rang Oui
Hwa Rang Yeh
Hwa Rang Ji
Hwa Rang Shin
Hwa Rang Sun
Hwa Rang Duk

Black Belt

Hwa Rang Chung
Hwa Rang Yong
Gum Gang Yang
Hyun Ki Um
Ho Sun
Su Am
Chun Ki

Armed

Dan Bong
Gum Moo
Yeuk Gum
Jang Bong
Sang Gum
Chul Sun
Cheung Ryong Do
Jang Chan
Hwan Do
On Wol Do

KUK SOOL WON (IN HYUK SUH)

Beginner

Ki Cho
Cho Keub

Intermediate

Joong Keub
?
Dai Keub

Black Belt

Kum Moo
Baik Phal Ki
Kyuk Pha
Sam Bang Cho (divided into two
   forms)
Woon Hak

Armed

Joong Bang (pole)
Jung Kum (sword)
Asang Dan Bong (two short sticks)
Dan Ssang Kum (two short swords)
Yuk Kum (sword)
Jang Ssang Kum (two long swords)

TAE KWON DO

American Taekwon-do Association (Haeng Ung Lee System)

Below Black Belt

Songahm I–V
Inwha I & II
Choongjung I & II

1st-Degree Black

Shimjun

2nd-Degree Black

Jungyul

3rd-Degree Black

Chungsan

4th-Degree Black

Sokbong

5th-Degree Black

Chunghae

International Taekwon-do Federation (Gen. Hong Hi Choi System)

Basic

Chon-Ji
Tan-Gun
To-San
Won-Hyo
Yul-Gok
Chung-Gun
Toi-Gye
Hwa-Rang
Chung-Mu

Black Belt

Kwan-Gae
Po-Eun
Gae-Baek

World Taekwon-do Federation (Poomse)

Basic

Tae Geuk Chang I–VIII

Black Belt

Koryo
Keum Gang
Tae Baek
Pyong Won
Sip Jin
Ji Tae
Cheon Kwon
Han Soo

OKINAWAN KARATE FORMS

Note: Most of the traditional karate styles throughout the world today trace their lineage to one or more of the three original orthodox styles of Okinawa-te: Naha-te, Shuri-te and Tomari-te.

CHUBU-SHORIN-RYU: SEE SHORIN-RYU

GOJU-RYU (OKINAWAN) (CHOJUN MIYAGI SYSTEM)

Sanchin
Fukyu I & II
Gekisai I & II
Saifa
Shisochin
Seisan
Seipai
Sanseru
Seiuchin
Kururunfa
Suparinpe; Pechurin
Tensho

ISHIMINE-RYU (ISHIMINE SYSTEM; SHINEI KANESHIMA)

Unarmed

Passai
Naihanchi
Sanchin

ISSHINRYU (TATSUO SHIMABUKU SYSTEM)

Unarmed

Seisan
Seiuchin
Naihanchi
Wansu
Chinto
Sanchin

Kusanku
Sunsu

Armed

Tokumine-No-Kun Bo
Urashi-Bo
Shishi-No-Kun-No-Dai Bo
Kusanku-Sai
Chatanyara-Sai
Bo-Sai Kumite

KOBAYASHI-RYU: SEE SHORIN-RYU

KOJO-RYU (KATOMI KOJO SYSTEM)

Unarmed

Shoshin-Kata; Ne Kata
Fudo-Kata; Ushi-Kata
Chinpu-Kata; Tora Kata
Jumonji-Kata; U Kata
Unryu-Kata; Tatsu Kata
Aiki-Kata; Mi Kata
Seigan-Kata; Uma Kata
Doko-Kata; Hitsuji Kata
Tenchi-Kata; Saru Kata
Fukka-Kata; Tori Kata
Chi Seigan-Kata; Inu Kata
Ichimonji-Kata; I Kata

MATSUMURA SEITO: SEE SHORIN-RYU

MOTOBU-RYU (CHOKI MOTOBU SYSTEM)

Unarmed

Moto-Te I–V
Te
Tori-Te
Tori-Te Kaeshi
Ura-Kaeshi
Gassen-Te
Gassen-Bo (weapon)
Ogami-Te
Kaeshi-Te
Karami-Te
Nuki-Te
Nage-Te
Anshi-Kata-No Mai-No Te

NAHA-TE (PRE-1900 SHOREI-RYU; KANRYO HIGASHIONNA, KENRI NAKAIMA & KAMADEUNCHU ARAKAKI)

Unarmed

Sanchin
Seisan
Sanseiru

Seipai
Seiunchin
Shisochin
Kururunfa
Suparinpei/Pechurim
Ohan
Pachu
Heiku
Anan
Paiho
Sochin
Unsu
Niseishi

RYUEI-RYU (KENRI NAKAIMA SYSTEM)

Unarmed

Seiunchin
Sanchin-Seisan
Niseishi
Sanseiru
Pachu
Ohan
Anan
Heiku
Paiho

SHOBAYASHI-RYU: SEE SHORIN-RYU

SHOREI-GOJU (ROBERT TRIAS SYSTEM)

Unarmed

Ananku
Bassai Dai
Dan En Sho
Empi Sho
Gopei Sho
Kanku Sho
Naihanchi I–III
Nan Dan Sho
Sanchin
Taikyoku I–III
Tegatana
Tensho
Tsue Sho
Wan Su

SHORINJI-RYU (OKINAWAN; JOEN NAKAZATO)

Unarmed

Naifanchi I–III
Pinan I–V
Seisan
Wanshu
Ananku
Rohai
Passai
Chinto
Gojushiho
Kusanku

SHORIN-RYU

Chubu-Shorin-Ryu ("Central Shorin-Ryu Karate Association" includes Ankeida, Seibukan, Shidokan and Shudokan Karate systems)

Unarmed

Naihanchi I–III
Pinan I–V
Ananku
Seisan
Wansu
Gojushiho
Kusanku
Passai Sho
Passai Dai
Chinto

Kobayashi-Ryu (Originally from Choshin Chibana)

Pinan I–V
Naifanchi I–III
Passai Dai
Passai Sho
Kusanku Dai
Kusanku Sho
Gojushiho
Chinto

Kobayashi-Ryu (Shugoro Nakazato System)

Unarmed

Naihanchi I–III
Pinan I–V
Passai Dai
Passai Sho
Kusanku Sho
Chinto
Kusanku Dai
Gojushiho

Armed

Bo I–III
Sai I–III
Kama I & II
Eiku I & II

Nunchaku I & II
Tonfa I & II

Matsubayashi-Ryu (Shoshin Nagamine System)

Unarmed

BASIC KATA
Fyukyugata I & II
INTERMEDIATE KATA
Pinan I–V
Naihanchi I–III
BLACK BELT KATA; SHODAN
Ananku
Wankan; O-Kan
Rohai*
NIDAN
Passai (Tomari version)
Chinto
SANDAN
Gojushiho
*Wanchu
YONDAN
Kusanku (Matsumura version)

Matsumura Seito; Matsumura Kenpo; Matsumura Shorin-Ryu; Matsumura-Ryu (Hohan Soken System)

Unarmed

Pinan I & II
Naihanchi I–III
Seisan
Passai Dai
Passai Sho
Chinto
Gojushiho
Kusanku
Rohai I–III
So Hakutsuru
Tan Hakutsuru
Hakutsuru

Seidokan (Toma System)

Unarmed

Seisan
Ananku
Wansu
Passai Dai
Passai Sho
Pinan I–V
Naihanchi
Chinto
Gojushiho
Kusanku

*Influenced by Tomari kata.

Shobayashi-Ryu (Eizo Shimabuku System)

Unarmed

BASIC KATA

Seisan
Naihanchin I–III
Ananku
Wanshu
Pinan I

INTERMEDIATE KATA

Pinan II–V
Gojushiho
Chinto

BLACK BELT KATA

Passai Dai
Passai Sho
Kusanku Sho
Kusanku Dai
Seiunchin
Sanchin

Armed

Chatanyara-No-Sai
Towata-No-Sai
Tokumini-No-Kun
Sakugawa-No-Kun

SHURI-TE (PRE-1900 SHORIN-RYU; SOKON "BUSHI" MATSUMURA SYSTEM)

Unarmed

Seisan
Channan Sho
Channan Dai
Naifanchi
Passai
Chinto
Chinte
Kusanku
Useishi (Gojushiho)
Chinsu

SHURI-TE (SHORIN-RYU)

Unarmed

Naihanchi I–III
Pinan I–V
Ananku
Aoyagi
Chinte
Chinto
Jiin
Jion

Jitte
Jyuroku
Kusanku I & II
Passai Dai
Passai Sho
Seisan
Useshi; Gojushiho

TOMARI-TE (PRE-1900 SHORIN-RYU; KOSAKU MATSUMORA SYSTEM)

Unarmed

Passai
Wanshu
Wando
Wankan
Jion
Jiin
Jitte
Naifanchi
Rohai
Chinto

UECHI-RYU (KANEI UECHI SYSTEM)

Unarmed

Sanchin
Kanshu
Kanshiwa
Seichin
Seisan
Seiruie; Seiryuie
Kanchin
Sanseiryu

SPORT APPLICATIONS

WUSHU; WU SHU

International Wushu Federation

Seven Standardized Forms for International Competition

Changquan Long Fist
Nanquan South Fist
Sword
Broadsword
Spear
Staff
Taijiquan

Competitive Wushu is divided into the following areas:

1. Compulsory Fist and Weapon Forms.
2. Optional Barehand Routine: Either Long Fist, Taiji or Nanquan.
3. Optional Short and Long Weapon: Either Sword or Broadsword and either Spear or Staff.
4. Open Barehand Routine (from three categories):
   A. Internal Forms: Bagua, Xingyi or Baji.
   B. Northern Long-Arm Forms: Tongbei, Fanzi or Pigua.
   C. Ditang (Tumbling) and Imitative Forms: Mantis, Eagle, Drunken, etc.
5. Open Weapons Routine (from three categories):
   A. Taiji Sword, Kwan Dao, Monkey Staff, Long-Tasseled Sword, etc.
   B. Double Weapons: Swords, Broad-swords, Hooks, Daggers, etc.
   C. Flexible Weapons: Whip, Three-Section Staff, Rope Dart, etc.
6. Sparring Routine: Two- or Three-Person Sets, with or without weapons.

World Union of Karate-Do Organizations

Official Compulsory Forms

Bassai Sho
Bassai Dai; Passai
Kanku Sho; Kushinku; Kosokun Sho
Kanku Dai; Kushanku; Kosokun Dai
Gojoshinho; Gojushi Ho
Gankaku; Chinto
Hangetsu
Seisan; Seishan
Unsu; Unshu
Seipai
Saifa
Enpi; Wanshu
Niju Shiho; Nisei Shi
Seienchin
Jion
Jitte; Jutte
Suparenpei; Pipporin
Gojushiho Dai; Useishi
Rohai

CHAPTER 4

WEAPONS OF THE WORLD

This chapter contains 444 weapons from 10 countries. Many of these weapons are centuries old, but still practiced today by various martial artists around the world. For inclusion in this work, a weapon had to have an Asian basis.

CHINA

The original Shaolin style of kung-fu had eighteen basic weapons. Over the centuries an incredible array of different weapons were integrated into the practice of kung-fu. Today the number and scope of Chinese weapons is truly mind-boggling; as well, the most colorful names in all martial arts nomenclature have been attached to them. To dramatically demonstrate that color, I've included the English translation of the weapon wherever possible.

Kung-fu students, for the most part, are required to learn far more weapons than their karate counterparts. One instructor alone, John Allen of Ohio, for example, teaches 72 classical kung-fu weapons.

JAPAN

The hundreds of Japanese weapons fall into two categories, the ancient Kobu-jutsu and its twentieth-century counterpart, the Kobu-do. Japan was not nearly as prolific in number of weapons, and by no means as colorful in name as China. Nevertheless, the Japanese spawned many ingenious devices of war, many of which have been employed in the popular movies featuring ninja warriors.

FORMAT

Listings appear alphabetically by country of origin. Weapons are categorized in alphabetical order under the art in which they are practiced. Each art appears in bold letters. Subcategories of major weapons are added when known.

Grandmaster Kenwa Mabuni, founder of Shito-ryu karate, practicing a defense against the katana. Courtesy of karate Master Anthony Mirakian

CHINA

KUNG-FU; GUNG-FU; WU SHU

Baat Gaw Lance
Broadsword
Butterfly Double Knives (Bot Jum Do; Hu-Tieh Dau)
Cane
Centipede Hook (Wu-Gung-Go)
Cern-Do; Swang-Tao (Paired Broadswords)
Chian; Chiang; Ko; Mao (Spear)
Chien; Gim; Jyan; Jien (Sword, double-edged)
Chinese Hoops
Chinese Waterpipe
Cold Night Knife (single and double)
Cold Night Sword (single and double)
Convenient Shovel (Fang Bian Tsang)
Copper Hammer
Crippled Man's Crutch
Cross Plum Flower Pole (Sap Tse Mui Fa Kwun)
Darn-Do; Ta-Tao (Long-Handled Halberd)
Deer-Horn Knife
Double-Edge Sword
Double-End Whirling Staff
Double-Handed Saber (Tang-Lang Jyan)
Double-Headed Spear (Shuang-Tou Chiang)
Double-Headed Staff
Double-Hooking Sword (Hu-Tou-Gou; Shuang-Gou)
Double-Long Daggers
Double Yin-Yang Axes
Dragon Sticks
Dragon Sword
Eight Diagram Stick
"18" Staff
Eight Trigrams Knife
Elephant Trunk Sword
Emei Daggers
Enchanted Staff
Eyebrow Height Staff
Eyebrow Spear
Fan
Farmer's Hoe
Fay Tian-Chi
Fingernail Razors
Five Tiger Spear (Ng Fu Chueng)

Flute
Flying Claw
Flying Crane Sword (single and double)
Flying Fork
Flying Meteor
Flying Ring
Fong-Bin-Charn
Gahn
Ghost Hat Sword
Ghostly Phoenix Big Spear
Gisarme
Gold Coin Halberd
Gold Coin Knife
Gold Coin Spade
Gold Coin Wheels (Chin-Chien Yueh)
Golden Helon Hammer
Gong Tin Spear
Goose-Feather Saber
Grain Leaf Saber
Green Dragon Knife
Ground Rolling Double Sabers
Gu-Tang
Hand-Breaking Fan
Hero Big Fork
Hidden Shoe Razor
Hook and Crescent Sword (Fou-Tou-Ou)
Hook Spear
Horn Big Fork
Horn Twin Daggers
Horse Bench
Horse Leg-Chopping Sword
Horse-Chopper (Ja Ma Do)
Hurricane Double Axes
I-Mao (Lance)
Inward-Pointed Tiger Fork (Niou-Tour Cha)
Iron Circle
Iron Ruler
Iron Thread
Justice Brush (Pan-Gwai-Bi)
King Dragon Heart Piercing Pole (Wong Loong Tsun Sum Kwun)
Knife and Rattan Shield
Kwan-Tao; Kwan-Do
Kwun (Staff)
Lau Gar Stick
Liu-Po Spear
Long Staff
Lung Chuan Dau
Lung Chuan Jiann
Ma Do
Marshal's Spear

Meteor Hammer
Miao Dao
Mixed Gold Twin Daggers
Monk's Crescent Spade
Monk's Rake
Monk's Spade (Yueh-Ya-Chaan)
Nine-Dragon Trident (Gao-Loon Cha)
Nine-Ring Big Sword
Nine-Ring Knife
Nine-Section Whip
Ox-Tail Knife
Pa-Kua Circular Knives
Phoenix Sword
Pike
Pirate's Twin Daggers
Plum Blossom Double Hook Swords
Plum Flower Spear
Poison Snake Staff
Pressure Point Fan
Razor Coins
Red-Tasseled Spear
Rope Dart (Sheng Biao)
San-Chien Liang-Ren-Tao (Three-Pointed, Double-Bladed Sword)
San Ts'ai Chien Sword
Scepter (Ju-I)
Seagull Sword (Yan-Ling-Tao)
Seven Stars Knife
Seven Stars Sword
Shaolin Monk's Blade
Shaolin Staff
Shepherd Staff (Kuan Yeung Kuan)
Shooting Star Rope Dart
Short Ax (single and double)
Silk Reeling Spear
Sin Bin Crutch
Single-End Whirling Staff
Single-Hand Spear
Six-Direction Saber (Lok Hop Do)
Six-Pointed Staff (Look-Dim-Buen)
Sleeve Arrow; Sleeve Dart (Sui-Jian)
Smoking Pipe
Snake Spear; Snake-Tongue Spear
Southern Tiger Fork (Nan-Fang Dah-Pa)
Spinning Spear
Spear (Jyang)
Spread the Water Knife
Spring and Autumn Knife (Chuen-Chiou Dah-Do)
Staff
Staff with Chain

Steel Flute
Stiff-Jointed Iron Whip
Sun-Moon Crescent Sickle
Sun-Moon Crescent Swords
Tai-Chi Ruler
Tai Pah (Trident)
Tamo Cane
Tao (Knife, single-edged)
Ta-Shao-Dz
Thorn Staff
Three-Section Staff (San-Chieh-Pang; Sam-Jeet-Gwun; San-Jay-Kun; Sam-Chit-Kwan)
Three-, Five-, Seven-, Nine-, and Eleven-Section Steel Whip
Tiger Fork (Hu-Cha)
Tiger's Head Double Hooks (Hu Tou Kon)
Tiger Tail Broadsword
Titjio
Twin Dragons Double Knives
Two-Section Cudgel (short and long)
Tuan-Tang
Unicorn-Horn Knives (Lin-Jeau-Shuang Dau)
Vagabond Fork
Wah-Shan Ax
Waist Sword
Wai-Tieh Spear
Walking Dragon Pole (Lung Hung Kwan)
Waterpipe
Weeping Willow Knife
Whip Chain
White Ghost Knife
White Jade Fan
White Lotus Double Iron Crutch
White Lotus Double Iron Ruler
White Lotus Fan
White Tiger Knife
White Tiger Sword (Pai Hu Chien)
Willow Leaf Double Swords
Willow Leaf Knife (single and double)
Wind and Fire Wheels (Fung-Huo Lun)
Wolf Teeth Cudgel
Wooden Bench
Ying Cheong (Spear)
Yueh-Ya-Tsan

FRANCE

Canne (Walking Stick)

INDIA

KALARI PAYAT

Kettukari; Allvadi (Long Stick)
Muchann (Small Stick)
Outta; Otta (Elephant Tusk)
Puliyangam (Sword and Shield)
Urumi

MISCELLANEOUS

Gadka
Lathi
Vita

SILAMBAM

Kambu; Kuchu (Staff)
Lathi (Cane)
Madai
Podi Kuchi (Double Sticks)
Surul (Spring Sword)
Veal Kambu (Spear)

VAJRAMUSHTI

Vajramusti; Bajarmutha

INDONESIA

PENTJAK SILAT; PENCAK SILAT

Arbir
Arit
Atjeh Rentjang
Badik
Barong
Batak Kapak
Batak Raut
Beladau
Bulu Ajam
Celurit
Enhero
Gadubong
Gatka; Gadka
Golok
Gontar
Halasan
Hui-Tho
Jengok
Kalus
Kapa; Kapak
Karambit
Karis
Kelewang
Kowlium
Kris; Keris
Kris Bahari
Kris Balengko
Kris Majapahit

Kris Pangang
Kris Pichit
Kujang
Kujungi
Kujur; Kunjur
Kukri
Lading
Lajatang
Lambing
Lopu
Luris Pedang
Mandau
Paku
Parang; Belo; Belo-Leong
Pamor
Pedang
Pendjepit
Pentjong
Petjat
Petjut
Peudeueng
Piau
Pisau
Pisau Bilati
Plong
Pringapus
Puttha
Rante
Rante Ber Gangedug
Raut
Rentjong; Rencong
Roti Kalong
Rudus
Sabit
Sakin
Sanokat
Sarpa Lumaku
Segu
Sewar
Sikim Gala
Sjang Sutai
Sumping; Sumpit; Sumpitan
Tadji
Talwar
Tapak Kudak
Thinin
Tjabang
Tjaluk
Tjelurit
Todo
Tombak; Korung (Spear)
Tongkat; Gada; Gala
Tongkat Pemukul
Toya
Toyak

JAPAN

KO-BUJUTSU; KO-BUDO

Aikuchi (Dagger)
Bo (Staff)
    Shin-bo (Heart staff)
    Tsuki-bo
Bokken (Wooden Sword)
Chigiriki (Weighted Chain)
Chisa-Katana (Intermediate Sword)
Daito (Sword)
Ham-bo; Hanbo; Hon-bo (Half-staff)
Hasaku-bo (Wooden Spear)
Hoko
Jo (Staff)
Juken (Bayonet)
Jutte; Jitte; Jittei; Jutta (Iron Truncheon)
Kaiken (Short Knife)
Kanzashi (Hairpin)
Katana (Long Sword)
Keibo
Keiko-Naginata
Kodachi; Kogusoku (Small Sword)
Ko-Gatana
Konsaibo
Kusari; Gusari (Chain)
Kusari-Gama (Chained Sickle)
Manriki-Gusari; Kusari-Bundo; Ryo-Bundo; Sode-Kusari; Tama-Kusari; Kusari-Jutte (Weighted Chain)
Mitsu-Dogu
    Sasu-mata
    Sode-Garami
    Tsukubo
Nage-Gama (Javelin Sickle)
Naginata (Reaping Sword)
    Jumon-ji Naginata
    Nagemaki
    Ta-No-Saki
    Tsukushi-Naginata
Nakamaki
Nakazashi
Nippon-to (Saber)
No-Dachi; Dai-Katana (Long Sword)
O-Dachi (Great Sword)
Shinai (Bamboo Sword)
Sasumata
So (Spear)
Tachi (Sword)
Tambo; Tanbo (Short Stick)
Tanjo (Club)

Tanto (Dagger)
Tessen (Iron Fan)
Tetsubo (Iron Staff)
Tokushu Keibo (Short Wooden Club)
Tsurugi
Wakizashi (Short Sword)
Yari (Spear)
    Futamata-Yari
    Hoko-Yari
    Kagi-Yari
    Kama-Yari
    Magari-Yari
    Omi-Gari
    Sasumata-Yari
    Sode-Garami
    Su-Yari
    Tsukubo
    Tsukushi-Boko
Yawara Stick
Yumi (Bow)

NINJUTSU

Bisento
Fukiya
Fukumi-Bari
Hankyu
Hyakurai-Ju
Igadama
Kumade
Kusarifundo
Kyoketsu-Shoge
Metsubushi
Nage Teppo
Nekode
Ninja-To; Shinobi-gatana
Shaken
Shikomi-Zue
Shinobi-Kai
Shinobi-Zue
Shuko
Shuriken
Tekagi
Tetsu Bishi
Tonki
Yumi and Ya

KOREA

Bong (Staff)
Chong Bong (Long Staff)
Dan Bong
Joong Bong
Kum-Do
Yuk Gum (Inverted Sword)

MALAYSIA

Gayung (quarter staff)

OKINAWA

OKINAWAN KO-BUDO; OKINAWAN KO-BUJUTSU; BUKI-HO

The following list includes all ancient and modern weapons.

Bo; Rokushakubo (Staff)
Boar Spear
Chize Kun Bo; Chizikunbo
Eku (Oar)
Kama (Sickle)
Magodi Spear
Manji-No-Sai
Nunchaku (Flail)
    Han-Kei (Half-Size)
    Hjakakuei (Octagonal)
    Maru-Gat (Round)
    San-Setsu-Kon (Three-Piece)
    So-Setsu-Kon (Long-Short)
    Yon-Setsu-Kon (Four-Piece)
Nunte
Nuntembo
Rochin (Short Spear)
Rokushaku-bo (Halberd)
Rokushaku-kama
Sai (Short Sword)
Surushin (Weighted Chain)
Tanbo
Te Chu
Teko; Tetsu (Knuckleduster)
Tetko; Tek Chu (Iron Claw)
Tetsu
Timbei (Shield)
Tonfa; Tuifa; Ton-Kwa (Handle)
Zinkasa (Knife and Shield)

PHILIPPINES

ARNIS; ARNIS DE MANO; ESCRIMA; ESTOCADA; ESTOGUE; FRAILE; KALI; SINAWALI

Badik
Bahi
Balaraw Tapic
Balisong
Bangkcon
Banjal
Barong
Baston

Bidio
Bolo
Cane
Espada y Daga (Stick and Dagger;
    Sword and Dagger)
Garrote
Gayang
Gunong
Itak
Kabaroan Stick
Kalis
Kampilan (Sword)

Karasaik
Lahot
Laring
Lcampilan
Muton
Panabas
Panan-Tukan
Pingga
Pira
Punal
Serrada Sticks
Sinawali Sticks

Tabak
Utak
Yantok

UNITED STATES

Handler
Prosecutor (Billy Club–Tonfa
    Combination)
Side-Handle Baton

FAMOUS
MARTIAL ARTISTS

This section lists the recipients of every known Hall of Fame for martial arts and sports from 1968 to 1992. An aggressive attempt was made to collect a full list of recipients for every such award, but in some cases was genuinely impossible. Some Hall of Fame founders did not keep complete records of past recipients, and at least one such awards founder did not respond to my repeated requests for a full list of recipients.

Nevertheless, this is the first book to assemble between two covers all the Hall of Fame recipients covering a period of twenty-five years.

CHAPTER 5

HALLS OF FAME AND OTHER AWARDS

FORMAT

Each award appears in alphabetical order by title, from the "All American Open Hall of Fame" to the "Walt Bone Memorial Award." A brief introduction explains the status and significance of each award. The recipients are then listed from the most recent, i.e., 1992, to the earliest.

ALL AMERICAN OPEN HALL OF FAME (1977–91)

Founded in New York by tae kwon do pioneer S. Henry Cho in conjunction with his long-running tournament, the All American Open, this award is included here because in most cases it honors recipients outside of those who won the tournament. This condition gives it a much broader definition and status.

1991
Kim Soo
Sam Naples

1990
Chae Bok Rhee
Yeon Hee Park

1989
Suh Chong Kang
Peter Urban

Distinguished martial artists, most of whom went on to become Hall of Famers, gather at the 1964 Internationals in Long Beach, California. Front row, left to right: J. Pat Burleson, Bruce Lee, Anthony Mirakian, Jhoon Rhee. Back row, left to right: Allen Steen, George Mattson, Ed Parker, Tsutomu Ohshima, Robert Trias. Courtesy of Keith D. Yates

Don Nagle
Alan Lee

1988
Hyun Ok Shin
Chun Shik Kim

1987
Tae Kwon Do Times Magazine
Ronald Duncan

1986
Richard Chun
David Charney

1985
Y.J. Chang
B.M. Lee
Gary Alexander

1984
Madison Square Garden
Joe Hayes

1983
Moon Sung Lee
Ray Martin
Ron Van Clief

1982
Dong Keun Park
Ralph Chirico

1981
Il Joo Kim
Suk Jong Chung
Nick Adler

1980
Ki Chung Kim
Toyotaro Miyazaki
Bill Chung
Mike Warren

1979
Official Karate Magazine

1978
Rainbow Publications (*Black Belt*,
  Karate Illustrated magazines)

1977
Ki Whang Kim

BLACK BELT HALL OF FAME (1968–92)

Founded in Los Angeles by Mito
Uyehara, publisher of *Black Belt*
magazine, the Black Belt Hall of
Fame is considered the world's
most prestigious martial arts award.

MAN OF THE YEAR

Curtis Sliwa (1992)
Joe Mirza (1991)
Wally Jay (1990)
Hwang Kee (1989)
Daniel Lee (1988)
Tsutomu Ohshima (1987)
Richard Kim (1986)
George Anderson (1985)
In Hyuk Suh (1984)
Jhoon Rhee (1983)
Teruyuki Okazaki (1982)
Roy Kurban (1981)
Hidy Ochiai (1980)
(No selection for 1979)
Bill Wallace (1978)
Chuck Norris (1977)
Ed Parker (1976)
Fumio Demura (1975)
Bruce Lee (1974)
Ernest Lieb (1973)
Dan Ivan (1972)

S. Henry Cho (1971)
Eichi Koiwai (1970)
Sam Allred (1969)
Frank Fullerton (1968)

WOMAN OF THE YEAR

Danielle Laney, Lynette Love,
  Diane Murray, Terry Poindexter
  (1992)
Kathy Long (1991)
Karyn Turner (1990)
Graciela Casillas (1989)
Dana Hee, Arlene Limas, Lynette
  Love (1988)
Lisa Sliwa (1987)

COMPETITOR OF THE YEAR

Herb Perez, Juan Moreno, Mari
  Kotaka (1992)
Chip Wright, Hosung Pak, Edna
  Lima (1991)
Michael Bernardo, Tsuyoshi
  Ishigami, Debbie Tang (1990)
Kevin Thompson, Christine
  Bannon, Ferdie Allas (1989)
Jimmy Kim (1988)
Dae Sung Lee, Lisa Kozak (1987)
Charlie Lee (1986)
Keith Hirabayashi (1985)
Arlene Limas (1984)
George Chung, Cynthia Rothrock
  (1983)
Steve Anderson, John Chung (1982)
Keith Vitali (1981)
Linda Denley (1980)
Ray McCallum (1979)
Benny Urquidez (1978)
Bill Wallace (1977)
Jeff Smith (1976)
Joe Lewis (1975)
Howard Jackson (1974)
Bill Wallace (1973)
Joe Hayes (1972)
Mike Stone (1971)
Ron Marchini (1970)
Thomas LaPuppet (1969)
Chuck Norris (1968)

INSTRUCTOR OF THE YEAR

Osamu Ozawa (1992)
Adriano Emperado (1991)
Takayuki Mikami (1990)
Hee Il Cho, Richard Bustillo (1989)

Ralph Castro, Steven Seagal (1988)
Ray Dalke, Arsenio Advincula
  (1987)
Joe Lewis, Masaaki Hatsumi (1986)
Stephen Hayes (1985)
Steve Sanders (1984)
Dan Inosanto (1983)
Remy Presas (1982)
Ernie Reyes, Sr. (1981)
Chuck Merriman (1980)
Richard Chun, Hidy Ochiai, Ed
  Parker, Lily Siou (1979)
Ken Funakoshi, Alan Lee (1978)
Al Dacascos, Glenn Keeney (1977)
Jay T. Will (1976)
Chuck Norris (1975)
Gary Alexander, Bucksam Kong
  (1974)
Richard Kim (1973)
Gosei Yamaguchi (1972)
Bob Yarnall (1971)
Ki Whang Kim, Ark Y. Wong (1970)
Fumio Demura (1969)
Tsutomu Ohshima (1968)

FULL-CONTACT FIGHTER OF THE YEAR

Kathy Long (1992)
Jerry Rhome (1986)
Brad Hefton (1985)
Don Wilson (1984)
Jean-Yves Theriault (1983)

KUNG-FU ARTIST OF THE YEAR

Richard Brandon (1992)
Doc-Fai Wong (1991)
Seng Jeong Au (1990)
Paulie Zink (1989)
Chan Pui (1988)
Ark Yuey Wong (1987)
Eric Lee (1986)
Adam Hsu (1985)
Brendan Lai (1984)
William Cheung (1983)
Roger Tung (1982)
Anthony Chan (1980)

JUDO INSTRUCTOR OF THE YEAR

Gene LeBell (1991)
Paul Maruyama (1983)
Yoshisada Yonezuka (1982)
Jack Williams (1981)
Ed Maley (1980)

Charles Chaves (1979)
Jimmy Pedro (1978)
Hayward Nishioka (1977)
Shag Okada (1976)
Willie Cahill (1975)
Pat Burris (1974)
Sachio Ashida (1973)
Taizo Sone (1972)
George Harris (1971)
George Wilson (1970)
Masato Tamura (1969)
Kiro Nagano (1968)

JUDO COMPETITOR OF THE YEAR

Jason Morris (1992)
Lynn Roethke (1989)
Kevin Asano (1988)
Eddie Liddie (1985)
Bob Berland (1984)
Leo White (1983)
Mike Swain (1982)
Jimmy Martin (1981)
Steve Seck (1980)
Brett Barron (1979)
Irwin Cohen (1978)
Allen Coage (1977)
Pat Burris (1976)
Tommy Martin (1975)
Karl Geis (1974)
Jim Bregman (1973)
Doug Graham (1972)
Paul Maruyama (1971)
Allen Coage (1970)
Ben Campbell (1969)
Hayward Nishioka (1968)

BLACK BELT HONORARY AWARD

Shogo Kuniba (1992)
Ed Parker (1990)
Robert Trias (1989)
William Chow (1988)
Masatoshi Nakayama (1987)
Ronald McNair (1986)
Demetrius Havanas (1983)

MISCELLANEOUS

Floro Villabrille, Weapons
   Instructor of the Year (1992)
Angel Cabales, Weapons Instructor
   of the Year (1991)
Takayuki Kubota, Weapons
   Instructor of the Year (1990)
Dan Inosanto, Weapons Instructor
   of the Year (1988)

Tadashi Yamashita, Weapons
   Expert of the Year (1987)
Tsutomu Ohshima, Publisher's
   Award (1979)
Robert Trias, *Black Belt* Editor's
   Award (1979)
Jhoon Rhee, *Karate Illustrated*
   Editor's Award (1979)
Chuck Norris, *Fighting Stars*
   Editor's Award (1979)
Bong Soo Han, Hapkido (1978)
Dan Inosanto, Jeet Kune Do (1977)
Marshall Ho'o, Tai Chi Chuan
   (1973)
Bruce Lee, Jeet Kune Do (1972)
Maki Miyahara, Kendo; Yoshimitsu
   Yamada, Aikido (1971)
Shinichi Suzuki, Aikido (1970)
Koichi Tohei and Yukiso
   Yamamoto, Aikido; Wally Jay,
   Jujutsu (1969)
Shuji Makami, Kendo (1968)

FLORIDA AFFILIATION OF MARTIAL ARTS EVENTS (FAME) HALL OF FAME (1986–92)

The FAME is a statewide organization of promoters whose purpose is to promote and support professional sport karate events and crown state champions. Each year it honors one accomplished individual who does not necessarily reside in the state of Florida.

1992
Steve Anderson

1991
John Pachivas

1990
John Prevatt

1989
Bill Wallace

1988
Mike Green

1987
Earl Harris & Bill Slinker

1986
Joe Lewis

THE "GOLDEN FIST" AWARDS (1973 & 1974)

A short-lived award conceived by retired national karate champion Mike Stone to honor outstanding California martial artists, the first event at which the Golden Fist Award was presented was produced by Stone on February 1, 1973, and the second by Stone and Stuart Sobel on March 14, 1974. The inaugural Golden Fist Awards also recognized those who had made earlier significant contributions to the arts and the sport.

The banquets at which these awards were presented were high-class affairs distinguished by formal attire and a host of Hollywood celebrities in attendance to present them.

1974

Best All-Around Competitor
Steve Fisher

Most Exciting Competitor
Benny Urquidez

Outstanding Weapons Kata
Ted Tabura

Outstanding Women's Kata
Beverly Romero (hard style)
April Hiraki (soft style)

Outstanding Men's Kata
Glen Rabago (hard style)
Albert Leong (soft style)

Best Tournament of the Year
International Karate
   Championships

Best Officials
Arnold Urquidez
Steve Sanders
Pat Johnson

Journalism Award
Official Karate Magazine

1973

Outstanding Chinese-Style Instructor
Steve Sanders

Outstanding Japanese-Style Instructor
Ron Marchini

Outstanding Korean-Style Instructor
Chuck Norris

Outstanding Okinawan-Style Instructor
Side Campbell

Outstanding Work with Children
Soloman Kaihewalu

Outstanding Tournament Officials
Fumio Demura
Soloman Esquivel
Pat Johnson
Ron Marchini
Tadashi Yamashita

Outstanding Demonstration
Tadashi Yamashita

Best Defensive Fighter
Ron Marchini (1966–70)
Ernest Russell (1971–73)

Best Offensive Fighter
Joe Lewis (1966–70)
John Natividad (1971–73)

Outstanding Chinese Forms Competitor
Al Dacascos (1966–70)
Eric Lee (1971–73)

Outstanding Japanese–Okinawan Forms Competitor
John Pereira (1966–70)
Steve Fisher (1971–73)

Outstanding Korean Forms Competitor
Chuck Norris (1966–70)
Byong Yu (1971–73)

Outstanding Weapons Competitor
Eric Lee

Outstanding Women's Fighting Competitor
Malia Dacascos (1966–70)
Mikie Rowe (1971–73)

Outstanding Women's Form Competitor
Malia Dacascos (1966–70)
Marlene Schumann (1971–73)

Pioneers of West Coast Karate
Dan Ivan
Hidetaka Nishiyama
Tsutomu Ohshima
Ed Parker

Magazine Award
Mito Uyehara (*Black Belt*)

Current National Fighters Award
Darnell Garcia
Howard Jackson

Best All-Around Female Competitor
Malia Dacascos (1966–70)
Marlene Schumann (1971–73)

Best All-Around Male Competitor
Chuck Norris (1966–70)
Byong Yu (1971–73)

THE "GOLDEN GREEK" AWARDS (1988)

Each year the Amateur Organization of Karate, a prominent Texas tournament-circuit sanctioning body, presents the "Golden Greek" Awards in honor of the late, great Demetrius "Golden Greek" Havanas, one of Texas's all-time great karate champions. Havanas was killed in a tragic plane crash on July 24, 1981, en route to a kickboxing event in Atlantic City, New Jersey.

At press time, only the recipients of the 1988 awards were available. Ishmael Robles, founder of the awards, attempted unsuccessfully to reconstruct a list of recipients. Regrettably, he reports that no records were kept of past recipients.

Black Belt Male
Brice Anthony (1988)

Black Belt Female
Alinda Maxwell (1988)

Junior Black Belt
Eva Ramerez (1988)

SPECIAL RECOGNITION
Male of the Year
Carlo Falco (1988)

Female of the Year
Aide Ramirez (1988)

Official of the Year
Brice Anthony (1988)

Instructor of the Year
Al Garza (1988)

Tournament of the Year
Hurricane Nationals (1988)

INSIDE KARATE HALL OF FAME (1983–89)

This award was created by Curtis Wong, publisher of *Inside Karate* magazine, *Inside Kung Fu's* sister publication, in the mid-1980s. Unfortunately, a full list of recipients was not available at press time.

OUTSTANDING CONTRIBUTIONS
1989
Jhoon Rhee

1988
Hee Il Cho

1984
Tsutomu Ohshima
Jhoon Rhee
Peter Urban
Jay T. Will

1983
Joe Lewis
Chuck Norris
Benny Urquidez
Bill Wallace

MAN OF THE YEAR
Jean-Claude Van Damme (1989)
Samuel Kuoha (1988)

WOMAN OF THE YEAR
Karyn Turner (1989)
Arlene Limas (1988)

INSTRUCTOR OF THE YEAR
Tae Yun Kim (1989)

Takayuki Kubota (1988)

COMPETITOR OF THE YEAR
Fighting

1984

Steve Anderson
Linda Denley

1983

Steve Anderson
Arlene Limas

Forms

1984

John Chung

1983

George Chung

Overall

Kevin Thompson (1989)
Jean Frenette (1988)

ARTICLE OF THE YEAR
"Training in Japan" by Dave
   Lowry (1989)
"The Infantilization of the Martial
   Arts" by Shirotatsu Nakamichi
   (1988)

INSIDE KUNG-FU HALL OF FAME (1982–93)

Founded in 1982 by Curtis Wong,
publisher of *Inside Kung Fu* magazine, this award was originally created to pay particular attention to
Chinese stylists, but in recent years
has blossomed into an indus-
trywide institution. Unfortunately, a
full list of recipients was not available at press time.

MAN OF THE YEAR

David Carradine (1993)
Jean-Claude Van Damme (1992)
Brendan Lai (1991)
Dr. Jwing Yang Ming (1990)
James McNeal (1989) ('90
   Honorable Mention)
Bruce Lee (1988)

WOMAN OF THE YEAR

Linda Lee (1993)

Kathy Long (1992)
Gini Lau (1991)
Cynthia Rothrock (1990); Chavela
   Aaron (Honorable Mention)
Arlene Limas (1988)

HUMANITARIAN OF THE YEAR

Glenn Wilson's Kung Fu Academy
   (1993)
Blinky Rodriguez (1992)
Chuck Norris (1991)
Sam Kuoha (1990)
James P. Lacy (1988)

INSTRUCTOR OF THE YEAR

Al Dacascos (1993)
Tat-Mau Wong (1992)
Blinky and Lily Rodriguez (1991)
Jimmy H. Woo (1990)
Joe Pina ('90 Honorable Mention)
William Cheung; Leung Ting (1988)
Adam Hsu (1984)
Ark Y. Wong (1983)
Chan Poi (1982)

WUSHU PERFORMER OF THE YEAR

Yu Shao-Wen, Li Xia, Dong Hong
   Lin, Zhou Jing-Ping (1984)
Anthony Chan (1983)
Don Yen (1982)

MALE COMPETITOR OF THE YEAR

Kevin Thompson (1990)
Christine Bannon ('90 Honorable
   Mention)
Keith Hirabayashi (1983)
Paulie Zink (1982)

FEMALE COMPETITOR OF THE YEAR

Arlene Limas (1983)
Cynthia Rothrock (1982)

COMPETITOR OF THE YEAR
Overall

Jason Yee (1993)
Christine Bannon-Rodrigues (1992)
Scott Parker (1991)
Alice Chang (1988)

KENPO INSTRUCTOR OF THE YEAR

Larry Tatum (1984)
Jay T. Will (1983)
Ed Parker (1982)

READERS' AWARD

Lew Illar (1983)
Nick Cerio (1982)

NEWCOMER OF THE YEAR

Jason Scott Lee (1993)
Brandon Lee (1992)
Qiuying Feng (1991)
John R. Allen (1990); Pixie Elmore
   (Honorable Mention)
Gene Chicoine (1988)

WRITER OF THE YEAR

Jane Hallander (1993)
Dr. John P. Painter (1992)
Lilia Howe (1990); John R. Allen,
   Glenn Hart (Honorable Mention)
William Barrett (1988)

OUTSTANDING CONTRIBUTION

John Paul Jones Dejoria (1993)
Phillip Starr (1992)
Dan Inosanto (1991)
Ed Parker (1989)
Robert Trias (1988)

KARATE/KUNG FU ILLUSTRATED'S AWARD FOR EXCELLENCE (1987)

This was a short-lived award, created by *Black Belt's* sister publication, that concentrated chiefly on
martial athletes.

COMPETITOR OF THE YEAR

Terry Creamer (1987)

RUNNER-UP
Keith Hirabayashi (1987)

MALE FIGHTER OF THE YEAR

Steve Anderson (1987)

FEMALE FIGHTER OF THE YEAR

Linda Denley (1987)

FORMS COMPETITOR OF THE YEAR

Keith Hirabayashi (1987)

WEAPONS COMPETITOR OF THE YEAR

Keith Hirabayashi (1987)

ROOKIE OF THE YEAR

Phillip Wong (1987)

NORTH AMERICAN SPORT KARATE ASSOCIATION'S (NASKA) HALL OF FAME (1990–92)

The NASKA is North America's foremost sanctioning body for open sport karate tournaments. Its prestigious annual Hall of Fame and Outstanding Achievement Awards was founded in 1990; the awards are presented in first-class fashion at a fancy awards banquet.

HALL OF FAME

Mike Stone (1992)
Ed Parker (1991)
George Chung (1990)
John Chung (1990)
Pat Johnson (1990)
Joe Lewis (1990)
Chuck Norris (1990)
Ernie Reyes, Sr. (1990)
Jeff Smith (1990)
Bill Wallace (1990)

OUTSTANDING ACHIEVEMENT AWARDS

OVERALL EXCELLENCE

MAN OF THE YEAR

Steve Anderson (1990)

WOMAN OF THE YEAR

Arlene Limas (1990)

ROOKIE OF THE YEAR—MALE

Saeed Delkash & Mike Smith (1990)

ROOKIE OF THE YEAR—FEMALE

Cindy Ingram & Laurie McCutcheon (1990)

ROOKIE OF THE YEAR—YOUTH

Tiffany Costello (1990)

BLACK BELT FIGHTING

FIGHTING COMPETITOR OF THE YEAR—MALE

Hakim Alston (1990)

FIGHTING COMPETITOR OF THE YEAR—FEMALE

Chavela Aaron (1990)

FIGHTING COMPETITOR OF THE YEAR—YOUTH

Robert Hendricks (1990)

BLACK BELT FORMS

FORMS COMPETITOR OF THE YEAR—MALE

Charlie Lee (1990)

FORMS COMPETITOR OF THE YEAR—FEMALE

Yungchu Kim (1990)

FORMS COMPETITOR OF THE YEAR—YOUTH

Jon Valera (1990)

BLACK BELT WEAPONS

COMPETITOR OF THE YEAR—MALE

Mike Bernardo (1990)

COMPETITOR OF THE YEAR—FEMALE

Kathy Quan (1990)

COMPETITOR OF THE YEAR—YOUTH

Jeff Sue (1990)

UNDER BLACK BELT

COMPETITOR OF THE YEAR—ADULT

Rob Tirollo (1990)

COMPETITOR OF THE YEAR—YOUTH

Nick Boccagno (1990)

DEMONSTRATIONS

GROUP PERFORMANCE OF THE YEAR

George Chung & the California Surfers, Diamond Nationals (1990)

INDIVIDUAL PERFORMANCE OF THE YEAR

Roy Williams, U.S. Open (1990)

PROMOTION

PROMOTER OF THE YEAR

Joe Corley (1990)

TOURNAMENT OF THE YEAR

Diamond Nationals (1990)

NIGHTTIME SHOW OF THE YEAR

Diamond Nationals (1990)

SPORTSMANSHIP

SPORTSMAN OF THE YEAR

Mike Bernardo (1990)

SPORTSWOMAN OF THE YEAR

Elsa Cordero & Kathy Quan (1990)

SPORTSYOUTH OF THE YEAR

Mike Chaturantabut & Jennifer Yanoff (1990)

OFFICIAL KARATE MAGAZINE'S LEGION OF HONOR (1979–86)

Founded by Al Weiss, publisher of *Official Karate* magazine, this award spanned 1979–86 and named general recipients without specific categorization.

1986
William K. S. Chow
Phil Koeppel
Chuck Merriman
Jay Trombley
Frank Van Lenten

1985
Edward Brown
Bill Dometrich
Takayuki Kubota
Bill McDonald
John Monczak
Masami Tsuroka

1984
David Barber
Roger Carpenter
Fumio Demura
Mike DePasquale, Sr.
John Nanay

1983
Larry Black
Adriano Emperado
Roger Greene
Fred Hamilton
Mike McNamara

1982
Demetrius Havanas
He-Young Kimm
Toyotaro Miyazaki
Tom Schlesinger
John Townsley
Keith Vitali

1981

Richard Chun
Steve Fisher
George Minshew
Parker Shelton
Jeff Smith

1980

Gary Alexander
Sam Chapman
Roy Kurban
Benny Urquidez
John Worley
Pat Worley

1979

Bruce Lee
Steve Armstrong
S. Henry Cho
Joe Corley
Mike Foster
Glenn Keeney
Jim Harrison
Joe Lewis
Chuck Norris
Ed Parker
Moses Powell
Jhoon Rhee
Allen Steen
Robert Trias
Peter Urban
Bill Wallace

PROFESSIONAL KARATE LEAGUE (PKL) HALL OF FAME (1988 & 1989)

Starting in the late 1980s, the PKL, a sanctioning body for American sport karate tournaments, created a hall of fame for its membership. Although I made a genuine attempt to collect a full list of these recipients from the PKL president, nothing was received by press time. All that could be found in research were parts of 1988 and 1989.

MALE COMPETITOR OF THE YEAR

Charlie Lee (1989)

FEMALE COMPETITOR OF THE YEAR

Chavela Aaron (1989)

BEST TOURNAMENT

Battle of Baltimore (1989)

COACH OF THE YEAR

Ed Budd (1989)
Chuck Merriman (1988)

MAN OF THE YEAR

Nick Cerio (1989)
John Duess (1988)

WOMAN OF THE YEAR

Lil Hasselman (1988)

PROMOTER OF THE YEAR

Don Rodrigues (1988)

PROFESSIONAL KARATE MAGAZINE HALL OF FAME (1973–75)

Founded by Mike Anderson, publisher of the short-lived but critically acclaimed *Professional Karate* magazine, this award paid tribute almost exclusively to the greatest sport karate champions.

Mike Stone
Joe Lewis
AlGene Caraulia
Bruce Lee
Byong Yu
Bill Wallace
Jhoon Rhee
Jim Harrison

THE STAR SYSTEM HALL OF FAME (1971–88)

The STAR (Standardized Tournaments and Ratings) System debuted as tournament rankings in the March 1980 issue of *Inside Kung Fu* magazine, while the world kickboxing rankings premiered a few months later as part of *Kick Illustrated* (now *Inside Karate* magazine). Eventually it focused solely on kickboxing and appeared regularly in more than fifty publications around the world, making it the most widespread literature in martial arts history.

The STAR System was created by journalists Paul Maslak and John Corcoran to rate fighters impartially in the same way that prominent players are rated in other professional individual and team sports. Cofounder Maslak solely carried on the STAR System from 1981 to January 1988, and for eight years it reigned as the world's premier kickboxing ratings. Each year it named recipients from every aspect of kickboxing to its comprehensive sport-oriented Hall of Fame, and included retrospective recognition for distinguished pioneers of the sport beginning in 1971.

FIGHTER OF THE YEAR

1988

Don Wilson (USA)

   RUNNERS-UP

   Christian Battesti (USA)
   Branimir Cikatic' (Yugoslavia)
   Troy Dorsey (USA)
   Rob Kamen (Holland)

1987

Pete Cunningham (Canada)
John Moncayo (USA)
Fred Royers (Holland)
Richard Sylla (France)

   RUNNERS-UP

   John Longstreet (USA)
   Jerry Rhome (USA)
   Rik van de Vathorst (Holland)

1986

Brad Hefton (USA)
Maurice Smith (USA)
Youssef Zenaf (France)

   RUNNERS-UP

   Ricky Haines (USA)
   Jerry Rhome (USA)
   Fred Royers (Holland)
   Benny Urquidez (USA)

1985

Rob Kamen (Holland)
Jean-Yves Theriault (Canada)
Don Wilson (USA)

RUNNERS-UP
Branimir Cikatic' (Yugoslavia)
Youssef Zenaf (France)

1984
Don Wilson (USA)

RUNNERS-UP
Pete Cunningham (Canada)
Anthony Elmore (USA)
Ron Kamen (Holland)
Jean-Yves Theriault (Canada)

1983
Alvin Prouder (USA)

RUNNER-UP
John Moncayo

1982
Graciela Casillas (USA)
Steve Sheperd (USA)
Jean-Yves Theriault (Canada)

1981
Bill Wallace (USA)

1980
Benny Urquidez (USA)

1979
Gordon Franks (USA)

1978
Benny Urquidez (USA)
Bill Wallace (USA)

1977
Benny Urquidez (USA)

1976
Jeff Smith (USA)
Benny Urquidez (USA)

1975
Isaias Duenas (Mexico)
Joe Lewis (USA)
Jeff Smith (USA)
Benny Urquidez (USA)
Bill Wallace (USA)

1974
Vacant

1973
Vacant

1972
Joe Lewis (USA)

1971
Joe Lewis (USA)

TRAINER–COACH OF THE YEAR

1988
Master Toddy (England)

1987
Thom Harinck (Holland)

1986
John Monczak (USA)

1985
Brooks Mason (USA)

1984
Jan Plas (Holland)

1983
Bill Packer (USA)

1982
Julio Flores (USA)

1981
Demetrius Havanas (USA)

1980
Hap Holloway (USA)

1979
Asa Gordon (USA)

1978
Toshio Kaneda (Japan)

1977
Arnold Urquidez (USA)

1976
Arnold Urquidez (USA)

1975
Joey Orbillo (USA)

1974
Vacant

1973
"Atlas" Jesse King (USA)

1972
Joey Orbillo (USA)

1971
Bruce Lee (USA)

**GREATEST BEHIND-THE-SCENES
CONTRIBUTORS**

1988
Karyn Turner (Promoter)
John Worley (Promoter)
Mike Sawyer (Promoter)

1987
Jim Abernethy (Financier)
Joe Corley (Promoter)
Toshio Kaneda (Financier/
    Matchmaker)

1986
Steve Bornstein (Cable TV
    Executive)

1985
Don Wilson (Kickboxer)
Jean-Yves Theriault (Kickboxer)

1984
Fred Royers (Kickboxer/Journalist)

1983
Ted Kopplar (TV Executive)
Renardo Barden (Editor)

1982
John Corcoran (Editor/Author)

1981
Richard Auerback (TV Executive)
Al Weiss (Publisher)
Alan Paul (Editor)
Bob Jones (Promoter)

1980
Barry Frank (TV Executive)
Joe Corley (Promoter)

1979
Thom Harinck (Promoter)
Jan Plas (Promoter)
Count Pierre Baruzy (Financier)
Jerome Canabate, Sr. (Promoter)

1978
Howard Hanson (Promoter)
Eiichi Kamimura (Promoter)
Stuart Goldman (Journalist)

1977

Al Weiss (Publisher)
John Corcoran (Journalist)

1976

Don Quine (Promoter)
Judy Quine (Promoter)
Chuck Norris (Promoter)
Tommy Lee (Promoter)
Mito Uyehara (Publisher/
    Promoter)
George Bruckner (Promoter)
Ennio Falsoni (Promoter)
Mike Anderson (Promoter)
Aaron Banks (Promoter)
Kenji Kurosaki (Promoter)

1975

Tom Tannanbaum (TV Executive)
Mike Anderson (Promoter)
Joe Lewis (Kickboxer)

1972–74

Vacant

1971

Joe Lewis (Kickboxer)
Lee Faulkner (Promoter)

TAEKWONDO TIMES HALL OF FAME (1988–90)

Created by *Tae Kwon Do Times* magazine, this award focused on successful individuals chiefly involved in the Korean martial arts. It was discontinued after three years, but in 1993 editor Rod Speidel was hopeful of resuming it in the near future.

MAN OF THE YEAR

Cheong Woo Lee (1990)
Gen. Choi Hong Hi (1989)
Dr. Un Yong Kim (1988)

INSTRUCTOR OF THE YEAR

Hee Il Cho (1990)
Dae Sup An (1989)
Dong Won Kang (1988)

SCHOOL OF THE YEAR

Cheung's Tae Kwon Do Center:
    Brampton, Ont., Canada (1990)
Yung Ho's Tae Kwon Do: Tampa,
    Florida (1989)

COMPETITOR OF THE YEAR

Professional Fighter

Troy Dorsey (1989)
John Longstreet (1988)

Male Amateur

Juan Moreno (1990)
Jay Warwick (1989)
Herbert Perez (1988)

Female Amateur

Anita Silsby (1990)
Lynette Love (1989)
Arlene Limas (1988)

Male Forms

John Godwin (1990)
Nguyen Phuoc (1989)
Mike Winegar (1988)

Female Forms

Kristy Connor (1990)
Susan Park (1989)
Cheryl Zaccagnini (1988)

YOUTH OF THE YEAR

Male

Ernie Reyes, Jr. (1988)

Female

Kristin Boyer (1988)

FOREIGN INSTRUCTOR OF THE YEAR

Dave Oliver (1988)

READER'S CHOICE AWARD

S.R. Mooreland (1990)

James Dussault (1989)
Maurice Elmalem (1988)

SPECIAL RECOGNITION

Dae Sung Lee (1990)

THE WALT BONE MEMORIAL AWARD (1984–92)

Named after the late martial artist and transplanted Texan who left a lasting impression on west central Florida martial arts, this annual award is administered by John Graden, Bone's senior black belt, and is presented to martial artists who have had a sizable impact on martial arts in Florida.

Starting in 1987, the award was presented to those who had a "national" impact on the martial arts, whether or not they resided in Florida. Since 1990 it has been presented at the prestigious U.S. Open International Karate Championships in Orlando, Florida.

1992
Kathy Marlor

1991
Hiatus

1990
Bill Wallace

1989
John Corcoran

1988
Joe Lewis

1987
Mike Sawyer

1986
Herbie Thompson

1985
Mike Green

1984
John Pachivas

CHAPTER 6

BIRTH AND DEATH DATES

Here in the first part of this chapter you will find 323 birth dates of prominent martial arts masters, film stars and champions. Exact dates appear in almost all cases except where they were virtually impossible to obtain; sometimes only the month and year could be found.

This chapter also features 125 years of birth and death for famous martial artists of the past. Here, precise dates were almost impossible to obtain, particularly since the eminent masters listed go back as far as the sixteenth century. Further, the life span of some prominent masters of the past are subject to multiple opinions, even from renowned historians.

Perhaps the worst-case scenario I encountered was for Okinawan karate master Sokon Matsumura. There were *four* contradictory dates. For each date I initially checked my earlier definitive work, *The Original Martial Arts Encyclopedia*, a book containing one thousand biographies and first published in 1983. A number of the dates for Okinawan masters published in that book were submitted by or taken from the works of Master Richard Kim, one of the martial arts' premier historians.

Two of the greatest fighters in their respective sports: karate's Joe Lewis (left) and boxing's Muhammad Ali. Photo by Ed Ikuta; courtesy of the John Corcoran Archives

So, after consulting the encyclopedia, I placed after Matsumura's name the following dates: (1797–1889). Then, as I undertook new research, I found the following dates submitted by the following people: Okinawan goju-ryu karate master Anthony Mirakian placed Matsumura 1805–93; Shotokan karate master Hidetake Nishiyama had it 1808–95; and Shorin-ryu karate historian Jerry Gould offered (1792–1884). These three masters are competent historians from diverse backgrounds, but not one of them agree.

To solve this problem, I have maintained the original dates that appeared in *The Original Martial Arts Encyclopedia*. I will correct any inaccurate dates in future editions of this book when convincing evidence to the contrary is presented.

People die unexpectedly and "contemporary" martial artists can literally become "late" martial artists overnight. Many times, too, a distinguished though low-profile foreign master can die, say, in Japan, and nobody outside of a handful of devoted disciples will be aware of it until months later. It is difficult to obtain exact dates of death, and the level of difficulty increases as time passes.

Many of these accomplished individuals, past and present, have made an impact in more than one area; most have had a major influence in several martial arts activities. In the interest of brevity, however, I have limited the identification line to the activity for which they are—or were—renowned.

All champions listed are no less than *national* champions, meaning they are or have been ranked in national top ten ratings polls or have won major tournaments. World champions are designated as such where appropriate. Note, too, that current champions can retire overnight; some have been known to oscillate interminably. Thus I have not defined anyone as a "former" champion.

FORMAT

All listings are in alphabetical order by last name.

CONTEMPORARY MASTERS, CHAMPIONS AND PERSONALITIES

Aaron, Chavela (Oct. 18, 1963)
American Semi-Contact Karate
Champion
Adkins, Caylor (May 15, 1934)
Former Chairman, AAU
Karate Committee
Akamine, Eisuke (May 1, 1925)
Okinawan Kobudo Master
Alexander, Gary (Feb. 12, 1938)
American Karate Pioneer
Alexio, Dennis (March 19, 1959)
American World Kickboxing
Champion
Ali, Muhammad (Jan. 17, 1942)
"The Greatest" Boxer of All
Time
Anderson, Steve (March 29, 1955)
American World Semi-Contact
Champion
Arakaki, Seiki (Dec. 1, 1923)
Okinawan Shorin-ryu Karate
Master
Babcock, Steve (May 1, 1964)
American WAKO National
Karate Champion
Baker, Greg (Feb. 7, 1965)
American Tae Kwon Do
Champion
Banks, Aaron (Aug. 12, 1928)
American Martial Arts Pioneer
Bannon-Rodrigues, Christine (Nov. 6, 1966)
American Karate World Forms
& Weapons Champion
Baptista, Rich (Jan. 20, 1953)
American Sport Karate
Promoter
Barefield, Richard (Sept. 29, 1965)
Member, WAKO American
World Championship Karate
Team
Beasley, Jerry (Dec. 7, 1950)
American Martial Arts Author
& Writer
Bernardo, Mike (May 28, 1964)
Canadian Karate Weapons
Champion
Blanck, Gerry (Aug. 22, 1954)
American World Kickboxing
Champion

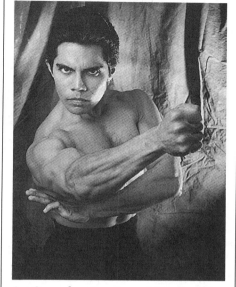

Art Camacho. Courtesy of Art Camacho

Blanks, Billy (Sept. 1, 1955)
American Semi-Contact Karate
Champion
Bobrow, Mitch (Dec. 28, 1950)
American Karate Champion
Brandon, Richard (Sept. 28, 1963)
American WAKO World
Weapons Champion
Brown, Dennis (Jan. 16, 1948)
American Sport Karate
Promoter
Bruno, Emilio (Aug. 30, 1914)
American Judo Pioneer
Buell, Martin (Aug. 3, 1942)
American Karate Coach
Burleson, J. Pat (April 27, 1936)
American Karate Pioneer &
Champion
Butin, Jim (Aug. 24, 1949)
American Semi-Contact Karate
Champion
Camacho, Art (June 3, 1960)
Martial Arts Movie
Choreographer
Campbell, Ben (April 13, 1933)
American Judo Coach &
Champion
Campbell, Sid (Sept. 29, 1944)
American Karate-do Pioneer
Canabate, Jerome (May 26, 1959)
Swiss World Kickboxing
Champion

Caraulia, AlGene (Dec. 22, 1940)
American Karate Pioneer &
Champion
Carnahan, Larry (Oct. 30, 1949)
American Sport Karate
Administrator
Carpenter, Roger (Dec. 21, 1940)
American Karate Pioneer
Carradine, David (Dec. 8, 1936)
American Actor & Kung-Fu
Expert
Casamassa, Chris (Jan. 17, 1965)
American National Forms
Champion
Casamassa, Louis (May 3, 1940)
American Karate Master
Casillas, Graciela (Aug. 22, 1956)
American Kickboxing
Champion
Castellanos, Ralph (Feb. 24, 1935)
American Kenpo Karate
Master
Castro, Ralph (Dec. 30, 1931)
American Kenpo Karate
Pioneer & Master
Cerio, Nick (July 9, 1936)
American Karate Pioneer
Chan, Jackie (April 17, 1954)
Chinese Martial Arts Film Star

Graciela Casillas. Courtesy of George Foon

Master Hee Il Cho. Courtesy of George Foon

Chang, Alice Chung (Jan. 6, 1963)
Chinese-Canadian Forms & Weapons Champion
Cheung, William (Oct. 10, 1940)
Chinese Wing Chun Kung-Fu Pioneer
Cho, Hee Il (Oct. 13, 1940)
Korean-American Tae Kwon Do Pioneer
Cho, S. Henry (Nov. 9, 1934)
Korean-American Tae Kwon Do Pioneer
Chong, Jun (April 9, 1952)
Korean-American Tae Kwon Do Master
Chun, Richard (Feb. 22, 1935)
Korean-American Tae Kwon Do Pioneer
Chung, John (Sept. 26, 1958)
Korean-American World Forms Champion
Cikatic', Branimir (Oct. 4, 1955)
Yugoslavian World Muay Thai Champion
Cofield, George (Oct. 13, 1935)
American Karate Pioneer
Cogliandro, Tony (Aug. 29, 1957)
American Sport Karate Promoter
Collins, David (Sept. 10, 1967)
Member, WAKO American

World Championship Karate Team
Conde, Francisco (Dec. 31, 1936)
American Karate Pioneer
Conroy, Mike (Sept. 21, 1966)
Member, WAKO American World Championship Karate Team
Corcoran, John (Nov. 27, 1948)
American Martial Arts Writer & Author
Corley, Joe (Feb. 21, 1947)
American Karate & Kickboxing Pioneer & Promoter
Creamer, Terry (June 7, 1956)
American Semi-Contact Karate Champion
Cunningham, Pete (March 25, 1963)
World Kickboxing Champion
Dacascos, Al (Sept. 6, 1942)
American Kung-Fu Pioneer
Dacascos (Bernal), Malia (Oct. 5, 1943)
American Kung-Fu Pioneer
Dacascos, Mark (Feb. 26, 1964)
American Martial Arts Film Star
Daniels, Gary (May 9, 1963)
British Martial Arts Film Star
Demura, Fumio (Sept. 15, 1938)
Japanese-American Karate-do Champion & Pioneer
DePasquale, Jr., Mike (Feb. 22, 1953)
American Martial Arts Writer & Author
DePasquale, Sr., Mike (Feb. 24, 1925)
American Jujutsu Pioneer
Deubner, Michael (Jan. 25, 1967)
German Martial Arts Editor & Writer
Dietze, Ludger (Oct. 1, 1960)
German European Semi-Contact Karate Champion
Dillard, Mike (Nov. 24, 1950)
American Martial Arts Businessman
DiRico, Rocky (Aug. 6, 1952)
American Karate Weapons Champion
Dorsey, Troy (Nov. 19, 1962)
World Kickboxing Champion

Master Al Dacascos. Courtesy of George Foon

Gary Daniels. Photo by Tang Trang/ Photo Pluz; courtesy of George Foon

Master Fumio Demura. Courtesy of Master Fumio Demura

James Dussault. Courtesy of James Dussault

Master Reylson Gracie. Courtesy of Master Reylson Gracie

Dussault, James (May 28, 1956)
American *Tae Kwon Do Times*
Hall of Fame Member

Emperado, Adriano Prof. (June 16, 1926)
American Kajukenbo
Grandmaster

Eubanks, Ken (Jan. 8, 1943)
American Sport Karate
Promoter

Evans, Flem (Oct. 7, 1945)
American Semi-Contact Karate
Champion

Farkas, Emil (April 20, 1946)
American Martial Arts
Author

Fisher, Steve (Feb. 14, 1953)
American National Forms &
Semi-Contact Champion

Fong, Leo T. (Sept. 23, 1928)
Chinese-American Martial Arts
Filmmaker

Forbach, Gary (May 1, 1951)
American National Forms
Champion

Foster, Mike (April 19, 1940)
American Karate Pioneer

Frenette, Jean (March 6, 1961)
French-Canadian World Forms
Champion

Frysz, Marek (April 20, 1964)
Polish Kickboxing Pioneer

Funakoshi, Ken (Sept. 4, 1938)
American Karate-do Champion

Furuya, Daniel (April 25, 1948)
Japanese-American Aikido
Master

Goldsmith, George (Nov. 30, 1954)
American Screenwriter &
Karate Black Belt

Gracenin, Nick (Dec. 5, 1958)
American Wushu
Administrator

Gracie, Reylson (Aug. 12, 1943)
Brazilian Jujutsu Pioneer

Graden, Jim (Sept. 18, 1963)
American World Kickboxing
Champion

Graden, John (Dec. 2, 1960)
Member, WAKO American
World Championship Karate
Team

Green, Ronnie (April 1, 1959)
British World Thai Boxing
Champion

Gyi, Dr. Maung (March 30, 1933)
Burmese-American Bando
Pioneer

Halliburton, Robert (Aug. 14, 1944)
American Karate Pioneer

Han, Bong Soo (Aug. 25, 1931)
Korean-American Hapkido
Pioneer

Harrison, Jim (Dec. 30, 1936)
American Karate Pioneer

Hart, Jr., Earnest (March 5, 1955)
American World Kickboxing
Champion

Hasan, Na'im (July 31, 1957)
American Tae Kwon Do
Champion

Hassell, Randall (June 5, 1948)
American Martial Arts Author
& Historian

Nick Gracenin. Courtesy of Nick Gracenin

John Graden. Courtesy of John Graden

Master Masaaki Hatsumi. Courtesy of Joe Hyams

Master Adam Hsu. Courtesy of George Foon

Goju-ryu masters Skipper Ingham (left) and Chuck Merriman. Courtesy of Master Skipper Ingham

Hasselmann, Lillian (July 7, 1954)
American PKL Hame of Fame Member
Hatsumi, Masaaki (Dec. 2, 1931)
Japanese Togakure-ryu Ninjutsu Grandmaster
Hayes, Stephen (Sept. 9, 1949)
American Ninjutsu Pioneer
Hee, Dana (Nov. 9, 1961)
American Olympic Tae Kwon Do Champion
Higa, Seikichi (Feb. 10, 1927)
Okinawan Karate Master
Higa, Seitoku (Jan. 20, 1921)
Okinawan Bugeikan Karate Master
Higa, Yuchoku (Feb. 8, 1910)
Okinawan Shorin-ryu Karate Master
Higaonna, Morio (Dec. 25, 1938)
Okinawan Goju-Ryu Karate Master
Hill, Tokey (July 11, 1957)
American World Karate Champion
Hirabayashi, Keith (Sept. 17, 1959)
Japanese-American World Forms & Weapons Champion
Ho, Steven (March 9, 1967)
Indonesian-American National Forms Champion

Hokama, Seikichi (Sept. 11, 1896)
Okinawan Oyadomari-ryu Karate Master
Holloway, Anthony (July 27, 1967)
American Semi-Contact Karate Champion
Holloway, Debra (Jan. 23, 1955)
American Tae Kwon Do Champion
Hsu, Adam (Dec. 14, 1941)
Chinese-American Kung-Fu Instructor
Hund, Brenda (June 7, 1969)
American Semi-Contact Karate Champion
Hurley, Carson (April 20, 1939)
American Karate Pioneer
Hwang, Jack (July 3, 1931)
Korean-American Tae Kwon Do Pioneer
Hwang, Kee (1912–)
Korean Tang Soo Do Grandmaster
In, Sun Seo (Aug. 1, 1942)
Korean Martial Arts Administrator
Inamine, Seijin (Jan. 2, 1937)
Okinawan Ryukyu Shorin-ryu Karate Master
Ingham, Skipper (Feb. 18, 1930)
Bermudian Karate Promoter

Inosanto, Dan (July 24, 1936)
Filipino-American Jeet Kune Do Pioneer
Isa, Shinyu (June 10, 1941)
Okinawan Kobudo Master
Ishikawa, Horoku (July 27, 1922)
Okinawan Shito-ryu Karate Master
Itokazu, Yoshio (Oct. 2, 1896)
Okinawan Goju-ryu Karate Master
Ivan, Dan (Nov. 20, 1929)
American Karate-do Pioneer
Jackson, Howard (June 27, 1951)
American World Kickboxing Champion
Jay, Wally (June 15, 1917)
American Jujutsu Pioneer
Jewell, Sharon (April 26, 1960)
American Tae Kwon Do Champion
Johnson, Pat (Dec. 31, 1939)
American Martial Arts Film Choreographer
Jones, Dr. A. Jose (Feb. 25, 1932)
American Karate Pioneer
Jones, Roger (March 8, 1946)
American Sport Karate Promoter
Jwing, Yang-Ming (Aug. 11, 1946)
Chinese-American Kung-Fu Pioneer

Kaihewalu, Sr., Soloman (Dec. 2, 1935)
American Martial Arts Promoter

Kalanoc, Cheryl (Oct. 2, 1958)
American Tae Kwon Do Champion

Kaneshima, Shinyei (Sept. 22, 1900)
Okinawan Ishimine-ryu Karate Master

Keeney, Glenn (May 6, 1941)
American Karate Pioneer

Kelly, Jim (May 5, 1946)
American Martial Arts Film Star

Kim, In Mook (March 29, 1934)
Korean-American Tae Kwon Do Pioneer

Kim, Jimmy (April 11, 1967)
Korean-American Olympic Tae Kwon Do Champion

Kim, Richard (Nov. 17, 1917)
Japanese-American Karate-do Pioneer

Kim, Yungchu (Sept. 12, 1965)
Korean-American Wu Shu Forms Champion

Kinjo, Akio (Nov. 2, 1936)
Okinawan Jukendo Master

Koda, Yuki (June 1, 1944)
Japanese-American Yoshukai Karate Master

Kojo, Kafu (Feb. 13, 1909)
Okinawan Kojo-ryu Karate Founder

Master Takayuki Kubota. Courtesy of George Foon

Kong, Bucksam (June 11, 1940)
Chinese-American Kung-Fu Pioneer

Kubota, Takayuki (Sept. 20, 1934)
Japanese-American Karate-do Pioneer

Kuhr, Michael (Feb. 26, 1962)
German World Amateur Kickboxing Champion

Kurban, Roy (Sept. 5, 1948)
American Semi-Contact Karate Champion

Lai, Brendan (Nov. 15, 1942)
Chinese-American Kung-Fu Pioneer

Lane, Danny (Jan. 3, 1949)
American Karate Administrator

Lantrip, Jim (Aug. 18, 1942)
American Kickboxing Administrator

Lantrip-Stanley, Lori (Dec. 20, 1962)
American Forms, Fighting & Weapons Champion

LaPuppet, Tom (Feb. 7, 1938)
American Karate Champion

Larson, Shawna (Feb. 24, 1974)
American Tae Kwon Do Champion

Lau, Jim (April 11, 1952)
Chinese-American Kung-Fu Master

LeBell, Gene (Oct. 9, 1932)
American Judo Pioneer

Lee, Charlie (Jan. 20, 1964)
Korean-American Forms Champion

Lee, Eric (July 30, 1948)
Chinese-American Forms Champion

Lee, Eric Tae Hyun (Aug. 20, 1971)
Korean-American Hwa Rang Do Master

Lee, Haeng Ung (July 21, 1936)
Korean-American Tae Kwon Do Pioneer

Lee, Han Won (May 18, 1962)
American Tae Kwon Do Champion

Lee, Henry Tae Joon (June 6, 1964)
Korean-American Hwa Rang Do Master

Guro Dan Inosanto. Courtesy of George Foon

Lori Lantrip-Stanley. Courtesy of Lori Lantrip-Stanley

Master Haeng Ung Lee. Copyright 1990, ATA Publications; courtesy of Milo Dailey

Lee, Jeong Sook (Jan. 13, 1947)
   Korean-American Tang Soo Do
   Pioneer
Lee, Dr. Joo Bang (Oct. 15, 1936)
   Korean-American Hwa Rang
   Do Grandmaster
Lee, Nam Suk (June 28, 1925)
   Chang Moo Kwan
   Grandmaster
Lew, James (Sept. 6, 1952)
   Chinese-American Actor &
   Forms Champion
Lewis, Alfie (Nov. 16, 1961)
   British World Semi-Contact
   Champion
Lewis, Joe (March 7, 1944)
   American Karate Pioneer &
   Champion
Limas, Arlene (Feb. 9, 1966)
   Olympic Tae Kwon Do
   Champion
Lizotte, Lou (Aug. 22, 1935)
   American Karate Pioneer
Llanos, Domingo (Sept. 30, 1957)
   American Semi-Contact &
   Forms Champion
Long, Kathy (April 21, 1964)
   American World Kickboxing
   Champion
Longstreet, John (March 8, 1959)
   American World Kickboxing
   Champion
Lundgren, Dolph (Oct. 17, 1959)
   Swedish-American Film Star

Luzzi, Cheech (April 8, 1960)
   American National Forms
   Champion
Mack, Ferdinand (Dec. 26, 1959)
   German World Kickboxing
   Champion
Macomber, Dave (Oct. 22, 1969)
   American Karate Forms
   Champion
Mamar, Romeo (Aug. 19, 1938)
   Filipino Tapado Founder
Mandris, Rick (May 21, 1952)
   Canadian Kickboxing &
   Boxing Trainer
Marchini, Ron (March 4, 1945)
   American Karate Champion
Mark, Bow Sim (July 24, 1942)
   Chinese-American Kung-Fu
   Master
Marlor, Kathy (Aug. 16, 1965)
   American Karate Forms
   Champion
Maslak, Paul (Nov. 28, 1951)
   American Kickboxing Ratings
   Pioneer
Matayoshi, Shinpo (Jan. 16, 1922)
   Okinawan Matayoshi Kobudo
   Grandmaster
Mather, Jim (Nov. 28, 1942)
   American Karate-do
   Administrator
McCallum, Ray (March 17, 1958)
   American World Semi-Contact
   Karate Champion

McCoy, Mike (July 3, 1957)
   American Sport Karate
   Promoter & Administrator
Merriman, Chad (March 16, 1965)
   American National Forms
   Champion
Merriman, Chuck (Jan. 8, 1933)
   American Forms Champion &
   Karate Pioneer
Mikami, Takayuki (Dec. 10, 1933)
   Japanese-American Karate-do
   Champion & Pioneer
Min, Ken (Aug. 14, 1936)
   Korean-American Tae Kwon
   Do Pioneer
Mirakian, Anthony (Nov. 12, 1933)
   American Karate Pioneer
Miyagi, Masakazu (Sept. 25, 1935)
   Okinawan Honshin-ryu Karate
   Master
Miyahira, Katsuya (Aug. 16, 1918)
   Okinawan Shorin-ryu Karate
   Master
Miyazaki, Toyotaro (Sept. 25, 1944)
   Japanese-American Point-
   Fighting & Forms Champ
Miyazato, Eiichi (July 5, 1922)
   Okinawan Goju-ryu Karate
   Master
Montrond, Alberto (Dec. 26, 1969)
   Member, WAKO American
   World Championship Karate
   Team
Moon, David (Jan. 19, 1943)
   Korean-American International
   Tae Kwon Do Pioneer
Moreno, Juan (April 1, 1971)
   American Tae Kwon Do
   Champion
Muller, Oliver (May 23, 1965)
   Swiss Kickboxing
   Administrator
Mullins, Skipper (April 25, 1946)
   American Karate Champion
Nagamine, Shoshin (July 15, 1906)
   Okinawan Shorin-ryu Karate
   Grandmaster
Nakaima, Kenko (Dec. 2, 1911)
   Okinawan Ryuei-ryu Karate
   Master

(Left to right) Master Ed Parker, Master Bow Sim Mark, Shik Kin (Han, the villain of *Enter the Dragon*) and Malia Bernal-Dacascos. Courtesy of Sid Campbell

David Moon. Courtesy of Keith D. Yates   Master Hidy Ochiai. Courtesy of Master Hidy Ochiai

Nakamura, Tadashi (Feb. 22, 1942)
Seido Karate Founder
Nakamura, Taketo (Jan. 2, 1934)
Okinawan Kenpo Karate
Master
Nakazato, Joen (April 13, 1922)
Okinawan Shorinji-ryu Karate
Master
Nakazato, Shugoro (Aug. 14, 1920)
Okinawan Shorin-ryu Karate
Grandmaster
Nance, Cheryl (Sept. 1, 1965)
American Semi-Contact Karate
Champion
Nishioka, Hayward (Jan. 4, 1942)
Japanese-American Judo
Champion
Nishiyama, Hidetaka (Nov. 21,
1928)
Japanese-American Karate-do
Pioneer
Norris, Chuck (March 10, 1940)
Film Star & Retired Karate
Champion
Ochiai, Hidy (Sept. 27, 1939)
Japanese-American Karate
Forms Champion
Ohshima, Tsutomu (Aug. 6, 1930)
Japanese-American Karate-do
Pioneer
Okada, Shag (Feb. 6, 1923)
Japanese-American Judo
Coach

Okamura, Gerald (Nov. 11, 1940)
American Actor & Weapons
Master
Onowo, Kazuo "Sonny" (July 28,
1954)
Japanese-American Forms
Champion
Osako, John (Dec. 22, 1921)
Japanese-American Judo
Administrator
Oyata, Seiyu (Oct. 19, 1928)
Okinawan Kempo
Grandmaster
Ozawa, Osamu (Nov. 25, 1925)
Japanese-American Karate
Pioneer
Pak, Hosung (Nov. 8, 1967)
Korean-American Wu Shu
Forms Champion
Pak, Hoyoung (Sept. 13, 1965)
Korean-American Wu Shu
Forms Champion
Panza, Derek (Feb. 16, 1971)
American National Semi-
Contact Karate Champion
Pariset, Eric (July 21, 1954)
French Jujutsu Pioneer
Payton, John (Dec. 4, 1968)
Member, WAKO American
World Championship Karate
Team
Pejo, Mayumi (June 9, 1972)
American Tae Kwon Do
Champion

Perez, Herb (Dec. 6, 1959)
American Olympic Tae Kwon
Do Champion
Petschler, Howard (Aug. 21, 1948)
American Kickboxing Pioneer
Plowden, Richard (Feb. 27, 1960)
American Semi-Contact Karate
Champion
Poi, Chan (Dec. 10, 1938)
Chinese Wah Lum Kung-Fu
Master
Porter, Phil (Nov. 27, 1924)
American Judo Pioneer
Price, Anthony (Sept. 13, 1959)
American Semi-Contact Karate
Champion
Quan, Kathy (Nov. 29, 1960)
American Karate Forms
Champion
Quan, Stuart (Oct. 17, 1962)
American Karate Forms
Champion
Rappold, Christopher (Aug. 22,
1969)
Member, WAKO American
World Championship Karate
Team
Reyes, Jr., Ernie (Jan. 15, 1972)
Martial Arts Film Star & Karate
Forms Champion
Reyes, Sr., Ernie (Feb. 12, 1947)
American Martial Arts Pioneer
Reynaga, Gabe (May 15, 1972)
American National Forms &

Grandmaster Jhoon Rhee. Courtesy of Grandmaster Jhoon Rhee

Master Shigetoshi Senaha. Courtesy of Karate Master Anthony Mirakian

Semi-Contact Karate
Champion
Rhee, Jhoon (Jan. 7, 1932)
American Tae Kwon Do
Pioneer
Rhee, Kang (Jan. 30, 1938)
Korean-American Tae Kwon
Do Master
Rhee, Phillip (Sept. 7, 1960)
Korean-American Film Star &
Producer

Rhee, Simon (Oct. 28, 1957)
Korean-American Forms
Champion
Roberts, Ted Jan (Sept. 24, 1979)
American Martial Arts Film
Star
Rodrigues, Don (March 18, 1955)
American Karate Coach &
Tournament Promoter
Romero, Pat (Dec. 16, 1963)
American Kickboxing
Champion
Roop, Kerry (Sept. 8, 1950)
American World Kickboxing
Champion
Santamaria, Joyce (Sept. 15, 1942)
American Sport Karate
Promoter
Sawyer, Mike (May 3, 1955)
American Kickboxing
Administrator
Saxon, John (Aug. 5, 1935)
American Actor & Karate
Black Belt
Seagal, Steven (April 10, 1952)
American Film Star & Aikido
Master
Sells, John (Nov. 23, 1949)
American Martial Arts
Historian
Senaha, Shigetoshi (Jan. 24, 1941)
Okinawan Goju-ryu Karate
Master
Sharkey, John (Feb. 27, 1956)
American Sport Karate
Promoter
Shepard, Karen (Nov. 12, 1953)
American Kung-Fu Forms
Champion
Shepherd, Steve (Oct. 10, 1950)
World Kickboxing Champion
Shimabuku, Kichiro (Feb. 15,
1938)
Okinawan Isshin-ryu Karate
Grandmaster
Shimabuku, Zenpo (Oct. 11, 1943)
Okinawan Chubu Shorin-ryu
Karate Master
Shinzato, Yoshihide (March 15,
1927)
Okinawan Shorin-ryu Karate
Master
Shioda, Gozo (Sept. 9, 1915)
Japanese Yoshinkai Aikido
Founder

Silliphant, Stirling (Jan. 16, 1918)
American Filmmaker &
Martial Arts Pioneer
Sims, Kierston (Aug. 29, 1963)
American Semi-Contact Karate
Champion
Sliwa, Curtis (March 26, 1954)
Guardian Angels Founder
Slocki, Wally (April 13, 1947)
Canadian Karate Champion
Smith, Jeff (Nov. 20, 1947)
World Kickboxing Champion
Sobel, Stuart (March 7, 1943)
American Martial Arts
Businessman
Soet, John (July 19, 1952)
American Martial Arts Editor
& Writer
Speakman, Jeff (Nov. 8, 1957)
American Martial Arts Film
Star
Speidel, Rod (Feb. 20, 1949)
American Tae Kwon Do Editor
& Black Belt
Steen, Allen (March 16, 1939)
American Karate Pioneer
Sternberg, Alex (Oct. 30, 1950)
American Karate Forms
Champion
Stone, Mike (June 29, 1943)
American Karate Champion
Sue, Jeff (April 2, 1977)
American Karate Forms
Champion
Swain, Michael (Dec. 21, 1960)
American World Judo
Champion
Swayze, Patrick (Aug. 18, 1952)
American Actor & Karate
Black Belt
Tabura, Ted (Aug. 26, 1940)
American Lima Lama Master
Takamine, Choboku (March 24,
1908)
Okinawan Goju-ryu Karate
Master
Terrill, Bruce (Feb. 10, 1942)
American Martial Arts
Pioneer
Thanos, George (March 1, 1952)
American National Open Tae
Kwon Do Champion
Theriault, Jean-Yves (Jan. 16, 1955)
Canadian World Kickboxing
Champion

Jean-Claude Van Damme (second from left) and Dolph Lundgren (third from left) in *Universal Soldier*. Courtesy of TriStar Pictures

Richard Roundtree (left) and Don Wilson in *Forced to Fight*. Courtesy of Paul Maslak and Don Wilson

Thomas, Cliff (Jan. 27, 1957)
    American World Kickboxing
    Champion
Thompson, Kevin (June 26, 1961)
    American Forms, Weapons &
    Semi-Contact Karate
    Champion
Thurman, Bob (Oct. 6, 1960)
    World Kickboxing Champion
Tippett, Andre (Dec. 27, 1959)
    All-Pro Football Linebacker &
    Karate Black Belt
Todd, Walter (Feb 1, 1927)
    American Karate Pioneer

Bill "Superfoot" Wallace. Photo by Panther Productions; courtesy of George Foon

Toddy, Master (a.k.a. Sitiwatjana, Thohsaphon) (May 4, 1953)
    Thai Muay Thai Master
Trejo, Frank (Dec. 24, 1952)
    American Kenpo Karate
    Master
Trimble, Jerry (May 12, 1961)
    American World Kickboxing
    Champion
Trinh, Kim-Du (Nov. 19, 1966)
    Canadian Karate Forms
    Champion
Uechi, Kanei (June 26, 1911)
    Okinawan Uechi-ryu
    Grandmaster
Uehara, Seikichi (March 24, 1904)
    Okinawan Motobu-ryu
    Kobujutsu Grandmaster
Urban, Peter (Aug. 14, 1934)
    American Karate Pioneer
Urquidez, Benny "The Jet" (June 20, 1952)
    American World Kickboxing
    Champion
Uyeshiba, Kisshomaru (1921–)
    Japanese Aikido Grandmaster
Van Clief, Ron (Jan. 25, 1943)
    American Chinese Goju Karate
    Master
Van Damme, Jean-Claude (Oct. 18, 1961)
    Belgian-American Martial Arts
    Film Star
Van Ryswyk, Saskia (Jan. 19, 1961)
    Dutch World Muay Thai
    Champion

Vitali, Keith (Dec. 24, 1952)
    American Semi-Contact Karate
    Champion
Wall, Bob (Aug. 22, 1939)
    American Martial Arts
    Businessman
Wallace, Bill "Superfoot" (Dec. 1, 1945)
    American World Kickboxing
    Champion
Wang, Madam Jurong (Nov. 4, 1928)
    Chinese Wushu Master
Warwick, Jay (Sept. 14, 1957)
    American Tae Kwon Do
    Champion
Weiss, Al (June 8, 1926)
    American Martial Arts
    Publisher & Writer
Will, Jay T. (March 10, 1942)
    American Karate Pioneer
Williams, Mark (Sept. 8, 1958)
    American National Tae Kwon
    Do Champion
Williams, Tommy (April 13, 1951)
    American World Kickboxing
    Champion
Wilson, Don "The Dragon" (Sept. 10, 1954)
    Japanese-American World
    Kickboxing Champion
Wong, Carrie Ogawa- (June 6, 1955)
    Japanese-American National
    Forms Champion

Curtis Wong. Courtesy of Curtis Wong

Master Douglas Wong. Courtesy of Master Douglas Wong

Wong, Curtis (Nov. 21, 1949)
    Chinese-American Martial Arts
    Publisher
Wong, Doc-Fai (June 10, 1948)
    Chinese-American Kung-Fu
    Master
Wong, Douglas (Dec. 7, 1948)
    Chinese-American Kung-Fu
    Pioneer
Wong, Phillip (July 28, 1962)
    Chinese-American Wushu
    Forms Champion
Worley, John (Jan. 22, 1944)
    American Sport Karate
    Promoter
Worley, Pat (Nov. 17, 1948)

    American Semi-Contact Karate
    Champion
Xavier, Pedro (Sept. 19, 1970)
    American WAKO World Semi-
    Contact Karate Champion
Yagi, Meitatsu (June 1944)
    Okinawan Karate Master
Yagi, Meitoku (March 6, 1912)
    Okinawan Goju-ryu Karate
    Grandmaster
Yamaguchi, Gosei (Jan. 15, 1936)
    Japanese-American Karate-do
    Pioneer
Yamashita, Tadashi (Feb. 5, 1942)
    Okinawan-American Karate &
    Kobudo Master

Yamazaki, Kiyoshi (Aug. 16, 1940)
    Japanese-American Karate-do
    Master
Yarnall, Bob (Nov. 3, 1942)
    American Karate Pioneer
Yates, Keith D. (Nov. 28, 1950)
    American Karate Author &
    Journalist
Yip, Shui (Oct. 1913)
    Chinese Chow Gar & Praying
    Mantis Grandmaster
Yoshizato, Shintaro (June 20, 1913)
    Okinawan Kushin-ryu Karate
    Master
Young, Tony (Sept. 8, 1962)
    American Semi-Contact Karate
    Champion
Yu, Byong (Jan. 17, 1935)
    Korean-American Karate &
    Forms Champion
Zaccagnini Norman, Cheryl
    (March 31, 1959)
    American Tae Kwon Do
    Champion

THE GREAT MASTERS OF THE PAST

Aragaki, Seiki (Dec. 1, 1923–April
    22, 1986)
    Okinawan Karate Master
Arakaki, Ankichi (1899–1927)
    Okinawan Karate Master

Rare historical photograph of great ka-rate masters and students taken on Okinawa on November 16, 1925. Seated in second row, left to right: Goju-ryu Master Seiko Higa, Yasuzo Tahara, Shito-ryu Grandmaster Kenwa Mabuni, Goju-ryu Grandmaster Cho jun Miyagi, Toon-ryu Grandmaster Juhatsu Kiyoda, Goju-ryu karate student Jinan Shinzato and Naha-te student Keiyo Madan-bashi. Standing, left to right: Kojun Yasuzama, Fumihara Tamashiro, Shin-genkai Nakai, Higa Okugi and Tat-sutoku Sen aba. All the named individuals were karate masters or ad-vanced practitioners; the unnamed peo-ple were their students. Courtesy of Karate Master Anthony Mirakian

Armstrong, Steve (Sept. 22, 1931–
?)
 American Karate Pioneer
Azato, Yasuato (c. 1864–c. 1929)
 Okinawan Kobudo Master
Azato, Yasutsune (1827–1906)
 Okinawan Karate Master
Bone, Walt (1944–82)
 American Karate Pioneer
Bruckner, Georg (July 30, 1937–
Dec. 30, 1992)
 German Martial Arts Pioneer
Canete, Eulogio (1900–88)
 Filipino Escrima Pioneer
Chang, Dung Sheng (d. June 18,
1986)
 Chinese Shuai Chao
 Grandmaster
Chang, San-Feng (1279–1368)
Chen, Yuan-Pin (a.k.a. Chin,
Gempin) (1587–1671)
 Reputed Founder of Jujutsu
Cheng, Man-Ching (1902–March
26, 1975)
 Chinese Tai-Chi Chuan Kung-
 Fu Grandmaster
Chibana, Choshin (1887–1969)
 Okinawan Karate Master &
 Pioneer
Chinen, Yamane (c. 1860–c. 1928)
 Okinawan Kobudo Master
Chitose, Tsuyoshi Dr. (1899–1984)
 Japanese Chito-ryu Karate-do
 Founder
Choi, D.H. (1932–89)
 Korean-American Tae Kwon
 Do Master
Choi, Yong Shul (1904–Nov. 1987)
 Korean Hapkido Founder
Chow, William Kwai-sun (July 13,
1913–Sept. 21, 1987)
 American Kenpo Grandmaster
Chuan, Tung Hai (d. Dec. 15, 1882)
 Chinese Pa-Kua Kung-Fu
 Founder
Church, Albert (1930–June 23, 1980)
 American Jujutsu Pioneer
Funakoshi, Gichin (1868–1957)
 Okinawan Father of Modern
 Karate
Gehlson, John (1936–72)
 American Shotokan Karate
 Champion
Gimu, Kanegawa (c. 1862–c. 1921)
 Okinawan Kobudo Master

Master Gichin Funakoshi (left) with Mel Bruno.
Courtesy of the John Corcoran Archives

Naha-te Grandmaster
Kanryo Higa(shi)onna.
Courtesy of Karate Master Anthony Mirakian

Hamahiga, Peichin (c. 1820–c. 1904)
 Okinawan Kobudo Master
Hamilton, Fred (Jan. 25, 1925–July
16, 1986)
 American Karate Pioneer
Hanashiro, Chomo (1869–1945)
 Okinawan Karate Master
Havanas, Demetrius (1950–81)
 American Karate Champion
Higa(shi)onna, Kanryo (March 10,
1852–Dec. 23, 1915)
 Okinawan Karate Master &
 Pioneer
Hisatake, Arthur Koji (1927–73)
 German Karate Pioneer
Hokama, Seikichi (Sept. 11, 1896–?)
 Okinawan Karate Master
Hsiung, Chien-Hsun (1895–1977)
 Chinese Tzu Men Chuan
 Master
Ichiun, Odagiri (1629–1706)
 Japanese Samurai
Inoue, Kinichi (a.k.a. "Azumafuji")
(1922–July 31, 1973)
 Japanese Sumo Grand
 Champion
Ishikawa, Harry (Dec. 25, 1928–Jan.
20, 1978)
 Japanese-American Aikido
 Pioneer

Ito, Kazuo (1898–1974)
 Japanese Judo Master
Itoh, Takasue (1897–1981)
 Japanese Judo Master
Itosu, Yasutsune "Ankoh" (1830–
Aug. 1915)
 Okinawan Karate Master &
 Pioneer
Jinsei, Kamiya (c. 1895–1964)
 Okinawan Kobudo Master
Kamadeunchu, Arakaki (1840–
1920)
 Okinawan Karate Master &
 Pioneer
Kaneshima, Shinsuke (1896–June
14, 1991)
 Okinawan Karate Master
Kaneshima, Shinyei (Sept. 22,
1900–?)
 Okinawan Karate Master
Kano, Jigoro (1860–1938)
 Japanese Judo Founder
Keehan, John (a.k.a. "Count
Dante") (1939–May 25, 1975)
 American Karate Pioneer .
Kim, Ki Whang (Nov. 20, 1920–
Sept. 16, 1993)
 Korean-American Tae Kwon
 Do Pioneer

Anthony Mirakian (left) with the late Toon-ryu Grandmaster Juhatsu Kiyoda, circa 1958. Courtesy of Karate Master Anthony Mirakian

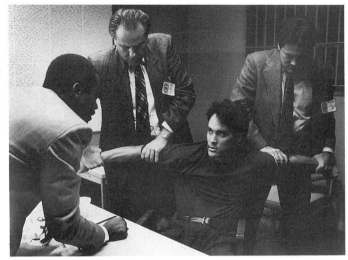

Brandon Lee (center) in *Rapid Fire*. Courtesy of Twentieth Century-Fox

Bruce Lee. Courtesy of the John Corcoran Archives

Kina, Shosei (1883–1980)
    Okinawan Karate Master
Kiyoda, Juhatsu (1887–1967)
    Okinawan Toon-ryu Karate
      Founder
Koizumi, Gunji (1885–1965)
    Japanese Judo Pioneer
Kraka, Chiken (c. 1829–c. 1898)
    Okinawan Kobudo Master
Kyan, Chotoku (Dec. 1870–1945)
    Okinawan Karate Master &
      Pioneer

Lam, Yui Kwai (1877–1968)
    Chinese Southern Dragon
      Kung-Fu Grandmaster
Lam, Yum Tong (1874–1971)
    Chinese Mok Gar Kung-Fu
      Master
Lee, Brandon (Feb. 2, 1965–March
   31, 1993)
    Chinese-American Film Star;
      son of Bruce Lee
Lee, Bruce (Nov. 27, 1940–July 20,
   1973)
    Chinese-American Martial Arts
      Pioneer
Lee, James Yimm (1920–72)
    Chinese-American Kung-Fu
      Pioneer
Lee, Jung Nam (d. Dec. 26, 1988)
    Korean-American Tae Kwon
      Do Master
Lee, Kwan Shan (a.k.a. Yuk Tong
   Lee) (1866–1948)
    Chinese Wah Lum Praying
      Mantis Grandmaster
Lefiti, Haumea (d. Feb. 18, 1973)
    Polynesian-American Kung-Fu
      Pioneer
Mabuni, Kenwa (1889–1952)
    Japanese Shito-ryu Karate-do
      Founder
Matayoshi, Shinko (1888–1947)
    Okinawan Kobudo Master
Matsumora, Kosaku (1820–98)

    Okinawan Shorin-ryu Karate
      Master
Matsumura, Nabe (c. 1860–1930)
    Okinawan Karate Master
Matsumura, Sokon (1797–1889)
    Okinawan Karate Master &
      Pioneer
Mifune, Kyuzo (1883–Jan. 27, 1965)
    Japanese Judo Pioneer
Mitose, James (Dec. 30, 1916–March
   26, 1981)
    Hawaiian Kempo/Karate
      Pioneer
Miyagi, Chojun (April 25, 1888–
   Oct. 8, 1953)
    Okinawan Goju-ryu Karate-do
      Grandmaster
Moden, Yabiku (c. 1867–c. 1940)
    Okinawan Karate Master

Grandmaster Kenwa Mabuni. Courtesy of Karate Master Anthony Mirakian

Motobu, Choki (Feb. 1871–1944)
　Okinawan Karate Master &
　　Pioneer
Musashi, Miyamoto (1584–1645)
　Japanese Samurai & Author
Nakaima, Kenko (Dec. 23, 1911–
　Sept. 21, 1989)
　Okinawan Karate Master
Nakama, Chozo (Dec. 1, 1898–197?)
　Okinawan Shorin-ryu Karate
　　Master
Nakamura, Shigeru (1892–1969)
　Okinawan Kempo
　　Grandmaster
Nakayama, Hakudo (1873–1959)
　Japanese Kendo Master
Nakayama, Masatoshi (1913–April
　14, 1987)
　Japanese Shotokan Karate-do
　　Master & Pioneer
No Tanme, Shingaki (c. 1848–
　c. 1911)
　Okinawan Kobudo Master
No Tanme, Sueyoshi (c. 1869–
　c. 1916)
　Okinawan Kobudo Master
No Tanme, Uhugushuku (c. 1850–
　c. 1945)
　Okinawan Kobudo Master
No Tanme, Yamachi (c. 1823–
　c. 1891)
　Okinawan Kobudo Master
Ohtsuka, Hironori (1892–1982)
　Japanese Wado-ryu Karate-do
　　Founder

Okazaki, Henry (Jan. 28, 1890–1951)
　Japanese Jujutsu Master
Okuyama, Ryuho (Yoshinobu)
　(Feb. 21, 1901–Nov. 25, 1987)
　Japanese Hakko-ryu Jujutsu
　　Founder
Oshiro, Choki (a.k.a. Ogusuku,
　Choen) (c. 1873–c. 1947)
　Okinawan Kobudo Master
Ota, Tsugiyoshi (1892–1984)
　Japanese Iaido Master
Oyadomari, Peichin (1831–1905)
　Okinawan Karate Master
Oyama, Mas (July 27, 1923–April
　25, 1994)
　Korean Karate Grandmaster
Pai, Daniel (April 4, 1930–June
　1993)
　American Kung-Fu Pioneer
Parker, Ed (March 19, 1931–Dec. 15,
　1990)
　American Karate Pioneer
Presley, Elvis (Jan. 8, 1935–August
　16, 1977)
　American Karate Pioneer
Reyes, Al (1927–79)
　Filipino-American Kajukenbo
　　Pioneer
Saigo, Tanomo (1829–1905)
　Japanese Aikijutsu Master
Sakugawa, Satonuku "Tode"
　(March 3, 1733–Aug. 17, 1815)
　Okinawan Karate Master &
　　Pioneer

Nanfah Seheradecho (left). Photo by Mark Van Schuyver

Master Tatsuo Shimabuku. Courtesy of the John Corcoran Archives

Grandmaster Chojun Miyagi (second from left) in 1950. Courtesy of Karate Master Anthony Mirakian

Ed Parker (left) with Jay T. Will in 1969. Courtesy of Jay T. Will

Seheradecho, Nanfah "Lot" (1961–
　Nov. 21, 1991)
　World Muay Thai Champion
Sekiun, Harigaya (1592–1662)
　Japanese Samurai
Shimabuku, Tatsuo (Sept. 19, 1908–
　May 30, 1975)
　Okinawan Isshin-ryu Karate
　　Founder
Shimabuku, Zenryo (1904–1969)
　Chubu Shorin-ryu Karate
　　Founder

One of the rare photographs taken of Grandmaster Taira Shinken (center, black gi) in the 1950s. Courtesy of Karate Master Anthony Mirakian

Shinjo, Masanobu (1938–Oct. 15, 1993)
    Okinawan Goju-ryu Karate Master
Shinken, Taira (1902–70)
    Okinawan Kobudo Master
Shinko, Matayoshi (c. 1873–c. 1925)
    Okinawan Kobudo Master
Shirata, Rinjiro (1912–May 29, 1993)
    Japanese Aikido Master
Soken, Hohan (May 25, 1890–Nov. 30, 1982)
    Okinawan Matsumura Shorin-ryu Karate Founder
Song, Duk Ki (1893–1987)
    Korean Tae Kyon Master
Takahara, Peichin (c. 1694–c. 1754)
    Okinawan Karate Master
Takano, Hiromasa (1900–87)
    Japanese Kendo Master
Takeda, Soemon (1758–1853)
    Japanese Aikijutsu Master
Takeda, Sokaku (1860–April 25, 1943)
    Japanese Aikijutsu Master
Tani, Yukio (1881–1950)
    Japanese Judo Pioneer

Tomiki, Kenji (1900–Dec. 25, 1979)
    Japanese Aikido Grandmaster
Toyama, Kanken (Sept. 24, 1888–1966)
    Japanese Founder of Shudokan Karate
Trias, Robert (March 18, 1922–July 11, 1989)
    American Karate Pioneer; Founder of Karate in America
Tung, Hai Chuan (1796–1880)
    Reputed Chinese Pa-Kua Kung-Fu Founder
Tung, Hu-Ling (1917–92)
    Chinese Tai-Chi Chuan Master
Uechi, Kanbum (May 5, 1877–1948)
    Okinawan Uechi-ryu Karate Founder
Uechi, Kanei (June 26, 1911–Feb. 24, 1991)
    Okinawan Uechi-Ryu Karate Grandmaster
Ufushiku, Kanakushiku (1841–1920)
    Okinawan Kobudo Master
Uyeshiba, Morihei (Dec. 14, 1883–April 26, 1969)

    Aikido Founder & Pioneer
Wang, Hsiang-Chai (1885–1963)
    Chinese I Chuan Master
Wong, Ark Y. (1900–Jan. 11, 1987)
    Chinese-American Kung-Fu Pioneer
Wong, Moon Toy (1907–60)
    Chinese-American Fu-Jow Pai Kung-Fu Master

Grandmaster Hohan Soken (right) with George Dillman in 1972. Courtesy of George Dillman

Wyatt, Pat (1941–April 1, 1974)
    American Karate Pioneer
Yabu, Kentsu (1863–1937)
    Okinawan Karate Master &
    Pioneer
Yagyu, Muneyoshi (1529–1606)
    Japanese Yagyu
    Swordsmanship Founder
Yagyu, Musemori (1571–1646)
    Japanese Swordsmanship
    Master
Yamaguchi, Gogen (Jan. 20, 1909–
    July 1989)
    Japanese Goju-ryu Karate-do
    Founder
Yip, Man (d. Dec. 1, 1972)
    Chinese Wing Chun Kung-Fu
    Pioneer
Yoshizato, Shintaro (June 20, 1913–
    Oct. 8, 1988)
    Okinawan Karate Master

Grandmaster Ark Yuey Wong. Courtesy
of Master Douglas Wong

PART III

CHAMPIONS OF THE MARTIAL ARTS

KICKBOXING COMPETITION RESULTS (1970–92)

This section is divided into two chapters, the first of which features box-score results of professional kickboxing world title fights from 1970 to 1992. The second chapter composing this section is a complete amateur kickboxing winner's list from every World Association of Kickboxing Organizations (WAKO) World, European and U.S. Championship.

The professional kickboxing chapter encompasses 516 world title fights from 14 various sanctioning bodies since the sport's inception in 1970. The full names of these sanctioning organizations precede the box-score listings.

In addition, an annual overview of global kickboxing activity appears at the end of some year's data but, unfortunately, was not available for each and every year.

The majority of the professional kickboxing data appearing here derives from the Standardized Tournaments and Ratings (STAR) System, a revolutionary ratings system originated by journalists Paul Maslak and John Corcoran (this book's author), and individually carried on by Maslak until 1988. The STAR System debuted as tournament rankings in the March 1980 issue of *Inside Kung Fu* magazine, while the world kickboxing rankings premiered a few months later in *Kick Illustrated* (now *Inside Karate* magazine).

Subsequently the STAR System focused exclusively on kickboxing, and eventually its ratings appeared regularly in more than fifty publications around the world.

The system was created to rate fighters impartially in the same way as are prominent players in other professional individual and team sports. Maslak, its chief architect, ceased publishing the STAR System in January 1988, but for eight years it reigned as the world's premier kickboxing ratings.

Additional data was provided by Joe Corley, president of the Professional Karate Association (PKA); Jay T. Will, who, from 1990 to 1992, input a vast amount of PKA data on computer; and Mike Sawyer, chairman of the International Sport Karate Association (ISKA).

I also wish to thank Frank Babcock, president of the Karate International Council of Kickboxing (KICK) for attempting to supply that organization's world championship data. Mr. Babcock's search into his archives, however, was unsuccessful, but the fighters belonging to his excellent organization should know that their president made every effort to make them a part of this official record book.

Muay Thai results are not featured in this chapter. Although a number of fighters from both sports have crossed over, Muay Thai is as different from kickboxing as karate is from kung-fu. Muay Thai rules permit elbow and knee blows, as well as holding and hitting, primary distinctions not found in conventional kickboxing. Included here are the results of a number of mixed bouts featuring "international rules," where fighters are permitted to use kicks to the legs. In recent years, too, the ISKA expanded its base to include separate "leg kick" divisions with so-called "international rules," which recognize kickboxers involved in this aspect of the sport.

CHAPTER 7

PROFESSIONAL KICKBOXING (1970–93)

FORMAT

Entries appear in reverse chronological order from 1993 to 1970. Where possible, each entry provides the date, site, producer, sanctioning body, TV coverage (if any), divisional title at stake, winner(s) and loser(s) and fight outcome. Some events feature multiple title-fight data.

Promoters are named only when that information was made available. The world championship results are preceded by a list of the STAR System's undisputed world champions, a data abbreviation table to explain how to read the results and a sanctioning body legend.

STAR SYSTEM UNDISPUTED WORLD CHAMPIONS (1974–87)

MEN

Heavyweights

1985: Maurice Smith (USA)
1984: Tony Palmore (USA)
1982: Anthony Elmore (USA)
1977: Ross Scott (USA)
1974: Joe Lewis (USA)

Cruiserweights

1987: James Warring (USA)
1986: Jerry Rhome (USA)
1984: Brad Hefton (USA)
1984: James Warring (USA)
1983: Don Wilson (USA)

Super Light-Heavyweights

1984: Don Wilson (USA)
1980: Dan Macaruso (USA)
1974: Jeff Smith (USA)

Light Heavyweights

1980: Don Wilson (USA)

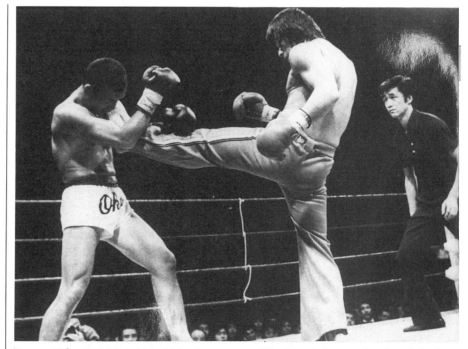

Benny "The Jet" Urquidez kicks Kunimatsu Okao in their 1977 landmark bout in Japan. Okao was undefeated and came out of retirement to challenge the American Urquidez, who had defeated his countrymen. The fight was a scorcher and Urquidez KOed Okao in the 4th round, thus establishing American kickboxers as respected world-class fighters. Courtesy of Stuart Sobel and Benny Urquidez

Super Middleweights

1987: Christian Battesti (France)
1983: Bob Thurman (USA)
1981: Jean-Yves Theriault (Canada)
1980: Bob Ryan (USA)
1974: Bill Wallace (USA)

Middleweights

1987: Dale Cook (USA)
1985: Fred Royers (Holland)
1984: Yasuo Tabata (Japan)
1983: Rob Kamen (Holland)
1982: John Moncayo (USA)
1979: Steve Shepherd (USA)
1978: Bob Ryan (USA)
1977: Earnest Hart, Jr. (USA)

Super Welterweights

1986: David Humphries (USA)
1978: Alvin Prouder (USA)
1974: Isaias Duenas (Mexico)

Welterweights

1985: Benny Urquidez (USA)
1984: Andre Brilleman (Holland)
1980: Howard Jackson (USA)
1975: Benny Urquidez (USA)

Super Lightweights

1986: Richard Sylla (France)
1986: Pete Cunningham (Canada)
1977: Benny Urquidez (USA)
1975: Gordon Franks (USA)

Lightweights

1986: Pete Cunningham (Canada)

1981: Paul Vizzio (USA)
1980: Cliff Thomas (USA)
1979: Gordon Franks (USA)
1977: Kunimasa Nagae (Japan)

Super Featherweights

1986: Dave Johnston (USA)
1984: Dave Johnston (USA)
1983: Gerry Blanck (USA)
1981: Dave Johnston (USA)

Featherweights

1987: Troy Dorsey (USA)
1986: Lawrence Miera (USA)
1984: Victor Solier (Puerto Rico)
1980: Felipe Garcia (USA)

Bantamweights

1986: Miloud El Geubli (Holland)
1986: Joao Vierra (Holland)

Super Flyweights

1987: Miguel Montoya (USA)
1986: Yuki Horiuchi (Japan)

Flyweights

1986: (Discontinued)
1983: Hiroshi Takahashi (Japan)

WOMEN

Catchweights

1985: Lucia Rijker (Holland)
1980: Lilly Rodriguez (USA)

Super Bantamweights

1986: (Discontinued)

Troy Dorsey poses with his daughter, his most admiring fan. Dorsey was the first man to hold world professional titles in two ring sports, boxing and kickboxing. Courtesy of Troy Dorsey

1984: Cheryl Wheeler (USA)

Bantamweights

1987: Leah Goldstein (Canada)
1979: Graciela Casillas (USA)

Super Flyweights

1986: Lisa Howarth (England)

DATA ABBREVIATION TABLE

DEC	Unanimous Decision
DRW	Draw
DSQ	Disqualification
KO	Knockout
MDEC	Majority Decision
MDRW	Majority Draw
NC	No Contest
SDEC	Split Decision
SDRW	Split Draw
TDEC	Technical Decision
TDRW	Technical Draw
TKO	Technical Knockout
TMDEC	Technical Majority Decision
TSDEC	Technical Split Decision

SANCTIONING BODIES

EPKA	European Professional Karate Association
FFKA	Fight Factory Karate Association
IKL	International Kickboxing League
ISKA	International Sport Karate Association
KICK	Karate International Council of Kickboxing
PKA	Professional Karate Association
PKC	Professional Karate Commission
PKO	Professional Karate Organization
SEPKA	South East Professional Karate Association
WBBL	World Black Belt League
WKA	World Karate Association/World Kickboxing Association

WKC   World Karate Commission
WPKO   World Professional Karate Organization
WSMAC   World Series of Martial Arts Championships

1992 WORLD PROFESSIONAL TITLE FIGHTS

February 5
Site: Honolulu, HI. Sanction: ISKA.
Division: Heavy. Winner: Dennis Alexio. KO-5. Loser: Clement Salles.

February 25
Site: Montreal, Canada. Sanction: ISKA. Television: RDS (Canada).
Division: Super Light. Winner: Michel Rochette. TKO-6. Loser: Viktor Aksyutin.

March 16
Site: Las Vegas, NV. Sanction: ISKA. Television: Viewer's Choice pay-per-view (live).
Division: Heavy. Winner: Dennis Alexio. TKO-3. Loser: Branimir Cikatic'.
Division: Super Light. Winner: Pete Cunningham. TKO-7. Loser: Chris Anderson.
Division: Bantam. Winner: Kathy Long. DEC-5. Loser: Kyoto Kamikaze.

March 21
Site: Mulhouse, France. Sanction: ISKA.
Division: Light Middle. Winner: Patrick Prando. Loser: Bernd Grew.

April 4
Site: Berlin, Germany. Sanction: ISKA.
Division: Light. Winner: Michael Kuhr. DEC-12. Loser: Santae Wilson.

April 25
Site: Atlanta, GA. Promoter: Joe Corley. Sanction: ISKA.
Division: Light Heavy. Winner: Rick Roufus. TKO-7. Loser: Henk Pelser.

Site: Geleen, Holland. Sanction: ISKA. Television: Eurosport.
Division: Super Welter. Winner: El-Kadir Saddouki. KO-10. Loser: Billy Murray.

May 17
Site: Moscow, Russia. Sanction: ISKA. Television: Russian National TV.

Division: Super Welter. Winner: Richard Hill. DEC-12. Loser: Vadim Ukraintsev.
Division: Fly. Winner: Ramona Gatto. DEC-10. Loser: Natalia Larionova.

June 12
Site: Solothurn, Switzerland. Sanction: ISKA.
Division: Super Welter. Winner: El-Kadir Saddouki. MDEC-12. Loser: Billy Murray.

June 20
Site: Corsica, France. Sanction: ISKA.
Division: Welter. Winner: Curtis Bush. DEC-12. Loser: Toussaint Andrarelli.

Site: Paris, France. Sanction: ISKA.
Division: Super Middle. Winner: Rob Kaman. TKO-6. Loser: Jean-Yves Theriault.

July 18
Site: Denver, CO. Sanction: ISKA.
Division: Super Light. Winner: David Cummings. KO-2. Loser: Ray Fernandez.

July 25
Site: Murfreesboro, TN. Sanction: ISKA.
Division: Light Welter. Winner: Cliff Thomas. KO-3. Loser: Thomas Chesterfield.

August 8
Site: San Juan, Puerto Rico. Sanction: ISKA.
Division: Bantam. Winner: Danny Melendez. KO-2. Loser: Curtis Evans.

August 14
Site: St. Raphael, France. Sanction: ISKA. Television: TFI (France).
Division: Middle. Winner: Christian Battesti. TDEC-12. Loser: Robert Harris.

September 6
Site: Las Vegas, NV. Sanction: ISKA. Television: Canal Plus (Europe); RDS (Canada).
Division: Super Heavy. Winner: Vitaly Klichko. DEC-12. Loser: Brad Hefton.
Division: Feather. Winner: Troy Dorsey. KO-6. Loser: Alexei Nechaev.

September 18
Site: San Jose, CA. Promoter: Scott Coker. Sanction: ISKA.
Division: Light Cruiser. Winner: Javier Mendez. MDEC-12. Loser: Mark Longo.

October 10
Site: Albuquerque, NM. Sanction: ISKA.
Division: Middle. Winner: Mike Winklejohn. TKO-4.
   Loser: Billy Murray.

October 16
Site: Pearl City, HI. Sanction: ISKA.
Division: Feather. Winner: Ramona Gatto. KO-6. Loser:
   Debbie Page.

October 24
Site: Cayenne, French Guyana. Sanction: ISKA.
Division: Light Middle. Winner: Andre Panza. DEC-12.
   Loser: Jacques Eugenie.

November 6
Site: Audincourt, France. Sanction: ISKA.
Division: Light Middle. Winner: Massimo Liberati.
   DEC-12. Loser: Patrick Prando.

November 10
Site: Honolulu, HI. Sanction: ISKA.
Division: Heavy. Winner: Dennis Alexio. KO-2. Loser:
   Laurence White.

November 13
Site: Marseille, France. Sanction: ISKA. Television: TFI
   (France).
Division: Light Heavy. Winner: Rick Roufus. DEC-12.
   Loser: Ernesto Hoost.

November 14
Site: Barcelona, Spain. Sanction: ISKA.
Division: Welter. Winner: Jose Equzquiza. KO-3. Loser:
   Jos Van Bejnen.
Division: Light Welter. Winner: Valerie Henin. DEC-10.
   Loser: Zelda Tekin.

November 21
Site: Paris, France. Sanction: ISKA. Television: Canal
   Plus-Europe (live).
Division: Light Heavy. Winner: Rob Kaman. TKO-7.
   Loser: Marek Piotrowski.
Division: Light Welter. Winner: Pete Cunningham.
   SDEC-12. Loser: Dida Diafat.
Division: Super Light. Winner: Cesar Joel. TKO-6.
   Loser: Fernando Calleros.

December 6
Site: Melbourne, Australia. Sanction: ISKA. Television:
   Australian National TV.
Division: Heavy. Dennis Alexio vs. Stan Longinidis.
   "No Decision" (Bout ended in six seconds when
   Alexio slipped on the canvas and broke two bones in
   his leg.)

Division: Welter. Winner: Hector Pena. DEC-12. Loser:
   Steve Vick.

December 18
Site: Montreal, Canada. Promoter: Joe Corley. Sanction:
   ISKA/PKC. Television: Showtime cable TV.
Division: Light Heavy. Winner: Rick Roufus. TKO-5.
   Loser: Jersey Long.
Division: Super Middle. Winner: Jean-Yves Theriault.
   DSQ-11. Loser: Leo De Snoo.

1991 WORLD PROFESSIONAL TITLE FIGHTS

January 12
Site: Anaheim, CA. Promoter: Ruben Urquidez/Steve
   Antonio/Dennis Warner. Sanction: WKA. Television:
   Pay-per-view; syndication.
Division: Light Heavy. Winner: Don Wilson. DEC-11.
   Loser: Gabe Carmichael.

March 8
Site: Gaillard, France. Promoter: Denis Fioraso.
   Sanction: ISKA.
Division: Light Middle. Winner: Denis Fioraso.
   MDEC-12. Loser: Curtis Bush.

March 15
Site: Marseille, France. Promoter: Erick Romeas.
   Sanction: ISKA.
Division: Super Middle. Winner: Jean-Yves Theriault.
   TKO-4. Loser: Michel Mangeot.

April 20
Site: Poznan, Poland. Promoter: Marek Frysz. Sanction:
   ISKA.
Division: Cruiser. Winner: Przemyslaw Saleta. DEC-12.
   Loser: Clement Salles.

May 5
Site: St. Gallen, Switzerland. Promoter: Petra Bruhin.
   Sanction: ISKA.
Division: Super Welter. Winner: Billy Murray. SDEC-12.
   Loser: Daniel Torre.

May 25
Site: Laughlin, NV. Promoter: Karyn Turner. Sanction:
   ISKA.
Division: Bantam. Winner: Kathy Long. DEC-10. Loser:
   Ramona Gatto.

June 11
Site: Virginia Beach, VA. Sanction: ISKA.

August 24, 1991: Dennis Alexio kicks Jerry Rhome. Courtesy of Jay T. Will

August 24, 1991: Rick Roufus (right) versus William Knorr. Courtesy of Jay T. Will

Division: Welter. Winner: Curtis Bush. KO-6. Loser: Piotr Falender.

June 15

Site: Dalton, GA. Promoter: Ben Kiker. Sanction: ISKA.
Division: Middle. Winner: Robert Harris. DEC-12. Loser: Michel Louart.

June 22

Site: Chicago, IL. Sanction: ISKA.
Division: Light Heavy. Winner: Rick Roufus. KO-2. Loser: Marek Piotrowski.
Division: Light Heavy. Winner: Paul Biafore. KO-6. Loser: Jose Santiago.

August 24

Site: Lake Tahoe, NV. Promoter: Joe Corley. Sanction: ISKA. Television: Showtime cable TV.
Division: Heavy. Winner: Dennis Alexio. TKO-4. Loser: Jerry Rhome.
Division: Light Heavy. Winner: Rick Roufus. DSQ-8. Loser: William Knorr.
Division: Super Heavy. Winner: Brad Hefton. DEC-12. Loser: Sergio Batarelli.

August 31

Site: St. Gallen, Switzerland. Promoter: Petra Bruhin. Sanction: ISKA.
Division: Super Welter. Winner: Billy Murray. TKO-5. Loser: Eric Melton.

September 21

Site: Warsaw, Poland. Promoter: Marek Frysz. Sanction: ISKA.
Division: Cruiser. Winner: Przemyslaw Saleta. DEC-12. Loser: Mark Longo.

October 4

Site: Gaillard, France. Promoter: Denis Fioraso. Sanction: ISKA.
Division: Light Middle. Winner: Denis Fioraso. TKO-8. Loser: Scott Ashley.

October 12

Site: Nashua, NH. Promoter: Frank Thiboutot. Sanction: ISKA.
Division: Bantam. Winner: Danny Melendez. TKO-3. Loser: Teddy Padilla.

October 16

Site: Honolulu, HI. Promoter: Tom Moffat. Sanction: ISKA.
Division: Heavy. Winner: Dennis Alexio. TKO-8. Loser: Clement Salles.

October 25

Site: Paris, France. Promoter: Pierre-Yves Benoliel. Sanction: ISKA.
Division: Super Middle. Winner: Jean-Yves Theriault. TKO-5. Loser: Klaus Nonnemacher.

November 5

Site: Audincourt, France. Sanction: ISKA.

Division: Light Middle. Winner: Patrick Prando. DEC-12. Loser: Curtis Bush.

November 23

Site: Marseille, France. Promoter: Erick Romeas. Sanction: ISKA.

Division: Super Middle. Winner: Jean-Yves Theriault. KO-4. Loser: Kevin Morton.

Site: Marseille, France. Promoter: Erick Romeas. Sanction: ISKA.

Division: Super Middle. Winner: Jean-Yves Theriault. KO-4. Loser: Kevin Morton.

December 8

Site: St. Gallen, Switzerland. Promoter: Petra Bruhin. Sanction: ISKA.

Division: Super Welter. Winner: El-Kadir Saddouki. DEC-12. Loser: Billy Murray.

December 20

Site: Paris, France. Promoter: Pierre-Yves Benoliel. Sanction: ISKA.

Division: Light Heavy. Winner: Rick Roufus. DEC-12. Loser: Rob Kaman.

1990 WORLD PROFESSIONAL TITLE FIGHTS

January 20

Site: Belfast, Northern Ireland. Promoter: Billy Murray. Sanction: ISKA.

Division: Welter. Winner: Billy Murray. KO-8. Loser: Farid Bennecer.

February 7

Site: Sacramento, CA. Sanction: ISKA.

Division: Heavy. Winner: Dennis Alexio. TKO-8. Loser: Dino Homsey.

February 20

Site: Montreal, Canada. Promoter: Michel Lavallee. Sanction: ISKA.

Division: Light Heavy. Winner: Jean-Yves Theriault. KO-4. Loser: Andy Mayo.

June 8

Site: Marseille, France. Promoter: Erick Romeas. Sanction: ISKA.

Division: Middle. Winner: Michel Mangeot. DEC-12. Loser: Rick Vathorst.

June 9

Site: Paris, France. Promoter: Emanuel Essesima. Sanction: ISKA.

Division: Light Middle. Winner: Curtis Bush. SDEC-12. Loser: Emanuel Essesima.

June 15

Site: Sopot, Poland. Promoter: Marek Frysz. Sanction: ISKA.

Division: Cruiser. Winner: Przemyslaw Saleta. TKO-11. Loser: Tom Hall.

August 6

Site: Lake Tahoe, NV. Promoter; Karyn Turner. Sanction: ISKA & KICK. Television: Pay-per-view (live).

Division: Heavy. Winner: Dennis Alexio, TKO-5. Loser: Darrell Henegan.

Division: Bantam. Winner: Kathy Long, DEC-12. Loser: Denise Taylor.

November 12

Site: Quebec City, Canada. Promoter: Serge Laflamme. Sanction: ISKA.

Division: Super Middle. Winner: Jean-Yves Theriault. DEC-12. Loser: Mark Longo.

Division: Super Light. Winner: Michel Rochette. DEC-12. Loser: Jerome Canabate.

November 29

Site: Virginia Beach, VA. Sanction: ISKA.

Division: Welter. Winner: Curtis Bush. KO-3. Loser: Bubba Walters.

December 17

Site: Montreal, Canada. Promoter: Michel Lavallee. Sanction: ISKA.

Division: Super Middle. Winner: Jean-Yves Theriault. KO-1. Loser: Yedidiah Judah.

1989 WORLD PROFESSIONAL TITLE FIGHTS

February 3

Site: Marseille, France. Promoter: Erick Romeas. Sanction: ISKA.

Division: Middle. Winner: Michel Mangeot. TKO-5. Loser: Jean May.

February 19

Site: Amsterdam, Holland. Promoter: Jan Plas. Sanction: ISKA.

Division: Feather. Winner: Lucia Rijker. KO-2. Loser: Martine Koukindji.

March 15

Site: Belfast, Northern Ireland. Promoter: Billy Murray. Sanction: ISKA.

Division: Super Welter. Winner: Richard Hill. SDEC-12. Loser: Billy Murray.

March 18

Site: Berlin, Germany. Promoter: Georg Bruckner. Sanction: PKO. Television: German TV.

Division: Light Heavy. Winner: Don Wilson. KO-9. Loser: Ferdinand Mack.

April 21

Site: Geneva, Switzerland. Promoter: Daniel Perioud. Sanction: ISKA.

Division: Super Middle. Winner: Jean-Yves Theriault. SDEC-12. Loser: Ernesto Hoost.

May 28

Site: Amsterdam, Holland. Promoter: Johan Vos. Sanction: ISKA.

Division: Feather. Winner: Lucia Rijker. KO-5. Loser: Bonnie Canino.

June 3

Site: Chattanooga, TN. Promoter: Ben Kiker. Sanction: ISKA.

Division: Middle. Winner: Robert Harris. DEC-12. Loser: John Longstreet.

June 10

Site: Lausanne, Switzerland. Sanction: ISKA.

Division: Light. Winner: Johnny Canabate. DEC-12. Loser: Pat Romero.

July 28

Site: LaHavre, France. Promoter: Jean Pieters. Sanction: ISKA.

Division: Light Heavy. Winner: Jean-Yves Theriault. Loser: Bob Thurman.

September 12

Site: Belfast, Northern Ireland. Promoter: Billy Murray. Sanction: ISKA.

Division: Super Welter. Winner: Billy Murray. DEC-12. Loser: Richard Hill.

October 20

Site: Marseille, France. Sanction: ISKA.

Division: Middle. Winner: Michel Mangeot. KO-1. Loser: Robert Harris.

December 12

Site: Montreal, Canada. Promoter: Michel Lavallee. Sanction: ISKA.

Division: Super Middle. Winner: Jean-Yves Theriault. KO-4. Loser: William Knor.

1988 WORLD PROFESSIONAL TITLE FIGHTS

February 2

Site: Lausanne, Switzerland. Promoter: Mohammad Hosseini. Sanction: ISKA.

Division: Feather. Winner: Jerome Canabate. DEC-12. Loser: Bilam Nesradine.

May 15

Site: Miami, FL. Promoter: Robert Heale. Sanction: ISKA.

Division: Heavy. Winner: Dennis Alexio. KO-4. Loser: Tommy Morton.

April 21

Site: Palermo, Italy. Sanction: IKL.

Division: Heavy. Title: World. Winner: Jim Graden. TKO-8. Loser: Bruno Campiglia.

August 12

Site: San Jose, CA. Promoter: Scott Coker. Sanction: ISKA. Television: SCORE.

Division: Light Middle. Winner: Sam Montgomery. DEC-12. Loser: Ricky Haynes.

August 19

Site: El Paso, TX. Promoter: Hilary Sandoval. Sanction: ISKA. Television: SCORE.

Division: Light Welter. Winner: Cliff Thomas. KO-4. Loser: Eric Melton.

Site: Chicago, IL. Sanction: ISKA. Television: SCORE.

Division: Cruiser. Winner: Rob Salazar. DEC-12. Loser: Lowell Nash.

October 1

Site: Rockford, IL. Promoter: Dave McGinty. Sanction: ISKA. Television: SCORE.

Division: Super Heavy. Winner: Jerry Rhome. MDEC-12. Loser: Brad Hefton.

October 8

Site: Lake Tahoe, NV. Promoter: Scott Coker. Sanction: ISKA. Television: SCORE.

Division: Cruiser. Winner: Don Wilson. SDEC-12. Loser: Rob Salazar.

October 15
Site: Miami, FL. Promoter: Robert Heale. Sanction: ISKA. Television: SCORE.
Division: Heavy. Winner: Dennis Alexio. TKO-3. Loser: Tommy Morton.

November 13
Site: New York, NY. Promoter: Louis Neglia. Sanction: ISKA. Television: SCORE.
Division: Heavy. Winner: Dennis Alexio. KO-3. Loser: Maurice Tornesi.

November 20
Site: Montreal, Canada. Promoter: Light Heavy. Sanction: ISKA. Television: SCORE.
Division: Light Heavy. Winner: Jean-Yves Theriault. KO-5. Loser: William Knorr.

(Coors Beer-sponsored ISKA fights began airing on the SCORE cable channel on March 7.)

1987 WORLD PROFESSIONAL TITLE FIGHTS

January 9
Site: Miami, FL. Promoter: Chip Post. Sanction: WKA.
Division: Cruiser. Winner: James Warring. DEC-12. Loser: Neil Singleton.

January 19
Site: Merrit Island, FL. Promoter: Chip Post. Sanction: WKA.
Division: Light Heavy. Winner: Don Wilson. TKO-6. Loser: Paul Ford.

January 21
Site: Perth, Australia. Promoter: Bob Jones. Sanction: WKA.
Division: Super Light Heavy. Stan Longinidis vs. Santiago Garza. DRW-12.
Division: Super Light. Winner: Ronnie Green. SDEC-12. Loser: Fuzimo Fujimoto.
Division: Super Heavy. Winner: Maurice Smith. KO-5. Loser: Dino Homsey.

February 1
Site: Amsterdam, Holland. Sanction: WKA.
Division: Super Feather. Winner: Joao Vierra. DEC-12. Loser: Dave Johnston.

February 6
Site: Vallejo, CA. Sanction: ISKA.

Division: Cruiser. Winner: Dennis Alexio. KO-4. Loser: Denny Reynolds.

February 14
Site: Memphis, TN. Promoter: Anthony Elmore. Sanction: KICK.
Division: Super Heavy. Winner: Anthony Elmore. DEC-12. Loser: Melvin Cole.

February 15
Site: Harbor Castle, Canada. Promoter: Mick McNamara. Sanction: ISKA.
Division: Welter. Winner: Paul Biafore. MDEC-12. Loser: Richard Hill.

February 27
Site: Tulsa, OK. Promoter: Dale Cook. Sanction: WKA.
Division: Middle. Winner: Dale Cook. DEC-12. Loser: Pascal LePlat.

March 1
Site: Istanbul, Turkey. Sanction: ISKA.
Division: Middle. Winner: John Longstreet. DEC-12. Loser: Refik Gocek.

March 9
Site: Vancouver, B.C., Canada. Sanction: WKA.
Division: Bantam. Winner: Leah Goldstein. DEC-7. Loser: Arlene Webber.

March 14
Site: El Paso, TX. Promoter: Hilary Sandoval. Sanction: ISKA.
Division: Light Welter. Winner: Cliff Thomas. TKO-9. Loser: Thomas Chesterfield.

March 20
Site: Twin Falls, IA. Promoter: Gene Starr. Sanction: ISKA.
Division: Fly. Winner: Carl Sklavos. MDEC-12. Loser: Jerry Clarke.

April 3
Site: Lausanne, Switzerland. Promoter: Richard Mayor. Sanction: ISKA.
Division: Feather. Winner: Jerome Canabate. DEC-12. Loser: Jorge Angot.

April 4
Site: Bradenton, FL. Promoter: John Ingram. Sanction: ISKA.
Division: Fly. Winner: Jerry Clarke. KO-1. Loser: David McGee.

April 17
Site: Richmond, CA. Sanction: ISKA.

Division: Cruiser. Winner: Dennis Alexio. DEC-8. Loser: Paul Madison.

April 22

Site: Cocoa Beach, FL. Promoter: Chip Post. Sanction: WKA.
Division: Light Heavy. Winner: Don Wilson. TKO-4. Loser: Roger Hurd.

April 25

Site: Atlanta, GA. Promoter: Abernethy Sports. Sanction: PKC. Television: ESPN cable.
Division: Middle. Winner: Rick Roufus. KO-7. Loser: John Moncayo.
Division: Welter. Winner: David Humphries, DEC-15. Loser: Dan Magnus.
Division: Super Heavy. Winner: Brad Hefton. TKO-12. Loser: Anthony Elmore.
Division: Heavy. Winner: James Warring, KO-4. Loser: Jerry Rhome.

May 3

Site: Toronto, Canada. Promoter: Mick and Mike McNamara. Sanction: ISKA.
Division: Welter. Winner: Richard Hill. DEC-12. Loser: Paul Biafore.

Site: Pueblo, CO. Promoter: Rocky Guererro. Sanction: WKA.
Division: Bantam. Winner: Lawrence Miera. DEC-12. Loser: Yuki Horiuchi.

May 5

Site: Montreal, Canada. Promoter: Richard Dufresne. Sanction: ISKA.
Division: Light Heavy. Winner: Jean-Yves Theriault. KO-1. Loser: C.L. Bergeron.

May 16

Site: San Juan, Puerto Rico. Sanction: WKA.
Division: Super Feather. Winner: Victor Solier. KO-2. Loser: John Melton.

Site: South Haven, MS. Promoter: Jimmy Blann. Sanction: KICK.
Division: Welter. Winner: Tom Laroche. DEC-12. Loser: Jimmy Blann.

May 30

Site: Birmingham, England. Promoter: Brown Promotions. Sanction: WKA.
Division: Bantam. Winner: Howard Brown. DEC-12. Loser: Ruben Valdarez.

Site: Denver, CO. Sanction: PKC.
Division: Feather. Winner: Felipe Garcia. DEC-15. Loser: Miguel Montoya.

June 3

Site: Lake Tahoe, NV. Promoter: Karyn Turner/John Worley. Sanction: ISKA. Television: ESPN cable.
Division: Fly. Winner: Carl Sklavos. DEC-12. Loser: Jerry Clarke.
Division: Cruiser. Winner: Dennis Alexio. DEC-12. Loser: Larry McFadden.

June 5

Site: Paris, France. Sanction: IKL.
Division: Middle. Winner: Christian Battesti. KO-3. Loser: Youssef Zenaf.

June 12

Site: Tulsa, OK. Promoter: Dale Cook. Sanction: WKA.
Division: Middle. Winner: Dale Cook. KO-1. Loser: Donald Tucker.

June 16

Site: Dalton, GA. Promoter: Ben Kiker. Sanction: PKC.
Division: Middle. Winner: Robert Harris. TKO-4. Loser: Michel Lupart.

June 19

Site: Nice, France. Sanction: PKC.
Division: Feather. Winner: Edmond Ardissone. DEC-12. Loser: Aldaberto Leal.

June 16, 1987: Referee Jay T. Will helps a stunned Michel Lupart of France back to his corner after being stopped by Robert Harris. Courtesy of Jay T. Will

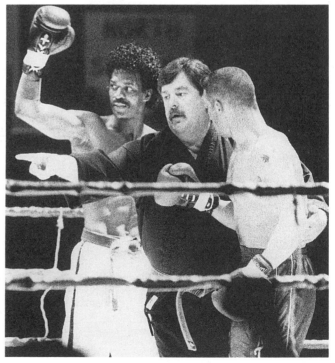

June 20

Site: Denver, CO. Promoter: Karyn Turner. Sanction: ISKA.

Division: Heavy. Winner: Dennis Alexio. DEC-12. Loser: Jeff Hollins.

June 26

Site: Geneva, Switzerland. Promoter: Claude Proz. Sanction: ISKA.

Division: Light Middle. Winner: Jean-Marc Tonus. DEC-12. Loser: Bob Thurman.

June 27

Site: San Juan, Puerto Rico. Sanction: WKA.

Division: Feather. Winner: Victor Solier. TKO-12. Loser: Lawrence Miera.

July 10

Site: Albuquerque, NM. Promoter: Bill Packer. Sanction: ISKA.

Division: Light. Winner: Pat Romero. TKO-4. Loser: Jimmy Tappia.

August 8

Site: Tulsa, OK. Promoter: Dale Cook. Sanction: WKA.

Division: Heavy. Winner: Maurice Smith. KO-8. Loser: Charles Archie.

Division: Feather. Winner: Rod Kei. DEC-12. Loser: Pee Wee Walker.

Site: El Paso, TX. Promoter: Hilary Sandoval. Sanction: ISKA.

Division: Light. Winner: Cliff Thomas. TKO-6. Loser: Dickie Jordan.

Division: Bantam. Winner: Troy Dorsey. DEC-12. Loser: Felipe Garcia.

Division: Atom. Winner: Rico Brockington. KO-2. Loser: Ricardo Rodarte.

August 16

Site: Lancaster, PA. Promoter: Terry Nye. Sanction: FFKA.

Division: Feather. Winner: Johnny Davis. KO-1. Loser: Jerry Smith.

August 30

Site: St. Paul, MN. Promoter: John Worley and Larry Carnahan. Sanction: ISKA.

Division: Middle. Winner: John Longstreet. KO-6. Loser: Jordan Keepers.

September 5

Site: Tokyo, Japan. Promoter: All Japan Promotions. Sanction: WKA.

Division: Fly. Winner: Miguel Montoya. KO-1. Loser: Tsuchida Kontaro.

September 26

Site: Southaven, MS. Promoter: Jimmy Blann. Sanction: KICK.

Division: Welter. Winner: Jimmy Blann. TKO-4. Loser: Chris Samples.

September 28

Site: Amsterdam, Holland. Sanction: WKA.

Division: Super Middle. Winner: Rob Kaman. KO-1. Loser: Roger Hurd.

October 14

Site: Lausanne, Switzerland. Sanction: ISKA.

Division: Feather. Winner: Jerome Canabate. MDEC-12. Loser: Santae Wilson.

October 16

Site: Paris, France. Sanction: WKA.

Division: Super Light. Winner: Richard Sylla. TKO-10. Loser: Brian Cullen.

October 17

Site: St. Paul, MN. Promoter: John Worley and Larry Carnahan. Sanction: ISKA.

Division: Middle. Winner: John Longstreet. DEC-12. Loser: Martin Friolet.

October 24

Site: Memphis, TN. Promoter: Melvin Cole. Sanction: WKA.

Division: Super Heavy. Winner: Raymond Horsey. TKO-7. Loser: Melvin Cole.

Division: Feather. Winner: Tanya Mackwood. TKO-2. Loser: Debbie Jones.

October 30

Site: Boynton Beach, FL. Promoter: Bill Berryman. Sanction: WKA.

Division: Cruiser. Winner: Ernest Simmons. TKO-2. Loser: Shawn Bonner.

November 7

Site: Denver, CO. Promoter: Karyn Turner. Sanction: ISKA.

Division: Heavy. Winner: Dennis Alexio. KO-2. Loser: Al Mims.

November 8

Site: Amsterdam, Holland. Promoter: Thom Harinck. Sanction: WKA.

Division: Super Welter. Winner: Ivan Hyppolyte. DEC-12. Loser: David Humphries.

Division: Light. Winner: Gilbert Ballantine. TKO-4. Loser: Norris Williams.

Division: Feather. Winner: Lucia Rijker. KO-4. Loser: Valerie Henin.

November 10

Site: Montreal, Canada. Promoter: Richard Dufresne. Sanction: ISKA.

Division: Light Heavy. Winner: Jean-Yves Theriault. KO-2. Loser: Larry McFadden.

November 11

Site: Atlanta, GA. Sanction: FFKA.

Division: Heavy. Winner: Jerry Rhome. SDEC-12. Loser: Darrell Henegan.

November 15

Site: Tokyo, Japan. Sanction: WKA.

Division: Fly. Winner: Miguel Montoya. DEC-12. Loser: Kimihiko Akatsuchai.

Site: El Paso, TX. Promoter: Hilary Sandoval. Sanction: ISKA.

Division: Light Welter. Winner: Cliff Thomas. KO-5. Loser: Lafayette Lawson.

November 17

Site: Las Vegas, NV. Promoter: Karyn Turner. Sanction: ISKA.

Division: Bantam. Winner: Troy Dorsey. TKO-8. Loser: Steve Demencuk.

November 21

Site: Lausanne, Switzerland. Promoter: Mohammad Hosseini. Sanction: ISKA.

Division: Feather. Winner: Santae Wilson. TKO-11. Loser: Jerome Canabate.

Site: Marseille, France. Promoter: Erick Romeas. Sanction: ISKA.

Division: Middle. Winner: Christian Battesti. SDEC-12. Loser: Johnny Davis.

December 12

Site: Orlando, FL. Promoter: Bob Heinkins. Sanction: KICK. Television: Pay-per-view; syndication.

Division: Light Heavy. Winner: Don Wilson. TKO-7. Loser: Branimir Cikatic.

1987 YEAR-END DATA

The STAR System documented the outcomes of 306 events in 1987 and estimated that some 415 kickboxing events in total were promoted worldwide, featuring 2,905 individual bouts (an average of seven bouts per event), which represents a 2% decrease compared with 1986.

1986 WORLD PROFESSIONAL TITLE FIGHTS

January 25

Site: Las Vegas, NV. Promoter: Jim Smith. Sanction: KICK.

Division: Middle. Winner: John Moncayo. DEC-12. Loser: Dale Cook.

Division: Light. Winner: Norris Williams. DEC-12. Loser: Tony Rosser.

February ?

Site: Denver, CO. Promoter: Karyn Turner. Sanction: PKA.

Division: Light Feather. Winner: Felipe Garcia. DEC-12. Loser: David Hamilton.

February 2

Site: Toronto, Canada. Promoter: Mike McNamara. Sanction: PKA.

Division: Light. Winner: Leo Loucks. DEC-12. Loser: Cliff Thomas.

February 21

Site: Edmonton, Canada. Promoter: Frank Lee. Sanction: WKA.

Division: Super Welter. Winner: Billy Chau. TKO-6. Loser: Daryl Penn.

February 28

Site: Hollywood, CA. Promoter: Ruben Urquidez. Sanction: WKA.

Division: Light. Winner: Pete Cunningham. KO-3. Loser: Phil Holdridge.

March 24

Site: Paris, France. Promoter: Gilles Belloni. Sanction: IKL.

Division: Super Middle. Winner: Rik v.d. Vathorst. KO-1.

April 26

Site: Atlanta, GA. Promoter: Jim Abernethy. Sanction: PKA.

Division: Middle. Winner: Jean-Yves Theriault. TKO-4. Loser: Bob Thurman.

Division: Heavy. Winner: Jerry Rhome. KO-7. Loser: Brad Hefton.

Division: Light Welter. Winner: Jerry Trimble. TSDEC-6. Loser: Leroy Taylor.

May 4

Site: Reseda, CA. Promoter: Ruben Urquidez. Sanction: WKA.

Division: Super Feather. Winner: Dave Johnston. DEC-12. Loser: Yohan Kim.

May 5

Site: Edmonton, Canada. Promoter: Frank Lee.
Sanction: WKA.

Division: Super Welter. Winner: David Humphries.
DEC-12. Loser: Billy Chau.

Site: Amsterdam, Holland. Promoter: Ampye Verkaart.
Sanction: WKA.

Division: Bantam. Winner: Joao Vierra. DEC-12. Loser:
Rod Kei.

May 10

Site: Tulsa, OK. Sanction: WKA.

Division: Super Middle. Winner: Dale Cook. DEC-12.
Loser: Tony Smith.

May 16

Site: Memphis, TN. Promoter: Pat Wrenn/Jim Smith.
Sanction: KICK.

Division: Light. Winner: Norris Williams. DEC-12.
Loser: Dale Frye.

May 17

Site: Atlanta, GA. Promoter: Jim Abernethy. Sanction:
PKC. Television: ESPN cable.

Division: Bantam. Winner: Edmond Ardissone. TKO-6.
Loser: Jorge Angot.

June 14

Site: Warner-Robbins, GA. Promoter: David Barber.
Sanction: WKA.

Division: Super Heavy. Winner: Raymond Horsey.
KO-4. Loser: Ray Williams.

June 28

Site: Reno, NV. Promoter: Howard Hanson. Sanction:
WKA.

Division: Super Light. Winner: Pete Cunningham.
DEC-12. Loser: Pat Romero.

Site: Memphis, TN. Promoter: Anthony Elmore.
Sanction: KICK.

Division: Super Heavy. Winner: Anthony Elmore.
DEC-12. Loser: Jeff Hollins.

August 8

Site: Denver, CO. Promoter: Karyn Turner. Sanction:
ISKA.

Division: Cruiser. Winner: Dennis Alexio. KO-4. Loser:
Lowell Nash.

Division: Bantam. Winner: Felipe Garcia. DEC-12.
Loser: Troy Dorsey.

August 15

Site: El Paso, TX. Promoter: Hilary Sandoval. Sanction:
ISKA.

Division: Light Welter. Tony Rosser vs. Cliff Thomas.
DRW-12.

August 30

Site: Memphis, TN. Promoter: Anthony Elmore.
Sanction: KICK.

Division: Super Heavy. Winner: Anthony Elmore.
TKO-12. Loser: Melvin Cole.

September 10

Site: Atlanta, GA. Promoter: Joe Corley. Sanction: PKC.
Division: Super Heavy. Winner: Jerry Rhome. TKO-1.
Loser: Philippe Coutelas.

September 22

Site: Cocoa Beach, FL. Promoter: Jim Wilson. Sanction:
WKA.

Division: Light Heavy. Winner: Don Wilson. KO-5.
Loser: Rich Lopez.

September 30

Site: Montreal, Canada. Promoter: Victor Theriault.
Sanction: PKC.

Division: Middle. Winner: Jean-Yves Theriault. KO-4.
Loser: Richard Green.

October 4

Site: Minneapolis, MN. Promoter: John Worley & Larry
Carnahan. Sanction: ISKA.

Division: Middle. Winner: John Longstreet. KO-8.
Loser: John Moncayo.

October 9

Site: Lausanne, Switzerland. Promoter: Mohammed
Hosseini. Sanction: ISKA.

Division: Feather. Winner: Jerome Canabate. TKO-4.
Loser: Jerry Clarke.

October 12

Site: Amsterdam, Holland. Sanction: WKA.
Division: Bantam. Winner: Miloud El Geubli. DEC-12.
Loser: Joao Vierra.

October 14

Site: Atlanta, GA. Promoter: Joe Corley. Sanction: PKC.
Television: ESPN cable.

Division: Light Welter. Jerry Trimble vs. Leroy Taylor.
DRW-12.

October 25

Site: Lake Tahoe, NV. Promoter: Karyn Turner.
Sanction: ISKA.

Division: Light. Winner: Pat Romero. KO-4. Loser:
Norris Williams.

Site: Daytona Beach, FL. Promoter: Mike Sawyer &
Mike McCoy. Sanction: ISKA.
Division: Welter. Winner: Richard Hill. TKO-9. Loser:
Curtis Bush.

October 26

Site: London, Canada. Sanction: PKA.
Division: Light. Winner: Leo Loucks. TMDEC-5. Loser:
Mark Gurley.

November ?

Site: Nice, France. Sanction: PKC.
Division: Light Feather. Winner: Aldaberto Leal.
TKO-6. Loser: Edmond Ardissone.

November 1

Site: Yuma, AZ. Sanction: WKA.
Division: Super Light. Winner: Pete Cunningham.
KO-7. Loser: Okubo Hirokawa.

Site: Kings Mountain, NC. Sanction: WKA.
Division: Super Welter. Winner: David Humphries.
TKO-4. Loser: Ray Rice.
Division: Cruiser. Winner: Gerald Murray. KO-1. Loser:
Jeff Robinson.

November 4

Site: Tulsa, OK. Promoter: Dale Cook. Sanction: WKA.
Division: Super Middle. Winner: Dale Cook. DEC-12.
Loser: Troy Howland.

November 21

Site: Marseille, France. Sanction: ISKA.
Division: Middle. Winner: Christian Battesti. SDEC-12.
Loser: Johnny Davis.
Division: Feather. Winner: Santae Wilson. KO-9. Loser:
Jerome Canabate.
(IKL Sanction)
Division: Super Middle. Winner: Youssef Zenaf.
DEC-10. Loser: Christian Battesti.

November 22

Site: Lake Helen, FL. Sanction: PKC. Television: ESPN
cable.
Division: Welter. Winner: David Humphries. DEC-12.
Loser: Ricky Haynes.

Site: Ponce, Puerto Rico. Sanction: WKA.
Division: Feather. Winner: Lawrence Miera. TKO-3.
Loser: Victor Solier.

Site: Atlanta, GA. Sanction: WKA.
Division: Super Heavy. Winner: Maurice Smith. TKO-6.
Loser: Raymond Horsey.

November 23

Site: London, England. Sanction: WKA.
Division: Bantam. Winner: Lisa Howarth. DEC-7.
Loser: Dayle Baykey.

November 28

Site: Paris, France. Sanction: WKA.
Division: Super Light. Winner: Richard Sylla. DEC-12.
Loser: Pete Cunningham.

1985 WORLD PROFESSIONAL TITLE FIGHTS

January 5

Site: Rockford, IL. Promoter: John Monczak. Sanction:
PKA. Television: Syndication.
Division: Heavy. Winner: Brad Hefton. Loser: KO-3.
Loser: Philippe Coutelas.
Division: Welter. Winner: Alvin Prouder. MDEC-12.
Loser: Ricky Haines.

January 12

Site: Reno, NV. Promoter: Howard Hanson. Sanction:
WKA.
Division: Heavy. Winner: Maurice Smith. TKO-8.
Loser: Jimmy Walker.
Division: Super Welter. Winner: Billy Chau. TKO-7.
Loser: Milt Bennett.

January 27

Site: Tokyo, Japan. Promoter: Kimio Akage. Sanction:
WKA.
Division: Middle. Winner: Yasuo Tabata. KO-2. Loser:
Garlic Philip.

February 2

Site: Denver, CO. Promoter: Karyn Turner. Sanction:
PKA. Television: Syndication.
Division: Welter. Winner: Johnny Davis. MDEC-12.
Loser: Alvin Prouder.

February 3

Site: Amsterdam, Holland. Promoter: Netherlands Kick
Boxing Bunde. Sanction: WKA.
Division: Super Middle. Winner: Rob Kaman. KO-3.
Loser: Larry McFadden.

February 16

Site: Atlantic City, NJ. Promoter: Howard Petschler.
Sanction: PKA. Television: NBC (live).
Division: Heavy. Winner: Brad Hefton. SDEC-12. Loser:
Tom Hall.

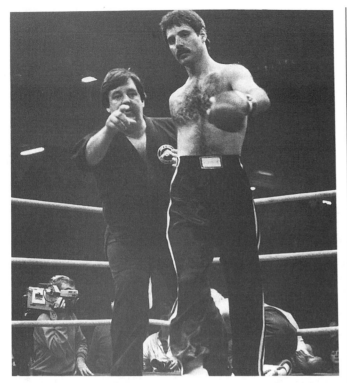

May 1, 1985: Referee Jay T. Will directs Jean-Yves Theriault to a neutral corner. A crumpled Andy Brewer lies behind them. Courtesy of Jay T. Will

March 1
Site: Nanaimo, B.C., Canada. Promoter: Don Arnott. Sanction: WKA.
Division: Heavy. Winner: Maurice Smith. SDEC-12. Loser: Gord Racett.

March 2
Site: El Paso, TX. Promoter: Hilary Sandoval. Sanction: PKA.
Division: Light. Winner: Cliff Thomas. TKO-8. Loser: Kevin Hillhouse.

March 30
Site: Kamloops, Canada. Promoter: Barry Adkins. Sanction: KICK.
Division: Welter. Winner: Tom Laroche. DEC-12. Loser: Rick Simerly.

April 6
Site: Sacramento, CA. Promoter: Sid Tanner/Tony Thompson/Ed Fong. Sanction: PKA. Television: ESPN cable.
Division: Light Heavy. Winner: Dennis Alexio. TKO-4. Loser: Bernard Clark.

Site: Northridge, CA. Promoter: Jet Center Productions. Sanction: WKA.

Division: Light. Winner: Pete Cunningham. TKO-2. Loser: Robert Visitacion.

May 1
Site: Hull, Canada. Promoter: John Therien. Sanction: PKA. Television: CTV.
Division: Middle. Winner: Jean-Yves Theriault. KO-1. Loser: Andy Brewer.

May 11
Site: Rockford, IL. Promoter: John Monczak. Sanction: PKA. Television: ESPN cable.
Division: Welter. Winner: Ricky Haynes. KO-10. Loser: Johnny Davis.

June 1
Site: Memphis, TN. Promoter: Anthony Elmore. Sanction: KICK.
Division: Heavy. Winner: Anthony Elmore. DEC-12. Loser: Bill Morrison.
Division: Light. Winner: Tony Rosser. DEC-12. Loser: Robert Visitacion.

June 7
Site: Rockford, IL. Promoter: John Monczak. Sanction: PKA. Television: ESPN cable.
Division: Heavy. Brad Hefton. KO-5. Loser: Curtis Crandall.

June 8
Site: El Paso, TX. Promoter: Hilary Sandoval. Sanction: PKA. Television: ESPN cable.

June 7, 1985: "Bad" Brad Hefton kicks Curtis Crandall. Courtesy of Jay T. Will

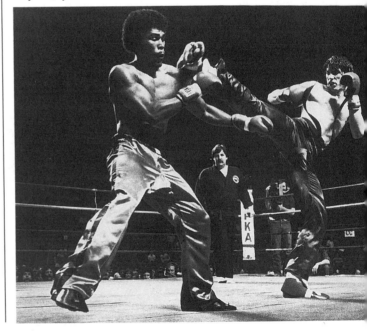

Division: Light. Winner: Cliff Thomas. TKO-8. Loser: Garry Garner.

Division: Light Welter. Winner: Leroy Taylor. TKO-5. Loser: Ishmael Robles.

Site: Victoria, B.C., Canada. Promoter: Don Arnott. Sanction: WKA.

Division: Super Heavy. Winner: Gord Racette. KO-4. Loser: John Jackson.

June 15

Site: West Palm Beach, FL. Promoter: Jim Abernethy. Sanction: PKA. Television: ESPN cable.

Division: Light Middle. Winner: Bob Thurman. DEC-12. Loser: John Moncayo.

Division: Light Welter. Winner: Jerry Trimble. DEC-7. Loser: Fred Arce.

June 29

Site: Atlantic City, NJ. Promoter: Howard Petschler. Sanction: PKA.

Division: Heavy. Winner: Brad Hefton. TKO-7. Loser: Jeff Hollins.

July 13

Site: London, England. Promoter: Master Toddy. Sanction: WKA.

Division: Light. Winner: Pat Romero. DEC-12. Loser: Ronnie Green.

August 3

Site: Rome, Italy. Sanction: IKL.

Division: Super Light. Winner: Rocky Benacef. MDEC-8. Loser: Giorgio Perreca.

August 24

Site: Las Vegas, NV. Promoter: Howard Hanson. Sanction: WKA.

Division: Heavy. Winner: Maurice Smith. KO-8. Loser: Bill Morrison.

September 7

Site: Cincinnati, OH. Promoter: Teresa Pryor. Sanction: PKA.

Division: Bantam. Winner: Jerry Clarke. DSQ-6. Loser: Rico Brockington.

October 4

Site: Tijuana, Mexico. Promoter: Paco Bazan/Angel Gutierrez. Sanction: WKA.

Division: Light. Winner: Pete Cunningham. KO-3. Loser: Angel Gutierrez.

October 5

Site: Nanaimo, B.C., Canada. Promoter: Don Arnott. Sanction: WKA.

Division: Feather. Winner: Victor Solier. DEC-12. Loser: Rod Kei.

October 6

Site: Amsterdam, Holland. Promoter: Thom Harinck. Sanction: ?. Television: ?.

Division: Feather. Winner: Lucia Rijker. DEC-7. Loser: Cheryl Wheeler.

October 10

Site: West Palm Beach, FL. Promoter: Joe Corley. Sanction: PKA. Television: ESPN cable.

Division: Light Middle. Winner: Bob Thurman. MDEC-12. Loser: John Moncayo.

October 11

Site: New Orleans, LA. Promoter: Jimmy Rodriguez. Sanction: WKA.

Division: Super Light Heavy. Winner: Curtis Crandall. KO-5. Loser: Al Mims.

October 16

Site: Nanaimo, Canada. Promoter: Don Arnott. Sanction: WKA.

Division: Feather. Winner: Victor Solier. DEC-12. Loser: Rod Kei.

October 19

Site: Manchester, England. Promoter: Master Toddy. Sanction: WKA.

Division: Super Feather. Winner: Ronnie Green. KO-1. Loser: Masahiro Nagohama.

October 20

Site: Amsterdam, Holland. Promoter: Ampye Verkaart. Sanction: WKA.

Division: Middle. Winner: Fred Royers. DEC-12. Loser: Yasuo Tabata.

November 2

Site: Rockford, IL. Promoter: John Monczak. Sanction: PKA. Television: ESPN cable.

Division: Heavy. Winner: Brad Hefton. KO-9. Loser: Curtis Crandall.

Division: Welter. Winner: Alvin Prouder. SDEC-12. Loser: Ricky Haynes.

November 16

Site: Northridge, CA. Promoter: Ruben Urquidez. Sanction: WKA.

Division: Welter. Winner: Benny Urquidez. DEC-12. Loser: Tom Laroche.

December 5

Site: Paris, France. Sanction: IKL.

Division: Super Middle. Winner: Youssef Zenaf.
DEC-9. Loser: Fred Royers.

Site: Tijuana, Mexico. Promoter: Eddie Mapula.
Sanction: WKA.
Division: Super Fly. Winner: Yuki Horiuchi. TKO-6.
Loser: Ricardo Rodarte.

December 15
Site: Montreal, Canada. Promoter: Real Masse.
Sanction: KICK.
Division: Welter. Winner: Ducarmel Cyrius. KO-4.
Loser: Billye Jackson.

December 16
Site: Northridge, CA. Promoter: Ruben Urquidez.
Sanction: WKA.
Division: Welter. Winner: Benny Urquidez. DEC-12.
Loser: Tom Laroche.

1985 YEAR-END DATA

The STAR System documented the outcomes of 277
events in 1985 and estimated that some 453 kickboxing
events in total were promoted worldwide, featuring
3,171 individual bouts (an average of seven bouts per
event), which represents a 29% decrease compared with
1984.

1984 WORLD PROFESSIONAL TITLE FIGHTS

January 7
Site: Reno, NV. Promoter: Howard Hanson/Richard
Lopushinsky. Sanction: WKA. Television: SPO cable.
Division: Heavy. Winner: Maurice Smith. TKO-8.
Loser: Dana Goodson.

January 15
Site: Amsterdam, Holland. Promoter: Thom Harinck.
Sanction: MTBN.
Division: Welter. Winner: Benny Urquidez. TKO-5.
Loser: Ivan Sprang.
Division: Feather. Winner: Lucia Rijker. KO-1. Loser:
Lilly Rodriguez.

January 20
Site: Juarez, Mexico. Sanction: WKA.
Division: Cruiser. Winner: James Warring. KO-3. Loser:
Don Nielsen.
Division: Super Fly. Winner: Ron Cisneros. TKO-9.
Loser: Ricardo Rodarte.

March 29, 1984: Don Wilson (right) on his way to defeating
Dennis Alexio. Courtesy of Paul Maslak and Don Wilson

Site: Nice, France. Promoter: Jean-Paul Ardissone;
Jean-Marie Delcort; Jean-Claude Wurstenburg.
Sanction: PKA. Television: French TV.
Division: Super Light. Winner: Edmond Ardissone.
TKO-12. Loser: Felipe Garcia.

January 26
Site: New York, NY. Promoter: Bruce Turnbull/Henry
Barbey. Sanction: PKA.
Division: Middle. Winner: Jean-Yves Theriault. KO-6.
Loser: Paul Ford.

February 25
Site: Duncan, OH. Sanction: WKA.
Division: Bantam. Winner: Rod Kei. KO-3. Loser: Lloyd
Anderson.

March 3
Site: Zurich, Switzerland. Sanction: IKL.
Division: Super Middle. Winner: Youssef Zenaf.
DEC-6. Loser: Franz Haller.

March 29
Site: Hollywood-by-the-Sea, FL. Promoter: Howard
Hanson. Sanction: WKA. Television: NBC.

Division: Super Light Heavy. Winner: Don Wilson. DEC-12. Loser: Dennis Alexio.

April 6

Site: El Paso, TX. Promoter: Hilary Sandoval. Sanction: PKA. Television: ESPN cable.
Division: Light. Winner: Cliff Thomas. TKO-9. Loser: Tommy Williams.
Division: Light Welter. Winner: Ishmael Robles. KO-1. Loser: Fermin Garcia.

April 10

Site: Verdun, Canada. Promoter: Real Masse. Sanction: PKA. Television: ESPN cable; CTV.
Division: Middle. Winner: Jean-Yves Theriault. KO-7. Loser: Rodney Batiste.

April 21

Site: Amsterdam, Holland. Sanction: WKA.
Division: Welter. Winner: Andre Brilleman. DEC-12. Loser: Howard Jackson.

May 5

Site: Atlantic City, NJ. Promoter: Howard Petschler. Sanction: PKA. Television: NBC; ESPN cable.
Division: Heavy. Winner: John Jackson. DEC-9. Loser: Randall Cobb.
Division: Feather. Winner: Yoel Judah. ?. Loser: Salerno.

April 10, 1984: Referee Jay T. Will counts over challenger Rodney Batiste after he was floored by Jean-Yves Theriault. Courtesy of Jay T. Will

May 12

Site: Rockford, IL. Promoter: John Monczak. Sanction: PKA. Television: ESPN cable.
Division: Heavy. Winner: Brad Hefton. TKO-8. Loser: Kerry Roop.

June 9

Site: Memphis, TN. Promoter: Anthony Elmore. Sanction: PKA. Television: ESPN cable.
Division: Super Heavy. Winner: Anthony Elmore. KO-9. Loser: Tracy Thomas.

June 10

Site: Kansas City, KS. Promoter: Steve Mackey. Sanction: PKA. Television: ESPN cable.
Division: Light Middle. Winner: Bob Thurman. TKO-6. Loser: Richard Green.

June 16

Site: Oak Park, MI. Promoter: Kerry Roop/Ron Day. Sanction: PKA. Television: ESPN cable.
Division: Light Welter. Winner: Leroy Taylor. MDEC-12. Loser: Leo Loucks.

Site: Denver, CO. Promoter: Karyn Turner. Sanction: PKA. Television: ESPN cable.
Division: Feather. Winner: Felipe Garcia. DEC-12. Loser: Edmond Ardissone.

Site: Kings Mountain, NC. Sanction: WKA.
Division: Super Bantam. Winner: David Barber. TKO-2. Loser: Charles Turner.

July 12

Site: Kamloops, Canada. Promoter: Barry Atkins. Sanction: KICK.
Division: Light Welter. Winner: Tom Larouche. SDEC-12. Loser: Ishmael Robles.

August 4

Site: Guayama, Puerto Rico. Sanction: WKA.
Division: Feather. Winner: Victor Solier. KO-1. Loser: Juan Valesquez.

August 11

Site: Little Rock, AR. Promoter: Cedric Rodgers. Sanction: PKA. Television: ESPN cable.
Division: Super Heavy. Winner: Anthony Elmore. KO-1. Loser: Rick Harris.

August 25

Site: Reno, NV. Promoter: Howard Hanson. Sanction: WKA.
Division: Heavy. Winner: Maurice Smith. KO-9. Loser: Jeff Hollins.

December 18, 1984: Don Wilson (left) kicks Jean-Yves Theriault in their landmark bout that ended in a controversial draw. Many observers, including the media, felt Wilson won the bout. Photo by Auman Photo Studio; courtesy of Paul Maslak and Don Wilson

Site: El Paso, TX. Promoter: Hilary Sandoval. Sanction: PKA. Television: ESPN cable.
Division: Light. Winner: Cliff Thomas. TKO-7. Loser: Mike McClelland.

Site: Muscle Shoals, AL. Sanction: WKA.
Division: Super Bantam. Winner: David Barber. TKO-3. Loser: Davey Jones.

September 8
Site: Denver, CO. Promoter: Karyn Turner. Sanction: PKA. Television: ESPN cable.
Division: Bantam. Winner: Felipe Garcia. DEC-12. Loser: Edmond Ardissone.

September 22
Site: Sacramento, CA. Promoter: Clint Robinson/Sid Tanner. Sanction: PKA. Television: ESPN cable.
Division: Light Heavy. Winner: Dennis Alexio. DEC-12. Loser: Rob Salazar.

September 27
Site: Edmonton, Canada. Sanction: WKA.
Division: Heavy. Winner: Jim Walker. DEC-12. Loser: Maurice Smith.

October 13
Site: Miami, FL. Promoter: Les Freedman. Sanction: PKA. Television: ESPN cable.
Division: Heavy. Winner: Tony Palmore. SDEC-12. Loser: Anthony Elmore.

October 20
Site: Tokyo, Japan. Sanction: WKA.

Division: Middle. Winner: Yasuo Tabata. KO-3. Loser: You Jakiu.

October 26
Site: New Westminster, Canada. Sanction: WKA.
Division: Bantam. Winner: Rod Kei. TKO-2. Loser: Alan Cunningham.

October 27
Site: Orlando, FL. Promoter: Mike Sawyer/Mike McCoy. Sanction: PKA. Television: ESPN cable.
Division: Bantam. Winner: Jerry Clarke. DEC-12. Loser: Everett Berry.

November 10
Site: Reno, NV. Promoter: Howard Hanson. Sanction: WKA.
Division: Super Light Heavy. Winner: Curtis Crandall. KO-1. Loser: Don Neilsen.
Division: Super Bantam. Winner: Cheryl Wheeler. TKO-1. Loser: Carol Lemos.

November 23
Site: Juarez, Mexico. Sanction: WKA.
Division: Fly. Winner: Ricardo Rodarte. TKO-6. Loser: Ron Cisneros.

November 24
Site: Kamloops, Canada. Sanction: WKA.
Division: Welter. Winner: Tom Laroche. KO-6. Loser: Alan Watson.

Site: Charlotte, NC. Sanction: WKA.

Division: Feather. Winner: David Barber. KO-2. Loser: Davey Jones.

November 27
Site: Orlando, FL. Sanction: PKA. Television: ESPN cable.
Division: Bantam. Winner: Jerry Clarke. DEC-12. Loser: Everett Berry.

December 8
Site: Sacramento, CA. Promoter: Bill Kerr/Sid Tanner. Sanction: PKA.
Division: Light Heavy. Winner: Dennis Alexio. TKO-8. Loser: Cedric Rodgers.

December 18
Site: Montreal, Canada. Promoter: Real Masse. Sanction: STAR System (fight was to decide the undisputed world champion between champions of two different sanctioning bodies.) Television: TSN-TV.
Division: Light Heavy (177 pounds). Don Wilson vs. Jean-Yves Theriault. SDRW-12.

December 29
Site: Memphis, TN. Promoter: Anthony Elmore. Sanction: KICK.
Division: Heavy. Winner: Anthony Elmore. TKO-10. Loser: Ray Williams.

1984 YEAR-END DATA

The STAR System documented the outcomes of 456 events in 1984 and estimated that some 644 kickboxing events in total were promoted worldwide, featuring some 4,500 individual bouts (an average of seven bouts per event), representing a 31% increase over 1983.

1983 WORLD PROFESSIONAL TITLE FIGHTS

January 8
Site: Tokyo, Japan. Sanction: WKA. Television: Ashai.
Division: Super Light. Winner: Benny Urquidez. KO-4. Loser: Kunimasa Nagae.
Division: Feather. Winner: Victor Solier. KO-1. Loser: Koji Ishikawa.
Division: Fly. Winner: Hiroshi Takahashi. DEC-11. Loser: Miguel Montoya.

January 20
Site: Toronto, Canada. Promoter: John Therien. Sanction: PKA. Television: ESPN cable.

Division: Middle. Winner: Jean-Yves Theriault. KO-4. Loser: Steve Mackey.

February 5
Site: St. Louis, MO. Sanction: KICK.
Division: Heavy. Winner: Tony Palmore. DEC-12. Loser: Demetrius Edwards.
Division: Super Welter. Winner: Billye Jackson. KO-6. Loser: Kelly Gallegos.
Division: Welter. Winner: Ishmael Robles. TKO-1. Loser: Alan Watson.

February 17
Site: Pearl Harbor, HI. Sanction: WKC.
Division: Cruiser. Winner: Maurice Smith. TKO-7. Loser: Tony Morelli.

March 15
Site: Montreal, Canada. Promoter: Real Masse. Sanction: PKA. Television: CTV.
Division: Middle. Winner: Jean-Yves Theriault. KO-4. Loser: Junior Bowden.

March 19
Site: Las Vegas, NV. Promoter: Ted Kopplar. Sanction: KICK. Television: Syndication.
Division: Light Heavy. Winner: Don Wilson. TKO-11. Loser: Curtis Crandall.
Division: Super Middle. Winner: Ray McCallum. KO-10. Loser: Gene McComb.

March 22
Site: El Paso, TX. Promoter: Hilary Sandoval. Sanction: PKA. Television: ESPN cable.
Division: Feather. Winner: Tony Rosser. DEC-12. Loser: Cliff Thomas.
Division: Light. Winner: Paul Vizzio. DEC-12. Loser: Joe Soto.

March 26
Site: Scranton, PA. Sanction: PKA. Television: ESPN cable.
Division: Light Heavy. Winner: Emilio Narvaez. DEC-12. Loser: Matt Lawrence.

April 29
Site: Coquitlam, Canada. Sanction: WKA.
Division: Cruiser. Winner: James Warring vs. Maurice Smith. DRW-10.

May 5
Site: Rockford, IL. Promoter: John Monczak. Sanction: PKA. Television: ESPN cable.
Division: Heavy. Winner: Brad Hefton. DEC-12. Loser: Tom Hall.

May 21

Site: Tokyo, Japan. Promoter: Kimio Akagi. Sanction: WKA. Television: Channel 12.

Division: Cruiser. Winner: Don Wilson. DEC-11. Loser: Maurice Smith.

Division: Super Middle. Winner: Yasuo Tabata. SDEC-11. Loser: Larry Nichols.

June 11

Site: Memphis, TN. Promoter: Anthony Elmore. Sanction: PKA. Television: ESPN cable.

Division: Super Heavy. Winner: Anthony Elmore. DEC-12. Loser: John Jackson.

June 12

Site: Edmonton, Canada. Sanction: WKA.

Division: Heavy. Winner: Jim Walker. DEC-10. Loser: Ted Anderson.

July 8

Site: Atlantic City, NJ. Promoter: Howard Petschler. Sanction: PKA. Television: NBC; ESPN cable.

Division: Welter. Winner: Alvin Prouder. DEC-12. Loser: Mike Brennan.

Division: Feather. Winner: Paul Vizzio. DEC-12. Loser: Yoel Judah.

Division: Fly. Winner: Jerry Clarke. DEC-12. Loser: Felipe Garcia.

July 14

Site: Nanaimo, Canada. Sanction: WKA.

Division: Super Feather. Winner: Gerry Blanck. SDEC-11. Loser: Dave Johnston.

July 16

Site: New York, NY. Promoter: Titan Sports. Sanction: KICK. Television: Syndication.

Division: Light Heavy. Winner: Don Wilson. TKO-4. Loser: Steve Valencia.

Division: Super Middle. Winner: John Moncayo. KO-2. Loser: Ray McCallum.

Division: Welter. Winner: Billye Jackson. SDEC-12. Loser: Danny Lopez.

August 4

Site: Mexico City, Mexico. Sanction: WKA.

Division: Heavy. Winner: Maurice Smith. KO-6. Loser: Travis Everett.

August 20

Site: Memphis, TN. Sanction: PKA. Television: ESPN cable.

Division: Super Heavy. Winner: Anthony Elmore. DEC-12. Loser: Bill Morrison.

August 27

Site: El Paso, TX. Promoter: Hilary Sandoval. Sanction: PKA. Television: ESPN cable.

Division: Super Light. Winner: Cliff Thomas. DEC-12. Loser: Tony Rosser.

September 12

Site: Tokyo, Japan. Sanction: WKA.

Division: Super Light. Winner: Benny Urquidez. KO-6. Loser: Iron Fujimoto.

Division: Bantam. Winner: Lloyd Anderson. TKO-2. Loser: Masayuki Yamazato.

Division: Fly. Winner: Hiroshi Takahashi. DEC-11. Loser: Miguel Montoya.

September 23

Site: Amsterdam, Holland. Sanction: WKA.

Division: Middle. Winner: Rob Kaman. TKO-3. Loser: John Moncayo.

September 24

Site: Denver, CO. Promoter: Karyn Turner. Sanction: PKA. Television: ESPN cable.

Division: Bantam. Winner: Felipe Garcia. DEC-12. Loser: Segy Robles.

October 10

Site: Bal Harbour, FL. Sanction: PKA. Television: ESPN cable.

Division: Super Heavy. Winner: Anthony Elmore. TKO-10. Loser: Tony Palmore.

October 15

Site: Kansas City, MO. Promoter: Rio DeGennaro. Sanction: PKA. Television: ESPN cable.

Division: Light Middle. Winner: Bob Thurman. TKO-4. Loser: Tom Dalton.

October 22

Site: West Palm Beach, FL. Promoter: Steve Shepherd. Sanction: WKA.

Division: Super Middle. Winner: Steve Shepherd. DEC-11. Loser: Yasuo Tabata.

November 5

Site: Quayama, Puerto Rico. Sanction: WKA.

Division: Feather. Winner: Victor Solier. KO-2. Loser: Rod Kei.

November 16

Site: Lake Charles, LA. Promoter: Rod Prejean. Sanction: PKA.

Division: Light Welter. Winner: Bob Thurman. TKO-3. Loser: Gene McComb.

November 19

Site: New Castle, Australia. Sanction: WKC.
Division: Cruiser. Winner: Tony Morelli. KO-1. Loser: Pat Peterson.

November 21

Site: Sydney, Australia. Sanction: WKA/KICK.
Division: Middle. Winner: John Moncayo. TKO-2. Loser: Chan Cheuk Fai.
Division: Super Feather. Winner: Dave Johnston. KO-1. Loser: Seng Chanh.

December 3

Site: Rockford, IL. Promoter: John Monczak. Sanction: PKA. Television: ESPN cable.
Division: Heavy. Winner: Brad Hefton. DEC-12. Loser: Al Mims.

Site: Nanaimo, Canada. Sanction: WKA.
Division: Light. Winner: Mike Bell. DEC-11. Loser: Mickey Griffin.
Division: Feather. Winner: Victor Solier. KO-4. Loser: Lloyd Anderson.

December 20

Site: Montreal, Canada. Promoter: Real Masse. Sanction: PKA. Television: CTV.
Division: Middle. Winner: Jean-Yves Theriault. TKO-8. Loser: Laroy Hopkins.

1983 YEAR-END DATA

The STAR System documented the outcomes of 446 events in 1983 and estimated that some 490 kickboxing events in total were promoted worldwide, featuring almost 4,000 individual kickboxing bouts (an average of eight bouts per event), representing a 44% increase over 1982.

1982 WORLD PROFESSIONAL TITLE FIGHTS

January 9

Site: Tokyo, Japan. Promoter: Kimio Akagi. Sanction: WKA. Television: Ashai-TV.
Division: Feather. Winner: Dave Johnston vs. Kunimasa Nagae. MDRW-11.

February 8

Site: Hong Kong. Promoter: Russ Choi. Sanction: WKA. Television: TVB-TV.
Division: Light Heavy. Winner: Don Wilson. TKO-4. Loser: James Sisco.

February 18

Site: Windsor, Canada. Sanction: PKA. Television: CTV.
Division: Middle. Winner: Jean-Yves Theriault. TKO-1. Loser: Mark Zackaratos.

February 20

Site: West Palm Beach, FL. Promoter: Steve Shepherd. Sanction: WKA.
Division: Middle. Winner: Steve Shepherd. KO-4. Loser: Daryl Croker.

April 2

Site: Topeka, KS. Promoter: Rio DeGennaro. Sanction: PKA. Television: ESPN cable.
Division: Super Middle. Winner: Bob Thurman. DEC-12. Loser: Alvin Prouder.

April 3

Site: Oklahoma City, OK. Promoter: Bill Cagle. Sanction: PKA. Television: ESPN cable.
Division: Super Welter. Winner: Tommy Williams. TKO-12. Loser: Tony Avalos.

April 4

Site: Amsterdam, Holland. Promoter: Thom Harinck. Sanction: MTBN.
Division: Super Bantam. Winner: Lilly Rodriguez. TKO-2. Loser: Saskia van Rijswijk.

April 8

Site: Hong Kong. Promoter: Russ Choi. Sanction: WKA. Television: TVB-TV.
Division: Light Heavy. Winner: Don Wilson. DEC-9. Loser: Panya Sornnoi.

April 8, 1982: Don Wilson (right) kicks Panya Sornnoi. Courtesy of Paul Maslak and Don Wilson

May 29, 1982: Anthony Elmore lands a concussive kick on Demetrius Edwards. Courtesy of Jay T. Will

July 24, 1982: Referee Jay T. Will sends Alvin Prouder to a neutral corner after he knocked down Jeff Gripper. Courtesy of Jay T. Will

April 24

Site: Atlanta, GA. Promoter: Joe Corley. Sanction: PKA. Television: NBC; ESPN cable.
Division: Welter. Winner: Jeff Gripper. SDEC-12. Loser: Mike Brennan.
Division: Super Light. Winner: Paul Vizzio. DEC-12. Loser: Richard Jackson.

April 25

Site: Montreal, Canada. Promoter: Real Masse. Sanction: PKA. Television: CTV.
Division: Middle. Winner: Jean-Yves Theriault. KO-4. Loser: Andy Brewer.

May 22

Site: Denver, CO. Promoter: Karyn Turner. Sanction: PKA. Television: ESPN cable.
Division: Feather. Winner: Felipe Garcia. DEC-12. Loser: Abel Macius.

May 23

Site: Atlantic City, NJ. Promoter: Howard Petschler. Sanction: PKA. Television: ESPN cable.
Division: Super Light. Winner: Roy Kleckner. DEC-9. Loser: Anthony Salerno.

May 29

Site: Memphis, TN. Promoter: Anthony Elmore. Sanction: PKA. Television: ESPN cable.
Division: Heavy. Winner: Anthony Elmore. SDEC-12. Loser: Demetrius Edwards.

June 14

Site: Detroit, MI. Promoter: Kerry Roop. Sanction: PKA. Television: ESPN cable.
Division: Light Heavy. Winner: Kerry Roop. DSQ-3. Loser: Dan Macaruso.

June 21

Site: Vancouver, Canada. Promoter: Cliff Loree. Sanction: WKA. Television: Canadian.
Division: Cruiser. Winner: Tony Morelli. TKO-6. Loser: Kung Pong Sarkonpitak.
Division: Super Light. Winner: Benny Urquidez. TKO-6. Loser: Yutaka Koshikawa.

June 25

Site: New Orleans, LA. Sanction: PKA. Television: ESPN cable.
Division: Heavy. Winner: Brad Hefton. TKO-5. Loser: Al Mims.

June 26

Site: Las Vegas, NV. Promoter: Howard Hanson/Ted Kopplar. Sanction: WKA. Television: Syndication.
Division: Middle. Winner: John Moncayo. TKO-9. Loser: Steve Shepherd.
Division: Super Feather. Winner: Dave Johnston. TKO-2. Loser: Victor Solier.
Division: Light. Winner: Mike Bell. DEC-11. Loser: Shinobu Onuki.

July 24
Site: Atlanta, GA. Promoter: Joe Corley. Sanction: PKA.
  Television: ESPN cable.
Division: Welter. Winner: Alvin Prouder. TKO-3. Loser:
  Jeff Gripper.

August 12
Site: Raleigh, NC. Sanction: PKA.
Division: Heavy. Winner: Demetrius Edwards. DEC-12
  (Later, No Contest). Loser: Anthony Elmore.

August 14
Site: El Paso, TX. Promoter: Hilary Sandoval. Sanction:
  PKA.
Division: Light. Winner: Cliff Thomas. TKO-10. Loser:
  Norris Williams.

August 20
Site: Fort Lauderdale, FL. Sanction: PKA.
Division: Feather. Winner: Jerry Clarke. KO-2. Loser:
  Vernon Mason.

September ?
Site: Anderson, IN. Promoter: Glenn Keeney. Sanction:
  PKA.
Division: Heavy: Winner: Ross Scott. KO-1. Loser:
  Melvin Cole.

September 4
Site: Tokyo, Japan. Promoter: Kimio Akagi. Sanction:
  WKA. Television: Ashai.

November 6, 1982: Don Wilson fires a kick at Demetrius Edwards. Courtesy of Paul Maslak and Don Wilson

Division: Fly. Winner: Hiroshi Takahashi. TKO-10.
  Loser: Chuntchang Yell.
Division: Light Heavy. Winner: Don Wilson. DEC-11.
  Loser: James Warring.

September 18
Site: Lake Charles, LA. Promoter: Rod Prejean.
  Sanction: PKA. Television: ESPN cable.
Division: Super Middle. Winner: Bob Thurman.
  TKO-12. Loser: Gene McComb.

Site: Gainesville, FL. Promoter: Mike Sawyer/Mike
  McCoy. Sanction: PKA.
Division: Feather. Winner: Jerry Clarke. TKO-4. Loser:
  Abel Macias.

September 27
Site: Boise, ID. Sanction: PKA.
Division: Super Light. Winner: Cliff Thomas. DEC-12.
  Loser: Tony Guiterrez.

October ?
Site: Bolzano, Italy. Promoter: Ennio Falsoni. Sanction:
  PKO.
Division: Middle. Winner: Franz Haller. SDEC-6. Loser:
  Ray McCallum.

October 16
Site: Topeka, KS. Promoter: Rio DeGennaro. Sanction:
  PKA. Television: ESPN.
Division: Super Light. Winner: Paul Vizzio. KO-1.
  Loser: Jeff Payne.

October 19
Site: London, Canada. Promoter: John Therien.
  Sanction: PKA. Television: CTV.
Division: Middle. Winner: Jean-Yves Theriault. KO-2.
  Loser: Bernard Clark.
Division: Light Welter. Winner: Leroy Taylor. TKO-7.
  Loser: Leo Loucks.

October 22
Site: Gainesville, FL. Promoter: Mike Sawyer/Mike
  McCoy. Sanction: PKA. Television: ESPN cable.
Division: Bantam. Winner: Felipe Garcia vs. Jerry
  Clarke. DRW-12.

November 6
Site: West Palm Beach, FL. Sanction: WKC.
Division: Light Heavy. Winner: Don Wilson. DEC-9.
  Loser: Demetrius Edwards.
Division: Middle. Winner: John Moncayo. DEC-11.
  Loser: Steve Shepherd.

November 17

Site: Montreal, Canada. Promoter: Real Masse.
   Sanction: PKA. Television: NBC.
Division: Middle. Winner: Jean-Yves Theriault. TKO-7.
   Loser: Kerry Roop.
Division: Super Middle. Winner: Bob Thurman. TKO-2.
   Loser: Eddie McCray.

December 2

Site: Cocoa Beach, FL. Promoter: Jim Wilson. Sanction:
   WKA.
Division: Light. Winner: Mike Bell vs. Jorge Angot.
   TDRW-11.

December 4

Site: Fort Worth, TX. Promoter: Jay Trombley. Sanction:
   PKA.
Division: Welter. Winner: Alvin Prouder. DEC-12.
   Loser: Billye Jackson.

April 25, 1981: Jean-Yves Theriault catches Rodney Batiste with a crushing left hook. Courtesy of Jay T. Will

1981 WORLD PROFESSIONAL TITLE FIGHTS

January 16

Site: Culver City, CA. Promoter: Don and Judy Quine.
   Sanction: PKA. Television: ESPN.
Division: Light. Winner: Tommy Williams. KO-6. Loser:
   Dave Johnston.

January 24

Site: El Paso, TX. Promoter: Hilary Sandoval. Sanction:
   PKA. Television: ESPN cable.
Division: Light. Winner: Cliff Thomas. DEC-12. Loser:
   Richard Jackson.

February 24

Site: Ottawa, Canada. Sanction: PKA. Television: ESPN
   cable.
Division: Middle. Winner: Jean-Yves Theriault. KO-5.
   Loser: Glenn McMorris.

March 10

Site: Westchester, NY. Promoter: Clay Teppenpau/Jim
   Wilson. Sanction: WKA.
Division: Light Heavy. Winner: Don Wilson. KO-8.
   Loser: Herbie Thompson.
Division: Bantam. Winner: Graciela Casillas. DEC-5.
   Loser: Elba Melendez.

April 9

Site: Hong Kong. Promoter: Russ Choi. Sanction:
   WKA. Television: TVB-TV.

Division: Super Light. Winner: Benny Urquidez.
   TKO-4. Loser: Kong Fu Tak.
Division: Bantam. Winner: Graciela Casillas. TKO-1.
   Loser: Chan Lai Yin.

April 25

Site: Ottawa, Canada. Promoter: John Therien.
   Sanction: PKA. Television: ESPN cable.
Division: Middle. Winner: Jean-Yves Theriault. DEC-12.
   Loser: Rodney Batiste.

May 1

Site: New York, NY. Sanction: PKA. Television: NBC;
   ESPN cable.
Division: Heavy. Winner: Demetrius Edwards. TKO-9.
   Loser: Ross Scott.

May 16

Site: Denver, CO. Promoter: Karyn Turner. Sanction:
   PKA. Television: ESPN cable.
Division: Feather. Winner: Felipe Garcia. DEC-12.
   Loser: Jerry Clarke.

May 18

Site: Atlanta, GA. Promoter: Joe Corley. Sanction: PKA.
   Television: ESPN cable.
Division: Welter. Winner: Earnest Hart, Jr. DEC-12.
   Loser: Jeff Gripper.

June 18

Site: Honolulu, HI. Promoter: V.C. Productions.
   Sanction: WKA. Television: ABC (local affiliate).
Division: Super Welter. Winner: Alvin Prouder.
   DEC-12. Loser: Marc Costello.

Division: Cruiser. Winner: Tony Morelli. TKO-3. Loser: Ted Anderson.

June 24

Site: Tokyo, Japan. Promoter: Kimio Akagi. Sanction: WKA. Television: Ashai.

Division: Light Heavy. Winner: Don Wilson. KO-2. Loser: Mohammed Ashraf Tai.

June 27

Site: Atlantic City, NJ. Promoter: Howard Petschler. Sanction: PKA. Television: ESPN cable.

Division: Super Light. Winner: Paul Vizzio. DEC-9. Loser: Roy Kleckner.

July 24

Site: Atlantic City, NJ. Promoter: Howard Petschler. Sanction: PKA. Television: NBC.

Division: Super Light. Winner: Cliff Thomas. TKO-5. Loser: Paul Vizzio.

Division: Welter. Winner: Earnest Hart, Jr. DEC-12. Loser: David Beckwith.

Site: Denver, CO. Promoter: Karyn Turner. Sanction: PKA. Television: ESPN cable.

Division: Bantam. Winner: Felipe Garcia. KO-6. Loser: Vernon Mason.

July 25

Site: West Palm Beach, FL. Promoter: Steve Shepherd. Sanction: WKA.

Division: Middle. Winner: Steve Shepherd. TKO-3. Loser: Dave Hedgecock.

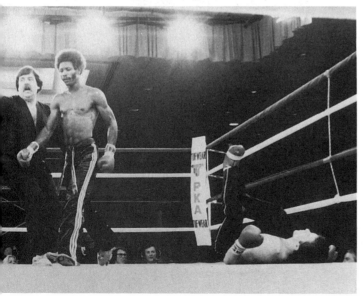

July 24, 1981: Cliff Thomas is directed to a neutral corner by referee Jay T. Will after knocking down Paul Vizzio.

August 15

Site: Providence, RI. Promoter: George Pesare. Sanction: PKA.

Division: Light Heavy. Winner: Dan Macaruso. DEC-12. Loser: Tom Hall.

August 29

Site: Las Vegas, NV. Promoter: Howard Hanson. Sanction: WKA.

Division: Super Feather. Winner: Dave Johnston. TKO-4. Loser: Jorge Angot.

Division: Feather. Winner: Refugio Flores vs. Craig Fossett. TDRW-4.

September 8

Site: Hong Kong. Promoter: Russ Choi. Sanction: WKA. Television: TVB-TV.

Division: Light Heavy. Winner: Don Wilson. SDEC-7 (three-minute rounds). Loser: Panya Sornnoi.

Division: Light. Winner: Mike Bell. SDEC-11. Loser: Kunimasa Nagae.

October 3

Site: Atlanta, GA. Promoter: Joe Corley. Sanction: PKA. Television: ESPN cable.

Division: Welter. Winner: Jeff Gripper. TKO-8. Loser: Earnest Hart, Jr.

October 8

Site: Chicago, IL. Promoter: Bob Oberg. Sanction: WKA. Television: Syndication.

Division: Welter. Winner: Howard Jackson. DEC-11. Loser: Bubba Walters.

Division: Heavy. Winner: Jim Walker. DEC-11. Loser: Jim Wallace.

Division: Bantam. Winner: Graciela Casillas. DEC-7 (disputed). Loser: Cheryl Wheeler.

October 10

Site: Seminole, OK. Sanction: PKA. Television: ESPN cable.

Division: Light Welter. Winner: Tommy Williams. KO-4. Loser: Tony Gutierrez.

October 24

Site: Las Vegas, NV. Promoter: Howard Hanson. Sanction: WKA.

Division: Light Heavy. Winner: Don Wilson. KO-3. Loser: Mark Zacharatos.

Division: Welter. Winner: Howard Jackson. SDEC-11. Loser: Ron Smith.

November 10

Site: Ft. Lauderdale, FL. Promoter: Jim Wilson. Sanction: WKA.

Division: Super Middle. Winner: Ted Pryor. SDEC-11. Loser: Steve Mackey.

November 13

Site: New York, NY. Sanction: PKA. Television: NBC; USA cable.

Division: Super Light. Winner: Paul Vizzio. DEC-12. Loser: Cliff Thomas.

November 19

Site: West Palm Beach, FL. Promoter: Steve Shepherd. Sanction: PKA.

Division: Heavy. Winner: Steve Shepherd. DEC-11. Loser: Demetrius Edwards.

December 5

Site: Gainesville, FL. Promoter: Mike Sawyer/Mike McCoy. Sanction: PKA. Television: ESPN cable.

Division: Feather. Winner: Jerry Clarke. DEC-9. Loser: Billy Taylor.

December 10

Site: Fort Lauderdale, FL. Sanction: PKA.

Division: Light Middle. Winner: Ted Pryor. SDEC-11. Loser: Steve Mackey.

1981 YEAR-END DATA

According to reports from the sport's two leading sanctioning bodies, the PKA and the WKA, there were exactly 100 televised events in 1981. Of its more than 200 sanctioned events in 70 cities, the PKA reportedly had 48 of them broadcast. Forty-five of those events were broadcast on ESPN cable-TV and the remaining three on NBC's *Sports World*, a network sports anthology program.

The WKA reportedly had 52 of its events in television syndication throughout the world.

1980 WORLD PROFESSIONAL TITLE FIGHTS

January 10

Site: Providence, RI. Promoter: George Pesare. Sanction: PKA. Television: ESPN cable.

Division: Light Heavy. Winner: Dan Macaruso. SDEC-12. Loser: Jeff Smith.

January 26

Site: Las Vegas, NV. Promoter: Howard Hanson. Sanction: WKA. Television: CBS.

Division: Welter. Winner: Howard Jackson. DEC-9. Loser: Yoshimitsu Tomashiro.

Division: Super Light. Winner: Benny Urquidez. KO-7. Loser: Shinobu Onuki.

March ?

Site: Denver, CO. Sanction: WKA.

Division: Feather. Winner: Felipe Garcia. DEC-9. Loser: Stewart Lauper.

March 8

Site: Brussels, Belgium. Sanction: PKA.

Division: Light Heavy. Winner: Dan Macaruso. KO-?. Loser: Dominic Valera.

March 29

Site: Las Vegas, NV. Promoter: Howard Hanson. Sanction: WKA. Television: USA cable.

Division: Super Middle. Winner: Bob Ryan. DEC-9. Loser: Blinky Rodriguez.

Division: Super Welter. Winner: Alvin Prouder. KO-5. Loser: Marc Costello.

Division: Super Middle. Winner: Bob Ryan. DEC-9. Loser: Blinky Rodriguez.

Division: Bantam. Winner: Graciela Casillas. TKO-2. Loser: Rochelle Raggsdale.

April 19

Site: Vancouver, B.C., Canada. Promoter: Jim Wright. Sanction: WKA. Television: USA cable.

Division: Super Light. Winner: Benny Urquidez. DEC-9. Loser: Frank Holloway.

Division: Super Light Heavy. Winner: Tony Morelli. KO-7. Loser: Travis Everett.

Division: Feather. Winner: Lily Rodriguez. DEC-5. Loser: Maureen Tatum.

May 17

Site: West Palm Beach, FL. Promoter: Steve Shepherd/Don Haines. Sanction: PKA.

Division: Welter. Winner: Steve Shepherd. TKO-12. Loser: Mike Brennan.

Division: Bantam. Winner: Larry Sanders. KO-4. Loser: Vernon Mason.

June 15

Site: Anderson, IN. Promoter: Glenn Keeney/Don and Judy Quine. Sanction: PKA. Television: CBS (the Wallace retirement fight was aired live).

Division: Middle. Winner: Bill Wallace. DEC-9. Loser: Robert Biggs.

Division: Heavy. Winner: Ross Scott. KO-2. Loser: Jacquet Bazemore.

August 9

Site: El Paso, TX. Promoter: Hilary Sandoval. Sanction: PKA. Television: ESPN cable.

Division: Super Light. Winner: Cliff Thomas. TKO-3. Loser: Gordon Franks.

August 12
Site: Ottawa, Canada. Promoter: John Therien/Don and Judy Quine. Sanction: PKA. Television: CBS.
Division: Heavy. Winner: Demetrius Edwards. KO-7. Loser: Ross Scott.

August 16
Site: Tijuana, Mexico. Sanction: WKA.
Division: Bantam. Winner: Graciela Casillas. DEC-7. Loser: Darlena Valdez.

October 13
Site: Cocoa Beach, FL. Promoter: Jim Wilson. Sanction: WKA.
Division: Light Heavy. Winner: Don Wilson. KO-2. Loser: Andy White.

October 30
Site: Providence, RI. Promoter: George Pesare. Sanction: PKA. Television: ESPN cable.
Division: Light Heavy. Winner: Dan Macaruso.DEC-12. Loser: Carl Beamon.

November 8
Site: West Palm Beach, FL. Promoter: Steve Shepherd/Don Haines. Sanction: PKA/WKA. Television: ESPN cable.

Bill "Superfoot" Wallace kicks at Robert Biggs and raises his hands in victory at the decision. This was Wallace's retirement fight and ended an era in which he reigned as the greatest kicking artist in his sport. Photos courtesy of Jay T. Will

Division: Welter. Winner: Steve Shepherd. KO-7. Loser: Earnest Hart, Jr.

November 15
Site: Ottawa, Canada. Promoter: John Therien/Don and Judy Quine. Sanction: PKA. Television: ESPN cable.
Division: Middle. Winner: Jean-Yves Theriault. TKO-1. Loser: Robert Biggs.

Site: Denver, CO. Promoter: Karyn Turner/Jim Hawkins. Sanction: PKA. Television: ESPN cable.
Division: Bantam. Winner: Felipe Garcia. TKO-1. Loser: Larry Sanders.

1979 WORLD PROFESSIONAL TITLE FIGHTS

Date: ?
Site: St. Paul, MN. Promoter: John and Pat Worley/Gary Hestilow. Sanction: PKA.
Division: Super Light. Winner: Gordon Franks. DEC-9. Loser: Tommy Williams.

Date: ?
Site: St. Paul, MN. Promoter: John and Pat Worley/Gary Hestilow. Sanction: PKA.
Division: Super Light. Winner: Gordon Franks. DEC-9. Loser: Richard Jackson.

March 3
Site: Las Vegas, NV. Promoter: Ron Holmes/Hap Holloway. Sanction: WKA.
Division: Super Welter. Winner: Alvin Prouder. DEC-9. Loser: Ken Okada.

April 20
Site: St. Paul, MN. Promoter: John and Pat Worley/Gary Hestilow. Sanction: PKA.
Division: Super Light. Winner: Gordon Franks. KO-5. Loser: Frank Corona.

May 2
Site: Lake Tahoe, NV. Promoter: Howard Hanson. Sanction: WKA. Television: NBC.
Division: Super Light. Winner: Benny Urquidez. KO-6. Loser: Rick Simerly.

May 26
Site: West Palm Beach, FL. Promoter: Steve Shepherd. Sanction: WKA.
Division: Middle. Winner: Steve Shepherd. DEC-9. Loser: Chris Gallegos.

August 25

Site: Hampton, VA. Promoter: Frank Hargrove.
  Sanction: PKA.
Division: Bantam. Winner: Vernon Mason. TKO-9.
  Loser: Sonny Onowo.

October 1

Site: Tokyo, Japan. Promoter: Tatsumi Okamura.
  Sanction: WKA. Television: Ashai (live).
Division: Light. Winner: Benny Urquidez. DEC-9.
  Loser: Yoshimitsu Tomashiro.
Division: Feather. Winner: Kunimasa Nagae. KO-2.
  Loser: Stewart Lauper.

November 7

Site: West Palm Beach, FL. Promoter: Steve Shepherd/
  Don Haines. Sanction: PKA. Television: ESPN cable.
Division: Welter. Winner: Steve Shepherd. KO-6. Loser:
  Earnest Hart, Jr.

December 21

Site: St. Paul, MN. Promoter: John and Pat Worley/
  Gary Hestilow. Sanction: PKA. Television: ESPN
  cable.
Division: Super Light. Winner: Gordon Franks.
  DEC-12. Loser: Tony Lopez.

December 23

Site: Las Vegas, NV. Promoter: Hap Holloway/Ron
  Holmes. Sanction: WKA.
Division: Super Welter. Winner: Alvin Prouder. TKO-1.
  Loser: Loser: Andy White.
Division: Bantam. Winner: Graciela Casillas. DEC-6.
  Loser: Irene Garcia.
Division: Light. Winner: Kunimasa Nagae. DEC-9.
  Loser: Daniel Hong.

1978 WORLD PROFESSIONAL TITLE FIGHTS

March 11

Site: Providence, RI. Promoter: George Pesare/Don
  and Judy Quine. Sanction: PKA. Television: CBS.
Division: Middle. Winner: Bill Wallace. DEC-9. Loser:
  Emilio Narvaez.
Division: Welter. Winner: Bob Ryan. DEC-9. Loser:
  Earnest Hart, Jr.

April 5

Site: Vancouver, Canada. Promoter: Jim Wright.
  Sanction: WKA.
Division: Super Light. Winner: Benny Urquidez.
  TKO-4. Loser: Dave Paul.

May 22, 1978: Champion Jeff Smith (right) versus challenger
Dominique Valera. Courtesy of Jay T. Will

April 10

Site: Osaka, Japan. Promoter: Kenji Kurosaki. Sanction:
  WKA.
Division: Super Light. Winner: Benny Urquidez. KO-1.
  Loser: Takeshi Naito.

May ?

Site: Tokyo, Japan. Promoter: Tatsumi Okamura.
  Sanction: WKA. Television: Ashai.
Division: Super Light. Winner: Benny Urquidez.
  TKO-3. Loser: Shinobu Onuki.

May 22

Site: Paris, France. Promoter: Guy Jugla and Marc
  Counil. Sanction: PKA.
Division: Light Heavy. Winner: Jeff Smith. DEC-9.
  Loser: Dominique Valera.

July 18

Site: Monte Carlo, Monaco. Sanction: PKA.
Division: Middle. Winner: Bill Wallace. TKO-6. Loser:
  Daryl Tyler.

July 22

Site: West Palm Beach, FL. Promoter: Steve Shepherd/
  Don Haines. Sanction: PKA.

Division: Welter. Winner: Steve Shepherd. DEC-9.
  Loser: Bob Ryan.

September 1

Site: Long Beach, CA. Promoter: Wally Emery/Hap
  Holloway. Sanction: WKA.
Division: Super Welter. Winner: Alvin Prouder. DEC-9.
  Loser: Brendan Leddy.

September 11

Site: Tokyo, Japan. Promoter: Tatsumi Okamura.
  Sanction: WKA. Television: NBC; Ashai.
Division: Welter. Winner: Alvin Prouder. TKO-6. Loser:
  Toshihiro Nishiki.

November 30

Site: Atlanta, GA. Promoter: Joe Corley. Sanction: PKA.
  Television: CBS.
Division: Super Light. Winner: Gordon Franks.
  DEC-12. Loser: Tony Lopez.
Division: Welter. Winner: Earnest Hart, Jr. SDEC-12.
  Loser: Steve Shepherd.

1977 WORLD PROFESSIONAL TITLE FIGHTS

March 12

Site: Los Angeles, CA. Promoter: Howard Hanson/
  Arnold Urquidez. Sanction: WKA.
Division: Light. Winner: Benny Urquidez vs.
  Narongnoi Kiatbandit. No Contest-9.

April 23

Site: Las Vegas, NV. Promoter: Don and Judy Quine.
  Sanction: PKA. Television: CBS—Wallace bout was
  the first live TV broadcast in the sport's history.
Division: Middle. Winner: Bill Wallace. DEC-9. Loser:
  Blinky Rodriguez.
Division: Heavy. Winner: Ross Scott. KO-1. Loser:
  Everett Eddy.
Division: Light. Winner: Benny Urquidez. TKO-4.
  Loser: Howard Jackson.

May 21

Site: Providence, RI. Promoter: Hee Il Cho. Sanction:
  PKA.
Division: Middle. Winner: Bill Wallace. TKO-6. Loser:
  Ron Thiveridge.
Division: Welter. Winner: Eddie Andujar. DEC-9. Loser:
  Thomas Dakalakis.

Site: Charlotte, NC. Promoter: Jerry Piddington.
  Sanction: PKA.
Division: Light Heavy. Winner: Jeff Smith. DEC-9.
  Loser: Keith Haflich.

July ?

Site: Tijuana, Mexico. Promoter: Angel Gutierrez.
  Sanction: WKA.
Division: Super Light. Winner: Benny Urquidez. KO-1.
  Loser: ?

July ?

Site: New York, NY. Promoter: Aaron Banks. Sanction:
  WPKO. Television: ABC.

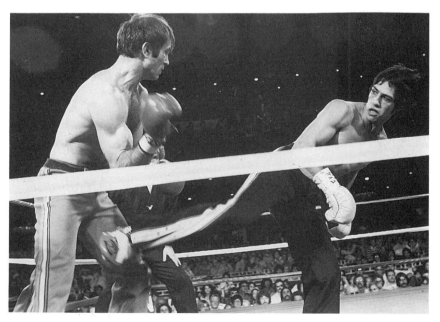

Bill "Superfoot" Wallace meets the biggest
challenge of his career in rugged Blinky
Rodriguez. The bout on April 23, 1977, marked
the first network television live broadcast of
the sport. Courtesy of Stuart Sobel and Benny
Urquidez

Division: Heavy. Winner: Everett Eddy. KO-? Loser: Joe Hess.

Division: Feather. Winner: Marion Bermudez. DEC-4. Loser: Lilly Rodriguez.

August 2

Site: Tokyo, Japan. Promoter: Howard Hanson/Ron Holmes/Hisashi Shima/Antonio Inoki. Sanction: WKA. Television: Ashai (live).

Division: Light. Winner: Benny Urquidez. KO-6. Loser: Katsuyuki Suzuki.

October 8

Site: Indianapolis, IN. Promoter: Don and Judy Quine. Sanction: PKA. Television: CBS.

Division: Middle. Winner: Bill Wallace. KO-2. Loser: Pat Worley.

November 14, 1977: Two-picture series of the landmark bout between Benny "The Jet" Urquidez and Kunimatsu Okao in Tokyo, the match that put American kickboxers on the world map. Photos courtesy of Stuart Sobel and Benny Urquidez

Division: Welter. Winner: Earnest Hart, Jr. DEC-9. Loser: Eddie Andujar.

November 14

Site: Tokyo, Japan. Promoter: Howard Hanson/Ron Holmes/Hisashi Shima. Sanction: WKA. Television: Ashai (live).

Division: Super Light. Winner: Benny Urquidez. KO-4. Loser: Kunimatsu Okao.

Division: Light. Winner: Kunimasa Nagae. DEC-9. Loser: Tony Lopez.

November 15

Site: St. Paul, MN. Promoter: John and Pat Worley/ Gary Hestilow. Sanction: PKA.

Division: Super Light. Winner: Gordon Franks. DEC-9. Loser: Frank Corona.

November 28

Site: Honolulu, HI. Promoter: Kip Russo. Sanction: PKA.

Division: Middle. Winner: Bill Wallace. DEC-9. Loser: Burnis White.

1976 WORLD PROFESSIONAL TITLE FIGHTS

February 8

Site: Atlanta, GA. Promoter: Joe Corley. Sanction: SEPKA. Television: Syndication.

Division: Light Heavy. Winner: Jeff Smith. DEC-9. Loser: Wally Slocki.

March 13

Site: Las Vegas, NV. Promoter: Don and Judy Quine. Sanction: PKA. Television: 90-minute syndication.

Division: Middle. Winner: Bill Wallace. TKO-2. Loser: Jem Echollas.

May 29

Site: Toronto, Ontario, Canada. Promoter: Jong Soo Park. Sanction: PKA. Television: Filmed by ABC, but not aired.

Division: Middle. Winner: Bill Wallace. TKO-3. Loser: Daniel Richer.

June ?

Site: Dallas, TX. Promoter: Tommy Lee. Sanction: WSMAC.

Division: Catchweight. Winner: Benny Urquidez. DEC-8. Loser: Sanun Plypoolsup.

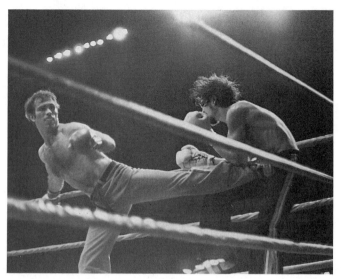

October 1, 1976: Bill Wallace (left) spears Gary Edens with a side kick. Courtesy of Stuart Sobel and Benny Urquidez

August 28

Site: Honolulu, HI. Promoter: Howard Hanson/Don and Judy Quine. Sanction: PKA.

Division: Light: Benny Urquidez. DEC-9. Loser: Earnest Hart, Jr.

Division: Heavy. Winner: Teddy Limoz. KO-2. Loser: Mike Arroyo.

October 1

Site: Los Angeles, CA. Promoter: Don and Judy Quine and Howard Hanson. Sanction: PKA. Television: CBS.

Division: Middle. Winner: Bill Wallace. DEC-9. Loser: Gary Edens.

Division: Welter. Winner: Benny Urquidez. TKO-8. Loser: Eddie Andujar.

1975 WORLD PROFESSIONAL TITLE FIGHTS

May 3

Site: Atlanta, GA. Promoter: Joe Corley. Sanction: PKA.
Division: Middle. Winner: Bill Wallace. TKO-9. Loser: Joe Corley.

May 10

Site: New York, NY. Promoter: Aaron Banks. Sanction: WPKO. Television: ABC.
Division: Light. Winner: Benny Urquidez. DEC-3. Loser: Tayari Casel.

May 16

Site: Los Angeles, CA. Promoter: Tommy Lee. Sanction: WSMAC.
Division: Catchweight. Winner: Benny Urquidez. KO-2. Loser: Roland Talton.

May 17

Site: Washington, DC. Promoter: Jhoon Rhee.
Division: Light Heavy. Winner: Jeff Smith. KO-2. Loser: Jim Butin.

May 30

Site: Honolulu, HI. Promoter: Tommy Lee. Sanction: WSMAC.
Division: Catchweight. Winner: Benny Urquidez. TKO-2. Loser: Sanun Plypoolsup.

June 20

Site: Honolulu, HI. Promoter: Tommy Lee. Sanction: WSMAC.
Division: Catchweight. Winner: Benny Urquidez. KO-2. Loser: Ken Riley.

July ?

Site: Honolulu, HI. Promoter: Tommy Lee. Sanction: WSMAC.
Division: Catchweight. Winner: Benny Urquidez. KO-4. Loser: Burnis White.
Division: Catchweight. Winner: Teddy Limoz. DEC-3. Loser: Joe Lewis.

September 21

Site: West Berlin, Germany. Promoter: Georg Bruckner. Sanction: Independent.
Division: Super Light. Winner: Gordon Franks. DEC-9. Loser: Ramiro Guzman.

July 1975: Joe Lewis (left) against Teddy Limoz. Courtesy of Joe Lewis

September 14, 1974: Joe Lewis (left) is presented his world heavyweight trophy from actor Telly Savalas as promoter Mike Anderson looks on. Lewis was responsible for putting together this inaugural kickboxing event with television executive and karate black belt Tom Tannenbaum. Courtesy of the John Corcoran Archives

October ?
Site: Los Angeles, CA. Promoter: Tommy Lee. Sanction: WSMAC.
Division: Catchweight. Winner: Benny Urquidez. KO-2. Loser: Bill Henderson.

October 1
Site: Washington, DC. Promoter: Jhoon Rhee. Sanction: WBBL. Television: Closed circuit feed into the Muhammad Ali–Joe Frazier "Thrilla in Manila."
Division: Light Heavy. Winner: Jeff Smith. SDEC-11. Loser: Karriem Allah.

September 14, 1974: Bill Wallace lands a kick on Germany's Bernd Grothe at the inaugural World Professional Karate Championships in Los Angeles, the event at which modern kickboxing was created. Wallace was the event's outstanding fighter. Courtesy of Mitchell Bobrow

1974 WORLD PROFESSIONAL TITLE FIGHTS

September 14
Site: Los Angeles, CA. Promoter: Mike Anderson. Sanction: PKA. Television: ABC-TV 90-minute special.
Division: Heavy. Winner: Joe Lewis. KO-2 Loser: Frank Brodar.
Division: Light Heavy. Winner: Jeff Smith. DEC-3. Loser: Wally Slocki.
Division: Middle. Winner: Bill Wallace. DEC-3. Loser: Daniel Richer.
Division: Light. Winner: Isiais Duenas. TKO-3. Loser: Ramon Smith.

December 21
Site: Honolulu, HI. Promoter: Tommy Lee. Sanction: WSMAC.
Division: Catchweight. Winner: Benny Urquidez. DEC-3. Loser: Dana Goodson.

1971 WORLD PROFESSIONAL TITLE FIGHTS

June 23
Site: New York, NY. Promoter: Aaron Banks. Sanction: None.
Division: Heavy. Winner: Joe Lewis. KO-1. Loser: Jesse King.

Date: ?
Site: Houston, TX. Promoter: George Minshew. Sanction: None.
Division: Heavy. Winner: Joe Lewis. KO-2. Loser: Ed Daniels.

1970 WORLD PROFESSIONAL TITLE FIGHTS

January 17

Site: Long Beach, CA. Promoter: Lee Faulkner. Sanction: None. (Note: This was the first kickboxing title fight in the United States.)

Division: Heavy. Winner: Joe Lewis. KO-2. Loser: Greg Baines.

1971: Joe Lewis (left) knocks out Ronnie Barkoot in New York City. Lewis is considered the father of full-contact karate, actually creating the sport as "American kickboxing" in 1970. Courtesy of the John Corcoran Archives

CHAPTER 8

AMATEUR KICKBOXING

~ · · ~

WORLD ASSOCIATION OF KICKBOXING ORGANIZATIONS (WAKO)

This chapter is composed of complete winners' lists from every World Association of Kickboxing Organizations (WAKO) World and European Championship. The WAKO is the world's leading amateur kickboxing organization. It also conducts, as an official part of its program, competitions in semi-contact, continuous contact and forms, the results of which all appear here. It is presently headquartered in Milan, Italy, under the direction of World President Ennio Falsoni.

FORMAT

Entries appear in reverse chronological order beginning with the most recent event in 1991. World championship results appear at the beginning of this chapter, followed by the European results. The United States has hosted only one national WAKO championship, the results of which were unavailable at press time.

The results of each event appear in this order: 1) overall medal standings; 2) men's kickboxing; 3) men's semi-contact; 4) women's semi-contact; 5) men's continuous contact; 6) women's continuous contact; 7) men's forms; and 8) women's forms. These are the standard types of competition conducted in all WAKO competitions today, but note that the organization's earliest events featured kickboxing exclusively.

Overall medal standings, by country, appear first only when they were available for publication. The overall medal standings are decided by this standard Olympic formula: three points are awarded for each individual gold medal, two per silver, one per bronze. In the event of a tie by total points, as was the case between Italy and the United States in the 1990 WAKO World Championships, the country with more gold medals wins the overall championship.

Each winners' list appears according to weight class, starting with the heaviest division and ending with the lightest. *In the case of a tie, no number will precede the second competitor or country listing. For example, the winners' lists typically feature three places with two competitors sharing the third position.* A dash following a placement number (for example, as in 3. —) indicates there were no winners at that place in that division. This usually occurs when there are insufficient competitors to complete a division, and/or when that division is newly introduced.

What the WAKO calls "light contact" I have instead designated *continuous contact*. In this event, contestants fight in the style of semi-contact, but are *not* stopped by officials after each point is scored. The latter designation was used to avoid confusing this event with the "light contact" typically conducted in traditional karate-do tournaments.

Lavish efforts were exerted to obtain the full (first and last) name of each winner. However, Europeans, like the Japanese, more often than not list a winner's last name and his or her country; occasionally, an initial is used for the first name. Nevertheless, through dogged determination and painstaking research, I constructed as many full names as possible.

WEIGHT DIVISION CONVERSION CHART

The following chart will help readers interested in weight divisions quickly determine exact kilos to pounds and vice versa.

Kilos	Pounds	Pounds	Kilos
48	105.82	112	50.8
50	110.23	113	51.25
51	112.44	115	52.16

Kilos	Pounds		Pounds	Kilos
54	119.05		118	53.53
55	121.25		119	53.98
57	125.66		122	55.34
58	127.87		126	57.15
60	132.28		130	58.97
62	136.69		133	60.33
63	138.89		135	61.24
66	145.51		140	63.50
67	147.71		147	66.68
70	154.32		148	67.13
71	156.53		154	69.85
72	158.73		156	70.76
74	163.14		160	72.58
75	165.35		164	73.94
76	167.55		167	75.75
79	174.17		172	78.47
80	176.37		175	79.38
81	178.57		180	79.38
82	180.78		182	82.56
85	187.39		190	86.18
86	189.60		195	86.18
91	200.62		200	90.72

Christine Bannon-Rodrigues, the only athlete in the history of WAKO competition to win three gold medals at a single event and set a new world record. In 1991 in London, England, she captured world titles in women's black belt fighting (110–121-pound division), women's black belt soft-style forms, and women's black belt weapons. The old record was shared by two other Americans: Troy Dorsey and Keith Hirabayashi, both of whom won two titles in 1987. Courtesy of Don Rodrigues

WAKO WORLD CHAMPIONSHIPS (1978–91)

8TH WAKO WORLD CHAMPIONSHIPS

Date: October 12–13, 1991.
Site: London, England.
Participants: 28 countries.

Note: Kickboxing competition was not conducted at this event, and a complete overall medal standing was unavailable. American Christine Bannon set a world record by becoming the first athlete ever to win three gold medals—in forms, fighting and weapons—at one WAKO World Championship.

Overall Medal Standing

1. United States

Fighting

Men's Semi-Contact

84+ kg:
1. Andrew Boyce (GRB)
2. Cruz (Brazil)
3. Barnabas Katona (Hungary)
   Valentini (Italy)

−84 kg:
1. Alfie Lewis (GRB)
2. Bettini (Italy)
3. Bettencourt (Cab)
   Zoltan Szucs (Hungary)

−79 kg:
1. P. Edwards (GRB)
2. Delaporte (France)
3. Flood (Canada)
   Richard Barefield (USA)

−74 kg:
1. Sergio Portaro (Italy)
2. Rappold (USA)
3. Lajos Hugyetz (Hungary)
   Martin (Switzerland)

−69 kg:
1. Pedro Xavier (USA)
2. Yves Lalonde (Canada)
3. Pfaffl (Germany)
   Billy Bryce (GRB)

−63 kg:
1. Kilgus (Germany)
2. Tierney (GRB)
3. Giersthoven (Nether)
   Peter Gilpin (Canada)

−57 kg:
1. Cucci (Italy)
2. Preece (GRB)
3. Beaudry (Canada)
   Piotr Siegoczynski (Poland)

Women's Semi-Contact

−60 kg:
1. Ribeiro (Brazil)
2. Stiegler (Germany)
3. Mirai (Turkey)
   Lawson (GRB)

−55 kg:
1. Christine Bannon (USA)
2. Hugyetz (Hungary)
3. Deyta (Turkey)
   Desrochlers (Canada)

−50 kg:
1. Karin Schiller (Germany)
2. Szepessi (Hungary)
3. Quansa (GRB)
   Derita (Canada)

Men's Continuous Contact

84+ kg:
1. Barnabas Katona (Hungary)
2. Morozow (CIS)
3. Reed (GRB)
   Jeff Roufus (USA)

−84 kg:
1. Wilkinson (GRB)
2. Lalos Szucs (Hungary)
3. Donet (France)
   Adamson (Nigeria)

−79 kg:
1. George McKenzie (GRB)
2. Flood (Canada)
3. Reichenbach (Germany)
   Csaszar (Austria)

−74 kg:
1. Lajos Hugyetz (Hungary)
2. Wubke (Germany)
3. Alberto Montrond (USA)
   Dushkin (CIS)

−69 kg:
1. Evelyn Dwyer (GRB)
2. David Wilson (USA)
3. Carvalho (Portugal)
   Drazdynski (Poland)

−63 kg:
1. Ivanov (CIS)
2. Charles Barron (USA)

3. Alan Johnson (Ireland)
   Peter Gilpin (Canada)

−57 kg:
1. Lantos (Hungary)
2. Jurgen Jakob (Germany)
3. Shawn Wheat (USA)
   Ind (GRB)

Women's Semi-Contact

60+ kg:
1. Bailey (GRB)
2. Lisa Crosby (USA)
3. Sasse (Germany)
   Tunde Kocsis (Hungary)

−60 kg:
1. Rylik (Poland)
2. Gabriella Bady (Hungary)
3. Justina Hall (USA)
   Gilpin (Canada)

−55 kg:
1. Proietti (Italy)
2. A. Joswig (Germany)
3. Kathy Carchia (USA)
   Carson (Nigeria)

−50 kg:
1. Leclerau (France)
2. Szepessi (Hungary)
3. Gabriel Damm (Germany)
   Neglia (Italy)

Forms

Men

Hard:
1. Richard Brandon (USA)
2. Sforza (Italy)
3. Simson (Germany)
   ?

Soft:
1. Jean Frenette (Canada)
2. David Collins (USA)
3. Stark (Germany)
   Guarnacci (Italy)

Women

Hard:
1. Lamoureux (Canada)
2. Ann Gregory (USA)
3. Soter (Switzerland)
   Alo (Italy)

Soft:
1. Christine Bannon
2. Waellapia (Nether)
3. Austin (GRB)
   Anzhenko (CIS)

Weapons

Hard:
1. Tony Orr (USA)
2. Jean Frenette (Canada)
3. Baba-Milis (Mar)
   Ghorbani (Ireland)

Soft:
1. Richard Brandon (USA)
2. Engelhardt (Nether)
3. Eismann (Germany)
   Sporka (Italy)

Women:
1. Christine Bannon (USA)
2. Desrochlers (Canada)
3. Anzhenko (CIS)
   Austin (GRB)

7TH WAKO WORLD CHAMPIONSHIPS

Date: January 19–21, 1990.
Site: Mestre, Italy.
Producer: Ennio Falsoni.
Participants: 28 countries.

Overall Medal Standings
1. USA
2. Italy
3. Hungary
4. W. Germany (FRG)
5. Canada
6. Poland
7. Great Britain
8. France
9. Sweden

Fighting

Men's Kickboxing

+91 kg:
1. Philippe Coutelas (France)
2. Paolo Zorello (Brazil)
3. Dusko Malovic (Yugoslavia)
   Angelo Spreafico (Italy)

−91 kg:
1. Saleta Przemyslaw (Poland)

2. Said Bechari (France)
3. Eirik Lutken (Norway)
Nik Askitis (Greece)

−81 kg:
1. David Taylor (GRB)
2. Pares Basilikos (Greece)
3. Alfonso Sgarro (Brazil)
Paul Thorsten (FRG)

−75 kg:
1. Ralph Kunzler (FRG)
2. Nasser Nassiri (France)
3. Steve Martin (GRB)
Tiziano Ubaldi (Switzerland)

−71 kg:
1. Paolo Liberati (Italy)
2. Horst Nether (FRG)
3. Chabanne Bouricha (Algeria)
Michael Lowengren (Sweden)

−67 kg:
1. Piotr Falender (Poland)
2. Sahah Alston (USA)
3. Roberto Rocchi (Italy)
Patrice Prando (France)

−63.5 kg:
1. Janos Gonczi (Hungary)
2. Dogan Sinan (Turkey)
3. Giorgio Perreca (Italy)
Wojciech Wiertel (Poland)

−60 kg:
1. Bogdan Sawicki (Poland)
2. Dennis Sigo (Sweden)
3. Nesradin Bilan (Belgium)
Alessandro Gatto (Brazil)

−57 kg:
1. Massimo Rizzoli (Italy)
2. Pascal Comaille (France)
3. Luis Diego (Spain)
Murat Comert (Turkey)

−54 kg:
1. Jonny Gevriye (Sweden)
2. Massimo Spinelli (Italy)
3. Gabriel Damm (FRG)
Oskar Balogh (Hungary)

Men's Semi-Contact

+84 kg:
1. Steve Anderson (USA)
2. Tony Syces (GRB)
3. Mick Dunleavy (N. Ireland)
Peter Hainke (FRG)

−84 kg:
1. Alfie Lewis (GRB)
2. Eric Depaite (Canada)
3. Hakim Alston (USA)
Peter Berndt (FRG)

−79 kg:
1. Anthony Holloway (USA)
2. Gianna Peruchetti (Switzerland)
3. Yaka Yilmaz (Turkey)
Milan Alessandro (Italy)

−74 kg:
1. Jay Bell (USA)
2. Andreas Lindemann (FRG)
3. Sergio Portaro (Italy)
Ibrahim Centintas (Turkey)

−69 kg:
1. Billy Bryce (GRB)
2. Ibrahim Triqui (Turkey)
3. Bobby O'Neil (N. Ireland)
Yves Lalonde (Canada)

−63 kg:
1. Peter Gilpin (Canada)
2. Polgar Zsolt (Hungary)
3. Hassin Chardbani (N. Ireland)
Joachin Weiphrdt (FRG)

−57 kg:
1. Piotr Siegoczynski (Poland)
2. Cuccu Maurizio (Italy)
3. Uc Abidin (Turkey)
Attila Balogh (Hungary)

Women's Semi-Contact

+60 kg:
1. Linda Denley (USA)
2. Tiziana Zennaro (Italy)
3. Tunde Kocsis (Hungary)
Nichole Corbett (N. Ireland)

−60 kg:
1. Betty Hills (Canada)
2. Gabriella Bady (Hungary)
3. Roberta Vitali (Italy)
Elsa Cordero (USA)

−55 kg:
1. Manon Desrochers (Canada)
2. Amabile Reasilvia (Italy)
3. Christine Bannon (USA)
Marta Bene (Hungary)

−50 kg:
1. Aquilano Eulalia (Italy)
2. Lori Lantrip (USA)
3. Katalin Lorinezi (Hungary)
Deya Yappak (Turkey)

Men's Continuous Contact

84+ kg:
1. Barnabas Katona (Hungary)
2. Torstein Fossnes (Norway)
3. Ray McKenzie (GRB)
Alex Edoo (France)

−84 kg:
1. Zoltan Szucs (Hungary)
2. Nori Carlo (Italy)
3. Mike Schuhmann (USA)
Carl-Heinz Martin (FRG)

−79 kg:
1. Lajos Hugyetz (Hungary)
2. Tim Flood (Canada)
3. Franz Haber (Austria)
Douglas Vincent (France)

−74 kg:
1. Heinz Bresser (FRG)
2. Istvan Toth (Hungary)
3. Giuseppe Paladino (Italy)
Warren Garrett (USA)

−69 kg:
1. Marek Drazdzynski (Poland)
2. Rodrigue Listoir (France)
3. Claudio Pattarino (Italy)
Christoph Walder (Austria)

−63 kg:
1. Ralph Nietto (GRB)
2. Peter Gilpin (Canada)
3. Polgar Zsolt (Hungary)
Jean Luc Kitoko (France)

−57 kg:
1. Piotr Siegoczynski (Poland)
2. Jurgen Jacob (FRG)
3. Attila Balogh (Hungary)
Uc Abidin (Turkey)

Forms

Hard Style
1. Jean Frenette (Canada)
2. Warren Garrett (USA)
3. Lino Guarnaccia (Italy)

Soft Style
1. Karl Romain (USA)
2. Enrico Giachero (Italy)
3. Kirstin Waldberg (FRG)

Weapons
1. Kevin Thompson (USA)
2. Mike Bernardo (Canada)
3. Bob Fermor (N. Ireland)

Women (Demonstration)*
1. Christine Bannon (USA)
2. Elsa Cordero (USA)
3. Kathy Quan (USA)

6TH WAKO WORLD CHAMPIONSHIPS

Date: October 10–11, 1987.
Site: Olympic Hall, Munich, West Germany.
Producers: George Bruckner and Carl Wiedmeier.
Participants: 290 competitors from 29 countries.
Spectators: 11,000.
Television Coverage: Hessische Rund Funk & TV (30 minutes).

Overall Medal Standings
1. USA
2. West Germany (FRG)
3. Canada
4. Hungary
5. France
6. Great Britain
7. Austria
8. Poland
9. Spain
10. Italy

Fighting
Men's Kickboxing

+91 kg:
1. Norbert Novengi (Hungary)
2. Jim Graden (USA)
3. Oskar Printster (Austria)
   Klaus Osterrieder (FRG)

−91 kg:
1. Jerry Rhome (USA)
2. Helmut Joder (FRG)
3. Bruno Campiglia (Italy)
   Oliver Turcan (Turkey)

*The women's forms competition was considered a "demonstration" only; their medals, therefore, were not included in the overall medal standings. These medalists are, however, recognized as legitimate world champions by the WAKO. This event will be an official competition in future WAKO world championships.

−81 kg:
1. Marek Piotrowski (Poland)
2. Karoly Haldsz (Hungary)
3. Jonny Andreasson (Sweden)
   Sokrates Karaites (Greece)

−75 kg:
1. Ferdinand Mack (FRG)
2. Nasser Nassiri (France)
3. Albi Bimpson (GRB)
   G. Anastasion (Greece)

−71 kg:
1. Jose Eguzquiza (Spain)
2. Slimane Hamzaoui (Algeria)
3. Norbert Fisch (Switzerland)
   Carl Whitaker (USA)

−67 kg:
1. Mario Dimitroff (FRG)
2. Romeo Charry (Netherlands)
3. Trevor Ambrose (GRB)
   Yazid Djahnit (Algeria)

−63.5 kg:
1. Djemal Rahilou (France)
2. Tommy Williams (USA)
3. Clemens Willner (FRG)
   Giorgio Perrecca (Italy)

−60 kg:
1. Mike Anderson (USA)
2. Hamed Sakraoui (France)
3. Bogdan Sawicki (Poland)
   Farid Agueni (Algeria)

−57 kg:
1. Troy Dorsey (USA)
2. Massimo Spinelli (Italy)
3. Brahim Rahal (Algeria)
   Oskar Balogh (Hungary)

−54 kg:
1. Peter Hierith (FRG)
2. Jonny Gevrie (Sweden)
3. Gabriel Damm (FRG)
   F. Haddoliche (France)

Men's Semi-Contact

+84 kg:
1. Steve Anderson (USA)
2. Peter Hainke (FRG)
3. Barnabas Katona (FRG)
   E. Bettancourt (Kap Verde)

−84 kg:
1. Alfie Lewis (USA)
2. Peter Bernd (FRG)

3. A. Edoo (Cameroun)
   Michele Surian (Italy)

−79 kg:
1. J. Heidinger (Austria)
2. Raymond Deschamps (Canada)
3. Donato Milani (Italy)
   Rudolf Soos (Hungary)

−74 kg:
1. Jay Bell (USA)
2. Lajos Hugyetz (Hungary)
3. G. Pelucchetti (Switzerland)
   Juergen Pelikan (FRG)

−69 kg:
1. Robert Ulbrich (FRG)
2. Evelyn Dwyer (GRB)
3. Daniel Kroepfl (Austria)
   Janos Hortobagyi (Hungary)

−63 kg:
1. Peter Gilpin (Canada)
2. Giuseppe Trucci (Italy)
3. Walter Lange (FRG)
   Tommy Williams (USA)

−57 kg:
1. Oliver Drexler (FRG)
2. Troy Dorsey (USA)
3. M. Caccu (Italy)
   K. Uzan (Turkey)

Women's Semi-Contact

+60 kg:
1. Linda Denley (USA)
2. Victoria Desantos (Canada)
3. T. Zennarro (Italy)
   Gabriella Bady (Hungary)

−60 kg:
1. Helen Chung (USA)
2. Ute Bernhard (FRG)
3. Diane Riley (GRB)
   Betty Hills (Canada)

−55 kg:
1. Angela Schmid (FRG)
2. Josee Blanchard (Canada)
3. K. Leclerc (France)
   M. Giagnioti (Italy)

−50 kg:
1. Lori Lantrip (USA)
2. Gerda Mack (FRG)
3. Lou Pauli (GRB)
   Elena Capitanio (Italy)

Forms

Hard Style
1. Jean Frenette (Canada)
2. John Chung (USA)
3. Antonio Caridi (Italy)

Soft Style
1. Keith Hirabayashi (USA)
2. Bui Duc Lai (Vietnam)
3. Christian Wolf (FRG)

Weapons
1. Keith Hirabayashi (USA)
2. Jean Frenette (Canada)
3. Nick Stratacos (Saudi Arabia)

5TH WAKO WORLD CHAMPIONSHIPS I

Note: Due to temporary political differences, the WAKO split into two factions and conducted two world championships on the same weekend in 1985. The split lasted only one year and the two factions merged again in 1986. For the purpose of thoroughness, the results of both events are presented here.

Neither event provided an overall medal standing, but both events for the first time added women's semi-contact competition. The London event also introduced forms competition for the first time.

Date: November 2, 1985.
Site: Wembley Centre, London, England.
Producer: Joe Johal.

Overall Medal Standing (Kickboxing)
1. Germany
2. United States
3. Great Britain
4. Italy
   Ireland
   Greece
   Wales
5. Switzerland
   Mexico

Men's Kickboxing

+91 kg:
1. Martin Roetzer (FRG)
2. Jim Graden (USA)
3. (Walkover)

−91 kg:
1. Alois Hoffman (FRG)
2. John Graden (USA)

−81 kg:
1. Ray McCallum (USA)
2. M. Montrasio (Italy)
3. Alexander Zoetl (FRG)

−75 kg:
1. Ferdinand Mack (FRG)
2. Eddie Butcher (USA)

−71 kg:
1. Daniel Bodo (FRG)
2. Brian Dorsey (USA)
3. Roland Gut (Switzerland)
   Pablo Delgado (Mexico)

−67 kg:
1. Chris McNeesh (GRB)
2. A. Trimble (Wales)
3. LeRoy Taylor (USA)

−63.5 kg:
1. Tommy Williams (USA)
2. L. Paerickios (Greece)

−60 kg:
1. Michael Kuhr (FRG)
2. Gerry Kidd (Ireland)

−57 kg:
1. Troy Dorsey (USA)
2. Jergen Jakob (FRG)

−54 kg:
1. Gabriel Damm (FRG)
2. J. Evans (GRB)

Overall Medal Standing (Semi-Contact)
1. United States
2. Germany
3. Great Britain
4. Scotland
5. Wales
6. India
7. Italy
   Ireland
8. Yugoslavia

Men's Semi-Contact

+84 kg:
1. Steve Anderson (USA)
2. Jeff Singh (India)
3. Peter Hainke (FRG)
   Jaime Cochrale (Wales)

−84 kg:
1. Rudy Smedley (USA)
2. Alfie Lewis (GRB)
3. M. Mladen (Yugo)
   Steve Brindley (Wales)

−79 kg:
1. John French (GRB)
2. Robert Jung (FRG)
3. Ray McCallum (USA)
   Baltramy (Italy)

−74 kg:
1. John Longstreet (USA)
2. George McKenzie (GRB)
3. George Canning (Ireland)
   Luzzi (Italy)

−69 kg:
1. Walter Reiner (FRG)
2. Jackson White (Wales)
3. John Chung (USA)
   Ian Ferguson (Scotland)

−63 kg:
1. Rod Sergiew (Scotland)
2. Walter Lange (FRG)
3. Tommy Williams (USA)
   Desi Murphy (Ireland)

−57 kg:
1. Troy Dorsey (USA)
2. Harold Roegner (FRG)
3. David Gee (Wales)

Women's Semi-Contact

+60 kg:
1. Linda Denley (USA)
2. D. Kelly (GRB)
3. Rascall (Wales)
   Hynes (Ireland)

−60 kg:
1. June Morson (Scotland)
2. Ute Bernhard (FRG)
3. Yvonne Alladice (Wales)

−55 kg:
1. Gerda Mack (FRG)
2. Hilliard (Scotland)
3. Jean Klink (Scotland)

−50 kg:
1. Chris Ganzmann (FRG)
2. L. Pavli (GRB)
3. Hamilton (Ireland)
   Hall (Wales)

Forms

Men
1. John Chung
2. (Walkover)
3. (Walkover)

5TH WAKO WORLD CHAMPIONSHIPS II

Date: November 2, 1985.
Site: Budapest, Hungary.
Producer: Hungarian Sport Karate
   Union.
Spectators: 20,000.

Fighting

Men's Kickboxing

+87 kg:
1. Chiarrochi (France)
2. Bruno Campiglia (Italy)
3. Mihaloydis (Greece)
   Jumasz (Hungary)

−87 kg:
1. Monaco (Belgium)
2. Vasilikos Kirarisson (Greece)
3. Halasz (Hungary)
   Slobodon Sokota (Yugoslavia)

−80 kg:
1. Othmar Felsberger (Austria)
2. Zolt (FRG)
3. Pino Bosco (Belgium)
   Dietmar (Austria)

−75 kg:
1. Judes (France)
2. Nasser Nassiri (France)
3. Caracho (Portugal)
   Dietmar (Austria)

−71 kg:
1. Norbert Fisch (Switzerland)
2. Olivier Gruner (France)
3. O'Loughlin (GRB)
   Ferrari (Italy)

−67 kg:
1. Massimo Liberati (Italy)
2. Torre (France)

3. Berrar (Switzerland)
   Nachife (Morocco)

−63.5 kg:
1. Giorgio Perreca (Italy)
2. Michael Duhs (Austria)
3. Jasch (Hungary)
   Ghoose (Belgium)

−60 kg:
1. Hawak (Hungary)
2. El Quandili (France)
3. Ulissi (Italy)
   Hartenberger (Austria)

−57 kg:
1. Kaidi (France)
2. Howard Brown (GRB)
3. Koczor (Hungary)

−54 kg:
1. Farid Agueni (France)
2. Dahak (Algeria)
3. Rechsteiner (Switzerland)
   Balog (Hungary)

Semi-Contact

Teams:
1. Great Britain
2. Italy
3. Hungary
4. Austria

Men

+84 kg:
1. Laurent Dably (Ivory Coast)
2. Neville Wray (GRB)
3. Szivak (Hungary)

−84 kg:
1. Kevin Brewerton (GRB)
2. Harrer (FRG)
3. Barnabas Katona (Hungary)

−79 kg:
1. Clive Parkinson (GRB)
2. Zimmerman (FRG)
3. Stelzl (Austria)

−74 kg:
1. Hans Hinz (FRG)
2. Nasser Nassiri (France)
3. Bencic (Yugoslavia)

−69 kg:
1. Bresser (Norway)
2. Haas (FRG)
3. Veres (Hungary)

−63 kg:
1. Massimo Galozzi (Italy)
2. Baleche (France)
3. Bobby O'Neil (Ireland)

−57 kg:
1. Syegoczinsky (Poland)
2. Gerhard Walde (Italy)
3. Ulrick (FRG)

Women
+60 kg:
1. Bruno (France)
2. Ujfallidi (Hungary)
3. Heinz (FRG)

−60 kg:
1. Szepessi (Hungary)
2. Spata (Italy)
3. Kiss Beata (Hungary)

4TH WAKO WORLD CHAMPIONSHIPS

Date: October 22, 1983.
Site: Wembley Centre, London,
   England.
Producer: Mike Haig.

Note: Only separate medal
standings were available for this
event.

Overall Medal Standings (Kickboxing)
1. Germany (FRG)
2. Netherlands
3. Italy
   Great Britain
   France
4. Yugoslavia
   Norway
   Switzerland

Fighting

Men's Kickboxing

+91 kg:
1. Chiarrochi (France)
2. Manfred Vogt (FRG)
3. Cipollaro (Italy)
   Prinster (Austria)

−91 kg:
1. M. Rotzer (FRG)
2. Brandenburger (France)

3. Taberner (GRB)
   Door (Austria)

−80 kg:
1. N. Heiderhoff (FRG)
2. Klause (Switzerland)
3. Maurizio Callegari (Italy)
   Othmar Felsberger (Austria)

−75 kg:
1. Barrett (GRB)
2. A. Zoltl (FRG)
3. Mathews (Ireland)
   Milakovinc (Yugo)

−71 kg:
1. Ferdinand Mack (FRG)
2. Ferrari (Italy)
3. Wolfgang Muller (Austria)
   Gomez (USA)

−67 kg:
1. Osborne (GRB)
2. Nygard (Norway)
3. Roberts (Ireland)
   Ramjanli (Portugal)

−63.5 kg:
1. Giorgio Perreca (Italy)
2. Sasha Stojanovic (Yugo)
3. Godfrey Butler (GRB)
   Bensalah (France)

−60 kg:
1. Romeo Charry (Netherlands)
2. Michael Kuhr (FRG)
3. Feene (GRB)
   Schoberl (Austria)

−57 kg:
1. Vieira (Netherlands)
2. Anderson (Norway)
3. Creawe (Ireland)
   Glover (GRB)

Overall Medal Standing (Semi-Contact)
1. USA
2. Great Britain
   Italy
3. Germany (FRG)

Men's Semi-Contact
+84 kg:
1. Steve Anderson (USA)
2. Colombo (Italy)
3. Neville Wray (GRB)
   Malinaishe (Wales)

−84 kg:
1. Alfie Lewis (GRB)
2. Donato Milani (Italy)
3. Rudy Smedley (USA)
   Grey (Ireland)

−79 kg:
1. Ludger Dietze (FRG)
2. Ray McCallum (USA)
3. Federico Milani (Italy)
   Vettler (Switzerland)

−74 kg:
1. John Longstreet (USA)
2. Wilson (GRB)
3. Gillot (France)
   Maller (FRG)

−69 kg:
1. John Chung (USA)
2. Davis (GRB)
3. Massimo Casula (Italy)
   Mark Aston (GRB)

−63 kg:
1. Tommy Williams (USA)
2. Brooms (GRB)
3. Losi (Italy)
   Lehmer (Switzerland)

−57 kg:
1. Giuliano Sartoni (Italy)
2. Rainer Knell (FRG)
3. Lee (USA)
   Stack (Ireland)

3RD WAKO WORLD CHAMPIONSHIPS

Date: 1981.
Site: Milan, Italy.
Producer: Ennio Falsoni.

Note: This event featured semi-contact competition only; no kickboxing. The forms results listed at the end are presumably unofficial in that the respective victories were not tallied as part of the overall medal count.

Overall Medal Standings
1. Germany (FRG)
2. United States
3. Italy
4. Switzerland
5. Canada
   San Marino

6. Austria
7. Yugoslavia

Fighting

Men's Semi-Contact
+84 kg:
1. Daryl Tyler (USA)
2. A. Miller (Canada)
3. T. Volken (Switzerland)

−84 kg:
1. Harald Edel (FRG)
2. Walter Meneghini (Italy)
3. Slobodon Sokota (Yugo)

−79 kg:
1. Ray McCallum (USA)
2. Ludger Dietze (FRG)
3. Federico Milani (Italy)

−74 kg:
1. Hans Gerd Hitz (FRG)
2. Riccardo Pavoni (Italy)
3. Billye Jackson (USA)

−69 kg:
1. Fritz Bibot (FRG)
2. Daniel Humbel (Switzerland)
3. John Chung (USA)

−63 kg:
1. Ulf Schmidt (FRG)
2. Tommy Williams (USA)
3. David Sirota (Austria)

−57 kg:
1. Ranier Knell (FRG)
2. Giuliano Sartoni (San Marino)
3. Peter Muller (Austria)

Forms

Men
1. John Chung (USA)
2. Ric Pascetta (USA)
3. Daryl Tyler (USA)

2ND WAKO WORLD CHAMPIONSHIPS

Date: November 3–4, 1979.
Site: Hillsborough Community College, Tampa, Florida.
Producer: Mike Anderson.

Overall Medal Standing (Kickboxing)
1. West Germany (FRG)
2. Italy

3. United States
4. Great Britain
5. Switzerland
6. Yugoslavia
7. Dominican Republic
8. Austria
9. Norway
   Belgium
   Sweden
   Netherlands

Fighting

Men's Kickboxing

+84 kg:
1. Tony Palmore (USA)
2. Harold Ehmann (Austria)
3. Mladen Carevic (Yugo)

−84 kg:
1. Flavio Galessi (Italy)
2. Branko Zgalijardic (Yugo)
3. Juan Ponce (Switzerland)
   Gary Sproule (USA)

−79 kg:
1. Jean Marc Tonus (Switzerland)
2. Dieter Herdel (FRG)
3. Benny Hedlund (Sweden)
   F. Okkonowiak (Netherlands)

−74 kg:
1. Franz Haller (Italy)
2. Harold Roth (USA)
3. Alfred Tommey (Switzerland)
   Branko Cikatic (Yugo)

−69 kg:
1. Ferdinand Mack (FRG)
2. Javier Reyes (Dominican)
3. Sandry Ravessoud (Switzerland)
   Walter Parlovic (Yugo)

−63 kg:
1. Ali Pehlivan (FRG)
2. Godfrey Butler (GRB)
3. Jonny Mirer (Switzerland)
   Jimmy Barletta (Belgium)

−57 kg:
1. Howard Brown (GRB)
2. Michael Kuhr (FRG)
3. Jesus Duran (Dominican)
   Max Mankowitz (Norway)

Overall Medal Standing (Semi-Contact)

1. West Germany (FRG)
2. Italy

3. Great Britain
4. Austria
5. USA
6. Netherlands
   Switzerland
7. Belgium
   Yugoslavia
8. Norway
   Morocco
   Dominican Republic

Men's Semi-Contact

+84 kg:
1. McKenzie (GRB)
2. Falk (Switzerland)
3. Anne Delis (Netherlands)

−84 kg:
1. Harold Edel (FRG)
2. Walter Meneghini (Italy)
3. Streicher (Austria)

−79 kg:
1. James Cisco (USA)
2. Ivan Wray (GRB)
3. Flavio Galessi (Italy)

−74 kg:
1. Weinhold (Austria)
2. Durovic (Yugo)
3. De la Cruz (Dominican)

−69 kg:
1. Andreas Brannasch (FRG)
2. Theugels (Belgium)
3. Goyvaerts (Morocco)

−63 kg:
1. A. Lindemann (FRG)
2. Jim Hakkens (Netherlands)
3. Thomas Volken (Switzerland)

−57 kg:
1. A. Ortelli (Italy)
2. Sarhan Salman (FRG)
3. F. Infantone (Norway)

1ST WAKO WORLD CHAMPIONSHIPS

Date: November 5, 1978.
Site: West Berlin, Germany.
Producer: Georg Bruckner.
Participants: Competitors from 18 countries.

Overall Medal Standing

1. USA
2. West Germany (FRG)

3. Dominican Republic
4. Netherlands
   Norway
5. Yugoslavia
6. France
7. Switzerland
8. Belgium
   Austria

Fighting

Men's Kickboxing

+84 kg:
1. Tony Palmore (USA)
2. Tom Rissman (FRG)
3. Harold Ehmann (Austria)

−84 kg:
1. Branko Zgaljardic (Yugo)
2. Dirk Peter (FRG)
3. Nils Hovlsrud (Norway)

−79 kg:
1. Daryl Tyler (USA)
2. Nelson Colon (Dominican)
3. Bernd Eggert (FRG)

−74 kg:
1. Peter Harbrecht (FRG)
2. Harold Roth (USA)
3. Enric Gunning (Nether)

−69 kg:
1. Omar Sahli (Norway)
2. Youssef Zenaf (France)
3. Heinz Klupp (FRG)

−63 kg:
1. Ivan Menes (Netherlands)
2. Chalabi Bennacef (France)

−57 kg:
1. Jose Caballos (Dominican)
2. Jonny Canabate (Switzerland)
3. Rachid Alitem (Belgium)

WAKO EUROPEAN CHAMPIONSHIPS (1977–90)

10TH WAKO EUROPEAN CHAMPIONSHIPS

Date: November 16–18, 1990.
Site: Madrid, Spain.
Participants: 24 countries.

Note: The Overall Medal Standing was unavailable for this event.

Fighting

Men's Full Contact

+91 kg:
1. Paolo Zorello (Italy)
2. Fucho (France)
3. Hubert Numrich (Germany)
   Sharapov (CIS)

−91 kg:
1. Premyslav Saleta (Poland)
2. Mutavlic (Yugo)
3. Lopez (Spain)
   Perreira (Portugal)

−81 kg:
1. Sanchez (Spain)
2. Jorge (Portugal)
3. Spiridon (Belgium)
   Pavel Rumas (Poland)

−75 kg:
1. Fernandez (Portugal)
2. Riccio (Italy)
3. Jozef Warchol (Poland)
   Sharepo (CIS)

−71 kg:
1. Gerd Dittrich (Germany)
2. Trones (Norway)
3. Ruggiero (France)
   Zelevic (Yugo)

−67 kg:
1. Klemens Willner (Germany)
2. Imed Matlouti (France)
3. Teixeira (Portugal)
   Hsaine (Belgium)

−63.5 kg:
1. Pinel (Spain)
2. Ivanov (CIS)
3. Chesnot (France)
   Carvalho (Portugal)

−60 kg:
1. Ivan Aksutin (CIS)
2. Helge Halvordsen (Norway)
3. Bogdan Sawicki (Poland)
   Diaz (Portugal)

−57 kg:
1. Alexeji Nechaev (CIS)
2. Erdogan (Turkey)
3. Lombardi (Italy)
   Pina (Portugal)

−54 kg:
1. Massimo Spinelli (Italy)
2. Oskar Balough (Hungary)

3. Demirkapu (Belgium)
   Huete (Spain)

Men's Semi-Contact

+89 kg:
1. Alfie Lewis (GRB)
2. Valentini (Italy)
3. O'Brian (Ireland)
   ?

−84 kg:
1. Peter Bernt (Germany)
2. Kevin Brewerton (GRB)
3. Riboud (France)
   Szulcs (Hungary)

−79 kg:
1. P. Edwards (GRB)
2. Zadra (Italy)
3. Ralf Kunzler (Germany)
   Flanagan (Ireland)

−74 kg:
1. Thompson (GRB)
2. Lajos Hugyetz (Hungary)
3. Sergio Portaro (Italy)
   Andreas Lindemann (Germany)

−69 kg:
1. Billy Bryce (GRB)
2. M. Niola (Italy)
3. Walder (Austria)
   Hortobagy (Hungary)

−63 kg:
1. Reiner Stadtmuller (Germany)
2. Lico (Italy)
3. Juan Perez (Portugal)
   Sosa (Spain)

−57 kg:
1. Abadin Uz (Turkey)
2. Oliver Drexler (Germany)
3. Piotr Siegoczynski (Poland)
   Tony Byrne (Ireland)

Women's Semi-Contact

+60 kg:
1. Tiziana Zennaro (Italy)
2. Moffett (Nether)
3. Mestar (France)
   Rivilla (Spain)

−60 kg:
1. Lahnsen (GRB)
2. Vitali (Italy)
3. Gabriella Bady (Hungary)
   Van Eetveld (Belgium)

−55 kg:
1. Hugyetz (Hungary)
2. Rotario (Italy)
3. Mahner (Germany)
   Smith (GRB)

−50 kg:
1. Karin Schiller (Germany)
2. Quansah (GRB)
3. Szepressi (Hungary)
   Diego (Spain)

Men's Continuous Contact

+84 kg:
1. Bruno Campiglia (Italy)
2. McKenzie (GRB)
3. Kabba (France)
   Barnabas Katona (Hungary)

−84 kg:
1. Zoltan Szucs (Hungary)
2. Wilkinson (GRB)
3. Colombo (Italy)
   Deveci (Turkey)

−79 kg:
1. George McKenzie (GRB)
2. Rigamonti (Italy)
3. Dunglas (France)
   Harald Zimmermann (Germany)

−74 kg:
1. Lajos Hugyetz (Hungary)
2. Robert Steiner (Switzerland)
3. Nicolo (Italy)
   Karpov (CIS)

−69 kg:
1. Pattarino (Italy)
2. Marough (France)
3. Surkovic (Yugo)
   Dimont (Belgium)

−63 kg:
1. Rafael Neito (GRB)
2. Axel Briesenich (Germany)
3. Duponchel (France)
   Eosentino (Italy)

−57 kg:
1. Abidin Uz (Turkey)
2. Jurgen Jacob (Germany)
3. Conrad (GRB)
   Melo (Portugal)

Women's Continuous Contact

+60 kg:
1. Claudia Schregele (Germany)

2. Bailey (GRB)
3. Byrne (Ireland)
   Szucs (Hungary)

−60 kg:
1. Bonazza (Italy)
2. Rylik (Poland)
3. Hebert (France)
   Harris (GRB)

−55 kg:
1. Le Clerq (France)
2. Smith (GRB)
3. Kirschbaum (Germany)
   Federico Milani (Italy)

−50 kg:
1. Szepessi (Hungary)
2. Alo (Italy)
3. Diego (Spain)
   Keogh (Ireland)

Forms

Soft:
1. Earl Blijd (Nether)
2. Simon Keith (GRB)
3. ? (Ireland)

Weapons:
1. ?
2. Earl Blijd (Nether)
3. ?

9TH WAKO EUROPEAN CHAMPIONSHIPS

Date: 1988.
Site: Venice, Italy.
Producer: Ennio Falsoni.

Note: This event did not feature a kickboxing competition.

Fighting

Men's Semi-Contact

+84 kg:
1. Andrew Boyce (GRB)
2. Thomas Brunnier (Switzerland))
3. Michael Dunleavy (Ireland)
   Edward Strand (Austria)

−84 kg:
1. Michele Surian (Italy)
2. Alfie Lewis (GRB)
3. Guner Lentz (Turkey)
   Barnabas Katoona (Hungary)

−79 kg:
1. Wayne Benoni (GRB)
2. Rudolph Soos (Hungary)
3. Stephan Plattner (Austria)
   Yilmaz Yaka (Turkey)

−74 kg:
1. Chris William (GRB)
2. Lajos Hugyetz (Hungary)
3. Massimo Galozzi (Italy)
   Roy Baker (Ireland)

−69 kg:
1. Francesco Arnone (Italy)
2. Robert Ulbricht (FRG)
3. Jones Hortobaji (Hungary)
   Bob Bodson (Belgium)

−63 kg:
1. Gaetano Sambataro (Italy)
2. Zsoltan Polgar (Hungary)
3. Isa Acar (Turkey)
   ?

−57 kg:
1. Maurizio Cuccu (Italy)
2. Oliver Drexler (FRG)
3. Gerhard Schatz (Austria)
   ?

Women's Semi-Contact

+60 kg:
1. Tiziana Zennaro (Italy)
2. Gabriella Bady (Hungary)
3. Margaret Dent (Ireland)
   Noleen Murphy (N. Ireland)

−60 kg:
1. Roberta Vitali (Italy)
2. Ute Howell (FRG)
3. Maria Bene (Hungary)
   Noleen Murphy (N. Ireland)

−55 kg:
1. Barbara Englert (FRG)
2. Sonia Bonazza (Italy)
3. Patricia Sager (Switzerland)
   Una Loughram (N. Ireland)

−50 kg:
1. Marian Egrich (Hungary)
2. Debbie Graham (GRB)
3. Antonella Aversano (Italy)
   Karin Schiller (FRG)

Men's Continuous Contact

+84 kg:
1. Raymond McKenzie (GRB)
2. Gerald Hellman (FRG)

3. Steve Makawaya (Belgium)
   Zoltan Szucs (Hungary)

−84 kg:
1. Karl-Heinz Martin (FRG)
2. Barnabas Katoona (Hungary)
3. Alessandro Milan (Italy)
   Jerje Nordal (Norway)

−79 kg:
1. George McKenzie (GRB)
2. Alain Lonnedy (Belgium)
3. Andreas Lindemann (FRG)
   Franz Haberl (Austria)

−74 kg:
1. Rolf Kunzler (FRG)
2. Lajos Hugyetz (Hungary)
3. Robert Steiner (Switzerland))
   Martin Gibbons (Ireland)

−63 kg:
1. Silvano Cosentino (Italy)
2. Axel Briesenik (FRG)
3. Alan Johnson (Ireland)
   Marek Drazosynski (Poland)

−57 kg:
1. Jakob Jurgen (FRG)
2. Gianni Morigi (Italy)
3. Michael Crane (Ireland)
   Attila Balough (Hungary)

8TH WAKO EUROPEAN CHAMPIONSHIPS

Date: November 29–30, 1986.
Site: Athens, Greece.
Producer: Simon Zahopoulos.

Note: Women's semi-contact competition was introduced at this event.

Overall Medal Standing
1. West Germany (FRG)
2. Great Britain
3. Greece
4. Poland
5. Scotland
6. Yugoslavia
7. Cyprus
8. Italy
9. Wales

Fighting

Men's Kickboxing

+91 kg:
1. Mladen Carevic (Yugo)

−91 kg:
1. G. Stefanopulos (Greece)
2. Miljenco Sarac (Yugo)
3. Franco Mondolo (Italy)

−80 kg:
1. Keith Wilson (Scot)
2. Peter Lowrie (GRB)
3. Raffaello Molino (Italy)
  Rudolf Dusan (Yugo)

−75 kg:
1. Ferdinand Mack (FRG)
2. Mick McCue (Eng)
3. Mario Pisk (Yugo)
  N. Papatheas (Greece)

−71 kg:
1. Martin Manaville (GRB)
2. Kostas Gogos (Greece)
3. Angelo Ciarafoni (Italy)
  Joachim Mainka (FRG)

−67 kg:
1. Mario Dimitroff (FRG)
2. Chris McNeesh (GRB)

−63.5 kg:
1. George Kotsis (Greece)
2. Joannis Zachos (Cyprus)

−60 kg:
1. Michael Kuhr (FRG)
2. Bogdan Sawicki (Poland)

−57 kg:
1. Rudolf Kainer (FRG)
2. Paul Monty (GRB)

−54 kg:
1. Darren Evans (GRB)
2. Gabriel Damm (FRG)

Men's Semi-Contact

+84 kg:
1. Peter Hainke (FRG)
2. Andrew Boyce (GRB)
3. M. Zapior (Poland)

−84 kg:
1. Alfie Lewis (GRB)
2. D. Muratithis (Greece)
3. Peter Opasca (Scot)
  M. Markesina (Yugo)

−79 kg:
1. Steve French (Eng)
2. Andreas Lindemann (FRG)
3. Basilio Basile (Italy)
  Irenevsz Jakubiak (Poland)

−74 kg:
1. Ralf Kunzler (FRG)

2. Carl Reynolds (Scot)
3. Vassilios Kapatais (Cyprus)
  George McKenzie (GRB)

−69 kg:
1. Reiner Walter (FRG)
2. Spiros Velios (Greece)
3. Artur Piekarz (Poland)
  Evelyn Dwyer (GRB)

−63 kg:
1. Walter Lange (FRG)
2. Bogdan Rudkowski (Poland)
3. Nikos Memos (Greece)
  Carlton Abbey (GRB)

−57 kg:
1. Piotr Siegoczynski (Poland)
2. Jurgen Jakob (FRG)

Women's Semi-Contact

+60 kg:
1. Diane Grimmer (Wales)
2. Dagmar Einwag (FRG)
3. M. Tzeffrakov (Greece)
  Monik Maughan (Scot)

−60 kg:
1. Margareta Niania (Greece)
2. Lisa Oliver (Scot)
3. Ute Bernhard (FRG)
  Jane Grey (GRB)

−55 kg:
1. Gerda Mack
2. Anna Pietryka (Poland)

−50 kg:
1. Angela Schmid (FRG)
2. Ewa Lysiak (Poland)

7TH WAKO EUROPEAN CHAMPIONSHIPS

Date: September 22, 1984.
Site: Graz, Austria.
Producer: Peter Land.

Overall Medal Standing (Kickboxing)
1. West Germany (FRG)
2. Austria
3. Italy
4. Belgium
  Yugoslavia
5. ?
  Ireland
6. Great Britain

7. Switzerland
8. Denmark
  Spain
  Greece

Fighting

Men's Kickboxing

87+ kg:
1. Martin Roetzer (FRG)
2. Manfred Hammerl (Austria)
3. Mladen Stanimirovic (Yugo)
  Bruno Campiglia (Italy)

−87 kg:
1. Ernest Ingdorr (Austria)
2. Stefano Bortoloni (Italy)
3. Alex Brodmann (Switzerland)
  Vasilikos Kirarisson (Greece)

−80 kg:
1. Pino Bosco (Belgium)
2. Laurence White (GRB)
3. Maurizio Callegari (Italy)
  Othmar Felsberger (Austria)

−75 kg:
1. Alexander Zotl (FRG)
2. Alfonso Sgarro (Italy)
3. Moreno Gallego (Spain)
  Gill Kashmir (GRB)

−71 kg:
1. Ferdinand Mack (FRG)
2. Derrick Edwards (GRB)
3. Wolfgang Muller (Austria)
  Paolo Liberati (Italy)

−67 kg:
1. Massimo Liberati (Italy)
2. Erich Gsellmann (Austria)
3. Aco Serafinovski (Denmark)
—

−63.5 kg:
1. Sasha Stojanovich (Yugo)
2. Andreas Richter (FRG)
3. Gaetano Scarpetta (Italy)
  Bruno Ferretti (Belgium)

−60 kg:
1. Gerard Kidd (Ireland)
2. Michael Duhs (Austria)
3. Branco Morellini (Switzerland)
  Zadravec Certomiz (Yugo)

−57 kg:
1. Kumur Raj (Denmark)
2. E. Muhlberger (FRG)
3. Gerhard Poms (Austria)
  Vladimir Sitar (Yugo)

−54 kg:
1. Jurgen Jakob (FRG)
2. Bogdan Stoijkovic (Austria)
3. Patrick Cammalleri (Belgium)
   Livio Carite (Italy)

Overall Medal Standing (Semi-Contact)

1. Germany (FRG)
2. Italy
3. Great Britain
4. Austria
5. Hungary
6. Yugoslavia
7. Spain
   Switzerland

Men

84+ kg:
1. Neville Wray (GRB)
2. Italo Piras (Italy)
3. Vojislav Car (Yugo)
   Roland Bleich (FRG)

−84 kg:
1. Robert Jung (FRG)
2. Alvin Mighty (GRB)
3. Barnabas Katowa (Hungary)
   Martin Golob (Yugo)

−79 kg:
1. Ludger Dietz (FRG)
2. Clive Parkinson (GRB)
3. Dejan Bancic (Yugo)
   Herald Raimond (Switzerland)

−74 kg:
1. Johann Heidinger (Austria)
2. Leonardo Pavoni (Italy)
3. Wolfgang Muller (FRG)
   Mark Aston (GRB)

−69 kg:
1. Massimo Casula (Italy)
2. Rudolf Soos (Hungary)
3. S. Bajraktarevic (Yugo)
   Reiner Walter (FRG)

−63 kg:
1. Walter Lange (FRG)
2. Manfred Frohwein (Austria)
3. G. DePablo Pedro (Spain)
   Kevin Green (GRB)

−57 kg:
1. Gerhard Walde (Italy)
2. Ozkan Kadiz (FRG)

3. Peter Muller (Austria)
   Istvan Fodoz (Hungary)

6TH WAKO EUROPEAN CHAMPIONSHIPS

Date: 1982.
Basel, Germany.

Note: This event featured only semi-contact competition.

Overall Medal Standing

1. Italy
2. Germany (FRG)
3. Great Britain
4. France
5. Austria
6. Belgium
7. Switzerland
   Ireland

Fighting

Men's Semi-Contact

84+ kg:
1. Neville Wray (GRB)
2. Hoffman (FRG)
3. Colombo (Italy)

−84 kg:
1. Windischbacher (Austria)
2. K. Konigsreuther (FRG)
3. Konig (Switzerland)

−79 kg:
1. Ludger Dietz (FRG)
2. Federico Milani (Italy)
3. Page (GRB)

−74 kg:
1. Leonardo Pavoni (Italy)
2. Clezardin (France)
3. Curry (Ireland)

−69 kg:
1. Matala (France)
2. Steinheuser (FRG)
3. v.d. Myunsbrugge (Belgium)

−63 kg:
1. Losi (Itali)
2. Asten (GRB)
3. Scherbaum (FRG)

−57 kg:
1. Giuliano Sartoni (Italy)
2. Rainer Knell (FRG)
3. Goppens (Belgium)

5TH WAKO EUROPEAN CHAMPIONSHIPS

Date: 1981.
Dublin, Ireland.
Producer: George Canning.

Overall Medal Standing (Kickboxing)

1. Great Britain
2. West Germany (FRG)
3. Yugoslavia
4. Switzerland
5. Italy

Fighting

Men's Kickboxing

84+ kg:
1. Greenwood (GRB)
2. Miljenco Sarac (Yugo)
3. Panseri (Italy)

−84 kg:
1. Flavio Galessi (Italy)
2. Spika (Yugo)
3. Cabo (Yugo)

−79 kg:
1. Branko Cikatic (Yugo)
2. Dieter Herdel (FRG)
3. Babbs (GRB)

−74 kg:
1. A. Tommei (Switzerland)
2. Wilson (GRB)
3. Barrett (GRB)

−69 kg:
1. Ferdinand Mack (FRG)
2. Sandry Ravessoud (Switzerland)
3. Wellington (GRB)

−63 kg:
1. Godfrey Butler (GRB)
2. Klaus Friedhaber (FRG)
3. Sasha Stojanovich (Yugo)

−57 kg:
1. Michael Kuhr (FRG)
2. Howard Brown (GRB)
3. Uguz (FRG)

Overall Medal Standing (Semi-Contact)

1. Germany (FRG)
2. Great Britain
3. Italy

4. Ireland
5. Yugoslavia
6. Switzerland

Men

84+ kg:
1. Rudiger Malzahn (FRG)
2. Leavey (Ireland)
3. Price (GRB)

−84 kg:
1. Harald Edel (FRG)
2. Alfie Lewis (GRB)
3. Walter Meneghini (Italy)

−79 kg:
1. H. Hirschganger (FRG)
2. Ivan Wray (GRB)
3. Sehic (Yugo)

−74 kg:
1. Hans Hinz (FRG)
2. Federico Milani (Italy)
3. Clive Parkinson (GRB)

−69 kg:
1. Fritz Bissot (FRG)
2. Panunzio (Italy)
3. Roberts (Italy)

−63 kg:
1. Mark Aston (GRB)
2. Mike Schiller (FRG)
3. Vosak (Yugo)

−57 kg:
1. Coughlan (GRB)
2. Luciano (Italy)
3. Paladino (Switzerland)

4TH WAKO EUROPEAN CHAMPIONSHIPS

Date: 1980.
Site: London, England.

Overall Medal Standing (Kickboxing)
1. West Germany (FRG)
2. Great Britain
3. Yugoslavia
4. Norway
5. Switzerland
6. Italy
7. Netherlands
8. Austria
   Wales

Fighting

Men's Kickboxing

84+ kg:
1. Commack (GRB)
2. Pusnik (Yugo)
3. Harold Ehmann (Austria)

−84 kg:
1. Participilio (Italy)
2. Spika (Yugo)
3. Oberhummer (Austria)

−79 kg:
1. Branko Cikatic (Yugo)
2. David (Netherlands)
3. Barrett (GRB)

−74 kg:
1. Havna (Norway)
2. Wilson (GRB)
3. Ruedisnehli (Switzerland)

−69 kg:
1. Sandry Ravessoud (Switzerland)
2. Sunde (Norway)
3. van Duin (Netherlands)

−63 kg:
1. Klaus Friedhaber (FRG)
2. Godfrey Butler (GRB)
3. Broom (Wales)

−57 kg:
1. Michael Kuhr (FRG)
2. Howard Brown (GRB)
3. Lloyd (Wales)

Overall Medal Standing (Semi-Contact)
1. Germany (FRG)
2. Italy
   Austria
3. Switzerland
4. Belgium
5. Great Britain
   Ireland
6. Netherlands

Men

84+ kg:
1. Ansberger (Austria)
2. Urich Falk (Switzerland)
3. Rudiger Malzahn (FRG)

−84 kg:
1. Harald Edel (FRG)
2. Streicher (Austria)
3. Walter Meneghini (Italy)

−79 kg:
1. Ivan Wray (GRB)
2. Facchinetti (Italy)
3. Ludger Dietz (FRG)

−74 kg:
1. Federico Milani (Italy)
2. Kropf (Switzerland)
3. De Koning (Netherlands)

−69 kg:
1. Andreas Brannasch (FRG)
2. Prelog (Austria)
3. De Koning (Netherlands)

−63 kg:
1. Scantlebury (GRB)
2. Kessels (Belgium)
3. Gerathy (Ireland)

−57 kg:
1. Christian Wulf (FRG)
2. A. Ortelli (Italy)
3. Coughlan (GRB)

3RD WAKO EUROPEAN CHAMPIONSHIPS

Date: 1978.
Site: Milan, Italy.
Producer: Ennio Falsoni.

Overall Medal Standing (Kickboxing)
1. West Germany (FRG)
2. Yugoslavia
3. Italy
4. Switzerland
5. Norway
   Belgium
6. Netherlands

Fighting

Men's Kickboxing

84+ kg:
1. Tom Rissman (FRG)
2. Manfred Vogt (FRG)
3. Rigo (Italy)

−84 kg:
1. Branko Zgaljardic (Yugo)
2. Flavio Galessi (Italy)
3. Hovelsrud (Norway)

−79 kg:
1. Branko Cikatic (Yugo)
2. Jean-Marc Tonus (Switzerland)
3. Roufs (Netherlands)

−74 kg:
1. Peter Harbrecht (FRG)
2. Erling (Norway)
3. A. Tommei (Switzerland)

−69 kg:
1. Ferdinand Mack (FRG)
2. Kemal Zeriat (FRG)
3. Colapietro (Belgium)

−63 kg:
1. Klaus Friedhaber (FRG)
2. Jimmie Barletta (Belgium)
3. Jorg Leuk-Emden (FRG)

−57 kg:
1. Jerome Canabate (Italy)
2. Boffa (Switzerland)
3. Jonny Canabate (Italy)

Overall Medal Standing (Semi-Contact)
1. Germany (FRG)
2. Great Britain
3. Austria
4. Netherlands
5. Italy
6. Belgium
   Yugoslavia
7. Switzerland

Men

84+ kg:
1. McKenzie (GRB)
2. Srienz (Austria)
3. Ulrich Falck (Switzerland)

−84 kg:
1. Harald Edel (FRG)
2. Facchinetti (Italy)
3. Walter Meneghini (Italy)

−79 kg:
1. H. Hirschganger (FRG)
2. Ivan Wray (GRB)
3. Norbert Schochl (Austria)

−74 kg:
1. Jurgen Gorak (FRG)
2. Slobodon Sokota (Yugo)
3. Wilson (GRB)

−69 kg:
1. Jochen Klapproth (FRG)
2. Andreas Brannasch (FRG)
3. Ronchiato (Italy)

−63 kg:
1. Dennis Wooter (Netherlands)
2. Goyvaerts (Belgium)
3. Antonio Loser (Austria)

−57 kg:
1. Sarhan Salman (FRG)
2. Christian Wulf (FRG)
3. Manfred Frohwein (Austria)

2ND WAKO EUROPEAN CHAMPIONSHIPS

Date: 1978.
Site: Wolfsburg, Germany.

Note: Semi-contact competition was introduced at this event.

Overall Medal Standing (Kickboxing)
1. West Germany (FRG)
2. Netherlands
3. Yugoslavia
4. Norway
5. Italy
6. Austria
   Switzerland

Fighting

Men's Kickboxing

87+ kg:
1. Tom Rissmann (FRG)
2. Milan Rokvic (Yugo)
3. Manfred Vogt (FRG)

−87 kg:
1. Maurice Moore (FRG)
2. Flavio Galessi (Italy)
3. Gianni Rugliancich (Italy)

−79 kg:
1. Daryl Tyler (FRG)
2. Dieter Herdel (FRG)
3. Bernd Eggert (FRG)

−74 kg:
1. Peter Harbrecht (FRG)
2. Klaus Lutze (FRG)
3. Slobodon Sokota (Yugo)

−69 kg:
1. Omar Salhi (Norway)
2. Javier Muniz (Netherlands)
3. Tone Spiljak (Yugo)

−63 kg:
1. Ivan Menes (Netherlands)
2. Rafik Jamali (FRG)
3. Gunter Dienstl (Austria)

−57 kg:
1. Ali Pehlivan (FRG)
2. Constantinos Goris (FRG)
3. Jonny Canabate (Switzerland)

Overall Medal Standing (Semi-Contact)
1. Germany (FRG)
2. Netherlands
3. Italy
4. Austria
5. Switzerland
6. Sweden

Men

84+ kg:
1. Anne Delis (Netherlands)
2. Federico Milani (Italy)
3. Howard Collins (Sweden)
   Ernest Lee Patton (FRG)

−84 kg:
1. Harald Edel (FRG)
2. Aldo Capra (Italy)
3. Albert Purschl (Austria)

−79 kg:
1. Alton Davis (Netherlands)
2. Herbert Schochl (Austria)
3. Walter Asche (FRG)

−74 kg:
1. Jurgen Gorak (FRG)
2. H. Hirschganger (FRG)
3. Luigi Franchi (Italy)

−69 kg:
1. Jochen Klapproth (FRG)
2. Andreas Brannasch (FRG)
3. Carlo Broccolli (Italy)

−63 kg:
1. J. Rothenbucher (FRG)
2. Dennis Wooter (Netherlands)
3. Johnny Mirer (Switzerland)

−57 kg:
1. Christian Wulf (FRG)
2. Sarhan Salman (FRG)
3. Dominique Rahm (Switzerland)

1ST WAKO EUROPEAN CHAMPIONSHIPS

Date: 1977.
Site: Wien, Germany.
Producer: Georg Bruckner.

Overall Medal Standing
1. Netherlands
2. West Germany (FRG)
3. Norway
4. Italy
5. Switzerland

Fighting

Men's Kickboxing

84+ kg:
1. Jan de Graf (Netherlands)
2. Kunibert Back (FRG)
3. Gianni Rugliancic (Italy)

−84 kg:
1. Gerad Bakker (Netherlands)
2. Maurice Moore (FRG)
3. Vittorio Caselli (Italy)

−79 kg:
1. H. Rompa (Netherlands)
2. Bert de Frel (Netherlands)
3. J. Schepers (Netherlands)

−74 kg:
1. Peter Harbrecht (FRG)
2. Serge Metz (Netherlands)
3. Aalstede (Netherlands)

−69 kg:
1. Ron Kuyt (Netherlands)
2. Kemal Zeriat (FRG)
3. Jorg Schmidt (FRG)

−63 kg:
1. Hansi Jaensch (FRG)
2. Martin Giesselmann (FRG)
3. Ivan Menes (Netherlands)

−57 kg:
1. Max Mankowitz (Norway)
2. Ali Pehlivan (FRG)
3. Jerome Canabate (Switzerland)

WAKO U. S. CHAMPIONSHIPS (1991 & 1993)

2ND WAKO UNITED STATES CHAMPIONSHIPS

Date: January 27–28, 1993.
Site: Green Convention Center, Evansville, Indiana.
Promoter: Jim Lantrip.
Sanctioned by: WAKO-USA.
Participants: 157 black belts from 39 states.

Note: Only first-place winners were available. Kickboxing competition was not conducted at this event.

Fighting

Men's Continuous Contact

89+ kg:
1. William Eaves (Alabama)

−89 kg:
1. Mark Graden

−84 kg:
1. Ric Pascetta (New Jersey)

−79 kg:
1. Tony Montanez (New Jersey)

−74 kg:
1. Chris McBride (Ohio)

−69 kg:
1. David Wilson (Illinois)

−63 kg:
1. Charles Barron (Illinois)

−57 kg:
1. Tuan Nguyen (New York)

Women's Continuous Contact

65+ kg:
1. Lisa Crosby (Connecticut)

−65 kg:
1. Justina Hall (Massachusetts)

−60 kg:
1. Linda Dice (Tennessee)

−55 kg:
1. Krishea Strayn (Kentucky)

−50 kg:
1. Lori Lantrip-Stanley (Indiana)

Men's Semi-Contact

91+ kg:
1. Richard Plowden (Michigan)

−91 kg:
1. Steve Babcock (Rhode Island)

−84 kg:
1. Jerry Fontanez (New York)

−79 kg:
1. E.J. Greer (Tennessee)

−74 kg:
1. Chris Rappold (Massachusetts)

−69 kg:
1. Pedro Xavier (Connecticut)

−63 kg:
1. Tony Young (Georgia)

−57 kg:
1. Jerry Maloney (California)

Women's Semi-Contact

65+ kg:
1. Sue Brazelton (North Carolina)

−65 kg:
1. Michelle Arango (New York)

−60 kg:
1. Kierston Sims (Massachusetts)

−55 kg:
1. Christine Bannon-Rodrigues (Rhode Island)

−50 kg:
1. Lori Lantrip-Stanley (Indiana)

Forms

Men

Hard Style:
1. Gabe Reynaga (California)

Soft Style:
1. Richard Brandon (Massachusetts)

Women

Hard Style:
1. Stacy Knight (Louisiana)

Soft Style:
1. Christine Bannon-Rodrigues (Rhode Island)

Weapons

Hard Style:
1. Tony Orr (Florida)

Soft Style:
1. Richard Brandon (Massachusetts)

Women:
1. Christine Bannon-Rodrigues (Rhode Island)

1ST WAKO UNITED STATES CHAMPIONSHIPS

Date: July 20–21, 1991.
Site: Green Convention Center, Evansville, Indiana.
Promoter: Jim Lantrip.
Sanctioned by: WAKO-USA.
Participants: 77 black belts from 19 states.

Note: Only first-place winners were available. Kickboxing competition was not conducted at this event.

Fighting

Men's Continuous Contact

84+ kg:
1. Jeff Roufus (Wisconsin)

−84 kg:
1. Jerry Fontanez (New York)

−79 kg:
1. Derrick Freijomil (New Jersey)

−74 kg:
1. Alberto Montrond (Rhode Island)

−69 kg:
1. David Wilson (Illinois)

−63 kg:
1. Charles Barron (Illinois)

−57 kg:
1. Shawn Wheat (Indiana)

Women's Continuous Contact

60+ kg:
1. Lisa Crosby (Massachusetts)

−60 kg:
1. Kellie Hausner (Missouri)

−55 kg:
1. Kathi Carchia (Massachusetts)

−50 kg:
1. Amy Corbin (Missouri)

Men's Semi-Contact

84+ kg:
1. Steve Babcock (Rhode Island)

−84 kg:
1. John Payton (Massachusetts)

−79 kg:
1. Richard Barefield (California)

−74 kg:
1. Chris Rappold (Massachusetts)

−69 kg:
1. Pedro Xavier (Massachusetts)

−63 kg:
1. Tony Young (Georgia)

−57 kg:
1. Jerry Maloney (California)

Women's Semi-Contact

60+ kg:
1. Kierston Sims (Massachusetts)

−60 kg:
1. Justina Hall (Massachusetts)

−55 kg:
1. Christine Bannon-Rodrigues (Rhode Island)

−50 kg:
1. Ann Gregory (Kentucky)

Forms

Men

Hard Style:
1. David Collins (Massachusetts)

Soft Style:
1. Richard Brandon (Massachusetts)

Women

Hard Style:
1. Ann Gregory (Kentucky)

Soft Style:
1. Christine Bannon-Rodrigues (Rhode Island)

Weapons

Hard Style:
1. Tony Orr (Florida)

Soft Style:
1. Richard Brandon (Massachusetts)

Women:
1. Christine Bannon-Rodrigues (Rhode Island)

BLACK BELT
COMPETITION RESULTS
(1957–92)

The following are the most comprehensive black belt winners' lists ever compiled for martial sports worldwide. Essentially, this section documents the entire history of martial sports around the world, excluding judo, beginning in Japan with the very first karate tournament held in 1957.

Black belt judo results are not included here because they are all listed in the excellent recently published book *Great Judo Championships of the World* by Oon Oon Yeoh. Publishing them here would just be robbing the foundation—and duplicating the painstaking research—of Mr. Yeoh's important work.

All winners' lists and results appear here as they originally appeared in martial arts magazines and other public and private sources. Many of them were submitted for publication by the promoter(s) or sanctioning bodies in the same fashion in which they appear here, other than necessary editorial changes.

Therefore, I cannot be responsible for misspellings or incomplete names. In numerous cases, the given and family names of Asian and European winners were transposed and I took the liberty of correcting them only when I was sure of the order. However, I was unsure of numerous foreign names, such as those from the Middle East who appear on various European winners' lists.

All of the tae kwon do results are compliments of the World Taekwon-do Federation in Seoul. All WUKO results are courtesy of the World Union of Karate-do Organizations and/or George Anderson, president of its official U.S. affiliate, the USA Karate Federation.

The World Association of Kickboxing Organizations (WAKO) also holds world championships in forms, semi-contact and continuous contact competition. All WAKO world and European event results, however, appear in the chapter on kickboxing since that sport is the organization's primary focus.

From these worldwide sanctioning bodies, I chose three areas of competitions to include in this book: world championships, European championships and U.S. championships. In each case the title of the event appears first, followed—ideally—by the date, site, promoter, and number of participants and spectators. The complete information was not always available. This is followed by a complete male and female winners' list in both forms and fighting, where applicable. Women's divisions and form competition are a relatively recent addition to several martial sports. In the case of Overall Medal Standings in international competitions, I have limited the listing to the top ten teams.

CHAPTER 9

JUJUTSU CHAMPIONSHIP RESULTS

Jujutsu (a.k.a. jujitsu) fighting competition is a relatively new activity. It is conducted much like karate's semi-contact point fighting. Although this chapter is noticeably incomplete, due to inadequate previously published results, I hope to correct this void in future editions of this book.

4TH WORLD JUJITSU CHAMPIONSHIPS

Date: September 1, 1990.
Site: Lawrence Joel Veteran's Memorial Coliseum, Winston-Salem, North Carolina.
Producer: Tony Maynard.
Sanctioned by: World Council of Jiu-Jitsu Organizations.

Overall Medal Standing
1. United States
2. Canada
3. Wales

Fighting
Teams:
1. Wales
2. United States
3. Canada

Men
Heavy:
1. Sean Stewart (Canada)
2. Terry Yanke (Canada)
3. Carl Spencer (Wales)

Light Heavy:
1. Chris Easley (Wales)
2. Paul Grant (England)
3. Scott Shamblin (USA)

Middle:
1. Ernie Boggs (USA)
2. Craig Oxley (USA)
3. John May (Australia)

Light:
1. Lew Walker (New Zealand)
2. Daniel Gimenez (Argentina)
3. David Eickenloff (Australia)

Seniors:
1. Gerry Knowles (Canada)
2. Bob Krantz (Canada)
3. Bob Long (USA)

Women
1. Elizabeth Hodgson (Wales)
2. Ruth Ann Shamblin (USA)
3. Katheryn Roe-Geurin (Canada)

Demonstrations
1. United States
2. Australia
3. England

3RD WORLD JUJITSU CHAMPIONSHIPS

Date: November 12, 1988.
Site: Sleeman Sports Complex, Brisbane, Australia.
Producer: Peter McAnalen.
Sanctioned by: World Council of Jiu-Jitsu Organizations.

2ND WORLD JUJITSU CHAMPIONSHIPS

Date: 1986.
Sanctioned by: World Council of Jiu-Jitsu Organizations.

1ST WORLD JUJITSU CHAMPIONSHIPS

Date: 1984.
Site: Canada.
Sanctioned by: World Council of Jiu-Jitsu Organizations.
Producer: Canadian Jiu Jitsu Association.

Fighting

Teams:
1. ?
2. ?
3. ?
4. Europe

Men

Heavy:
1. Martin Clarke (England)
2. ?
3. Ken Wright (Scotland)

Light:
1. ?
2. ?
3. ?

CHAPTER 10

KARATE-DO CHAMPIONSHIP RESULTS (1957–93)

Karate competition officially started with the All-Japan Karate Championships, founded and sanctioned by the Japan Karate Association in 1957 in Tokyo, Japan. This was the world's first organized karate tournament. Not only was this tournament the most prestigious in Japan but it was the basis for spreading sport karate throughout the world.

Like the early tournaments in the United States, these were rugged, sometimes "blood-'n'-guts" affairs where only the most intrepid warriors emerged in the winner's circle. That many of the same names appear frequently in the following results attests to their skill, for this event was loaded with competitive talent. Many of these All-Japan Champions went on to become renowned karate-do instructors and pioneers in countries across the world.

The following list begins in the year of the tournament's founding, 1957, and continues only until 1970, when the World Union of Karate-do Organizations (WUKO) conducted its first world championships in Tokyo, Japan. The WUKO is the world's foremost sanctioning body for traditional karate competitions and is working toward Olympic acceptance for its sport. *In the case of a tie, no number will precede the second competitor or country listing. For example, the winners' lists typically feature three places with two competitors sharing the third position.*

I would like to thank Randall G. Hassell, the world's leading karate-do writer, for permission to excerpt the following results from his excellent book, *Shotokan Karate: Its History and Evolution.*

Tokey Hill (center platform), the only American ever to win a gold medal in WUKO competition, in 1980. Courtesy of Tokey Hill

WEIGHT DIVISION CONVERSION CHART

The following chart will help readers interested in weight divisions quickly determine exact kilos to pounds and vice versa.

Kilos	Pounds	Pounds	Kilos
48	105.82	112	50.80
50	110.23	113	51.25
51	112.44	115	52.16
54	119.05	118	53.53
55	121.25	119	53.98
57	125.66	122	55.34
58	127.87	126	57.15
60	132.28	130	58.97
62	136.69	133	60.33
63	138.89	135	61.24
66	145.51	140	63.50
67	147.71	147	66.68
70	154.32	148	67.13
71	156.53	154	69.85
72	158.73	156	70.76
74	163.14	160	72.58
75	165.35	164	73.94
76	167.55	167	75.75
79	174.17	172	78.47
80	176.37	175	79.38
81	178.57	180	79.38
82	180.78	182	82.56
85	187.39	190	86.18
86	189.60	195	86.18
91	200.62	200	90.72

ALL-JAPAN KARATE CHAMPIONSHIPS (1957–70)

1957

Kumite/Fighting:

1. Hirokazu Kanazawa
2. Katsunori Tsuyama
3. Masahide Nakamura

Kata/Forms:

1. Hiroshi Shoji
2. Masaru Sakamoto
3. Shojiro Koyama

1958

Kumite/Fighting:

1. Hirokazu Kanazawa
   Takayuki Mikami
2. Masahiro Sato

Kata/Forms:

1. Hirokazu Kanazawa
2. Takayuki Mikami
3. Shigeru Saito

1959

Kumite/Fighting:

1. Takayuki Mikami
2. Hirokazu Kanazawa
3. Masahiro Sato

Kata/Forms:

1. Takayuki Mikami
2. Hirokazu Kanazawa
3. Shigeru Saito

1960

Kumite/Fighting:

1. Masahiro Sato
2. Takayuki Mikami
3. Tetsuhiko Asai
   Toru Iwaizumi

Kata/Forms:

1. Hiroshi Shoji
2. Takayuki Mikami
3. Hirokazu Kanazawa

1961

Kumite/Fighting:

1. Tetsuhiko Asai
2. Hiroshi Shirai
3. Takayuki Mikami
   Keinosuke Enoeda

Kata/Forms:

1. Takayuki Mikami
2. Tetsuhiko Asai
3. Hiroshi Shirai

1962

Kumite/Fighting:

1. Hiroshi Shirai
2. Keinosuke Enoeda
3. Takayuki Mikami
   Yutaka Yaguchi

Kata/Forms:

1. Hiroshi Shirai
2. Takayuki Mikami
3. Toru Iwaizumi

1963

Kumite/Fighting:

1. Keinosuke Enoeda
2. Hiroshi Shirai
3. Hirokazu Kanazawa
   Yutaka Yaguchi

Kata/Forms:

1. Tetsuhiko Asai
2. Toru Iwaizumi
3. Ken Nakaya

1964

Kumite/Fighting:

1. Katsuya Kisaka
2. Masaaki Ueki
3. Tetsu Miyagi
   Toru Miyazaki

Kata/Forms:

1. Masaaki Ueki
2. Hideo Ochi
3. Noriaki Sasakuma

1965

Kumite/Fighting:

1. Hideo Ochi
2. Masaaki Ueki
3. Yoshimasa Takahashi

Kata/Forms:

1. Hideo Ochi
2. Masaaki Ueki
3. Yoshimasa Takahashi

1966

Kumite/Fighting:

1. Hideo Ochi
2. Takeshi Oishi
3. Yukichi Tabata
   Keigo Abe

Kata/Forms:

1. Masaaki Ueki
2. Hideo Ochi
3. Yoshimasa Takahashi

1967

Kumite/Fighting:
1. Masaaki Ueki
2. Hideo Ochi
3. Yukichi Tabata
   Keigo Abe

Kata/Forms:
1. Masaaki Ueki
2. Yoshimasa Takahashi
3. Hideo Ochi

1968

Kumite/Fighting:
1. Takeshi Oishi
2. Norihiko Iida
3. Hideo Ochi
   Akihito Isaka

Kata/Forms:
1. Hideo Ochi
2. Yoshimasa Takahashi
3. Akihito Isaka

1969

Kumite/Fighting:
1. Takeshi Oishi
2. Yoshimasa Takahashi
3. Toru Yamaguchi
   Yukichi Tabata

Kata/Forms:
1. Yoshimasa Takahashi
2. Toru Yamaguchi
3. Shigeru Takashina

1970

Kumite/Fighting:
1. Takeshi Oishi
2. Masaaki Ueki
3. Norihiko Iida
   Yukichi Tabata

Kata/Forms:
1. Masaaki Ueki
2. Yoshimasa Takahashi
3. Toru Yamaguchi

WORLD UNION OF KARATE-DO ORGANIZATIONS (WUKO) WORLD CHAMPIONSHIP RESULTS (1970–92)

11TH WUKO WORLD KARATE CHAMPIONSHIPS

Date: November 19–22, 1992.
Site: Granada, Spain.
Sanction: World Union of Karate-
   do Organizations.

Kumite/Fighting

Men

Team:
1. Spain
2. Sweden
3. Japan
   France

+80 kg:
1. B. Peakall (Australia)
2. S. Tomao (France)
3. J. Hernandez (Spain)
   H. Roovers (Neth)

−80 kg:
1. J. Egea (Spain)
2. M. Gachulinec (Czech)
3. D. Josepa (Curacao)
   Christophe Pinna (France)

−75 kg:
1. W. Otto (GRB)
2. J. Hansen (Norway)
3. T. Herrero (Spain)
   B. Burkel (Germany)

−70 kg:
1. W. Thomas (GRB)
2. J. Watenabe (Japan)
3. R. Rivano (Neth)
   M. Oggianu (Italy)

−65 kg:
1. Juan Rubio (Spain)
2. B. Kandaz (Turkey)
3. J. Timonen (Finland)
   M. Uysal (Germany)

−60 kg:
1. V. Bugur (Turkey)
2. D. Luque (Spain)
3. N. Fujita (Japan)
   Damien Dovy (France)

Women

Team:
1. Great Britain
2. Netherlands
3. France
   Italy

+60 kg:
1. Catherine Belhriti (France)
2. M. Firat (Turkey)
3. Y. Yoneda (Japan)
   S. Wiegartners (Germany)

−60 kg:
1. M. Samuel (GRB)
2. C. Bux (Italy)
3. T. Petrovic (?)
   C. Garcia (Spain)

−53 kg:
1. C. Machin (Australia)
2. J. Toney (GRB)
3. D. Yaman (Turkey)
   M. Mazurier (France)

Kata/Forms

Men

Team:
1. Japan
2. Spain
3. France

Individual:
1. L. Sanz (Spain)
2. R. Abe (Japan)
3. L. Riccio (France)

Women

Team:
1. Japan
2. United States
3. Spain

Individual:
1. Y. Mimura (Japan)
2. M. Genung (USA)
3. San Narciso (Spain)

One Point

Men's Ippon Shobu
1. A. Hayashi (Japan)
2. ?
3. J. Dietl (Germany)
   ?

10TH WUKO WORLD KARATE CHAMPIONSHIPS

Date: 1990.
Site: Mexico City, Mexico.
Sanction: World Union of Karate-do Organizations.
Participants: 792.

Kumite/Fighting

Men

Team:
1. Great Britain
2. France
3. Spain
   Netherlands

+80 kg:
1. Marc Pyree (France)
2. I. Cole (GRB)
3. R. Brachmann (Germany)
   I. Ercin (Turkey)

−80 kg:
1. J. Egea (Spain)
2. M. Alstadsaether (Norway)
3. O. Pokoeni (Sweden)
   R. Hernandez (Mexico)

−75 kg:
1. H. Tamaru (Japan)
2. G. Francis (GRB)
3. P. Alderson (GRB)
   G. Talarico (Italy)

−70 kg:
1. H. Alagas (Turkey)
2. V. Aminconi (Italy)
3. Y. Anzai (Japan)
   W. Thomas (GRB)

−65 kg:
1. T. Azumi (Japan)
2. G. Romic (Yugo)
3. B. Kandaz (Turkey)
   J. Puertas (Spain)

−60 kg:
1. S. Ronning (Norway)
2. H. Nakano (Japan)
3. H. Yagli (Turkey)
   V. Bugur (Turkey)

Women

+60 kg:
1. Catherine Belhriti (France)
2. M. Sartirani (Italy)
3. B. Brogan (Australia)
   K. Kawano (Japan)

−60 kg:
1. M. Amghar (France)
2. C. Bux (Italy)
3. C. Dorrie (Germany)
   M. Samuel (GRB)

−53 kg:
1. Y. Hasama (Japan)
2. A. Flores (Mexico)
3. Y. Senff (Neth)
   E. Chamarro (Spain)

Kata/Forms

Men's Team
1. Italy
2. Japan
3. France

Women's Team
1. Japan
2. USA
3. France

Men
1. T. Aihara (Japan)
2. D. Marchini (Italy)
3. L. Sanz (Spain)

Women
1. Y. Mimura (Japan)
2. H. Yokoyama (Japan)
3. D. Tang (USA)

One Point

Ippon
1. G. Tramontini (France)
2. V. Micovic (Yugo)
3. Y. Uchida (Japan)
   M. Hamon (Canada)

Sanbon
1. W. Otto (GRB)
2. S. Jez (Australia)
3. A. Leitto (Neth)
   M. Alvarado (Spain)

9TH WUKO WORLD KARATE CHAMPIONSHIPS

Date: October 13–16, 1988.
Site: Egyptian National Police Academy, Cairo, Egypt.
Sanction: World Union of Karate-do Organizations.

Participants: 1,157 competitors from 54 countries.

Kumite/Fighting

Team
1. Great Britain
2. Netherlands
3. Spain
   Italy

Men

+80 kg:
1. Emmanuel Pinda (France)
2. V. Charles (GRB)
3. J. Tell (Sweden)
   C. Guazzaroni (Italy)

−80 kg:
1. Josepa (Neth)
2. M. Etiene (GRB)
3. W. Rauch (FRG)
   J. Egea (Spain)

−75 kg:
1. K. Hayashi (Japan)
2. T. Hallman (Sweden)
3. T. Dietl (FRG)
   J. Galan (Spain)

−70 kg:
1. T. Masci (France)
2. F. Egea (Spain)
3. Y. Anzai (Japan)
   B. Pellicer (France)

−65 kg:
1. T. Stephens (GRB)
2. R. Doran (Neth)
3. Juan Rubio (Spain)
   F. Muffato (Italy)

−60 kg:
1. A. Shaher (GRB)
2. N. Simmi (Italy)
3. S. Reonning (Norway)
   H. Nozaki (Japan)

Women

+60 kg:
1. Guus Van Mourik (Neth)
2. Y. Wickberg (Sweden)
3. M. Legros (France)
   M. Sartirani (Italy)

−60 kg:
1. A. Kimura (Japan)
2. J. Kurata (Japan)

3. Regina Halterman (USA)
   R. Hahn (FRG)

−53 kg:
1. Y. Hasama (Japan)
2. C. Girardet (France)
3. M. Capechi (Venezuela)
   S. Graham (GRB)

Kata/Forms
Men's Team
1. Japan
2. Italy
3. France
4. Spain

Women's Team
1. Japan
2. USA
3. Italy
4. Chinese Taipei

Men
1. Tsuguo Sakumoto (Japan)
2. T. Aihara (Japan)
3. D. Marchini (Italy)
   P. Acri (Italy)

Women
1. Y. Mimura (Japan)
2. H. Yokoyama (Japan)
3. Kathy Jones (USA)
   C. Restelli (Italy)

One Point
Open Ippon
1. G. Guazzaroni (Italy)
2. V. Charles (GRB)
3. Y. Hyashi (Japan)
   K. Aktepe (Neth)

Open Sanbon
1. J. Egea (Spain)
2. M. Sailsman (GRB)
3. Y. Shimitzu (Japan)
   Emmanuel Pinda (France)

8TH WUKO WORLD KARATE CHAMPIONSHIPS

Date: October 3–6, 1986.
Site: Sydney, Australia.
Sanction: World Union of Karate-do Organizations.

Participants: 890 competitors from 48 countries.
Spectators: 8,000.

Kumite/Fighting
Team
1. Great Britain
2. France
3. Italy

Men
Open:
1. Daggfelt (Sweden)
2. C. Guazzaroni (Italy)
3. Josepa (Neth)
   J. Egea (Spain)

+80 kg:
1. Charles (GRB)
2. Thompson (GRB)
3. Bura (Denmark)
   Rauchi (Germany)

−80 kg:
1. Tapol (France)
2. McKay (GRB)
3. C. Guazzaroni (Italy)
   J. Egea (Spain)

−75 kg:
1. Leeuwin (Neth)
2. De Oliviera (Brazil)
3. Napier (Australia)
   Lilovac (Australia)

−70 kg:
1. Masci (France)
2. Hayashi (Japan)
3. Monzon (Canada)
   Megro (Switzerland)

−65 kg:
1. Kondo (Japan)
2. Suzuki (Japan)
3. Piispa (Finland)
   Reybroek (Belgium)

−60 kg:
1. Nakano (Japan)
2. Uchi (Japan)
3. McKinnon (GRB)
   Valle (France)

Women
+60 kg:
1. Guus Van Mourik (Neth)
2. Lunde (Norway)
3. Kawano (Japan)
   Bryan (GRB)

−60 kg:
1. Varelius (Finland)
2. Samuel (GRB)
3. Hansen (Norway)
   Furguson (Australia)

−50 kg:
1. Kauria (Finland)
2. Yanagisawa (Japan)
3. Hazama (Japan)
   Lane (Finland)

Kata/Forms
Men
Team:
1. Great Britain
2. France
3. Italy
   Sweden

Individual:
1. Tsuguo Sakumoto (Japan)
2. Alhara (Japan)
3. D. Marchini (Italy)

Synchronized:
1. Japan
2. France
3. Yugoslavia

Women
Individual:
1. Mie Nakayama (Japan)
2. Hashimoto (Japan)
3. Seymour (Australia)

Synchronized:
1. Chinese Taipei
2. Japan
3. USA

7TH WUKO WORLD KARATE CHAMPIONSHIPS

Date: October 18–21, 1984.
Site: The Eurohall, Maastricht, Netherlands.
Sanction: World Union of Karate-do Organizations.
Participants: 930 competitors from 49 countries.

Kumite/Fighting
Men
Team:
1. Great Britain
2. Sweden

3. France
Spain

Open:
1. Emmanuel Pinda (France)
2. Patrice Ruggiero (France)
3. Victor Charles (GBR)
V. Charles (GRB)

+80 kg:
1. Jerome Atkinson (GBR)
2. C. Guazzaroni (Italy)
3. M. Pyree (France)
M. Diluigi (Italy)

−80 kg:
1. Pat McKay (GBR)
2. Otti Roethoff (Neth)
3. G. Sacchi (Italy)
D. Josepa (Neth)

−75 kg:
1. T. Stelling (Neth)
2. J. Gomez (Switzerland)
3. S. Sarfati (France)
Y. Uchida (Japan)

−70 kg:
1. Jimmy Collins (GRB)
2. G. Rodriquez (Spain)
3. F. Hita (Spain)
C. Hackett (GRB)

−65 kg:
1. Ramon Malave (Sweden)
2. Ignacio Lugo (Mexico)
3. Mark Van Reybroeck (Belgium)
R. Van Loon (Neth)

−60 kg:
1. D. Betzien (Germany)
2. Nicola Simmi (Italy)
3. Shinichi Hasegawa (Japan)
I. Alberto (Neth)

Women
+60 kg:
1. Guus Van Mourik (Neth)
2. Yvette Bryan (GRB)
3. Stine Nygard (Norway)
K. Lunde (Norway)

−60 kg:
1. Tomoko Konishi (Japan)
2. Kuei-Yuan Wang (China)
3. S. Nyback (Finland)
B. Morris (GRB)

−53 kg:
1. Sophie Berger (France)

2. Anita Myhren (Norway)
3. Geradet (France)
K. Friedr (USA)

Kata/Forms
Men
1. Tsuguo Sakumoto (Japan)
2. M. Koyama (Japan)
3. E. Karamitsos (Germany)

Women
1. Mie Nakayama (Japan)
2. Setsuko Takagi (Japan)
3. Mei-Yeh Chu (China)

6TH WUKO WORLD KARATE CHAMPIONSHIPS

Date: November 26–28, 1982.
Site: Taipei, Taiwan.
Sanction: World Union of Karate-do Organizations.
Participants: 850 competitors from 46 countries.

Kumite/Fighting
Men
Team:
1. Great Britain
2. Italy
3. Japan
4. Spain

Open:
1. H. Murase (Japan)
2. Amillo (Spain)
3. J. Atkinson (GBR)
P. Pinard (France)

+80 kg:
1. J. Thompson (GBR)
2. P. Rugiero (France)
3. M. Garofoli (Luxembourg)
J. R. Reeberg (Neth)

−80 kg:
1. Pat McKay (GBR)
2. J. Pirtosa (Finland)
3. J. Tapol (France)
J. Holm (Den)

−75 kg:
1. J. Gomei (Surinam)
2. A. Borg (GBR)

3. C. M. Lin (Taipei)
Fred Royers (Neth)

−70 kg:
1. S. Nishimura (Japan)
2. M. Mika (Finland)
3. T. Masci (France)
B. Raffaele (Italy)

−65 kg:
1. Y. Suzuki (Japan)
2. G. Carcangiu (Italy)
3. T. Maeda (Japan)
R. Sanz (Spain)

−60 kg:
1. J. Vayrinen (Finland)
2. R. Vallee (France)
3. R. Castillo (Venezuela)
S. McKinnon (GBR)

Women
+60 kg:
1. Guus Van Mourik (Neth)
2. T. Yamafuku (Japan)
3. N. Ferluga (Italy)
J. Argyle (GBR)

−60 kg:
1. Y. Yamakawa (Japan)
2. Tomoko Konishi (Japan)
3. W. T. Chang (Taipei)
B. Morris (GBR)

−53 kg:
1. Sophie Berger (France)
2. Y. Li (Taipei)
3. F. Fillios (France)
S. T. Chiang (Taipei)

Kata/Forms
Men
1. M. Koyama (Japan)
2. Domingo Llanos (USA)
3. M. Marangoni (Italy)
T. Tabata (Japan)

Women
1. Mie Nakayama (Japan)
2. Mei-Yeh Chu (Taipei)
3. M. Tabata (Japan)
A. Starling (Australia)

5TH WUKO WORLD KARATE CHAMPIONSHIPS

Date: November 27–30, 1980.
Site: Palacio dello Sport, Madrid, Spain.
Sanction: World Union of Karate-do Organizations.
Participants: 800 competitors from 48 countries.

Kumite/Fighting

Men

Team:
1. Spain
2. Netherlands
3. Great Britain
4. France

Open:
1. Ricciardi (Italy)
2. Billy Blanks (USA)
3. H. Murase (Japan)
   J. Pedro Carvila (Spain)

+80 kg:
1. Montama (France)
2. Whyte (USA)
3. Billy Blanks (USA)
   Sias (Mexico)

−80 kg:
1. Tokey Hill (USA)
2. Amarilla (Paraguay)
3. Otti Roethoff (Neth)

−75 kg:
1. Tajima (Japan)
2. Imamatsu (Japan)
3. Aguilar (Mexico)
   Fred Royers (Neth)

−70 kg:
1. Gonzales (Spain)
2. T. Masci (France)
3. Schenker (Neth)

−65 kg:
1. Maeda (Japan)
2. Ono (Japan)
3. Arsenal (Spain)
   Hita (Spain)

−60 kg:
1. Abad (Spain)
2. Granet (France)
3. Sugiyama (Japan)
   Rosuero (Spain)

Kata/Forms

Men
1. K. Okada (Japan)
2. M. Koyama (Japan)
3. Romero (Spain)

Women
1. S. Okamura (Japan)
2. Mie Nakayama (Japan)
3. Moreno (Spain)

4TH WUKO WORLD KARATE CHAMPIONSHIPS

Date: December 3–4, 1977.
Site: Budokan Hall, Tokyo, Japan.
Sanction: World Union of Karate-do Organizations.
Participants: 316 competitors from 47 countries.
Spectators: 10,000.

Team
1. Netherlands
2. West Germany
3. France
   Iran

Men's Kumite
1. Otti Roethoff (Neth)
2. Eugene Codrington (GBR)
3. J. Pedro Carvila (Spain)
   C. Chien (Taipei)

Men's Kata
1. K. Okada (Japan)
2. H. Miyano (Japan)
3. G. Tsutsui (USA)

3RD WUKO WORLD KARATE CHAMPIONSHIPS

Date: October 4–5, 1975.
Site: Long Beach, California.
Sanction: World Union of Karate-do Organizations.
Participants: 300 competitors from 30 countries.

Team
1. Great Britain
2. Japan

3. Netherlands
4. Philippines

Men's Kumite
1. Kunio Murakami (Japan)
2. Junichiro Hamaguchi (Japan)
3. Pedro Rivera (Dominica)

2ND WUKO WORLD KARATE CHAMPIONSHIPS

Date: April 21–22, 1972.
Site: Coubertine Hall, Paris, France.
Sanction: World Union of Karate-do Organizations.
Participants: 220 competitors from 22 countries.

Team
1. France
2. Italy
3. Great Britain
   Singapore

Men's Kumite
1. L. Watanabe-Taske (Brazil)
2. W. Higgins (GBR)
3. Schupter (Yugo)
   Guy Sauvin (France)

1ST WUKO WORLD KARATE CHAMPIONSHIPS

Date: October 10–13, 1970.
Site: Tokyo, Japan.
Sanction: World Union of Karate-do Organizations.
Participants: 178 competitors from 33 countries.

Team
1. Japan E Team
2. Japan C Team
3. Japan B Team

Men's Kumite
1. K. Wada (Japan)
2. J. Carnio (Canada)
3. Tonny Tulleners (USA)
   Dominique Valera (France)

EUROPEAN KARATE-DO UNION (EKU) EUROPEAN CHAMPIONSHIPS (1966–93)

27TH EUROPEAN KARATE CHAMPIONSHIPS

Date: May 7, 1993.
Site: Prague, Czechoslovakia.
Sanctioned by: European Karate Union.
Medal standing unavailable.

Kumite/Fighting

Men

Team:
1. France
2. Finland
3. Great Britain
   Germany

Individuals:

+80 kg:
1. Idrizi (Croatia)
2. Cole (GRB)
3. Benetello (Italy)
   Kleinekathofer (Austria)

−80 kg:
1. Alstadsaether (Norway)
2. Gillan (Scotland)
3. Nitschmann (Germany)
   Talarico (Italy)

−75 kg:
1. Sariyannis (Germany)
2. Amicone (Italy)
3. Meana (Spain)
   W. Otto (GRB)

−70 kg:
1. Oggianu (Italy)
2. W. Thomas (GRB)
3. Anselmo (France)
   Azadi (Germany)

−65 kg:
1. S. Ronning (Norway)
2. Uysal (Germany)
3. Stephens (GRB)
   Muffato (Italy)

−60 kg:
1. Luke (Spain)
2. Simmi (Italy)
3. Damien Dovy (France)
   McCulloch (Scotland)

Women

Team:
1. Spain
2. Great Britain
3. France
   Austria

Individuals

+60 kg:
1. Olsson (Sweden)
2. Sykorova (Czech)
3. Jean-Pierre (France)
   Dougeni (Greece)

−60 kg:
1. Schafer (Germany)
2. Lyel (Austria)
3. Petrovic (CIS)
   Gedik (Turkey)

−53 kg:
1. Mazurier (France)
2. Laine (Finland)
3. Tuccito (Italy)
   Senff (Neth)

Ippon Shobu

Men:
1. Le Hetet (France)
2. Herrero (Spain)
3. Tiainen (Finland)
   Petrovic (Sweden)

Women:
1. Firat (Turkey)
2. Laine (Finland)
3. Christel (Germany)
   Hotinga (Neth)

Kata/Forms

Men

Team:
1. France
2. Spain
3. Italy

Individual:
1. L. Sanz (Spain)
2. Acri (Italy)
3. Riccio (France)

Women

Team:
1. Spain
2. Italy
3. France

Individual:
1. San Narciso (Spain)
2. Schreiner (Germany)
3. Giacomo (Italy)
   ?

26TH EUROPEAN KARATE CHAMPIONSHIPS

Date: May 3–5, 1991.
Site: Hanover, Germany.
Sanctioned by: European Karate Union.

Overall Medal Standing
1. Spain
2. Great Britain
3. France
4. Turkey

Kumite/Fighting

Men

Team:
1. Spain
2. Great Britain
3. Scotland

Individuals

+80 kg:
1. Roddie (Scotland)
2. Garcia (Spain)
3. Petrovic (Sweden)
   Brachmann (Germany)

−80 kg:
1. Etienne (GRB)
2. Hallman (Sweden)
3. Cherdieu (France)
   Moldner (Germany)

−75 kg:
1. Blanco (Spain)
2. Doula (Switzerland)
3. Dedios (Spain)
   Leito (Neth)

−70 kg:
1. Alagas (Turkey)
2. Martinez (Spain)
3. Rivano (Neth)
   Degli Abbati (Italy)

−65 kg:
1. Stephens (GRB)
2. S. Ronning (Norway)
3. Kandaz (Turkey)
   Cunningham (Scotland)

−60 kg:
1. Gomez (Spain)
2. Sigillo (Switzerland)
3. Luque (Spain)
   Chang (Neth)

One Point

Open Sanbon Shobu:
1. W. Otto (GRB)
2. Cengiz (Turkey)
3. Gomis (France)
   Amiconni (Italy)

Open Ippon Shobu:
1. K. Aktepe (Neth)
2. Tramontini (France)
3. Kleinekathofer (Austria)
   Juan Rubio (Spain)

Kata/Forms

Men
Team:
1. France
2. Spain
3. Germany

Individual:
1. L. Sanz (Spain)
2. Acri (Italy)
3. Morris (Scotland)

Women
Team:
1. Spain
2. France
3. Italy

Individual:
1. Schreiner (Germany)
3. A. San Narciso (Spain)
   M. San Narciso (Spain)

25TH EUROPEAN KARATE CHAMPIONSHIPS

Date: May 1990.
Sanctioned by: European Karate
   Union.

24TH EUROPEAN KARATE CHAMPIONSHIPS

Date: May 1989.
Sanctioned by: European Karate
   Union.

23RD EUROPEAN KARATE CHAMPIONSHIPS

Date: 1988.
Site: Genova, Italy.
Sanctioned by: European Karate
   Union.
Participants: 22 countries; 350
   competitors.

Kumite/Fighting

Men
Team:
1. Norway
2. Italy
3. Great Britain
   Scotland

Individuals
Open:
1. Daggfelt (Sweden)
2. J. Egea (Spain)
3. Sailsman (GRB)
   Cole (GRB)

+80 kg:
1. Marc Pyree (France)
2. Emmanuel Pinda (France)
3. Hjerpaasen (Norway)
   Hernandez (Spain)

−80 kg:
1. J. Egea (Spain)
2. Josepa (Neth)
3. Peinella (France)
   Guazzaroni (Italy)

−75 kg:
1. Gibson (Scotland)
2. Leewin (Neth)
3. Giacenti (France)
   Serfati (France)

−70 kg:
1. W. Otto (GRB)
2. K. Aktepe (Neth)
3. Masci (France)
   Degli Abbati (Italy)

−65 kg:
1. Muffato (Italy)
2. Lee Sang (GRB)
3. Juan Rubio (Spain)
   Stephens (GRB)

−60 kg:
1. S. Ronning (Norway)
2. Fiarclough (GRB)
3. Damien Dovy (France)
   Criado (Spain)

One Point
1. Reuss (Germany)
2. Tramontini (France)
3. Veysel (Turkey)
   Lentini (Italy)

Kata/Forms

Men
Team:
1. Italy
2. France
3. Spain

Individual:
1. D. Marchini (Italy)
2. L. Sanz (Spain)
3. Morris (Scotland)

Women
Team:
1. Italy
2. France
3. Spain

Individual:
1. Restelli (Italy)
3. Svenssen (Sweden)
   Rosalin (Spain)

22ND EUROPEAN KARATE CHAMPIONSHIPS

Date: May 1987.
Site: Glasgow, Scotland.
Sanctioned by: European Karate
   Union.
Participants: 21 countries; 310
   competitors.

21ST EUROPEAN KARATE CHAMPIONSHIPS

Date: May 1986.
Site: Madrid, Spain.
Sanctioned by: European Karate
   Union.
Participants: 20 countries; 300
   competitors.

20TH EUROPEAN KARATE CHAMPIONSHIPS

Date: May 1985.
Site: Oslo, Norway.

Sanctioned by: European Karate
Union.
Participants: 18 countries; 292
competitors.

Kumite/Fighting

Men

Team:
1. Great Britain
2. Spain
3. France

Individuals
Open:
1. Emmanuel Pinda (France)
2. Sailsman (GRB)
3. Josepa (Neth)
   Daggfelt (Sweden)

+80 kg:
1. Zazo (Spain)
2. Daggfelt (Sweden)
3. Marc Pyree (France)
   Guazzaroni (Italy)

−80 kg:
1. J. Egea (Spain)
2. Cornwall (GRB)
3. Mossel (Neth)
   Etienne (GRB)

−75 kg:
1. Martinez (Spain)
2. Dietl (Germany)
3. Serfati (France)
   Leewin (Neth)

−70 kg:
1. Mossel (Neth)
2. Negro (Switzerland)
3. Francis (GRB)
   Rodriguez (Spain)

−65 kg:
1. Abad (Spain)
2. Royo Garcia (Spain)
3. Heinrich (Germany)
   Ramon Malave (Sweden)

−60 kg:
1. S. Ronning (Norway)
2. Betzien (Germany)
3. Lassen (Germany)
   R. Vallee (France)

Kata/Forms

Men

Team:
1. Great Britain
2. Spain
3. France

Individual:
1. Karamitsos (Germany)
2. Escolastica (Spain)
3. D. Marchini (Italy)
   De La Sanz (Spain)

Women

Team:
1. Spain
2. Italy
3. Germany

Individual:
1. Svensson (Sweden)
2. Restelli (Italy)
3. Moreno (Spain)

19TH EUROPEAN KARATE CHAMPIONSHIPS

Date: May 1984.
Site: Paris, France.
Producer: French Karate Union.
Sanctioned by: European Karate
Union.
Participants: 17 countries; 268
competitors.

Kumite/Fighting

Men

Team:
1. Scotland
2. Great Britain
3. Netherlands

Individuals
Open:
1. Patrice Ruggiero (France)
2. Emmanuel Pinda (France)
3. Dietl (Germany)
   Guazzaroni (Italy)

+80 kg:
1. Charles (GRB)
2. Patrice Ruggiero (France)
3. Nisman
   Akinlami (Scotland)

−80 kg:
1. Pettinella (France)
2. Otti Roethoff (Neth)
3. Cornwall (GRB)
   J. Egea (Spain)

−75 kg:
1. Le Cuwin (Neth)
2. Santhier (Swiss)
3. Morean (France)
   Fred Royers (Neth)

−70 kg:
1. Rodriguez (Spain)
2. T. Masci (France)
3. Lindstrom (Finland)
   Bruns (Scotland)

−65 kg:
1. Timonen (Finland)
2. Coulter (Scotland)
3. Abad (Spain)
   Dorville (France)

−60 kg:
1. D'Agostino (Italy)
2. Shaer (GRB)
3. Stephen (GRB)
   Criado (Spain)

Kata/Forms

Men

Team:
1. Italy
2. Spain
3. West Germany

Individual:
1. D. Marchini (Italy)
2. Luis Maria (Spain)
3. Chan Liat (France)

Women

Team:
1. Spain
2. England
3. Italy

Individual:
1. Helen Raye (GRB)
2. Marisa Rozalem (Spain)
3. Sonja Sanchez (Spain)

18TH EUROPEAN KARATE CHAMPIONSHIPS

Date: May 1983.
Site: Madrid, Spain.
Sanctioned by: European Karate Union.
Participants: 17 countries; 261 competitors.

Kumite/Fighting

Men

Team:
1. Great Britain
2. France
3. Spain
   Sweden

Individuals

Open:
1. J. Egea (Spain)
2. Thompson (GRB)
3. Patrice Ruggiero (France)
4. Pirttiosa (Finland)

Heavy:
1. Patrice Ruggiero (France)
2. Marc Pyree (France)
3. Carbila (Spain)
   Atkinson (GRB)

Light Heavy:
1. Pirttiosa (Finland)
2. Manzano (Spain)
3. Prince (GRB)
   Guazzaroni (Italy)

Middle:
1. Merino (Spain)
2. Pinar (France)
3. Spaarto (Belgium)
   Gomez (Switzerland)

Light Middle:
1. Kaunismaki (Finland)
2. Bernadi (Italy)
3. Danatelli (Sweden)
   Hita (Spain)

Light:
1. Coulter (GRB)
2. Goffin (France)
3. Lupo (France)
   Abad (Spain)

Super Light:
1. Stephens (GRB)
2. MacKinnon (GRB)

3. Khatiri (France)
   R. Vallee (France)

17TH EUROPEAN KARATE CHAMPIONSHIPS

Date: May 1982.
Site: Goteborg, Sweden.
Sanctioned by: European Karate Union.
Participants: 18 countries; 278 competitors.

16TH EUROPEAN KARATE CHAMPIONSHIPS

Date: May 1981.
Site: Venice, Italy.
Sanctioned by: European Karate Union.
Participants: 19 countries; 245 competitors.

15TH EUROPEAN KARATE CHAMPIONSHIPS

Date: May 1980.
Site: Barcelona, Spain.
Sanctioned by: European Karate Union.
Participants: 21 countries; 345 competitors.

14TH EUROPEAN KARATE CHAMPIONSHIPS

Date: May 1979.
Site: Helsinki, Finland.
Sanctioned by: European Karate Union.
Participants: 17 countries; 240 competitors.

13TH EUROPEAN KARATE CHAMPIONSHIPS

Date: May 1978.
Site: Geneva, Switzerland.
Sanctioned by: European Karate Union.
Participants: 17 countries; 286 competitors.

12TH EUROPEAN KARATE CHAMPIONSHIPS

Date: May 1977.
Site: Paris, France.
Sanctioned by: European Karate Union.
Participants: 17 countries; 279 competitors.

11TH EUROPEAN KARATE CHAMPIONSHIPS

Date: May 1976.
Site: Teheran, Iran.
Sanctioned by: European Karate Union.
Participants: 15 countries; 225 competitors.

10TH EUROPEAN KARATE CHAMPIONSHIPS

Date: May 1975.
Site: Ostend, Belgium.
Sanctioned by: European Karate Union.
Participants: 16 countries.
Participants: 21 countries; 260 competitors.

Kumite/Fighting

Teams:
1. France
2. Switzerland
3. Scotland
   West Germany (FRG)

Men

Open:
1. Jacques Abdurraman (France)
2. Von Johnson (Wales)
3. Dominique Valera (France)
   Pasquale La Cassia

Heavy:
1. Eugene Codrington (GRB)
2. John Roel Reeberg (Neth)
3. Dominique Valera (France)
   Brian Fitkin (GRB)

Middle:
1. William Higgins (GRB)
2. William Millerson (Neth)
3. Christian Alifax (France)
   Wolfgang Zierbart (FRG)

Light:
1. Roger Paschy (France)
2. Willy Voss (FRG)
3. Jacques Bonvin (Switzerland)
   Marc Soli (Belgium)

9TH EUROPEAN KARATE CHAMPIONSHIPS

Date: May 9, 1974.
Site: Crystal Palace, London, England.
Sanctioned by: European Karate Union.
Participants: 15 countries; 130 competitors.

Kumite/Fighting

Teams:
1. France
2. Belgium
3. ?
   ?

Men

Open:
1. Jan Kallenbach (Neth)
2. Jean Luc Mami (France)
3. Pasquale La Cassia (Italy)

Heavy:
1. Robin McFarlane (Scotland)
2. Francois Petitdemange (France)
3. Brian Fitkin (GRB)

Middle:
1. William Higgins (GRB)
2. Geert Lemmens (Belgium)
3. Unknown

Light:
1. Richard Scherer (FRG)
2. Antonio Oliva (Spain)
3. Unknown

8TH EUROPEAN KARATE CHAMPIONSHIPS

Date: May 26–27, 1973.
Site: Valencia, Spain.
Sanctioned by: European Karate Union.
Participants: 14 countries; 210 competitors.

Kumite/Fighting

Teams:
1. Scotland
2. Switzerland
3. West Germany (FRG)
   Italy

Men

Open:
1. Francis Didier (France)
2. Patrice Lanoir (France)
3. Alfonso Rivilla (Spain)
   Willy Voss (FRG)

Heavy:
1. Francois Petitdemange (France)
2. Robin McFarlane (Scotland)
3. Gerard Boukhezer (France)
   Tom Van Heuman (Neth)

Middle:
1. Christian Alifax (France)
2. William Millerson (Neth)
3. Giorgio Schiappagasse (Italy)
   William Higgins (GRB)

Light:
1. Roger Paschy (France)
2. Steve Cattle (GRB)
3. Richard Scherer (FRG)
   Paolo Ciotoli (Italy)

7TH EUROPEAN KARATE CHAMPIONSHIPS

Date: May 1972.
Site: Brussels, Belgium.
Sanctioned by: European Karate Union.
Participants: 13 countries; 195 competitors.

6TH EUROPEAN KARATE CHAMPIONSHIPS

Date: May 1971.
Site: Coubertine Hall, Paris, France.
Producer: French Karate Union.
Sanctioned by: European Karate Union.
Participants: 15 countries; 135 competitors.
Spectators: 7,000.

Kumite/Fighting

Men

Team:
1. France
2. Belgium
3. Yugoslavia
   West Germany (FRG)

Individuals:
1. Dominique Valera (France)
2. Gilbert Gruss (France)
3. Francis Didier (France)
   Joachim Otremba (FRG)

5TH EUROPEAN KARATE CHAMPIONSHIPS

Date: May 3–4, 1970.
Site: Paris, France.
Sanctioned by: European Karate Union.
Participants: 14 countries; 119 competitors.

4TH EUROPEAN KARATE CHAMPIONSHIPS

Date: May 10, 1969.
Site: London, England.
Sanctioned by: European Karate Union.
Participants: 13 countries; 117 competitors.

Kumite/Fighting

Men

Team:
1. France
2. Great Britain
3. Yugoslavia
   Belgium

Individuals:
1. Dominique Valera (France)
2. Gilbert Gruss (France)
3. Jorga (Yugoslavia)
   Scherer (FRG)

3RD EUROPEAN KARATE CHAMPIONSHIPS

Date: May 4, 1968.
Site: Paris, France.
Producer: French Karate Union.

Sanctioned by: European Karate
Union.
Participants: 10 countries; 90
competitors.

Kumite/Fighting

Men

Team:
1. France
2. Belgium
3. Yugoslavia
   Italy

Individuals:
1. Guy Sauvin (France)
2. Dominique Valera (France)
3. Richard Kozakiewitcz (Belgium)
   Gerard Grossetete (Switzerland)

2ND EUROPEAN KARATE CHAMPIONSHIPS

Date: May 6, 1967.
Site: London, England.
Sanctioned by: European Karate
Union.
Participants: 10 countries; 70
competitors.

1ST EUROPEAN KARATE CHAMPIONSHIPS

Date: May 7, 1966.
Site: State de Coubertin, Paris,
France.
Sanctioned by: European Karate
Union.
Participants: 6 countries; 54
competitors.

Kumite/Fighting

Men

Team:
1. France
2. Switzerland
3. Italy
   Great Britain

Individuals:
1. Patrick Baroux (France)
2. Guy Sauvin (France)
3. Setrouk (France)
   Gerometta (Italy)

UNITED STATES OF AMERICA KARATE FEDERATION (USAKF) & AMATEUR ATHLETIC UNION (AAU) NATIONAL CHAMPIONSHIPS (1975–89)

15TH USAKF NATIONAL KARATE CHAMPIONSHIPS

Date: 1989.
Orlando, Florida.
Sanction: USA Karate Federation.
Participants: 2,200.

Kumite/Fighting

Men

Open:
1. Jerry Kattawar, Jr.

80+ kg:
1. Glen West

−80 kg:
1. Bob Oliveri

−75 kg:
1. Jerry Kattawar, Jr.

−70 kg:
1. David Cheung

−65 kg:
1. Derik Ochiai

Women

Open:
1. Tracey Day

60+ kg:
1. Mary Tripp

−60 kg:
1. Tracey Day

−53 kg:
1. Gwen Hoffman

Kata/Forms

Men

Advanced Open:
1. Kent Kim

Mandatory:
1. Ferdie Allas

Weapons:
1. Michael Pomeroy

Women

Advanced Open:
1. Debbie Tang

Mandatory:
1. Debbie Tang

Weapons:
1. Gwen Hoffman

14TH USAKF NATIONAL KARATE CHAMPIONSHIPS

Date: 1988.

13TH USAKF NATIONAL KARATE CHAMPIONSHIPS

Date: 1987.
Site: Columbus, Ohio.
Producer: George Anderson.
Sanction: USA Karate Federation.
Participants: 800 competitors.

Kumite/Fighting

Men

Open:
1. Jerry Kattawar

+80 kg:
1. John Hill

−80 kg:
1. Dan Deere

−75 kg:
1. Dale Beam

−70 kg:
1. Paul Cortright

−65 kg:
1. Hector Torres

−60 kg:
1. Scott Rosak

Women

Open:
1. Regina Halteman

+60 kg:
1. Chris Dawson

−60 kg:
1. Gwenna Black

−53 kg:
1. Gwen Hoffman

Kata/Forms

Empty Hand

Men
1. Julio Martinez

Women
1. Kathy Jones

Weapons

Men
1. James Devenne

Women
1. Debbie Tang

12TH USAKF NATIONAL KARATE CHAMPIONSHIPS

Date: August 22–24, 1986.
Site: Westin Peachtree Plaza,
    Atlanta, Georgia.

Note: This was the first year this annual event came under the auspices of the USA Karate Federation.

Kumite/Fighting

Men

Open:
1. John Caluda
2. Saha Alston

+80 kg:
1. Eddie Partain
2. John Caluda

−80 kg:
1. Mark Heyerdahl
2. Glen Evans

−75 kg:
1. Dale Beam
2. Tony Fournier

−70 kg:
1. Paul Cortright
2. Keith Taylor

−65 kg:
1. David Crockett
2. John Montalto

−60 kg:
1. Joe Minney
2. Blair Portier

Women

Open:
1. Faith Barbera
2. Benilda Otley

+60 kg:
1. Carol Trenga
2. Ana Plunkett

−60 kg:
1. Gina Halterman
2. Gwenna Black

−53 kg:
1. Oretha Jeffers
2. Denise Bradley

Kata/Forms

Men

Mandatory:
1. Julio Martinez

Open:
1. Julio Martinez

Weapons:
1. Norman Lacaden

Women

Mandatory:
1. Faith Barbera

Open:
1. Faith Barbera

Weapons:
1. Gwenna Black
2. Gwen Hoffman

11TH AAU NATIONAL KARATE CHAMPIONSHIPS

Date: August 24–25, 1985.
Site: New Orleans, Louisiana.
Producer: Louisiana Karate
    Association.
Participants: Less than 500.
Spectators: 1,500.

Fighting

Men

Team:
1. Southern Region

Individuals
+80 kg:
1. John Caluda
2. Asa Herring

−80 kg:
1. Mark Prudhomme

−75 kg:
1. Jerry Kattaway
2. Dale Beam

Women

Open:
1. Nicki Allen
2. Christella Dawson

Forms

Mandatory:
1. Julio Martinez

Open:
1. Julio Martinez

10TH AAU NATIONAL KARATE CHAMPIONSHIPS

Date: 1984.
Site: San Diego, California.

Kumite/Fighting

Men

Team:
1. Southern
2. Central
3. Arizona
    Florida

Open:
1. Asa Herring
2. Dan Anderson
3. John Caluda
    Mark Prudhomme

80+ kg:
1. John Caluda
2. Randall Nelson
3. Anthony DiSardi
    Glenn West

−80 kg:
1. Mark Prudhomme
2. Ken Ferguson
3. Richard Sutherland
    David Fricks

−75 kg:
1. Dale Beam
2. Brad Marineau
3. Chun Mon Isang
    Dan Anderson

−70 kg:
1. Paul Cortright
2. Marvin Coleman
3. Julio Martinez
   Dennis Wanless

−65 kg:
1. David Crockett
2. Hiroshi Morimoto
3. L. Jay Castellano
   Noriaki Hamasaki

−60 kg:
1. Yoshiaki Inoue
2. Jim Sornito
3. Joseph Minney
   Norman Sandler

Women

Team:
1. Virginia
2. Allegheny Mountain
3. Ohio
   Central

Open:
1. Debbi Aguirre
2. Gina Halteman
3. Antoinette Chavez
   Tammy Harwood

60+ kg:
1. Gale Egeland
2. Roberta Huskin
3. Cindy Johnson
   Cindy Watson

−60 kg:
1. Gwenna Black
2. Gina Halteman
3. Tina Noble
   Marla Cohen

−53 kg:
1. Stephanie Johnson
2. Kim Friedl
3. Gwen Hoffman
4. Debbi Aguirre

Kata/Forms

Men

Mandatory:
1. Julio Martinez
2. Ron Mizusawa
3. Jim Sornito
   Domingo Llanos

Open:
1. Julio Martinez

2. Somingo Llanos
3. Ron Mizusawa
   Jim Sornito

Synchronized:
1. Pacific Southwest
2. Southern
3. Florida Gold Coast
   Lake Erie

Weapons:
1. Mark Heyerdahl
2. Jay Castellano
3. Scott Hoganson
   Steve Woodward

Women

Mandatory:
1. Kathy Baxter
2. Pam Glaser
3. Tilly Garcia
   Kathy Jones

Open:
1. Kathy Jones
2. Kathy Baxter
3. Linda Marquardt
   Pam Glaser

Synchronized:
1. Pacific Northwest

Team:
1. New York

Weapons:
1. Gwenna Black
2. Kathy Baxter
3. Lea Sukenik
   Gwen Hoffman

9TH AAU NATIONAL KARATE CHAMPIONSHIPS

Date: 1983.
Site:
Producer: Unknown.
Participants: Unknown.

8TH AAU NATIONAL KARATE CHAMPIONSHIPS

Date: July 23–25, 1982.
Site: Chicago, Illinois.
Participants: 800 competitors.

7TH AAU NATIONAL KARATE CHAMPIONSHIPS

Date: June 26–28, 1981.
Site: Hyannis, Massachusetts.
Director: Glenn Hart.
Participants: 1,000+ from 31 states.

Kumite/Fighting

Senior Advanced Men

Open:
1. Steve Black
2. Alberto Pena
3. Traylon Smith
4. Hector Gomez

80.1+ kg:
1. Billy Blanks
2. Sonny Daniels
3. William Huber
4. Jordan Berry

−80 kg:
1. Tokey Hill
2. Ken Ferguson
3. John DiPasquale
4. Richard Faustini

−75 kg:
1. John Almeida
2. Keith Hanson
3. Charles Stack
4. Dale Beam

−70 kg:
1. Domingo Llanos
2. Mark Wilson
3. Hector Gomez
4. Tom O'Brien

−65 kg:
1. Michael Sledge
2. Lawrence Calloway
3. Ray Jenkins
4. Eric Griffin

−60 kg:
1. William Matthews
2. Louis Reyes
3. Rolando Mirandilla
4. David Crocket

Senior Advanced Women

120+ lbs:
1. Gail Egeland
2. Julie Deal
3. Cindy Watson
4. Regina Floyd

–120 lbs:

1. Gina Schavone
2. Patricia Booth
3. Katherine Baxter
4. Gwen Hoffman

Kata/Forms

Senior Advanced Men:

1. Domingo Llanos
2. Jim Sornito
3. Alberto Pena
4. Mike Bakala

Senior Advanced Women:

1. Pamela Glaser
2. Lea Sukenik
3. Katherine Baxter
4. Gina Schavone

Men's Weapons:

1. Glenn Hart
2. Jim Bornito
3. Alberto Pena
4. Kavell Kalamtari

Women's Weapons:

1. Katherine Baxter
2. Gwen Hoffman
3. Gina Schavone
4. Becky Smith

6TH AAU NATIONAL KARATE CHAMPIONSHIPS

Date: July 26–27, 1980.
Virginia Beach, Virginia.
Producer: Noel Smith.

5TH AAU NATIONAL KARATE CHAMPIONSHIPS

Date: July 6–8, 1979.
Site: University of Akron, Akron, Ohio.
Producer: George Anderson.

4TH AAU NATIONAL KARATE CHAMPIONSHIPS

Date: July 22–23, 1978.
Site: Hackensack, New Jersey.
Producer: Jerry Thomson.

3RD AAU NATIONAL KARATE CHAMPIONSHIPS

Date: June 24–26, 1977.
Site: Norfolk, Virginia.
Producer: Dan Montgomery.
Participants: 294 competitors from 18 states.

Kumite/Fighting

Senior Advanced Men:

1. Ken Ferguson
2. Dana Billings
3. Roberto Marcello

Senior Advanced Women:

1. Pam Wansker
2. Joanna Needham
3. Karen Session

Kata/Forms

Senior Advanced Men:

1. Domingo Llanos
2. Roberto Marcello
3. Joe Lamelas

Senior Advanced Women:

1. Pamela Glaser
2. Mildred Kuttawar
3. Mary Gaeta

Men's Weapons:

1. Jerry Serino
2. Curtis Smith
3. Don Page

Women's Weapons:

1. Bonnie McGinley
2. Ellen Beal
3. Mildred Kuttawar

2ND AAU NATIONAL KARATE CHAMPIONSHIPS

Date: August 5–7, 1976.
Site: Missouri Southern State University, Joplin, Missouri.
Producer: Errin Wright.

1ST AAU NATIONAL KARATE CHAMPIONSHIPS

Date: 1975.
Site: Cleveland, Ohio.

Kumite/Fighting

Senior Advanced Men:

1. Billy Blanks
2. Walter Fagan
3. Huey Daniels

Senior Advanced Women:

1. Sandra Watter
2. Margie Pessin
3. Marilyn Putt

Kata/Forms

Senior Advanced Men:

1. Will Haynie
2. Hiroshi Hamada
3. James Cook, Jr.

Senior Advanced Women:

1. S. Anne Small
2. Ellen Beal
3. Kathleen Garrity

Men's Weapons:

1. Wayne Wellings
2. Robert Sparks
3. James Cook, Jr.

Women's Weapons:

1. Karen Tolczyk
2. Janet Beer
3. S. Anne Small

CHAPTER 11

TAE KWON DO CHAMPIONSHIP RESULTS

All of the following black belt results are based on competitions sanctioned by the World Taekwon-do Federation (WTF), the world's leading tae kwon do organization and the only one with an Olympic connection. Included here, with only a few exceptions, are all of the World, U.S. and European Championship results from 1972 to 1992.

Note that some of the divisional places marked "?" were chiefly from the earliest tae kwon do competitions. It is very possible that there were insufficient competitors to fill a particular division. In those cases, it is not the fault of any contributors to this section; all winners' lists supplied by the various contributors to this section were as complete as possible. *In the case of a tie, no number will precede the second competitor or country listing. For example, the winners' lists typically feature three places with two competitors sharing the third position.*

A mass board-breaking demonstration at the Olympic Stadium brought a standing ovation at the 1988 Olympic Games in Seoul, Korea. The demo was broadcast worldwide as part of the Olympic festivities. Courtesy of Dr. Un Yong Kim and the World Taekwon-do Federation

WEIGHT DIVISION CONVERSION CHART

The following chart will help readers interested in weight divisions quickly determine exact kilos to pounds and vice versa.

Kilos	Pounds	Pounds	Kilos
48	105.82	112	50.8
50	110.23	113	51.25
51	112.44	115	52.16
54	119.05	118	53.53
55	121.25	119	53.98
57	125.66	122	55.34
58	127.87	126	57.15
60	132.28	130	58.97
62	136.69	133	60.33
63	138.89	135	61.24
66	145.51	140	63.50
67	147.71	147	66.68
70	154.32	148	67.13
71	156.53	154	69.85
72	158.73	156	70.76
74	163.14	160	72.58
75	165.35	164	73.94
76	167.55	167	75.75
79	174.17	172	78.47
80	176.37	175	79.38
81	178.57	180	79.38
82	180.78	182	82.56
85	187.39	190	86.18
86	189.60	195	86.18
91	200.62	200	90.72

WORLD TAEKWON-DO FEDERATION (WTF) WORLD AND OLYMPIC CHAMPIONSHIP RESULTS (1973–92)

OLYMPIC TAE KWON DO RESULTS (1992 SUMMER OLYMPIC GAMES)

Date: July 26–27, 1992.
Site: Barcelona, Spain.
Producer: World Taekwon-do Federation.

Overall Medal Standing

1. South Korea
2. Spain
3. Taiwan
4. United States
5. Canada
6. Indonesia
7. Mexico
8. Turkey
9. Venezuela
10. Italy
    France

Fighting

Men

183+ pounds:
1. Kim Je Kyoung (South Korea)
2. Emmanuel Oghenejobo (Nigeria)
3. Amr Hassan (Egypt)
   Simon Hosking (Australia)

183 pounds:
1. Herbert Perez (United States)
2. Juan Solis Godoy (Spain)
3. Ammar Sbeihi (Jordan)
   Khalad Ibrahim (Egypt)

168 pounds:
1. Ha Tae Kyoung (South Korea)
2. Jae Hun Lee (Canada)
3. Mohammad Al Qaimi (Kuwait)
   Reza Somesarayi (Iran)

154 pounds:
1. Jose Santolaria Martos (Spain)
2. Fariboz Askari (Iran)
3. Kuei-Ming Chou (Taiwan)
   Djamel Khali (France)

141 pounds:
1. Kim Byong Cheol (South Korea)
2. Ekrem Boyali (Turkey)
3. Luca Massaccesi (Italy)
   Woo Yong Jung (Canada)

128 pounds:
1. William Santamaria (Mexico)
2. Sayed Youssef Najem (Canada)
3. Domenico D'Allise (Italy)
   Stephen Fernandez (Philippines)

119 pounds:
1. Arlindo L. Gouvela Colina (Venezuela)
2. Dirc Richard Talumewo (Indonesia)
3. Ming-Sung Wang (Taiwan)
   Seo Sung Kyo (South Korea)

110 pounds:
1. Gergely Salim (Denmark)
2. Juan Moreno (United States)
3. Javier Argudo Sesmilo (Spain)
   Jefi Tri Aji (Indonesia)

Women

154+ pounds:
1. Coral Astrid Bistuer Ruiz (Spain)
3. Susan Graham (New Zealand)
   Adriana Carmona (Venezuela)
   Lynnette Love (United States)

154 pounds:
1. Lee Sun Hee (South Korea)
3. Marcia Catherine King (Canada)
   Morfou Drosidou (Greece)
   Denise Angela Parmley (Australia)

143 pounds:
1. Elena Benitez Morales (Spain)
2. Brigitte Geffroy (France)
3. Sheliey Vettese-Baert (Canada)
   Danielle Laney (United States)

132 pounds:
1. An Chen (Taiwan)
2. Susilawati (Indonesia)
3. Hafida El Ouacef (Morocco)
   Jeung Eun Ok (South Korea)

121 pounds:
1. Ya-Ling Tung (Taiwan)
2. Aysegul Ergin (Turkey)
3. Beatriz Lucero (Philippines)
   Dolores Ann Knolle Weaver (Mexico)

112 pounds:
1. Hwang Eun Suk (South Korea)
2. Diane Murray (United States)
3. Hii King Hung (Malaysia)
   Catherine Noble (France)

104 pounds:
1. Elisabet Delgado Cazorla (Spain)
2. Piera Muggiri (Italy)
3. Arzu Tan (Turkey)
   Terry Poindexter (United States)

95 pounds:
1. Yueh-Ying Lo (Taiwan)
2. Rahmi Kumia (Indonesia)
3. Monica Torres Amarillas (Mexico)
   Amanda Broadbent (Britain)

10TH WTF WORLD TAEKWON-DO CHAMPIONSHIPS

Date: October 28–November 3, 1991.
Site: Athens, Greece.
Sanctioned by: World Taekwon-do Federation.
Medal standing unavailable.

Fighting

Men

Team:
1. Korea
2. Denmark
3. Spain

Heavy (+83 kg):
1. Tony Sorensen (Denmark)
2. Oliver Schawe (Germany)
3. Jordan (Spain)
   Khairy Arm (Egypt)

Middle (−83 kg):
1. Yoon (S. Korea)
2. Alam Yehya (Egypt)
3. Sahin Metin (Turkey)
   Herb Perez (USA)

Welter (−76 kg):
1. Park (S. Korea)
2. Villisana (USA)
3. Kondo (Japan)
   Garcia Hugo (Mexico)

Light (−70 kg):
1. Dae Doung Yang (S. Korea)
2. Abratique (Philippines)
3. Collinson (Australia)
   Hiang (C. Taipei)

Feather (−64 kg):
1. Chang (S. Korea)
2. Tapilatu (Neth)
3. Concalves (?)
   El Monen (Egypt)

Bantam (−58 kg):
1. Angel Alonso (Spain)
2. Najen Sayen (Canada)
3. Seon (S. Korea)
   Boyali Ekrem (Turkey)

Fly (−54 kg):
1. Chul Ho Kim (S. Korea)
2. Salim (Denmark)
3. Esparza (Spain)
   Tapilatu (Neth)

Fin (−50 kg):
1. Gergely Salim (Denmark)
2. Jung San Chang (C. Taipei)
3. Rezaei Syrous (Iran)
   Kang (S. Korea)

Women

Team:
1. Korea
2. USA
3. Spain

Heavy (+70 kg):
1. Lynette Love (USA)
2. Yvonne Franssen (Canada)
3. Widehov (Sweden)
   ?

Middle (−70 kg):
1. Yang (S. Korea)
2. Chavela Aaron (USA)
3. Del Real (Mexico)
   Ketesidou (Greece)

Welter (−65 kg):
1. Arlene Limas (USA)
2. Bistuer (Spain)
3. Cho (S. Korea)
   Drosidou (Greece)

Light (−60 kg):
1. Jeong (S. Korea)
2. Yi An Chen (C. Taipei)
3. Thielman (Neth)
   Knoll (Mexico)

Feather (−55 kg):
1. Ya Lin Tung (C. Taipei)
2. Aysegul (Turkey)
3. Lopez (Spain)
   Adel Azaa (Egypt)

Bantam (−51 kg):
1. Park (S. Korea)
2. Sahim Dondu (Turkey)
3. Walker (GRB)
   Solis (Spain)

Fly (−47 kg):
1. Tan Arzu (Turkey)
2. Van der Pas (Neth)
3. Valenzuela (Argentina)
   Wen Tanghui (C. Taipei)

Fin (−43 kg):
1. Delgado (Spain)
2. Gulmur (Turkey)
3. Shan Chen Wu (C. Taipei)
   Jee Hyang Kim (S. Korea)

9TH WTF WORLD TAEKWON-DO CHAMPIONSHIPS

Date: October 9–14, 1989.
Site: Seoul, Korea.
Producer: World Taekwon-do
   Federation.
Medal standing unavailable.

Fighting

Men

Heavy:
1. Amr Khairy Mahmoud (Egypt)
2. Sang Jin Choi (S. Korea)
3. Victor Bateman (Australia)
   Farzad Zarakhsh (Iran)

Middle:
1. Yong Suk Jeong (S. Korea)
2. Renzo Zenteno (Chile)
3. S.H. Zahedi H.G. (Iran)
   Jarl Kaila (Finland)

Welter:
1. Hyun Suk Lee (S. Korea)
2. Humberto Norabuena (Chile)
3. Dante Pena (Philippines)
   Khaled Mahmoud Fawzi
   (Egypt)

Light:
1. Dae Doung Yang (S. Korea)
2. Nusret Ramazanoglu (Turkey)
3. Jae Hoon Lee (Canada)
   Joseph Rocamora (France)

Feather:
1. Hyuk Jang (S. Korea)
2. Hubert Sinegre (France)
3. Cicek Musa (FRG)
   Dhanaraj Rassiah (Malaysia)

Bantam:
1. Jun Ham (S. Korea)
2. D'Alise Domenico (Italy)
3. Herbert Christian (FRG)
   Abdullah Nagrani (Saudi
   Arabia)

Fly:
1. Chul Ho Kim (S. Korea)
2. Turgut Ucan (Turkey)
3. Salah Abdel Hamid (Egypt)
   Fariborz Danesh (Iran)

Fin:
1. Tae Ho Kwon (S. Korea)
2. Jung San Chang (C. Taipei)
3. Juan Moreno (USA)
   Harun Ates (Turkey)

Women

Heavy:
1. Wan Sook Jung (S. Korea)
2. Yvonne Franssen (Canada)
3. Hoi Chun Yang (C. Taipei)
   Yolanda Santana (Spain)

Middle:
1. Lydia Zele (USA)
2. Marcie King (Canada)
3. Antonia Vega (Spain)
   Ju Ya Hsy (C. Taipei)

Welter:
1. Anita Silsby (USA)
2. A. Buys (Netherlands)
3. Ayse Alkaya (Turkey)
   Jee Sook Kim (S. Korea)

Light:
1. Eun Young Lee (S. Korea)
2. Chao Chin Liu (C. Taipei)
3. Elena Benitez (Spain)
   Seyda Serefoglu (Turkey)

Feather:
1. So Young Kim (S. Korea)
2. Kim Dotson (USA)
3. Raquel Palacios (Spain)
   Patricia Mariscal (Mexico)

Bantam:
1. Nam Suk Jung (S. Korea)
2. Diane Murray (USA)
3. Yi An Chen (C. Taipei)
   Aysin Haktanir (Turkey)

Fly:
1. Sun Jin Weon (S. Korea)
2. Yun Yao Pai (C. Taipei)
3. Mayumi Pejo (USA)
   Anita Falieros (Australia)

Fin:
1. Yu Fang Chin (C. Taipei)
2. Monica Amarilla (Mexico)
3. Jee Hyang Kim (S. Korea)
   Sita Kumari Rai (Nepal)

1988 OLYMPIC TAEKWON-DO CHAMPIONSHIPS (WTF)

Date: September 17–20, 1988.
Site: Seoul, Korea;
24th Summer Olympic Games.
Participants: 192 competitors from 51 countries.
Sanctioned by: World Taekwon-do Federation.
Television Coverage: NBC; global broadcast.
Status: Taekwon-do's entry into the Olympics as a Demonstration Sport.
Spectators: Up to 7,000 daily.

For the Record: Olympic Team Selection Process

Phase One

Athlete must qualify for National Championship:

1st through 3rd place winners from respective state championships.
1st through 3rd place winners from most recent official nationally sanctioned collegiate championship.
1st through 3rd place winners from the official national championship.

Phase Two

National Championships:
Top four athletes per weight class plus two alternates qualify for Olympic trials/eliminations.

Phase Three

Olympic Trials/Eliminations:
Top two athletes per weight class qualify for Olympic trials/finals.

Phase Four

Olympic Trials/Finals:
Top two athletes from trials/eliminations vie for Olympic team slot.

Overall Medal Standing
1. South Korea
2. USA
3. Spain
4. Taiwan
5. Germany (FRG)
6. Turkey
   Mexico
7. Denmark
   Netherlands
   Jordan
8. Italy
   Egypt
   Bahrain
   Canada
   Iran
   Malaysia
   Nepal
   Saudi Arabia

Fighting

Men

Heavy/+183 lbs:
1. Jimmy Kim (USA)
2. Jong-sun Kim (S. Korea)
3. Jose Alvarez (Spain
   Michael Arnet (FRG)

Middle/−183 lbs:
1. Kye-Haeng Lee (S. Korea)
2. Amr Hussein (Egypt)
3. Markus Woznicki (FRG)
   Metin Sahin (Turkey)

Welter/−167 lbs:
1. Kook-Hyun Chung (S. Korea)
2. Luigi DiOriano (Italy)
3. Jay Warwick (USA)
   Tsung-che Wu (Taiwan)

Light/−154 lbs:
1. Bong-Kwon Park (S. Korea)
2. Jose Sanchez (Spain)
3. Greg Baker (USA)
   Manuel Jurado (Mex)

Feather/−140 lbs:
1. Myung-sam Chang (S. Korea)
2. Cengiz Yagiz (Turkey)
3. Ibrahim Al Gafar (S. Arabia)
   Samar Kamal (Jordan)

Bantam/−128 lbs:
1. Yong-Suk Ji (S. Korea)
2. Jose Sanabria (Spain)
3. Han Won Lee (USA)
   Feisal Danesh (Iran)

Fly/−119 lbs:
1. Tae-Kyung Ha (S. Korea)
2. Gabriel Garcia (Spain)
3. Ihsan Abushekha (Jordan)
   Adel Darraj (Bahrain)

Fin/−110 lbs:
1. Tae-Ho Kwon (S. Korea)
2. Juan Moreno (USA)
3. Enrique Torroella (Mex)
   Bidhan Lama (Nepal)

Women

Heavy/+154 lbs:
1. Lynette Love (USA)
2. Youn-Jung Jang (S. Korea)
3. Ute Guessen (FRG)
   Yvonne Fransser (Canada)

Middle/−154 lbs:
1. Hyun-Hee Kim (S. Korea)

2. Mandy De Jongh (Neth)
3. Sharon Jewell (USA)
   Elena Navay (Spain)

Welter/−143 lbs:
1. Arlene Limas (USA)
2. Jee Sook Kim (S. Korea)
3. Coral Bistuer (Spain)
   Sonny Seidel (FRG)

Light/−132 lbs:
1. Dana Hee (USA)
2. Karin Schwartz (Den)
3. Jiun-Feng Chen (Taiwan)
   Jolanda Van Duren (Neth)

Feather/−121 lbs:
1. Annemette Christiansen (Den)
2. Zuleyha Tan (Turkey)
3. So-Young Kim (S. Korea)
   Amparo Dolls (Spain)

Bantam/−112 lbs:
1. Yi-an Chen (Taiwan)
2. Debra Holloway (USA)
3. Josefina Lopez (Spain)
   Sun-Young Park (S. Korea)

Fly/−103 lbs:
1. Nan-Yool Choo (S. Korea)
2. Maria Naranjo (Spain)
3. Mayumi Pejo (USA)
   Yun-Yao Pai (Taiwan)

Fin/−94 lbs:
1. Yu-Fang Chin (Taiwan)
2. Hwa-Jin Lee (S. Korea)
3. Vasugi Marathamuthu (Malay)
   Monica Torres (Mex)

8TH WTF WORLD TAEKWON-DO CHAMPIONSHIPS AND 1ST WOMEN'S WORLD TAEKWON-DO CHAMPIONSHIPS

Date: October 7–11, 1987.
Site: Palau Municipal D'Esports, Barcelona, Spain.
Producer: Federacion Espanola de Tae Kwon Do.
Participants: 434 competitors from 62 countries.

Men

Overall Medal Standing
1. South Korea
2. West Germany (FRG)
3. Chinese Taipei
4. Spain
5. USA
6. Turkey
7. Mexico
8. Indonesia
9. France
10. Jordan

Fighting

Heavy/+83 kg:
1. Michael Arndt (FRG)
2. Jimmy Kim (USA)
3. Carmelo Medina (Spain)
   M. Boukrouh (France)

Middle/−83 kg:
1. Gye-Haeng Lee (S. Korea)
2. Francisco Jimenez (Spain)
3. Herb Perez (USA)
   Ammar Sbeihi (Jordan)

Welter/−76 kg:
1. Kuk-Hyun Jeong (S. Korea)
2. John Wright (Spain)
3. Gernhardt Torsten (FRG)
   Jay Warwick (USA)

Light/−70 kg:
1. Dea-Seung Yang (S. Korea)
2. Jesus Tortosa (Spain)
3. Steve Capener (USA)
   Georg Streif (FRG)

Feather/−64 kg:
1. Chian-Hsiang Lee (CHT)
2. Luis Torner (Spain)
3. Mustafa Elmali (Turkey)
   Chris Spence (USA)

Bantam/−58 kg:
1. Myung-Sik Yoo (S. Korea)
2. Nakhr Bezch (Turkey)
3. Nuno Damaso (Swiss)
   Alfie Dellorso (Austria)

Fly/−54 kg:
1. Chang Moo Kang (S. Korea)
2. Budi Setiawan (Indo)
3. Geremia DiCostanzo (Italy)
   Younousse Bathily (Ivory Coast)

Fin/−50 kg:
1. Sung-Wook Lim (S. Korea)
2. Enrique Torroella (Mexico)
3. Dae Sung Lee (USA)
   Bidhan Lama (Nepal)

Women

Overall Medal Standing
1. Korea
2. Chinese Taipei
3. Spain
4. USA
5. Netherlands
6. Turkey
7. Mexico
8. West Germany (FRG)
9. Canada
10. France

Fighting

Heavy/+70 kg:
1. Lynette Love (USA)
2. Yi Ling Liu (CHT)
3. Yoon-Jung Chang (S. Korea)
   A. Buys (Neth)

Middle/−70 kg:
1. M. De Jongh (Neth)
2. Chih Yu Wang (CHT)
3. Sharon Jewell (USA)
   Angelika Biegger (FRG)

Welter/−65 kg:
1. Coral Bistuer (Spain)
2. Jee-Sook Kim (S. Korea)
3. Tessa Gordon (Canada)
   Huey Ting Tang (CHT)

Light/−60 kg:
1. Eun-Young Lee (S. Korea)
2. Feng Lien Hsien (CHT)
3. Evanno (France)
   Elena Navaz (Spain)

Feather/−55 kg:
1. So-Young Kim (S. Korea)
2. Kim Dotson (USA)
3. Zuleyha Tan (Turkey)
   Anne Christensen (Denmark)

Bantam/−51 kg:
1. Tennur Yerlhsu (Turkey)
2. Josefina Lopez (Spain)
3. Margarita Ogarrio (Mexico)
   Ya Lin Torng (CHT)

Fly/−47 kg:
1. Yun Yiao Pai (CHT)
2. Young Lee (S. Korea)
3. Ginean Hatter (USA)
   Antonia Cayetano (Spain)

Fin/−43 kg:
1. Ei-Suk Jang (S. Korea)
2. Monica Torres (Mexico)

3. Rosa Moreno (Spain)
   Yu Fang Chin (CHT)

7TH WTF WORLD TAEKWON-DO CHAMPIONSHIPS

Date: September 4–8, 1985.
Site: Chamshil Gym, Seoul, Korea.
Producer: WTF.
Participants: 63 countries.
Medal standing unavailable.

Fighting

Men

Heavy:
1. Henk Meijer (Neth)
2. Seung Woo Kang (S. Korea)
3. Mostafa El-Abrak (Egypt)
   Cisse Abdoulaye (Ivory Coast)

Middle:
1. Dong Joon Lee (S. Korea)
2. S.H. Zahedi (Iran)
3. Amr Khairy (Egypt)
   Doug Crowder (USA)

Welter:
1. Hyun Jeong Kook (S. Korea)
2. Metin Sahin (Turkey)
3. Patrice Remark (Ivory Coast)
   Jay Warwick (USA)

Light:
1. Bong Kwon Park (S. Korea)
2. Carrieri Pietro (Italy)
3. R. Thijs (Neth)
   Manuel Del Rosaio (Phil)

Feather:
1. Jae Koo Han (S. Korea)
2. Ahmet Ercan (Turkey)
3. Manuel I. Tejeda (Dom Rep)
   Lucio Couzzo (Italy)

Bantam:
1. Sik Yoo Myeong (S. Korea)
2. Gustavo Sanciprian (Mexico)
3. Feisal Danesh (Iran)
   Cengiz Yagiz (Turkey)

Fly:
1. Yeong Sik Kim (S. Korea)
2. Bethily Younousse (Ivory Coast)
3. Geremia DiCostanzo (Italy)
   Hon Cha Sang (USA)

Fin:
1. Sun Jang Lee (S. Korea)
2. Dae Sung Lee (USA)

3. Koidio Konan (Ivory Coast)
   Abdula Eliamy (Saudi Arabia)

Women

Heavy:
1. Lynette Love (USA)
2. Ute Guster (FRG)
3. Andrea Cooke (Canada)
   Yoon Jeong Jang (S. Korea)

Middle:
1. Hyun Hee Kim (S. Korea)
2. Sharon Jewell (USA)
3. M. DeJongh (Neth)
   Olga Majua (Spain)

Welter:
1. Coral Distuer (Spain)
2. Doris Fuchsrcifer (FRG)
3. Tessa Gordan (Canada)
   A. Smeet Ouda Lvttikhuis
   (Neth)

Light:
1. Ji Sook Kim (S. Korea)
2. Paz Gordillo (Spain)
3. Lene Lauridsen (Denmark)
   Tamberlain Connelly (USA)

Feather:
1. Rocio Valverde (Spain)
2. Patricia Mariscal (Mexico)
3. So Young Kim (S. Korea)
   Valerie Long (USA)

Bantam:
1. Im Shin Ja (S. Korea)
2. Debra Holloway (USA)
3. Pietra (Italy)
   Susan Greuves (GRB)

Fly:
1. Lucia Martinez (Spain)
2. Pietra (Italy)
3. Marion Gal (FRG)
   Jeong Im Kim (S. Korea)

Fin:
1. Sook Sin (S. Korea)
2. Cheryl Kalanoc (USA)
3. Claudia Vieg (FRG)
   Rosa Moreno (Spain)

6TH WTF WORLD TAEKWON-DO CHAMPIONSHIPS

Date: October 20–23, 1983.
Site: Brondby Hall, Copenhagen,
   Denmark.

Organizers: Danish Taekwon-do
   Federation.
Participants: 353 competitors from
   51 countries.

Overall Medal Standing
1. South Korea
2. Spain
3. Turkey
4. Germany (FRG)
5. Netherlands
6. Mexico
7. Canada
8. Great Britain
9. Italy
10. USA

Fighting

Men

Heavy:
1. Seung Hwa Jang (S. Korea)
2. Dirk Jung (FRG)
3. H. Meijer (Neth)
   Fonseca Feco (Spain)

Light Heavy:
1. Fargas Inreno (Spain)
2. Eugen Nefedow (FRG)
3. John Lee (USA)
   Michael Knudsen (Den)

Middle:
1. Dong Jun Lee (S. Korea)
2. Jersey Long (Canada)
3. Charles Bayou (Ivory Coast)
   Jay Warwick (USA)

Light Middle:
1. Dong Jun Lee (S. Korea)
2. H. Brugsmans (Neth)
3. Patrice Remark (Ivory Coast)
   Luigi D'Oriano (Italy)

Welter:
1. Yilmaz Helvacioglu (Turkey)
2. Lawrence Lindsay (GRB)
3. Kwang Keun Choi (S. Korea)
   Harold Schrmann (FRG)

Light:
1. Jae Ku Han (S. Korea)
2. Navarrete (Spain)
3. Della Negra (France)
   Po Nhu Ly (Austral)

Feather:
1. Jae Bong Lee (S. Korea)
2. Thomas Fabula (FRG)

3. Ahmet Ercan (Turkey)
   Gustavo Sanciprian (Mex)

Bantam:
1. Hong Sik Han (S. Korea)
2. Luis Torner (Spain)
3. Nadar Khodamoradi (Iran)
   Geremia DiConstanzo (Italy)

Fly:
1. Jeong Ho Ko (S. Korea)
2. Turgut Ucan (Turkey)
3. Javier Benito (Spain)
   Guiseppe Flotti (Italy)

Fin:
1. Kwang Yeon Wang (S. Korea)
2. Cesar Rodriquez (Mex)
3. Chan Ok Choi (FRG)
   Emilio Azofra (Spain)

Women (Demonstration Tournament)

Heavy:
1. Ute Guter (FRG)
2. Lynette Love (USA)
3. Else Marie Olsen (Den)

Middle:
1. Petra Urban (FRG)
2. A. Smeets (Neth)
3. Sharon Jewell (USA)

Welter:
1. Savine Hunkel (FRG)
2. Lene Lauridsen (Den)
3. Chiou Tzs Ru (Chin. Taipei)

Light:
1. Dorothea Kapkowski (FRG)
2. A. Hubers van Assenraad (Neth)
3. Valerie Long (USA)
   Helle Petermann (Den)

Feather:
1. Cheng Chun Feng (Chin. Taipei)
2. Susan Greaves (GRB)
3. Marion Gal (FRG)
   J. Loots (Neth)

Bantam:
1. Antonella LaPietra (Italy)
2. A. van de Pas (Neth)
3. Bettina Engelkin (FRG)

Fly:
1. Claudia Vleg (FRG)
2. Luisa Domingo (Italy)

Fin:
1. Emilia Guerra (Italy)

5TH WORLD TAEKWON-DO CHAMPIONSHIPS

Date: February 24–27, 1981.
Site: Coliseo Cerrado, Guayaquil, Ecuador.
Participants: 50 countries.
Medal standing unavailable.

Fighting

Men

Heavy:
1. Dirk Jung (FRG)
2. Kim Royce (USA)
3. Rafael Devesa (Spain)
   Dario Scalella (Italy)

Light Heavy:
1. Yong Seong Ha (S. Korea)
2. Medhat Mansy Fahim (Egypt)
3. B. O. Luttik Huis (Neth)
   Ireno Fargas (Spain)

Middle:
1. Sang Cheon Kim (S. Korea)
2. Rashid Hassan (Bahrain)
3. Javier Mayen Mena (Mexico)
   Earl Taylor (USA)

Light Middle:
1. Kuk Hyeon Jeong (S. Korea)
2. Duvan Canga (Ecuador)
3. A. Garrido (Spain)
   Helmut Gartner (FRG)

Welter:
1. Cheon Jae Park (S. Korea)
2. Oscar Mendiola Cruz (Mexico)
3. Jose Alonso (Spain)
   Lindsay Lawrence (GRB)

Light:
1. Oh Seong Park (S. Korea)
2. Juan Rosales (Spain)
3. Alfonso Qahhaar (USA)
   Bouedo (France)

Feather:
1. Myeong Sam Jang (S. Korea)
2. Ignacio F. Blanco A. (Mexico)
3. Raffaele Marchione (Italy)
   Kao-Ming Lu (Chinese Taipei)

Bantam:
1. Jong Ki Kim (S. Korea)
2. Jesus Benito (Spain)
3. J. DeFretes (Neth)
   Chung Sik Choi (USA)

Fly:
1. Woong Hwan Jeon (S. Korea)
2. Chen Chia Su (Chinese Taipei)
3. Ertugrul Turgay (FRG)
   Fernando Celada Cruz (Mexico)

Fin:
1. Jose Cedeno (Ecuador)
2. Cesar Rodriguez Luna (Mexico)
3. Dae Sung Lee (USA)
   Emilio Azofra (Spain)

4TH WTF WORLD TAEKWON-DO CHAMPIONSHIPS

Date: October 26–28, 1979.
Site: Sindelfingen Sports Hall, Stuttgart, West Germany.
Participants: 52 countries.

Overall Medal Standing

1. South Korea
2. Mexico
3. West Germany (FRG)
4. Netherlands
5. United States
6. Spain
7. England
8. Australia
   Ivory Coast
9. Morocco

Fighting

Men

Heavy:
1. Sjaf Vos (Neth)
2. Thomas Seabourne (USA)
3. Keith Whittemore (Austral)
   Carlos Obregon (Mexico)

Light Heavy:
1. Chan Chung (S. Korea)
2. E. Nefedow (FRG)
3. Scott Rohr (USA)
   Abdoulaye Cisse (Ivory Coast)

Middle:
1. San Chun Kim (S. Korea)
2. R. Schultz (FRG)
3. Byl Be Yao (Ivory Coast)
   John Holloway (USA)

Light Middle:
1. Rainer Muller (FRG)
2. Guillermo Aragonez (Mexico)
3. Chung Ho Park (S. Korea)
   Hans Brugmans (Neth)

Welter:
1. Oscar Mendiola (Mexico)
2. Lindsay Lawrence (GRB)
3. H. Garthner (FRG)
   Moo Chun Kim (S. Korea)

Light:
1. Oh Sung Park (S. Korea)
2. Greg Fears (USA)
3. Henk Horsten (Neth)
   Hubert Leuchter (FRG)

Feather:
1. Dai Taik Yim (S. Korea)
2. Reynaldo Salazar (Mexico)
3. B. Barth (FRG)
   Martin Hall (Austral)

Bantam:
1. Chong Ki Kim (S. Korea)
2. Pablio Arismendi (Mexico)
3. Chung Shik Choi (USA)
   D. Veljovic (FRG)

Fly:
1. Ki Mo Yang (S. Korea)
2. Jesus Benito (Spain)
3. Ramiro Guzman (Mexico)
   Bachir (Morocco)

Fin:
1. Seung Kyung Lee (S. Korea)
2. Jaime de Pablos (Mexico)
3. Dae Sung Lee (USA)
   Emilio Azofra (Spain)

3RD WTF WORLD TAEKWON-DO CHAMPIONSHIPS

Date: September 15–17, 1977.
Site: Amphitheater, Chicago,
   Illinois.
Producer: Kyung S. Shin.
Participants: 37 countries.

Overall Medal Standing
1. South Korea
2. Chinese Taipei
3. United States
4. Mexico
5. Ivory Coast
6. Ecuador
7. West Germany (FRG)
8. Spain
9. Netherlands

Fighting
Men

Heavy:
1. Shik Ahn Jang (S. Korea)
2. Lin Ying Peng (Chin. Taipei)
3. Dirk Jung (FRG)
   John Holloway (USA)

Middle:
1. Hur Song (S. Korea)
2. James Kirby (USA)
3. M. Salcedo (Spain)
   Carlos Obregon (Mexico)

Welter:
1. Hap Yu Yong (S. Korea)
2. Theophile Dossou (Ivory Coast)
3. Manuel Jurado (Mexico)
   Rainer Muller (FRG)

Light:
1. Ming Der Hwang (Chin. Taipei)
2. Jae Chun Choi (S. Korea)
3. Ernie Reyes, Sr. (USA)
   Eduardo Merchair (Spain)

Feather:
1. Ho Park Chung (S. Korea)
2. Greg Fears (USA)
3. P. Salm (Neth)
   Fredirec Kouassi (Ivory Coast)

Bantam:
1. Ki Kim Chong (S. Korea)
2. H. Shing (Chin. Taipei)
3. H. Stoppe (FRG)
   R. Salzar (Mexico)

Fly:
1. Kwang Ha Suk (S. Korea)
2. Jorge Ramirez (Ecuador)
3. Moritz von Macher (Mexico)
   Francisco Garcia (Spain)

Fin:
1. Ki Yul Song (S. Korea)
2. Jaime de Pablos (Mexico)
3. Jiom Shi Sheu (Chin. Taipei)
   Ertugrul Turgay (FRG)

2ND WTF WORLD TAEKWON-DO CHAMPIONSHIPS

Date: August 28–31, 1975.
Site: Kukkiwon and Jangchoong
   Gym, Seoul, Korea.
Participants: 30 countries.

Overall Medal Standing
1. South Korea
2. Chinese Taipei
3. Mexico
4. West Germany (FRG)
5. Australia
6. Guam
7. Ivory Coast
8. United States

Fighting
Men

Heavy:
1. Jeong Do Choi (S. Korea)
2. Lutecken Meincif (FRG)
3. Lim Ying Teng (Chin. Taipei)
   Carl Pluekham (Austral)

Middle:
1. Young Kwan Yang (S. Korea)
2. Steve Pound (Guam)
3. Aleiandro Zumibado (Costa
   Rica)
   Ksiang Hsing Chang (Chin.
   Taipei)

Welter:
1. Hur Song (S. Korea)
2. Ping Hui Liang (Chin. Taipei)
3. A.F. Odut (Uganda)
   The Phile Dossou (Ivory Coast)

Light:
1. Young Hab You (S. Korea)
2. Michael Adey (Austral)
3. Tieh Cheng Wang (Chin. Taipei)
   Emmanuel Paman (Ivory Coast)

Feather:
1. Gyeo Sung Lee (S. Korea)
2. Wolfgang Dahmen (FRG)
3. Martin Hall (Austral)
   Reya Arab (Iran)

Bantam:
1. Tae Whan Son (S. Korea)
2. Ramiro Guzman (Mexico)
3. Dennis Robinson (USA)
   Hubert Leuchter (FRG)

Fly:
1. You Keum Han (S. Korea)
2. Chin Chien Liu (Chin. Taipei)
3. Jaime Martin (Phil)
   Moritz von Macher (Mexico)

Fin:
1. Yong Soo Whang (S. Korea)
2. Jaime de Pablos (Mexico)

3. Ching Wen Liu (Chin. Taipei)
   Hidesi Yamane (Japan)

1ST WTF WORLD TAEKWON-DO CHAMPIONSHIPS

Date: May 25–27, 1973.
Site: Kukkiwon, Seoul, Korea.
Producer: WTF.
Participants: 18 countries.
Spectators: 4,500.

Overall Team Standing
1. South Korea
2. United States
3. Chinese Taipei
4. Mexico

Fighting

Men

Teams:
1. South Korea
2. United States
3. Chinese Taipei
4. Mexico

Heavy:
1. Jeong Tae Kim (S. Korea)
2. Mike Warren (USA)
3. Albert Cheeks (USA)
   Raimond (USA)

Light:
1. Ki Hyung Lee (S. Korea)
2. Chabero (FRG)
3. Joe Hayes (USA)
   George Karrenberg (FRG)

EUROPEAN TAEKWON-DO FEDERATION (ETF) EUROPEAN CHAMPIONSHIP RESULTS (1976–92)

9TH WTF EUROPEAN TAEKWON-DO CHAMPIONSHIPS

Date: May 1992.
Site: Valencia, Spain.
Sanctioned by: European Taekwon-do Union.

Fighting

Men:
Heavy (+83 kg):
1. Oliver Schawe (Germany)
2. Jose Luis Alvarez (Spain)
3. Cezmi Zizilay (Turkey)

Middle (−83 kg):
1. Mickael Melloul (France)
2. Ivan Brjlevic (Sweden)
3. Markus Nitschke (Germany)
   Jos Bouwhuis (Neth)

Welter (−76 kg):
1. Marcello Pezzolla (Italy)
2. Antonio Perez (Spain)
3. Eric Halejcio (France)
   Sten Knuth (Denmark)

Light (−70 kg):
1. Jose Santolaria (Spain)
2. Mustafa Elmali (Turkey)
3. Erkan Ozkuru (Germany)
   John Kelly (GRB)

Feather (−64 kg):
1. Musa Cicek (Germany)
2. Eknem Boyali (Turkey)
3. Youssef Lharraki (Denmark)
   ?

Bantam (−58 kg):
1. Josef Salim (Denmark)
2. Kader Yagiz (Turkey)
3. Angel Alonso (Spain)
   Leonardo Glasnovic (Sweden)

Fly (−54 kg):
1. Gabriel Esparza (Spain)
2. Arbor Haider (Denmark)
3. Marc Wennamann (Germany)
   Sedat Bekdemir (Turkey)

Fin (−50 kg):
1. Gergely Salim (Denmark)
2. Harem Ates (Turkey)
3. ?
   ?

Women

Heavy (+70 kg):
1. Sandra Martin (Spain)
2. Abbe Kiurik (Turkey)
3. ?
   ?

Middle (−70 kg):
1. Coral Bisteur (Spain)

2. Anke Girg (Germany)
3. ?
   ?

Welter (−65 kg):
1. Sonny Seidel (Germany)
2. Drosidou Evmorfia (Greece)
3. Brigitte Geffroy (France)
   Hellen Jakobsen (Denmark)

Light (−60 kg):
1. Patricia Reynois (France)
2. Minouschka Thielman (Neth)
3. Judit Pirchmoser (Austria)
   Karin Schwarz (Denmark)

Feather (−55 kg):
1. Nuray Deliktas (Turkey)
2. Josefina Lopez (Spain)
3. Marian Engrich (Hungary)
   Stephanie Dhaeye (France)

Bantam (−51 kg):
1. Rosario Solis (Spain)
2. Doudo Sahin (Turkey)
3. Kattrin Vetter (Germany)
   Trine Nielsen (Denmark)

Fly (−47 kg):
1. Elisabet Delgado (Spain)
2. Anzu Tan (Turkey)
3. Christelle Hamon (France)
   ?

Fin (−43 kg):
1. Gulmun Yerlisu (Turkey)
2. Helle Panzieri (Denmark)
3. ?
   ?

8TH WTF EUROPEAN TAEKWON-DO CHAMPIONSHIPS

Date: 1990.
Site: Copenhagen, Denmark.
Producer: ?
Sanctioned by: European Taekwon-do Union.

7TH WTF EUROPEAN TAEKWON-DO CHAMPIONSHIPS

Date: May 26–29, 1988.
Site: Ataturk Spor Salonu, Ankara, Turkey.
Sanctioned by: European Taekwon-do Union.
Participants: 265 competitors from 19 countries.

Fighting

Men:

Heavy:
1. Tonny Sorensen (Denmark)
2. Ali Sahin (Turkey)
3. Jose Alvarez (Spain)
   Henk Meijer (Neth)

Middle:
1. Markus Woznicki (FRG)
2. Metin Sahin (Turkey)
3. Miguel Jordan (Spain)
   Jarl Kaila (Finland)

Welter:
1. Osman Ozsoy (Turkey)
2. Juan Wright (Spain)
3. Robert Tomasevic (Yugo)
   Marcello Pezzolla (Italy)

Light:
1. Nusret Ramazanoglu (Turkey)
2. Jose Elez (Spain)
3. Ruben Thijs (Neth)
   Markku Parviainen (Finland)

Feather:
1. Jesus Tortosa (Spain)
2. Cengiz Yagiz (Turkey)
3. Thomas Filyo (Denmark)
   Hubert Sinegre (France)

Bantam:
1. Jose Sanabria (Spain)
2. Damaso Nuno (Sui)
3. Christian Herberth (FRG)
   Sakir Bezci (Turkey)

Fly:
1. Geremia DiCostanza (Italy)
2. Reinhard Langer (FRG)
3. Josef Salim (Denmark)
   Thomas Mayr (Austria)

Fin:
1. Harun Ates (Turkey)
2. Vickey Rumeon (Neth)
3. Dario Manca (Italy)
   Oscar Blanco (Spain)

Women

Heavy:
1. Anne-Mieke Buijs (Neth)
2. Mine Ardinc (Turkey)
3. Ute Guster (FRG)
   —

Middle:
1. Mandy de Jongh (Neth)
2. Elena Navaz (Turkey)

3. Seyda Serefoglu (Turkey)
   Michaela Huber (Austria)

Welter:
1. Coral Bistuer (Spain)
2. Sonny Seidel (FRG)
3. Petra Adler (Sui)
   Sabina Lucina (Denmark)

Light:
1. Sibel Dincer (Turkey)
2. Jolanda van Duren (Neth)
3. Karin Schwartz (Denmark)
   Juana Usurbil (Spain)

Feather:
1. Zuleyha Tan (Turkey)
2. Kerstin Aaslepp (FRG)
3. Anne-M. Christensen (Denmark)
   Amparo Dols (Spain)

Bantam:
1. Sultan Demir (Turkey)
2. Roberta Parisella (Italy)
3. Fatma Kayadelen (FRG)
   Josefina Lopez (Spain)

Fly:
1. Piera Muggiri (Italy)
2. Anita van de Pas (Neth)
3. Regina Singer (Austria)
   Bettina Engelking (FRG)

Fin:
1. Rosa Moreno (Spain)
2. Emine Guler (Turkey)
3. Charlotte Konig (FRG)
   Sonia Calvano (Italy)

6TH WTF EUROPEAN TAEKWON-DO CHAMPIONSHIPS

Date: October 3–5, 1986.
Site: WM Hall, Seefeld, Austria.
Sanctioned by: European Taekwon-do Union.
Participants: 313 competitors from 19 countries.

Overall Medal Standing

1. West Germany
2. Turkey
3. Netherlands
4. Spain
5. Denmark
6. France
7. Italy
8. Austria
9. Yugoslavia
10. Finland

Fighting

Men

Team:
1. West Germany
2. Denmark
3. Turkey

+83 kg:
1. Michael Arndt (FRG)
2. Tonny Sorensen (Den)
3. Ali Sahin (Turkey)
   Kimmo Tirkkonen (Fin)

−83 kg:
1. Metin Sahin (Turkey)
2. Martin Bernhofer (FRG)
3. Erich Zaller (Austria)
   Francesco Genetile (Italy)

−76 kg:
1. Helmuth Kock (Austria)
2. Rob. Beckenbauer (FRG)
3. Luigi DiOriano (Italy)
   Christ. Sawyer (GRB)

−70 kg:
1. R. Thijs (Neth)
2. Ahmet Ercan (Turkey)
3. Georg Streif (FRG)
   Pietro Carricri (Italy)

−64 kg:
1. Frank Cribaillet (France)
2. Andreas Holflehner (Austria)
3. Cengiz Yagiz (Turkey)
   Lucio Cuozzo (Italy)

−58 kg:
1. Ole Nielsen (Den)
2. Sakir Bezcir (Turkey)
3. Eduardo Rodriguez (Spain)
   E. Goewie (Neth)

−54 kg:
1. Josef Salim (Den)
2. Turgut Ucan (Turkey)
3. Jose Guerra (Spain)
   Geremia DiCostanza (Italy)

−50 kg:
1. Chan-Ok Choi (FRG)
2. Harun Ates (Turkey)
3. Dario Manca (Italy)
   Jan Hansen (Den)

Women

Team:
1. Netherlands
2. Turkey
3. West Germany

+70 kg:
1. A. Buys (Neth)
2. Ute Guster (FRG)
3. Christine Six (Austria)
   Mia Karunen (Finland)

−70 kg:
1. Mandy De Jogh (Neth)
2. Angelika Biegger (FRG)
3. Michaela Huber (Austria)
   Fatima Mir (Spain)

−65 kg:
1. Coral Bistuer
2. Sema Kaya (Turkey)
3. A. Reniers (Neth)
   Bente Mathiesen (Den)

−60 kg:
1. Brigitte Evano (France)
2. Maria Horman (FRG)
3. Elena Benitez (Spain)
   Y. Klaver (Neth)

−55 kg:
1. Zulyma Tan (Turkey)
2. Rocio Valverde (Spain)
3. Anna Ciampaglia (Italy)
   Anne Christensen (Den)

−51 kg:
1. Marion Gal (FRG)
2. Roberta Parisella (Italy)
3. Veronika Six (Austria)
   Rafaela Velasco (Spain)

−47 kg:
1. Anita Van de Pas (Neth)
2. Bettina Engelking (FRG)
3. Aytul Ucan (Turkey)
   Regina Singer (Austria)

−43 kg:
1. Nejla Demirel (Turkey)
2. Maria Moreno (Spain)
3. G. Aidelsburger (FRG)
   Sonja Galvano (Italy)

Juniors

Team:
1. West Germany
2. Turkey
3. Italy

+76 kg:
1. Josef Strobl (FRG)
2. Carlo Guadalup (Italy)
3. Francisco Franco (Spain)
   Viktor Romancuk (Yugo)

−76 kg:
1. Dirk Nadolny (FRG)
2. Reza Iran-Nejad (Austria)
3. Ibrahim Ozturk (Turkey)
   Jorge Lago (Spain)

−70 kg:
1. Thomas Bollin (FRG)
2. Luigi Masiello (Italy)
3. G. Josefzoon (Neth)
   Anton Drmic (Yugo)

−64 kg:
1. Fernandez Santiago (Spain)
2. Mustafa Elmali (Turkey)
3. Marc Pisane (Belgium)
   Hubert Sinegre (France)

−58 kg:
1. Sinan Gonzelrazi (Turkey)
2. Domenico D'Akuse (Italy)
3. Carlos Gomez (Spain)
   Michael Haus (FRG)

−54 kg:
1. Andreas Platz (FRG)
2. M. Rijvers (Neth)
3. Mario Hunjak (Yugo)
   Luca Bertone (Italy)

−50 kg:
1. Ibrahim Ipek (Turkey)
2. P. Meels (Neth)
3. Angelo Casaburi (Italy)
   Erci Perez (France)

−45 kg:
1. Luigi Sarmataro (Italy)
2. Jesus Balmonte (Spain)
3. Frank Pfeiffer (Austria)
   Dirk Grasler (FRG)

5TH WTF EUROPEAN TAEKWON-DO CHAMPIONSHIPS

Date: October 26–28, 1984.
Site: Hans-Martin-Schleyer-Halle, Stuttgart, West Germany.
Producer: European Taekwon-do Union.
Organizer: Deutsche Taekwon-do Union.
Medal standing unavailable.

Fighting
Men
Heavy:
1. Anton Ginhart (FRG)

2. Alain Molle (France)
3. K. Tirkkonen (Finland)
   F. Stollberger (Austria)

Light Heavy:
1. Eugen Nefedow (FRG)
2. Jens Stephansen (Denmark)
3. C. Montjean (France)
   Medona (Spain)

Middle:
1. Richard Schulz (FRG)
2. Metin Sahin (Turkey)
3. Angel Donadei (France)
   R. Tomasevic (Yugo)

Light Middle:
1. A. Scheffler (FRG)
2. Anton Maras (Yugo)
3. P. Madsen (Denmark)
   Luigi D'Oriano (Italy)

Welter:
1. R. Thijs (Neth)
2. N. Ramazanoglu (Turkey)
3. Peter Ebenfeldt (Sweden)
   N. Toskovic (Yugo)

Light:
1. Lucio Cuozza (Italy)
2. Thomas (France)
3. Navarette (Spain)
   Daniel Stoll (Swiss)

Feather:
1. R. Marchione (Italy)
2. Erik Nissen (Denmark)
3. Ahmet Ercan (Turkey)
   Nuno Damaso (Swiss)

Bantam:
1. Geremia DiCostanza (Italy)
2. Yagiz Cengiz (Turkey)
3. Benito (Spain)
   Baker (GRB)

Fly:
1. Reinhard Langer (FRG)
2. Rumeon (Belgium)
3. Turgut Ucan (Turkey)
   Aldo Codazzo (Italy)

Fin:
1. Halit Avci (Turkey)
2. Chan Choi (FRG)
3. Trabazos (Spain)
   deFretes (Neth)

4TH WTF EUROPEAN TAEKWON-DO CHAMPIONSHIPS

Date: September 23–26, 1982.
Site: Rome, Italy.
Sanctioned by: European Taekwon-do Union.

Overall Medal Standing

1. West Germany
2. Spain
3. Italy
4. Netherlands
5. Turkey
6. Denmark
7. France
8. United Kingdom
9. Belgium
10. Greece
    Norway

Fighting

(Only First-Place Winners Available)

Heavy:
1. H. Meijer (Neth)

Light Heavy:
1. Ireno Fargas (Spain)

Middle:
1. Richard Schulz (FRG)

Light Middle:
1. H. Brugmans (Neth)

Welter:
1. R. Thijs (Neth)

Light:
1. Karl Wohlfahrt (FRG)

Feather:
1. Thomas Fabula (FRG)

Bantam:
1. Geremia DiCostanzo (Italy)

Fly:
1. Reinhard Langer (FRG)

Fin:
1. Emilio Azofra (Spain)

Women

Heavy:
1. Else Marie Olsen (Denmark)

Middle:
1. Anita Sanita (Italy)

Welter:
1. Coval Vistuer (Spain)

Light:
1. Brigitte Evanno (France)

Feather:
1. Nurten Yalcinkaya (Turkey)

Bantam:
1. Ilona Ersinger (FRG)

Fly:
1. Yerlisu Tennur (Turkey)

Fin:
1. Maria Jose Diaz (Spain)

Youth

Welter:
1. J.C. Costa (Spain)

Light:
1. Lucio Cuozzo (Italy)

Feather:
1. Jesus Tortosa (Spain)

Bantam:
1. Franko Ernsten (FRG)

Fly:
1. Achille Caruso (Italy)

Fin:
1. Frank Spieker (FRG)

3RD WTF EUROPEAN TAEKWON-DO CHAMPIONSHIPS

Date: October 14–17, 1980.
Site: Copenhagen, Denmark.
Sanctioned by: European Taekwon-do Union.
Medal standing unavailable.

Fighting

Men

Heavy:
1. M. Arndt (FRG)
2. H. Prijs (Neth)
3. F. Senen (Spain)
    M. Corsaro (Italy)

Light Heavy:
1. D. Jung (FRG)
2. B.O. Luttik Huis (Neth)
3. Walter Cacciatore (Italy)
    Rafael Devesa (Spain)

Middle:
1. Richard Schulz (FRG)
2. John Pedersen (Denmark)

3. Stanzack (France)
    Ireno Fargas (Spain)

Light Middle:
1. Christopher Sawyer (GRB)
2. Per H. Madsen
3. H. Spierings
    Jose Ma Elez (Spain)

Welter:
1. Lindsay Lawrence (GRB)
2. A. Yilmaz (Turkey)
3. R. Thijs (Neth)
    Kent Jakobsen (Denmark)

Light:
1. H. Horsten (Neth)
2. Daniel Pirchmoser (Austria)
3. Antonio Caldora (Italy)
    ?

Feather:
1. Raffaele Marchione (Italy)
2. C. Nakel (Denmark)
3. A.V. Esch (Neth)
    A. Vieches (Spain)

Bantam:
1. Geremia DiCostanzo (Italy)
2. Jesus Benito (Spain)
3. Christian Aubert (Belgium)
    M. Przcybilla (FRG)

Fly:
1. K.S.R. Wong Fat (Neth)
2. John Villy Hansen (Denmark)
3. A. Straube (FRG)
    A. Barbatol (Italy)

Fin:
1. Reinhard Langer (FRG)
2. Roberto Pettineo (Italy)
3. Emilio Azofra (Spain)
    ?

Women

Heavy:
1. S. Pool (Neth)
2. Anna Costa (Italy)
3. Jutta Gauss (FRG)
    ?

Middle:
1. Sivia Winkelmann (FRG)
2. Anita Sanma (Italy)
3. Helle Peterman (Denmark)
4. Linda Michielsen (Belgium)

Welter:
1. Sabine Hunkel (FRG)
2. J. Basten-Crapels (Neth)

3. Filomena LaMarca (Italy)
Gerda Hendrix (Belgium)

Light:
1. Dorothea Kapowski (FRG)
2. Mirabella Pascaline (Italy)
3. Lene Lauridsen (Denmark)
?

Feather:
1. Elvira Trovato (Italy)
2. Ursula Mach (FRG)
3. J. Kottelaar (Neth)
Una Petersen (Denmark)

Bantam:
1. Antonietta LaPietra (Italy)
2. Marion Gal (FRG)
3. ?
?

Fly:
1. Laila Jensen (Denmark)
2. Chiara Mastroianni (Italy)
3. ?
?

2ND WTF EUROPEAN TAEKWON-DO CHAMPIONSHIPS

Date: October 20–22, 1978.
Site: Munich, West Germany.
Sanctioned by: European Taekwon-do Union.
Participants: 14 countries.

Note: In the official results published in the World Taekwon-do Federation's publications, the results for this event are a duplication of the same results for the 3rd European Taekwon-do Championships. Consequently, these results have been omitted until the confusion is eliminated.

1ST WTF EUROPEAN TAEKWON-DO CHAMPIONSHIPS

Date: May 22–23, 1976.
Site: Barcelona, Spain.
Sanctioned by: European Taekwon-do Union.
Medal standing unavailable.

Fighting

Men

Heavy:
1. Jose Izquierdo (Spain)

2. A. Vamemerik (Neth)
3. Reza Zademonamed (Austria)
Francisco Vallecillo (Spain)

Middle:
1. M. Dona (Neth)
2. Wolfgang Schindl (Austria)
3. Ben V.D. Wal (Neth)
Pedro Secorum (Spain)

Welter:
1. W. Vamemerik (Neth)
2. Antonio Vicent (Spain)
3. Josef Steinberger (FRG)
Francesco Sanila (Italy)

Light:
1. Lindsay Lawrence (GRB)
2. J.U. Wanrooy (Neth)
3. Eric Gancylus (France)
Hubert Lanchter (FRG)

Feather:
1. Christian Stizysch (FRG)
2. Hauswald (Belgium)
3. Hugo Villamide (Spain)
Wolfgang Dahman (FRG)

Bantam:
1. Josef Ascanto (FRG)
2. Kaya Kirac (Turkey)
3. Eugenio Castro (Spain)
Helmut Schneider (FRG)

Fly:
1. Murat Gollo (Turkey)
2. Fernando Vadillo (Spain)
3. Eduardo Merchan (Spain)
Ost Irwald Gisbert (FRG)

Fin:
1. Eddi Klimt (FRG)
2. Osman Kara (Turkey)
3. Jesus Martin (Spain)
Domingo Martinez (Spain)

UNITED STATES TAEKWON-DO UNION (USTU) AND AMATEUR ATHLETIC UNION (AAU) NATIONAL CHAMPIONSHIPS (1975–93)

19TH USTU NATIONAL TAEKWON-DO CHAMPIONSHIPS

Date: May 27–29, 1993.
Site: Civic Center, St. Paul, Minnesota.

Producer: Kun Yoo Park.
Sanctioned by: United States Taekwon-do Union.
Participants: Nearly 1,000 competitors.

Fighting

Men

Heavy:
1. George Weissfisch
2. Kwame Adwere-Boamah
3. Shelbert Creech
Barry Partridge

Middle:
1. Panagiotis Bardatsos
2. Roland Ferrer
3. Glenn Warren
James Choi

Welter:
1. Garth Cooley
2. Adalberto Arajo
3. Javier Sanches
Kenneth Hance

Light:
1. Nicholas Terstenjak
2. Emory Rowe
3. George Bell
Gordon White

Feather:
1. Dong Lee
2. Sam Visconti
3. David Kang
David Johnson

Bantam:
1. Shawn Evenson
2. Robert Leach
3. Steve Lee
Clayton Barber

Fly:
1. Angel Aranzamendi
2. Justin Poos
3. Criag DeRosa
Ho Yong Lee

Fin:
1. Lai Vo
2. Logan Matsuoka
3. Daniel Kim
David Montalvo

Women

Heavy:
1. Christina Bayley

2. Jean Podskalan
3. Michelle Hogan
   Gwenevere Teague

Middle:
1. Rhonda Juarez
2. Yvonne Kerno
3. Barbara Kunkel
   Laurie Blum

Welter:
1. Regina Pluth
2. Rachael Ridenour
3. Lisa Thrower
   Laurinda Tysor

Light:
1. Gail Hinshaw-Wright
2. Simona Hradil
3. Kristin Ehrmantraut
   Elizabeth Evans

Feather:
1. Janet Yi
2. Kimberly Jo Wakefield
3. Darcy Dekriek
   Tiffany Norris

Bantam:
1. Rachel Moenich
2. Yolanda Bennett
3. Jennifer Mohamed
   Tammy Stamps

Fly:
1. Sharon Hough
2. Karen Hough
3. Sayuri Kelly
   Justina Wu

Fin:
1. Akiko Catacutan
2. Stephanie Park
3. Vicki Slane

Male Competitor of the Year

Garth Cooley

Female Competitor of the Year

Christine Bayley

Coach of the Year

Jay Warwick

18TH USTU NATIONAL TAEKWON-DO CHAMPIONSHIPS

Date: 1992.

17TH USTU NATIONAL TAEKWON-DO CHAMPIONSHIPS

Date: 1991.

16TH USTU NATIONAL TAEKWON-DO CHAMPIONSHIPS

Date: May 24–26, 1990.
Site: Dane County Coliseum,
   Madison, Wisconsin.
Producer: Dr. Paik.

Note: Although the results were unavailable, this event featured three major innovations: divisions for Executive Seniors (35 years old and over), and competitions in Kyukpa ("breaking") and Creative Poomse ("forms").

Fighting

Men

Heavy:
1. Paris Amani
2. Dimitri Diatchenko

Middle:
1. Doyen Wilson

Welter:
1. Kun Tae Kim

Light:
1. Doug Baker
2. Reginald Hughes

Feather:
1. Clayton Barber

Bantam:
1. Jose Dilag

Fly:
1. Sam Pejo

Fin:
1. Juan Moreno

Women

Heavy:
1. Kathy Wagner

Middle:
1. Sharon Jewell
2. Danielle Laney

Welter:
1. Arlene Limas

Light:
1. Kristi Koch

Feather:
1. Mary Horvith

Bantam:
1. Diane Murray

Fly:
1. Ginean Hatter

Fin:
1. Shawna Larson

Poomse

Women's Heavy Creative:

Arlene Limas

15TH USTU NATIONAL TAEKWON-DO CHAMPIONSHIPS

Date: 1989.
Site: ?
Producer: ?
Sanctioned by: United States
   Taekwon-do Union.

Fighting

Men

Heavy:
1. Scott Miranti
2. Greg Tubbs
3. George Weissfisch
   Emmett Tademy

Middle:
1. Rory Vierra
2. Herb Perez
3. Mike Pejo
   Victor Clark

Welter:
1. Greg Baker
2. ?
3. Brian Laney
   ?

Light:
1. Garth Cooley
2. Tim Connolly
3. Rich Ahn
   Bobby Clayton

Feather:
1. Clay Barber
2. Sung Kang
3. Heath Watson
   Rodney Stum

Bantam:
1. Yun Won Jung

2. Leon Lynn
3. Donald Jackson
   Chris Berlow

Fly:
1. Luong Pham
2. Hyon Lee
3. Jeff Cofrey
   John Monroe

Fin:
1. Juan Moreno
2. Young Lee
3. Hoang Ly
   Andrew Young

Women
Heavy:
1. Kathy Wagner
2. Cindy Anglemyer
3. Rhonda Juarez
   Gwen Teague

Middle:
1. Lydia Zele
2. Sharon Jewell
3. Diana Mason
   Michelle Smith

Welter:
1. Kristi Koch
2. Teresa Naddour
3. Anita Silsby
   Arlene Limas

Light:
1. Julie Werhnyak
2. Stephanie Magid
3. Angela Wolbert
   Kristin Ehrmantraut

Feather:
1. Kim Dotson
2. Rose Chaplin
3. Mary Horvith
   Ayoka Brown

Bantam:
1. Diane Murray
2. Ani Ahn
3. Tammy Stamps
   Yolanda Bennett

Fly:
1. Mayumi Pejo
2. Terry Poindexter
3. Maria Gonzalez
   Thu Nguyen Smith

Fin:
1. Helen Yee

2. Cheryl Kalanoc
3. Cathy Gravelin
   Bonnie Watts

Forms/Poomse
Men

140.8+ pounds:
1. Kum Tae Kim
2. Jim Bowles
3. Edison Park

−140.8 pounds:
1. Boo Hong Kim
2. Ki Jan Chang
3. Edmond Wiggins

Women

121+ pounds:
1. Amy Simpler
2. Rhonda Juarez
3. Carla Fortney

−121 pounds:
1. Susan Park
2. Josephine Nyland
3. Shawna Larson

14TH USTU NATIONAL TAEKWON-DO CHAMPIONSHIPS
Date: April 14–16, 1988.
Site: James L. Knight Center, Miami, Florida.
Sanctioned by: United States Taekwon-do Union.
Participants: 1,100.

Fighting
Men

Heavy/+83 kg:
1. Jimmy Kim
2. Won Yang
3. Scott Miranti
   Glenn Warren

Middle/−83 kg:
1. Roland Ferrer
2. Joon Yang
3. Na'im Hasan
   Ed Shorter

Welter/−76 kg:
1. Doug Baker
2. Charles Thompson
3. Mike Demkowski
   Eric Hampton

Light/−70 kg:
1. Bobby Clayton
2. Garth Cooley
3. Steve Shinn
   Kareem Jabbar

Feather/−64 kg:
1. Raphael Park
2. Tuoi Nguyen
3. John Kim
   Dong Sun Lee

Bantam/−58 kg:
1. Chris Spence
2. Clay Barbar
3. Britney Combs
   Hee Chan Chung

Fly/−54 kg:
1. Hyon Lee
2. John Monroe
3. Jeffrey Coffey
   Craig DeRosa

Fin/−50 kg:
1. Juan Moreno
2. Robert Leach
3. Chuck Flayler
   Jeff Pinaroc

Women

Heavy/+70 kg:
1. Kathy Wagner
2. Gwen Teague
3. Emma Cottini
   Kelly Schroeder

Middle/−70 kg:
1. Lydia Zele
2. Sharon Jewell
3. Rhonda Juarez
   Diana Mason

Welter/−65 kg:
1. Michele Pellegrini
2. Diane Saiev
3. Susana Mirjanic
   Terri Bolduc

Light/−60 kg:
1. Carolyn Raimondi
2. Dana Hee
3. Gail Hinshaw-Wright
   Anne Louise Long

Feather/−55 kg:
1. Kim Dotson
2. Ayoka Brown
3. Josephine Nyland
   Mai Nguyen

Bantam/−51 kg:
1. Nosrat Elyasai
2. Susan Kim
3. Jennifer Gray
   Heather Byrom

Fly/−47 kg:
1. Ginean Hatter
2. Arabella Naguit
3. Theresa Alvey
   Susan Park

Fin/−43 kg:
1. Helen Yee
2. Cheryl Kalanoc
3. Susan Palmer
   Diana Radakovic

Forms/Poomse

Men
1. Chung Hee Chan
2. Tony Stinson
3. Robert Rhone
   Hyon Lee

Women
1. Susan Park
2. Lisa Kosal
3. Debra Holloway
   Marlo Ruilova

Male Competitor of the Year

Jimmy Kim

Female Competitor of the Year

Kim Dotson

Coach of the Year

Chan-Yong Kim

USTU First President Award

Chris Spence

13TH USTU NATIONAL TAEKWON-DO CHAMPIONSHIPS

Date: April 3–4, 1987.
Site: Anaheim Convention Center
   Arena, Anaheim, California.
Sanctioned by: United States
   Taekwon-do Union.

Fighting

Men

Heavy/+83 kg:
1. Jimmy Kim
2. Scott Miranti

3. Brian Knechtges
   Won Yang

Middle/−83 kg:
1. Herbert Perez
2. Na'im Hasan
3. Stephen Dorhorst
   John Lyman

Welter/−76 kg:
1. Jay Warwick
2. Michael Canda
3. Eric Hampton
   Timothy Thornburg

Light/−70 kg:
1. Greg Baker
2. Stephen Carpenter
3. Brian Parker
   Kazuto Augustus

Feather/−64 kg:
1. Chris Spence
2. Doug Baker
3. Dave Mabiz
   Gerald Winn

Bantam/−58 kg:
1. Han Lee
2. Bob Hong
3. John Beaupre
   Leon Lynn

Fly/−54 kg:
1. Joseph Chang
2. Hyon Lee
3. Paul Lee
   Esmaeil Torabpour

Fin/−50 kg:
1. Dae Sung Lee
2. Robert Leach
3. Juan Moreno
   Thang Vuong

Women

Heavy/+70 kg:
1. Lynette Love
2. Rhonda Juarez
3. Beverly Rios
   Kelly Schroeder

Middle/−70 kg:
1. Michelle Smith
2. Jennifer Laney
3. Ida Church
   Marie Gollin

Welter/−65 kg:
1. Arlene Limas

2. Heather Tallman
3. Alison Henderson
   Sharon Jewell

Light/−60 kg:
1. Leslie Losinger
2. Dana Hee
3. Debbie Pendegraft
   Gail Hinshaw-Wright

Feather/−55 kg:
1. Ann Ryerson
2. Kim Dotson
3. Diane Buhison
   Judith Kilger

Bantam/−51 kg:
1. Debra Holloway
2. Yolanda Bennett
3. Terry Poindexter
   Rochelle Perlysky

Fly/−47 kg:
1. Ginean Hatter
2. Arabella Naguit
3. Theresa Alvey
   Mayumi Pejo

Fin/−43 kg:
1. Cheryl Kalanoc
2. Rachael Licht
3. Sheila Donnelly
   Melissa Gromoll

Forms/Poomse

Men:
1. Dae Sung Lee
2. Hyon Lee
3. Chien Vuong
   John Krizan

Women:
1. Debra Holloway
2. Susan Park
3. Susan Kim
   Rhonda Juarez

Male Competitor of the Year

Chris Spence

Female Competitor of the Year

Leslie Losinger

Ken Min Award

Han Won Lee

Coach of the Year

Hong Kang Kim

12TH USTU NATIONAL TAEKWON-DO CHAMPIONSHIPS

Date: April 4–5, 1986.
Site: Dayton, Ohio.
Sanctioned by: United States
Taekwon-do Union.

Fighting

Men

Heavy:
1. Kim Royce
2. Jimmy Kim
3. Jeffrey Wachter
   Brent Jordheim

Middle:
1. Herb Perez
2. John Lee
3. Douglas Crowder
   Na'im Hasan

Welter:
1. Jay Warwick
2. Patrice Remark
3. Chris Thomburg
   Craig Peeples

Light:
1. Kareem Ali Jabbar
2. Bobby Clayton
3. Greg Baker
   Lawrence Sakies

Feather:
1. Chris Spence
2. Doug Baker
3. Hee Chan Chung
   Darryl Henderson

Bantam:
1. Han Won Lee
2. David Perez
3. Clay Barber
   Rannel Thompson

Fly:
1. Luong Pham
2. Esmaeil Torabpour
3. Jungsik Chang
   Jon Bryant

Fin:
1. Dae Sung Lee
2. Ismael Aponte
3. Sung Yoon Chung
   John Chong

Women

Heavy:
1. Lynette Love
2. Rhonda Juarez
3. Diana Mason
   Kim Ward

Middle:
1. Sharon Jewell
2. Jennifer Laney
3. Cynthia Gaeth
   Michelle Smith

Welter:
1. Coral Bistuer
2. Allison Henderson
3. Heather Tallman
   Diane Shaieb

Light:
1. Leslie Losinger
2. Dana Hee
3. Gail Hinshaw
   Carolyn Raimondi

Feather:
1. Kim Dotson
2. Josephine Nyland
3. Diane Buhisan
   Silvia Jabbar

Bantam:
1. Deborah Holloway
2. Charisse Garwood
3. Joan McLaughlin
   Lisa Gagnon

Fly:
1. Catherine Lee
2. Lori Mong
3. Sandra Meyer
   Mayumi Pejo

Fin:
1. Andree Leveque
2. Rachel Licht
3. Cheryl Kalanoc
   Min Jin Sung

Forms/Poomse

Men:
1. Dae Sung Lee
2. Hyon Kwi Lee
3. Hee Chan Chung
   Myung Chan Kim

Women:
1. Deborah Holloway

2. Joyce Thom
3. Charisse Garwood
   Sandra Meyer

11TH USTU NATIONAL TAEKWON-DO CHAMPIONSHIPS

Date: June 7–8, 1985.
Site: Hartford, Connecticut.
Sanctioned by: United States
Taekwon-do Union.

Fighting

Men

Heavy:
1. Jimmy Kim
2. Christopher Galloway
3. Na'im Hasan

Middle:
1. Douglas Crowder
2. John Lee
3. Herb Perez

Welter:
1. Patrice Remark
2. Jay Warwick
3. Mike Pejo

Light:
1. Christopher Spence
2. Ruben Figueroa
3. Steven Capener

Feather:
1. Greg Baker
2. Darryl Henderson
3. John Min Kim

Bantam:
1. Chung Sik Choi
2. Kil Sop Hong
3. Han Won Lee

Fly:
1. Esmaeil Torapour
2. Sang Hon Cha
3. Jon Drew Bryant

Fin:
1. Dae Sung Lee
2. Lueng Pham
3. Robert Leach

Women

Heavy:
1. Lynette Love

2. Chelle Mebane
3. Rita Winborne

Middle:
1. Sharon Jewell
2. Henrietta Robinson
3. Lynn Ann Malinowski

Welter:
1. Heather Tallman
2. Alison Henderson
3. Linda Kajisa

Light:
1. Shadrene Howard
2. Tamberlain Connelly
3. Gail Hinshaw

Feather:
1. Valerie Long
2. Anne Ryerson
3. Kim Dotson

Bantam:
1. Debra Holloway
2. Laura Bonner
3. Joan McLaughlin

Fly:
1. Catherine Lee
2. Ginean Hatter
3. Andree Leveque

Fin:
1. Cheryl Kalanoc
2. Young Mi Park
3. Tracy Bjomeby

10TH USTU NATIONAL TAEKWON-DO CHAMPIONSHIPS

Date: June 15–17, 1984.
Site: River Grove, Illinois.
Sanctioned by: United States
    Taekwon-do Union.

Fighting

Men

Heavy:
1. Na'im Hasan
2. Christopher Galloway
3. James Thompson

Light Heavy:
1. Philip Samotshozo
2. Il Young Choi
3. John Lee

Middle:
1. Earl Taylor

2. Jay Warwick
3. L. Wayne Jones

Light Middle:
1. Patrice Remark
2. Kareem Ali Jabbar
3. Mark Shuter

Light:
1. Darryl Henderson
2. Oren Gautreaux
3. Daniel Jackson

Feather:
1. Thomas Marshall
2. Gerald Wynn
3. Tony Lewis

Bantam:
1. Moritz von Nacher
2. Han Won Lee
3. Ranell Thompson

Fly:
1. Frederick Lewis
2. Clive Afflick
3. Chung Sik Choi

Fin:
1. Dae Sung Lee
2. Song Hu So
3. Esmaeil Torabpour

Women

Heavy:
1. Lynette Love
2. Chelle Mebane
3. Christine Bair

Middle:
1. Sharon Jewell
2. Lydia Zele
3. Gwen Toney

Light:
1. Leslie Cone
2. Deborah Torregrosa
3. Gail Hinshaw

Feather:
1. Valerie Long
2. Maria Leguel
3. Tamberlain Connelly

Bantam:
1. Anne Ryerson
2. Kim Dotson
3. Carrenia Mathews

Fly:
1. Catherine Lee

2. Barbara Brand
3. Kim Miller

Fin:
1. Cheryl Kalanoc
2. Lori Mong
3. Irene Santiago

Forms/Poomse

Men:
1. Thomas Mitchell
2. Soo Am Cho
3. Dae Sung Lee

Women:
1. Wendy Suddard
2. Letty Reifel
3. Sharon Jewell

9TH USTU NATIONAL TAEKWON-DO CHAMPIONSHIPS

Date: June 9–12, 1983.
Site: Washington, DC.
Sanctioned by: United States
    Taekwon-do Union.

Fighting

Men

Heavy:
1. Christopher Galloway
2. Darryl Smith
3. Sylvester James

Light Heavy:
1. John Lee
2. Sumorry Alpha
3. Scott Miranti

Middle:
1. Jay Warwick
2. Earl Tayler
3. Robert Huskey

Light Middle:
1. John Glee
2. Suk Won Kang
3. Michael Canada

Welter:
1. Young Joon Kong
2. Steven Silz
3. Chris Hawkins

Light:
1. Pablo Arizmendi-Kalb
2. Tony Lewis
3. Michael Choi

Feather:
1. Greg Baker
2. Bobby Hong
3. Alphonso Aguilar

Bantam:
1. Frederick Lewis
2. Han Won Lee
3. Chung Sik Choi

Fly:
1. Wendell Lee
2. Sung Yoon Chong
3. Jamie Hernandez

Fin:
1. Dae Sung Lee
2. My Tan Nguyen
3. ?

Women

Heavy:
1. Lynette Love
2. Chelle Mebane
3. Susan Roth

Middle:
1. Sharon Jewell
2. Lydia Zele
3. Megan Dineen

Welter:
1. Leslie Cone
2. Kimberly Soloman
3. Melinda Bair

Light:
1. Valerie Trott
2. Tamberlain Connelly
3. Roberta Prosser

Feather:
1. Kim Dotson
2. Ayoka Brown
3. Diane Ellis

Bantam:
1. Soretha Eldredge
2. Kim Miller
3. Diana Khabiri

Fly:
1. Cheryl Kalanoc
2. ?
3. ?

8TH USTU NATIONAL TAEKWON-DO CHAMPIONSHIPS

Date: May 15–16, 1982.
Site: University of Michigan, Ann Arbor, Michigan.
Producer: Hwa Chong.
Sanctioned by: United States Taekwon-do Union.

Fighting

Men

Heavy:
1. Kim Royce
2. Christopher Galloway
3. Mike Zebalza

Light Heavy:
1. Scott Rohr
2. Scott Miranti
3. Mat Davis

Middle:
1. Jay Warwick
2. Chris Thornbure
3. John Lee

Light Middle:
1. Chul Kim
2. Kareem Ali Jabbar
3. Tony Pulido

Welter:
1. Alfonso Qahhaar
2. Randy Micheletti
3. Bob Cafarella

Light:
1. Tom Marshall
2. Michael Choi
3. Tony Lewis

Feather:
1. Greg Baker
2. Fred Choy
3. Bob Hong

Bantam:
1. Han Won Lee
2. Terry Lee
3. Joseph Hernandez

Fly:
1. Chris Spense
2. Dale Green
3. Alphonso Ogivlar

Fin:
1. Dae Sung Lee
2. Jamie Hernandez
3. So Sung Hu

Women

Heavy:
1. Lynette Love
2. Georgina Pezzella
3. Joyce Jones

Middle:
1. Rosetta Jahlaar
2. Sharon Jewell
3. Lydia Zele

Welter:
1. Gail Hinslaw
2. Maria Fauser
3. Alison Parker

Light:
1. Kristine Hamilton
2. Carrenia Mathew
3. Tami Cornelly

Feather:
1. Karen Brown
2. Hang Ya Kim
3. Debra Kopp

Bantam:
1. Sunny Graff
2. Barbara Brand
3. Diana Khabiri

Fly:
1. Cheryl Kalanoc
2. Lori Mong
3. Lisa Davy

Forms/Poomse

Men
1. Dae Sung Lee
2. Kwang Yong Lee
3. Doug Quan

Women
1. Kathy Lee
2. Shirley Smiley
3. Angie Miller

Breaking

Men
1. Darryl Smith
2. Doug Quan
3. Norman Salang

Women
1. Hun Ya Kim
2. Gloria DuBissette
3. Janett Weller

Male Competitor of the Year
Chul Kim

Female Competitor of the Year
Lynette Love

Ken Min Award
Scott Rohr

Coach of the Year
Dong Keun Park

7TH USTU NATIONAL TAEKWON-DO CHAMPIONSHIPS

Date: May 2–3, 1981.
Site: Sun Dome, Tampa, Florida.
Producer: Yung Ho Jun.
Sanctioned by: United States
    Taekwon-do Union.

Note: This marked the first year this event was sanctioned by the USTU and not the AAU.

Fighting

Men
Heavy:
1. Kim Royce
2. Robert Connally
3. Thomas Seabourne

Light Heavy:
1. Tom Federle
2. Edward Smith
3. Kenneth Dye

Middle:
1. Earl Taylor
2. Edward Harnen
3. Myung Chan Kim

Light Middle:
1. Chul Kim
2. Kareem Jabbar
3. Daniel Jackson

Welter:
1. Michael O'Malley
2. Randy Micheletti
3. Gerald Wynn

Light:
1. Alfonso Qahhaar
2. Jae Hon Kim
3. Scott Littke

Feather:
1. Marvin McMillion
2. Richard Lee
3. Victor Oritz

Bantam:
1. Chung Sik Choi
2. Greg Baker
3. Joseph Hernandez

Fly:
1. Young Kim
2. Mike Vasquez
3. Dak Sung Lee

Fin:
1. Dae Sung Lee
2. Joe Martin
3. Ricky Garcia

Women
Heavy:
1. Lynette Love
2. Sharon Jewell
3. Jerelyn Taubert

Middle:
1. Jo Ann Hamelin
2. Connie Rice
3. Candie Williams

Welter:
1. Nancy Ferguson
2. Gloria DuBisset
3. Leslie Losinger

Light:
1. Karen Brown
2. Terri Treaster
3. Stacy Jackson

Feather:
1. Deborah Holloway
2. Ayoka Brown
3. Diane Ellis

Bantam:
1. Sunny Graf
2. Dale Jun
3. Mercedes Morales

Fly:
1. Cheryl Kalanoc
2. Helen Yee
3. Lorilyn Mong

Fin:
1. Diana Hill
2. ?
3. ?

Forms/Poomse

Men:
1. Dae Sung Lee
2. Myung Chan Kim
3. Mark Moore

Women:
1. Dale Jun
2. Karen Brown
3. Shelly Smiley

Breaking

Men:
1. Phillip Cunningham
2. Gary Werder
3. Dong Quam

Women:
1. Gloria Dubissette
2. Dale Jun
3. Sharon Jewell

Male Competitor of the Year
Kim Royce

Female Competitor of the Year
Sunny Graf

Ken Min Award
Dae Sung Lee

Coach of the Year
Hwa Chong

6TH AAU NATIONAL TAEKWON-DO CHAMPIONSHIPS

Date: May 3, 1980.
Site: University of California,
    Berkeley, California.
Producer: Ken Min.
Sanctioned by: Amateur Athletic
    Union.
Participants: 1,000+.

Fighting

Men
Heavy:
1. Tom Seabourne
2. Kim Royce
3. Dennis Dallas

Light Heavy:
1. Scott Rohr
2. Earl Taylor
3. Leroy Charbonnet

Middle:
1. Jay Warwick
2. Mike Kim
3. Edward Harner

Light Middle:
1. Michael Canada
2. Kareem Jabbar
3. Donald Cottee

Welter:
1. Mike O'Malley
2. Randy Micheletti
3. Gerald Wynn

Light:
1. Tom Marshall
2. Marc Williams
3. Oren Gautreaux

Feather:
1. Marvin McMillion
2. Victor Oritz
3. Jack Grisius

Bantam:
1. Chungsik Choi
2. Sang Han
3. Fred Choy

Fly:
1. Mike Vasquez
2. Young Kim
3. Joe Hernandez

Fin:
1. Dae Sung Lee
2. My Nguyen
3. James Martin

Women

Heavy:
1. Lynette Love
2. Debbie Pederson
3. Shelley Gehman

Middle:
1. Marcia Hall
2. Rosetta Quahhaar
3. Jeanne Davis

Welter:
1. Monique Heckler
2. Connie Miller
3. Nancy Ferguson

Light:
1. Belinda Davis
2. Jip Brunner
3. Kay Canavino

Feather:
1. Theresa Jun
2. Karen Osborne
3. Sarah Strand

Bantam:
1. Jodene Goldenring
2. ?
3. ?

Fly:
1. Cheryl Kalanoc
2. ?
3. ?

Fin:
1. Dianna Hill
2. ?
3. ?

Male Competitor of the Year
Dae Sung Lee

Female Competitor of the Year
Belinda Davis

Ken Min Award
Michael O'Malley

Coach of the Year
Jung Nam Lee

5TH AAU NATIONAL TAEKWON-DO CHAMPIONSHIPS

Date: June 2–3, 1979.
Site: Dayton Convention Center, Dayton, Ohio.
Producer: Young Chi Kim.
Sanctioned by: Amateur Athletic Union.

Fighting

Men

Heavy:
1. Thomas Seabourne
2. Gerard Robinson
3. Na'im Hasan

Light Heavy:
1. Scott Rohr
2. Neil Singleton
3. William Smith

Middle:
1. John Holloway
2. Joseph Salvino
3. Timothy Dunphy

Light Middle:
1. Frank Calderon
2. James Ridley
3. Roger Gilbreath

Welter:
1. Michael O'Malley
2. Ernest Robinson
3. Kadil Bibbs

Light:
1. Greg Fears
2. Yong Sung Choi
3. Muhammed Abdul Jabar

Feather:
1. Oren Gautreaux
2. Bobby Hong
3. Dennis Robinson

Bantam:
1. Chung Sik Choi
2. Sun Woong Park
3. Ronald Lough

Fly:
1. Michael Vasquez
2. Don Stowers
3. Larry Rogers

Fin:
1. Dae Sung Lee
2. My Tan Nguyen
3. Dayton Pang

Women

Heavy:
1. Lynette Love
2. Debbie Pederson
3. Christine Coleman

Middle:
1. Marcia Hall
2. Marcella Byrd
3. Dawniza Scott

Welter:
1. Melinda Aynes
2. Penny Bero
3. Nancy Johnson

Light:
1. Kathy Jones
2. Jane Freese
3. Belinda Davis

Feather:
1. Ayoka Brown
2. Sharon Tatum
3. Sheila Mullins

Bantam:
1. Sunny Graff
2. Anne Top
3. Beverly Vining

Fly:
1. Brenda Waller
2. Elsie Harrison
3. ?

Fin:
1. Elaine Chung
2. ?
3. ?

Male Competitor of the Year
Michael O'Malley

Female Competitor of the Year
Sunny Graff

Ken Min Award
John Holloway

Coach of the Year
Joon Pyo Choi

4TH AAU NATIONAL TAEKWON-DO CHAMPIONSHIPS

Date: April 6–8, 1978.
Site: Howard University,
    Washington, DC.
Producer: Dong Ja Yang.
Sanctioned by: Amateur Athletic
    Union.

Fighting

Men

Open:
1. Gerald Robbins
2. Ken Nicholson
3. Tony Thompson

Heavy:
1. John Holloway
2. Ken Ferguson
3. Pete Brown

Light Heavy:
1. Leroy Hopkins
2. Ernest McAllister
3. Gordon Graaff

Middle:
1. Larry Nelle
2. Kun Young Lee
3. Peter Paik

Welter:
1. Michael O'Malley
2. Ernie Reyes, Sr.
3. Myung Chan Kim

Light:
1. Greg Fears
2. Muhammed Abdul Jabar
3. William Polk

Feather:
1. Oren Gautreaux

2. Nicholas Fusco
3. Marc Haag

Bantam:
1. William Kim
2. James Boykins
3. Timothy Reddick

Fly:
1. Mike Vasquez
2. Tony Lewis
3. Larry Rodgers

Fin:
1. My Tan Nguyen
2. Don Hardesty
3. Thomas Gonzalez

Women

Open:
1. Darlene Jeffries
2. Cynthia Darling
3. Karen Fergus

Heavy:
1. Christine Coleman
2. Lauren McCrorey
3. ?

Middle:
1. Marcia Hall
2. Angela Townes
3. Terry Wahls

Welter:
1. Thedia Jones
2. Jackie Jones
3. Connie Miller

Light:
1. Kathy Jones
2. Letty Reiffel
3. Myung Paik

Feather:
1. Ayoka Brown
2. Patricia Fraser
3. Vickie Swatford

Bantam:
1. Sunny Graff
2. Amani Jordan
3. Manuela Nitsche

Fly:
1. Brenda Waller
2. ?
3. ?

Fin:
1. Mary Hostetler
2. Elsie Harrison
3. ?

3RD AAU NATIONAL TAEKWON-DO CHAMPIONSHIPS

March 5, 1977.
Site: University of California,
    Berkeley, California.
Producer: Ken Min.
Sanctioned by: Amateur Athletic
    Union.

Fighting

Men

Heavy:
1. Percy Woods
2. Steve Littrell
3. Larry Hampton

Middle:
1. James Kirby
2. Scott Ruhr
3. Marcus Davis

Welter:
1. Asa Knowles
2. Jay Warwick
3. William Scott

Light:
1. Ernie Reyes, Sr.
2. Howard Davis
3. Paul Beauchesne

Feather:
1. Greg Fears
2. Daniel Smith
3. Doug Weaver

Bantam:
1. Oren Gautreaux
2. Sang Chon
3. Mike Hwang

Fly:
1. Michael Vasquez
2. Tae Sung Lee
3. Eric Best

Fin:
1. Daryl O'Neal
2. Peter Lee
3. Gervase Flipping

Women

Heavy:
1. Debbie Sloan
2. Debbie Sharpe
3. Lannea Vonahn

Middle:
1. Patricia Filinick

2. Antonia Ricks
3. Linda Kirk

Welter:
1. Gloria DuBissette
2. Jackie Jones
3. Connie Miller

Light:
1. Debra Hooper
2. Terry Edel
3. Wendy Thompson

Feather:
1. Ayoka Brown
2. Jaymayne Gross
3. ?

Bantam:
1. Donna Stockman
2. Beverly Vining
3. Vickie Swatford

Fly:
1. Laurie Frymine
2. ?
3. ?

2ND AAU NATIONAL TAEKWON-DO CHAMPIONSHIPS

Date: March 28, 1976.
Site: Penn Valley Community College, Kansas City, Missouri.
Producer: Won Suk Kim.
Sanctioned by: Amateur Athletic Union.
Participants: 300+ competitors.

Note: Women's competition was added to this event for the first time.

Fighting

Men

Open:
1. Charles Chandler
2. David Parris
3. Luther Gold

Heavy:
1. John Holloway
2. Tom Seabourne
3. Robert Chaney

Middle:
1. Joseph Salvino

2. Robert Phillips
3. Bobby Smith

Welter:
1. Curtis Airall
2. Anthony Alvarez
3. Joseph Turner

Feather:
1. Howard Davis
2. George Salvino
3. Joel Thone

Bantam:
1. Terry Drennen
2. Daniel Smith
3. Kirby Schnebly

Fly:
1. Yong Woo Choi
2. Clark Murphy
3. Roger Brown

Fin:
1. Oren Gautreaux
2. Richard Smith
3. Mark Hazen

Women

Heavy:
1. Debra Hooper
2. Susan Catallo
3. Beverly Acton

Middle:
1. Cheryl Lowry
2. Lori Arnold
3. Sally Cornelison

Welter:
1. Wendy Thompson
2. Julie Kellogg
3. Deborah Pendleton

Feather:
1. Cheryl Rodgers
2. Jo A. Brennick
3. ?

Bantam:
1. Ayoka Brown
2. Joyce Weddle
3. Alice Yip

Fly:
1. Jean Nelson
2. Jean Kropp
3. ?

Fin:
1. Joan Meyer
2. ?
3. ?

1ST AAU NATIONAL TAEKWON-DO CHAMPIONSHIPS

Date: April 25–26, 1975.
Site: Yale University, New Haven, Connecticut.
Producer: In-Soo Hwang.
Sanctioned by: Amateur Athletic Union.

Fighting

Men

Heavy:
1. Gerald Robbins
2. John Holloway
3. Steven Chambliss

Middle:
1. Terrance Watson
2. J.A. Lee
3. Jeff Haney

Welter:
1. Bob Phillips
2. Dan Dixon
3. Carlos Ramos

Light:
1. Joe Hayes
2. Michael Ajay
3. Frank Calderon

Feather:
1. Gary Mule
2. Eric Scott
3. Neil Pease

Bantam:
1. Dennis Robinson
2. Ramkumar Singh
3. William Foushee

Fly:
1. William Felton
2. Andy Hahn
3. Michael Berland

Fin:
1. Clark Murphy
2. Kerry Yankowy
3. Frank Roche

CHAPTER 12

MAJOR U.S. OPEN KARATE TOURNAMENTS (1963–92)

The most challenging problem for the Martial Sports section, if not for this entire book, was researching America's major open tournaments. Unlike the martial arts and sports in most countries, American sport karate is not government regulated and, consequently, the "official" national open tournaments are independently produced by karate entrepreneurs.

Tracing thirty years of U.S. tournament dates and black belt results was a monumental undertaking. On numerous occasions, when winners' lists went unpublished for certain major tournaments, the top-ten rankings in magazine yearbooks had to be consulted. Then, using the data appearing in each rated fighter or form competitor's biography, major tournament results had to be virtually reconstructed from scratch. This mired me in months of full-time research. When I explained the process to Tony Cogliandro, promoter of a major U.S. tournament and a contributor here, it led him to facetiously dub this chapter "Winners' Lists from Hell." There were times when, I must admit, I agreed with him.

National tournaments in America were instituted with the 1st World Karate Tournament in 1963, the results of which appear at the end of this chapter. Since 1963, national tournaments have sprung up all over the country. Some of them are one-shot promotions that lasted but a single year. Most of the major karate tournaments retained their national status for numerous years and then faded into regional obscurity only because the promoter's interest waned or because of an inability to keep up with progress, such as when safety equipment, semicontact competition and $1,000 grand championship purses were instituted, all in 1973.

Some tournaments, too, are large regional events—like Ed Parker's Internationals in Long Beach, California—which sporadically go "national" only when top-ten-rated competitors show up unexpectedly to participate. Occasionally, too, a long-standing national event will become overshadowed by a bigger, better event conducted within the same region.

From 1975 to 1980, the martial arts industry suffered a dismal business slump after riding the unprecedented crest of prosperity during the Bruce Lee era of the early to mid-1970s. In 1975, too, *Professional Karate* magazine, the ratings and promotional kingpin of the industry for two years, suspended publication. For these reasons, national tournaments were at an all-time low from 1975–80 and few winners' lists from national tournaments appear here from that period. The sport gathered momentum again when *Karate Illustrated* magazine, under the inspired reign of editor Renardo Barden, launched its national ratings in 1980.

In 1987, the landmark Atlantic Oil sponsorship emerged under its chairman, John Duess, an avid karate student. Karate pioneer Chuck Merriman of Connecticut was named Atlantic's sports director, and under the banner of this massive sponsorship—rumored to be in the seven figures annually—he assembled the greatest competitive team in karate history.

With so many great forms and fighting champions—about two dozen of them—the Atlantic Oil Karate Team's presence at a tournament could determine its status as a genuine national-caliber event. Duess eventually sold Atlantic Oil and in 1989 continued his support under a personal sponsorship. At that time, the former Atlantic team became the Transworld Oil Karate Team.

CRITERIA

The criterion distinguishing between a national and regional tournament is simple: the former attracts a number of nationally rated black belts, which adds prestige to the tournament. That qualification has not changed since 1963, even though tournaments themselves have changed dramatically.

The criteria I considered for acceptance of a major tournament varied from the 1960s to the late 1980s as sport karate grew in size and scope. In the 1960s, the participation of as few as two top-ten-ranked fighters, depending on their status (such as Joe Lewis and Chuck Norris), could constitute a major tournament. Any combination of four rated fighters and/or forms competitors in the 1970s to the mid-1980s were needed, and six of that combination beginning in 1987 as independent ratings services came of age. In the late 1980s, ratings services began expanding the overall top ten competitors into weight divisions and forms subdivisions, greatly increasing the number of national champions each year.

Currently, there are two established ratings circuits to which national-caliber open karate tournaments belong. (There's also a third, budding organization which, as of 1992, was yet to prove itself.) Each issues a series of published regional and national ratings, as well as a final set of year-end ratings (see the chapter on Top Ten Champions). The North American Sport Karate Associa-

tion (NASKA), composed of most of America's major promoters, has since its inception in the late 1980s been the foremost circuit for American sport karate. The Professional Karate League (PKL) oversees a second nationwide circuit. Its qualifications are reportedly more relaxed and it is known to award "national" status to large regional tournaments.

FORMAT

I have attempted to trace the black belt winners of as many national open tournaments as possible from 1963 to 1992. This includes the "Tournament of Champions" events prevalent in the 1960s and 1970s, in which seeded national fighters competed in an elimination apart from the regular tournament competition. Not represented here are closed, invitational, interstyle and regional tournaments. Also excluded are the majority of team championships, which enjoyed a brief vogue in the late 1960s and early 1970s.

The listings appear in reverse chronological order from 1992 to 1963. Each year, however, proceeds in chronological order from January to December.

My ideal format—naming the date of the event and the black belt grand champions and divisional champions in both forms and fighting—has been accomplished only intermittently. For one, there were periods when grand championships went out of vogue and tournaments featured only first through third divisional places. Second—and most unfortunately—many of the winners' lists have been lost to time or were subject to only sporadic publishing; third, the major promoters have, understandably, long ago discarded aging winners' lists that apparently had no use or value.

In the case of a tie, no number will precede the second competitor or country listing. For example, the winners' lists often feature these places with two competitors sharing the third position.

For the record, I have listed all the national tournaments each year even when the results of those tournaments were *not* available. Hence, some tournaments appear *without* a winners' list.

Notice, too, that junior black belts begin appearing here in the late 1980s. Thanks to the immense success of the *Karate Kid* films, children enrolled in martial arts schools in huge waves in the 1980s. Now they have their own black belt divisions and national champions and must be recognized for their terrific competitive achievements.

Billy Blanks (left) and Steve Anderson, two of the greatest American karate champions of all time. Courtesy of George Foon

Exact event dates are not published in tournament results; these had to be located in separate research in calendar listings.

As a final note, this chapter can also be cross-referenced to the one on Top Ten Champions to see how various champions fared in the year-end ratings.

LONG-RUNNING NATIONAL TOURNAMENTS

To avoid constantly repeating the same information for current national tournaments, here's an alphabetical list of all the national tournaments that are annually ongoing, their promoters and sites, and how to reach them by phone.

NORTH AMERICAN SPORT KARATE ASSOCIATION (NASKA)

AKA Grand Nationals
John Sharkey, Producer
Chicago, IL
(815) 472-4259

Battle of Atlanta
Joe Corley, Producer
Atlanta, GA
(404) 998-4610

Bluegrass Nationals
Ken Eubanks, Producer
Louisville, KY
(502) 842-9495

Compete Nationals
Mohamad Jahan-vash
Irvine, CA
(714) 595-4550

Diamond Nationals
Larry Carnahan and John Worley,
    Producers
(Founding coproducers included
    Pat Worley, Gordon Franks and
    Gary Hesilow)

Minneapolis, MN
(612) 770-0490

Empire State Nationals
Joyce Santamaria, Producer
St. James, NY
(516) 541-6887

Mile High Karate Classic
Peter Morales and Steven Oliver,
    Producers
Denver, CO
(303) 986-5468

New England Open Nationals
Richard and Maria Baptista,
    Producers
Boston, MA
(617) 567-4989

North American Championships
Lewis Lizotte, Producer
Detroit, MI
(203) 745-1495

Ocean State Nationals
Don Rodrigues, Producer
Warwick, RI
(401) 739-0302

U.S.A. Nationals
Roger Jones, Producer
Charlotte, NC
(704) 252-4192

U.S. Capital Classics
Dennis Brown, Producer
Washington, DC
(202) 882-4435

U.S. Open
Mike Sawyer and Mike McCoy,
    Producers
Orlando, FL
(904) 375-8144

World Pro-Am
Steve Curran, Producer
Tacoma, WA
(206) 759-4262

PROFESSIONAL KARATE LEAGUE (PKL)

All-Star Karate Nationals
Tony Young, Producer
Atlanta, GA
(404) 997-3165

Battle of Baltimore
John Burdyck, Producer
Baltimore, MD
(301) 676-1776

Boston Internationals
(Formerly Boston Open)
Tony and Doreen Cogliandro,
    Producers
Boston, MA
(617) 233-8135

Bruce Lee Junior Nationals
Richard Morris, Producer
Ft. Worth, TX
(817) 346-7811

L.A.M.A. Nationals
Tom Letuli, Producer
Chicago, IL
(312) 562-5316

Niagara Nationals
Boice Lydell
Buffalo, NY
(716) 763-1111

Pan-Am Nationals
Manny Reyes, Producer
Miami, FL
(305) 681-4952

SPORADIC NATIONAL TOURNAMENTS

All-American Championships
S. Henry Cho, Producer
New York, NY
(212) 245-4499

Long Beach Internationals
Ed Parker, Jr., Producer
Long Beach, CA
(213) 682-2456

USKA Grand Nationals
[Sanctioned by the United States Karate Association, founded by the late Robert Trias (d. 1989), this tournament was the longest running annual karate event in the U.S. until Mr. Trias's death. It had different locations and producers each year.]
Contact: Roberta Trias-Kelly
Phoenix, AZ
(602) 277-9505

Brian Ruth at the New England Nationals. Courtesy of Rich Baptista

1992 NATIONAL TOURNAMENTS

COMPETE NATIONALS: FEBRUARY 16, 1992

Fighting

Men's Grand Champions:

HEAVY:
  Chris Daley
1. Jeff Newton

MIDDLE:
  Chris McBride
1. Jose Pacheco

LIGHT:
  Shah Alston
1. Tony Young

EXECUTIVE:
  Joe Swift

EXECUTIVE HEAVY (35–42):
1. Joe Swift

EXECUTIVE LIGHT (35–42):
1. Troy McKaskell

SENIORS (43 & OVER):
1. Bob Dillard
2. Robert Hurt

Women's Grand Champion:
  Michelle Arango

MIDDLE:
1. Dawn Allen

LIGHT MIDDLE:
1. Michelle Arango

LIGHT:
1. Laura Armes

SUPER LIGHT:
1. Elsa Cordero

Youth (Boys)

(15–17):
1. Mark Reyes
2. Adilson Baptista
3. Brian Ruth

(13–14):
1. Mario Hirose
2. Albert Anon

(11–12):
1. Jay Hirleman
2. Nick Baccagno

(9–10):
1. Kody Gilbow
2. Justin Sheppard

Youth (Girls)

(15–17):
1. Krista Shearer

(13–14):
1. Bernadette Ambrosia

(11–12):
1. Jamie Mueller

Forms

Men's Grand Champion:
  Gabe Reynaga

Men

AMERICAN (CO-ED):
1. Richard Brandon

CHINESE:
1. Hoyoung Pak

JAPANESE/OKINAWAN:
1. Gabe Reynaga

KOREAN:
1. Dave Macomber

MUSICAL (CO-ED):
1. Chris Casamassa

EXECUTIVE/SENIOR (CO-ED):
1. Terry Creamer
2. Dennis Kelly

Women's Grand Champion:
  Elsa Cordero

Bernadette Ambrosia at the U.S. Open. Photo by Cheryl Henson; courtesy of Mike McCoy

HARD STYLE:
1. Elsa Cordero

SOFT STYLE:
1. Geri James

Youth Grand Champion:
Bernadette Ambrosia

(MUSICAL 17 & UNDER CO-ED):
1. Kim Do

(15–17 Co-Ed):
1. Jon Valera
2. Anne Hsu

(13–14 CO-ED):
1. Bernadette Ambrosia
2. Omar Guerrero

(11–12 CO-ED):
1. Henry Rodrigues

(9–10 CO-ED):
1. Emily Pokora
2. Anthony Stewart

(8 & UNDER CO-ED):
1. Joseph Tran
2. Ashley Kohler

Adult Weapons Grand Champion:
Chris Casamassa

Men

HARD STYLE:
1. Chris Casamassa

SOFT STYLE:
1. Richard Brandon

WOMEN:
1. Michelle Arango

EXECUTIVE/SENIOR CO-ED:
1. Rocky DiRico

Youth Weapons Grand Champion:
Bernadette Ambrosia

(15–17 CO-ED):
1. Mike Chaturantabut

(13–14 CO-ED):
1. Bernadette Ambrosia

(11–12 CO-ED):
1. Kim Do

(10 & UNDER CO-ED):
1. Kody Gilbow

MILE HIGH KARATE CLASSIC: MARCH 7, 1992

Fighting

Men's Grand Champions:

HEAVY:
Hakim Alston
1. Mark Baier

MIDDLE:
Marty Eubanks
1. Carl Bradford

LIGHT:
Tony Young
1. John Marshall

EXECUTIVE:
Terry Creamer

EXECUTIVE HEAVYWEIGHT (35–42):
1. Terry Creamer

EXECUTIVE LIGHTWEIGHT (35–42):
1. Troy McKaskell

SENIORS (43 & OVER):
1. John Prevatt

Women's Grand Champion:
Laura Armes

MIDDLE:
1. Dawn Allen

LIGHT MIDDLE:
1. Cheryl Corman

LIGHT:
1. Laura Armes

SUPER LIGHT:
1. Elsa Cordero

Youth (Boys)

(15–17):
1. Brian Ruth

(13–14):
1. Hector Santiago

(11–12 CO-ED):
1. Jay Hirleman

(9–10 CO-ED):
1. Justin Sheppard

Youth (Girls)

(15–17):
1. Ming Tran

(13–14):
1. Kari Linden

Forms

Men's Grand Champion
Gabe Reynaga

Men

AMERICAN (CO-ED):
1. Richard Brandon

CHINESE:
1. Woody Wong

JAPANESE/OKINAWAN:
1. Gabe Reynaga

Elsa Cordero at the U.S. Open. Photo by Cheryl Henson; courtesy of Mike McCoy

(Left to right) Brian Ruth, Bernadette Ambrosia, Carmichael Simon and Krista Shearer. Photo by Cheryl Henson; courtesy of Mike McCoy

KOREAN:
1. Dave Macomber

MUSICAL (CO-ED):
1. Chris Casamassa

EXECUTIVE/SENIOR (CO-ED):
1. Terry Creamer

Women's Grand Champion:
Elsa Cordero

HARD STYLE:
1. Elsa Cordero

SOFT STYLE:
1. Geri James

Youth Grand Champion:
Joseph Tran

(MUSICAL 17 & UNDER CO-ED):
1. Ming Tran

(15–17 CO-ED):
1. Michael Sales

(13–14 CO-ED):
1. Hector Santiago

(11–12 CO-ED):
1. Justin Margotto

(9–10 CO-ED):
1. Emily Pokora

(8 & UNDER CO-ED):
1. Joseph Tran

Adult Weapons Grand Champion:
Richard Brandon

HARD STYLE:
1. Chris Casamassa

SOFT STYLE:
1. Richard Brandon

WOMEN:
1. Elsa Cordero

EXECUTIVE/SENIOR CO-ED:
1. Rocky DiRico

Youth Weapons Grand Champion:
Brian Ruth

(15–17 CO-ED):
1. Brian Ruth

(13–14 CO-ED):
1. Hector Santiago

(11–12 CO-ED):
1. Michael Butts

(10 & UNDER CO-ED):
1. Kody Gilbow

EMPIRE STATE NATIONALS: MARCH 28–29, 1992

Fighting

Men's Grand Champions:

HEAVY:
Anthony Holloway
1. Steve Babcock

MIDDLE:
James Boogie
1. Marty Eubanks

LIGHT:
Donald Brady
1. Akbar Alston

EXECUTIVE:
Terry Creamer

EXECUTIVE HEAVYWEIGHT (35–42):
1. Terry Creamer

SENIORS (43 & OVER):
1. John Prevatt

Women's Grand Champion:

HEAVY:
Michelle Arango
1. Jessica Robeson

LIGHT:
Christine Bannon-Rodrigues
1. Angela Webb

Christine Bannon-Rodrigues. Courtesy of Don Rodrigues

Youth (Boys)

(15–17):
1. Mike Shurina
2. Naim Alston

(13–14):
1. Jason Shapiro
2. Barry Gonzales

(11–12):
1. Peter Allende
2. Jamie Perry

(9–10 CO-ED):
1. Kody Gilbow
2. Anthony Stewart

(8 & UNDER CO-ED):
1. Amir Hoskins

Youth (Girls)

(15–17):
1. Kyria Gallagher

(13–14):
1. Angela Richards

(11–12):
1. Christine LaCasse

Forms

Men's Grand Champion:
  Hoyoung Pak

Men

AMERICAN (CO-ED):
1. Richard Brandon

CHINESE:
1. Hoyoung Pak

JAPANESE/OKINAWAN:
1. Grant Campbell

KOREAN:
1. Dave Macomber

MUSICAL (CO-ED):
1. Chris Casamassa

EXECUTIVE/SENIOR (CO-ED):
1. Rocky DiRico

Women's Grand Champion:
  Elsa Cordero

HARD STYLE:
  Elsa Cordero

SOFT STYLE:
1. Christine Bannon-Rodrigues

Youth Grand Champion:
  Mike Chaturantabut

(MUSICAL 17 & UNDER CO-ED):
1. Carmichael Simon

(15–17 CO-ED):
1. Mike Chaturantabut

(13–14 CO-ED):
1. Bernadette Ambrosia

(11–12 CO-ED):
1. Peter Allende

(9–10 CO-ED):
1. Kody Gilbow

(8 & UNDER CO-ED):
1. Joseph Tran

Adult Weapons Grand Champion:
  Richard Brandon

HARD STYLE:
1. Chris Casamassa

SOFT STYLE:
1. Richard Brandon

WOMEN:
1. Christine Bannon-Rodrigues

EXECUTIVE/SENIOR CO-ED:
1. Dan McFarland

Youth Weapons Grand Champion:
  Bernadette Ambrosia

(15–17 CO-ED):
1. Don Therathada

(13–14 CO-ED):
1. Bernadette Ambrosia

(11–12 CO-ED):
1. Peter Allende

(10 & UNDER CO-ED):
1. Kody Gilbow

Richard Brandon. Photo by Cheryl Henson; courtesy of Mike McCoy

Carmichael Simon at the New England Nationals. Courtesy of Rich Baptista

(Left to right) Truman Irving, Charlie Lee, Steve Anderson, J. Pat Burleson, Larry Carnahan, John Chung and John Longstreet. Photo by Cheryl Henson; courtesy of Mike McCoy

BATTLE OF ATLANTA: APRIL 25, 1992

Fighting

Men's Grand Champions:
Steve Anderson

HEAVY:
1. Steve Anderson
2. Gerald Dawson

LIGHT HEAVY:
1. Eric Jones
2. Gregg White

MIDDLE:
Alberto Montrond

MIDDLE:
1. Joe Rivera
2. Jeff Gears
3. Mike Burton

LIGHT MIDDLE:
1. Alberto Montrond
2. E.J. Greer
3. Omar Olumee

LIGHT:
Shah Alston

LIGHT:
1. Shah Alston
2. Todd Singleton

SUPER LIGHT:
1. Akbar Alston
2. Tony Young
3. Roland Murdock

EXECUTIVE:
Terry Creamer

EXECUTIVE HEAVYWEIGHT (35–42):
1. Terry Creamer

EXECUTIVE LIGHTWEIGHT (35–42):
1. Charles Fears

SENIORS (43 & OVER):
1. Bob Nucera

Women's Grand Champion:

MIDDLE:
Michelle Arango

MIDDLE:
1. Nicki Carlson
2. Michelle Griffin
3. Dawn Allen

LIGHT MIDDLE:
1. Michelle Arango
2. Claire Moscone
3. Dee Dee Villalona

LIGHT:
Laura Armes

LIGHT:
1. Laura Armes

2. Angela Webb

SUPER LIGHT:
1. Amy Corbin
2. Shelly Taylor
3. Elsa Cordero

Youth (Boys)

(15–17):
1. Brian Ruth
2. Naim Alston
3. Michael Terrace

(13–14):
1. Barry Gonzales
2. Adam Keister
3. Clint Darden

(11–12):
1. Trip Ferguson
2. Andrew Brown
3. Nathan Loftis

(9–10 CO-ED):
1. Emily Pokora
2. Amy Pokora
3. Charles Youmans

(8 & UNDER CO-ED):
1. Eboni Adams
2. Joseph Tran
3. Kalman Csoka

Youth (Girls)

(15–17):
1. Kyria Gallagher
2. Krishea Strayn

Terry Creamer. Photo by Cheryl Henson; courtesy of Mike McCoy

(13–14):
1. Heather Preston
2. Bernadette Ambrosia

(11–12):
1. Jennifer Dinger
2. Tifanie Matthews

Forms

Men's Grand Champion:
Hoyoung Pak

Men

AMERICAN (CO-ED):
1. Richard Brandon

CHINESE:
1. Hoyoung Pak
2. James Hobby
3. Willie Johnson

JAPANESE/OKINAWAN:
1. Gabe Reynaga
2. Marty Eubanks

KOREAN:
1. Dave Macomber

MUSICAL (CO-ED):
1. Todd Allen

EXECUTIVE/SENIOR (CO-ED):
1. Janice Adamson
2. Mie Matsuoka
3. Rocky DiRico

Women's Grand Champion:
Stacey Demejia

HARD STYLE:
1. Stacey Demejia
2. Michelle Maizis
3. Michelle Arango

SOFT STYLE:
1. Colleen Kouyoujian

Youth Grand Champion:
Carmichael Simon

(MUSICAL 17 & UNDER CO-ED):
1. Carmichael Simon
2. Kim Do
3. Gary Waugh

(15–17 CO-ED):
1. Mike Chaturantabut

(13–14 CO-ED):
1. Bernadette Ambrosia

(11–12 CO-ED):
1. Justin Margotto

(9–10 CO-ED):
1. Kody Gilbow

(8 & UNDER CO-ED):
1. Joseph Tran

Adult Weapons Grand Champion:
Chris Casamassa

HARD STYLE:
1. Chris Casamassa

SOFT STYLE:
1. Richard Brandon

WOMEN:
1. Michelle Arango

EXECUTIVE/SENIOR CO-ED:
1. Dorothy Wright
2. Michelle Darbro
3. Art Sands

Youth Weapons Grand Champion:
Mike Chaturantabut

(15–17 CO-ED):
1. Mike Chaturantabut

(13–14 CO-ED):
1. Bernadette Ambrosia

(11–12 CO-ED):
1. Kim Do

(10 & UNDER CO-ED):
1. Kristopher Katira
2. Joseph Tran

NEW ENGLAND OPEN: MAY 30, 1992

Fighting

Men's Grand Champions:

HEAVY:
Steve Babcock
1. Jeff Newton

MIDDLE:
Ronald Brady
1. Calvin Thomas

LIGHT:
Donald Brady
1. Akbar Alston

EXECUTIVE:
Wali Islam

EXECUTIVE HEAVYWEIGHT (35–42):
1. Terry Creamer

EXECUTIVE LIGHTWEIGHT (35–42):
1. Leroy Taylor

SENIORS (43 & OVER):
1. Wali Islam

Women's Grand Champion:
Kierston Sims

MIDDLE:
1. Jessica Robeson

LIGHT MIDDLE:
1. Kierston Sims

LIGHT:
1. Lydia Amaya

SUPER LIGHT:
1. Christine Bannon-Rodrigues

Youth (Boys)

(15–17):
1. Mike Shurina

(13–14):
1. Hector Santiago

(11–12 CO-ED):
1. Andrew Brown

(9–10 CO-ED):
1. Joseph Guarneri

(8 & UNDER CO-ED):
1. Eboni Adams

Youth (Girls)

(15–17):
1. Jennifer Yanoff

Gabe Reynaga. Photo by Cheryl Henson; courtesy of Mike McCoy

(13–14):
1. Angela Richards

Forms

Men's Grand Champion:
Gabe Reynaga

Men

AMERICAN (CO-ED):
1. Richard Brandon

CHINESE:
1. Hoyoung Pak

JAPANESE/OKINAWAN:
1. Gabe Reynaga

KOREAN:
1. Guy Hankins

MUSICAL (CO-ED):
1. Todd Allen

EXECUTIVE/SENIOR (CO-ED):
1. Rocky DiRico

Women's Grand Champion:
Stacey Demejia

HARD STYLE:
1. Stacey Demejia

SOFT STYLE:
1. Christine Bannon-Rodrigues

Youth Grand Champion:
Carmichael Simon

(MUSICAL 17 & UNDER CO-ED):
1. Carmichael Simon

(15–17 CO-ED):
1. Krista Shearer

(13–14 CO-ED):
1. Bernadette Ambrosia

(11–12 CO-ED):
1. Peter Allende

(9–10 CO-ED):
1. Kody Gilbow

(8 & UNDER CO-ED):
1. Eboni Adams

Adult Weapons Grand Champion:
Richard Brandon

HARD STYLE:
1. Dave Macomber

SOFT STYLE:
1. Richard Brandon

WOMEN:
1. Christine Bannon-Rodrigues

EXECUTIVE/SENIOR CO-ED:
1. Rocky DiRico

Youth Weapons Grand Champion:
Bernadette Ambrosia

(15–17 CO-ED):
1. Don Therathada

(13–14 CO-ED):
1. Bernadette Ambrosia

(11–12 CO-ED):
1. Andrew Brown

(10 & UNDER CO-ED):
1. Kody Gilbow

BLUEGRASS NATIONALS: JUNE 20, 1992

Fighting

Men's Grand Champions:

HEAVY:
Anthony Price
1. Hakim Alston

MIDDLE:
Marty Eubanks
1. Karl Bradford

LIGHT:
Pedro Xavier
1. Gabe Reynaga

EXECUTIVE:
Terry Creamer

EXECUTIVE HEAVYWEIGHT (35–42):
1. Terry Creamer
2. Marty Knight

EXECUTIVE LIGHTWEIGHT (35–42):
1. Joshua Harper
2. Larry Tankson

SENIORS (43 & OVER):
1. Larry Bulard
2. J.C. Copeland

Women's Grand Champion:

MIDDLE:
Nicki Carlson
1. Kierston Sims

LIGHT:
Christine Bannon-Rodrigues
1. Dawn Santamaria

Youth (Boys)

(15–17):
1. Derek Pendergrass
2. Brian Ruth

(13–14):
1. Hector Santiago
2. Randy Glover

(11–12):
1. Jason Bourelly
2. Andrew Brown

(9–10 CO-ED):
1. Anthony Stewart
2. Paul Goins

(8 & UNDER CO-ED):
1. Eboni Adams
2. Adam Mitchell

Youth (Girls)

(15–17):
1. Krista Shearer

(13–14):
1. Aisha Thornton

(11–12):
1. Jamie Caskey

Forms

Men's Grand Champion:
Gabe Reynaga

Men

AMERICAN (CO-ED):
1. Richard Brandon

CHINESE:
1. Hoyoung Pak

JAPANESE/OKINAWAN:
1. Gabe Reynaga

KOREAN:
1. Dave Macomber

MUSICAL (CO-ED):
1. Chris Casamassa

EXECUTIVE/SENIOR (CO-ED):
1. Phil Morgan
2. Lynn Gregory

Women's Grand Champion:
Christine Bannon-Rodrigues

HARD STYLE:
1. Stacey Demejia

SOFT STYLE:
1. Christine Bannon-Rodrigues

Hosung Pak. Photo by Cheryl Henson; courtesy of Mike McCoy

Youth Grand Champion:
    Jon Valera

(MUSICAL 17 & UNDER CO-ED):
1. Carmichael Simon
2. Kris Khamvongsa

(15–17 CO-ED):
1. Jon Valera

(13–14 CO-ED):
1. Bernadette Ambrosia

(11–12 CO-ED):
1. Li-Ling Li

(9–10 CO-ED):
1. Kody Gilbow

(8 & UNDER CO-ED):
1. Eboni Adams

Adult Weapons Grand Champion:
    Chris Casamassa

HARD STYLE:
1. Chris Casamassa

SOFT STYLE:
1. Hoyoung Pak

WOMEN:
1. Christine Bannon-Rodrigues

EXECUTIVE/SENIOR CO-ED:
1. Dan McFarland

Youth Weapons Grand Champion:
    Jon Valera

(15–17 CO-ED):
1. Jon Valera

(11–14 CO-ED):
1. Bernadette Ambrosia

(10 & UNDER CO-ED):
1. Justin Margotto

U.S. OPEN: JULY 18, 1992

Fighting

Men's Grand Champions:

HEAVY:
    Anthony Price
1. Anthony Holloway

MIDDLE:
    Ronald Brady
1. Calvin Thomas

LIGHT:
    Pedro Xavier
1. Tony Young

EXECUTIVE:
    Terry Creamer

EXECUTIVE HEAVYWEIGHT (35–42):
1. Terry Creamer
2. Leroy Taylor

EXECUTIVE LIGHTWEIGHT (35–42):
1. Earl Harris
2. M. Page

SENIORS (43 & OVER):
1. Wali Islam
2. John Prevatt

Women's Grand Champion:
    Laura Armes

MIDDLE:
1. Mitzi Tyler

LIGHT MIDDLE:
1. Megyesi

LIGHT:
1. Laura Armes

SUPER LIGHT:
1. Christine Bannon-Rodrigues

Youth (Boys)

(15–17):
1. Brian Ruth
2. Gerry Iamunno

(13–14):
1. Adam Keister
2. Shawn Viceroy

(11–12):
1. Andrew Brown
2. Trip Gerguson

(9–10 CO-ED):
1. Joseph Guarneri

(8 & UNDER CO-ED):
1. Eboni Adams

Youth (Girls)

(15–17):
1. Krista Shearer

(13–14):
1. Lona Love

(11–12):
1. Tiffany Matthews

Forms

Men's Grand Champion:
    Richard Brandon

Men

AMERICAN (CO-ED):
1. Richard Brandon

CHINESE:
1. Hoyoung Pak

JAPANESE/OKINAWAN:
1. Gabe Reynaga
2. J. Marshall

Hoyoung Pak. Courtesy of Mike McCoy

KOREAN:
1. Michael Dietrich

MUSICAL (CO-ED):
1. Chris Casamassa

EXECUTIVE/SENIOR (CO-ED):
1. Rocky DiRico
2. Terry Creamer
3. M. Matsuoka

Women's Grand Champion:
Stacey Demejia

HARD STYLE:
1. Stacey Demejia

SOFT STYLE:
1. Christine Bannon-Rodrigues

Youth Grand Champion:
Carmichael Simon

(MUSICAL 17 & UNDER CO-ED):
1. Carmichael Simon

(15–17 CO-ED):
1. Brian Ruth

(13–14 CO-ED):
1. Jake Cohen

(11–12 CO-ED):
1. Justin Margotto

(9–10 CO-ED):
1. Vince Cohen

(8 & UNDER CO-ED):
1. Joseph Tran

Adult Weapons Grand Champion:
Richard Brandon

HARD STYLE:
1. Chris Casamassa

SOFT STYLE:
1. Richard Brandon

WOMEN:
1. Elsa Cordero

EXECUTIVE/SENIOR CO-ED:
1. Rocky DiRico

Youth Weapons Grand Champion:
Bernadette Ambrosia

(15–17 CO-ED):
1. Brian Ruth

(13–14 CO-ED):
1. Bernadette Ambrosia

(11–12 CO-ED):
1. Peter Allende

(10 & UNDER CO-ED):
1. Justin Margotto

U.S. CAPITAL CLASSICS: AUGUST 8, 1992

Fighting

Men's Grand Champions:

HEAVY:
Hakim Alston
1. Stephen Babcock

MIDDLE:
Chris Rappold
1. Marty Eubanks

LIGHT:
Tony Young
1. Shah Alston

EXECUTIVE:
Terry Creamer

EXECUTIVE HEAVYWEIGHT (35–42):
1. Terry Creamer
2. Laymor Williamson

EXECUTIVE LIGHTWEIGHT (35–42):
1. Dan Boccagno
2. Leroy Taylor

SENIORS (43 & OVER):
1. John Prevatt

Women's Grand Champion:

MIDDLE:
Sue Brazelton
1. Mary Corrigan

LIGHT:
Laura Armes
1. Elsa Cordero

Youth (Boys)

(15–17):
1. Brian Ruth

(13–14):
1. Hector Santiago

(11–12):
1. Andrew Brown

(9–10 CO-ED):
1. Anthony Stewart

(8 & UNDER CO-ED):
1. Eboni Adams

Youth (Girls)

(15–17):
1. Krishea Strayn

(13–14):
1. Dawn Biancaniello

(11–12):
1. Li-Ling Li

Forms

Men's Grand Champion:
Gabe Reynaga

Men

AMERICAN (CO-ED):
1. Tsao Tsao

CHINESE:
1. Hoyoung Pak

JAPANESE/OKINAWAN:
1. Gabe Reynaga

KOREAN:
1. Dave Macomber

MUSICAL (CO-ED):
1. Chris Casamassa

EXECUTIVE/SENIOR (CO-ED):
1. Phil Morgan

Women's Grand Champion:
Elsa Cordero

HARD STYLE:
1. Elsa Cordero

SOFT STYLE:
1. Christine Bannon-Rodrigues

Youth Grand Champion:
Carmichael Simon

(MUSICAL 17 & UNDER CO-ED):
1. Carmichael Simon

(15–17 CO-ED):
1. Brian Ruth

(13–14 CO-ED):
1. Bernadette Ambrosia

(11–12 CO-ED):
1. Justin Margotto

(9–10 CO-ED):
1. Vince Cohen

(8 & UNDER CO-ED):
1. Jennifer Santiago

Adult Weapons Grand Champion:
Richard Brandon

HARD STYLE:
1. Chris Casamassa

SOFT STYLE:
1. Richard Brandon

WOMEN:
1. Michelle Arango

EXECUTIVE/SENIOR CO-ED:
1. Dan McFarland

Youth Weapons Grand Champion:
Carmichael Simon

(15–17 CO-ED):
1. Carmichael Simon

(13–14 CO-ED):
1. Bernadette Ambrosia

(11–12 CO-ED):
1. Peter Allende

(10 & UNDER CO-ED):
1. Eboni Adams

DIAMOND NATIONALS: OCTOBER 10, 1992

Fighting

Men's Grand Champions:

HEAVY:
Richard Plowden
1. Anthony Holloway

MIDDLE:
Joe Rivera
1. Ronald Brady

LIGHT:
Donald Brady
1. Gabe Reynaga

EXECUTIVE:
Terry Creamer

EXECUTIVE HEAVYWEIGHT (35–42):
1. Terry Creamer

EXECUTIVE LIGHTWEIGHT (35–42):
1. Leroy Taylor
2. Earl Harris

SENIORS (43 & OVER):
1. Wali Islam
2. John Prevatt

Women's Grand Champion:
Christine Bannon-Rodrigues

MIDDLE:
1. Carrie Fuerstenberg

LIGHT MIDDLE:
1. Michelle Arango

LIGHT:
1. Sue Lomasney

SUPER LIGHT:
1. Christine Bannon-Rodrigues

Youth (Boys)

(15–17):
1. Mike Shurina

2. Gerry Iamunno

(13–14):
1. Shawn Vickery
2. Bruce Cervantez

(11–12 CO-ED):
1. Kris Khamvongsa
2. Jay Hirleman
3. L. Dobbins

(9–10 CO-ED):
1. Joe Guarneri
2. Michael Adams

(8 & UNDER CO-ED):
1. Jennifer Santiago
2. Amir Hoskins

Youth (Girls)

(15–17):
1. Krista Shearer

(13–14):
1. Bernadette Ambrosia

Forms

Men's Grand Champion:
Gabe Reynaga

Men

AMERICAN (CO-ED):
1. Richard Brandon

CHINESE:
1. Hosung Pak

JAPANESE/OKINAWAN:
1. Gabe Reynaga

KOREAN:
1. Dave Macomber

MUSICAL (CO-ED):
1. Chris Casamassa

EXECUTIVE/SENIOR (CO-ED):
1. Rocky DiRico
2. Mie Matsuoka

Women's Grand Champion:
Elsa Cordero

HARD STYLE:
1. Elsa Cordero

SOFT STYLE:
1. Christine Bannon-Rodrigues

Youth Grand Champion:
Carmichael Simon

(MUSICAL 17 & UNDER CO-ED):
1. Carmichael Simon
2. Kris Khamvongsa

(15–17 CO-ED):
1. Mike Chaturantabut

(13–14 CO-ED):
1. Bernadette Ambrosia

(Left to right) Stacey Knight, Terry Creamer (background), Gabe Reynaga, Laura Armes and Tony Young. Photo by Cheryl Henson; courtesy of Mike McCoy

(11–12 CO-ED):
1. Justin Margotto

(9–10 CO-ED):
1. Vince Cohen

(8 & UNDER CO-ED):
1. Joseph Tran

Adult Weapons Grand Champion:
Richard Brandon

HARD STYLE:
1. John Marshall

SOFT STYLE:
1. Richard Brandon

WOMEN:
1. Michelle Arango

EXECUTIVE/SENIOR CO-ED:
1. Terry Creamer

Youth Weapons Grand Champion:
Bernadette Ambrosia

(15–17 CO-ED):
1. Brian Ruth

(13–14 CO-ED):
1. Bernadette Ambrosia

(11–12 CO-ED):
1. Justin Margotto

(10 & UNDER CO-ED):
1. Vince Cohen

NORTH AMERICAN: NOVEMBER 7, 1992

Fighting

Men's Grand Champions:

HEAVY:
Richard Plowden
1. Richard Barefield

MIDDLE:
Jeff Gears
1. E.J. Greer

LIGHT:
Pedro Xavier
1. Tony Young

EXECUTIVE:
Terry Creamer

EXECUTIVE HEAVYWEIGHT (35–42):
1. Terry Creamer

EXECUTIVE LIGHTWEIGHT (35–42):
1. Ronnie Moore

SENIORS (43 & OVER):
1. Bill Mason

Women's Grand Champion:
Laura Armes

MIDDLE:
1. Dawn Allen

LIGHT MIDDLE:
1. Laura Armes

LIGHT:
1. Emily Cooper

SUPER LIGHT:
1. Elsa Cordero

Youth (Boys)

(15–17):
1. Brian Ruth

(13–14):
1. Hector Santiago

(11–12):
1. Andrew Brown

(9–10 CO-ED):
1. Joe Guarneri

(8 & UNDER CO-ED):
1. Eboni Adams

Youth (Girls)

(15–17):
1. Krista Shearer

(13–14):
1. Aisha Thornton

(11–12):
1. Salin McDaniel

Forms

Men's Grand Champion:
Dave Macomber

Men

AMERICAN (CO-ED):
1. Richard Brandon

CHINESE:
1. Hoyoung Pak

JAPANESE/OKINAWAN:
1. Gabe Reynaga

KOREAN:
1. Dave Macomber

MUSICAL (CO-ED):
1. Chris Casamassa

EXECUTIVE/SENIOR (CO-ED):
1. Terry Creamer

Women's Grand Champion:
Stacey Demejia

Youth Grand Champion:
Bernadette Ambrosia

(MUSICAL 17 & UNDER CO-ED):
1. Carmichael Simon

(15–17 CO-ED):
1. Brian Ruth

(13–14 CO-ED):
1. Bernadette Ambrosia

(11–12 CO-ED):
1. Justin Margotto

(9–10 CO-ED):
1. Kody Gilbow

(8 & UNDER CO-ED):
1. Joseph Tran

Adult Weapons Grand Champion:
Mike Bernardo

HARD STYLE:
1. Mike Bernardo

SOFT STYLE:
1. Richard Brandon

WOMEN:
1. Michelle Arango

EXECUTIVE/SENIOR CO-ED:
1. Rocky DiRico

Youth Weapons Grand Champion:
Brandon Kersey

(15–17 CO-ED):
1. Brandon Kersey

(13–14 CO-ED):
1. Mike Franze

(11–12 CO-ED):
1. Justin Margotto

(10 & UNDER CO-ED):
1. Kody Gilbow

1991 NATIONAL TOURNAMENTS

COMPETE NATIONALS: FEBRUARY 17, 1991

MILE HIGH KARATE CLASSIC: MARCH 7, 1991

EMPIRE STATE NATIONALS: APRIL 14, 1991

Fighting

Men's Grand Champions:

HEAVY:
Hakim Alston
1. Paul Pinnock

MIDDLE:
Anthony Holloway
1. Chris McBride

LIGHT:
Gabe Reynaga
1. Pedro Xavier

EXECUTIVE HEAVYWEIGHT (35–42):
1. Michael Fields

EXECUTIVE LIGHTWEIGHT (35–42):
1. Lee Ireland

SENIORS (UNDER 43):
1. Gary Nichols

Women's Grand Champion:

HEAVY:
Nicki Carlson
1. Michelle Arango

LIGHT:
Brenda Lee
1. Elsa Cordero

Youth (Boys)

(15–17):
1. Niam Alston
2. Denis DeBranche

(13–14):
1. Brian Ruth
2. Carmichael Simon

(11–12):
1. Adam Keister

(9–10 CO-ED):
1. Andre Velez
2. Milan Costich

(8 & UNDER CO-ED):
1. Maurice Bradford

Youth (Girls)

(15–17):
1. Cherie Ground

(13–14):
1. Kyria Gallagher

(11–12):
1. Bernadette Ambrosia

(Left to right) Bill "Superfoot" Wallace, Charlie Lee, Jeff Smith, Chris Casamassa and Hakim Alston. Photo by Cheryl Henson; courtesy of Mike McCoy

Forms

Men's Grand Champion:
Chris Casamassa

Men

CHINESE:
1. Greg Walraven

JAPANESE/OKINAWAN:
1. Grant Campbell

KOREAN:
1. Dave Macomber

AMERICAN (CO-ED):
1. Mike Bernardo

MUSICAL (CO-ED):
1. Chris Casamassa

EXECUTIVE/SENIOR (CO-ED):
1. Rocky DiRico

Women's Grand Champion:
Elsa Cordero

HARD STYLE:
1. Elsa Cordero

Youth Grand Champion:
Carmichael Simon

(MUSICAL 17 & UNDER CO-ED):
1. Clay Morton

(15–17 CO-ED):
1. Jon Valera

(13–14 CO-ED):
1. Carmichael Simon

(11–12 CO-ED):
1. Bernadette Ambrosia

(9–10 CO-ED):
1. Matthew Hayes

(8 & UNDER CO-ED):
1. Maurice Bradford

Adult Weapons Grand Champion:
Mike Bernardo

HARD STYLE:
1. Mike Bernardo

SOFT STYLE:
1. Javonne Holmes

WOMEN:
Michelle Arango

EXECUTIVE/SENIOR CO-ED:
1. Rocky DiRico

Youth Weapons Grand Champion:
Brian Ruth

(15–17 CO-ED):
1. Jon Valera

(11–14 CO-ED):
1. Bernadette Ambrosia/Brian Ruth

(10 & UNDER CO-ED):
1. Kody Gilbow

BATTLE OF ATLANTA: APRIL 27, 1991

Fighting

Men's Grand Champions:

HEAVY:
Hakim Alston
1. Ernest Miller

MIDDLE:
Anthony Holloway
1. Alberto Montrond

LIGHT:
Pedro Xavier
1. Jose Pacheco

EXECUTIVE:
John Turner

EXECUTIVE HEAVYWEIGHT (35-42):
1. Michael Avent

EXECUTIVE LIGHTWEIGHT (35-42):
1. John Turner
2. Joey Shiflett

SENIORS (43 & OVER):
1. John Prevatt
2. J.C. Copeland

Women's Grand Champion:
Kierston Sims

HEAVY:
1. Kierston Sims
2. Nicki Carlson

LIGHT:
1. Christine Bannon-Rodrigues
2. Elsa Cordero

Youth (Boys)

(15-17):
1. Steven Sosa
2. Paul Kirton

(13-14):
1. Brian Ruth

(11-12):
1. Adam Keister
2. Jaime Perry

(9-10 CO-ED):
1. Matthew Hayes

(8 & UNDER CO-ED):
1. Mike Pete

Youth (Girls)

(15-17):
1. Tiffany Costello

(13-14):
1. Rosalind Russell

(11-12):
1. Bernadette Ambrosia

Forms

Men's Grand Champion:
Hosung Pak

Men

AMERICAN (CO-ED):
1. Mike Bernardo

CHINESE:
1. Hosung Pak

JAPANESE/OKINAWAN:
1. Gabe Reynaga

KOREAN:
1. Eric San Jose

MUSICAL (CO-ED):
1. Eric Lee

EXECUTIVE/SENIOR (CO-ED):
1. Phil Morgan

Women's Grand Champion:
Christine Bannon-Rodrigues

HARD STYLE:
1. Elsa Cordero

SOFT STYLE:
1. Christine Bannon-Rodrigues

Youth Grand Champion:
Kim Do

(MUSICAL 17 & UNDER CO-ED):
1. Kim Do
2. Justin Sheppard
3. Mike Chanturantabut

(15-17 CO-ED):
1. Griff Tester

(13-14 CO-ED):
1. Carmichael Simon

(11-12 CO-ED):
1. Bernadette Ambrosia
2. Jennifer Yanoff
3. Randy Dugas

(9-10 CO-ED):
1. Lance Guillermo
2. Kody Gilbow

(8 & UNDER CO-ED):
1. Ashley Kohler
2. Michael Pete

Adult Weapons Grand Champion:
Mike Bernardo

HARD STYLE:
1. Mike Bernardo

SOFT STYLE:
1. Hoyoung Pak

WOMEN:
1. Christine Bannon-Rodrigues

EXECUTIVE/SENIOR CO-ED:
1. Rocky DiRico

Youth Weapons Grand Champion:
Jon Valera

(15-17 CO-ED):
1. Jon Valera
2. Mike Chaturantabut

(11-14 CO-ED):
1. Mike Franze
2. Brian Ruth

(10 & UNDER CO-ED):
1. Kody Gilbow
2. Matthew Hayes

NEW ENGLAND OPEN: JUNE 1, 1991

Fighting

Men's Grand Champions:

HEAVY:
Hakim Alston
1. Steve Babcock

MIDDLE:
Anthony Holloway
1. Chris Rappold

LIGHT:
Pedro Xavier
1. Gabe Reynaga

EXECUTIVE:
Joshua Harper

EXECUTIVE (35-42):
Joshua Harper

SENIORS (43 & OVER):
1. Bill Rowling

Women's Grand Champion:
Nicki Carlson

HEAVY:
1. Nicki Carlson
2. Michelle Arango

LIGHT:
1. Christine Bannon-Rodrigues
2. Michelle Maizis

Youth (Boys)

(15–17):
1. Joe Rivera
2. Paul Kirton

(13–14):
1. Brian Ruth

(11–12):
1. Jaime Perry

(9–10 CO-ED):
1. Lance Guillermo

(8 & UNDER CO-ED):
1. Ashley Kohler

Youth (Girls)

(15–17):
1. Tiffany Costello

(13–14):
1. Jennifer Yanoff

(11–12):
1. Bernadette Ambrosia

Forms

Men's Grand Champion:
Gabe Reynaga

Men

AMERICAN (CO-ED):
1. Mike Bernardo

CHINESE:
1. Richard Brandon

JAPANESE/OKINAWAN:
1. Gabe Reynaga

KOREAN:
1. Eric San Jose

MUSICAL (CO-ED):
1. Dan McFarland

EXECUTIVE/SENIOR (CO-ED):
1. Phil Morgan

Women's Grand Champion:
Christine Bannon-Rodrigues

HARD STYLE:
1. Michelle Arango

SOFT STYLE:
1. Christine Bannon-Rodrigues

Youth Grand Champion:
Bernadette Ambrosia

(MUSICAL 17 & UNDER CO-ED):
1. Mike Chaturantabut

(15–17 CO-ED):
1. Michael Reid

(13–14 CO-ED):
1. Brian Ruth

(11–12 CO-ED):
1. Bernadette Ambrosia

(9–10 CO-ED):
1. Kody Gilbow

(8 & UNDER CO-ED):
1. Ashley Kohler

Adult Weapons Grand Champion:
Mike Bernardo

HARD STYLE:
1. Mike Bernardo

SOFT STYLE:
1. Richard Brandon

WOMEN:
1. Christine Bannon-Rodrigues

SENIOR (CO-ED)/SENIOR CO-ED:
1. Rocky DiRico

Youth Weapons Grand Champion:
Bernadette Ambrosia

(15–17 CO-ED):
1. Mike Chaturantabut

(11–14 CO-ED):
1. Bernadette Ambrosia

(10 & UNDER CO-ED):
1. Kody Gilbow

BLUEGRASS NATIONALS: JUNE 22, 1991

Fighting

Men's Grand Champions:
HEAVY:
Hakim Alston
1. Steve Boyles
MIDDLE:
Anthony Holloway
1. Alberto Montrond
LIGHT:
Shah Alston
1. Akbar Alston

SENIOR (CO-ED):
Joshua Harper

EXECUTIVE HEAVYWEIGHT (35–42):
1. Laymor Williamson

SENIOR (CO-ED) LIGHTWEIGHT (35–42):
1. Joshua Harper

SENIORS (43 & OVER):
1. John Prevatt

Women's Grand Champion:
Christine Bannon-Rodrigues

HEAVY:
1. Laura Armes
2. Nicki Carlson

LIGHT:
1. Christine Bannon-Rodrigues
2. Elsa Cordero

Youth (Boys)

(15–17):
1. Jon Valera
2. Jessie Wray

(13–14):
1. Brian Ruth
2. Hector Santiago

(11–12):
1. Jerry Moseley
2. Adam Keister

(9–10 CO-ED):
1. Jennifer Dinger
2. Anthony Stewart

(8 & UNDER CO-ED):
1. Amy Pokora

Youth (Girls)

(15–17):
1. Cherie Ground

(13–14):
1. Jennifer Yanoff

(11–12):
1. Bernadette Ambrosia

Forms

Men's Grand Champion:
Hosung Pak

Men

AMERICAN (CO-ED):
1. Mike Bernardo

CHINESE:
1. Hosung Pak

JAPANESE/OKINAWAN:
1. Gabe Reynaga

KOREAN:
1. Eric San Jose

MUSICAL (CO-ED):
1. Chris Casamassa

EXECUTIVE/SENIOR (CO-ED):
1. Rocky DiRico
2. Lynn Gregory

Women's Grand Champion:
Elsa Cordero

HARD STYLE:
1. Elsa Cordero

SOFT STYLE:
1. Christine Bannon-Rodrigues

Youth Grand Champion:
Jon Valera

(MUSICAL 17 & UNDER CO-ED):
1. Mike Chaturantabut

(15–17 CO-ED):
1. Jon Valera

(13–14 CO-ED):
1. Carmichael Simon

(11–12 CO-ED):
1. Bernadette Ambrosia

(9–10 CO-ED):
1. Kody Gilbow

(8 & UNDER CO-ED):
1. Amy Pokora

Adult Weapons Grand Champion:
Mike Bernardo

HARD STYLE:
1. Mike Bernardo

SOFT STYLE:
1. Hoyoung Pak

WOMEN:
1. Christine Bannon-Rodrigues

EXECUTIVE/SENIOR CO-ED:
1. Dan McFarland

Youth Weapons Grand Champion:
Brian Ruth

(15–17 CO-ED):
1. Mike Chaturantabut

(11–14 CO-ED):
1. Brian Ruth

(10 & UNDER CO-ED):
1. Matthew Hayes

U.S. OPEN: JULY 20, 1991

Fighting

Men's Grand Champions:
HEAVY:
Anthony Holloway
1. Barry Grizzard

MIDDLE:
Alberto Montrond
1. Calvin Thomas

LIGHT:
Pedro Xavier
1. Ronald Brady

SENIOR (CO-ED):
Joshua Harper

SENIOR (CO-ED) HEAVYWEIGHT (35–42):
1. Neville Wray
2. Manny Reyes

SENIOR (CO-ED) LIGHTWEIGHT (35–42):
1. Joshua Harper
2. Earl Harris

SENIORS (UNDER 43):
1. John Prevatt
2. J.C. Copeland

Women's Grand Champion:
Nicki Carlson
1. Brenda Lee

Youth (Boys)

(15–17):
1. Joe Rivera
2. Frank DeCaria

(13–14):
1. Brian Ruth
2. Hector Santiago

(11–12):
1. Jaime Perry
2. Jerry Mosley

(9–10 CO-ED):
1. Lori Sojack

(8 & UNDER CO-ED):
1. Mike Pete

Youth (Girls)

(15–17):
1. Cherie Ground

(13–14):
1. Jennifer Yanoff

(11–12):
1. Bernadette Ambrosia

Forms

Men's Grand Champion:
Hosung Pak

Men

AMERICAN (CO-ED):
1. Hoyoung Pak

CHINESE:
1. Hosung Pak

OKINAWAN/OKINAWAN:
1. Mike Hunter
2. Grant Campbell

KOREAN:
1. Eric San Jose

MUSICAL (CO-ED):
1. Chris Casamassa

EXECUTIVE/SENIOR (CO-ED):
1. Phil Morgan

Women's Grand Champion:
Christine Bannon-Rodrigues

HARD STYLE:
1. Elsa Cordero

SOFT STYLE:
1. Christine Bannon-Rodrigues

Youth Grand Champion:
Bernadette Ambrosia

(MUSICAL 17 & UNDER CO-ED):
1. Mike Chaturantabut

(15–17 CO-ED):
1. Michael Reid

(13–14 CO-ED):
1. Carmichael Simon

(11–12 CO-ED):
1. Bernadette Ambrosia

(9–10 CO-ED):
1. Kody Gilbow

(8 & UNDER CO-ED):
1. Emily Pokora

Adult Weapons Grand Champion:
Mike Bernardo

HARD STYLE:
1. Mike Bernardo

SOFT STYLE:
1. Richard Brandon

WOMEN:
Michelle Arango

EXECUTIVE/SENIOR CO-ED:
1. Dan McFarland

Youth Weapons Grand Champion:
Mike Chaturantabut

(15–17 CO-ED):
1. Mike Chaturantabut

(11–14 CO-ED):
1. Brian Ruth

(10 & UNDER CO-ED):
1. Kody Gilbow

U.S. CAPITAL CLASSICS: AUGUST 10, 1991

Fighting

Men's Grand Champions:
Hakim Alston
1. Derek Panza

MIDDLE:
Alberto Montrond
1. Karl Bradford

LIGHT:
Pedro Xavier
1. Donald Brady

SENIOR (CO-ED):
Joshua Harper

EXECUTIVE HEAVY (35–42):
1. Terry Creamer

SENIOR (CO-ED) LIGHT (35–42):
1. Joshua Harper

SENIORS (43 & OVER):
1. J.C. Copeland

Women's Grand Champion:
Brenda Lee

HEAVY:
1. Amy Plante
2. Michelle Arango

LIGHT:
1. Brenda Lee
2. Dawn Santamaria

Youth (Boys)

(15–17):
1. Joe Rivera

(13–14):
1. Chris Goldberg

(11–12):
1. Adam Keister

(9–10 CO-ED):
1. Milan Costich

(8 & UNDER CO-ED):
1. Emily Pokora

Youth (Girls)

(15–17):
1. Cherie Ground

(13–14):
1. Jennifer Yanoff

(11–12):
1. Bernadette Ambrosia

Forms

Men's Grand Champion:
Hosung Pak

Men

AMERICAN (CO-ED):
1. Mike Bernardo

CHINESE:
1. Hosung Pak

JAPANESE/OKINAWAN:
1. Grant Campbell

KOREAN:
1. Dave Macomber

MUSICAL (CO-ED):
1. Chris Casamassa

EXECUTIVE/SENIOR (CO-ED):
1. Phil Morgan

Women's Grand Champion:
Elsa Cordero

HARD STYLE:
1. Elsa Cordero

SOFT STYLE:
1. Christine Bannon-Rodrigues

Youth Grand Champion:
Mike Chaturantabut

(MUSICAL 17 & UNDER CO-ED):
1. Mike Chaturantabut

(15–17 CO-ED):
1. Jon Valera

(13–14 CO-ED):
1. Carmichael Simon

(11–12 CO-ED):
1. Bernadette Ambrosia

(9–10 CO-ED):
1. Kody Gilbow

(8 & UNDER CO-ED):
1. Ashley Kohler

Adult Weapons Grand Champion:
Mike Bernardo

Men

HARD STYLE:
1. Mike Bernardo

SOFT STYLE:
1. Richard Brandon

WOMEN:
1. Christine Bannon-Rodrigues

EXECUTIVE/SENIOR CO-ED:
1. Rocky DiRico

Youth Weapons Grand Champion:
Brian Ruth

(15–17 CO-ED):
1. Mike Chaturantabut

(11–14 CO-ED):
1. Brian Ruth

(10 & UNDER CO-ED):
1. Kody Gilbow

A.K.A. GRAND NATIONALS: SEPTEMBER 7, 1991

Fighting

Men's Grand Champions:
Hakim Alston
1. David Kiss

MIDDLE:
Mike Bernardo
1. Marino Jones

LIGHT:
Shah Alston
1. David Wilson

EXECUTIVE:
Joshua Harper

EXECUTIVE HEAVY (35–42):
1. Rudy Sayers

EXECUTIVE LIGHT (35–42):
1. Joshua Harper

SENIORS (43 & OVER):
1. J.C. Copeland

Women's Grand Champion:
Nicki Carlson
1. Laura Armes

Youth (Boys)

(15–17):
1. Joe Rivera
2. Mike Chaturantabut

(13–14):
1. Brian Ruth
2. Hector Santiago

(11–12):
1. Adam Keister
2. Jay Hirleman

(9–10 CO-ED):
1. Kody Gilbow
2. Melvin Hayes

(8 & UNDER CO-ED):
1. Emily Pokora
2. Ashley Kohler

Youth (Girls)

(15–17):
1. Krysta Shearer

(13–14):
1. Jennifer Yanoff

(11–12):
1. Bernadette Ambrosia

Forms

Men's Grand Champion:
Hosung Pak

Men

AMERICAN (CO-ED):
1. Hoyoung Pak

CHINESE:
1. Hosung Pak

JAPANESE/OKINAWAN:
1. John Marshall

KOREAN:
1. Michael Dietrich

MUSICAL (CO-ED):
1. Chris Casamassa

EXECUTIVE/SENIOR (CO-ED):
1. Phil Morgan

Women's Grand Champion:
Elsa Cordero

HARD STYLE:
1. Elsa Cordero

SOFT STYLE:
1. Michelle Griffin

Youth Grand Champion:
Mike Chaturantabut

(MUSICAL 17 & UNDER CO-ED):
1. Mike Chaturantabut
2. Adam Keister
3. Clay Morton

(15–17 CO-ED):
1. Jon Valera

(13–14 CO-ED):
1. Carmichael Simon

(11–12 CO-ED):
1. Bernadette Ambrosia

(9–10 CO-ED):
1. Kody Gilbow

(8 & UNDER CO-ED):
1. Emily Pokora

Adult Weapons Grand Champion:
Mike Bernardo

Men

HARD STYLE:
1. Mike Bernardo

SOFT STYLE:
1. Hosung Pak

WOMEN:
1. Stacy Demejia

EXECUTIVE/SENIOR CO-ED:
1. Phil Morgan

Youth Weapons Grand Champion:
Brian Ruth

(15–17 CO-ED):
1. John Valera

(11–14 CO-ED):
1. Brian Ruth

(10 & UNDER CO-ED):
1. Kody Gilbow

**WORLD PRO-AM:
SEPTEMBER 21, 1991**

Fighting

Men's Grand Champions:
Richard Triplett
1. Chris Daley

MIDDLE:
Mike Bernardo
1. Marino Jones

LIGHT:
Shah Alston
1. Gabe Reynaga

SENIOR (CO-ED)
J.C. Copeland

EXECUTIVE HEAVY (35–42):
1. James Hobby

SENIOR (CO-ED) LIGHT (35–42):
1. Dan Trailing

SENIORS (43 & OVER):
1. J.C. Copeland
2. Tom Levak

Women's Grand Champion:
Nicki Carlson
1. Elsa Cordero

Youth (Boys)

(15–17):
1. Mike Chaturantabut

(13–14):
1. Brian Short

(11–12):
1. Adam Keister

(9–10 CO-ED):
1. Kody Gilbow

(8 & UNDER CO-ED):
1. Ashley Kohler

Youth (Girls)

(15–17):
1. Sadie Brower

(13–14):
1. Maria Bovacqua

(11–12):
1. Tarha Gableman

Forms

Men's Grand Champion:
Chris Casamassa

Men

AMERICAN (CO-ED):
1. Mike Bernardo

CHINESE:
1. Hoyoung Pak

JAPANESE/OKINAWAN:
1. Gabe Reynaga

KOREAN:
1. Dave Macomber

MUSICAL (CO-ED):
1. Chris Casamassa

EXECUTIVE/SENIOR (CO-ED):
1. Mike Powser

Women's Grand Champion:
Elsa Cordero

HARD STYLE:
1. Elsa Cordero

SOFT STYLE:
1. Irene Chen

Youth Grand Champion:
Mike Chaturantabut

(MUSICAL 17 & UNDER CO-ED):
1. Mike Chaturantabut

(15–17 CO-ED):
1. Jon Valera

(13–14 CO-ED):
1. Brian Short

(11–12 CO-ED):
1. Adam Keister

(9–10 CO-ED):
1. Kody Gilbow

(8 & UNDER CO-ED):
1. Ashley Kohler

Adult Weapons Grand Champion:
Hoyoung Pak

Men

HARD STYLE:
1. Mike Bernardo

SOFT STYLE:
1. Hoyoung Pak

WOMEN:
1. Elsa Cordero

EXECUTIVE/SENIOR CO-ED:
1. Steve Carlson

Youth Weapons Grand Champion:
Mike Chaturantabut

(15–17 CO-ED):
1. Mike Chaturantabut

(11–14 CO-ED):
1. Brian Short

(10 & UNDER CO-ED):
1. Kody Gilbow

DIAMOND NATIONALS: OCTOBER 12, 1991

Fighting

Men's Grand Champions:

HEAVY:
Steve Boyles
1. Hakim Alston

MIDDLE:
Ibby Abdalla
1. Calvin Thomas

LIGHT:
Shah Alston
1. Akbar Alston

EXECUTIVE:
J.C. Copeland

EXECUTIVE HEAVY (35–42):
1. James Hobby

EXECUTIVE LIGHT (35–42):
1. Joshua Harper

SENIORS (43 & OVER):
1. J.C. Copeland

Women's Grand Champion:
Nicki Carlson

HEAVY:
1. Nicki Carlson
2. Michelle Arango

LIGHT:
1. Brenda Lee
2. Andrea Spitz

Youth (Boys)

(15–17):
1. Joe Rivera
2. Frank DiCaria

(13–14):
1. Brian Ruth
2. Hector Santiago

(11–12):
1. Jay Hirleman
2. Travis Abicht

(9–10 CO-ED):
1. Jay Lindeman
2. Justin Sheppard

(8 & UNDER CO-ED):
1. Emily Pokora

Youth (Girls)

(15–17):
1. Tiffany Costello

(13–14):
1. Jennifer Yanoff

(11–12):
1. Bernadette Ambrosia

Forms

Men's Grand Champion:
Hosung Pak

Men

AMERICAN (CO-ED):
1. Hoyoung Pak

CHINESE:
1. Hosung Pak

OKINAWAN/OKINAWAN:
1. Gabe Reynaga

KOREAN:
1. Michael Dietrich

MUSICAL (CO-ED):
1. Chris Casamassa

EXECUTIVE/SENIOR (CO-ED):
1. Phil Morgan

Women's Grand Champion:
Elsa Cordero

HARD STYLE:
1. Elsa Cordero

SOFT STYLE:
1. Geri James

Youth Grand Champion:
Kim Do

(MUSICAL 17 & UNDER CO-ED):
1. Kim Do
2. Mike Chaturantabut
3. Justin Sheppard

(15–17 CO-ED):
1. Jon Valera

(13–14 CO-ED):
1. Carmichael Simon

(11–12 CO-ED):
1. Bernadette Ambrosia

(9–10 CO-ED):
1. Kody Gilbow

(8 & UNDER CO-ED):
1. Christopher Katera

Adult Weapons Grand Champion:
Mike Bernardo

Men

HARD STYLE:
1. Mike Bernardo

SOFT STYLE:
1. Hosung Pak

WOMEN:
1. Michelle Arango

EXECUTIVE/SENIOR CO-ED:
1. Rocky DiRico

Youth Weapons Grand Champion:
Mike Chaturantabut

(15–17 CO-ED):
1. Mike Chaturantabut

(11–14 CO-ED):
1. Bernadette Ambrosia

(10 & UNDER CO-ED):
1. Kody Gilbow

NORTH AMERICAN KARATE CHAMPIONSHIPS: OCTOBER 26, 1991

Fighting

Men's Grand Champions:

HEAVY:
Richard Plowden
1. Hakim Alston

MIDDLE:
Ibby Abdalla
1. Calvin Thomas

LIGHT:
Akbar Alston
1. Shah Alston

EXECUTIVE:
J.C. Copeland

EXECUTIVE HEAVY (35–42):
1. Terry Creamer

EXECUTIVE LIGHT (35–42):
1. Lamon Kersey

SENIORS (43 & OVER):
1. J.C. Copeland

Women's Grand Champion:
Laura Armes
1. Michelle Arango

Youth (Boys)

(15–17):
1. Andre Hodge

(13–14):
1. Brian Ruth

(11–12):
1. Mike Franze

(9–10 CO-ED):
1. Jeff Lindeman

(8 & UNDER CO-ED):
1. Emily Pokora

Youth (Girls)

(15–17):
1. Krista Shearer

(13–14):
1. Jennifer Yanoff

(11–12):
1. Bernadette Ambrosia

Forms

Men's Grand Champion:
Hosung Pak

Men

AMERICAN (CO-ED):
1. Hoyoung Pak

CHINESE:
1. Hosung Pak

JAPANESE/OKINAWAN:
1. Gabe Reynaga

KOREAN:
1. Eric San Jose

MUSICAL (CO-ED):
1. Chris Casamassa

EXECUTIVE/SENIOR (CO-ED):
1. Rocky DiRico

Women's Grand Champion:
Christine Bannon-Rodrigues

HARD STYLE:
1. Michelle Arango

SOFT STYLE:
1. Christine Bannon-Rodrigues

Youth:

(MUSICAL 17 & UNDER CO-ED):
1. Mike Chaturantabut

(15–17 CO-ED):
1. Jon Valera

(13–14 CO-ED):
1. Carmichael Simon

(11–12 CO-ED):
1. Bernadette Ambrosia

(9–10 CO-ED):
1. Kody Gilbow

(8 & UNDER CO-ED):
1. Ashley Kohler

Adult Weapons Grand Champion:
Mike Bernardo

Men

HARD STYLE:
1. Mike Bernardo

SOFT STYLE:
1. Hosung Pak

WOMEN:
1. Christine Bannon-Rodrigues

EXECUTIVE/SENIOR CO-ED:
1. Rocky DiRico

Youth Weapons Grand Champion:
Bernadette Ambrosia

(15–17 CO-ED):
1. Brandon Kersey

(11–14 CO-ED):
1. Bernadette Ambrosia

(10 & UNDER CO-ED):
1. Kody Gilbow

1990 NATIONAL TOURNAMENTS

BOSTON INTERNATIONALS: FEBRUARY 3, 1990

Fighting

Men

HEAVY:
1. Richard Plowden
2. Chris Brookens
3. Matthew Babine

LIGHT HEAVY:
1. Anthony Price
2. Steve Babcock
3. Raven Lee Smith

MIDDLE:
1. "Stingo" Garcia
2. Anthony Holloway
3. Jeff Gears

LIGHT MIDDLE:
1. Chris Rappold
2. Rupert Daniel
3. Bob Lamattina

LIGHT:
1. Kevin Thompson
2. Pedro Xavier
3. Alberto Montrond

SUPERLIGHT:
1. Tony Young
2. Waymon Beavers
3. Manny Reyes, Jr.

EXECUTIVE:
1. Terry Creamer
2. Frank Perry
3. Steve McGill

SENIORS:
1. Wali Islam
2. Doug Peoples
3. Bill Bryant

Women

HEAVY:
1. Linda Denley
2. Kierston Sims
3. Lisa Crosby

MIDDLE:
1. Cheryl Nance
2. Rose Moscato
3. Michelle Delgiorno

LIGHT:
1. Christine Bannon
2. Robin Tierney

Junior Boys

(16–17):
1. Yanick Turgeon
2. Michael Baez
3. Fredric Matte

(14–15):
1. Jean Tessel
2. Yanick Marcote
3. Adilson Baptista

(12–13):
1. Mike Freed
2. Steve Guerrero
3. Hector Santiago

(10–11 CO-ED):
1. Jonathan DiPina
2. Nick Gingras
3. Brian Shean

Junior Girls

(16–17):
1. Christina Muccini
2. Melissa Souza
3. Isabelle Tessier

(14–15):
1. Jenn Gambardella
2. Laura Barletta

(12–13):
1. Jennifer Yanoff
2. Jessica Calderon
3. Lisa Colby

Forms

Grand Champion
Hosung Pak
2. Kevin Thompson

Men

CHINESE:
1. Hosung Pak
2. Richard Brandon
3. Greg Walraven

JAPANESE:
1. Kevin Thompson
2. Vincent Rigueros
3. Papo Villarrubia

KENPO:
1. Terry Creamer
2. Chris Columbo
3. Mark Sheeley

KOREAN:
1. David Collins
2. Steve Magill
3. Albano DaSilva

OKINAWAN:
1. Domingo Llanos
2. Cheech Luzzi
3. Anthony Jadarola

OPEN/MUSICAL:
1. Jean Frenette
2. Harold DeSauguste
3. Bill Marr

SENIOR MEN:
1. Sonny Onowo

2. Rocky DiRico
3. Brian Ricci

Women

HARD STYLE:
1. Cheryl Nance
2. Sue Brazelton
3. Denise Rouleau

SOFT STYLE:
1. Christine Bannon
2. Alice Chung
3. Holly Olson

Juniors

(16–17):
1. Mark Bonaquisto
2. Christina Muccini
3. Melissa Sanza

(14–15):
1. Chris Alibrandi
2. Mike Terrace
3. Paul Mayo

(12–13):
1. Jessica Calderon
2. Jennifer Yanoff
3. Eric Pare

(11 & UNDER):
1. Nick Gingras
2. Corey Remon
3. Brian Shea

Weapons

HARD STYLE:
1. Kevin Thompson
2. Jean Frenette
3. Domingo Llanos

SOFT STYLE:
1. Hosung Pak
2. Christine Bannon
3. Richard Brandon

SENIOR WEAPONS:
1. Rocky DiRico
2. Sonny Onowo
3. Brian Ricci

JUNIORS (17 & UNDER):
1. Chris Aligrandi
2. Jennifer Yanoff
3. Mark Bonaquisto

COMPETE NATIONALS: FEBRUARY 17, 1990

Fighting

Men

HEAVY:
1. Shon Adams

LIGHT HEAVY:
1. Mike Smith

MIDDLE:
1. Hakim Alston

LIGHT MIDDLE:
1. Joey Escobar

LIGHT:
1. Marty Eubanks

SUPER LIGHT:
1. Jose Pacheco

SENIORS (HEAVY):
1. Johnny Gyro

SENIORS (LIGHT):
1. Dan Boccagno

EXECUTIVE (42 & OVER):
1. Steve Curran

Women

HEAVY:
1. Chavela Aaron

MIDDLE:
1. Elsa Cordero

LIGHT:
1. Brenda Hund

SENIOR:
1. Phyllis McNeal

Forms

Men's Grand Champion:
Steven Ho

AMERICAN:
1. Steve Ho

CHINESE:
1. Javonne Holmes

JAPANESE:
1. Mike Bernardo

KENPO/KAJUKENBO:
1. Manuel Mendez

KOREAN:
1. Dave Macomber

MUSICAL:
1. Chris Casamassa

OKINAWAN:
1. Gabe Reynaga

SENIORS:
1. Phil Morgan

Women's Grand Champion
Elsa Cordero
2. Yungchu Kim

Weapons

GRAND CHAMPION:
Mike Bernardo

HARD STYLE:
1. Mike Bernardo

SOFT STYLE:
1. Hoyoung Pak

SENIOR MEN:
1. Phil Morgan

WOMEN:
1. Kathy Quan

BREAKING:
1. Frank Aguilar

GREATER METROPOLITAN NATIONALS: MARCH 11, 1990

Tom Festa, Producer
Hempstead, NY

EMPIRE STATE NATIONALS: APRIL 1, 1990

BATTLE OF ATLANTA: APRIL 28, 1990

OCEAN STATE NATIONALS: May 5, 1990

U.S.A. NATIONALS: MAY 19, 1990

NEW ENGLAND OPEN: JUNE 2, 1990

Fighting

Men

HEAVY:
1. Shon Adams

LIGHT HEAVY:
1. Hakim Alston

MIDDLE:
1. Anthony Holloway

LIGHT MIDDLE:
1. Alberto Montrond

LIGHT:
1. Pedro Xavier

SUPER LIGHT:
1. Gabe Reynaga

SENIOR (HEAVY):
1. Steve Anderson

SENIOR (LIGHT):
1. Marty Knight

SENIOR (43 & OVER):
1. Wali Islam

Women's Grand Champion:
Brenda Hund
2. Angela Webb

HEAVY:
1. Doreen Cogliandro

MIDDLE:
1. Angela Webb

LIGHT:
1. Brenda Hund

Junior Boys

(16–17):
1. Brian Smith

(14–15):
1. Jon Valera

(12–13):
1. Brian Ruth

(10–11 CO-ED):
1. Adam Keister

(8–9 CO-ED):
1. Jason Dawson

Junior Girls

(16–17):
1. Tiffany Costello

(14–15):
1. Krista Shearer

(12–13):
1. Jennifer Yanoff

Forms

Men's Grand Champion:
Hoyoung Pak
2. Saeed Delkash

AMERICAN:
1. Saeed Delkash

CHINESE/KENPO:
1. Will Allen

JAPANESE/OKINAWAN:
1. Grant Campbell

KOREAN:
1. David Macomber

MUSICAL:
1. Hoyoung Pak

SENIORS:
1. Phil Morgan

Women

GRAND CHAMPION:
Elsa Cordero
2. Yungchu Kim

HARD STYLE:
1. Elsa Cordero

SOFT STYLE:
1. Yungchu Kim

Juniors

GRAND CHAMPION:
Jon Valera
2. Carmichael Simon

(16–17):
1. Brian Smith

(14–15):
1. Jon Valera

(12–13):
1. Carmichael Simon

(8–9):
(10–11):
1. Bernadette Ambrosia
1. Jason Dawson

Weapons

GRAND CHAMPION:
Hoyoung Pak
2. Rocky DiRico

HARD STYLE:
1. Dan McFarland

SENIORS:
1. Rocky DiRico

SOFT STYLE:
1. Hoyoung Pak

WOMEN:
1. Kathy Quan

Juniors

GRAND CHAMPION
Jon Valera
2. Brian Ruth

(14–17):
1. Jon Valera

(10–13):
1. Brian Ruth

(9 & UNDER):
1. Jason Dawson

**BLUEGRASS NATIONALS:
JUNE 16, 1990**

**TOP TEN NATIONALS:
JULY 14, 1990**

Dr. Eddie Andujar, Producer
Atlantic City, NJ

U.S. OPEN: JULY 28, 1990

**KEYSTONE NATIONALS:
AUGUST 5, 1990**

Jerry & Candy Otto, Producers
Easton, PA

**U.S. CAPITAL CLASSICS:
AUGUST 11, 1990**

**WORLD PRO-AM:
SEPTEMBER 15, 1990**

**ALAMANCE NATIONALS:
SEPTEMBER 15, 1990**

Hamilton Perkins, Producer
Greensboro, NC

**A.K.A. GRAND NATIONALS:
SEPTEMBER 30, 1990**

**DIAMOND NATIONALS:
OCTOBER 13, 1990**

**BATTLE OF BALTIMORE:
OCTOBER 21, 1990**

**PAN-AM NATIONALS:
NOVEMBER 3, 1990**

Manny Reyes, Producer
Miami, FL

**MILE HIGH CLASSIC:
NOVEMBER 10, 1990**

**NORTH AMERICAN
CHAMPIONSHIPS:
DECEMBER 1, 1990**

**1989 NATIONAL
TOURNAMENTS**

Note: A new grand championship policy was instituted in 1989 for national tournaments. For years, complaints had been raised about pitting a lightweight fighter against bigger and heavier opponents for the grand championship. The bigger fighter usually won the title and the additional purse.

To solve this problem, several subdivisional grand championships were created and the traditional overall grand title was eliminated. Now the lightweight winner, for example, would fight the super lightweight champion for a grand championship. Likewise for the middle- and light-middleweight winners and the heavy- and light-heavyweight winners. To conserve space and eliminate even longer sets of winners' lists, these subdivisional grand champions are not listed.

**GOLDEN DESERT CLASSIC:
FEBRUARY 25, 1989**

Toni Lee, Producer
Palm Springs, CA

Fighting

Men's Grand Champion:
Satch Williams
2. Anthony Halloway
3. Hakim Alston
Joey Shiflett

HEAVY:
1. Satch Williams

LIGHT HEAVY:
1. Alvin Prouder
2. Mike Smith
3. Steve Rice

MIDDLE:
1. Atakin Alston
2. Mike Green
3. Ray Wizard

LIGHT MIDDLE:
1. Anthony Holloway

2. Berry Garbon
3. Joey Escobar

LIGHT:
1. Joey Shiflett
2. Shah Alston
3. Randy Pumputus

SUPER LIGHT:
1. Leonard Cree
2. Don Crenshaw
3. Glen Yawn

FLY:
1. Jose Pacheco
2. Michael Dietrich
3. Willie King

FEATHER:
1. John Palitti
2. Steven Ho

SENIORS (35–42):
1. Joe Swift
2. Mr. T.
3. Carl Clary

SENIORS (43+):
1. Steve Curran
2. Gary Nichols
3. Dave Hicks

Women's Grand Champion:
Chavela Aaron
2. Elsa Cordero
3. Kierston Sims

HEAVY:
1. Chavela Aaron
2. Nikki Carlson
3. Michonne Keeble

MIDDLE:
1. Kierston Sims
2. Sharon Floyd
3. Cynthia Prouder

LIGHT:
1. Elsa Cordero
2. Kathy Marlor
3. Lisa Cerda

EXECUTIVE:
1. Georgia Lipvak
2. Irene Herrera
3. Terry Reynaga

Junior Grand Champion:
Todd Finney
2. Sean Green

Junior Boys

(15–17, HEAVY):
1. Sean Green

(15–17, LIGHT):
1. Gabe Reynaga

(12–14):
1. Jason Gandy

(9–11):
1. Nicholas Gringas

(8 & UNDER):
1. Seth Anapolsky

Junior Girls

(15–17):
1. Kim Duran

(12–14):
1. Jessica Stevens

Forms

Grand Champion:
Charlie Lee
2. Steven Ho
3. Barron Tabura

CHINESE:
1. Ken Perez

JAPANESE/OKINAWAN:
1. Mike Bernardo

KENPO:
1. Manuel Mendez

KOREAN:
1. Charlie Lee

MUSICAL:
1. Chris Casamassa

OPEN:
1. Steven Ho

SENIORS:
1. Steve Curran

Women's Grand Champion:
Elsa Cordero
2. Yungchu Kim

Junior Grand Champion:
Jeff Sue
2. Dodger Villiers
3. Eddie Landa

(17+):
1. Eddie Landa

(15–17):
1. Joey Uyeda

(12–14):
1. Mike Chatarantabut

(9–11):
1. Jeff Sue

(8 & UNDER):
1. Nicholas Sheats

Weapons

HARD STYLE:
1. Barron Tabura

JUNIORS (13–17):
1. Dodger Villiers

JUNIORS (12 & UNDER):
1. Jeff Sue

SENIORS:
1. Steve Curran

SOFT STYLE:
1. Phillip Wong

WOMEN:
1. Kathy Quan

MILLER LITE GREATER METRO NATIONALS: MARCH 5, 1989

Tom Festa, Producer
Flushing, NY

Fighting

Men

HEAVY:
1. Anthony Price

LIGHT HEAVY:
1. Chip Wright

MIDDLE:
1. Anthony Holloway

LIGHT:
1. Kevin Thompson

SUPER LIGHT:
1. Tony Young

SENIORS:
1. Wali Islam

Women

HEAVY:
1. Chavela Aaron

LIGHT:
1. Christine Bannon

Forms

Grand Champion

Jean Frenette
2. Kevin Thompson
3. Hosung Pak

CHINESE:
1. Hosung Pak

JAPANESE:
1. Sonny Onowo

KOREAN:
1. Michael Dietrick

OKINAWAN:
1. Cheech Luzzi

OPEN/MUSICAL:
1. Jean Frenette

SENIORS:
1. Terry Maccarrone

Women

HARD STYLE:
1. Cheryl Nance

SOFT STYLE:
1. Christine Bannon

Weapons

HARD STYLE:
1. Kevin Thompson

SOFT STYLE:
1. Hosung Pak

SENIORS:
1. Felix Vasquez

JUNIOR CO-ED (13–17):
1. Chris Schroder

JUNIOR CO-ED (12 & UNDER):
1. Jennifer Yanoff

MONTREAL INTERNATIONALS: MARCH 11, 1989

Jean Frenette, Producer
Montreal, Canada

EMPIRE STATE NATIONALS: MARCH 12, 1989

Fighting

Men's Grand Champion:

Hakim Alston
2. Anthony Holloway

HEAVY:
1. Mike Smith

LIGHT HEAVY:
1. Shon Adams

MIDDLE:
1. Hakim Alston

LIGHT MIDDLE:
1. Anthony Holloway

LIGHT:
1. Marty Eubanks

SUPER LIGHT:
1. Jose Pacheco

SENIORS (35–42):
1. ?

SENIORS (43+):
1. Wali Islam

Women's Grand Champion:

Kierston Sims
2. Brenda Hund

Forms

Grand Champion

Michael Bernardo

CHINESE:
1. Richard Brandon

JAPANESE/OKINAWAN:
1. ?

KOREAN:
1. Michael Dietrick

MUSICAL:
1. Hoyoung Pak

OPEN:
1. Joon Bak Lee

Women

HARD STYLE:
1. Kathy Quan

SOFT STYLE:
1. Yungchu Kim

Junior Grand Champion:

Jeff Sue

(15–17):
1. Michael Saxon

(12–14):
1. Jon Valera

(11 & UNDER):
1. Jeff Sue

Weapons

HARD STYLE:
1. Michael Bernardo

JUNIORS:
1. Jeff Sue

SENIORS:
1. Rocky DiRico

SOFT STYLE:
1. Hoyoung Pak

COORS SILVER BULLET GRAND NATIONALS: APRIL 9, 1989

Harold Halterman, Producer
Harrisonburg, VA

Fighting

Men's Grand Champion:

Steve Anderson
2. Hakim Alston
3. Billy Bryant

Women's Grand Champion:

Chavela Aaron
2. Cheryl Nance

Forms

Grand Champion:

Jean Frenette
2. Charlie Lee
3. Kevin Thompson

Weapons Grand Champion:

Kevin Thompson

NEW ENGLAND OPEN: APRIL 15, 1989

Fighting

Men

HEAVY:
1. Andre Richardson

LIGHT HEAVY:
1. Michael Smith

MIDDLE:
1. Hakim Alston

LIGHT MIDDLE:
1. Anthony Holloway

LIGHT:
1. David Randall

SUPER LIGHT:
1. Donald Brady

Women's Grand Champion:

1. Chavela Aaron
2. Kierston Sims

HEAVY:
1. Chavela Aaron

MIDDLE:
1. Kierston Sims

LIGHT:
1. Kathy Marlor

Junior Boys

(15–17):
1. Robert Hendricks

(12–14):
1. Eddie Abrantes

(9–11 CO-ED):
1. Jonathan DiPina

Junior Girls

(15–17):
1. Shellie Blanks

(12–14):
1. Shannon Ashby

Forms

Grand Champion:
1. Charlie Lee
2. Richard Brandon

AMERICAN/OPEN:
1. Steven Ho

CHINESE/KENPO:
1. Richard Brandon

JAPANESE/OKINAWAN:
1. Mike Bernardo

KOREAN:
1. Charlie Lee

MUSICAL/OPEN:
1. Dan McFarland

SENIORS:
1. Steve Curran

WEAPONS (HARD-STYLE):
1. Mike Bernardo

WEAPONS (SENIOR):
1. Steve Curran

WEAPONS (SOFT-STYLE):
1. Richard Brandon

Women

HARD STYLE:
1. Elsa Cordero

SOFT STYLE:
1. Yungchu Kim

Junior Grand Champion:
1. Jon Valera
2. Jeff Soo

(15–17):
1. Michael Saxon

(12–14):
1. Jon Valera

(11 & UNDER):
1. Eddie Landa

WEAPONS (17 & UNDER):
1. Jeff Soo

BATTLE OF ATLANTA: APRIL 29, 1989

OCEAN STATE NATIONALS: MAY 6, 1989

Fighting

Men

HEAVY:
1. Richard Plowden
2. Terry Creamer

LIGHT HEAVY:
1. Anthony Price
2. Steve Babcock

MIDDLE:
1. Cheech Luzzi
2. Chip Wright

LIGHT MIDDLE:
1. Anthony Holloway
2. David Collins

LIGHT:
1. Kevin Thompson

SUPERLIGHT:
1. Tony Young

SENIOR HEAVY:
1. Doug Peoples
2. Wali Islam

SENIOR LIGHT:
1. Billy Bryant

Women

HEAVY:
1. Linda Denley
2. Chavela Aaron

MIDDLE:
1. Cheryl Nance
2. Kierston Sims

LIGHT:
1. Christine Bannon

Forms

Grand Champion:
　Jean Frenette
2. Kevin Thompson
3. Hosung Pak
　Richard Brandon

Junior Grand Champion:
　Jon Valera

USA JUNIOR NATIONALS: MAY 20, 1989

Roger Jones, Producer
Asheville, NC

Fighting

Divisional Winners

(16–17):
　David Oakley

(14–15):
　Mike Saxon

(12–13):
　Phillip Pippin

(10–11):
　Seneca Luther

(8–9):
　Jarrett Weeks

(7 & UNDER):
　Jimmy Fritsch

Forms

Grand Champion:
　Jon Valera
2. Seneca Luther
3. Mike Chaturantabut
4. Jimmy Fritsch

Weapons Grand Champion:
　Jon Valera
2. Jeff Sue
3. Mike Saxon
　Adam Keister

BLUEGRASS NATIONALS: JUNE 17, 1989

Fighting

Men

HEAVY:
1. Steve Anderson

LIGHT HEAVY:
1. Marino Jones

MIDDLE:
1. Hakim Alston

LIGHT MIDDLE:
1. Anthony Holloway

LIGHT:
1. Pedro Xavier

SUPER LIGHT:
1. Jose Pacheco

SENIORS:
1. Joe Pina

EXECUTIVE:
1. Ken Eubanks

Women's Grand Champion:
Chavela Aaron
2. Brenda Hund

Senior Men's Grand Champion:
Harold Burrage

LIGHT (35–42):
1. Harold Burrage

HEAVY (35–42):
1. Steve Curran

(42+):
1. James Hobby

Junior

CO-ED (15–17):
1. Dietra Spencer

CO-ED (13–14):
1. Brian Craig

CO-ED (11–12):
1. Brian Ruth

CO-ED (9–10):
1. Nick Gimgras

GIRLS (15–17):
1. Christina Muccini

GIRLS (12–14):
1. Jennifer Yanoff

GIRLS (9–11):
1. Eva Ramirez

Forms

Grand Champion:
Hoyoung Pak
2. Charlie Lee

Men

CHINESE:
1. Hoyoung Pak

CREATIVE:
1. Jerry Prince

JAPANESE/OKINAWAN:
1. Mike Bernardo

KOREAN:
1. Charlie Lee

MUSICAL:
1. Dan McFarland

SENIORS:
1. Steve Curran

Women

HARD STYLE:
1. Elsa Cordero

SOFT STYLE:
1. Yungchu Kim

Juniors

MUSICAL (15–17):
1. Gaffar Adam

(15–17):
1. Michael Saxon

MUSICAL (12–14):
1. Jon Valera

(12–14):
1. Mike Chatarantabut

MUSICAL (10–11):
1. Eddie Landa

(10–11):
1. Bernadette Ambrosia

MUSICAL (9 & UNDER):
1. Jason Webb

(9 & UNDER):
1. Jarrett Weeks

Weapons

HARD STYLE:
1. Mike Bernardo

SOFT STYLE:
1. Hoyoung Pak

SENIORS:
1. Steve Curran

JUNIOR GRAND CHAMPION:
Michael Saxon
2. Jon Valera
3. Seneca Luther

**TOP TEN NATIONALS:
JULY 15, 1989**

**Dr. Eddie Andujar, Producer
Atlantic City, NJ**

Fighting

Men's Grand Champion:
Steve Anderson

HEAVY:
1. Steve Anderson

LIGHT HEAVY:
1. Stingo Garcia

MIDDLE:
1. Hakim Alston

LIGHT MIDDLE:
1. Marc Jones

LIGHT:
1. Marty Eubanks

SUPER LIGHT:
1. Don Brady

SENIORS (HEAVY):
1. Wali Islam

SENIORS (LIGHT):
1. Dan Boccagneo

Women's Grand Champion:
Chavela Aaron
2. Lori McCutcheon

Junior Boys

(15–17):
1. Gaffar Adam

(12–14):
1. Mike Shurina

(9–11):
1. Jonathan DePina

Junior Girls

(15–17):
1. Christina Muccini

(12–14):
1. Rashnia Scott

(9–11):
1. Marina Kallergis

Forms

Grand Champion:
Charlie Lee
2. Steven Ho
3. Mike Bernardo

CHINESE:
1. Hoyoung Pak

CREATIVE:
1. Steven Ho

JAPANESE/OKINAWAN:
1. Mike Bernardo

KOREAN:
1. Charlie Lee

MUSICAL:
1. Chris Casamassa

Women

HARD STYLE:
1. Elsa Cordero

SOFT STYLE:
1. Yungchu Kim

Junior Grand Champion:
Seneca Luther
2. Jon Valera
3. Mike Saxon

Weapons

HARD STYLE:
1. Mike Bernardo

SOFT STYLE:
1. Hoyoung Pak

SENIORS:
1. Dewey Earwood

JUNIORS:
1. Bernadette Ambrosia

U.S. OPEN:
JULY 29, 1989

Fighting

Men

HEAVY:
1. Shon Adams

LIGHT HEAVY:
1. Michael Smith

MIDDLE:
1. Mike Green

LIGHT MIDDLE:
1. Anthony Holloway

LIGHT:
1. Marty Eubanks

SUPER LIGHT:
1. Jerry Price

SENIOR HEAVY:
1. Laymor Williamson

SENIOR MIDDLE:
1. Joshua Harper

SENIOR LIGHT:
1. Dan Boccagneo

OVER 42:
1. Steve Curran

Women

MIDDLE:
1. Chavela Aaron

LIGHT MIDDLE:
2. Cindy Ingram

LIGHT:
1. Lori McCutcheon

SUPER LIGHT:
1. Lori Lantrip

Forms

Grand Champion:
Charlie Lee
2. Hoyoung Pak
3. Mike Bernardo

Men

CHINESE:
1. Anthony Marquez

CREATIVE:
1. Jerry Prince

JAPANESE/OKINAWAN:
1. Mike Bernardo

KOREAN:
1. Charlie Lee

MUSICAL:
1. Hoyoung Pak

SENIORS:
1. Dewey Earwood

Women

HARD STYLE:
1. Elsa Cordero

SOFT STYLE:
1. Yungchu Kim

Weapons

HARD STYLE:
1. Mike Bernardo

SENIORS:
1. Rocky DiRico

SOFT STYLE:
1. Anthony Marques

Junior Grand Champion:
Michael Saxon
1. Jon Valera
2. Jeff Sue

(15–17):
1. Michael Saxon

(12–14):
1. Jon Valera

(11 & UNDER):
1. Eddie Landa

WEAPONS (13–17):
1. Michael Saxon

WEAPONS (12 & UNDER):
1. Jeff Sue

LONG BEACH INTERNATIONALS:
AUGUST 5–6, 1989

U.S. CAPITAL CLASSICS:
AUGUST 12, 1989

Fighting

Men

HEAVY:
1. Steve Anderson

LIGHT HEAVY:
1. Edward Littlejohn

MIDDLE:
1. Hakim Alston

LIGHT MIDDLE:
1. Anthony Holloway

LIGHT:
1. Ibbie Abdula

SENIORS (35–42):
1. Laymor Williamson

SENIORS (42+):
1. Steve Curran

Women

HEAVY:
1. Kierston Sims

MIDDLE:
1. Michelle Deigiorno

LIGHT:
1. Brenda Hund

SENIORS:
1. Linda Ranson

Forms

Grand Champion:
Mike Bernardo
2. Charlie Lee
3. Steve Ho

Men

CHINESE:
1. Phillip Wong

CREATIVE:
1. Steven Ho

JAPANESE/OKINAWAN:
1. Mike Bernardo

KOREAN:
1. Charlie Lee

MUSICAL:
1. Hoyoung Pak

SENIORS:
1. Rocky DiRico

Women

HARD STYLE:
1. Elsa Cordero

SOFT STYLE:
1. Yungchu Kim

Weapons

HARD STYLE:
1. Mike Bernardo

SOFT STYLE:
1. Hoyoung Pak

SENIORS:
1. Steve Curran

Junior Grand Champion:
Seneca Luther
2. Jon Valera

(15–17):
1. Mike Saxon

(12–14):
1. Jon Valera

(9–11):
1. Seneca Luther

(6–8):
1. Adam Garris

Weapons (17 & Under):
1. Jon Valera

BOSTON SUMMER OPEN: AUGUST 19, 1989

Fighting

Men

HEAVY:
1. Richard Plowden
2. Terry Creamer
3. Andre Richardson

LIGHT HEAVY:
1. Anthony Price
2. Richard Byrd
3. Jack Vigliotti

Kevin Thompson. Courtesy of Mike McCoy

MIDDLE:
1. "Stingo" Garcia
2. Cheech Luzzi
3. Ken Osborne

LIGHT MIDDLE:
1. Anthony Holloway
2. Lamart Tolusan
3. Brian Crumb

LIGHT:
1. Pedro Xavier
2. Mike Conroy
3. Kevin Thompson

SUPER LIGHT:
1. Tony Young
2. Waymon Beavets
3. Ronald Brady

SENIORS:
1. Wali Islam
2. Doug Peoples
3. Lee Ireland

Women

HEAVY:
1. Chavela Aaron
2. Linda Denley
3. Kierston Sims

MIDDLE:
1. Michelle Delgiorno
2. Cheryl Nance
3. Kristina Heap

LIGHT:
1. Christine Bannon
2. Dawn Santamaria
3. Isabelle Tessier

Junior Boys

(16–17):
1. Eric Caswell
2. Blaine D'Acci
3. Frederic Matte

(14–15):
1. Yanick Marcotte
2. Mark Bonaquisto
3. Arthur Gee

(12–13):
1. Will Howes
2. Chris Goldberg
3. Adilson Baptista

(10–11 CO-ED):
1. Jonathan DiPina
2. Nick Gringas
3. Jessica Calderon

(9 & UNDER CO-ED):
1. Christopher Lee
2. Daniel Schwartz
3. Brian Knowles

Junior Girls

(16–17):
1. Melissa Souza

(14–15):
1. Melanie Segal

(12–13):
1. Jennifer Yanoff
2. Melissa Knight
3. Heather Knowles

Forms

Men

CHINESE:
1. Hosung Pak
2. Richard Brandon
3. Karl Romain

JAPANESE:
1. Kevin Thompson
2. Grant Campbell
3. Gilles Cloutier

KENPO:
1. Terry Creamer
2. Hien Nguyen
3. Raven Lee Smith

KOREAN:
1. Pedro Xavier
2. Garrett Warren
3. Seroj Benjanian

OKINAWAN:
1. Cheech Luzzi
2. Domingo Llanos
3. Chad Merriman

OPEN:
1. Jean Frenette
2. Bill Marr
3. Tony Young

SENIORS:
1. Jerry Otto
2. Brian Ricci
3. Rocky DiRico

Women

HARD STYLE:
1. Justina Hall
2. Sue Brazelton
3. Cheryl Nance

SOFT STYLE:
1. Christine Bannon
2. Alice Chung
3. Cori Ertha

Juniors (Co-Ed)

(16–17):
1. Eric Caswell
2. Melissa Souza
3. —

(14–15):
1. Chris Alibrandi
2. James Gomes
3. Arthur Gee

(12–13):
1. Jennifer Yanoff
2. Melissa Knight
3. Adilson Baptista

(11 & UNDER):
1. Jessica Calderon
2. Daniel Schwartz
3. Ari Welkon

Weapons

HARD STYLE:
1. Kevin Thompson
2. Jean Frenette
3. Domingo Llanos

SOFT STYLE:
1. Hosung Pak
2. Richard Brandon
3. Alice Chung

SENIORS:
1. Jerry Otto
2. Rocky DiRico
3. Brian Ricci

JUNIORS:
1. Jennifer Yanoff
2. Chris Alibrandi
3. Mark Bonaquisto

BRUCE LEE JUNIOR NATIONALS: SEPTEMBER 9, 1989

**Richard Morris, Producer
Ft. Worth, TX**

WORLD PRO-AM: SEPTEMBER 16, 1989

Fighting

Men

HEAVY:
1. Shon Adams

LIGHT HEAVY:
1. Chris Daley

MIDDLE:
1. Hakim Alston

LIGHT MIDDLE:
1. Marc Jones

LIGHT:
1. Sahah Alston

SUPER LIGHT:
1. Jose Pacheco

SENIORS (35–42):
1. James Hobby

SENIORS (43+):
1. Chuck Timmons

Women's Grand Champion:
   Brenda Hund
2. Chavela Aaron

MIDDLE:
1. Chavela Aaron

LIGHT:
1. Brenda Hund

Forms

Grand Champion:
   Mike Bernardo
2. Hoyoung Pak
3. Chris Casamassa

Men

CHINESE:
1. Tony Martinez

CREATIVE:
1. Steven Ho

JAPANESE/OKINAWAN:
1. Mike Bernardo

KOREAN:
1. Michael Dietrick

MUSICAL:
1. Chris Casamassa

Women

HARD STYLE:
1. Elsa Cordero

SOFT STYLE:
1. Yungchu Kim

Junior Grand Champion:
   Seneca Luther

(15–17):
1. David Oakley

(12–14):
1. Jeff Sue

(11 & UNDER):
1. Seneca Luther

ALAMANCE NATIONALS: SEPTEMBER 23, 1989

**Hamilton Perkins, Producer
Greensboro, NC**

ALL-STAR NATIONALS: SEPTEMBER 30, 1989

**Tony Young, Producer
Atlanta, GA**

Fighting

Men's Grand Champion:
   Richard Plowden
2. Anthony Price
3. E.J. Greer

HEAVY:
1. Anthony Price

LIGHT HEAVY:
1. Marcal Lazenby

MIDDLE:
1. E.J. Greer

LIGHT:
1. Kevin Thompson

SUPER LIGHT:
1. Terry Heard

SENIORS (HEAVY):
1. Chip Wright

SENIORS (LIGHT):
1. Marty Knight

Women

HEAVY:
1. Linda Denley

MIDDLE:
1. Nicki Carlson

LIGHT:
1. Brenda Hund

Juniors

(15–17):
1. Brian Smith

(13–14):
1. Damon Jones

(11–12):
1. Brian Ruth

(9–10):
1. Jerry Mosley

(7–8):
1. Jason Dawson

(6 & UNDER):
1. Bryce Henson

Forms

Grand Champion:
Hosung Pak
2. Sonny Onowo
3. Kevin Thompson

CHINESE:
1. Hosung Pak

JAPANESE/OKINAWAN:
1. Domingo Llanos

KOREAN:
1. Pedro Xavier

MUSICAL:
1. Jean Frenette

SENIORS:
1. Sonny Onowo

Women

HARD STYLE:
1. Cheryl Nance

SOFT STYLE:
1. Christine Bannon

Juniors

(15–17):
1. Sean Green

(13–14):
1. Mike Chatarantabut

(11–12):
1. Brian Ruth

(9–10):
1. Eric Vonherbulis

(7–8):
1. Jason Dawson

(6 & UNDER):
1. Matt Tanner

Weapons

HARD STYLE:
1. Kevin Thompson

SOFT STYLE:
1. Hosung Pak

SENIORS:
1. Sonny Onowo

JUNIORS:
1. Brian Smith

L.A.M.A. NATIONALS: OCTOBER 8, 1989

Fighting

Men

HEAVY:
1. Richard Plowden

LIGHT HEAVY:
1. Marino Jones

MIDDLE:
1. Jeff Williams

LIGHT:
1. Joseph Santiago

SENIORS:
1. Harold Burrage

Women

HEAVY:
1. Linda Denley

MIDDLE:
1. Christine Bannon

LIGHT:
1. Laurie McCutcheon

Forms

Grand Champion:
Hosung Pak

CHINESE:
1. Hosung Pak

SENIORS (35+):
1. Skipper Ingham

Women's Grand Champion:
Alice Chung
2. Cheryl Nance
3. Christine Bannon

Weapons

Grand Champion:
Kevin Thompson
2. Hosung Pak

HARD STYLE:
1. Kevin Thompson

SOFT STYLE:
1. Hosung Pak

DIAMOND NATIONALS: OCTOBER 14, 1989

Fighting

Men's Grand Champion:
Hakim Alston
2. Harold Burrage

HEAVY:
1. Shon Adams

LIGHT HEAVY:
1. Mike Smith

MIDDLE:
1. Hakim Alston
2. Mike Green
3. Anthony Holloway

LIGHT:
1. Joey Shiflett
2. Donald Brady

EXECUTIVES:
1. Harold Burrage

SENIORS:
1. Steve Curran

Women's Grand Champion:
Chavela Aaron
2. Andrea Spitz

MIDDLE:
1. Chavela Aaron
2. Denise Green

LIGHT:
1. Cindy Ingram

SUPER LIGHT:
1. Andrea Spitz

Forms

Grand Champion:
Charlie Lee

2. Mike Bernardo
3. Richard Brandon

CHINESE:
1. Richard Brandon

KOREAN:
1. Charlie Lee

MUSICAL:
1. Hoyoung Pak

SENIORS:
1. Steve Curran

WOMEN'S HARD STYLE:
1. Elsa Cordero

WOMEN'S SOFT STYLE:
1. Yungchu Kim

Weapons

MEN'S HARD STYLE:
1. Mike Bernardo

MEN'S SOFT STYLE:
1. Anthony Marquez

SENIORS:
1. Rocky DiRico

WOMEN'S HARD STYLE:
1. Kathy Quan

Juniors
Grand Champion:
Jon Valera
2. Seneca Luther

(10–11):
1. Bernadette Ambrosia

(12–13):
1. Jeff Sue

(14–15):
1. Jon Valera

(16–17):
1. Michael Saxon

WEAPONS:
1. Seneca Luther

A.K.A. GRAND NATIONALS: OCTOBER 21, 1989

BATTLE OF BALTIMORE: OCTOBER 22, 1989

NORTH AMERICAN CHAMPIONSHIPS: OCTOBER 28, 1989

Note: This event awarded $52,000 in prize money, to date the largest amount in karate tournament history.

Fighting

Men

HEAVY:
1. Anthony Price
2. Marino Jones
3. Steve Anderson
4. Terry Creamer

LIGHT HEAVY:
1. Marcal Lazenby
2. ?
3. Paul Garcia
4. Tom Smith

MIDDLE:
1. Jeff Gears
2. Ronnie Moore
3. David Collins
4. Curtis Butler, Jr.

LIGHT MIDDLE:
1. Anthony Holloway
2. Karl Richard
3. Robert Perry
4. Bob Lamatina

LIGHT:
1. Pedro Xavier
2. Kevin Brown
3. Marty Eubanks
4. Mike Conroy

SUPER LIGHT:
1. Tony Young
2. Jose Pacheco
3. John Palitti
4. Michael Dietrich

EXECUTIVE:
1. Harold Burrage
2. Chip Wright
3. Doug Peoples
4. James Hoby

SENIORS:
1. Johnny Copeland
2. Steve Curran
3. Ken Eubanks
4. Harrison White

Women

HEAVY:
1. Linda Denley
2. Chavela Aaron
3. Dagmar White
4. Lisa Crosby

MIDDLE:
1. Eva Jones
2. Terrell Davis
3. Justina Hall
4. Robyn Covino

LIGHT:
1. Cheryl Nance
2. Christine Bannon
3. Laurie McCutcheon

Forms

Men

AMERICAN/OPEN:
1. Hoyoung Pak
2. Kevin Brown
3. Andre Sack
4. David Collins

CHINESE/KENPO:
1. Hosung Pak
2. Richard Brandon
3. Anthony Marquez
4. Tommie Smith

EXECUTIVE:
1. Sonny Onowo
2. Larry Isaac
3. Phil Morgan
4. Steve Curran

JAPANESE:
1. Mike Bernardo
2. Norman Lacaden
3. N. Stanolodis
4. Denolius Cain

KOREAN:
1. Charlie Lee
2. Dave Macomber
3. Michael Dietrich
4. Pedro Xavier

MUSICAL:
1. Jean Frenette
2. Chris Casamassa
3. Dan McFarland
4. Jose Pacheco

OKINAWAN:
1. Domingo Llanos
2. Terry Creamer
3. Cheech Luzzi

4. John Palitti

Women

HARD STYLE:
1. Cheryl Nance
2. Kathy Quan
3. Justina Hall
4. Karen Rothgeb

SOFT STYLE:
1. Alice Chung
2. Christine Bannon
3. Yungchu Kim
4. Geraldine James

Weapons

EXECUTIVE:
1. Steve Curran
2. Dan McFarland
3. Sonny Onowo
4. Phil Morgan

HARD:
1. Mike Bernardo
2. Kevin Brown
3. Dave Macomber
4. Denolius Cain

SOFT:
1. Hosung Pak
2. Hoyoung Pak
3. Richard Brandon
4. Christine Bannon

**PAN-AM NATIONALS:
OCTOBER 28, 1989**

**Manny Reyes, Producer
Miami, FL**

**MILE HIGH CLASSIC:
NOVEMBER 18, 1989**

**NIAGARA NATIONALS:
NOVEMBER 18–19, 1989**

**Boice Lydell, Producer
Niagara Falls, NY**

**BOSTON NATIONALS:
NOVEMBER 19, 1989**

1988 NATIONAL TOURNAMENTS

GOLDEN DESERT CLASSIC: JANUARY 16, 1988

**Toni Lee, Producer
Palm Springs, CA**

Fighting

Men's Grand Champion:
   Leonard Creer
2. Shon Adams

Women's Grand Champion:
   Joanna Brownell
2. Joyce Libert

Forms

Grand Champion:
   Charlie Lee
2. Kathy Quan
3. Stuart Quan
4. Chris Casamassa

ATLANTIC GRAND SLAM: JANUARY 23–24, 1988

**Chuck Merriman, Producer
Boston, MA**

Note: As part of the Atlantic Richfield Oil-sponsored karate circuit, this event awarded over $40,000 in prize money.

Fighting

Men's Grand Champion:
   Randall DeLoach
2. Billy Blanks
3. Anthony Holloway
4. Steve Anderson

HEAVY:
1. Steve Anderson
2. Anthony Price
3. Richard Plowden

LIGHT HEAVY:
1. Billy Blanks
2. Jerry Fontanez
3. Ray Wizard

MIDDLE:
1. Anthony Holloway
2. Kevin Thompson
3. Tony Morrison

LIGHT:
1. Randall DeLoach
2. Jessie Thornton
3. Tony Young

Women's Grand Champion:
   Chavela Aaron
2. Veronica DeSantos
3. Kim-Du Trinh
4. Cheryl Nance

LIGHT HEAVY:
1. Veronica DeSantos
2. Kelee Anderson
3. Doreen Cogliandro

MIDDLE:
1. Chavela Aaron
2. Nicola Quist
3. Linda Denley

LIGHT:
1. Kim-Du Trinh
2. Josee Blanchard
3. Lisa Cerda

SUPER LIGHT:
1. Cheryl Nance
2. Christine Bannon
3. Brenda Hund

Forms

Men's Grand Champion:
   Hosung Pak
2. Charlie Lee
3. Domingo Llanos
4. Keith Hirabayashi

CHINESE:
1. Hosung Pak
2. Keith Hirabayashi
3. Richard Brandon

JAPANESE/OKINAWAN:
1. Domingo Llanos
2. Stuart Quan
3. Kevin Thompson

KOREAN:
1. Jean Frenette
2. Stuart Quan
3. George Calderon

OPEN:
1. Charlie Lee
2. Kevin Thompson
3. Hosung Pak

WUSHU:
1. Keith Hirabayashi
2. Javonne Holmes
3. Hosung Pak

Women's Grand Champion:

Alice Chung
2. Kim-Du Trinh
3. Christine Bannon
4. Cheryl Nance

HARD STYLE:
1. Kim-Du Trinh
2. Cheryl Nance
3. Nicola Quist

OPEN:
1. Alice Chang Chung
2. Christine Bannon
3. Kim-Du Trinh

SOFT STYLE:
1. Christine Bannon
2. Alice Chung
3. Kelee Anderson

Weapons Grand Champion:

Jean Frenette
2. Keith Hirabayashi
3. Stuart Quan
4. Richard Brandon

HARD STYLE:
1. Stuart Quan
2. Jean Frenette
3. Baron Tabura

SOFT STYLE:
1. Richard Brandon
2. Keith Hirabayashi
3. Alice Chung

BOSTON NATIONALS: FEBRUARY 6, 1988

Rocky DiRico, Producer
Boston, MA

Fighting

Men's Grand Champion:

Jerry Fontanez
2. Anthony Holloway

HEAVY:
1. Kirrik Jenness

LIGHT HEAVY:
1. Jerry Fontanez

MIDDLE:
1. Anthony Holloway

LIGHT:
1. Marty Eubanks

SUPER LIGHT:
1. Donald Brady

SENIORS (HEAVY):
1. Wali Islam

SENIORS (LIGHT):
1. Clarence Reeves

Women's Grand Champion:

Chavela Aaron
2. Kierston Sims
3. Christine Bannon
Kim-Du Trinh

Forms

Grand Champion:

Charlie Lee
2. Richard Brandon
3. Christine Bannon
4. Kim-Du Trinh

Men

CHINESE:
1. Richard Brandon

JAPANESE:
1. Bill Beason

KENPO:
1. David Collins

KOREAN:
1. Charlie Lee

OKINAWAN:
1. Adriel Muniz

SENIORS (35–40):
1. Jerry Otto

SENIORS (41+):
1. Steve Curran

Women

CHINESE:
1. Christine Bannon

JAPANESE:
1. Kathy Quan

KENPO:
1. Sheri Mahoney

KOREAN:
1. Kim-Du Trinh

OKINAWAN:
1. Helen Giragosian

Weapons

HARD STYLE:
1. Cheech Luzzi

OPEN:
1. Chris Casamassa

SOFT STYLE:
1. Richard Brandon

SENIORS (35–40):
1. Jerry Otto

ATLANTIC GRAND SLAM: FEBRUARY 20–21, 1988

Chuck Merriman, Producer
Philadelphia, PA

Note: As part of the Atlantic Richfield Oil-sponsored karate circuit, this event awarded over $40,000 in prize money.

Christine Bannon (right) versus Kierston Sims. Courtesy of Rich Baptista

Fighting

Men's Grand Champion:
Billy Blanks
2. Steve Anderson
3. Ibraham Abdalla
4. Jeff Gears

HEAVY:
1. Steve Anderson
2. Terry Creamer
3. Anthony Price

LIGHT HEAVY:
1. Billy Blanks
2. Ray Wizard
3. Hakim Alston

MIDDLE:
1. Jeff Gears
2. Jay Bell
3. Kevin Thompson

LIGHT:
1. Ibraham Abdalla
2. Tony Young
3. Gary Landreth

Women's Grand Champion:
Chavela Aaron
2. Christine Bannon
3. Kim-Du Trinh
4. Doreen Cogliandro

LIGHT HEAVY:
1. Doreen Cogliandro
2. Michonne Keeble
3. Lisa Crosby

MIDDLE:
1. Chavela Aaron
2. Linda Denley
3. Sue Wineinger

LIGHT:
1. Kim-Du Trinh
2. Cheryl Nance
3. Elsa Cordero

SUPER LIGHT:
1. Christine Bannon
2. Brenda Hund
3. Eva Jones

Forms

Men's Grand Champion:
Keith Hirabayashi
2. Charlie Lee
3. Richard Brandon
4. Domingo Llanos

CHINESE:
1. John Sarmousakis
2. Keith Hirabayashi
3. Richard Brandon

JAPANESE/OKINAWAN:
1. Domingo Llanos
2. Kevin Thompson
3. Charlie Lee

KOREAN:
1. Charlie Lee
2. David Randall
3. Jean Frenette

OPEN:
1. Richard Brandon
2. Charlie Lee
3. Jean Frenette

WUSHU:
1. Keith Hirabayashi
2. Javonne Holmes
3. Kenny Perez

Women's Grand Champion:
Alice Chung
2. Christine Bannon
3. Kathy Quan
4. Elsa Cordero

HARD STYLE:
1. Elsa Cordero
2. Kathy Quan
3. Regina Gonzales

OPEN:
1. Alice Chung
2. Kim-Du Trinh
3. Christine Bannon

SOFT STYLE:
1. Alice Chung
2. Christine Bannon
3. Yungchu Kim

Weapons Grand Champion:
Keith Hirabayashi
2. Kevin Thompson
3. Alice Chung
4. Charlie Lee

HARD STYLE:
1. Kevin Thompson
2. Charlie Lee
3. Jean Frenette

SOFT STYLE:
1. Alice Chung
2. Keith Hirabayashi
3. Javonne Holmes

CANADIAN NATIONALS: MARCH 19, 1988

**Cezar Borkowski, Producer
Toronto, Canada**

Fighting

Men's Grand Champion:
Jerry Fontanez
2. Don Griffith

HEAVY:
1. Tony Marshall

LIGHT HEAVY:
1. Jerry Fontanez

MIDDLE:
1. Don Griffith

LIGHT:
1. Peter Gilpin

SUPER LIGHT:
1. John Palitti

Women

HEAVY:
1. Josee Blanchard

The two all-time greatest American point fighters strike a pose at the 1988 Bermuda International Grand Championships: Linda Denley (left) and Steve Anderson. Courtesy of Don Rodrigues

LIGHT:
1. Dawn Warner

Juniors

1. Jason Consoli
2. Young Park
3. Tim Manes

Forms

Grand Champion:
   Charlie Lee
2. Dan McFarland

CHINESE:
1. Doug Lee

JAPANESE:
1. Mike Bernardo

KOREAN:
1. Don Dunkan

OPEN:
1. Dan McFarland

SENIORS:
1. Humberto Medeiros

Women

HARD STYLE:
1. Vicki Donovan

SOFT STYLE:
1. Edie Styles

Juniors

1. Jeff Sue
2. Dodger Villiers
3. Randy Sharma

Weapons

HARD STYLE:
1. Dan McFarland

SOFT STYLE:
1. Chi Wai Lee

MONTREAL NATIONALS: 1988

**Jean Frenette, Producer
Quebec, Canada**

Fighting

Men's Grand Champion:
   Billy Blanks
2. Terry Creamer
3. Danny Griffith
4. Felisberto Fernandes

Women's Grand Champion:
   Chavela Aaron
2. Veronica DeSantos
3. Lyne Chatelain
4. Linda Denley

Forms

Men's Grand Champion:
   Keith Hirabayashi

Junior Grand Champion:
   Dodger Devilliers

BERMUDA INTERNATIONAL: APRIL 2–3, 1988

**Kristina & Skipper Ingham, Producers
Hamilton, Bermuda**

Note: As part of the Atlantic Richfield Oil-sponsored karate circuit, this event awarded over $40,000 in prize money.

Fighting

Men's Grand Champion:
   Chip Wright
2. Terry Creamer
3. Jeff Gears
4. Tony Young

HEAVY:
1. Terry Creamer
2. Richard Plowden

LIGHT HEAVY:
1. Chip Wright
2. Anthony Holloway

MIDDLE:
1. Jeff Gears
2. Tony Morrison

LIGHT:
1. Tony Young
2. Randall DeLoach

Women's Grand Champion:
   Chavela Aaron
2. Linda Denley
3. Christine Bannon
4. Josee Blanchard

LIGHT HEAVY:
1. Linda Denley
2. Veronica DeSantos

MIDDLE:
1. Chavela Aaron

2. Nicole Quist

LIGHT:
1. Josee Blanchard
2. Manon Desrochers

SUPER LIGHT:
1. Christine Bannon
2. Eva Jones

Forms

Men's Grand Champion:
   Keith Hirabayashi
2. Hosung Pak
3. Phillip Wong
4. Charlie Lee

OPEN:
1. Phillip Wong
2. Charlie Lee

WUSHU:
1. Hosung Pak
2. Phillip Wong

KOREAN:
1. Charlie Lee
2. Jerry Fontanez

CHINESE:
1. Keith Hirabayashi
2. Javonne Holmes

JAPANESE/OKINAWAN:
1. Kevin Thompson
2. Stuart Quan

Women's Grand Champion:
   Alice Chung
2. Christine Bannon
3. Regina Gonzalez
4. Kathy Quan

OPEN:
1. Alice Chung
2. Regina Gonzalez

SOFT STYLE:
1. Alice Chung
2. Christine Bannon

HARD STYLE:
1. Kathy Quan
2. Regina Gonzalez

Weapons Grand Champion:
   Keith Hirabayashi
2. Mike Bernardo
3. Hosung Pak

SOFT STYLE:
1. Hosung Pak
2. Keith Hirabayashi

HARD STYLE:
1. Kevin Thompson
2. Mike Bernardo

NEW ENGLAND OPEN: APRIL 9, 1988

Fighting

Men's Grand Champion:
Anthony Price
2. Chip Wright
3. Steve Anderson
4. Gary Eblan

HEAVY:
1. Steve Anderson

LIGHT HEAVY:
1. Anthony Price

MIDDLE:
1. Chip Wright

LIGHT MIDDLE:
1. Anthony Holloway

LIGHT:
1. David Randall

SUPER LIGHT:
1. Gary Eblan

SENIOR HEAVY:
1. Wali Islam

SENIOR LIGHT:
1. Edwin Rhodes

Women's Grand Champion:
Linda Denley
2. Christine Bannon

HEAVY:
1. Linda Denley

LIGHT:
1. Christine Bannon

Juniors Boys

(13–15):
1. Yawick Marcotte

(10–12):
1. Adilson Baptista

(8–9):
1. Jonathan DiPina

Junior Girls

(13–15):
1. Jean Gambardella

(10–12):
1. Melanie Segal

Forms

Grand Champion:
Jean Frenette
2. Kevin Thompson
3. Richard Brandon
4. Christine Bannon

Men

AMERICAN/OPEN:
1. Jean Frenette

CHINESE/KENPO:
1. Richard Brandon

JAPANESE/OKINAWAN:
1. Kevin Thompson

KOREAN:
1. David Randall

SENIORS:
1. Jerry Otto

Women

HARD STYLE:
1. Cheryl Nance

SOFT STYLE:
1. Christine Bannon

Juniors

(13–15):
1. Jean Marc Quellet

(10–12):
1. Chad Smith

(8–9):
1. Jonathan DiPina

(7 & UNDER):
1. Chad Kapusta

Weapons

HARD STYLE:
1. Kevin Thompson

SOFT STYLE:
1. Christine Bannon

SENIORS:
1. Brian Ricci

JUNIORS (15 & UNDER):
1. Todd Humes

COORS SILVER BULLET: APRIL 10, 1988

**Harold Halterman, Producer
Harrisonburg, VA**

BATTLE OF ATLANTA: APRIL 16, 1988

Fighting

Men's Grand Champion:
Hakim Alston

Women

LIGHT:
1. Christine Bannon

Forms

Grand Champion:
?

Women

CHINESE:
1. Christine Bannon

EMPIRE STATE NATIONALS: APRIL 24, 1988

Fighting

Men's Grand Champion:
Hakim Alston
2. Tony Morrison

Women's Grand Champion:
Elsa Cordero
2. Kim McCrorey

Forms

Grand Champion:
Richard Brandon

OCEAN STATE NATIONALS: MAY 7, 1988

Fighting

Men

HEAVY:
1. Steve Anderson

MIDDLE:
1. Anthony Holloway

LIGHT:
1. Kevin Thompson

SENIORS:
1. Wali Islam

Women

HEAVY:
1. Linda Denley

LIGHT:
1. Brenda Hund
2. Christine Bannon

Forms

Grand Champion:
   Richard Brandon
2. Jean Frenette
3. Christine Bannon
4. Domingo Llanos

A.K.A. GRAND NATIONALS: MAY 22, 1988

Fighting

Men

HEAVY:
1. Terry Creamer

LIGHT HEAVY:
2. Anthony Price

MIDDLE:
1. Jeff Gears

LIGHT MIDDLE:
1. Anthony Holloway

LIGHT:
1. Larry Tankson

SUPER LIGHT:
1. Jerry Prince

SENIORS (HEAVY):
1. Steve Curran

SENIORS (LIGHT):
1. Harold Burrage

Women's Grand Champion:
   Brenda Hund
2. Linda Denley

HEAVY:
1. Linda Denley
2. Chavela Aaron

LIGHT:
1. Brenda Hund

Forms

Grand Champion:
   Mike Bernardo

CHINESE:
1. Hosung Pak

JAPANESE/OKINAWAN:
1. Mike Bernardo

OPEN:
1. Andre Sack

SENIORS:
1. Jerry Otto

Women

HARD STYLE:
1. Kathy Quan

SOFT STYLE:
2. Christine Bannon

Junior Grand Champion:
   Mike Carrenda
2. Eddie Landa
3. Jon Valera
   Seneca Luther

BLUEGRASS NATIONALS: JUNE 18, 1988

TOP TEN NATIONALS: JULY 16, 1988

**Dr. Eddie Andujar, Producer
Atlantic City, NJ**

Note: This was the first major American tournament to feature a "continuous contact" team fight, similar to that pioneered by Europe's WAKO. The most outstanding fighters in it were Kevin Thompson and Billy Blanks.

Fighting

Men's Grand Champion:
   Steve Anderson

HEAVY:
1. Steve Anderson

LIGHT HEAVY:
1. Anthony Price

MIDDLE:
1. Eddie Butcher

LIGHT MIDDLE:
1. Anthony Holloway

LIGHT:
1. Pedro Xavier

SUPER LIGHT:
1. Keith McKinley

Women's Grand Champion:
   Linda Denley
2. Cheryl Nance

Seniors

HEAVY:
1. Wally Islam

LIGHT:
1. Jeff Wright

Continuous Contact:
1. Atlantic Oil Team
2. Miller Lite Team

Forms

Grand Champion:
   Jean Frenette
2. Hosung Pak
3. Young Bok Lee
4. Alice Chung

Weapons Grand Champion:
   Alice Chung
2. Jean Frenette
3. Hosung Pak
4. Jerry Otto

U.S.A. JUNIOR NATIONALS

**Roger Jones, Producer
Asheville, NC**

U.S. CAPITAL CLASSICS: AUGUST 13, 1988

Fighting

Men's Grand Champion:
   Billy Blanks
2. Marty Eubanks

Women's Grand Champion:
   Linda Denley
2. Christine Bannon

Forms

Grand Champion:
   Jean Frenette
2. Charlie Lee

BOSTON SUMMER OPEN: AUGUST 20, 1988

Fighting

Men

HEAVY:
1. Richard Plowden
2. Steve Anderson
3. Terry Creamer

LIGHT HEAVY:
1. Billy Blanks
2. Chip Wright
3. Jeff Doyle

MIDDLE:
1. Anthony Holloway
2. Rocky Silva
3. Paul Garcia

LIGHT:
1. Pedro Xavier
2. Felberto Fernandes
3. Tony Young

Women

HEAVY:
1. Linda Denley
2. Nicola Quist
3. Kelee Anderson

MIDDLE:
1. Kierston Sims
2. Chavela Aaron
3. Robyn Covino

LIGHT:
1. Christine Bannon
2. Maureen Cecil
3. Cathy Digiovanni

Forms

Grand Champion:
Jean Frenette

HARD STYLE:
1. Jean Frenette
2. Domingo Llanos
3. Cheech Luzzi

SENIORS:
1. Brian Ricci
2. Rocky DiRico
3. Manny Neves

SOFT STYLE:
1. Richard Brandon
2. Terry Creamer
3. Patric Barbieri

WEAPONS (HARD STYLE):
1. Kevin Thompson

2. Jean Frenette
3. Domingo Llanos

WEAPONS (SOFT STYLE):
1. Christine Bannon
2. Richard Brandon
3. Alice Chung

WOMEN:
1. Christine Bannon
2. Alice Chung
3. Cathy Digiovanni

WORLD PRO-AM: SEPTEMBER 10, 1988

Fighting

Men's Grand Champion:
Jerry Fontanez
2. Jessie Thornton

Women's Grand Champion:
Brenda Hund
2. Kelly Rae Marrs

Forms

Adult Grand Champion:
Charlie Lee
2. Chris Casamassa
3. Carla Fortney

Junior Grand Champion:
Jeff Sue
2. Matt Emery

DIAMOND NATIONALS: OCTOBER 15, 1988

Fighting

Men

HEAVY:
1. Vernon Johnson
2. Steve Anderson

LIGHT HEAVY:
1. Anthony Price

MIDDLE:
1. Fred Nicklaus

LIGHT:
1. Sahah Alston

SUPER LIGHT:
1. Tony Young

SENIOR (HEAVY):
1. Carl Clary

SENIORS (LIGHT):
1. Derek Reid

Women's Grand Champion:
Chavela Aaron
2. Cheryl Nance

LIGHT:
1. Cheryl Nance
2. Christine Bannon

Juniors

(15–17):
1. Keith Scott

(13–14):
1. Matt Bentram

(11–12):
1. Bob Guzinski

(9–10):
1. Seneca Luther

(8 & UNDER):
1. Jason Webb

Forms

Grand Champion:
Kevin Thompson
2. Charlie Lee
3. Hosung Pak

Men

CHINESE:
1. Hosung Pak

JAPANESE/OKINAWAN:
1. Sonny Onowo

KOREAN:
1. Charlie Lee

OPEN:
1. Andre Sack

SENIORS:
1. Jerry Otto

Women

HARD STYLE:
1. Regina Gonzales

SOFT STYLE:
1. Christine Bannon

Juniors

Grand Champion:
Seneca Luther

(14–15):
1. Michael Saxon

(13 & UNDER):
1. Jeff Sue

Weapons

HARD STYLE:
1. Kevin Thompson

SOFT STYLE:
1. Hosung Pak

SENIORS:
1. Jerry Otto

JUNIORS:
1. Michael Saxon

A.K.A. GRAND NATIONALS: OCTOBER 16, 1988

BATTLE OF BALTIMORE: OCTOBER 22, 1988

U.S. OPEN: NOVEMBER 5, 1988

1987 NATIONAL TOURNAMENTS

BOSTON NATIONALS: FEBRUARY 7, 1987

Rocky DiRico, Producer
Boston, MA

CANADIAN NATIONALS: MARCH 14, 1987

Cezar Borkowski, Producer
Toronto, Canada

BERMUDA INTERNATIONAL: APRIL 4–5, 1987

Kristina & Skipper Ingham,
Producers
Hamilton, Bermuda

Note: $24,000 in prize money was awarded at this event.

Fighting

Men's Grand Champion:
Billy Blanks
2. Kevin Thompson
3. Terry Creamer

HEAVY:
1. Billy Blanks
2. Mike Stiegerwald

Women
1. Nicola Quist
2. Helen Chung
3. Lisa Crosby

BATTLE OF ATLANTA: APRIL 25, 1987

EMPIRE STATE NATIONALS: APRIL 26, 1987

Fighting

Men's Grand Champion:
Steve Anderson

Women's Grand Champion:
Nicola Quist
2. Kim-Du Trinh

Forms

Grand Champion:
Jean Frenette

Weapons

HARD STYLE:
1. Tommy Chen

SOFT STYLE:
1. Javonne Holmes

OCEAN STATE NATIONALS: MAY 9, 1987

Fighting

Men's Grand Champion:
Steve Anderson
2. Tony Young
3. Billy Blanks
Walli Islam

Women's Grand Champion:
Linda Denley
2. Christine Bannon

Forms

Grand Champion:
Keith Hirabayashi

2. Jean Frenette
3. Jerry Prince

A.K.A. GRAND NATIONALS: MAY 24, 1987

K.I.C.K. NATIONALS: JUNE 1987

Alan Kelly, Producer
Tulsa, OK

BLUEGRASS NATIONALS: JUNE 19, 1987

Fighting

Men's Grand Champion:
Billy Blanks
2. Anthony Holloway
3. Robert Harris
4. Jessie Thornton

Women's Grand Champion:
Linda Denley
2. Christine Bannon

Forms

Grand Champion:
Keith Hirabayashi
2. Charlie Lee
3. Jean Frenette
4. Deno Cain

WESTERN U.S. NATIONALS: JULY 7, 1987

Al Dacascos, Producer
Portland, OR

BOSTON SUMMER OPEN: AUGUST 15, 1987

Fighting

Men

SUPER HEAVY:
1. Fred DePalma
2. Wally Geary
3. Lewis Reynolds

HEAVY:
1. Mike White
2. Larry Kelley
3. Chad Merriman

LIGHT HEAVY:
1. Chip Wright
2. Doug Peoples
3. Bob Daigle

MIDDLE:
1. Tony Morrison
2. Anthony Holloway
3. Bob Lamattina

LIGHT:
1. Kevin Thompson
2. Ray Jenkins
3. Pedro Xavier

SUPER LIGHT:
1. Tony Young
2. Ron Brady
3. Anthony Trotman

EXECUTIVE:
1. Robert Veno
2. Robert Parker
3. Carlos Chardone

Women

HEAVY:
1. Chavela Aaron
2. Doreen Cogliandro
3. Kelee Anderson

MIDDLE:
1. Annette Nagode
2. Rhonda Alexander
3. Maureen Cecil

LIGHT:
1. Christine Bannon
2. Tricia Humphrey
3. Cathy Digiovanni

Forms

Men

CHINESE:
1. Richard Brandon
2. Javonne Holmes
3. Raven Lee Smith

EXECUTIVE:
1. Carol Dupont
2. Manny Neves
3. Bill Newcombe

JAPANESE/OKINAWAN:
1. Sonny Onowo
2. Kevin Thompson

3. Domingo Llanos

KOREAN:
1. Pedro Xavier
2. David Collins
3. Waleed Yousef

OPEN:
1. Jean Frenette
2. Tom Bouchard
3. Steve Best

Women

HARD STYLE:
1. Tricia Humphrey
2. Cathy Digiovanni
3. Annette Nagode

SOFT STYLE:
1. Christine Bannon
2. Cori Ertha
3. Kelee Anderson

Weapons

HARD STYLE:
1. Cheech Luzzi
2. Jean Frenette
3. Kevin Thompson

SOFT STYLE:
1. Christine Bannon
2. Javonne Holmes
3. Richard Brandon

U.S. CAPITAL CLASSICS: AUGUST 15, 1987

Fighting

Men's Grand Champion:
Steve Anderson
2. Ibraham Abdulla

HEAVY:
1. Richard Plowden

LIGHT HEAVY:
1. Hakim Alston

MIDDLE:
1. Henry Grant

LIGHT:
1. Ibraham Abdulla

SUPER LIGHT:
1. David Wilson

Women's Grand Champion:
Linda Denley
2. Nicola Quist

3. Carolyn Jenkins
Diedra Cole

HEAVY:
1. Nicole Quist

MIDDLE:
1. Diedra Cole

LIGHT:
1. Carolyn Jenkins

Forms

Grand Champion:
Keith Hirabayashi
1. Charlie Lee

CHINESE:
1. Hosung Pak

JAPANESE/OKINAWAN:
1. Andrei Sack

KOREAN:
1. Charlie Lee

OPEN:
1. Michael Dietrich

HARD-STYLE WEAPONS:
1. Adriel Muniz

SOFT-STYLE WEAPONS:
1. Keith Hirabayashi

HARD-STYLE WOMEN:
1. Helen Chung Vasiliadis

SOFT-STYLE WOMEN:
1. Yungchu Kim

CALIFORNIA NATIONALS: AUGUST 24, 1987

Rose Casamassa, Producer
Covina, CA

WORLD PRO-AM: SEPTEMBER 12, 1987

L.A.M.A. NATIONALS: OCTOBER 4, 1987

Tom Letuli, Producer
Chicago, IL

DIAMOND NATIONALS: OCTOBER 17, 1987

Fighting

Men's Grand Champion:
Steve Anderson
2. Anthony Price

HEAVY:
1. Steve Anderson

LIGHT HEAVY:
1. Anthony Price

MIDDLE:
1. Jeff Gears
2. Mark Jones

LIGHT:
1. Jerry Prince
2. Keith Bowers

SENIORS:
1. Steve Curran
2. Belvin Eaves

Women's Grand Champion:
Linda Denley
2. Cheryl Nance

FORMS

Grand Champion:
Charlie Lee
2. Jean Frenette
3. Keith Hirabayashi

BATTLE OF BALTIMORE: OCTOBER 25, 1987

Forms

Grand Champion:
Keith Hirabayshi
2. Charlie Lee
3. Phillip Wong

ATLANTIC GRAND SLAM: DECEMBER 5–6, 1987

**Chuck Merriman, Producer
New York, NY**

Note: As part of the Atlantic Rich-field Oil-sponsored karate circuit, this event awarded over $40,000 in prize money.

Fighting

Men's Grand Champion:
Richard Plowden
2. Anthony Holloway
3. Anthony Price
4. Kevin Thompson

HEAVY:
1. Richard Plowden
2. Steve Anderson
3. Steve Boyles

LIGHT HEAVY:
1. Anthony Price
2. Jerry Fontanez
3. Raynald Campbell

MIDDLE:
1. Anthony Holloway
2. Jeff Gears
3. Chip Wright

LIGHT:
1. Kevin Thompson
2. Tony Young
3. Ibraham Abdalla

Women's Grand Champion:
Linda Denley
2. Nicola Quist
3. Cheryl Nance
4. Doreen Cogliandro

LIGHT HEAVY:
1. Doreen Cogliandro
2. Veronica DeSantos
3. Sandra Rice

MIDDLE:
1. Linda Denley
2. Chavela Aaron
3. Kelee Anderson

LIGHT:
1. Nicola Quist
2. Kim-Du Trinh

SUPER LIGHT:
1. Cheryl Nance
2. Christine Bannon
3. Elsa Cordero

Forms

Men's Grand Champion:
Jean Frenette
2. Domingo Llanos
3. Keith Hirabayashi
4. William Chung

CHINESE:
1. Keith Hirabayashi
2. William Chung
3. Javonne Holmes

JAPANESE/OKINAWAN:
1. Domingo Llanos
2. Adriel Muniz
3. William Beason

KOREAN:
1. Jean Frenette
2. Yves Lavigne
3. Anthony Price

OPEN:
1. Jean Frenette
2. Hoyoung Pak
3. Kevin Thompson

WUSHU:
1. William Chung
2. Javonne Holmes
3. Keith Hirabayashi

Women's Grand Champion:
Alice Chang
2. Kathy Quan

HARD STYLE:
1. Kathy Quan
2. Nicola Quist
3. Kim-Du Trinh

OPEN:
1. Alice Chang
2. Elsa Cordero
3. Kathy Quan

SOFT STYLE:
1. Alice Chang
2. Christine Bannon
3. Yungchu Kim

Weapons Grand Champion:
Keith Hirabayashi
2. Alice Chang
3. Kim-Du Trinh
4. Jean Frenette

HARD STYLE:
1. Jean Frenette
2. Kim-Du Trinh
3. Kevin Thompson

SOFT STYLE:
1. Alice Chang
2. Keith Hirabayashi
3. Yavonne Holmes

1986 NATIONAL TOURNAMENTS

BOSTON NATIONALS: FEBRUARY 22, 1986

Rocky DiRico, Producer
Watertown, MA

BERMUDA INVITATIONAL: MARCH 15–16, 1986

Skipper & Kristina Ingham, Producers
Hamilton, Bermuda

Fighting

Men's Grand Champion:
Steve Anderson
2. Anthony Holloway

Women's Grand Champion:
Arlene Limas
2. Linda Denley
3. Cheryl Nance

Forms

Open:
1. John Chung
2. Jean Frenette
3. Charlie Lee

Traditional (Men):
1. Keith Hirabayashi
2. Domingo Llanos
3. Stuart Quan

Traditional (Women):
1. Kathy Baxter
2. Kathy Quan
3. Arlene Limas

Weapons:
1. Keith Hirabayashi
2. Stuart Quan
3. Javonne Holmes

BATTLE OF ATLANTA: APRIL 1986

EMPIRE STATE NATIONALS: APRIL 1986

Fighting

Men's Grand Champion:
Kevin Thompson
2. Anthony Holloway

Women's Grand Champion:
Cheryl Nance
2. Linda Denley
3. Nicola Quist

Forms

Grand Champion:
Jean Frenette
2. Javonne Holmes
3. Richard Brandon

Weapons:
1. (tie) Cezar Bowkowski
1. (tie) Javonne Holmes

Youth Grand Champion:
Jeff Sue

OCEAN STATE NATIONALS MAY 4, 1986

Fighting

Men's Grand Champion:
Billy Blanks
2. Steve Anderson

Women's Grand Champion:
Christine Bannon
2. Linda Denley

Forms

Co-Ed Grand Champion:
Richard Brandon
CHINESE:
1. Richard Brandon
JAPANESE/OKINAWAN:
1. Chad Merriman
KENPO:
1. Richard Demas
KOREAN:
1. Gene Hong

Weapons Grand Champion:
Brian Ricci
2. Richard Brandon

BLUEGRASS NATIONALS: JUNE 7, 1986

Jim Lantrip, Producer
Louisville, KY

Fighting

Men's Grand Champion:
Steve Anderson
2. Robert Harris

HEAVY:
1. Steve Anderson
2. Billy Blanks
3. Terry Creamer

MIDDLE:
1. Robert Harris

TEAM:
1. Budweiser
2. British National

Women's Grand Champion:
Linda Denley
2. Arlene Limas

Forms

AMERICAN:
1. Kevin Thompson

CHINESE:
1. Keith Hirabayashi

KOREAN:
1. David Gonzalez

WEAPONS (HARD):
1. Cezar Borkowski

EASTERN AMERICAN SUPERSTAR: 1986

Chuck Merriman, Producer
East Lyme, CT

Fighting

Men's Grand Champion:
Terry Creamer
2. Anthony Holloway

OPEN:
1. Terry Creamer
2. Wali Islam

HEAVY:
1. Billy Blanks
2. Wali Islam

MIDDLE:
1. Anthony Holloway

LIGHT:
1. Gary Baynes

Women's Grand Champion:
Cheryl Nance
2. Doreen Cogliandro

LIGHT:
1. Doreen Cogliandro
2. Kim McCrorey

FLY:
1. Cheryl Nance
2. Christine Bannon

Forms

CHINESE:
1. Terry Creamer

JAPANESE:
1. Chad Merriman

KOREAN:
1. Jerry Fontanez

MUSICAL:
1. Jean Frenette

OPEN:
1. Andre Sack

TRADITIONAL:
1. Sonny Onowo

WEAPONS:
1. Terry Creamer
2. Christine Bannon

WOMEN (HARD):
1. Helen Chung
2. Cheryl Nance

LIBERTY CLASSIC:
AUGUST 3, 1986

Harry Krebs, Producer
New York, NY

Fighting

Men's Grand Champion:
Billy Blanks

TEAM:
1. Budweiser
2. Canada

Women's Grand Champion:
Linda Denley
2. Arlene Limas

Forms

Grand Champion:
Keith Hirabayashi
2. Charlie Lee
3. David Gonzalez

U.S. CAPITAL CLASSICS:
AUGUST 16, 1986

Fighting

Men's Grand Champion:
Steve Anderson

Women's Grand Champion:
Linda Denley

CALIFORNIA GRAND
NATIONALS:
AUGUST 24, 1986

Rose Marie Casamassa, Producer
Covina, CA

U.S. WORLD:
SEPTEMBER 13, 1986

Steve Curran, Producer
Tacoma, WA

DIAMOND NATIONALS:
OCTOBER 4, 1986

Fighting

Men's Grand Champion:
Terry Creamer
2. Steve Anderson
3. Joey Shiflett

Women's Grand Champion:
Arlene Limas
2. Linda Denley

Forms

Grand Champion:
Charlie Lee
2. Kim-Du Trinh

U.S. OPEN:
OCTOBER 25, 1986

L.A.M.A. NATIONALS:
NOVEMBER 9, 1986

Fighting

Men's Grand Champion:
Harold Burrage
2. Terry Creamer
3. Anthony Gipson
Larry Tankson

Women's Grand Champion:
Eva Jones
2. Veronica DeSantos

Forms

Grand Champion:
Jean Frenette
2. Kim-Du Trinh
3. Cezar Borkowski

1985 NATIONAL
TOURNAMENTS

CANADIAN NATIONALS:
MARCH 16, 1985

Cezar Borkowski, Producer
Toronto, Canada

BATTLE OF ATLANTA:
APRIL 13, 1985

Forms

Grand Champion:
Charlie Lee

BERMUDA INTERNATIONAL: APRIL 27–28, 1985

Kristina & Skipper Ingham, Producers
Hamilton, Bermuda

Note: This was the first tournament ever to offer $5,000 purses to winners of men's and women's fighting. Forms competitors won $1,000 for first place.

Fighting

Men's Grand Champion:
  Billy Blanks
2. Randall De Loach
3. Larry Kelley
4. Chip Wright

Note: Two competitors from each of the following divisions were selected to participate in the semi-finals.

HEAVY:
1. Steve Anderson
2. Billy Blanks

LIGHT HEAVY:
1. Larry Kelley
2. Kenneth De Loach

MIDDLE:
1. Gordon Franks
2. Chip Wright

LIGHT:
1. Anthony Holloway
2. Randall De Loach

Women's Grand Champion:
  Linda Denley
2. Josee Blanchard
3. Mitzi Tyler

LIGHT:
1. Linda Denley
2. Mitzi Tyler

FLY:
1. Lori Lantrip
2. Josee Blanchard

Forms

OPEN:
1. Jean Frenette
2. George Chung
3. John Chung
4. Charlie Lee

MALE TRADITIONAL:
1. Keith Hirabayashi
2. John Chung
3. Domingo Llanos
4. George Chung

OPEN:
1. Jean Frenette

WEAPONS (HARD):
1. Keith Hirabayashi
2. Stuart Quan
3. Cynthia Rothrock
4. Cesar Borkowski

WOMEN:
1. Cynthia Rothrock
2. Kathy Baxter
3. Helen Chung

A.K.A. GRAND NATIONALS: MAY 5, 1985

Fighting

Men's Grand Champion:
  Harold Burrage
2. Larry Tankson

HEAVY:
1. Terry Creamer

LIGHT HEAVY:
1. Harold Burrage

MIDDLE:
1. Anthony Gipson

LIGHT:
1. Larry Tankson

SUPER LIGHT:
1. Anthony Coleman

SENIORS:
1. Dale Kirby
2. Ken Eubanks
3. J. Ovjetkwick

Women's Grand Champion:
  Linda Denley
2. Lori Lantrip

HEAVY:
1. Linda Denley
2. Mitzi Tyler

LIGHT:
1. Lori Lantrip
2. Diane McGaughey

Forms

Grand Champion:
  Charlie Lee
2. Jean Frenette
3. Tony Orr
4. Cynthia Rothrock

CHINESE:
1. William Chung
2. Javonne Holmes
3. Jimee Choi

JAPANESE/OKINAWAN:
1. Deno Cain
2. Norman LaCaden
3. John Palitti

KOREAN:
1. Chun Siev
2. Chris Casamassa
3. Dave Hilton

SENIORS:
1. Jim Lantrip
2. Tom Heriaud
3. Tom Jakubczyk

WEAPONS (HARD):
1. Cezar Borkowski
2. Chun Siev
3. Dan McFarland

WEAPONS (SOFT):
1. Javonne Holmes
2. William Chung
3. Jimee Choi

BLUEGRASS NATIONALS: JUNE 15, 1985

Forms

Grand Champion:
  Jean Frenette

U.S. CAPITAL CLASSICS: AUGUST 10, 1985

Forms

Grand Champion:
  Keith Hirabayashi

U.S. WORLD: SEPTEMBER 14, 1985

Steve Curran, Producer
Tacoma, WA

DIAMOND NATIONALS: SEPTEMBER 28, 1985

Fighting

Men's Grand Champion:
Steve Anderson
2. Billy Blanks

HEAVY:
1. Steve Anderson
2. Richard Plowden
3. "Mongoose" Gipson

MIDDLE:
1. Billy Blanks
2. Chip Wright

Women's Grand Champion:
Linda Denley
2. Karen Cole
3. Arlene Limas

Forms

Grand Champion:
Keith Hirabayashi
2. Cynthia Rothrock
3. Jean Frenette
4. Charlie Lee

L.A.M.A. NATIONALS: OCTOBER 19, 1985

Fighting

Men's Grand Champion:
Harold Burrage

HEAVY:
1. Harold Burrage
2. Don Purdue

LIGHT HEAVY:
1. Anthony Gipson
2. Rick Roufus

MIDDLE:
1. Larry Tankson
2. Randall DeLoach

LIGHT:
1. Jeff Gears
2. Jessie Thornton

Women's Grand Champion:
Arlene Limas
2. Cheryl Nance

Senior Grand Champion:
Dale Kirby

2. Mike Cujetkovich

HEAVY:
1. Mike Cujetkovich
2. Jaami Dawan
3. Bill Schuch

LIGHT:
1. Tom Jakubczyk
2. Tom Nehring

Forms

Grand Champion:
Charlie Lee

The following are the 1st place winners; divisions were not available:

1. Charlie Lee
1. Jean Frenette
1. Cezar Borkowski
1. Kim Warner
1. Anthony Marquez
1. John Dufrense

WOMEN:
1. Diane McCaughey

U.S. OPEN: NOVEMBER 2, 1985

Fighting

Men's Grand Champion:
Terry Creamer
2. Anthony Gibson

HEAVY:
1. Mike Green
2. Mike Smith
3. Arnold White
4. Tony Palmore

LIGHT HEAVY:
1. Chip Wright
2. Harold Burrage
3. Paul Motley
4. Jay Bell

MIDDLE:
1. Anthony Gibson
2. Robert Harris
3. Jerome Johnson
4. Jeff Gears

LIGHT:
1. Johnny Gyro
2. Peter Gilpin
3. Joey Shiflett
4. Marty Eubanks

SUPER LIGHT:
1. Deno Cain
2. Randall DeLoach
3. Tony Young
4. Jerry Prince

SENIORS:
1. Steve Curran
2. Dale Kirby
3. Doc Roberts

Women's Grand Champion:
Veronica DeSantos
2. Diane McCaughey

HEAVY:
1. Veronica DeSantos
2. Louise Rivet
3. Donna Judge
4. Tamerah Hudgins

LIGHT:
1. Diane McCoughey
2. Rhonda Alexander
3. Cheryl Nance
4. Karen Cole

Forms

Grand Champion:
Charlie Lee
2. Jean Frenette

CHINESE:
1. Andy Horne

JAPANESE/OKINAWAN:
1. Norman Lacaden

KENPO:
1. Brian Fung

KOREAN:
1. Charlie Lee

OPEN:
1. Jean Frenette

SENIORS:
1. Chuck Merriman

WEAPONS (HARD):
1. Dale Kirby
2. Tony Orr
3. Cezar Borkowski
4. Cory Orr

WEAPONS (SOFT):
1. Keith Hirabayashi
2. William Chung
3. John DeFresne
4. Kim Warner

WOMEN (HARD):
1. Tricia Humphrey
2. Diane McCaughey

3. Lori Lantrip
4. Cheryl Nance

WOMEN (SOFT):
1. Alice Chang
2. Kim Warner
3. Christine Bannon
4. Rose Marie Casamassa

NATIONAL FINALS: NOVEMBER 9, 1985

Jim Butin, Producer
Oklahoma City, OK

1984 NATIONAL TOURNAMENTS

U.S. NATIONAL TOP TEN MARCH 3, 1984

Leo Fong & Ron Marchini, Producers
Stockton, CA

BATTLE OF ATLANTA: MARCH 31, 1984

EMPIRE STATE: APRIL 22, 1984

A.K.A. GRAND NATIONALS: MAY 6, 1984

WEST COAST NATIONALS: JUNE 2, 1984

Ernie Reyes, Sr., Producer
San Jose, CA

Fighting

Men's Grand Champion:
Steve Anderson
2. Dexter Brooks
3. Chip Wright

HEAVY:
1. Steve Anderson
2. Richard Plowden
3. Tony Williams

MIDDLE:
1. Chip Wright

LIGHT:
1. Larry Tankson

SUPER LIGHT:
1. Deno Cain
2. Tony Young
3. Brian Johnson

SENIORS:
1. Alexander Archie
2. Bob Hernandez
3. David Davis

Women's Grand Champion:
Linda Denley
2. Cissy Baird

HEAVY:
1. Linda Denley
2. Arlene Limas

LIGHT:
1. Cissy Baird
2. Lori Lantrip

Forms

Grand Champion:
John Chung
2. Keith Hirabayashi
3. Cynthia Rothrock
4. Stuart Quan

KOREAN:
1. John Chung

JAPANESE:
1. Stuart Quan

WOMEN (HARD):
1. Margie Betke
2. Lori Lantrip

WOMEN (SOFT):
1. Cynthia Rothrock

CHINESE:
1. Keith Hirabayashi

WEAPONS:
1. Keith Hirabayashi
2. Stuart Quan
3. Cynthia Rothrock

SENIORS:
1. Bill Grossman
2. Steve Curran
3. Bob Hernandez

FT. WORTH NATIONAL PRO-AM: JUNE 23, 1984

Roy Kurban, Producer
Ft. Worth, TX

Fighting

Men's Grand Champion:
Ray McCallum
1. Al Garza

Women's Grand Champion:
Linda Denley
2. Christy Moss

Forms

Grand Champion:
Tim Kirby

CHINESE:
1. Kazumasa Yokohama

JAPANESE/OKINAWAN:
1. Steve Powell

KOREAN:
1. Tim Kirby

OPEN:
1. Frances LeBlanc

WEAPONS:
1. Ken Nelms

DIAMOND NATIONALS: SEPTEMBER 22, 1984

Fighting

Men's Grand Champion:
Steve Anderson
2. Joey Shiflett

HEAVY:
1. Arnold White

LIGHT HEAVY:
1. Billy Blanks

MIDDLE:
1. Robert Harris

LIGHT:
1. Joey Shiflett

SUPER LIGHT:
1. Gary Michak

Women's Grand Champion:
Linda Denley
2. Stacey Duke

HEAVY:
1. Linda Denley
2. Arlene Limas

LIGHT:
1. Stacey Duke

Forms

Grand Champion:
   John Chung
2. Charlie Lee

CHINESE:
1. Keith Hirabayashi
2. Scott Dinger

JAPANESE/OKINAWAN:
1. Stuart Quan
2. Mike McCoy

KOREAN:
1. John Chung

WOMEN:
1. Cynthia Rothrock

U.S. WORLD:
SEPTEMBER 29, 1984

Steve Curran, Producer
Tacoma, WA

Fighting

Men's Grand Champion:
   Steve Anderson
2. Alvin Prouder

HEAVY:
1. Steve Anderson

LIGHT HEAVY:
1. Chip Wright
2. Jay Bell

MIDDLE:
1. ?

LIGHT:
1. Jessie Thornton

SUPER LIGHT:
1. ?

Women's Grand Champion:
   Arlene Limas
2. Lori Lantrip

HEAVY:
1. Arlene Limas
2. Janesa Kruse

LIGHT:
1. Lori Lantrip
2. Diane McCaughey

Forms

Grand Champion:
   Keith Hirabayashi
2. Cynthia Rothrock

CHINESE:
1. Keith Hirabayashi

JAPANESE/OKINAWAN:
1. Mike McCoy

WOMEN:
1. Cynthia Rothrock

L.A.M.A. NATIONALS:
OCTOBER 20, 1984

Fighting

Men's Grand Champion:
   Steve Anderson
2. Freddie Letuli

HEAVY:
1. Donald Purdue
2. Darryl Albanese
3. Terry Creamer

LIGHT HEAVY:
1. Harold Burrage
2. Chip Wright
3. Jay Bell

MIDDLE:
1. "Magic" Johnson
2. Robert Harris
3. Steve Curran

LIGHT:
1. Joey Shiflett
2. Charlie Fears
3. Marty Eubanks

SUPER LIGHT:
1. David Wilson
2. Deno Cain
3. Randall DeLoach

SENIORS:
1. David Deaton
2. Dale Kirby
3. Dean Bergman

Women's Grand Champion:
   Linda Denley
2. Lori Lantrip

HEAVY:
1. Linda Denley
2. Arlene Limas
3. Andrea DeCant

LIGHT:
1. Lori Lantrip
2. Diane McCaughey
3. Rebecca Novak

Forms

Grand Champion
   Charlie Lee

CHINESE:
1. Keith Hirabayashi

MUSICAL:
1. John Chung

OPEN:
1. Charlie Lee

WEAPONS (HARD STYLE):
1. Stuart Quan

WEAPONS (SOFT STYLE):
1. Cynthia Rothrock

WOMEN:
1. Mitzi Tyler

U.S. OPEN: OCTOBER 27, 1984

U.S. CAPITAL CLASSICS:
NOVEMBER 17, 1984

Fighting

Men's Grand Champion:
   Steve Anderson
2. Jessie Thornton
3. Henry Grant

Women's Grand Champion:
   Linda Denley
2. Rita Hundley

Forms

Grand Champion:
   Charlie Lee
2. George Chung

WEAPONS:
1. Keith Hirabayashi
2. Cynthia Rothrock
3. Calvin Bascomb

1983 NATIONAL TOURNAMENTS

BATTLE OF ATLANTA: MARCH 19, 1983

Fighting

Men's Grand Champion:
Johnny Davis
2. Marcal Lazenby

HEAVY:
1. Freddie Williams
2. Richard Plowden
3. Billy Blanks

LIGHT HEAVY:
1. Johnny Davis
2. Sid Gee

MIDDLE:
1. Robert Harris
2. Bobby Tucker
3. Mike Warren

LIGHT:
1. Charles Fears
2. Sam Montgomery

SUPER LIGHT:
1. Marcal Lazenby
2. Tony Young

Women's Grand Champion:
Linda Denley
2. Lori Lantrip

HEAVY:
1. Linda Denley
2. Arlene Limas
3. Rhonda Alexander

LIGHT:
1. Lori Lantrip
2. Stacey Duke

Forms

Grand Champion:
George Chung
2. Ernie Reyes, Jr.
3. Charlie Lee
4. Cynthia Rothrock

JAPANESE/OKINAWAN:
1. Sonny Onowo

KOREAN:
1. Charlie Lee

OPEN:
1. Ernie Reyes, Jr.

WOMEN:
1. Cynthia Rothrock

Weapons Grand Champion:
George Chung
2. Dale Kirby
3. Vic Coffin

A.K.A. GRAND NATIONALS: 1983

Fighting

Men's Grand Champion:
Steve Anderson
2. Billy Blanks
3. Harold Burrage
4. Richard Plowden

HEAVY:
1. Arnold White

LIGHT HEAVY:
1. ?
2. Steve Curran

MIDDLE:
1. ?

LIGHT:
1. Tony McCaskell
2. Larry Tankson
3. Gary Michak

SUPER LIGHT:
1. ?
2. Tony Young
3. Rick Roufus

Women's Grand Champion:
Linda Denley
2. Lori Lantrip

HEAVY:
1. ?
2. Arlene Limas

LIGHT:
1. ?
2. Rhonda Alexander
3. Stacey Duke

Forms

Grand Champion:
Cynthia Rothrock
2. Keith Hirabayashi
3. Charlie Lee
4. George Chung

WEAPONS (HARD):
1. George Chung

2. Stuart Quan
3. Toyotaro Miyazaki

WEAPONS (SOFT):
1. Keith Hirabayashi
2. Cynthia Rothrock

DIAMOND NATIONALS: MAY 7, 1983

Fighting

Men's Grand Champion:
Ray McCallum
2. Steve Anderson

HEAVY:
1. Richard Plowden
2. Kenny Blanche
3. Satch Williams

LIGHT HEAVY:
1. Harold Burrage
2. Steve Curran
3. Mike Steigerwald

MIDDLE:
1. Terry Norblem
2. Anthony Gipson
3. Johnny Gyro

LIGHT:
1. Sam Montgomery
2. Odis Richmond
3. Curtis Butler

SUPER LIGHT:
1. Gary Michak
2. Rick Roufus
3. Tony Overton

Women's Grand Champion:
Arlene Limas
2. Lois Jones

HEAVY:
1. Arlene Limas
2. Linda Denley

LIGHT:
1. Lois Jones
2. Stacey Duke

Forms

Grand Champion:
Keith Hirabayashi
2. Charlie Lee
3. ?
4. Ernie Reyes, Jr.

CHINESE:
1. Keith Hirabayashi

JAPANESE/OKINAWAN:
1. Sonny Onowo
2. Toyotaro Miyazaki
3. George Michak

KOREAN:
1. Charlie Lee
2. George Chung

OPEN:
1. Ernie Reyes, Jr.
2. Stuart Quan
3. Gary Michak

WOMEN:
1. Cynthia Rothrock
2. Kim Du-Trinh
3. Shelly Chacon

Weapons Grand Champion:
  Keith Hirabayashi
2. Cynthia Rothrock
3. Toyotaro Miyazaki

WEST COAST NATIONALS: JUNE 4, 1983

**Ernie Reyes, Sr., Producer
San Jose, CA**

Fighting

Men's Grand Champion:
  Mark Foster
2. Steve Anderson
3. Billy Blanks

HEAVY:
1. Billy Blanks
2. Arnold White

LIGHT HEAVY:
1. Steve Anderson
2. Ronnie Moore

MIDDLE:
1. Mark Foster
2. Barry Gordon

LIGHT:
1. Chris Ost
2. ?
3. Larry Tankson

SUPER LIGHT:
1. Tony Young
2. Gary Michak

Women's Grand Champion:
  Arlene Limas
2. Lynice Mills

HEAVY:
1. Arlene Limas
2. Linda Denley
3. Rhonda Alexander

LIGHT:
1. Lynice Mills
2. Lori Lantrip
3. Stacey Duke

Forms

Grand Champion:
  Ernie Reyes, Jr.
2. Cynthia Rothrock
3. Dayton Pang

CHINESE:
1. Dayton Pang

JAPANESE/OKINAWAN:
1. Gary Michak

KOREAN:
1. John Chuk

OPEN:
1. Brian Fung

WOMEN:
1. Cynthia Rothrock

Weapons Grand Champion:
  Cynthia Rothrock
2. Gary Michak
3. Dale Kirby

FT. WORTH NATIONAL PRO-AM: JUNE 18, 1983

**Roy Kurban, Producer
Ft. Worth, TX**

Note: Four nationally ranked male fighters were automatically seeded into the finals.

Fighting

Men's Grand Champion:
  Ray McCallum
2. Tim Kirby
3. Billy Blanks

HEAVY:
1. Lee McDowell
2. Daryl Albanese

LIGHT HEAVY:
1. Rudy Smedley
2. Sid Gee

MIDDLE:
1. Billy Kelly
2. Robert Hartfield

LIGHT:
1. Tim Kirby
2. David Deaton
3. Sam Montgomery

SUPER LIGHT:
1. Al Garza
2. Rick Roufus
3. Tony Young

Women's Grand Champion:
  Linda Denley
2. Stacey Duke

HEAVY:
1. Linda Denley
2. Kim Taylor
3. Rebecca Novak

LIGHT:
1. Stacey Duke
2. Lori Lantrip

Forms

Grand Champion:
  George Chung
2. Cynthia Rothrock
3. Keith Hirabayashi
4. Stuart Quan

CHINESE:
1. Keith Hirabayashi

JAPANESE/OKINAWAN:
1. Stuart Quan

KOREAN:
1. George Chung

OPEN:
1. Ernie Reyes, Jr.

WOMEN:
1. Cynthia Rothrock

Weapons Grand Champion:
  Stuart Quan
2. Cynthia Rothrock
3. Keith Hirabayashi

L.A.M.A. NATIONALS: JULY 16, 1983

Fighting

Men's Grand Champion:
  Billy Blanks

2. Larry Tankson
3. Richard Plowden
   Harold Burrage

HEAVY:
1. Richard Plowden
2. Zip White
3. Melvin Atkins

LIGHT HEAVY:
1. Billy Blanks
2. Freddie Letuli
3. Spider Kennedy

MIDDLE:
1. Robert Harris
2. George Bodie
3. Anthony Linson

LIGHT:
1. Larry Tankson
2. Peter Gilpin
3. Rick Roufus

SUPER LIGHT:
1. David Wilson
2. Deno Cain
3. Tony Young

Women's Grand Champion:
   Linda Denley
2. Lori Lantrip

HEAVY:
1. Linda Denley
2. Arlene Limas
3. Mitzi Tyler

LIGHT:
1. Lori Lantrip
2. Cheryl Nance
3. Rhonda Alexander

Forms

Grand Champion:
   George Chung
2. Charlie Lee
3. Keith Hirabayashi

CHINESE KENPO:
1. Keith Hirabayashi
2. Arthur Keith
3. Ishmael Lee

JAPANESE/OKINAWAN:
1. Stuart Quan
2. Gary Michak
3. Tony Orr

KOREAN:
1. Charlie Lee

OPEN:
1. George Chung
2. Jean Frenette

WOMEN:
1. Sophia Kikuchi
2. Arlene Limas
3. Margie Betke

Weapons Grand Champion:
   Stuart Quan
2. Keith Hirabayashi
3. George Chung

U.S. TOP 10 NATIONALS: 1983

Fighting

Men's Grand Champion:
   Steve Anderson
2. Billy Blanks
3. Alvin Prouder
4. Harold Burrage

HEAVY:
1. Kenny Blanche
2. Arnold White

LIGHT HEAVY:
1. Steve Anderson

MIDDLE:
1. ?
2. ?
3. Steve Curran

LIGHT:
1. Sam Montgomery

Women's Grand Champion:
   Arlene Limas
2. Linda Denley

HEAVY:
1. Rhonda Alexander
2. ?
3. Rebecca Novak

LIGHT:
1. Lori Lantrip
2. Stacey Duke

Forms

Grand Champion:
   Jean Frenette
2. Toyotaro Miyazaki
3. George Chung

WEAPONS (HARD):
1. Toyotaro Miyazaki
2. Stuart Quan

WEAPONS (SOFT):
1. ?
2. Cynthia Rothrock

PKA NATIONALS: SEPTEMBER 1983

Akron, OH

Fighting

Men's Grand Champion:
   Richard Plowden

Women's Grand Champion:
   Linda Denley

Forms

Grand Champion:
   Charlie Lee

PORTLAND PRO-AM: OCTOBER 8, 1983

**Dan Anderson & Tom Levak, Producers
Portland, OR**

Fighting

Men's Grand Champion:
   Steve Anderson
2. Dexter Brooks
3. Alvin Prouder
4. Billy Blanks

HEAVY:
1. Arnold White

LIGHT HEAVY:
1. Steve Anderson
2. Chip Wright

MIDDLE:
1. Anthony Linson
2. ?
3. Steve Curran

LIGHT:
1. Mel Cherry
2. Larry Tankson

SUPER LIGHT:
1. Dexter Brooks
2. ?
3. Troy McCaskell

Women's Grand Champion:
Arlene Limas
2. Tania Matthews

Forms

Grand Champion:
Keith Hirabayashi
2. Cynthia Rothrock
3. Jean Frenette
4. Stuart Quan

JAPANESE/OKINAWAN:
1. Jean Frenette

KOREAN:
1. Stuart Quan

OPEN:
1. Mark Heyerdahl

WOMEN:
1. Cynthia Rothrock

Weapons Grand Champion:
Keith Hirabayashi
2. Stuart Quan

U.S. OPEN:
OCTOBER 22, 1983

Charlie Brown, Producer
St. Petersburg, FL

Fighting

Men's Grand Champion:
Billy Blanks
2. Jessie Thornton
3. Tony Young

HEAVY:
1. Freddie Williams
2. Daryl Albanese

LIGHT HEAVY:
1. ?
2. ?
3. Sid Gee

MIDDLE:
1. Jerome Johnson

LIGHT:
1. Jessie Thornton

SUPER LIGHT:
1. Tony Young

Women's Grand Champion:
Linda Denley
2. Rhonda Alexander

HEAVY:
1. Linda Denley
2. Arlene Limas

LIGHT:
1. Rhonda Alexander
2. Lori Lantrip
3. Stacey Duke

Forms

Grand Champion:
George Chung
2. Stuart Quan
3. Gary Michak

JAPANESE/OKINAWAN:
1. Gary Michak

WOMEN:
1. Cynthia Rothrock

Weapons Grand Champion:
Stuart Quan
2. Cynthia Rothrock
3. Dale Kirby

NATIONAL FINALS:
NOVEMBER 5, 1983

Roger Green, Jim Butin & Terry Smith, Producers
Oklahoma City, OK

Fighting

Men's Grand Champion:
Billy Blanks
2. Larry Tankson
3. Ray McCallum

HEAVY:
1. Billy Blanks
2. Daryl Albanese
3. Arnold White
Terry Creamer

LIGHT HEAVY:
1. Ray McCallum
2. Steve Anderson
3. Chip Wright
Sid Gee

MIDDLE:
1. Tony Georgides
2. Ron Hill
3. Rick Arnold
Anthony Linson

LIGHT:
1. Larry Tankson
2. Tim Kirby
3. Allen Kelly
Joey Shifflet

SUPER LIGHT:
1. Tommy Williams
2. Tony Young
3. Keith Hirabayashi
Gary Michak

Women's Grand Champion:
Linda Denley
2. Stacey Duke

HEAVY:
1. Linda Denley
2. Arlene Limas
3. Kim Taylor
Rebecca Novak

LIGHT:
1. Stacey Duke
2. Cheryl Nance
3. Betsy Rimes
Rhonda Alexander

Forms

Grand Champion:
Stuart Quan

CHINESE:
1. Dayton Pang

JAPANESE/OKINAWAN:
1. Gary Michak

KOREAN:
1. John Chung

MUSICAL:
1. Brian Fung

OPEN:
1. George Chung

WEAPONS (HARD):
1. Stuart Quan
2. Gary Michak
3. George Chung

WEAPONS (SOFT):
1. Cynthia Rothrock
2. Keith Hirabayashi

WOMEN:
1. Cynthia Rothrock

OFFICIAL CALIFORNIA KARATE CHAMPIONSHIPS: NOVEMBER 19, 1983

Leo Fong & Ron Marchini, Producers
Stockton, CA

Fighting

Men's Grand Champion:
  Billy Blanks
2. Steve Anderson
3. Alvin Prouder
4. Larry Tankson

HEAVY:
1. Steve Anderson
2. Arnold White

LIGHT HEAVY:
1. Alvin Prouder
2. Chip Wright

MIDDLE:
1. Anthony Linson
2. Sam Montgomery

LIGHT:
1. Larry Tankson

SUPER LIGHT:
1. Gary Michak
2. Willy Mills

Women's Grand Champion:
  Arlene Limas
2. Lynice Mills

LIGHT:
1. Cheryl Nance
2. Lori Lantrip
3. Rhonda Alexander

Forms

Grand Champion:
  Dayton Pang
2. Keith Hirabayashi
3. Stuart Quan
4. Brian Fung

JAPANESE/OKINAWAN:
1. Gary Michak

KENPO:
1. Brian Fung

KOREAN:
1. Dayton Pang

MUSICAL:
1. Jean Frenette

OPEN:
1. Stuart Quan

WOMEN:
1. Lori Lantrip

Weapons Grand Champion:
  Stuart Quan
2. Keith Hirabayashi
3. Gary Michak

1982 NATIONAL TOURNAMENTS

SUPERSTAR NATIONALS: MARCH 6, 1982

Tom Schlesinger & Steve LaBounty, Producers
Oakland, CA

Fighting

Men's Grand Champion:
  Steve Anderson
2. Ray McCallum

HEAVY:
1. ?
2. Billy Blanks

LIGHT HEAVY:
1. Fred King

MIDDLE:
1. Dexter Brooks

LIGHT:
1. ?
2. Johnny Gyro

Women's Grand Champion:
  Linda Denley
2. Arlene Limas

HEAVY:
1. Linda Denley
2. ?
3. Mary Stark-Owens

LIGHT:
1. Lynice Mills

Forms

Grand Champion:
  Cynthia Rothrock

2. ?

KENPO:
1. Brian Fung

WOMEN:
1. Cynthia Rothrock
2. ?
3. Arlene Limas

BATTLE OF ATLANTA: APRIL 24, 1982

Note: Although this event was B-rated by *Karate Illustrated* magazine this year, it nevertheless drew enough nationally rated competitors to have a major impact.

Fighting

Men's Grand Champion:
  John Longstreet
2. Robert Harris

HEAVY:
1. Vernon Johnson
2. Felix Snoddy
3. Robert Ray

LIGHT HEAVY:
1. Mike Genova
2. Cedric Rodgers
3. Marty Knight

MIDDLE:
1. Jay Bell
2. James Hobby
3. Bobby Wilson

LIGHT:
1. Lewis Wilson
2. Joey Shiflett
3. Gary Landreth

SUPER LIGHT:
1. Tony Young
2. Eric Ekholm
3. Jessie Thornton

Women's Grand Champion:
  Linda Denley
2. Becky Chapman

LIGHT:
1. Linda Denley
2. Rhonda Alexander
3. Donna Judge

FEATHER:
1. Becky Chapman

2. Stacey Duke
3. Julia Ledbetter

Forms

Grand Champion:
George Chung
2. John Chung

CHINESE:
1. George Chung
2. Arthur Keith
3. Dennis Brown

JAPANESE:
1. Toyotaro Miyazaki
2. Hidy Ochiai
3. Dale Kirby

KOREAN:
1. John Chung
2. Philip Chung
3. Jamie Hooper

OKINAWAN:
1. Sonny Onowo
2. Bill Pickels
3. Vic Coffin

OPEN:
1. Charlie Lee
2. Ernie Reyes, Jr.
3. Stuart Quan

WEAPONS:
1. Cynthia Rothrock
2. Toyotaro Miyazaki
3. Dale Kirby

WOMEN:
1. Karen Sheperd
2. Cynthia Rothrock
3. Helen Chung

DIAMOND NATIONALS: MAY 8, 1982

Fighting

Men's Grand Champion:
John Longstreet
2. Robert Harris
3. Steve Anderson

HEAVY:
1. Billy Blanks
2. Richard Plowden
3. Steve Perry

LIGHT HEAVY:
1. Alvin Prouder
2. Ray McCallum

MIDDLE:
1. Harold Burrage
2. Terry Norblom
3. Fred Letuli

LIGHT:
1. Chris Ost

SUPER LIGHT:
1. Jessie Thornton
2. Gary Michak

Women's Grand Champion:
Linda Denley

Forms

Grand Champion:
John Chung

HARD STYLE:
1. ?
2. Sonny Onowo

OPEN:
1. Ernie Reyes, Jr.

SOFT STYLE:
1. ?
2. Brian Fung

WEAPONS:
1. ?
2. Dale Kirby
3. Cynthia Rothrock

WOMEN:
1. ?
2. Karen Sheperd

J. PARK EAST COAST NATIONALS: MAY 15, 1982

**J. Park, Producer
Springfield, MA**

Fighting

Men's Grand Champion:
Steve Anderson
2. Joey Shiflett

HEAVY:
1. Billy Blanks
2. Steve Perry
3. Terry Norblom

LIGHT HEAVY:
1. Fred Letuli
2. Larry Kelley

MIDDLE:
1. John Longstreet

2. Sam Roberts

LIGHT:
1. Joey Shiflett

SUPER LIGHT:
1. Gary Michak

Women's Grand Champion:
Arlene Limas

Forms

Grand Champion:
John Chung

WOMEN:
1. Cynthia Rothrock
2. Shelly Vhacon

A.K.A. GRAND NATIONALS: 1982

Fighting

Men's Grand Champion:
Richard Plowden
2. Larry Tankson

HEAVY:
1. Richard Plowden
2. Russ Mapes
3. Arnold White
Steve Perrey

LIGHT HEAVY:
1. Lonnie Pierce
2. Freddie Letuli
3. Steve Anderson
Jay Bell

MIDDLE:
1. Larry Tankson
2. Joey Shifflet
3. Mel Cherry
George Michak

LIGHT:
1. Charles Fears
2. Sonny Onowo
3. Gary Michak
Jonathan Wright

Women's Grand Champion:
Arlene Limas
2. Rhonda Alexander

HEAVY:
1. Arlene Limas
2. Linda Denley
3. Diedra Cole
Mitzi Tyler

LIGHT:
1. Rhonda Alexander
2. Loru Lantrip
3. Adriana Chacon
   Christine Sims

Forms

Grand Champion:
   John Chung
2. Dale Kirby
3. Toyotaro Miyazaki

MEN'S HARD STYLE:
1. John Chung
2. Sonny Onowo
3. George Chung
   Charlie Lee

MEN'S SOFT STYLE:
1. George Chung
2. Arthur Keith
3. K. Vita
   Jack Soderberg

OPEN:
1. Toyotaro Miyazaki
2. Cynthia Rothrock
3. Gary Michak
   Charlie Lee

WEAPONS (HARD):
1. Dale Kirby
2. George Chung
3. Vic Coffin
   Toyotaro Miyazaki

WEAPONS (SOFT):
1. Cynthia Rothrock
2. Shelly Chacon
3. Arthur Keith
   K. Vita

WOMEN:
1. Cynthia Rothrock
2. Shelly Chacon
3. Helen Chung
   Arlene Limas

WEST COAST NATIONALS:
JUNE 5, 1982

Ernie Reyes, Sr., Producer
San Jose, CA

Fighting

Men's Grand Champion:
   Steve Anderson
2. John Longstreet

3. Larry Kelley
   Joey Shiflett

HEAVY:
1. Steve Anderson
2. Billy Blanks

LIGHT HEAVY:
1. Larry Kelley
2. Alvin Prouder
3. Fred King

MIDDLE:
1. ?
2. Dexter Brooks

LIGHT:
1. Joey Shifflet
2. Keith Hirabayashi
3. Chris Ost
   Sonny Onowo

Women's Grand Champion:
   Linda Denley
2. Lois Jones

LIGHT:
1. Lynice Mills

Forms

Grand Champion:
   John Chung
2. George Chung
3. Anthony Chan

JAPANESE/OKINAWAN:
1. George Chung
2. Sonny Onowo

KENPO:
1. Brian Fung

KOREAN:
1. Dayton Pang

MUSICAL:
1. John Chung

OPEN:
1. Cynthia Rothrock
2. Ernie Reyes, Jr.

WEAPONS (HARD):
1. Anthony Chan

WEAPONS (SOFT):
1. Cynthia Rothrock

WOMEN (HARD):
1. Helen Chung
2. Margie Betke
3. Lori Lantrip

WOMEN (SOFT):
1. Cynthia Rothrock

2. Sophia Kikuchi
3. Belinda Davis

FT. WORTH NATIONAL PRO-AM:
JUNE 19, 1982

Roy Kurban, Producer
Ft. Worth, TX

Fighting

Men's Grand Champion:
   Ray McCallum
2. Steve Anderson

HEAVY:
1. Steve Perrey
2. Jerry Jones
3. Arnold White
   Billy Blanks

LIGHT HEAVY:
1. Steve Anderson
2. Rudy Smedley
3. Cedric Rodgers
   Larry Kelley

MIDDLE:
1. Ray McCallum
2. Harold Burrage
3. Terry Norblom
   Tommy Bloom

LIGHT:
1. Joey Shifflet
2. Tim Kirby
3. Erik Alexander
   David Deaton

SUPER LIGHT:
1. Al Garza
2. Troy Dorsey
3. Don Hill
   Troy McCaskell

EXECUTIVE:
1. Jerry Francis
2. J.W. Dunn

WOMEN:
1. Linda Denley
2. Arlene Limas
3. Cindy Benavidez
4. Lori Lantrip

Forms

Grand Champion:
   John Chung
2. George Chung
3. Cynthia Rothrock

HARD STYLE:
1. George Chung
2. John Chung
3. Charlie Lee
4. Toyotaro Miyazaki

SOFT STYLE:
1. George Chung
2. Mark Nakona
3. Robert Hartfield
4. Gary Lee

MUSICAL:
1. John Chung
2. Stuart Quan
3. Cynthia Rothrock
4. Charlie Lee

WEAPONS:
1. Cynthia Rothrock
2. George Chung
3. Toyotaro Miyazaki
4. Gary Michak

WOMEN:
1. Cynthia Rothrock
2. Helen Chung
3. Lori Lantrip
4. Cessy Pierson

L.A.M.A. NATIONALS: JULY 11, 1982

Fighting

Men's Grand Champion:
Steve Anderson
2. Harold Burrage
3. Richard Plowden
    Fred Letuli

HEAVY:
1. Richard Plowden

LIGHT HEAVY:
1. Fred King

MIDDLE:
1. Harold Burrage

LIGHT:
1. Joey Shiflett
2. Chris Ost
3. Johnny Gyro

Women's Grand Champion:
Arlene Limas
2. ?

HEAVY:
1. Arlene Limas
2. Kathy Faust
3. Mitzi Tyler

LIGHT:
1. Stacey Duke
2. Lori Lantrip

Forms

Grand Champion:
George Chung
2. John Chung
3. Cynthia Rothrock

JAPANESE/OKINAWAN:
1. Gary Michak
2. Sonny Onowo

KOREAN:
1. John Chung
2. Dayton Pang

OPEN:
1. ?
2. Ernie Reyes, Jr.

WEAPONS (SOFT):
1. Cynthia Rothrock

WOMEN (HARD):
1. Margie Betke
2. ?
3. Lori Lantrip

WOMEN (SOFT):
1. Cynthia Rothrock
2. Shelly Chacon

U.S. TOP TEN NATIONALS: SEPTEMBER 4, 1982

**Ron Marchini, Producer
Stockton, CA**

Fighting

Men's Grand Champion:
Alvin Prouder
2. John Longstreet

HEAVY:
1. Billy Blanks

LIGHT HEAVY:
1. ?
2. Larry Kelley
3. Fred King

MIDDLE:
1. Dexter Brooks

LIGHT:
1. Chris Ost
2. Johnny Gyro

SUPER LIGHT:
1. Jessie Thornton

Women's Grand Champion:
Arlene Limas
2. Lynice Mills

LIGHT:
1. Stacey Duke

Forms

Grand Champion:
John Chung
2. Charlie Lee

KENPO:
1. Brian Fung

WEAPONS:
1. Cynthia Rothrock

WOMEN (HARD):
1. ?
2. Margie Betke
3. Arlene Limas

WOMEN (SOFT):
1. Cynthia Rothrock
2. Sophia Kikuchi

PORTLAND PRO-AM: SEPTEMBER 18, 1982

**Dan Anderson & Tom Levak, Producers
Portland, OR**

Fighting

Men's Grand Champion:
Steve Anderson
2. Larry Kelley
3. Ray McCallum

HEAVY:
1. Steve Anderson
2. ?
3. Billy Blanks

LIGHT HEAVY:
1. Harold Burrage

MIDDLE:
1. Terry Norblom

LIGHT:
1. Joey Shiflett
2. Chris Ost

Women's Grand Champion:
Linda Denley

LIGHT:
1. Lynice Mills
2. Stacey Duke
3. Lori Lantrip

Forms

Grand Champion:

John Chung
2. George Chung
3. Toyotaro Miyazaki

JAPANESE/OKINAWAN:
1. Toyotaro Miyazaki

OPEN:
1. Ernie Reyes, Jr.

WOMEN:
1. Cynthia Rothrock
2. Sophia Kikuchi
2. Lori Lantrip

WEAPONS (HARD):
1. Dale Kirby

WEAPONS (SOFT):
1. ?
2. Cynthia Rothrock

U.S. OPEN: OCTOBER 23, 1982

**Charles Brown, Producer
St. Petersburg, FL**

Fighting

Men's Grand Champion:

Larry Kelley
2. ?
3. Robert Harris

HEAVY:
1. ?
2. Billy Blanks

LIGHT HEAVY:
1. Harold Burrage
2. Sam Roberts

MIDDLE:
1. ?
2. ?
3. John Longstreet

LIGHT:
1. ?
2. ?
3. Jessie Thornton

SUPER LIGHT:
1. Gary Michak

Women's Grand Champion:

Linda Denley
2. Stacey Duke

HEAVY:
1. Donna Judge
2. ?
3. Mitzi Tyler

LIGHT:
1. Stacey Duke
2. Lori Lantrip

Forms

Grand Champion:

John Chung

CHINESE:
1. ?
2. Brian Fung

OPEN:
1. ?
2. Ernie Reyes, Jr.

WEAPONS:
1. Dale Kirby

WOMEN (HARD):
1. Margie Betke

WOMEN (SOFT):
1. Cynthia Rothrock

NATIONAL FINALS KARATE TOURNAMENT: NOVEMBER 6, 1982

**Mike Dillard, Producer
Oklahoma City, OK**

Fighting

Men's Grand Champion:

Ray McCallum

HEAVY:
1. Billy Blanks
2. Fred King
3. Steve Perry

LIGHT HEAVY:
1. ?

MIDDLE:
1. Robert Harris
2. Sam Roberts

LIGHT:
1. ?
2. Chris Ost

Women's Grand Champion:

Arlene Limas
2. Lynice Mills

Forms

Grand Champion:

John Chung
2. ?
3. Cynthia Rothrock

CHINESE:
1. ?
2. Brian Fung

OPEN:
1. Ernie Reyes, Jr.

WOMEN:
1. Cynthia Rothrock

OFFICIAL CALIFORNIA KARATE CHAMPIONSHIPS: NOVEMBER 27, 1982

**Leo Fong, Joe Meyer & Ron Marchini, Producers
Stockton, CA**

Fighting

Men's Grand Champion

Steve Anderson
2. David Deaton

HEAVY:
1. Billy Blanks
2. Larry Kelley

LIGHT HEAVY:
1. Sam Montgomery
2. Freddie Letuli

MIDDLE:
1. Barry Gordon
2. Dexter Brooks
3. Sam Roberts

LIGHT:
1. Chris Ost
2. Joey Shiflett
3. Eduardo Ayuso

SUPER LIGHT:
1. Gary Michak
2. Willie Mills

Women's Grand Champion:

Arlene Limas
2. Linda Denley

HEAVY:
1. Rhonda Alexander

LIGHT:
1. Lynice Mills

Forms

Grand Champion:
George Chung
2. Toyotaro Miyazaki
3. Cynthia Rothrock

CHINESE:
1. Benson Lee
2. Josie Candolita

JAPANESE/OKINAWAN:
1. Toyotaro Miyazaki
2. Stuart Quan
3. Jean Frenette

KENPO:
1. Brian Fung

KOREAN:
1. George Chung
2. Dayton Pang

OPEN:
1. Charlie Lee

WEAPONS:
1. Benson Lee
2. Cynthia Rothrock

WOMEN (HARD):
1. ?
2. Margie Betke

WOMEN (SOFT):
1. Cynthia Rothrock
2. Sophia Kikuchi

1981 NATIONAL TOURNAMENTS

STEVE FISHER'S KARATE CHAMPIONSHIPS: FEBRUARY 7, 1981

**Steve Fisher, Producer
Culver City, CA**

Fighting

Men's Grand Champion:
Dwain Magett
2. Barry Gordon
3. Steve Anderson
Alvin Prouder

EXECUTIVE (35 & OVER):
1. Lloyd Francis
2. Dick Willett

Women's Grand Champion:
Arlene Limas

Forms

Grand Champion:
George Chung
2. Dayton Pang

WOMEN:
1. Carrie Ogawa
2. Sophia Kikuchi
3. Margie Betke
Belinda Davis

SUPERSTAR NATIONALS: MARCH 7, 1981

**Tom Schlesinger & Steve LaBounty, Producers
Oakland, CA**

Note: Keith Vitali, America's three-time number-one semi-contact champion, retired after this event.

Fighting

Men's Grand Champion:
Alvin Prouder
2. Keith Vitali
3. Ray McCallum
4. Steve Fisher

HEAVY:
1. ?
2. Dwain Magett

MIDDLE:
1. Ray McCallum
2. Barry Gordon

LIGHT:
1. ?
2. David Deaton

Women's Grand Champion:
Mary Stark-Owens

Forms

Grand Champion:
?
2. George Chung

HARD STYLE:
1. Dayton Pang

ALL-AMERICAN CHAMPIONSHIPS: MARCH 21, 1981

PRAIRIE STATES: MARCH 29, 1981

**Burley Wagner, Producer
Kankakee, IL**

Fighting

Men's Grand Champion:
John Longstreet
2. Richard Plowden
3. Larry Tankson
4. Al Campbell

HEAVY:
1. Richard Plowden
2. George Willis
3. Russ Mapes

LIGHT HEAVY:
1. John Longstreet
2. Sid Gee
3. Terry Norblom

MIDDLE:
1. Al Campbell
2. Fred Letuli
3. Terry Norblom

LIGHT:
1. Larry Tankson
2. Larry Sanders
3. Tyrone Cox

Forms

Grand Champion:
Steve Perry
2. K. Vita
3. Kelly Wencel

HARD STYLE:
1. Steve Perry
2. Kieron Davis
3. Herb Johnson

SOFT STYLE:
1. K. Vita
2. Charlie Webb
3. Lee Wedlake

WEAPONS:
1. K. Vita
2. Mike Bukala
3. Arlene Limas

WOMEN:
1. Kelly Wencel
2. Mary Amelotts
3. Arlene Limas

DIAMOND NATIONALS: MAY 2, 1981

Fighting

Men's Grand Champion:
Robert Harris
2. Ray McCallum
3. Steve Anderson
4. Joey Shiflett

HEAVY:
1. Steve Perry
2. Russ Mapes
3. Richard Plowden
Dan Martin

LIGHT HEAVY:
1. Larry Kelley
2. Chip Wright
3. Alvin Prouder
Sid Gee

MIDDLE:
1. John Longstreet
2. Harold Burrage
3. Dexter Brooks
Doug Jones

LIGHT:
1. Joey Shiflett
2. Hollywood Fever
3. Charles Fears
Allan Kelley

SUPER LIGHT:
1. Gary Michak
2. Larry Tankson
3. Mike Genova
Billy Mathews

Women
1. Arlene Limas
2. Joanna Needham
3. Linda Denley
Sue Wineinger

Forms

Grand Champion:
George Chung
2. John Chung
3. Gary Michak
4. Peter Morales

HARD STYLE:
1. John Chung
2. Sonny Onowo
3. Gary Nakahama
4. Gary Michak

MUSICAL:
1. Gary Michak
2. Helen Chung
3. Joseph Shahady
4. Gary Nakahama

SOFT STYLE:
1. George Chung
2. Peter Morales
3. Toru Kellam
4. Cynthia Rothrock

WEAPONS:
1. Peter Morales
2. George Chung
3. Karen Sheperd
4. Gary Michak

WOMEN:
1. Karen Sheperd
2. Belinda Davis
3. Lori Clapper
4. Cynthia Rothrock

A.K.A. GRAND NATIONALS: MAY 24, 1981

Note: Finalists in each weight division were pitted against seeded, nationally rated fighters.

Fighting

Men's Grand Champion:
John Jackson
2. Harold Burrage

HEAVY:
1. Dan Martin
2. Richard Plowden
3. Arnold White

LIGHT HEAVY:
1. Peter Paik
2. Steve Echtinaw
3. Mike Genova

MIDDLE:
1. Fred Letuli
2. Joey Shiflett
3. Matthew Glasper

LIGHT:
1. Larry Tankson
2. Sonny Onowo
3. Robert Madison

Women
1. Arlene Limas
2. Jennifer Hampton
3. Cathy Turrell

Forms

Grand Champion:
John Chung
2. Peter Morales
3. Dale Kirby

HARD STYLE:
1. John Chung
2. Gary Michak
3. Sonny Onowo
4. Jeff Carroll

SOFT STYLE:
1. Peter Morales
2. Cynthia Rothrock
3. Glenn Wilson
4. Lee Wedlake

WEAPONS (HARD):
1. Dale Kirby
2. Marty Fick
3. George Michak
4. Gary Michak

WEAPONS (SOFT):
1. Peter Morales
2. Cynthia Rothrock
3. Glenn Wilson

WOMEN:
1. Cynthia Rothrock
2. Helen Chung
3. Arlene Limas
4. Kim Cochin

WEST COAST NATIONALS: JUNE 6, 1981

**Ernie Reyes, Sr., Producer
San Jose, CA**

Fighting

Men's Grand Champion:
Steve Anderson
2. ?
3. John Longstreet

HEAVY:
1. Ricky Chambers
2. Arnold White

MIDDLE:
1. Bobby Wilson

LIGHT:
1. Ceric Hunt
2. Mills
3. De La Cruz

Women's Grand Champion:
Mary Stark-Owens

Forms

Grand Champion:
George Chung
2. Chuckie Curry
3. Simon Rhee

HARD STYLE:
1. Simon Rhee
2. Mark Mashiro & Dayton Pang
3. Henry Martinez

OPEN:
1. Karen Sheperd
2. Ernie Reyes, Jr.

SOFT STYLE:
1. Timmy Lovie
2. John Baymont
3. Ray Lozado

WOMEN:
1. Karen Sheperd
2. Belinda Davis
3. Josie Candalito

FT. WORTH NATIONAL PRO-AM: JUNE 20, 1981

Roy Kurban, Producer
Ft. Worth, TX

Fighting

Men's Grand Champion:
Ray McCallum
2. Zip White
3. Sam Montgomery
Larry Kelley

HEAVY:
1. Zip White
2. Steve Anderson
3. Russ Mapes

LIGHT HEAVY:
1. Larry Kelley

MIDDLE:
1. Ray McCallum
2. John Longstreet
3. Fred Letuli

LIGHT:
1. Sam Montgomery

Women's Grand Champion:
Linda Denley
2. Arlene Limas

Forms

Grand Champion:
John Chung

HARD STYLE:
1. John Chung
2. Dayton Pang

SOFT STYLE:
1. ?
2. Christian Wulf

WEAPONS:
1. Christian Wulf
2. ?
3. Cynthia Rothrock

WOMEN:
1. Cynthia Rothrock
2. Margie Betke
3. Sophia Kikuchi

L.A.M.A. NATIONALS: JULY, 1981

Fighting

Men's Grand Champion:
Harold Burrage
2. Steve Anderson

HEAVY:
1. Steve Anderson
2. John Jackson
3. Russ Mapes

MIDDLE:
1. Harold Burrage
2. ?
3. Robert Harris

SUPER LIGHT:
1. Jessie Thornton
2. Gary Michak

Women's Grand Champion:
Arlene Limas

HEAVY:
1. Arlene Limas
2. Mitzi Tyler

Forms

Grand Champion:
George Chung
2. John Chung
3. Christian Wulf

HARD STYLE:
1. Sonny Onowo
2. Gary Michak

KOREAN:
1. John Chung

SOFT STYLE:
1. Christian Wulf

WEAPONS:
1. Dale Kirby
2. Cynthia Rothrock
3. Christian Wulf

WOMEN:
1. Cynthia Rothrock
2. Arlene Limas
3. Mitzi Tyler

PORTLAND PRO-AM: SEPTEMBER 19, 1981

Tom Levak & Dan Anderson, Producers
Portland, OR

Fighting

Men's Grand Champion:
John Longstreet
2. Fred Letuli
3. Ray McCallum

LIGHT HEAVY:
1. Ray McCallum

MIDDLE:
1. John Longstreet

LIGHT:
1. David Deaton

SUPER LIGHT:
1. Fred Letuli

Women's Grand Champion:
Arlene Limas
2. Janesa Kruse

Forms

Grand Champion:
?

KOREAN:
1. Dayton Pang

OPEN:
1. Roger Tung

SOFT STYLE:
1. ?
2. ?
3. Roger Tung

WOMEN:
1. Karen Sheperd
2. Belinda Davis
3. Arlene Limas

U.S. TOP TEN NATIONALS: SEPTEMBER 19, 1981

Leo Fong & Ron Marchini, Producers
Stockton, CA

Fighting

Men's Grand Champion:
Steve Anderson
2. Sam Montgomery
3. Robert Harris

Women's Grand Champion:
Mitzi Tyler
LIGHT:
1. Rhonda Alexander

Forms

Grand Champion:
John Chung
2. Sonny Onowo
HARD STYLE:
1. John Chung
WOMEN:
1. Cynthia Rothrock
2. ?
3. Carrie Ogawa

BATTLE OF ATLANTA: OCTOBER 10, 1981

Fighting

Men's Grand Champion:
Sam Montgomery
2. David Deaton
3. Robert Harris
Tokey Hill
HEAVY:
1. Ernie Smith
2. Zip White
3. Richard Plowden
4. John Orck
LIGHT HEAVY:
1. Jarvis Suddreth
2. James Sisco
3. Jerry Rhome
4. Mike Genova
MIDDLE:
1. Fred Letuli

2. Jeff Farmer
3. Jay Bell
LIGHT:
1. David Deaton
2. Joey Shiflett
3. Speedy Wilson
4. Sherman Miller
SUPER LIGHT:
1. Marcal Lazenby
2. Ken Privette
3. Gary Michak
4. Tony Young

Women's Grand Champion:
Linda Denley
2. Becky Chapman
HEAVY:
1. Linda Denley
2. Mitzi Tyler
3. Rhonda Alexander
4. Tina Hamilton
LIGHT:
1. Becky Chapman
2. Donna Judge
3. Arlene Limas
4. Lori Lantrip

Forms

Grand Champion:
John Chung
2. ?
3. Sonny Onowo
CHINESE:
1. Roger Tung
2. George Chung
3. Peter Morales
4. Arthur Keith
JAPANESE:
1. Toyotaro Miyazaki
2. Gary Michak
3. George Michak
4. William Oliver
KOREAN:
1. John Chung
2. Jamie Hooper
3. Peter Lulgsurat
4. Archie Mullins
OKINAWAN:
1. Sonny Onowo
2. Steve Perry
3. Dwain Vaughns
4. Mike Day

OPEN:
1. Charlie Lee
2. Christopher Hardy
3. Mike Johnson
4. Carl West
WEAPONS:
1. Cynthia Rothrock
2. Vic Coffin
3. Dale Kirby
4. Jesse Bowen
WOMEN:
1. Karen Sheperd
2. Cynthia Rothrock
3. Arlene Limas
4. Helen Chung

U.S. OPEN: OCTOBER 24, 1981

Charles Brown, Producer
St. Petersburg, FL

Fighting

Men's Grand Champion:
Steve Anderson
2. Robert Harris
3. Jessie Thornton
Steve Perry
HEAVY:
1. Steve Perry
2. Zip White
3. Russ Mapes
LIGHT HEAVY:
1. ?
2. Larry Kelley
MIDDLE:
1. Robert Harris
2. Sam Montgomery
LIGHT:
1. Jessie Thornton
SUPER LIGHT:
1. ?
2. Gary Michak

Women's Grand Champion:
Linda Denley
2. Rhonda Alexander

Forms

Grand Champion:
John Chung

JAPANESE:
1. Sonny Onowo

KOREAN:
1. John Chung
2. Dayton Pang

OKINAWAN:
1. Sonny Onowo
2. ?
3. Gary Michak

OPEN:
1. ?
2. ?
3. Ernie Reyes, Jr.

WEAPONS:
1. Dale Kirby

WOMEN:
1. Lori Clapper
2. Cynthia Rothrock
3. Karen Sheperd

SOUTHERN CALIFORNIA NATIONALS: NOVEMBER 1, 1981

Steve Anderson & Larry McGraw, Producers
Chula Vista, CA

Fighting

Men's Grand Champion:
  Steve Anderson
2. Barry Gordon

LIGHT:
1. Al Francis

Women's Grand Champion:
  Linda Denley
2. Mary Stark-Owens

Forms

Grand Champion:
  John Chung

HARD STYLE:
1. John Chung

OPEN:
1. Gary Michak

WOMEN:
1. Cynthia Rothrock
2. ?
3. Sophia Kikuchi

NATIONAL KARATE CIRCUIT FINALS: NOVEMBER 7, 1981

Mike Dillard, Producer
Oklahoma City, OK

Fighting

Men's Grand Champion:
  Steve Anderson
2. Zip White
3. John Longstreet
  Larry Kelley

HEAVY:
1. Zip White
2. ?
3. Steve Perry

LIGHT HEAVY:
1. ?
2. ?
3. Russ Mapes

MIDDLE:
1. John Longstreet
2. Terry Norblom
3. Fred Letuli

LIGHT:
1. Tommy Williams

Women's Grand Champion:
  Linda Denley

Forms

Grand Champion:
  John Chung

JAPANESE:
1. Sonny Onowo

KOREAN:
1. John Chung
2. Dayton Pang

OPEN:
1. ?
2. Ernie Reyes, Jr.
3. Peter Morales

SOFT STYLE:
1. ?
2. ?
3. Peter Morales

WEAPONS:
1. ?
2. ?
3. Cynthia Rothrock

WOMEN:
1. Cynthia Rothrock

2. Belinda Davis
3. Carrie Ogawa

CALIFORNIA KARATE CHAMPIONSHIPS: NOVEMBER 14, 1981

Ron Marchini & Leo Fong, Producers
San Francisco, CA

Fighting

Men's Grand Champion:
  ?
2. Tommy Williams
3. Russ Mapes

LIGHT HEAVY:
1. ?
2. Larry Kelley

Women's Grand Champion:
  Mary Stark-Owens

Forms

Grand Champion:
  John Chung

HARD STYLE:
1. John Chung

1980 NATIONAL TOURNAMENTS

SUPERSTAR NATIONALS: MARCH 1, 1980

Tom Schlesinger & Steve LaBounty, Producers
Oakland, CA

Fighting

Men's Grand Champion:
  Sam Montgomery
2. Keith Vitali
3. Jimmy Tabares

HEAVY:
1. Tommy Gilbert
2. Steve Anderson

LIGHT HEAVY:
1. Keith Vitali
2. Fred King

MIDDLE:
1. Sam Montgomery
2. Dan Anderson

LIGHT:
1. Jimmy Tabares
2. Bobby Wilson

Women's Grand Champion:
 Mary Owens
2. Janesa Kruse

Forms

Grand Champion:
 George Chung
2. Ernie Reyes, Jr.

CHINESE:
1. Anthony Chan

JAPANESE:
1. Henry Martinez

KOREAN:
1. George Chung

MUSICAL:
1. George Chung

OPEN:
1. Ernie Reyes, Jr.

WEAPONS:
1. Tayari Casel

ALL-AMERICAN CHAMPIONSHIPS: MARCH 15, 1980

PRAIRIE STATES: MARCH 30, 1980

**Burley Wagner, Producer
Kankakee, IL**

EAST COAST NATIONALS: APRIL 19, 1980

**J. Park, Producer
Springfield, MA**

Fighting

Men's Grand Champion:
 Larry Kelley
2. John Longstreet
3. Dan Anderson
4. Jimmy Tabares

DIAMOND NATIONALS: MAY 3, 1980

Fighting

Men's Grand Champion:
 Ray McCallum
2. Keith Vitali
3. Larry Kelley
 Jimmy Tabares

HEAVY:
1. Vernon Johnson
2. John Orck
3. Steve Fisher
 Kevin Kastelle

LIGHT HEAVY:
1. Larry Kelley
2. Mike Genova
3. Woodrow Speed
 Dan Swenson

MIDDLE:
1. Robert Harris
2. John Longstreet
3. Harold Burrage
 Terry Norblom

LIGHT:
1. Al Francis
2. Fred Letuli
3. Erik Alexander
 Jesse Thornton

Women's Grand Champion:
 Joanna Needham
2. Linda Denley

Forms

Grand Champion:
 John Chung
2. George Chung
3. Peter Morales
 Karen Sheperd

MEN:
1. Tayari Casel
2. Sonny Onowo
3. John Chung

MUSICAL:
1. John Chung
2. George Chung
3. Peter Morales
 Karen Sheperd

WEAPONS:
1. Peter Morales
2. George Chung

3. George Michak
 Dennis Brown

WOMEN:
1. Karen Sheperd
2. Helen Chung
3. Lori Clapper
 Virginia Benavenidez

A.K.A. GRAND NATIONALS: MAY 25, 1980

Fighting

Men's Grand Champion:
 Keith Vitali
2. Steve Fisher
3. Bobby Tucker
 John Jackson

HEAVY:
1. Dwain Maggett
2. Richard Plowden

LIGHT HEAVY:
1. Chip Wright
2. Larry Kelley
3. Steve Anderson

MIDDLE:
1. Erik Alexander
2. Matt Glasper

LIGHT:
1. Bobby Tucker
2. Gary Michak
3. Darrell Lassiter

Women's Grand Champion:
 Linda Denley
2. Joanna Needham

Forms

Grand Champion:
 Anthony Chan
2. Steve Fisher
 Dale Kirby

HARD STYLE:
1. Steve Fisher
2. Ernie Reyes
3. Sonny Onowo

SOFT STYLE:
1. Anthony Chan
2. Glenn Wilson
3. Karen Sheperd

WEAPONS (HARD):
1. Dale Kirby

2. George Chung
3. Gary Michak

WEAPONS (SOFT):
1. Anthony Chan
2. George Chung
3. Tayari Casel

WOMEN:
1. Karen Sheperd

WEST COAST NATIONALS:
JUNE 1, 1980

Ernie Reyes, Sr., Producer
San Jose, CA

Fighting

Men's Grand Champion:
    Eddie Newman
2. Orned Gabriel
3. John Jackson
    Steve Fisher

HEAVY:
1. John Jackson
2. Steve Anderson

LIGHT HEAVY:
1. Steve Fisher
2. Luther Secrease

MIDDLE:
1. Orned Gabriel
2. Keith Vitali

LIGHT:
1. Eddie Newman
2. Harold Burrage

Forms

Grand Champion:
    Anthony Chan
2. George Chung
3. Karen Shepard
    Belinda Davis

HARD STYLE:
1. Chuckie Currie

SOFT STYLE:
1. Victor Chew

WEAPONS:
1. Janet Gee/Rick Farmer

WOMEN:
1. Sharman Wong

FT. WORTH NATIONAL PRO-AM:
JUNE 28, 1980

Roy Kurban, Producer
Ft. Worth, TX

Fighting

Men's Grand Champion:
    Ray McCallum
2. ?
3. Larry Kelley

HEAVY:
1. Jim Butin
2. Dan Martin
3. Tony Thompson
    Sal Narvarez

LIGHT HEAVY:
1. Larry Kelley
2. Steve Fisher
3. Steve Anderson
    Larry Hartman

MIDDLE:
1. Ray McCallum
2. Sam Montgomery
3. Tokey Hill
    John Longstreet

LIGHT:
1. Keith Vitali
2. Norris Williams
3. Dan Anderson
    Louis Vasquez

Women's Grand Champion:
    Becky Perkins
2. Margaret Beasley

Forms

Grand Champion:
    George Chung
2. Steve Fisher
3. Belinda Davis

HARD STYLE:
1. George Chung
2. Ernie Reyes, Sr.

WEAPONS:
1. George Chung
2. Peter Morales

WOMEN:
1. Belinda Davis
2. Martgie Betke

WORLD TOURNAMENT:
AUGUST 17, 1980

Sid Campbell, Producer
Oakland, CA

Fighting

HEAVY:
1. Steve Anderson
2. Fred King

LIGHT HEAVY:
1. Alvin Prouder
2. Percy Woods

MIDDLE:
1. Keith Vitali
2. Doug Jones
3. Eddie Newman

WELTER:
1. Sam Montgomery
2. Bobby Wilson
3. Andreas Brannsck

LIGHT:
1. Jimmy Tabares
2. Newby Lazado
3. Chris Estes

Forms

Grand Champion:
    Roger Tung
2. Tat May Wong

CHINESE:
1. Tat May Wong

JAPANESE:
1. Joyce Sauvain

KOREAN:
1. Steve Valente

OKINAWAN:
1. Joyce Sauvain

WEAPONS:
1. Roger Tung

PORTLAND PRO-AM:
SEPTEMBER 19, 1980

Tom Levak & Dan Anderson,
Producers
Portland, OR

U.S. TOP TEN NATIONALS: SEPTEMBER 20, 1980

Leo Fong & Ron Marchini, Producers
San Jose, CA

Fighting

Men's Grand Champion:
Eddie Newman
2. Steve Anderson
3. Keith Vitali
Alvin Prouder

1st-Round Winners After Automatic Seeding:
Keith Vitali
Alvin Prouder
Steve Fisher
Dan Anderson
Dave Brock
Eddie Newman
Steve Anderson
Robert Harris
Dexter Brooks
John Longstreet
Steve Anderson

Forms

Grand Champion:
Chuckie Currie
CHINESE:
1. Ed Solis
OKINAWAN:
1. Don Davis
OPEN:
1. Chuckie Currie
OTHER:
1. Tayari Casel
WEAPONS:
1. Tony Hemenes

BATTLE OF ATLANTA: OCTOBER 4, 1980

Note: Event featured a Tournament of Champions in which the 1st place winners of each weight division were pitted against seeded, nationally rated fighters.

Fighting

Tournament of Champions
Grand Champion:
Robert Harris
2. Bobby Tucker
3. Vernon Johnson
Jay Bell

Men's Grand Champion:
Jeff Farmer
2. Jessie Thornton
3. John Orck
HEAVY:
1. John Orch
2. Arnold White
3. Lee McDowell
4. Grey Irvin
LIGHT HEAVY:
1. Eugene Upshaw
2. James Hobley
3. Woodrow Speed
4. Fred King
MIDDLE:
1. ?
LIGHT:
1. Jerome Johnson
2. Chester Greene
3. Chris Couch
4. Donald Roberts
SUPER LIGHT:
1. Jessie Thornton
2. Fred Letuli
3. Tony Lopez
4. Rusty Gray

Women's Heavyweight
Grand Champion:
Linda Denley
2. Joanna Needham
HEAVY:
1. Joanna Needham
2. Dawn Tribbett
3. Mary Stark-Owens
4. Rhonda Alexander

Women's Lightweight
Grand Champion:
Becky Chapman
2. Julia Ledbetter
LIGHT:
1. Julia Ledbetter
2. Donna Judge
3. Velma Boykins
4. Mary Lou Michaels

Forms

Grand Champion:
John Chung
OPEN:
1. Gary Dillingham
2. Charlie Lee
3. James White
4. Al Garza
CHINESE:
1. Roger Tung
2. Dennis Brown
3. George Chung
4. Peter Morales
JAPANESE:
1. Hidy Ochiai
2. Vic Coffin
3. David Deaton
4. Gary Michak
KOREAN:
1. John Chung
2. Tony Lopez
3. Gary Nakahama
4. Tyler Kirby
OKINAWAN:
1. Sonny Onowo
2. Steve Perry
3. Herb Johnson
4. Fred Letuli
MUSICAL:
1. George Chung
2. John Chung
WOMEN:
1. Karen Sheperd
2. Judy Kolesar
3. Lori Clapper
4. Julia Ledbetter

Weapons Grand Champion:
Dale Kirby
2. Peter Morales
WEAPONS:
1. Dale Kirby
2. George Chung
3. Vic Coffin
4. Roger Tung

U.S. OPEN: NOVEMBER 1, 1980

Ted Kresge, Producer
St. Petersburg, FL

Fighting

Men's Grand Champion:
Steve Anderson
2. Keith Vitali

Forms

Grand Champion:
Karen Sheperd

KOREAN:
1. John Chung

NATIONAL KARATE CIRCUIT FINALS: NOVEMBER 8, 1980

Mike Dillard, Producer
Oklahoma City, OK

Fighting

Men's Grand Champion:
Keith Vitali
2. Robert Harris
3. Al Francis
Dave Ruppart

HEAVY:
1. Dave Ruppart
2. Russell Mapes
3. Steve Anderson
Dan Swenson

LIGHT HEAVY:
1. Robert Harris
2. Chip Wright
3. Larry Kelly
Rudy Smedley

MIDDLE:
1. Keith Vitali
2. Billye Jackson
3. Tommy Williams
William Powell

LIGHT:
1. Al Francis
2. Norris Williams
3. Brent Fabacher
Tim Jones

WOMEN:
1. Linda Denley
2. Joyce Brown

Forms

Grand Champion:
George Chung
2. Karen Sheperd

HARD STYLE:
1. George Chung

OPEN:
1. George Chung

WOMEN:
1. Karen Sheperd

PKA NATIONALS: NOVEMBER 1980

Glen Keeney, Producer
Anderson, IN

1979 NATIONAL TOURNAMENTS

ALL-AMERICAN CHAMPIONSHIPS: 1979

Fighting

Men's Grand Champion:
Mike Warren
2. Roy Buchanan
3. Gerald Robbins
George Aschkar

HEAVY:
1. George Aschkar
2. Richard Cooper
3. Barry Brown

MIDDLE:
1. Mike Warren
2. Stanley Halcomb
3. Alton Wilkinson

LIGHT:
1. Roy Buchanan
2. William Oliver
3. Greg Fears

Women
1. Sadie White
2. Marcella Byrd
3. Toni Mitchell

Forms

TAE KWON DO:
1. Jim Roberts, Jr.
2. Alton Wilkinson

KARATE:
1. Ian Rugel
2. William Oliver

CO-ED KUNG-FU:
1. David Wong
2. Benson Lee
3. Cynthia Rothrock

WOMEN (TAE KWON DO):
1. Milagro Van Clief
2. Debbie Knoeferl

WOMEN (KARATE):
1. Gina Schiaroni
2. Lorna Peterson

DIAMOND NATIONALS: MAY 5, 1979

Fighting

Men's Grand Champion:
Dan Anderson
2. Larry Kelley
3. John Orck
John Longstreet

HEAVY:
1. John Orck
2. Jim Butin
3. Shorty Mills

LIGHT HEAVY:
1. Larry Kelley
2. Woodrow Speed
3. Herb Johnson

MIDDLE:
1. John Longstreet
2. Peter Paik
3. Ray McCallum

LIGHT:
1. Dan Anderson
2. Keith Vitali
3. John Carini
David Deaton

Women:

1. Kris Grayson
2. Allison Baker
3. Jennifer Hampton

Forms

Grand Champion:

George Chung
2. Karen Choy
3. Peter Morales
Belinda Davis

Men:

1. George Chung
2. Peter Morales
3. Hidy Ochiai
Sonny Onowo

Weapons:

1. George Chung
2. Peter Morales
3. Karen Choy
Bobby Barongan

Women:

1. Karen Choy
2. Belinda Davis
3. Debbie Feierer
Margie Betke

BATTLE OF NASHVILLE: SUMMER 1979

Roy Hinkle, Producer
Nashville, TN

Fighting

Men:

HEAVY:
1. Ronnie Vowell
2. Benny Green
3. Herb Johnson

LIGHT HEAVY:
1. Gary Basinger
2. Ralph Smith
3. Jerry Potts

MIDDLE:
1. Robert Harris
2. Jay Bell
3. Ron Walker

LIGHT:
1. Keith Vitali
2. Tony Bell
3. Rusty Ceray

Women:

HEAVY:
1. Susan Morris
2. Dorothy Kirkland White
3. Nancy Toby

LIGHT:
1. Becky Chapman
2. Julia Ledbetter
3. Denice Coulter

Forms

Men:

1. Vic Greene

Weapons:

1. Dale Kirby

Seniors:

1. Jack Pippin

PKA NATIONALS: JUNE 9, 1979

John Corcoran, Producer
Los Angeles, CA

Fighting

Men's Grand Champion:

Keith Vitali
2. Ray McCallum
3. Eddie Newman

HEAVY:
1. John Orck

LIGHT HEAVY:
1. Lionel Seals
2. Mike Genova
3. Glen McMorris

MIDDLE:
1. Robert Harris

LIGHT:
1. Eddie Newman
2. Sam Montgomery
3. Jimmy Tabares

Women:

1. Linda Denley

Forms

CHINESE:
1. Anthony Chan

JAPANESE/OKINAWAN:
1. Hidy Ochiai

KOREAN:
1. George Chung
2. ?
3. Ray McCallum

WEAPONS:
1. Roger Tung

WOMEN:
1. Karen Sheperd

A.K.A. GRAND NATIONALS: JUNE 16, 1979

Chicago, IL

Fighting

Men's Grand Champion:

Harold Burrage
2. Richard Plowden
3. Steve Fisher
Michael Redman

HEAVY:
1. Richard Plowden

LIGHT HEAVY:
1. Steve Fisher
2. Fred Miller
3. Lee Wedlake

MIDDLE:
1. Harold Burrage
2. James Banks
3. Pete Neal

LIGHT:
1. Michael Redman
2. Kirby McDonald
3. Kieron Davis

SUPER LIGHT:
1. Steve Neal
2. Fred Letuli
3. Tippy Croton

Women:

1. Earnistine Morgan
2. Jennifer Hampton
3. Kathy Turrell

Forms

MEN'S HARD STYLE:
1. Steve Fisher
2. Kieron Davis
3. Buzz Basile

MEN'S SOFT STYLE:
1. Jack Soderberg
2. Lee Wedlake
3. K. Vita

WOMEN:
1. Jennifer Hampton
2. Benita Fornero
3. Kathy Turrell

HARD-STYLE WEAPONS:
1. Fred Letuli
2. Jennifer Hampton
3. Rocco Grimaldi

SOFT-STYLE WEAPONS:
1. K. Vita
2. Karl Knoble
3. Arlene Limas

FT. WORTH NATIONAL PRO-AM: JUNE 23, 1979

Roy Kurban, Producer
Ft. Worth, TX

Note: The grand championship was decided by cumulative points in divisional fights and not by one-on-one bouts.

Fighting

Men's Grand Champion:
Steve Fisher
2. Ray McCallum

LIGHT HEAVY:
1. Steve Fisher

MIDDLE:
1. Ray McCallum
2. ?
3. Mike Genova

LIGHT:
1. ?
2. Jimmy Tabares

Women:
1. Linda Denley

Forms

HARD STYLE:
1. Steve Fisher

LONG BEACH INTERNATIONALS: AUGUST 4–5, 1979

Ed Parker, Producer
Long Beach, CA

Fighting

Men's Grand Champion:
Eddie Newman
2. Lionel Seals

Women's Grand Champion:
Linda Denley

Forms

Grand Champion:
Anthony Chan
2. Ernie Reyes, Sr.
3. Karen Sheperd

WOMEN (HARD STYLE):
1. Belinda Davis

WOMEN (SOFT STYLE):
1. Karen Sheperd

BATTLE OF ATLANTA: OCTOBER 13, 1979

Note: Event featured a Tournament of Champions in which the 1st place winners of each weight division were pitted against seeded, nationally rated fighters.

Fighting

Men's Grand Champion:
Keith Vitali
2. Robert Harris
3. Jimmy Tabares
4. Steve Fisher

HEAVY:
1. Vernon Johnson

LIGHT HEAVY:
1. ?
2. Jay Bell
3. Harold Burrage

LIGHT:
1. Al Francis

SUPER LIGHT:
1. Jimmy Tabares

Women's Grand Champion:
Linda Denley
2. Julia Ledbetter
3. Becky Chapman

Forms

Grand Champion:
John Chung
2. George Chung
3. Tayari Casel
4. Tony Lopez

WEAPONS:
1. Peter Morales
2. Dennis Brown

U.S. OPEN: OCTOBER 27, 1979

Ted Kresge, Producer
St. Petersburg, FL

Note: Event featured a Battle of the Superstars in which the 1st place winners in fighting and forms were pitted against seeded, nationally rated champions.

Fighting

Men's Grand Champion:
Tony Palmore
2. Robert Harris
3. Jimmy Tabares
James Sisko

HEAVY:
1. Tony Pakmore
2. Oren Smith
3. Abdul Mutakabbir
Herb Johnson

LIGHT HEAVY:
1. James Sisko
2. Larry Kelley
3. Alphonso Gabbidon

MIDDLE:
1. Robert Harris
2. Doug Adamson
3. Craig Clinton
Leslie Lee

LIGHT:
1. Jimmy Tabares
2. Dan Anderson
3. Jackie Mole
   Mike Bell

Women:
1. Linda Denley
2. Oretha Grant

Forms

Grand Champion:
   John Chung

MEN'S CHINESE:
1. Manual Tanigco
2. Peter Morales

MEN'S JAPANESE:
1. Toyotaro Miyazaki
2. Gene Fry
3. Leslie Lee

MEN'S KOREAN:
1. John Chung
2. George Chung
3. Ernie Reyes
4. Jimmy Tabares

MEN'S OKINAWAN:
1. Sonny Onowo
2. Bill Pickells

Women:
1. Karen Sheperd
2. Julia Ledbetter
3. Millie Schreiner

Weapons (Co-Ed):
1. Peter Morales
2. Jerry Lee

1978 NATIONAL TOURNAMENTS

MID-AMERICA NATIONALS (A.K.A. DIAMOND NATIONALS): APRIL 29, 1978

Pat Worley, John Worley, Larry Carnahan, Gary Hestilow & Gordon Franks, Producers
Minneapolis, MN

Fighting

Men's Grand Champion:
   Keith Vitali

2. Mac Jaggers
3. John Longstreet
   Mike Genova

HEAVY:
1. Mac Jaggers
2. Gerald Robbins
3. Herb Johnson
   Robert Salazar

LIGHT HEAVY:
1. Mike Genova
2. Terry Norblom
3. Mark Hurst
   Rio DeGennaro

MIDDLE:
1. John Longstreet
2. Randy Reid
3. Jose Verdeja
   Peter Paik

LIGHT:
1. Keith Vitali
2. John Carini
3. Bobby Tucker
   Mark Hicks

EXECUTIVE (39 & OVER):
1. John Haaland
2. Joe Muellner
3. Russell Williams
   Floyd Isle

Women:
   (Insufficient competitors)

Forms

Men:
1. Sonny Onowo
2. Bill Pickells
3. Mark Hurst
   Kirk Notsch

Women:
   (Insufficient competitors)

Weapons:
1. Gary Donatell
2. Bobby Barongan
3. Richard Smith
   Gary Chanstier

MARTIAL ARTS RATING SYSTEM NATIONALS: JUNE 24–25, 1978

Cecil Kitchens, Producer
Cleveland, OH

Fighting

Men's Grand Championship:
   Dan Anderson
2. Robert Edwards
3. Ken Ferguson
   Jimmy Tabares

HEAVY:
1. Robert Edwards
2. Bill Hannah
3. Dennis Conatser
4. Karl Petro

LIGHT HEAVY:
1. Ken Ferguson
2. Steve Fisher
3. Mike Shintaku
4. Charlie Webb

MIDDLE:
1. Dan Anderson
2. Sheldon Wilkins
3. Earl Squalls
4. James Cook

LIGHT:
1. Jimmy Tabares
2. Lorenzo Scott
3. Nikya Yamashita
4. Karlas Mauzy

Women:
1. Linda Denley
2. Denise Garcia
3. Joanna Needham
4. Vicki Meade

Forms

Men's Grand Champion:
   John Sarmousakis

Men:
1. John Sarmousakis
2. Steve Fisher
3. Raul Hernandez
4. James Cook

Women:
1. Karen Ulmer
2. Judy Clapp
3. Roxanne Marcum
4. Michele Roberts

Weapons:
1. Don Murname
2. James Cook

3. Nikya Yamashita
4. John Sarmousakis

FT. WORTH NATIONAL PRO-AM: JUNE 24, 1978

Roy Kurban, Producer
Ft. Worth, TX

Fighting

Men's Grand Champion:
   Ray McCallum
   2. Willie Holland

HEAVY:
1. Ernie Smith
   Glenn McMorris
3. George Arnold
   Sal Narvaez

MIDDLE:
1. Ray McCallum
2. Tom Genova
3. Willie Holland
   Clarence Brown

LIGHT:
1. Keith Vitali
2. Ishmael Robles
3. D.P. Hill
   Al Francis

Women:
1. Kim Hyde
2. Jill Keith
3. Bobby Niemeyer

Forms

Men:
1. Glenn Rabago
2. Ray McCallum
3. Billy Burke
   Tim Kirby

Women:
1. Jill Swann
2. Kelly Hyde
3. Kim Hyde
   Judy Frye

Weapons:
1. Christian Wulf
2. Kevin Grimes & John Brame
3. Jill & Gary Swann

PKA NATIONALS: JULY 15, 1978

Francisco Conde & John Corcoran, Producers
Baltimore, MD

Fighting

Men's Grand Champion:
   Bobby Tucker
   2. Keith Vitali

BATTLE OF ATLANTA: OCTOBER 7, 1978

Note: Event featured a Tournament of Champions in which the 1st place winners of each weight division were pitted against seeded, nationally rated fighters.

Fighting

Men's Grand Champion:
   Keith Vitali
   2. Bobby Tucker
   3. Robert Harris
      Glenn McMorris

HEAVY:
1. Rory Bussey
2. Shorty Mills
3. Bruce Brutschy

LIGHT HEAVY:
1. Woodrow Speed
2. Roger Stamp
3. Emanuel Howard

MIDDLE:
1. James White
2. Jarvis Suddreth
3. Tom Genova

LIGHT:
1. Tony Bell
2. David Deaton
3. Bennie Lawrence

SUPER LIGHT:
1. Mike Goldman
2. Larry Logan
3. Alonzo Hall

Women:

Women's Grand Champion:
   Julia Ledbetter
   2. Becky Chapman

HEAVY:
1. Mary Barnett
2. Susan Shephard
3. Kathleen Garrity

LIGHT:
1. Becky Chapman
2. Lynn Scott
3. Millie Schreiner

Forms

CO-ED:
1. Hidy Ochiai
2. John Chung
3. Tony Lopez

CO-ED WEAPONS:
1. Peter Morales
2. Dale Kirby
3. George Chung

BATTLE OF THE SUPERSTARS (A.K.A. U.S. OPEN): OCTOBER 28, 1978

Ted Kresge, Producer
St. Petersburg, FL

Fighting

Men's Grand Champion:
   James Sisco
   2. Rory Bussey

Forms

JAPANESE:
1. Hidy Ochiai

OKINAWAN:
1. Sonny Onowo

CHINESE:
1. Jerry Lee

KOREAN:
1. Earl Harris

WOMEN:
1. Millie Schreiner

WEAPONS:
1. Jerry Lee

SOUTHWEST REGIONALS: OCTOBER 28, 1978

Gilbert Velez & Ed Parker, Producers
Tucson, AZ

Fighting

Men's Grand Champion:
Eddie Newman
2. Glenn McMorris
3. Alvin Prouder
Steve Fisher

Women

1. Linda Denley
2. Carlotta Lee
3. Sharon Scott
Valerie Ganther

Forms

Grand Champion:
Nancy McDonald
2. Jimmy Tabares
3. Alex Santamaria
4. Saul Tallbear

1977 NATIONAL TOURNAMENTS

Due to a mid-1970s industry business slump, a lack of national ratings, and an increased interest in kickboxing, tournament karate in the U.S. slumped dramatically. In 1977, there were fewer national karate tournaments than there had been back in 1965.

BATTLE OF ATLANTA: APRIL 2, 1977

Fighting

Men:

HEAVY:
1. Ernie Smith
2. Dan McCall
3. Rory Bussey

LIGHT HEAVY:
1. Glenn McMorris
2. Gary Basinger
3. Mike Cass

MIDDLE:
1. Tom Genova
2. Daryl Wilson

LIGHT:
1. Melvin Winn
2. Mike McNamara
3. Keith Vitali

SUPER LIGHT:
1. Jackie Mole
2. Chico Hill
3. Sonny Young

Women:

HEAVY:
1. Linda Denley
2. Margie Waller
3. Rhonda Alexander

LIGHT:
1. Julia Ledbetter
2. Tessie Jefferson
3. Millie Schreiner

Forms

Men:
1. Roger Tung
2. Sonny Onowo
3. Tony Lopez
4. Sang Han Kim

Weapons:
1. Roger Tung
2. Dennis Brown
3. Angel Rivera
4. Karyn Turner

Women:
1. Karyn Turner
2. Cynthia Rothrock
3. Julia Ledbetter
4. Millie Schreiner

ARLINGTON PRO-AM: JUNE 18, 1977

Roy Kurban, Producer
Arlington, TX

Fighting

Men's Grand Champion:
Ray McCallum
2. Louis Arnold

HEAVY:
1. Louis Arnold

2. Rufus Carpenter

MIDDLE:
1. Ray McCallum
2. Clyde Dennis
3. Steve Fisher

LIGHT:
1. D.P. Hill
2. Jimmy Tabares
3. Kwang Chon

WOMEN:
1. Linda Denley

Forms

Men:
1. Glenn Rabago
2. Steve Fisher

Weapons:
1. John Brame
Keven Grimes

Women:
1. Sandie McKenzie

U.S.K.A. GRAND NATIONALS: JUNE 18–19, 1977

Robert Trias, Producer
Pittsburgh, PA

Fighting

Men's Grand Champion:
James Cook
2. Mike Sheen
3. John Jackson
Woodrow Fairbanks

HEAVY:
1. John Jackson
2. Bruce Brietsky
3. Mike Awad

LIGHT HEAVY:
1. James Cook
2. Tokey Hill
3. Murray Sutherland

MIDDLE:
1. Woodrow Fairbanks
2. Stan Oussett
3. Don Felt

LIGHT:
1. Mike Sheen
2. Mike Isreal
3. Ron Nichols

WOMEN:
1. Wendi Weinshel
2. Pam Evans

Forms

Grand Champion:
  Barbara Niggel

Men:
1. Mike Isreal
2. Frank Kushner
3. Ian Rugel

Masters:
1. Randy Holman
2. Akio Minakami
3. Frank Caliguri

Weapons:
1. James Cook
2. Akio Minakami

Women:
1. Barbara Niggel
2. Vicki Johnson
   Rosie Rotz
3. Wendi Wenshell

EASTERN U.S. GRAND NATIONALS (A.K.A. U.S. OPEN): OCTOBER 29, 1977

Ted Kresge, Producer
St. Petersburg, FL

Fighting

Men's Grand Champion:
  Tony Palmore
2. Jackie Mole
3. Robert Harris

HEAVY:
1. Tokey Hill

LIGHT HEAVY:
1. Emanuel Howard

MIDDLE:
1. Mike Green

LIGHT:
1. Sang Hun Kim

Women:
1. Renee Smith
2. Kim Thompson

Forms

Grand Champion:
  Mike Isreal

CHINESE:
1. Jerry Lee
2. Orned Gabriel

JAPANESE:
1. Gene Fry
2. Leslie Lee
3. Bill Pickells

KOREAN:
1. Sang Hun Kim
2. Earl Harris
3. Millie Schreiner

OKINAWAN:
1. Mike Isreal
2. David Basile

Women:
1. Renee Smith
2. Pat Militelle

BATTLE OF ATLANTA: NOVEMBER 12, 1977

Note: 1) Producer Joe Corley held two Battles of Atlanta this year in order to permanently move its annual date to this time of year. In this way, he avoided conflicting dates with other national tournaments usually held in the spring. 2) Event featured a Tournament of Champions in which the 1st place winners of each weight division were pitted against seeded, nationally rated fighters.

Fighting

Men's Grand Champion:
  Glenn McMorris
2. Robert Harris
3. Rory Bussey

HEAVY:
1. Al Fiore
2. Robert Willis
3. John Orch

LIGHT HEAVY:
1. Gary Basinger
2. Herbie Thompson
3. Mike Cass

MIDDLE:
1. Jerry Smith

2. Bill Clark
3. Leslie Lee

LIGHT:
1. William McLarin
2. Bobby Tucker
3. Paul Bryant

SUPER LIGHT:
1. Mike Goldman
2. Steve Vitali
3. John Carini

Women:

HEAVY:
1. Linda Denley
2. Margie Waller

LIGHT:
1. Julia Ledbetter
2. Evelyn Vaughn

Forms

Women:
1. Barbara Niggel
2. Tayari Casel
3. Mike Isreal

TEXAS STATE: NOVEMBER 19, 1977

J. Pat Burleson, Producer
Ft. Worth, TX

Fighting

Men:

HEAVY:
1. Louis Arnold
2. Willie Holland
3. Ray Marshall

LIGHT:
1. Ray McCallum
2. Jimmy Tabares
3. Rudy Smedley

Women:
1. Linda Denley
2. Robin Miles
3. V. Meade

Forms

Co-Ed:
1. Karyn Turner
2. James Cook
3. Jimmy Tabares

EASTERN GRAND NATIONALS & U.S. BATTLE OF CHAMPIONS: 1977

Ted Kresge, Producer
St. Petersburg, FL

Fighting

Battle of Champions

MEN'S GRAND CHAMPION:
  Tony Palmore
2. Jackie Mole
3. Robert Harris
4. Emanuel Howard

Forms

Grand Champion:
  Mike Isreal
2. Jerry Lee

CHINESE:
1. Jerry Lee
2. Orned Gabriel

JAPANESE:
1. Gene Fry
2. Leslie Lee

KOREAN:
1. Sang Han Kim
2. Earl Harris

OKINAWAN:
1. Mike Isreal
2. Dave Basile

WEAPONS:
1. George Salis
2. Jerry Lee

WOMEN:
1. Renee Smith
2. Pat Militello

1976 NATIONAL TOURNAMENTS

U.S. CHAMPIONSHIPS: FEBRUARY 5, 1976

Allen Steen, Producer
Dallas, TX

Fighting

Men:

HEAVY:
1. Ed Williams
2. Cal Williams

3. Don Fritte
   Bob Halliburton

LIGHT HEAVY:
1. Ralph Alegria
2. Fred Wren
3. David Powell
   Ken Cagle

MIDDLE:
1. Ray McCallum
2. Rudy Smedley
3. David Archer
   Al Francis

LIGHT:
1. Ishmael Robles
2. Robert Arguelles
3. Dennis Gotcher
   Barry Gordon

Women:
1. Linda Denley
2. Joi Green
3. Gerrie Daniels
   Victoria Johnson

MARDI GRAS NATIONALS: FEBRUARY 21, 1976

Jenice Miller, Producer
New Orleans, LA

Fighting

Men:

HEAVY:
1. Pat Hardy
   Ernie Smith
3. Gerald Giles

LIGHT HEAVY:
1. Harold Roth
2. Glenn McMorris
3. Emanuel Howard

MIDDLE:
1. Glenn Mehlman
2. Gary Lloyd
3. John Shraver

LIGHT:
1. Demetrius Havanas
2. D.P. Hill
3. Steve Mazinzo

Women:
1. Karen Rooney
2. Tessie Jefferson
3. Linda Denley

Forms

Men:
1. Ray McCallum
2. Gary Lloyd
3. Larry Dreher

Women:
1. Karyn Turner
2. Audry Wallace
3. Patti Coleman

Weapons:
1. Gary Lloyd
2. John Wong
3. Don Castillo

BATTLE OF ATLANTA: FEBRUARY 8, 1976

Fighting

Men:

HEAVY:
1. Ernie Smith
2. Dave Ruppart
3. Larry Reinhardt
4. Tom McGhee

LIGHT HEAVY:
1. Jim Butin
2. Mike Cass
3. Gary Basinger
4. Herb Johnson

MIDDLE:
1. Bill Clark
2. Mike Moore
3. N. Davis
4. Wayne Lorance

LIGHT:
1. Mike McNamara
2. John Jesson
3. Bobby Tucker
4. Ken Dallas

SUPER LIGHT:
1. Jackie Mole
2. Sonny Onowo
3. Charles June
4. Rick Smith

Women:

HEAVY:
1. Sheila Davis
2. Margie Waller

LIGHT:
1. Evelyn Vaughn
2. Rhonda Alexander

Forms

Men:
1. Tayari Casel
2. Hidy Ochiai
3. ?

Weapons:
1. Jerry Lee
2. ?
3. ?

Women:
1. Evelyn Vaughn
2. Maryanne Corcoran
3. Margie Waller
4. Julia Ledbetter

U.S.K.A. GRAND NATIONALS: JUNE 18–20, 1976

Don Smith & Walt Fegan, Producers
Cincinnati, OH

Fighting

Men:

HEAVY:
1. Dave Ruppart
2. Ross Scott
3. Mike Awad

LIGHT HEAVY:
1. Mike Cass
2. Ernest Starr
3. William Scott

MIDDLE:
1. Flem Evans
2. William Powell
3. Woodrow Fairbanks

LIGHT:
1. John Carini
2. Sam Nichols
3. Howard Fox

Women:
1. Denise DeHaven
2. Kathleen Brewer
3. Earnestine Morgan

Forms

Masters:
1. James Cook
2. Hidy Ochiai
3. Randy Webb

Men:
1. Roger Tung
2. Randy Holman
3. Mike Day

Women:
1. Vicki Johnson
2. Barbara Niggel
3. Julie Meyers

Weapons:
1. Roger Tung

1975 NATIONAL TOURNAMENTS

MARDI GRAS NATIONALS: FEBRUARY 1, 1975

Jim & Jenice Miller, Producers
New Orleans, LA

Fighting

Men:

HEAVY:
1. Ernie Smith
2. Daryl Stewart
3. Shorty Mills

LIGHT HEAVY:
1. Harold Roth
2. Glenn McMorris
3. Dennis Gotcher

MIDDLE:
1. Fred Wren
2. Samuel Rubin
3. David Blunt

LIGHT:
1. D.P. Hill
2. Chuck Beard
3. Al Francis

Women:
1. Phyllis Evetts
2. Linda Denley
3. Karen Rooney

National Forms Champion Maryanne Corcoran at the 1975 Internationals. Courtesy of the John Corcoran Archives

Forms

Men:
1. Alex Kwok
2. Dan Smith
3. Roy Montalbano

Weapons:
1. Alex Kwok
2. Samuel Rubin
3. Roy Osborne

Women:
1. Shelly Williams
2. Kim Russell
3. Debbie King

U.S. CHAMPIONSHIPS: FEBRUARY 7, 1975

Allen Steen, Producer
Dallas, TX

Fighting

Men:

HEAVY:
1. Pat Hardy
2. Louis Arnold
3. Parker Shelton
Ross Scott

LIGHT HEAVY:
1. Glenn McMorris
2. Harold Roth
3. Robert Batie
   Paul Vasquez

MIDDLE:
1. Pat Worley
2. Ray McCallum
3. Mark Payne
   Flem Evans

LIGHT:
1. Demetrius Havanas
2. D.P. Hill
3. Alvin Robinson
   John Jessen

Women:
1. Phyllis Evetts
2. Linda Denley
3. April Cunningham
   Debbie Foreman

Forms

Weapons:
1. Alex Kwok

BATTLE OF ATLANTA:
MAY 3, 1975

Note: This tournament was the site of the first world title defense of the new sport of full-contact karate; it also marked the first time a full-contact event was incorporated into the finals of a karate tournament.

Fighting

Men:

HEAVY:
1. Parker Shelton
2. Ross Scott
3. Ernie Smith
4. Willie Ross

LIGHT HEAVY:
1. Dennis Tempe
2. George Thanos
3. Glenn McMorris
4. Wayne Van Buren

MIDDLE:
1. Ron Shaw

2. Huey Daniels
3. Leslie Lee
4. George Reynolds

LIGHT:
1. Bobby Tucker
2. Keith Vitali
3. Larry Carnahan
4. Mike Coles

SUPER LIGHT:
1. Charles June
2. Steve Stavroff
3. Sal Militello
4. Larry Pate

Women:

HEAVY:
1. Sheila Davis
2. Phyllis Evetts

LIGHT:
1. Evelyn Vaughn
2. Mary Lou Michael

Forms

Grand Champion:
   Alex Kwok
2. Hidy Ochiai
3. Lawrence Kuss
4. Ron Shaw

Women:
1. Myung Salee
2. Debbie Bone
3. Maryanne Corcoran

Weapons:
1. Paul Keller
2. Glenn Premru
3. Ron Shaw
4. Alex Kwok

U.S.K.A. GRAND NATIONALS:
JUNE 28–29, 1975

**AlGene Caraulia, Producer
Milwaukee, WI**

Fighting

Men's Grand Champion:
   Flem Evans
2. Mike Awad

Women:
1. Mary Barnette

Forms

Grand Champion:
   Akio Minakami
2. Hidy Ochiai

U.S. OPEN PRO-AM:
JULY 13, 1975

**Bob Maxwell, Producer
Catonsville, MD**

LONG BEACH
INTERNATIONALS:
AUGUST 2–3, 1975

Fighting

Men's Grand Champion:
   Lenny Ferguson
2. Ernie Smith

HEAVY:
1. Ernie Smith
2. Ray Sua

LIGHT HEAVY:
1. Ernest Russell
2. David Costillo

MIDDLE:
1. Lenny Ferguson
2. Bill Henry

LIGHT:
1. Cecil Peoples
2. Ray Davis

Women:
1. Terry Dent
2. Mary Stark-Owens
3. Charlotte Hoffman

Forms

Grand Champion:
   Hidy Ochiai
2. Jeannie Lau
3. Alex Kwok

CHINESE:
1. Alex Kwok

JAPANESE/OKINAWAN:
1. Hidy Ochiai

WEAPONS:
1. Jeannie Lau

WOMEN:

1. Jeannie Lau
2. Maryanne Corcoran

NORTHERN STATES: SUMMER 1975

Curtis Herrington, Producer
Cleveland, OH

Note: Fifteen top black belts fought in the professional semi-contact division, two of which were 1st place winners from the day's amateur competition.

Fighting

Men's Grand Champion:

Ross Scott
2. Ken Dallas
3. Dave Ruppart
4. Bob Harris
5. Truman Irving

Forms

Men:

1. Randy Holman
2. James Cook
3. Phil Fichera

Women:

1. Barbara Niggel
2. Vicki Johnson
3. Teri Betchel

TOP TEN NATIONALS: OCTOBER 25–26, 1975

Mike Anderson & Glenn Keeney, Producers
Anderson, IN

Fighting

HEAVY:
1. Dave Ruppart
2. Walter Fegan

LIGHT HEAVY:
1. George Thanos
2. Flem Evans
3. ?
    ?

MIDDLE:
1. Ernest Hart, Jr.
2. Bob Harris
3. ?
    ?

LIGHT:
1. Mike McNamara
2. Darrell Lassiter
3. Miguel Sanders
    Jeff Gripper

SUPER LIGHT:
1. Sam Nichols
2. Frederick Walker
3. Larry Logan
    Terry Campbell

Forms

Grand Champion:

Randy Holman
2. Bob Bowles
3. Hidy Ochiai
4. James Cook

Weapons:

1. Larry Logan
2. Paul Keller
3. Jawara Kenyata
4. Bob Bowles

Women:

1. Barbara Niggel

Pentathalon:

1. Hidy Ochiai
2. Bob Bowles
3. James Cook

1974 NATIONAL TOURNAMENTS

WESTERN U.S. CHAMPIONSHIPS: JANUARY 13, 1974

Tony Sartor, Producer
Anaheim, CA

Fighting

Grand Champion:

Darnell Garcia
2. Benny Urquidez
3. Ruben Urquidez

Women's Champion:

Margie Thompson

Forms

Men:

1. Al Leong

Women:

1. Maryanne Corcoran

Weapons:

1. James Lew

YAMASHITA OPEN: JANUARY 20, 1974

Tadashi Yamashita, Producer
Fountain Valley, CA

Fighting

Men's Grand Champion:

Darnell Garcia
2. John Natividad (defending champ)
3. Howard Jackson
    Eric Schuman

HEAVY:
1. Eric Schuman
2. Ray Sua
3. Buck Pao Pao

MIDDLE:
1. Darnell Garcia
2. Smiley Urquidez
3. Ernest Russell

LIGHT:
1. Howard Jackson
2. Cecil Peoples
3. Chong Lee

Women:

1. Yolanda Chapel
2. Sandy Garcia
3. Gigi Whitfield

Forms

Men:

1. Chong Lee
2. Byong Yu
3. Steve Fisher

Weapons:

1. Ted Tabura

2. Robin Kane
3. James Lew

Women:
1. Marlene Schuman
2. Leilani Kaihewalu
3. Beverly Romero

U.S. KARATE CHAMPIONSHIPS: FEBRUARY 2, 1974

Allen Steen, Producer
Dallas, TX

Note: Highlights of the finals were televised on ABC-TV's *Wide World of Sports.*

Fighting

Men:
TEAM:
1. Washington, DC
2. South East Karate Association
HEAVY:
1. Ernie Smith
2. Parker Shelton
3. Louis Arnold
   Larry Mosig
LIGHT HEAVY:
1. Wayne Van Buren
2. Ernest Russell
3. Steve Kijewski
   Darnell Garcia
MIDDLE:
1. Bill Wallace
2. Flem Evans
3. Pat Worley
   Fred Wren
LIGHT:
1. Howard Jackson
2. Larry Carnahan
3. Dan Anderson
   B. Caswell

Women:
1. Phyllis Evetts
2. Pam Watson
3. Bernice Downs
   Marsha Owens

Forms

Women:
1. Malia Dacascos

MARDI GRAS NATIONALS: FEBRUARY 23, 1974

Jim & Jenice Miller, Producers
Metairie, LA

Fighting

Men's Grand Champion:
   Fred Wren
2. Gerald Giles
3. Wade Bergeron
HEAVY:
1. Gerald Giles
2. Ernie Smith
3. Jim Butin
MIDDLE:
1. Fred Wren
2. Jeff Smith
3. Jack Motley
LIGHT:
1. Wade Bergeron
2. Demetrius Havanas
3. Ken Lambert

Women:
1. Gina Romano
2. Joy Turberville
3. Lyn Scott

Forms

Men:
1. Malia Dacascos
2. Maso Tatashi
3. Travis Everett

Women:
1. Cindy Peterson
2. Jenice Miller
3. April Cunningham

Weapons:
1. Mike Radulovich
2. Chuck Gleavis
3. Albert Christman

SOUTHERN COAST PRO-AM: MARCH 1974

Dave Adams, Producer
Belmont, NC

Fighting

Men's Grand Champion:
   Darnell Garcia

2. Howard Jackson
3. Jeff Smith

BATTLE OF ATLANTA: APRIL 20, 1974

Fighting

Tournament of Champions:
MEN'S GRAND CHAMPION:
   Howard Jackson
2. Jeff Smith
3. Bill Wallace
   Everett Eddy

Men:
HEAVY:
1. Johnny Lee
2. Jerry Piddington
3. Larry Reinhardt
4. Will Wright
LIGHT HEAVY:
1. Ernest Russell
2. Wayne Van Buren
3. Boyd
   Burnham
MIDDLE:
1. Aaron Norris
2. David Archer
3. Charles Henry
LIGHT:
1. Larry Carnahan
2. Gary Felder
3. Ray Nikiel

Women:
1. Jenice Miller
2. Malia Dacascos
3. Cooper

Forms

Men:
1. Hank Farrah
2. Greyman
3. Jim Henry

Women:
1. Vikki Morrow
2. Malia Dacascos
3. Bobbie Long

U.S.K.A. GRAND NATIONALS: JUNE 15–16, 1974

Robert Trias & AlGene Caraulia, Producers
Milwaukee, WI

Fighting

Men's Grand Champion:
Flem Evans
2. Parker Shelton
3. Ross Scott
4. Demetrius Havanas
HEAVY:
1. Ross Scott
2. Wayne Washington
3. Everett Eddy
LIGHT HEAVY:
1. Parker Shelton
2. Jeff Smith
3. Steve Kijewski
MIDDLE:
1. Flem Evans
2. Bill Wallace
3. Robert Harris
LIGHT:
1. Demetrius Havanas
2. Dan Anderson
3. Ken Kolodziej

Women:
1. Jeannette Janecek
2. Phyllis Evetts
3. Jenice Miller

Forms

Masters:
1. Hidy Ochiai
2. Bob Bowles
3. Akio Minakami

Men:
1. Shintaro Takahashi
2. Pete Rabino
3. Randy Holman

Weapons:
1. Paul Keller
2. Ron Shaw
3. Bob Bowles

Women:
1. Barbara Niggel
2. Teri Bechtel
3. Elizabeth Contreras

ROCKY MOUNTAIN: JUNE 15, 1974

Ralph Krause, Producer
Denver, CO

Fighting

Men's Grand Champion:
1. Benny Urquidez
2. Butch Batie
3. Ralph Alegria
Cecil Peoples

Women:
1. Marion Bermudez
2. Karyn Turner
3. Veronica Martinez

Forms

Men:
1. Steve Fisher

Women:
1. Marion Bermudez

Weapons:
1. Mike Radulovich

KARATE OLYMPICS: 1974

George Minshew, Producer
Houston, TX

Fighting
HEAVY:
1. Joe Lewis
2. Jim Butin
3. Ernie Smith
Glen Dicus
MIDDLE:
1. Jeff Smith
2. Fred Wren
3. Demetrius Havanas
LIGHT:
1. James Stevens
2. Wade Bergeron
3. Billy Singletary
Kidd Beard

Advanced Women:
1. Jenice Miller
2. Gina Romano

3. Dossy Morris
Phyllis Evetts

WESTERN U.S. NATIONALS: 1974

Al Dacascos, Producer
Denver, CO

Men's Grand Champion:
Bill Wallace
2. Bill Owens
HEAVY:
1. Bill Wallace
2. Parker Shelton
LIGHT:
1. Bill Owens
2. Ken Lambert

Advanced Women:
1. Mikey Rowe
2. Mary Stark

U.S. OPEN PRO-AM: JULY 13–14, 1974

Bob Maxwell & Harvey Hastings, Producers
Ocean City, MD

Fighting

Men's Grand Champion:
Jeff Smith

Forms

Grand Champion:
Tayari Casel
2. Lawrence Kuss
3. Hidy Ochiai
4. Malia Dacascos

TOP TEN NATIONALS: JULY 27, 1974

Mike Anderson, Producer
St. Louis, MO

Note: Professional kata was launched at this event.

Fighting
HEAVY:
1. Everett Eddy

2. Joe Lewis
3. John Bell
   Ernie Smith

LIGHT HEAVY:
1. Jim Butin
2. Jeff Smith
3. Roger Carpenter
   John Natividad

MIDDLE:
1. Bill Wallace
2. Flem Evans
3. Demetrius Havanas
   Pat Worley

LIGHT:
1. Cecil Peoples
2. Gordon Franks
3. Howard Jackson
   Al Dacascos

Women:
1. Cheryl Mainenti
2. JoAnne Duran

Forms

Men:
1. Hidy Ochiai
2. Tayari Casel
3. Minobu Miki
4. Malia Dacascos

Women:
1. Cindy Peterson

LONG BEACH INTERNATIONALS: AUGUST 10–11, 1974

Fighting

Men's Grand Champion:
   Jeff Smith
2. Darnell Garcia
3. Dave Brock
4. Ray Sua

HEAVY:
1. Bob Halliburton
2. Ray Sua
3. Flency
4. Sammy Pace

LIGHT HEAVY:
1. Jeff Smith
2. Lionel Seals

3. Roy Kurban
4. John Natividad

MIDDLE:
1. Darnell Garcia
2. Gary Goodman
3. Dan Esquivel
4. Ernest Russell

LIGHT:
1. Dave Brock
2. Ray Davis
3. Benny Urquidez
4. Vernelc Anderson

Women:
1. Marian Bermudez
2. Mikie Rowe
3. Pauline Short

Forms

Grand Champion:
   Chong Lee
2. Alex Kwok

CHINESE:
1. Al Leong
2. James Lew
3. Richard Cherge

JAPANESE:
1. John Stevenson
2. Minobu Miki
3. Mel Sugino

KENPO:
1. T. Barrow
2. Robbie Castro
3. Sol Kaihewalu

KOREAN:
1. Chong Lee
2. Arnold Corley
3. Sung Woo

WEAPONS:
1. Alex Kwok
2. Al Leong
3. James Lew

Women:
1. Malia Dacascos
2. Marlene Schumann
3. Maryanne Corcoran

SOUTHEAST TEXAS OPEN: OCTOBER 26, 1974

**Fred Simon, Producer
Beaumont, TX**

Fighting

Men:

HEAVY:
1. Ernie Smith
2. Parker Shelton
3. Louis Arnold

MIDDLE:
1. Harold Roth
2. David McMurray
3. Mike Coles
   Ken Spell

LIGHT:
1. Ishmael Robles
2. Rick Cook
3. D.P. Hill
   Jack LaCoco

Forms

Men:
1. Ralph Jaschke
2. Bob Griffin
3. Steve Powell
   Rick Morris

WESTERN PRO-AM: NOVEMBER 23, 1974

**Produced by Eight Co-op
Promoters
Oakland, CA**

Fighting

Men's Grand Champion:
   Roy Kurban
2. Darnell Garcia
3. Benny Urquidez
4. Flem Evans

1973 NATIONAL TOURNAMENTS

U.S. CHAMPIONSHIPS: FEBRUARY 10, 1973

**Allen Steen, Producer
Dallas, TX**

Fighting

Men's Grand Champion:
   Bill Wallace
2. Roy Kurban

3. Bob Dunek
   Dan Anderson

HEAVY:
1. Bill Wallace
2. Jim Butin
3. Dennis Gotcher
4. Kirby Fugate

MIDDLE:
1. Roy Kurban
2. Bill McCoy
3. Mike Usleton
4. Steve Kijewski

LIGHT:
1. Dan Anderson
2. Demetrius Havanas
3. Al Dacascos
4. Jim Harkins

Women:
1. Pam Watson
2. Phillis Evetts
3. April Cunningham
   Malia Dacascos

Forms

Men:
1. Demetrius Havanas
2. Walt Bone
3. Bob Campbell
4. Hank Farrah

Women:
1. Ruby Lazano
2. Debbie Bone
3. Cynthia Violet
4. Joy Turberville

Weapons:
1. Bob Campbell
2. Walt Bone
3. Mike Gassaway
4. Darrell Craig

ALL-AMERICAN OPEN: 1973

S. Henry Cho, Producer
New York, NY

Fighting

Men's Grand Champion:
   Albert Cheeks
2. Mike Warren

HEAVY:
1. Albert Cheeks
2. James Lee
3. Mike Arroyo

LIGHT:
1. Mike Warren
2. William Oliver
3. Ray Nikiel

Forms

Men:
1. Jim Roberts, Jr.

Women:
1. Angela Brown

ALL-AMERICAN OPEN: MARCH 1973

Jack Hwang, Producer
Oklahoma City, OK

Fighting

Men's Grand Champion:
   Roy Kurban
2. Demetrius Havanas
3. Fred Wren

HEAVY:
1. Jim Butin
2. Roger Carpenter
3. Billy Simmons
   Chuck Loven

MIDDLE:
1. Roy Kurban
2. Fred Wren
3. David Archer

LIGHT:
1. Demetrius Havanas
   James Stevens
2. Jim Harkins
   Mark Payne

Women:
1. Charlotte Hoffman
2. Malia Dacascos

Forms

Men:
1. Demetrius Havanas

TOURNAMENT OF CHAMPIONS: 1973

J. Pat Burleson, Producer
Ft. Worth, TX

Fighting

Grand Champion:
   Jim Miller
2. Bill Watson
3. Jim Butin
   Mike Anderson

MARDI GRAS NATIONALS: MARCH 3, 1973

Jim & Jenice Miller, Producers
New Orleans, LA

Fighting

Men's Grand Champion:
   Fred Wren
2. Al Dacascos

HEAVY:
1. Fred Wren
2. Dan Smith
3. Ernie Smith
4. James Stevenson

LIGHT:
1. Al Dacascos
2. Wade Bergeron
3. Jim Stevens
4. Jim Harkins

Women:
1. Cindi Peterson
2. Debbie Foreman
3. Carol Minshew
4. Malia Dacascos

Forms

Men:
1. Al Dacascos
2. Dan Smith
3. Wade Bergeron
4. Ben Edwards

Women:
1. Cindy Peterson
2. Malia Dacascos
3. Yvonne Arceneaux
4. Tammie Clemons

NATIONAL BLACK BELT GRAND CHAMPIONSHIPS: MARCH 24, 1973

Sam Allred, Producer
Albuquerque, NM

Fighting

Tournament of Champions

MEN'S GRAND CHAMPION:
Bill Wallace
2. Byong Yu
3. Al Dacascos
4. Fred Wren

Men:

HEAVY:
1. Ralph Alegria
2. Dave Pettigrew
3. Bob Barrow
4. Dick Douglas

MIDDLE:
1. Lionel Seals
2. Jim Harkins
3. Dan Esquivel
4. Harold Roth

LIGHT:
1. Howard Jackson
2. Dan Anderson
3. Stuart Rowe
4. Dick Hamilton

Forms

Men:
1. Eric Lee
2. Byong Yu
3. Tom Hyer
4. Dan Esquivel

YAMASHITA OPEN: MAY 20, 1973

Tadashi Yamashita, Producer
Gardena, CA

Fighting

Men's Grand Champion:
John Natividad
2. Howard Jackson

HEAVY:
1. John Natividad
2. Roy Kurban
3. Bob Alegria

LIGHT:
1. Howard Jackson
2. John Towns
3. Steve Fisher

Forms

Men:
1. Eric Lee
2. Hidy Ochiai
3. Fred Aviles

Women:
1. Marlene Schumann
2. Leilani Kaihewalu
3. Beverly Romero

Weapons:
1. Brian Fong
2. Steve Fisher
3. Ted Tabura

U.S.K.A. GRAND NATIONALS: JUNE 16–17, 1973

AlGene Caraulia, Producer
Cleveland, OH

Fighting

Men's Grand Champion:
Fred Wren
2. Everett Eddy
3. Robert Bowles

HEAVY:
1. Everett Eddy
2. Parker Shelton
3. Artis Simmons

MIDDLE:
1. Fred Wren
2. Flem Evans
3. Steve Kijewski

LIGHT:
1. Robert Bowles
2. Pete Rabino
3. Frank Caliguri

Women:
1. Jenice Miller
2. Alfreda Lindsey
3. Bernice Downs

Forms

Masters:
1. Hidy Ochiai

2. Glenn Premru
3. Byong Yu

Men:
1. Bob Bowles
2. Wally Slocki
3. Mike Awad

Weapons:
1. Bob Bowles
2. Hidy Ochiai
3. John Hamilton

Women:
1. Barbara Niggel
2. Janet Berry
3. Lorraine Lewis

U.S. OPEN PRO-AM: 1973

Bob Maxwell & Harvey Hastings, Producers
Ocean City, MD

Fighting

Men's Grand Champion:
Jeff Smith
2. Howard Jackson
3. Pat Worley
Marshall Collins

Women:
1. Jenice Miller

TOP TEN NATIONALS: JULY 7, 1973

Mike Anderson, Producer
St. Louis, MO

Note: This was the tournament at which semi-contact competition and $1,000 grand title purses were created.

Fighting

Men's Grand Champion:
Howard Jackson
2. Johnny Lee
3. Jeff Smith
Steve Kijewski

HEAVY:
1. Johnny Lee

2. Jim Miller
3. Everett Eddy
   Ralph Alegria

LIGHT HEAVY:
1. Jeff Smith
2. Jim Butin
3. John Natividad
   Larry Adams

MIDDLE:
1. Steve Kijewski
2. Pat Worley
3. Bob Burbidge
   Darnell Garcia

LIGHT:
1. Howard Jackson
2. Al Dacascos
3. Carl Nelapovitz
   Dennis Passaretti

Women:
1. Joy Turberville
2. Marsha Owens
3. Phyllis Evetts
   Bernice Downs

Forms

Men:
1. Eric Lee
2. Byong Yu
3. Hidy Ochiai
4. Steve Fisher

FOUR SEASONS NATIONALS: JULY 21, 1973

**Mike Stone, Producer
Las Vegas, NV**

Note: A pool of sixteen fighters were seeded as finalists and were eliminated to four winners.

Fighting

Men's Grand Champion:
   Darnell Garcia
2. Howard Jackson
3. Steve Kijewski
   John Bell

LONG BEACH INTERNATIONALS: AUGUST 5, 1973

Fighting

Men's Grand Champion:
   John Natividad
2. Benny Urquidez
3. Ralph Alegria
   Bob Burbidge

HEAVY:
1. Ralph Alegria
2. Cortez
3. Ruben Urquidez

LIGHT HEAVY:
1. John Natividad
2. C. C. Mayes
3. Thomas

MIDDLE:
1. Bob Burbidge
2. Smiley Urquidez
3. Pient

LIGHT:
1. Benny Urquidez
2. Kraiger Smith
3. Stuart Rowe

Women:
1. Mary Castro
2. Sharon Spremich
3. Mikie Rowe

Forms

Grand Champion:
   Eric Lee

CHINESE:
1. Eric Lee
2. David Chan
3. Brigida Villalon

JAPANESE/OKINAWAN:
1. Fred Aviles
2. Mel Sugino
3. Steve Fisher

KENPO:
1. Steve Sanders
2. Dan Esquivel
3. Nat Dominguez

KOREAN:
1. Byong Yu
2. Chong Lee
3. B. Gold

WEAPONS:
1. Albert Leong
2. Wing Wong & Tod Takeuchi
   (duo)
3. Ted Tabura

WOMEN:
1. Malia Dacascos
2. April Castro
3. Ruby Luzano

One of the most intensely fought grand championship bouts in sport karate history took place at the 1973 Internationals between Benny Urquidez (left) and John Natividad. Natividad won the double-overtime match, 13–12. Courtesy of Stuart Sobel and Benny Urquidez

BATTLE OF ATLANTA: NOVEMBER 1973

Fighting

Tournament of Champions:

MEN'S GRAND CHAMPION:
Howard Jackson
2. Jeff Smith
3. Everett Eddy
4. Bill Wallace

Men:

HEAVY:
1. Frank Hargrove
2. Larry Huff
3. Willie Ross

LIGHT HEAVY:
1. Mike Cass
2. Phil Waters
3. Steve Fisher

MIDDLE:
1. Andy Selcer
2. Steve Kijewski
3. Pat Duncan

LIGHT:
1. Ken Dallas
2. Steve Stavroff
3. Ray Nikiel

All-time great forms champion Chuck Merriman in 1972. The next year he was ranked in the first top ten national forms ratings.

Women:
1. Jenice Miller

Forms

Men:
1. Walt Bone
2. Daniel Richer
3. Steve Fisher

Women:
1. Vicki Morrow
2. Malia Dacascos

1972 NATIONAL TOURNAMENTS

U.S. CHAMPIONSHIPS: FEBRUARY 12–13, 1972

Allen Steen, Producer Dallas, TX

Fighting

Men's Grand Champion:
Bob Dunek
2. Roy Kurban

HEAVY:
1. Bob Dunek
2. Max Alsup
3. Jim Miller

MIDDLE:
1. Roy Kurban
2. John Costaldo
3. Raul Vasquez

LIGHT:
1. Demetrius Havanas
2. Walt Bone
3. Al Dacascos

Women:
1. Jenice Miller
2. Phyllis Evetts
3. Debbie Foreman

Forms

Men:
1. Walt Bone

2. Kazuo Kuriyama
3. Pete Rabino

Women:
1. Keating
2. Edwards
3. Robinson

ALL-AMERICAN OPEN: MARCH 11, 1972

Jack Hwang, Producer Oklahoma City, OK

Fighting

Grand Champion:
Skipper Mullins (defending champion)
2. Roger Carpenter

HEAVY:
1. Roger Carpenter
2. Jim Miller
3. ?

MIDDLE:
1. Fred Wren
2. Jim Floyd
3. Roy Kurban

LIGHT:
1. Ramiro Guzman
2. Larry Carnahan
3. Byong Yu

Forms

Men:
1. Byong Yu
2. Douglas San Lin
3. Keith Yates

Women:
1. Kimie Kawakami
2. Marsha Owens
3. Jenice Miller

ALL-AMERICAN OPEN: SPRING 1972

S. Henry Cho, Producer New York City

Fighting

Men's Grand Champion:
Mike Warren

NATIONAL BLACK BELT GRAND CHAMPIONSHIPS: MARCH 18, 1972

Sam Allred, Producer
Albuquerque, NM

Fighting

Men's Grand Champion:
1. Bill Wallace
2. Darnell Garcia
3. Al Dacascos
   Fred Wren

Forms

Men:
1. Eric Lee
2. Joe Hayes
3. Byong Yu
4. Roy Kurban

TOP TEN NATIONALS: APRIL 29, 1972

Mike Anderson, Producer
St. Louis, MO

Fighting

Men's Grand Champion:
   Ken Knudson
2. Steve Kijewski
3. Jeff Smith
   Byong Yu

Women:
1. Malia Dacascos
2. Cindy Berardino

Forms

Men:
1. Pat Worley

U.S.K.A. GRAND NATIONALS: JUNE 17–18, 1972

Bill Gardo, Producer
Memphis, TN

Fighting

Men's Grand Champion:
   Bill Wallace
2. Joe Lewis

Roy Kurban (left) versus Bob Dunek at the 1972 U.S. Karate Championships. Courtesy of Keith D. Yates

HEAVY:
1. Joe Lewis
2. Jerry Piddington

LIGHT:
1. Bill Wallace
2. Glenn Keeney

WESTERN U.S. NATIONALS: SUMMER 1972

Al Dacascos, Producer
Denver, CO

Fighting

Men's Grand Champion:
   Bill Wallace
2. Rick Alemany
3. Jim Hawks

Women:
1. Rose Rodriquez
2. Alfreda Lindsey
3. Camille Scurlock

Forms

Men:
1. Eric Lee
2. Jack Adair
3. Mike DeHart

Women:
1. Cindi Peterson
2. Sue Hawks
3. Debbie DeHart

LONG BEACH INTERNATIONALS: AUGUST 5–6, 1972

Fighting

Men's Grand Champion:
   Darnell Garcia
2. Joe Lewis (defending champ)
3. Byong Yu

LIGHT:
1. Byong Yu
2. Dan Anderson

Forms

Grand Champion:
1. ?

KOREAN:
1. Byong Yu

A.K.A. NATIONALS: 1972

Ken Knudson, Producer
Chicago, IL

Fighting

Men's Grand Champion:
   Flem Evans
2. Ken Kolokziej
3. John Bell

BATTLE OF ATLANTA: OCTOBER 1972

Fighting

Men's Grand Champion:
   Jack Motley and Phil Waters
   (Instructor Motley and his
   student Waters split the award)

HEAVY:
1. Phil Waters
2. Keith Haflich
3. Lawrence Huff
4. Andy Selcer

The Tracys Competition Team at the 1971 East Coast vs. West Coast Championships. (Left to right) promoter Aaron Banks, Ray Klingenberg, John Korab, Joe Lewis, Jay T. Will and Jack Morris. Courtesy of Jay T. Will

LIGHT:
1. Jack Motley
2. Charles June
3. Gary Ramsey
4. Joe Redmon

Forms

Men:
1. Charles Henry
2. Bill Clark
3. Chuck Blackburn

1971 NATIONAL TOURNAMENTS

U.S. CHAMPIONSHIPS: FEBRUARY 6, 1971

**Allen Steen, Producer
Dallas, TX**

Fighting

Men's Grand Champion:
1. Bill Wallace
2. Skipper Mullins
MIDDLE:
1. Bill Wallace
LIGHT:
1. Skipper Mullins
2. Fred Wren

ALL-AMERICAN CHAMPIONSHIPS AND TOURNAMENT OF CHAMPIONS: MARCH 6–7, 1971

**S. Henry Cho, Producer
New York, NY**

Fighting

Tournament of Champions:

Men's Grand Champion:
    Byong Yu
2. Joe Hayes
3. ?
4. Mitchell Bobrow

All-American Grand Champion:
    Byong Yu
2. Mike Warren
    HEAVY:
    1. Byong Yu
    2. Ernest Mickens
    3. Mike Arroyo
    LIGHT:
    1. Mike Warren
    2. Robert McAuyfle
    3. Jeff Smith

Women:
    HEAVY:
    1. Annette Ramson
    2. Leona Schauble
    3. Penny DeJan

LIGHT:
1. Tiney Pringle
2. Victoria Wilson
3. Susan Hart

Forms

Men:
1. Jim Roberts, Jr.
2. Glenn Premru
3. Alex Sternberg

Women:
1. Susan Hart
2. Jamison

ALL-AMERICAN OPEN: MARCH 13–14, 1971

**Jack Hwang, Producer
Oklahoma City, OK**

Fighting

Men's Grand Champion:
    Skipper Mullins
2. Bill Cagle

HEAVY:
1. Sam Price
2. Ken McDowell
3. Vance McNeal
4. Larry Whitener

MIDDLE:
1. Skipper Mullins
2. Fred Wren
3. Jim Butin
4. Larry Evans

LIGHT:
1. Bill Cagle
2. Walt Bone
3. Russell Perrone
4. Demetrius Havanas

Women:

HEAVY:
1. Phyllis Evetts
2. Pam Watson
3. Carlotta Johnson
4. Jan Williams

LIGHT:
1. Emma Harris
2. Charlotte Thompkins
3. Mary Coffman
4. Eva Warren

Forms

Men:
1. Santamaria
2. Tusi
3. Mike Anderson
4. Craig Henry

Women:
1. Holly Rader
2. Phyllis Evetts
3. Janell Emery
4. Jeanice Edwards

ALL-AMERICAN OPEN: SPRING 1971

**S. Henry Cho, Producer
New York City**

Fighting

Men's Grand Champion:
Byong Yu

NATIONAL BLACK BELT GRAND CHAMPIONSHIPS: MARCH 20, 1971

**Sam Allred, Producer
Albuquerque, NM**

Fighting

Men's Grand Champion:
Ron Marchini
2. Bill Wallace
3. Joe Hayes
Fred Wren

Forms

Men:
1. Malia Dacascos

AMERICAN INVITATIONAL (TOURNAMENT OF CHAMPIONS): 1971

**Ki Whang Kim, Producer
Washington, DC**

Fighting

Men's Grand Champion:
Mike Warren

2. Albert Cheeks
3. Jeff Smith

Forms

Men:
1. James Roberts, Jr.
2. Albert Cheeks
3. Neil Ehrlich

Women:
1. Susan Hart
2. Laima Simanavichus
3. Leslie Haller

KARATE OLYMPICS: 1971

**George Minshew, Producer
Houston, TX**

Fighting

Men's Grand Champion:
Rick Vaughn
2. Demetrius Havanas
HEAVY:
Rick Vaughn
2. Ed Daniel
3. Mike Uselton
LIGHT:
1. Demetrius Havanas
2. Fred Wren
3. James Stevens

U.S.K.A. GRAND NATIONALS: JUNE 26–27, 1971

**Glenn Keeney, Producer
Anderson, IN**

Fighting

Men's Grand Champion:
Bill Wallace
2. Ken Knudson
3. Mike Anderson

Forms

Men:
1. Hidy Ochiai
2. Bob Bowles
3. Glenn Premru
4. Al Dacascos

Women:
1. Malia Dacascos

LONG BEACH INTERNATIONALS: AUGUST 1971

Fighting

Men's Grand Champion:
Joe Lewis

Women:
1. Malia Dacascos

The 1971 Texas Karate Team Champions: (Left to right) Candy Simpson, Demetrius Havanas, Skipper Mullins and Keith Yates. Courtesy of Keith D. Yates

Forms

Women:

1. Malia Dacascos

MIDWEST CHAMPIONSHIPS: 1971

Mike Anderson, Producer
St. Louis, MO

Fighting

Men's Grand Champion:

Ken Knudson
2. Pat Worley

HEAVY:
1. Ken Knudson
2. Chuck Loven
3. Parker Shelton

MIDDLE:
1. Pat Worley
2. John Castaldo
3. George Reynolds

LIGHT:
1. Bill Cagle
2. Wayne Booth
3. Bob Bowles

Women:

1. Carol Strebler
2. Michele Currie
3. Kathy Hillen

BATTLE OF ATLANTA: 1971

Fighting

Men's Grand Champion:

Mike Warren

HEAVY:
1. Albert Cheeks

LIGHT:
1. Mike Warren

CENTRAL NORTH AMERICAN: OCTOBER 16, 1971

Sam Allred, Producer
Albuquerque, NM

Fighting

Men's Grand Champion:

Al Dacascos
2. Ralph Alegria

HEAVY:
1. Bob Alegria
2. Steve Miretti
3. Terry Forga

LIGHT HEAVY:
1. Ralph Alegria
2. Rick Vaughn
3. Dennis Gotcher

MIDDLE:
1. Roy Kurban
2. Ron McCormick
3. Gary Purdue

LIGHT:
1. Jack Adair
2. Fred Lauretta
3. Ed Cruz

Forms

Co-Ed:

1. Malia Dacascos
2. Don Anderson
3. Jack Adair

1970 NATIONAL TOURNAMENTS

1ST PROFESSIONAL TEAM CHAMPIONSHIPS: JANUARY 17, 1970

Lee Faulkner, Producer
Long Beach, CA

Note: This event was a historic turning point for numerous reasons: 1) It marked Chuck Norris's last fight before retiring; 2) it was the first and last time the great early fighters—Lewis, Norris, Stone and Mullins—fought as one team; 3) it was accompanied by America's first kickboxing match, in which Joe Lewis beat Greg Baines by 2nd round KO; and 4) it marked one of only two losses in the career of Mike Stone, when he pulled his shoulder and was

unable to continue against Victor Moore.

Fighting

Team Champions:

West Coast	Points
Joe Lewis	90
Skipper Mullins	90
Mike Stone	30
Chuck Norris	90
Bob Wall	77

East Coast	Points
Chuck Lovin	64
Walt Mattson	57
Victor Moore	86
Al Dacascos	40
Billy Watson	83

U.S. CHAMPIONSHIPS: FEBRUARY 7, 1970

Allen Steen, Producer
Dallas, TX

Fighting

Men's Grand Champion:

Fred Wren
2. Bill Watson

HEAVY:
1. Bill Watson
2. Chuck Loven
3. James Butin

LIGHT:
1. Fred Wren
2. Larry Mosig
3. Bill Wallace

Women:

1. Candy Simpson
2. Mary Ann Daniel
3. Shane Bondurant

Forms

Men:

1. Pat Worley
2. B. Wykspisz
3. Pete Rabino

Women:

1. Candy Simpson
2. Jenice Lester
3. Betty Cropper

ALL-AMERICAN OPEN: MARCH 8, 1970

S. Henry Cho, Producer
New York, NY

Fighting

Grand Champion:
William Swift
2. Thomas LaPuppet

HEAVY:
1. Thomas LaPuppet
2. Mitchell Bobrow
3. Norman Fouler

LIGHT:
1. William Swift
2. Mike Warren
3. Regie Simanca

Forms

Men:
1. Toyotaro Miyazaki
2. Adolfo Velasco

Women:
1. Dennie Dejan
2. Carmen Velasquez

SOUTHEAST U.S. OPEN: APRIL 1970

Joe Corley & Chris McLoughlin, Producers
Atlanta, GA

Fighting

Men's Grand Champion:
Joe Lewis
2. Joe Hayes

HEAVY:
1. Joe Lewis
2. Mitchell Bobrow
3. Hector Eugui

LIGHT:
1. Joe Hayes
2. Joe Corley
3. Thomas LaPuppet

Women:
1. Diane Smith
2. Ann Marie Wasilewski
3. Leara Rhodes

UNIVERSAL OPEN & TOURNAMENT OF CHAMPIONS: APRIL 18, 1970

Richard Chun, Producer
New York, NY

Fighting

Tournament of Champions

MEN'S GRAND CHAMPION:
Joe Hayes
2. Joe Corley
3. Byron Jones
Robert Engle

Forms

Men:
1. Toyotaro Miyazaki
2. Joe Hayes

Breaking

Men:
1. ?
2. Joe Hayes

1ST WORLD PRO-AM: MAY 2–3, 1970

Chuck Norris, Producer
Santa Monica, CA

Fighting

Men

HEAVY:
1. Vic Guerrera
2. Jerry Piddington
3. Joe Lewis
4. Ron Marchini

LIGHT HEAVY:
1. Jim Bottoms
2. Bill Wildman
3. Harold Gross
4. Ralph Castellanos

MIDDLE:
1. Skipper Mullins
2. Clyde Mills
3. Curtis Pulliam
4. Pete Rubino

LIGHT:
1. Byong Yu
2. Enrique Ordonez

3. Louis Delgado
4. Chris Oki

Forms

JAPANESE/OKINAWAN:
1. Louis Delgado
2. Dan Esquival
3. Jim Honaker

KOREAN:
1. Pat Johnson
2. Chris Oki

Women:
1. Ruby Luzano
2. Louise LaFosse
3. Joyce Shuman

U.S. NATIONALS: MAY 1970

Jhoon Rhee, Producer
Washington, DC

Fighting

Men's Grand Champion:
1. Pat Worley
2. Mike Warren
3. Byron Jones
4. Tommy Mickens

SOUTHWEST KARATE CHAMPIONSHIPS: 1970

Sam Allred, Producer
Albuquerque, NM

Fighting

Men's Grand Champion:
Louis Delgado
2. Roy Kurban

HEAVY:
1. Roy Kurban
2. Pete Ramacciotti
3. Russell Perrone

LIGHT:
1. Louis Delgado
2. Al Dacascos
3. Jim Harkins

U.S.K.A. GRAND NATIONALS: JUNE 6–7, 1970

Glenn Keeney, Producer
Anderson, IN

Fighting

Men's Grand Champion:
Bill Wallace
2. Joe Lewis (Defending Champ)

Men:
1. Bill Wallace
2. Victor Moore
3. Mike Posey
4. Dirk Mosig

Forms

Men:
1. George Dillman
2. Larry Pomilio
3. Tadashi Yamashita
4. Thomas St. Charles

Women:
1. Kathy Sullivan
2. Hilda Keloha
3. Linda Reyna
4. Linda Bennett

Weapons:
1. George Dillman
2. Tadashi Yamashita
3. Bob Dalgleish
4. Doug Gerrard

LONG BEACH INTERNATIONALS: AUGUST 1–2, 1970

Fighting

Men's Grand Champion:
Joe Lewis
2. Byong Yu
3. Arnold Urquidez
Harold Gross

HEAVY:
1. Arnold Urquidez
2. Quinn Frazier
3. Bob Halliburton

MIDDLE:
1. Harold Gross

2. Phil Cornin
3. Louis Delgado

LIGHT:
1. Byong Yu
2. Benny Urquidez
3. Steve Sanders

Women:

MIDDLE:
1. Malia Bernell
2. Lilly Urquidez
3. Yolanda Wollrabe

LIGHT:
1. Barbara Marez
2. Pat Lou
3. Diane Freeman

Forms

Grand Champion:
Mike Stone

CHINESE:
1. Mike Stone

JAPANESE:
1. Louis Delgado

KOREAN:
1. Chuck Norris

WOMEN:
1. Malia Bernell

CALIFORNIA CAPITAL CHAMPIONSHIPS: 1970

Ron Marchini & Leo Fong, Producers
Sacramento, CA

Note: This tournament is noteworthy only for its forms winners.

Forms

MEN (HARD STYLE):
1. Louis Delgado

MEN (SOFT STYLE):
1. Al Dacascos

WOMEN (HARD STYLE):
1. Cynthia Ajay

WOMEN (SOFT STYLE):
1. Malia Bernal

ALL-STATES OPEN: AUTUMN 1970

Youngstown, OH

Note: This tournament was noted for its forms competitors only.

Forms

BLACK BELT (CO-ED):
1. Mike Stone
2. George Dillman
3. Bobbi Snyder

WEAPONS:
1. George Dillman
2. Nate Cowger

AMERICAN TANG SOO DO INVITATIONAL: 1970

Ki Whang Kim, Producer
Washington, DC

Fighting

Men's Grand Champion:
Joe Hayes

2ND WORLD PRO-AM: NOVEMBER 1, 1970

Chuck Norris, Producer
Santa Monica, CA

Fighting

Men

HEAVY:
1. Joe Lewis
2. Jerry Piddington
3. Jerry Taylor

LIGHT HEAVY:
1. Jim Bottoms
2. Bob Dunek
3. Hugh Van Putten

MIDDLE:
1. Ron Marchini
2. Skipper Mullins
3. Bob Barrow

LIGHT:
1. Steve Sanders
2. Phil Cornin
3. Byong Yu

1969 NATIONAL TOURNAMENTS

AMERICAN INVITATIONAL (TOURNAMENT OF CHAMPIONS): 1969

Ki Whang Kim, Producer
Silver Springs, MD

Fighting

Men's Grand Champion:
   Joe Hayes
2. Riley Hawkins

HEAVY:
1. Riley Hawkins
2. Mitchell Bobrow
3. Robert Atkins
4. Robert Faulk

MIDDLE:
1. Joe Hayes
2. Bill Keefer
3. Phil Cunningham
4. Glenn Hawkins

Forms

Men:
1. Art Findling
2. Hector Eugui
3. Gary Cobin

Breaking

Men:
1. Lynn Jackson
2. Ron Collins
3. Joe Hayes

U.S. KARATE CHAMPIONSHIPS: FEBRUARY 8, 1969

Allen Steen, Producer
Dallas, TX

Fighting

Men's Grand Champion:
   Fred Wren
2. Jim Harrison

ALL-AMERICAN OPEN: FEBRUARY 22, 1969

S. Henry Cho, Producer
New York, NY

Fighting

Men's Grand Champion:
   Mitchell Bobrow
2. Toyotaro Miyazaki

HEAVY:
1. Mitchell Bobrow
2. Albert Cheeks
3. Ray Martin

LIGHT:
1. Toyotaro Miyazaki
2. Adolfo Velasco
3. Pete Ross

Forms

Men:
1. Toyotaro Miyazaki
2. Calvin Wilder
3. Melvin Wilder

Women:
1. Valerie McLean
2. Penny DeJan
3. Cote Lennie

GULF COAST KARATE CHAMPIONSHIP: 1969

Curtis Herrington, Producer
Galveston, TX

Fighting

Men's Grand Champion:
   David Moon
2. Jim Harrison

HEAVY:
1. Jim Harrison
2. Ed Daniel

LIGHT:
1. David Moon
2. Sigetada Tegima

KARATE WORLD TOURNAMENT OF CHAMPIONS: APRIL 12, 1969

Mills Crenshaw, Producer
Salt Lake City, UT

Fighting

Men:
1. Bill Wallace
2. Al Dacascos

UNIVERSAL TOURNAMENT OF CHAMPIONS: APRIL 19, 1969

Richard Chun, Producer
New York, NY

Fighting

Men's Grand Champion:
   Joe Hayes
2. Mitchell Bobrow
3. Bob Engel
4. Carlos Molina

Forms

Men:
1. Calvin Wilder
2. Melvin Wilder
3. William Hart

Women:
1. Nona Kamai
2. Lorraine Rodriguez
3. Debbie Kernahan

U.S. NATIONALS: MAY 10–11, 1969

Jhoon Rhee, Producer
Washington, DC

Note: A Tournament of Champions was conducted on the second day of this event, in which Nationals grand champ Joe Lewis did not compete.

Mitchell Bobrow (right) kicks David Moon in the 1969 U.S. Nationals Tournament of Champions, and appears in a double-exposure shot from the same event. Both photos courtesy of Mitchell Bobrow

Fighting

Men's Grand Champion:
Joe Lewis
2. Bill Keefer

HEAVY:
1. Joe Lewis
2. Bob Fowler
3. Riley Hawkins
   Bill Oliver

LIGHT:
1. Bill Keefer
2. Phil Cunningham
3. Don Cooper
   Mike Camberiate

Tournament of Champions
1. Chuck Norris
2. David Moon

U.S.K.A. GRAND NATIONALS: JUNE 14–15, 1969

**Jim Harrison, Producer
Kansas City, KS**

Fighting

Men's Grand Champion:
1. Joe Lewis
2. Artis Simmons

HEAVY:
1. Bill Wallace
2. Dirk Mosig

LIGHT:
1. Artis Simmons
2. Victor Moore

Women:
1. Kathy Sullivan
2. Kathy Merriman

Forms

Men:
1. Victor Moore
2. Dirk Mosig
3. Jim Hawkes

LONG BEACH INTERNATIONALS: AUGUST 3, 1969

Fighting

Men's Grand Champion:
Joe Lewis
2. Steve Sanders
3. Jim Bottoms

HEAVY:
1. Joe Lewis
2. Willie Norris
3. Steve LaBounty

MIDDLE:
1. Jim Bottoms
2. Bob Wall
3. Pat Johnson

LIGHT:
1. Steve Sanders
2. Richard Arviso
3. LeRoy Ruiz

Women:

MIDDLE:
1. Malia Riberio
2. Mahi Morales
3. Carole Hurley

LIGHT:
1. Silvana Salamone
2. Nan Schwartz
3. Cathy Chavez

Forms

Grand Champion:
Louis Delgado

CHINESE:
1. Armando Urquidez
2. Ed Keays

JAPANESE:
1. Kazuo Kuriyama
2. Louis Delgado

KOREAN:
1. Chuck Norris
2. Richard Niver

WEAPONS:
1. Nobuhiro Shinohara
2. James Steele

WOMEN:
1. Malia Riberio
2. Jeannie Luz

TOURNAMENT OF CHAMPIONS: AUGUST 24, 1969

J. Pat Burleson, Producer
Ft. Worth, TX

Fighting

Men's Grand Champion:

Roger Carpenter
2. Fred Wren
3. Bob Wall
4. Steve Stavroff

WORLD PROFESSIONAL KARATE CHAMPIONSHIPS: NOVEMBER 15, 1969

Aaron Banks, Producer
New York, NY

Fighting

HEAVY:
1. Joe Lewis

LIGHT HEAVY:
1. Mike Stone

MIDDLE:
1. Chuck Norris

LIGHT:
1. Skipper Mullins

GATEWAY OPEN: 1969

Bob Yarnall, Producer
St. Louis, MO

Fighting

Men's Grand Champion:

Bill Wallace
2. Mike Sheahon
3. Joel Ward

BLACK BELT:
1. Bill Wallace
2. Glenn Keeney
3. Fred Wren
4. Ridgely Abele

Women:
1. Kathy Sullivan
2. Linda Mikulich
3. Sunny Oliver
4. Kathy Fischer

1968 NATIONAL TOURNAMENTS

U.S. CHAMPIONSHIPS: 1968

Allen Steen, Producer
Dallas, TX

The team champions from the 1968 U.S. Championships: (Left to right) Demetrius Havanas, Ed Daniel, Ronny Cox and Skipper Mullins. Courtesy of Keith D. Yates

Fighting

Men's Grand Champion:

Joe Lewis
2. Chuck Norris

Women:

1. Phyllis Evetts

Skipper Mullins (left) versus Joe Lewis in 1968. Courtesy of Keith D. Yates

Marian Erickson (right) kicks an unidentified opponent at the 1968 U.S. Championships. Courtesy of Keith D. Yates

ALL-AMERICAN CHAMPIONSHIPS & TOURNAMENT OF CHAMPIONS: MARCH 30–31, 1968

S. Henry Cho, Producer
New York, NY

Note: Chuck Norris had to leave the tournament before defending his "Tournament of Champions" title.

Fighting

All American Men's Grand Champion:
 Chuck Norris
2. Carlos Farrell

HEAVY:
1. Carlos Farrell
2. Jeff Goldberg
3. Robert Engle
4. David Claudio

LIGHT:
1. Dwight Frazier
2. John Dinkens
3. Woodrow Fairbanks, Jr.
4. Leon Wallace

Women:
1. Joyce Phillips
2. Joyce Zinno
3. Maureen Brazil
4. Carol Buckley

Forms

Men:
1. Toyotaro Miyazaki
2. Arturo Aviles, Jr.

TOURNAMENT OF CHAMPIONS:

Men's Grand Champion:
 Ron Marchini
2. Mitchell Bobrow
3. Dwight Frazier
4. Thomas LaPuppet
Source

U.S.K.A. GRAND NATIONALS: JUNE 8–9, 1968

Jim Harrison, Producer
Kansas City, KS

Fighting

Men's Grand Champion:
 Joe Lewis

2. Roger Carpenter
3. Jay Garrett
4. George Smith

Women:
1. Tangia Abernathy
2. Janet Walgren

Forms

Men:
1. Rich Hootselle

Women:
1. Tangia Abernathy

U.S. NATIONALS: MAY 25, 1968

Jhoon Rhee, Producer
Washington, DC

Fighting

Men's Grand Champion:
 Joe Lewis

Forms

Men:
1. Lynn Jackson
2. James Jones

Bruce Lee presents the tournament flag to Joe Lewis, grand champion of the 1968 U.S. Nationals. Courtesy of Joe Lewis

Joe Lewis (below) on his way to being disqualified at the 1968 Internationals. Courtesy of Joe Lewis. At the same event, Chuck Norris (left side of picture at right) seems to be getting the worst of this exchange with Skipper Mullins. Courtesy of Keith D. Yates

A line-up of dignitaries and champions at the 1968 All American Invitational: (Left to right) Soo Wong Lee, Il Joo Kim, Phil Cunningham, grand champ Mitchell Bobrow, Muhn Soo Park, Ki Whang Kim, Joe Hayes, Mike Jack and James Roberts, Sr. Courtesy of Mitchell Bobrow

LONG BEACH INTERNATIONALS: AUGUST 3–4, 1968

Fighting

Grand Champion:
Chuck Norris
2. Skipper Mullins
3. AlGene Caraulia
3. Greg Baines

Forms

Grand Champion:
Mariano Estioka

JAPANESE:
1. John Pereira
2. Delroy Griffiths

KOREAN:
1. Mariano Estioka
2. Chuck Norris

CHINESE:
1. Sterling Peacock

2. Mario Magoangal

WEAPONS:
1. Ping Chin
2. Albert Avala

SAN ANTONIO PRO-AM: AUGUST 26, 1968

Robert Trias & Atlee Chittim, Producers
San Antonio, TX

Note: This was the first professional karate tournament in America.

Fighting

Professional Men:
1. Victor Moore
2. Joe Lewis
3. George Smith

Amateur Men:
1. Artis Simmons
2. Joe Alvarado

AMERICAN INVITATIONAL: SEPTEMBER 14, 1968

Ki Whang Kim, Producer
Silver Spring, MD

Fighting

Men's Grand Champion:
Mitchell Bobrow
2. Joe Hayes

HEAVY:
1. Hector Eugui
2. Barry Figard
3. Albert Cheeks

LIGHT:
1. Phil Cunningham
2. Thomas Lewis
3. Mike Jacks

Forms

Men:
1. Toyotaro Miyazaki
2. Joe Hayes
3. James Roberts, Jr.

Mitchell Bobrow (right) versus Jack Dutcher at the 1968 All American Invitational. Courtesy of Mitchell Bobrow

TAE GYUN OPEN: SEPTEMBER 1968

Mahn Suh Park, Producer
Philadelphia, PA

Note: This two-day event featured a "Tournament of Champions."

Fighting

Tournament of Champions

Men's Grand Champion:
John Dutcher
2. Mitchell Bobrow
3. Joe Lewis
Joe Hayes

PROFESSIONAL KARATE TOURNAMENT: OCTOBER 1968

Allen Steen, Producer
Dallas, TX

Fighting

Men's Grand Champion:
Joe Lewis
2. Skipper Mullins

At the 1967 U.S. Nationals. (Left to right) Jhoon Rhee (bending over stage), Bruce Lee, unidentified tournament queen, Senator Hiram Fong presenting grand champion trophy to Joe Lewis. Senator Howard Cannon stands behind the trophy. Courtesy of Grandmaster Jhoon Rhee

HEAVY:
1. Joe Lewis
2. Phil Ola
3. Larry Whitener

LIGHT:
1. Skipper Mullins
2. Harold Gross

Women:
1. Carol Cooper
2. Tanya Abernathy

WORLD PROFESSIONAL KARATE CHAMPIONSHIPS: NOVEMBER 24, 1968

Aaron Banks, Producer
New York, NY

HEAVY:
1. Joe Lewis

LIGHT HEAVY:
1. Mike Stone

MIDDLE:
1. Chuck Norris

LIGHT:
1. Skipper Mullins

1967 NATIONAL TOURNAMENTS

U.S. CHAMPIONSHIPS: 1967

Allen Steen, Producer
Dallas, TX

Fighting

Men's Grand Champion:
    David Moon
2. Terry Conner

Women:
1. Marian Erickson
2. Karen Taylor
3. Cherry Kirby

TOURNAMENT OF CHAMPIONS: 1967

S. Henry Cho, Producer
New York, NY

Note: 1) This was the first event to feature just ten fighters, half of them nationally rated. 2) The finals ended in a tie between Chuck Norris and Joe Lewis, each having

won four bouts and lost one. Norris was declared grand champion by a vote of the judges.

Fighting

Men's Grand Champion:
    Chuck Norris
2. Joe Lewis
3. Skipper Mullins
4. Bob Engle
5. Julio LaSalle

U.S. NATIONALS: MAY 1967

Jhoon Rhee, Producer
Washington, DC

Fighting

Men's Grand Champion:
    Joe Lewis

NATIONAL TOURNAMENT OF CHAMPIONS: JUNE 3, 1967

Cleveland, OH

Fighting

Men's Grand Champion:
    Chuck Norris

Joe Lewis (left) versus Mitchell Bobrow at the 1967 U.S. Nationals. Courtesy of Mitchell Bobrow

ALL-AMERICAN CHAMPIONSHIPS: JUNE 24, 1967

S. Henry Cho, Producer
New York, NY

Fighting

Men's Grand Champion:
Julio LaSalle

HEAVY:
1. Joe Lewis

U.S.K.A. NATIONALS: 1967

Robert Trias, Producer
Miami, FL

Fighting

Men's Grand Champion:
Jimmy Jones

LONG BEACH INTERNATIONALS: JULY 29–30, 1967

Fighting

Men's Grand Champion:
Chuck Norris
2. Joe Lewis

Two of sport karate's all-time great champions meet at the 1967 Internationals: Joe Lewis (right) and Chuck Norris. Courtesy of Joe Lewis

A referee's meeting for the 1967 American Invitational, at a time when officials had to show up in suits and ties on the eve of the event. (Seated, left to right): Chuck Norris, Mr. Ahn, Jhoon Rhee, Ki Whang Kim, S. Henry Cho, San Dak Sop and Richard Chun. Second row (standing, left to right): Neil Erlich, Hector Eugui, Frank Fuentes, Bill Keefer, John Molton, Quinton Conroy, Mitchell Bobrow, unidentified, Francis Conde, Riley Hawkins, Lynn Jackson, unidentified, unidentified and Bob Maxwell. Top row (left to right): unidentified, unidentified, Joe Hayes, unidentified, Pat Johnson and unidentified. Courtesy of Mitchell Bobrow

HEAVY:
1. Joe Lewis
2. Frank Noel
3. Jim Harrison

MIDDLE:
1. Chuck Norris
2. Arnold Urquidez
3. Victor Moore

LIGHT:
1. Steve Sanders
2. Jake Sabori
3. Carlos Bunda

Forms

Grand Champion:
Leroy Rodrigues

CHINESE:
1. Al Dacascos
2. Carlos Bunda

OKINAWAN:
1. Kazuo Kuriyama
2. Leroy Rodrigues

KOREAN:
1. Chuck Norris
2. Boung Kwak

AMERICAN TANG SOO DO INVITATIONAL: SEPTEMBER 30, 1967

Ki Whang Kim, Producer
Washington, DC

Fighting

Men's Grand Champion:
Chuck Norris
2. Skipper Mullins

HEAVY:
1. Chuck Norris
2. Riley Hawkins
3. Mitchell Bobrow

MIDDLE:
1. Skipper Mullins
2. Furman Marshall
3. Robert Maxwell

Line-up of champions and officials of the 1967 All American Invitational. (Left to right): Mr. Shin, Ki Whang Kim, Jhoon Rhee, Riley Hawkins, Mitchell Bobrow, grand champion Chuck Norris, Skipper Mullins, Bob Maxwell, Furman Marshall, Richard Chun, Glenn Premru and Gary Alexander. Courtesy of Mitchell Bobrow

Forms

Men:

1. Glenn Premru
2. Ron Collins
3. Frank Fuentes

1966 NATIONAL TOURNAMENTS

CALIFORNIA STATE KARATE CHAMPIONSHIPS: 1966

Ralph Castro & Ed Parker, Producers
San Francisco, CA

Fighting

Men:

1. Tonny Tulleners
2. Chuck Norris

U.S. CHAMPIONSHIPS (A.K.A. THE SOUTHWEST CHAMPIONSHIPS): 1966

Allen Steen, Producer
Dallas, TX

Note: A women's fighting division was introduced here for the first time in American sport karate.

Fighting

Men's Grand Champion:
    David Moon
2. J. Pat Burleson

Women:
    1. Marian Erickson
    2. ?
    3. Cherry Kirby

ALL-AMERICAN OPEN: 1966

S. Henry Cho, Producer
New York City

Fighting

Men's Grand Champion:
    Thomas LaPuppet

U.S. NATIONALS: MAY 7, 1966

Jhoon Rhee, Producer
Washington, DC

Fighting

Men:
    1. Joe Lewis
    2. Richard Sheppard
    3. Victor Moore

Women:
    1. Deborah Wear

2. Judith Clark
3. Cherry Kirby

Forms

Co-Ed:
    1. Joe Lewis

LONG BEACH INTERNATIONALS: JULY 31, 1966

Fighting

Men's Grand Champion:
    Allen Steen
2. Chuck Norris

HEAVY:
1. Allen Steen

MIDDLE:
1. Chuck Norris
2. Skipper Mullins

LIGHT:
1. ?

U.S.K.A. NATIONALS: SEPTEMBER 4, 1966

Robert Trias & John Pachivas, Producers
Miami, FL

Fighting

Men's Grand Champion:
    Mike Foster
2. Victor Moore

AMERICAN TANG SOO DO INVITATIONAL: 1966

Ki Whang Kim, Producer
Washington, DC

Note: The participation of Chuck Norris and Skipper Mullins gave this event a national impact. Norris lost in the eliminations.

Fighting

Men's Grand Champion:
  Skipper Mullins
  2. Lloyd Davis
  HEAVY:
  1. Lloyd Davis
  2. Jose Jones
  3. Riley Hawkins
  MIDDLE:
  1. Skipper Mullins
  2. Marcos Solo
  3. John Camanse

Forms

Men:
  1. Frank Fuentes
  2. Bruce Turner
  3. Victor Guererra

NATIONAL WINTER KARATE CHAMPIONSHIPS: 1966

San Jose, CA

Fighting

Men's Grand Champion:
  Chuck Norris

1965 NATIONAL TOURNAMENTS

SOUTHWEST KARATE CHAMPIONSHIPS: 1965

Allen Steen, Producer
Dallas, TX

Fighting

Men's Grand Champion:
  David Moon
  2. AlGene Caraulia
  3. Mike Steen

WORLD KARATE TOURNAMENT: 1965

Robert Trias & John Pachivas, Producers
Miami, FL

Fighting

Men's Grand Champion:
  Victor Moore
  2. Mike Foster

U.S. NATIONALS: APRIL 10, 1965

Jhoon Rhee, Producer
Washington, DC

Note: This tournament was the first in American karate to be filmed by ABC-TV's *Wide World of Sports*, but the footage was not aired, allegedly due to the violence displayed in the grand championship match.

Fighting

Men's Grand Champion:
  Mike Stone
  2. Walt Worthy

Forms

Champion:
  1. Mike Stone

ALL-AMERICAN CHAMPIONSHIPS: 1965

Fighting

Men's Grand Champion:
  Thomas LaPuppet

LONG BEACH INTERNATIONALS: AUGUST 1, 1965

Fighting

Men's Grand Champion:
  Mike Stone
  2. Tonny Tulleners
  3. AlGene Caraulia
  Art Pelela
  HEAVY:
  1. Art Pelela
  2. Harry Keolanni
  3. Allen Steen
  MIDDLE:
  1. Tonny Tulleners
  2. Richard Lee
  3. Leonard Mau
  LIGHT:
  1. AlGene Caraulia
  2. Earl Boles
  3. Jack Hwang

Forms

Champion:
  1. Mike Stone

1964 NATIONAL TOURNAMENTS

1ST SOUTHWEST KARATE CHAMPIONSHIPS: 1964

Allen Steen, Producer
Dallas, TX

Note: Team sparring competition was introduced here for the first time in American sport karate.

Fighting

Men's Individual:
  1. Keith See
  2. Allen Steen
  3. Hans Borgman

Men's Team:
  1. Jhoon Rhee Institute, Dallas (Mike Steen, Bill Bosworth, Allen Steen)

Four sport karate pioneers from 1964. (Left to right): J. Pat Burleson, Jhoon Rhee, Skipper Mullins and Allen Steen. Courtesy of Keith D. Yates

1963: AMERICA'S FIRST NATIONAL TOURNAMENT

1ST WORLD KARATE TOURNAMENT

Date: July 28, 1963. Site: University of Chicago Fieldhouse, Chicago, Illinois. Producers: John Keehan and Robert Trias. Sanctioned by: United States Karate Association. Participants: 311 competitors. Spectators: 4,500+.

Note: Despite its lofty title, this was actually the first genuinely *national* tournament conducted in the U.S. (It was later renamed the USKA Grand Nationals.) It attracted most of America's prominent martial artists of the time who came to compete or officiate. This event set a dual precedent: 1) It was the foundation for subsequent large-scale, national-caliber karate competitions; and 2) It marked the official birth of "American karate" by attracting America's premiere competitors who, according to retired karate champion J. Pat Burleson (who competed in it), "began integrating techniques. It was the first time you saw the marriage of kicking and punching in competition."

In essence, the '63 World Championships was the starting point for American karate tournaments as we know them today. Because of its historical importance, the winners in all divisions are listed.

2. Army, Ft. Chaffe, Arkansas (Herbert Peters, Mike Stone, James Keaneo)
3. Jhoon Rhee Institute, Ft. Worth (J. Pat Burleson, Steve Stavroff, Ron Moffet)

Forms

Men:

1. Keith See
2. Herbert Peters
3. John Nash

U.S. NATIONALS: MAY 1964

**Jhoon Rhee, Producer
Washington, DC**

Fighting

Men's Individual:

    J. Pat Burleson (National Champion)

1. Herbert Peters
2. Joe Pennywell
3. Raymond Cooper

Men's Team:

1. Chicago Karate Center
2. Jhoon Rhee Institute, Washington, DC
3. Chi Duk Kwan, Jacksonville, FL

LONG BEACH INTERNATIONALS: AUGUST 2, 1964

Fighting

Men's Grand Champion:
    Mike Stone

Forms

Champion:
    1. Mike Stone

WORLD KARATE TOURNAMENT: SEPTEMBER 6, 1964

    **Robert Trias & John Keehan, Producers
Chicago, IL**

Fighting

Men's Grand Champion:
    Mike Stone
    2. Ray Cooper

Fighting

Grand Champion:
    AlGene Caraulia
    2. Dan Lynch
    3. Ray Cooper

BLACK BELT:
1. Lewis Lizotte

2. Allen Steen
3. Jim Chapman

BROWN BELT:
1. AlGene Caraulia
2. Bob Fujimoto
3. J. Pat Burleson

WHITE BELT:
1. Joe Pennywell
2. Ron Harris

Kata/Forms

BLACK BELT:
1. Jerry Fasbender

2. Roberta Trias
3. Anthony Mirakian

BROWN BELT:
1. Murray Sutherland
2. Al Curatolo
3. Ron Taylor

WHITE BELT:
1. Ralph Curatolo
2. Bill Foster

OTHER 1963 TOURNAMENTS:

Tulsa Southwest Championships, Tulsa, OK

Fighting & Forms Champion:
Mike Stone

Fighting Runner-Up:
J. Pat Burleson

Southwest Karate Championships

**Allen Steen, Producer
Dallas, TX**

Fighting Champion:
Allen Steen
2. Elby McCoy

CHAPTER 13

WUSHU CHAMPIONSHIP RESULTS

Although there have been many kung-fu championships, including those which claim to be "world championships," most of them have been conducted in Asia without the participation of a multitude of Western nations, especially the United States. Only in recent years has that changed.

The first truly international wushu championship was conducted in 1985 and the first bona fide world championship in 1991. Here you will find the results of all the international and the single world championships so far.

Likewise, in the United States there have been only two bona fide "national" championships specifically for Chinese stylists. Those results appear here as well.

In the case of a tie,, no number will precede the second competitor or country listing. For example, the winners' lists may feature three places with two competitors sharing the third position.

WORLD CHAMPIONSHIPS (1991)

1ST WORLD WUSHU CHAMPIONSHIPS

Date: October 1991. Site: Capital Gymnasium, Beijing, China. Producer: Chinese Wushu Association. Sanctioned by: International Wushu Federation. Participants: 400+ athletes from 32 countries.

Note: Two types of competition took place at this event: 1) six sessions of "taolu" or "routines" (forms) and 2) "san shou" or "full-contact" sparring.

Men's Overall Medal Standing:
1. China
2. Japan
3. Japan
4. Philippines
5. Malaysia
6. Malaysia

Men's All-Around Champions:
1. Gao Huanbo (China)
2. Kazunari Hirota (Japan)
3. Hideo Ninomiya (Japan)

Women's Overall Medal Standing:
1. China
2. Hong Kong
3. Hong Kong
4. Japan
5. Japan
6. Philippines

Women's All-Around Champions:
1. Zhang Shaoyi (China)
2. Ng Siu Ching (Hong Kong)
3. Li Fai (Hong Kong)

Forms

Men

LONG FIST, BROADSWORD, STAFF:
1. Gao Huanbo (China)

SOUTHERN FIST:
1. Leung Yat Ho (Hong Kong)

SPEAR:
1. Choy Ching Chi (Philippines)

SWORD:
1. Kazunari Hirota (Japan)
2. Andrew Hartono (USA)

TAIJIQUAN:
1. Ryoji Ito (Japan)
2. ?
3. David Ross (USA)

Women

BROADSWORD:
1. Geng Zhenhui (China)

LONG FIST, SWORD, SPEAR:
1. Zhang Shaoyi (China)

SOUTHERN FIST:
1. Liang Yanhua (China)

TAIJIQUAN:
1. Gao Jiamin (China)

San Shou

Men

90 KG:
1. Dzaparov Kazbek (CIS)

85 KG:
1. James Ayres (Brazil)

80 KG:
1. Javier Moya (Spain)

75 KG:
1. Ramazanov Ramazan (CIS)

70 KG:
1. Pan Xiongqi (Chinese Taipei)

65 KG:
1. Yang Rui (China)

60 KG:
1. Wang Jianming (China)

56 KG:
1. Zeng Qingfeng (China)

52 KG:
1. Wang Shiying (China)

INTERNATIONAL CHAMPIONSHIPS (1985–88)

3RD INTERNATIONAL WUSHU INVITATIONAL TOURNAMENT

Date: October 1988. Site: Hangzhou, People's Republic of China. Sanctioned and Produced by: Chinese Wushu Association. Participants: 29 countries.

Men's All-Around Champions:
1. Yuan Wenching (China)
2. Hai Choi Lam (Hong Kong)
3. Manabu Hayashi (Japan)

Women's All-Around Champions:
1. Peng Ying (China)
2. Atsuko Maehigashi (Japan)
3. Ng Siu Ching (Hong Kong)

Forms

Men

LONG FIST, BROADSWORD, STAFF:
1. Yuan Wenching (China)

SOUTHERN FIST:
1. Chan Pangfei (Hong Kong)

SPEAR:
1. Wu Shu Kin (GRB)

SWORD:
1. Li Zhizhou (China)

TAIJIQUAN:
1. Toyohiko Kimura (Japan)

Women

BROADSWORD:
1. Wu Qiuhua (China)

LONG FIST, SWORD, SPEAR:
1. Peng Ying (China)

SOUTHERN FIST:
1. Tan Ailan (Singapore)

STAFF:
1. Shi Ruifen (China)

TAIJIQUAN:
1. Lin Qiuping (China)

2ND INTERNATIONAL WUSHU INVITATIONAL TOURNAMENT

Date: November 1986. Site: Tianjin, People's Republic of China. Sanctioned and Produced by: Chinese Wushu Association. Participants: 19 countries.

Men's All-Around Champions:
1. Zhao Changjun (China)
2. Phillip Wong (USA)
3. Nick Gracenin (USA)

Women's All-Around Champions:
1. Zhang Yuping (China)
2. Alice Chang (Canada)
3. Gillian Barber (GRB)

Forms

Men

BAGUAZHANG:
1. Nigel Sutton (GRB)

LONG FIST, BROADSWORD, STAFF:
1. Zhao Changjun (China)

SOUTHERN FIST:
1. Yang Shiwen (China)

SWORD, SPEAR:
1. Jia Ping (China)

TAIJIQUAN:
1. Ding Jie (China)

XINGYIQUAN:
1. Zhang Chengzhong (China)

Women

LONG FIST, BROADSWORD, STAFF:
1. Zhang Yuping (China)

SWORD, SPEAR:
1. Fang Jian (China)

TAIJIQUAN:
1. Lin Qiuping (China)

1ST INTERNATIONAL WUSHU INVITATIONAL TOURNAMENT

Date: August 1985. Site: Xian, People's Republic of China. Sanctioned and Produced by: Chinese Wushu Association. Participants: 14 countries.

Men's All-Around Champions:
1. Zhao Changjun (China)
2. Hideo Ninomiya (Japan)
3. Richard Vechiolla (USA)

Women's All-Around Champions:
1. Zhang Yuping (China)
2. Paule Bertrand (Canada)
3. Chi Ching Yen (USA)

Forms

Men

LONG FIST, BROADSWORD, STAFF:
1. Zhao Changjun (China)

SOUTHERN FIST:
1. Yang Shiwen (China)

SWORD, SPEAR:
1. Jia Ping (China)

TAIJIQUAN:
1. Chen Xiaowang (China)

Women

LONG FIST, BROADSWORD, STAFF:
1. Zhang Yuping (China)

SPEAR:
1. Lin Qiuping (China)

SWORD:
1. Zhang Hongmei (China)

TAIJIQUAN:
1. Lin Qiuping (China)

UNITED STATES

2ND U.S. NATIONAL CHINESE MARTIAL ARTS COMPETITION

Date: 1992. Site: Lake Buena Vista, FL. Producer: Jeff Bolt.

Grand Champions

Traditional Forms (Men)

Tracy Fleming

Traditional Forms (Women)
Patty Sun

Wushu Forms (Men)
Woody Wong

Wushu Forms (Women)
Cori Fukuchi

Internal Forms (Men)
Tai Ngo

Internal Forms (Women)
Kelly Maclean

Full-Contact Fighting

Advanced Men

180–189 LBS:
1. Expedito de Silva
2. Mikem Sutton

170–179 LBS:
1. Dana Rucker
2. Phillip LeGault

160–169 LBS:
1. Raul Moreno
2. Anthony Codron

150–159 LBS:
1. Mark Hurley
2. Pablo Han

140–149 LBS:
1. Silvanio de Silva
2. Jakub Cuzlog

130–139 LBS:
1. Anthony Sims
2. Raul Benavidez

120–129 LBS:
1. Piotr Siegocysup
2. Hung Stewart

Advanced Women

115–125 LBS:
1. Angela Finlay
2. Jean Luntz

Light Contact Free Fighting

Men's Advanced

HEAVY:
1. James Carinio
2. Ted Robaezewski
3. Arnold Nunez

MIDDLE:
1. Troy Provenzano

2. John Wai
3. Jeff Wooten

LIGHT:
1. Jimmy Lamon
2. Robert Desario

Women's Advanced

LIGHT:
1. Kris Jarrard
2. Rosemarie Clifford
3. Angela Finlay

Shuai Chiao

Advanced Men
1. Michael Seto
2. Manuel Rodriguez
3. Richard Wise

Push Hands

MOVING

Advanced Men

HEAVY:
1. Thomas Winkler-Parenty
2. Jeff Pratt
3. James Bessette

MIDDLE:
1. George Harris
2. Charles Cashell
3. Lauren Smith

LIGHT:
1. Joseph Soiza
2. Bill Perison
3. Tai Ngo

Women

MIDDLE:
1. Silvia Robinson
2. Pamela Conrad
3. Suzanne Harrison

LIGHT:
1. Donna Oliver
2. Wendy Miller

STATIONARY

Advanced Men

SUPER HEAVY:
1. Jeff Pratt

HEAVY:
1. Roger Whidden
2. Jim O'Leary
3. Sam Edwards

MIDDLE:
1. Robert Alexander

LIGHT:
1. Bill Perison
2. Tai Ngo
3. Joseph Soiza

Women

MIDDLE:
1. Adrian Wheeler
2. Sheila Todd
3. Pamela Conrad

LIGHT:
1. June Fukushima
2. Donna Oliver
3. Wendy Miller·

Forms

NORTHERN TRADITIONAL

Advanced Men
1. Sean Cochran
2. Dean Wong
3. Tai Ngo
4. Tracy Fleming
   Ryan Watson

Women
1. Debbie Wong
2. Cheryl Crawford
3. Katherine Williams
4. Jennifer Menefree

LONG/SHORT HAND

Advanced Men
1. Jason Yee
   Daniel Tanazake
3. Hung Stewart
4. Rick Wong

Women
1. Karin Sanjuan
2. Milani Elena
3. Shelly Kivera
4. Kelly Cramp

SOUTHERN SHORT HAND

Advanced Men
1. John Wai
2. Manuel Rodriquez
3. Tony Caucci
4. Jeff Larson

Women
1. Daisy Taylor
2. Rosemarie Clifford

3. Angela Finlay
4. Denise Smith

OPEN BAREHAND

Advanced Men
1. Tracy Fleming
2. Sean Cochran
3. Tu Truong
4. Siu Hung Huen

Women
1. Daisy Taylor
2. Janet Donahue
3. Patty Sun
4. Jean Luntz

CHANGQUAN

Advanced Men
1. Scott Parker
2. Woody Wong
3. Andrew Hartono
4. Brian Capps

NANQUAN

Advanced Men
1. Jason Yee
2. Greg Walraven
3. Jeff O'Donnell
4. Brian Capps

Women
1. Cheryl Vanatsky
2. Cori Fukuchi

TAIJIQUAN

Men
1. Joshua Grant
2. David Ross
3. Joel Timmons
4. Tor Lo

Women
1. Kelly Maclean
2. Doria Cook-Nelson
3. Theresa Rinehart
4. Suzanne Lojko

WUSHU OPEN BAREHAND

Advanced Men
1. Scott Parker
2. Joel Timmons

3. Woody Wong
4. Jeff O'Donnell

WUSHU STAFF

Advanced Men
1. Scott Parker
2. Brian Capps
3. Jeff O'Donnell
4. Mike Tom

Women
1. Amy Chow
2. Cori Fukuchi
3. Cheryl Vanatsky
4. Kelly Cramp

WUSHU SPEAR

Advanced Men
1. Woody Wong
2. Andrew Hartono
3. Joel Timmons
4. Luca Piazza

Women
1. Miresi Delendatl
2. Patty Sun
3. Kim Hardiman

WUSHU STRAIGHT SWORD

Advanced Men
1. Andrew Hartono
2. Thomas Domey
3. Joel Timmons
4. Luca Piazza

Women
1. Amy Chow
2. Miresi Delendatl
3. Patty Sun
4. Kristine Kent

WUSHU BROAD SWORD

Advanced Men
1. Woody Wong
2. Brian Capps
3. Scott Parker
4. Jeff O'Donnell

Women
1. Cori Fukuchi
2. Cheryl Vanatsky

3. Kelly Cramp
4. Kim Hardiman

WUSHU OPEN WEAPONS

Advanced Men
1. Woody Wong
2. Joel Timmons
3. Jeff O'Donnell
4. Thomas Domey

Women
1. Cori Fukuchi
2. Amy Chow
3. Kim Hardiman
4. Cheryl Vanatsky

YANG TAI CHI

Advanced Men
1. Tai Ngo
2. Herb Rich
3. Joel Timmons
4. David Ross

Women
1. Theresa Rinehart
2. Chantal Fafard
3. Suzanne Harrison
4. Donna Oliver

CHEN TAI CHI

Men
1. Herb Rich
2. Jian Xiong Liang
3. David Ross
4. John Vanko

Women
1. Kelly Maclean
2. Chantal Fafard
3. Theresa Rinehart

WU STYLE

Advanced Men
1. Gary Lee
2. Greg Guerin
3. Jack Creighton
4. Brian Weatherly

Women
1. Cheryl Rocco
2. Jayne Cobb

3. Diane Waters
4. Sheila Todd

OTHER INTERNAL STYLES

Advanced Men

1. Ramel Rones
2. Joel Timmons
3. David Ross
4. Herb Goldberg

Women

1. Daisy Taylor
2. Chantal Fafard
3. Kelly Maclean
4. Doria Cook-Nelson

PAQUA

Advanced Men

1. Joel Timmons
2. Tai Ngo
3. Siu HungHuen
4. Brian Weatherly

Women

1. June Fukushima
2. Rosemarie Reuben

HSING-I

Advanced Men

1. Siu Hung Huen
2. Joel Timmons
3. Tai Ngo
4. Rick Wong

Women

1. Kelly Maclean
2. Iva Peck

INTERNAL WEAPONS

Advanced Men

1. Jian Liang
2. Tai Ngo
3. Herb Rich
4. Joel Timmons

Women

1. Kelly Maclean
2. Jayne Cobb
3. Chantal Fafard
4. Theresa Rinehart

1ST U.S. NATIONAL CHINESE MARTIAL ARTS COMPETITION

Date: September 1–4, 1989. Site: Wyndham Hotel, Houston, TX. Participants: 300 competitors from eight countries. Promoter: Jeff Bolt.

Grand Champions

**All-Around External Events
Grand Champion:**

Javonne Holmes

**All-Around Internal
Grand Champion:**

Al-Waalee Muhammed
2. John Camp
3. Ramel Rones

All-Around Competitor Award:

Patrick Kelly

Fighting

SUPER HEAVY:
No competitors qualified

HEAVY:
No competitors qualified

MIDDLE:
1. Son Ok Cho

LIGHT:
1. Javonne Holmes
2. Jai Hyung Yu
3. Floyd Lifton

Men's Forms

All-Around Champion:

1. Javonne Holmes
   Hung Stewart
2. Patrick Kelly
   Wil Allen

Bare Hand

CHEN'S TAI-CHI:
1. Bomani Magharibi
2. Russell Sauls
3. Patrick Kelly

CHOREOGRAPHED SPARRING SETS:
1. George Kee, Jesse Vaughn, Sean Cochran
2. Hung Stewart, Linh Thai
3. Michael Reighard, Tommy Ngyuen

GROUP:
1. Wah Lum Kung-Fu School
2. South Africa Team

HSING-I:
1. Bomani Magharibi
2. Al-Waalee Muhammed
3. Peter Dinh

LONG/SHORT HAND:
1. Hung Stewart
2. Pedro Cepero
3. Jai Hyung Yu

OPEN:
1. Javonne Holmes
2. Patrick Kelly
3. Wil Allen

OTHER TAI-CHI:
1. John Camp
2. Russell Sauls
   Al-Waalee Muhammed

PA-QUA:
1. Bomani Magharibi
2. Patrick Kelly
3. Russell Sauls

SOUTHERN SHORT HAND:
1. Andrew Chung
2. Wen-Ching Wu
3. Floyd Lifton

TRADITIONAL NORTHERN:
1. Art D'Agostino
2. Wen-Ching Wu
3. John Cheng
4. James Au

WUSHU LONG FIST:
1. Patrick Kelly
2. Javonne Holmes
3. Woody Wong

YANG'S TAI-CHI:
1. Alex Kiesel
   John Camp
2. Andrew Chu
   Ramel Rones

Men's Moving Push Hands

SUPER HEAVY:
1. Dale Ward
2. Steven Conner
3. Daniel Leonard

HEAVY:
1. Christopher Clark
2. Paul Ramos
3. Gary Clyman

MIDDLE:
1. John Camp
2. Chris Luth
3. Tom Otterness

LIGHT:
1. Charles Blodgett
2. Heinz Rottman
3. Johnny Ortiz

Men's Stationary Push Hands

SUPER HEAVY:
1. Dale Ward
2. Steven Conner
3. Al-Waalee Muhammed

HEAVY:
1. Alex Kiesel
2. Andrew Chung
3. Paul Ramos

MIDDLE:
1. John Camp
2. Chris Moran
3. Philip Chao

LIGHT:
1. Daniel Zal
2. Charles Blodgett
3. Heinz Rottman

Men's Weapons

BROADSWORD:
1. Hung Stewart
2. Wil Allen
3. Greg Walraven

GROUP:
1. South Africa Team

OPEN:
1. Tracy Fleming
2. Javonne Holmes
3. Wil Allen

SOFT STYLE:
1. Al-Waalee Muhammed
2. Art D'Agostino
3. Russell Sauls

SPEAR:
1. Art D'Agostino
2. Andrew Hartono
3. Woody Wong

STAFF:
1. Javonne Holmes
2. Hung Stewart
3. Pedro Cepero

STRAIGHT SWORD:
1. Patrick Kelly
2. Ramel Rones
3. Joel Timmons

Women's Forms

Bare Hand

CHEN'S TAI-CHI:
1. Cherie Dijamco

LONG/SHORT HAND:
1. Stephanie Dea

WUSHU LONG FIST:
1. Debbie Seefelt
2. Cheryl Vanatsky

OPEN:
1. Cheryl Bussart

2. Cynthia Humphrey

OTHER TAI-CHI:
1. Cherie Dijamco

YANG'S TAI-CHI:
1. Terry Morgan
2. Cherie Dijamco
3. Adeera Muhammed

Women's Moving Push Hands

MIDDLE:
1. Kim Furry
2. Susan Leonard
3. Terry Morgan

Women's Stationary Push Hands

MIDDLE:
1. Susan Leonard
2. Carolyn Mills
3. Katherine Robertson

Women's Weapons

BROADSWORD:
1. Cheryl Vanatsky
2. Cheryl Bussart

OPEN:
1. Stephanie Dea
2. Cori Ertha

STAFF:
1. Cheryl Vanatsky
2. Pi-Gi Brite

STRAIGHT SWORD:
1. Debbie Seefelt

DISTINGUISHED CHAMPIONS (1967–92)

This section traces every top-ten-ranked fighter and forms champion in American and European sport karate since 1967, when heavyweight karate king Joe Lewis verbally named the first set of top-ten U.S. karate champions for *Black Belt* magazine. Also included, based on availability, are the top-ten ratings for European karate and judo champions, as well as for Japanese judo and karate champions.

A multitude of sources have instituted such ratings over the years. Incorporated here are the annual ratings first initiated by *Black Belt* magazine, the quarterly ratings of *Professional Karate* magazine from the mid-1970s, then considered the ultimate source, and the annual ratings launched by *Karate Illustrated* magazine during its influential heyday in the late 1970s and early 1980s.

In the mid-1970s, beginning with *Professional Karate* magazine, ratings services began ranking twenty of America's best karate competitors instead of ten. Purely for consistency and to maintain an accepted standard, I have limited the ratings in this chapter to just ten people when at least ten are listed.

Beginning in the late 1980s, as interest in sport karate swelled to an all-time high with more tournaments and participants than ever before, so did the size of the annual ratings. To keep up with increased demand, the ratings services added more subdivisions—such as the top five in various weight and forms divisions—in addition to the typical overall top tens. Too, separate national ratings in fighting and forms were instituted for youth. These extra classifications all are included in this chapter.

CHAPTER 14

TOP TEN U.S., EUROPEAN AND JAPANESE CHAMPIONS (1967–92)

FORMAT

Ratings appear from the latest, i.e., 1992, to the earliest, grouped by ratings body. For example, if the year 1985 had two sets of different ratings, *Karate Illustrated's* would appear before those of the North American Sport Karate Association.

At the time of this writing, mid-1993, there were two major national ratings services for American martial arts tournaments. (A third ratings service, the National Black Belt League, was still in its infancy.) Their names and contacts are: North American Sport Karate Association (NASKA), Mike McCoy, Ratings Chairman, 3501 S.W. 2nd Ave., Suite 2200, Gainesville, FL 32607, (904) 375-8144; and the Professional Karate League; Amateur Karate League (PKL; AKL), Glenn Hart, President, P.O. Box 1269, Sandwich, MA 02563.

I made repeated attempts to obtain all the PKL/AKL ratings, but was unsuccessful by the deadline for this book. Consequently, the PKL ratings are the only ones that do not appear in their entirety here.

In the case of a tie, no number will precede the second competitor or country listing. For example, the winners' lists may feature three places with two competitors sharing the third position.

1992 NATIONAL RATINGS

NORTH AMERICAN SPORT KARATE ASSOCIATION (NASKA)

Overall National Champions

Male Fighting
Tony Young

Female Fighting
Laura Armes

Executive Fighting
Terry Creamer

Youth Fighting—Boys
Brian Ruth

Youth Fighting—Girls
Krista Shearer

Male Forms
Gabe Reynaga

Female Forms
Stacey Demejia

Youth Forms
Carmichael Simon

Male Weapons
Richard Brandon

Female Weapons
Michelle Arango

Executive Weapons
Rocky DiRico

Youth Weapons
Bernadette Ambrosia

Best All-Around Male
Hoyoung Pak

Best All-Around Female
Michelle Arango/Elsa Cordero

Best All-Around Executive
Terry Creamer

Best All-Around Youth—Boys
Kody Gilbow

Best All-Around Youth—Girls
Bernadette Ambrosia

Male Rookie of the Year
Tsao Tsao

Female Rookie of the Year

Cheryl Cornman

Youth Rookie of the Year

Jennifer Santiago

Adult Fighting

Men's Superlightweight

1. Tony Young
2. Gabe Reynaga
3. Stewart Lauper
4. Manny Reyes
5. Willie Johnson
6. Dave Henson
7. Brian Nixon
8. Jaime Sabourin
9. Christian Tomooka
10. Larry Swartz

Men's Lightweight

1. Shah Alston
2. Pedro Xavier
3. John Marshall
4. Hoyoung Pak
5. David Macomber
6. Ricky Guinn
7. Phil Baroody
   Frank Decario
8. Eric Don Sheets
9. Derek MotschenBacher
10. Chris Bruner
    Jonathan Wright

Men's Lightmiddleweight

1. Marty Eubanks
2. David Collins
3. E.J. Greer
4. Allen Horner
5. Mike Conroy
   Omar Olumee
6. Alberto Montrond
7. Christopher Rappold
8. Terry Lee
   Frank Baker
9. David Roth

Men's Middleweight

1. Joseph Rivera
2. Karl Bradford
3. Calvin Thomas
4. Jose Pacheco
5. Jeff Gears
6. Jon Rackley
7. Greg Maye

8. Christopher Rappold
   Carl Soriano
9. Greg Burton
10. Paul Edwards

Men's Lightheavyweight

1. Jeff Newton
2. Hakim Alston
3. Tsao Tsao
4. Richard Triplett
5. John Payton
6. Chris Craighead
7. Gary Landreth
8. Ron Richman
9. Abundio Munoz
10. Michael Tull
    Burton Maben

Men's Heavyweight

1. Stephen Babcock
2. Gerald Dawson
3. Anthony Price
4. Mark Baier
5. Chris Daley
6. Derek Panza
   William Eaves
7. Jerry Roberts
8. Chuck Wyant
9. Jeff Newton
10. Rick Bivens
    Samuel Scott

Women's Superlightweight

1. Christine Bannon-Rodrigues
2. Elsa Cordero
3. Amy Corbin
4. Shelly Taylor
5. Lori Lantrip
6. Dawn Santamaria

Women's Lightweight

1. Laura Armes
2. Dawn Santamaria
3. Michelle Maizis
4. Kellie Hausner
5. Linda Dice
6. Emily Cooper
7. Holly York
8. Shelly Taylor

Women's Lightmiddleweight

1. Michelle Arango
2. Cheryl Cornman
3. Laura Armes
4. Chris McConnell

Women's Middleweight

1. Dawn Allen
2. Michelle Griffin
3. Mitzi Tyler
4. Nicole Adams

Senior Men (43 & Over)

1. John Prevatt
2. Bill Mason
3. Wali Islam
4. Gary Nichols
5. J.C. Copeland
6. Dennis Kelly
7. Nelson Jones
8. Darrell Richardson
9. Richard Schnapper
10. Bob Dillard
    Larry Bullard

Senior Men (35–42)

LIGHTWEIGHT

1. Leroy Taylor
2. Joshua Harper
3. Jay Hirleman
4. Joseph Zander
5. Roy Johns
6. Anthony Gallo
7. Troy McCaskell
   Marty Knight
8. Donnie Danner
9. Lamon Kersey
10. Ronnie Moore

HEAVYWEIGHT

1. Terry Creamer
2. Dave Holman
3. Barry Grizzard
4. Glenn Mehlman
5. Laymon Williamson
6. Tony Baker
   Robert Easley
7. Bill Brassette
8. Leonard Horger
9. Phil Morgan
10. Jose Jordan

Adult Forms

Men

AMERICAN

1. Richard Brandon
2. Tsao Tsao
3. Christian Tomooka
4. Phil Baroody
5. Larry Swartz
6. John Mason

7. David Collins
8. Willie Johnson
9. Mark Baier
10. Chris Bruner

CHINESE
1. Hoyoung Pak
2. Willie Johnson
3. Allen Horner
4. Woody Wong
5. Shaun Hahn
6. Phaun Phan

JAPANESE/OKINAWAN
1. Gabe Reynaga
2. John Marshall
3. Marty Eubanks
4. Mark Fletcher
5. Richard Triplett
6. E.J. Greer
7. David Roth
8. Larry Maddin
9. Pedro Xavier
   Cheech Luzzi
   Louis Clay

KOREAN
1. Dave Macomber
2. Eric San Jose
3. Guy Hankins
4. Karl Bradford
5. Michael Tull
6. Anthony Rockwell
7. Pedro Xavier
8. Abundio Munoz

MUSICAL (CO-ED)
1. Chris Casamassa
2. Abundio Munoz
3. Todd Allen
4. Dan McFarland
5. Dave Henson
6. Terry Lee
7. Rich Fukumoto
8. Scot Shannon
9. Francis Pineda
10. Hoyoung Pak
    Woody Wong

SENIOR WEAPONS (CO-ED)
1. Rocky DiRico
2. Dan McFarland
3. Terry Creamer
4. Arthur Sands
5. Phil Morgan
6. Lamon Kersey
7. Jeffrey Levitt
8. Nelson Jones

9. Bill Mason
10. Wali Islam

SENIORS
1. Terry Creamer
2. Rocky DiRico
3. Phil Morgan
   Mie Matsuoka
4. Lynn Gregory
5. Arthur Sands
6. Jeffrey Levitt
7. Jimmy Edwards
8. Lamon Kersey
9. Dennis Kelly
10. Donnie Danner

HARD-STYLE WEAPONS
1. Chris Casamassa
2. Dave Macomber
3. John Marshall
4. David Collins
5. Todd Allen
6. Mark Fletcher
7. Marty Eubanks
8. Terry Lee
   Rich Fukumoto
   Pedro Xavier
9. Cheech Luzzi
10. Tsao Tsao
    Dave Henson
    Bob Lamattina

SOFT-STYLE WEAPONS
1. Richard Brandon
2. Hoyoung Pak
3. Mark Baier
4. Willie Johnson
5. Allen Horner
6. Woody Wong

Women
HARD STYLE
1. Stacey Demejia
2. Elsa Cordero
3. Michelle Arango
4. Dawn Santamaria
5. Michelle Maizis
6. Amy Corbin
7. Kellie Hausner
8. Linda Dice
9. Laura Armes
10. Becky Kobrowski

SOFT STYLE
1. Christine Bannon-Rodrigues
2. Geri James
3. Michelle Boutin

WEAPONS
1. Michaelle Arango
2. Stacey Demejia
3. Elsa Cordero
4. Christine Bannon-Rodrigues
5. Michelle Maizis
6. Dawn Santamaria
7. Amy Corbin

Youth Fighting

Males (15–17)
1. Brian Ruth
2. Michael Shurina
3. Gerry Iamunno
4. Chris Goldberg
5. Chad Stevens
6. Jon Valera
7. Michael Terrace
8. Carmichael Simon
9. Diego Lopez
10. Philip Quinones

Males (13–14)
1. Hector Santiago
2. Barry Gonzalez
3. Jason Shapiro
4. Bruce Cervantez
5. Louis Puleo
6. Clint Darden
7. Evan Smith
8. Michael Butts
9. Todd Humes
10. Jack Cohen

Males (11–12)
1. Andrew Brown
2. Jay Hirleman
3. Trip Ferguson
4. Jerrod Choate
5. Peter Allende
6. Nick Boccagno
7. Kris Khamvongsa
8. Nathan Loftis
9. Josh Pilquist
10. Cory Parsons

Females (15–17)
1. Krista Shearer
2. Jennifer Yanoff
3. Krishea Strayn
4. Ming Tran
5. Jennifer Katz
6. Denise Moore
   Amy Giesler

Females (13–14)
1. Bernadette Ambrosia
2. Angela Richards
3. Meadow Maze
4. Aisha Thornton
5. Dawn Biancaniello
6. Roshanna Malone
7. Shatevia Allen

Females (11–12)
1. Li-Ling Li
2. Salim McDaniel
3. Christine LaCasse
4. Greer Martin

Co-Ed (9–10)
1. Joseph Guarneri
2. Michael Adams
   Kody Gilbow
3. Anthony Stewart
4. Emily Pokora
5. Amy Pokora
6. Vincent Cohen
7. Justin Sheppard
8. Michelle Evans
9. Jaime Tutton
   Robert McNeill
   Paul Goins
10. Kristopher Katira

Co-Ed (8 & Under)
1. Eboni Adams
2. Jennifer Santiago
3. Amir Hoskins
4. Ashley Kohler
5. Joseph Tran
6. Kalman Csoka
7. Ryan Gregory
8. Jessica Goldberg

Youth Forms

Co-Ed Musical (17 & Under)
1. Carmichael Simon
2. Don Theerathada
3. Kim Do
4. Ming Tran
5. Kris Khamvongsa
   Bruce Cervantez
6. Krishea Strayn
7. Justin Sheppard
8. Chris Goldberg
9. Evan Smith
10. Eboni Adams
    Clint Darden

Co-Ed (15–17)
1. Brian Ruth
2. Chad Stevens
   Krista Shearer
3. Mike Chaturantabut
4. Jon Valera
5. Diego Lopez
6. Brandon Kersey
7. Brian Spiess
   Can-Ye Wong
8. Jeffrey Lamb
   Jennifer Yanoff
   Michael Terrace
9. Brian Brunelle
   Gary Waugh
   Philip Quinones
   Ming Tran

Co-Ed (13–14)
1. Bernadette Ambrosia
2. Jason Shapiro
3. Hector Santiago
4. Jack Cohen
5. Louis Puleo
6. Meadow Maze
7. Aaron Gestl
8. Todd Humes
9. Michael Butts
   David Proctor
10. David Alderson
    Roshanna Malone

Co-Ed (11–12)
1. Justin Margotto
2. Trip Ferguson
3. Peter Allende
4. Li-Ling Li
5. Nick Boccagno
6. Jerrod Choate
7. Jarrod Newsome
8. Josh Pilquist
9. Michael Butts
10. Randall Dugas
    Jeff Lindeman

Co-Ed (9–10)
1. Kody Gilbow
2. Emily Pokora
3. Anthony Stewart
4. Vincent Cohen
5. Amy Pokora
6. William Hillmuth
7. Joseph Guarneri
   Kristoph Katira
8. Michael Adams

9. Paul Goins
10. Nathan Kollath
    Jimmy Fritsch

Co-Ed Weapons (15–17)
1. Brian Ruth
2. Carmichael Simon
3. Don Theerathada
4. Mike Chaturantabut
5. Jon Valera
6. Brandon Kersey
7. Chad Stevens
8. Jennifer Yanoff
   Brian Spiess
9. Brian Brunelle
10. Zachary Day
    Gary Waugh

Co-Ed Weapons (13–14)
1. Bernadette Ambrosia
2. Hector Santiago
3. Jason Shapiro
4. David Alderson
5. Michael Butts
6. Louis Puleo
7. Bruce Cervantez
8. David Proctor
9. Clint Darden
10. Todd Humes
    Dawn Biancaniello

Co-Ed Weapons (11–12)
1. Justin Margotto
2. Andrew Brown
3. Peter Allende
4. Jerrod Choate
5. Josh Pilquist
6. Kim Do
7. Michael Butts
8. Lyle Hull
9. Michael Lightfoot
10. Li-Ling Li

Co-Ed Weapons (10 & Under)
1. Kody Gilbow
2. Jennifer Santiago
3. Emily Pokora
4. Joseph Tran
5. Eboni Adams
6. Joseph Guarneri
7. William Hillmuth
8. Amy Pokora
   Anthony Stewart
9. Kristopher Katira
10. Vincent Cohen
    Thomas Lucas

1990 NATIONAL RATINGS

NORTH AMERICAN SPORT KARATE ASSOCIATION (NASKA)

Overall National Champions

Male Fighting
Mike Smith

Female Fighting
Brenda Hund

Executive Fighting
Steve Anderson

Youth Fighting—Boys
Adam Keister

Youth Fighting—Girls
Krysta Shearer

Male Forms
Saeed Delkash

Female Forms
Elsa Cordero

Youth Forms
Jon Valera

Male Weapons
Mike Bernardo

Female Weapons
Kathy Quan

Executive Weapons
Rocky DiRico

Youth Weapons
Jon Valera

Best All-Around Male
Mike Bernardo

Best All-Around Female
Elsa Cordero

Best All-Around Executive
Phil Morgan

Best All-Around Youth—Boys
Jon Valera

Best All-Around Youth—Girls
Bernadette Ambrosia

Male Rookie of the Year
Gabe Reynaga

Female Rookie of the Year
Michelle Arango

Youth Rookie of the Year
Jason Dawson

Adult Fighting

Men's Superlightweight
1. Gabe Reynaga
2. Jose Pacheco
3. Keith Scott
4. Barry Shackelford
5. Charles Rice
6. Michael Dietrich
   Patrick Van Landingham
7. Waymon Beavers
8. George Connelly
9. Terrance Hightower
10. Cliff Strand
    Eddie Thomas

Men's Lightweight
1. Marty Eubanks
2. Erik Ireland
3. Ricardo Desouza
4. Shah Alston
5. Orlando Gonzalez
6. Marc Jones
7. Joey Imperatori
8. John Bonilla
9. Mondo Reyes
10. Bill Young
    Craig Curran

Men's Lightmiddleweight
1. Mike Green
2. Saeed Delkash
3. Mike Bernardo
4. Joey Escobar
5. E.J. Greer
6. Marc Jones
7. Papo Villarrubia
8. Jessie Thornton
9. Bob Lamattina
   John Townsend
   Scott McIntosh
10. Marty Eubanks

Men's Middleweight
1. Anthony Halloway
2. Calvin Thomas
3. Hakim Alston
4. Paul Edwards
5. Willie Floyd
6. Carl Soriano
7. Bob Lamattina
8. Kenneth Osborne
9. Karl Bradford
10. Joey Escobar

Men's Lightheavyweight
1. Michael Smith
2. Hakim Alston
3. Curtis Jordan
4. Richard Triplett
5. Jack Foster
6. Edward Littlejohn
7. Zarko Stojanovich
8. Steve Magill

Men's Heavyweight
1. Shon Adams
2. Derek Panza
3. David Kiss
4. Gerald Dawson
5. Steve Boyles
6. Robert Franklin
7. John Douvris
8. Norman Wray
9. Mel Gutic
10. Berry Grizzard

Women's Lightweight
1. Brenda Hund
2. Elsa Cordero
3. Dawn Santamaria
4. Michelle Arango
5. Karen Kenley
6. Kim Curran
7. Jessica Robeson
8. Carolyn Jenkins
   Cynthia Silvestre
   Vickie Holobaugh
   Patty House
9. Linda Dice
   Meredith Sawers

Women's Heavyweight
1. Nicki Carlson
2. Kierston Sims
3. Angela Webb
4. Chavela Aaron
5. Dawn Allen

6. Lori Bennett
7. Kathleen LeBlanc
8. Sue Brazelton
9. Melanie Johnson
10. T'anna Baird

Executive Men

1. Steve Anderson
2. Dan Boccagno
3. Marty Knight
4. Joshua Harper
   James Hobby
5. Lewis Wilson
6. Laymon Williamson
   Paul Haroian
7. Ron Jenkins
8. Phil Morgan
9. Derek Reid
   Hector Santiago
10. J.C. Copeland

Senior Men

1. Gary Nichols
2. Wali Islam
3. William Rowling
4. B.J. Allen
5. Calvin Thomas
   B.J. Lewis
6. David Johnson
7. Emile Wright
8. Stewart Lauper
   Jack Morris

Adult Forms

Men

AMERICAN (CO-ED)

1. Saeed Delkash
2. Mondo Reyes
3. Keith Scott
4. James Hardy
   Hoyoung Pak
   Larry Lam
5. Glen Willis
6. David Collins
   Brian Curran
7. Ricardo Desouza
   George Connelly
8. Ron Richman
   John Mason
9. Jason Buckland

CHINESE

1. Phillip Wong
2. Anthony Marquez

3. Wil Allen
4. Javonne Holmes
5. Kyle MacArthur
6. Ben Salas
7. Greg Walraven
8. Brian Crowe
9. Hoyoung Pak
10. William Gaudette
    Woody Wong

JAPANESE/OKINAWAN

1. Gabe Reynaga
2. Mike Bernardo
3. Grant Campbell
4. Papo Villarrubia
5. Erik Ireland
6. Marty Eubanks
7. John Palitti
8. Todd Dunphy
   Miguel Hernandez
9. Charles Rice
10. Kevin Taylor

KOREAN

1. Dave Macomber
2. Michael Dietrich
3. Eric San Jose
4. Barry Shackelford
5. Steve Torres
6. Young Bok Lee
7. Joe Gelling
8. Steve Magill
9. Ricardo Desouza
10. John Townsend
    Orlando Gonzalez

MUSICAL (CO-ED)

1. Hoyoung Pak
2. Chris Casamassa
3. Dan McFarland
4. David Tu
5. Larry Lam
6. Chris Henderson
7. Geraldine James
8. Harold DeSauguste
   Craig Curran
9. Rich Fukumoto
10. Andrew Hartono

SENIOR WEAPONS (CO-ED)

1. Rocky DiRico
   Phil Morgan
2. John Gallaugher
3. James Hobby
4. Hector Santiago
5. Larry Isaac
6. Brian Ricci
7. Eric Chen

8. Dewey Earwood
   William Rowling
9. Dan McFarland
   Mary Smale
10. Wali Islam

SENIORS (CO-ED)

1. Phil Morgan
2. Vincent Riqueros
3. Rocky DiRico
4. John Gallaugher
5. Hector Santiago
6. James Hobby
7. Brian Ricci
8. Larry Isaac
9. Skipper Ingram
10. Dewey Earwood
    Hayme Serrato
    Efon Chen
    Bill Young
    Patrick Petitjean

HARD-STYLE WEAPONS

1. Mike Bernardo
2. Dan McFarland
3. Dave Macomber
4. Chris Casamassa
5. Mondo Reyes
6. Erik Ireland
7. John Palitti
8. Rich Fukumoto
9. John Townsend
10. Saeed Delkash

SOFT-STYLE WEAPONS

1. Hoyoung Pak
2. Phillip Wong
3. Kyle MacArthur
4. Andrew Hartono
5. Wil Allen
6. Greg Walraven
   Anthony Marquez
   Carl Romain
7. Brian Crowe
   Javonne Holmes
8. Woody Wong
9. William Gaudette
10. Chris Henderson

Women

HARD STYLE

1. Elsa Cordero
2. Michelle Arango
3. Kathy Quan
4. Dawn Santamaria
5. Kathleen LeBlanc
6. Jessica Robeson

7. Carolyn Jenkins
8. Melanie Johnson
9. T'anna Baird
10. Susan Suinn

SOFT STYLE
1. Yungchu Kim
2. Geraldine James
3. Ava Powell
4. Nancy Allen
5. Jeannie Dunn
6. Deborah Chen
7. Elsa Cordero
   Michelle Griffin
8. Mer-Mer Chen
9. Sue Skaroupka

WEAPONS
1. Kathy Quan
2. Yungchu Kim
3. Michelle Arango
4. Kathleen LeBlanc
5. Dawn Santamaria
6. Geraldine James
7. Elsa Cordero
8. Mer-Mer Chen
9. Jeannie Dunn
   Karen Kenley
10. Nancy Allen

Youth Fighting

Males (16–17)
1. Robert Hindricks
2. Brin Smith
3. John Marshall
4. Frank Decria
5. Griff Tester
6. Jack Lloyd
7. Steven Sos
8. Shawn Balentine
9. Jason Jones
10. Mike Posano
    Jeff Liotta

Males (14–15)
1. Todd Finney
2. Mike Chaturantabut
3. Jon Valera
4. Larry Brown
5. Phillip Pippin
6. Chad Love
7. Joe Deatherage
8. Bobby Barnett
9. Ben Hund
10. Mike Shurina
    Jose Cordero

Males (12–13)
1. Brian Ruth
2. Hector Santiago
3. Clint Darden
4. Carmichael Simon
5. Rich Costello
6. Chris Goldberg
7. Otis Hooper
8. Steve Guerrero
9. Mike Pulliam
10. Jeremy Martin

Females (16–17)
1. Tiffany Costello
2. Lori Temple
3. Soo Park

Females (14–15)
1. Krista Shearer
2. Rashia Scott
3. Lana Mosley
4. Cherie Ground
5. Kristy Adams
6. Nicole Cifarelli
7. Charity Girt
8. Leann Williams
9. Kristen McLaughlin

Females (12–13)
1. Jennifer Yanoff
2. Rosiland Russell
3. Lona Love
4. Karen McLaughlin

Co-Ed (10–11)
1. Adam Keister
2. Jerry Mosley
3. Nick Boccagno
4. Bernadette Ambrosia
5. Louis Puleo
6. Jarrett Weeks
7. Matthew Tiller
8. Todd Humes
9. Billy Linkwald
   Lindsey Huff
   Ari Welkom
10. Scott Serbin

Co-Ed (8–9)
1. Jason Dawson
2. Matt Gordon
3. Lori Sojack
4. Lace Guillermo
5. David Kline
6. Georgie Dominguez

7. Matthew Hayes
   Jennifer Dinger
8. David Lumpkin
9. Tiffany Williams
   Christopher Byrd
   Kevin McGrath
10. Seth Anapolsky
    Tim Knight
    Justin Sheppard

Co-Ed (6–7)
1. Mandy Gordon
2. Sean Jones
3. Jimmy Fritsch
4. James Kapner
5. Justin Goodge

Youth Forms

Co-Ed Musical (17 & Under)
1. Mike Chaturantabut
2. Scott Parker
3. Clint Darden
4. David Kline
5. Jerry Mosley
6. Jarrett Weeks
   Hiro Koda
7. Scot Shannon
   David Lumpkin
8. Eddie Landa
   Joseph Swayne
9. Arthur Gee
10. Matthew Hayes

Co-Ed (16–17)
1. Brian Smith
2. Jeff Liotta
3. John Marshall
4. Robert Hendricks
5. Griff Tester
6. Jennifer Schwartz
7. Jack Lloyd
8. Leo Nakatani
9. Eddie Gomez
10. Shawn Balentine

Co-Ed (14–15)
1. Jon Valera
2. Krista Shearer
3. Phillip Pippin
4. Lana Mosley
5. Scott Parker
6. Inki Kim
7. Larry Brown
8. Kristy Adams

9. Rashia Scott
10. Cherie Ground
    Mike Terrace

Co-Ed (12–13)

1. Carmichael Simon
2. Brian Ruth
3. Hector Santiago
4. Jennifer Yanoff
   Jeremy Martin
5. Mike Pulliam
6. Russell Taylor
7. Thomas Woodring
8. Brian Short
   Ben Wides
9. Mae Hsu
   Ari Welkom
10. Brian Spiess
    Otis Hooper

Co-Ed (10–11)

1. Adam Keister
2. Bernadette Ambrosia
3. Nick Boccagno
4. Louis Puleo
5. Jerry Mosley
6. Todd Humes
7. Jarrett Weeks
8. Michael Smith
   Lindsey Huff
9. David Lumpkin
   Ari Welkom
10. Nicole Forel
    Christian Racine

Co-Ed (8–9)

1. Jason Dawson
2. Lance Guillermo
3. Lori Sajack
4. Matt Gordon
5. Justin Margotto
   Georgie Dominguez
6. Justin Sheppard
7. Christopher Byrd
8. Benjamin Nivison
   Kevin McGrath
   Thomas Price
   Ben Wides
9. Tiffany Williams
10. Jennifer Dinger

Co-Ed (6–7)

1. Sean Jones
   Mandy Gordon
2. Jimmy Fritsch

3. James Kapner
   Ben Wides
4. Justin Goodge

Co-Ed Weapons (14–17)

1. Jon Valera
2. Brian Smith
3. Mike Chaturantabut
4. John Marshall
5. Robert Hendricks
6. Hiro Koda
7. Soo Park
8. Jeff Liotta
9. Jennifer Schwartz
10. Scott Parker

Co-Ed Weapons (10–13)

1. Bernadette Ambrosia
2. Brian Ruth
3. Adam Keister
4. Carmichael Simon
5. Jeremy Martin
6. Nick Boccagno
7. Eddie Landa
8. Thomas Woodring
9. Jennifer Yanoff
10. Jerry Mosley

Co-Ed Weapons (9 & Under)

1. Jason Dawson
2. Lance Guillermo
3. Jimmy Fritsch
4. Ben Wides
5. David Lumpkin
6. Georgie Dominguez
7. Benjamin Nivison
8. James Kapner
   Justin Sheppard
9. Sean Jones
10. Jason Longo
    Christopher Byrd

1989 NATIONAL RATINGS

NORTH AMERICAN SPORT KARATE ASSOCIATION (NASKA)

Adult Fighting

Men Overall

1. Hakim Alston
2. Shon Adams

3. Mike Smith
4. Anthony Holloway
5. Steve Anderson
6. Mike Green
7. Marty Eubanks
8. Shah Alston
9. Jose Pacheco
10. Joey Shiflett

Women Overall

1. Chavela Aaron
2. Kierston Sims
3. Brenda Hund
4. Elsa Cordero
5. Laurie McCutcheon
6. Kathy Marlor
7. Cindy Ingram
8. Nicki Carlson
9. Melanie Johnson
10. Kathleen Leblanc

Senior Men's Overall

1. Steve Curran
2. Dan Baccagno
3. James Hobby
4. Laymon Williamson
5. Harold Burrage

Divisional Ratings

Men's Superlightweight

1. Jose Pacheco
2. Donald Brady
3. Michael Dietrich
4. Jarry Prince
5. Leonard Creer

Men's Lightweight

1. Marty Eubanks
2. Shah Alston
3. Joey Shiflett
4. Jessie Thornton
5. Pedro Xavier

Men's Light Middleweight

1. Anthony Holloway
2. Marc Jones
3. Greg Greer
4. Saeed Delkash
5. Mike Bernardo

Men's Middleweight

1. Hakim Alston
2. Mike Green
3. Jerry Fontanez

4. Paul Edwards
5. Anthony Holloway

Men's Lightheavyweight
1. Mike Smith
2. Curtis Jordan
3. Edward Littlejohn
4. Marino Jones
5. Alvin Prouder

Men's Heavyweight
1. Shon Adams
2. Steve Anderson
3. Andre Richardson
4. Bruce Leamer
5. Satch Williams

Women's Lightweight
1. Brenda Hund
2. Elsa Cordero
3. Laurie McCutcheon
4. Kathy Marlor
5. Cindy Ingram

Women's Heavyweight
1. Chavela Aaron
2. Kierston Sims
3. Nicki Carlson
4. Melanie Johnson
5. Kathleen LeBlanc

Senior Men (43 & Over)
1. Steve Curran
2. Ken Eubanks
3. Gary Nickols
4. Chuck Timmons
5. Wali Islam

Senior Men (35–42)
LIGHTWEIGHT
1. Dan Boccagno
2. Lee Ireland
3. Joe Pina
4. Geoffrey Canada
5. Joshua Harper

HEAVYWEIGHT
1. James Hobby
2. Laymon Williamson
3. Harold Burrage
4. Paul Haroian
5. Carl Clary

Adult Forms

Men Overall
1. Charlie Lee

2. Hoyoung Pak
3. Mike Bernardo
4. Steven Ho
5. Michael Dietrich
6. Chris Casamassa
7. Saeed Delkash
8. Dave Macomber
9. Norman Lacaden
10. Anthony Marquez

Women Overall
1. Yung Chi Kim
2. Elsa Cordero
3. Kathy Quan
4. Kathy Marlor
5. Ava Powell
6. Geri James
7. Susan Suinn
8. Toni Lee
9. Michelle Delgiorno
10. Trudy Briker

Co-Ed Weapons Overall
1. Mike Bernardo
2. Hoyoung Pak
3. Dan McFarland
4. Anthony Marquez
5. Charlie Lee
6. Kathy Quan
7. Dave Macomber
8. Chris Casamassa
9. Gary Dezarn
10. Phillip Wong

Divisional Ratings

American
1. Steven Ho
2. Saeed Delkash
3. Andre Sack
4. Jerry Prince
5. Yong Bok Lee

Chinese
1. Hoyoung Pak
2. Anthony Marquez
3. Richard Brandon
4. Gary Dezarn
5. Karl Romain

Japanese/Okinawan
1. Mike Bernardo
2. Norman Lacaden
3. John Palitti
4. Papo Villarubia
5. Cheech Luzzic

Korean
1. Charlie Lee
2. Michael Dietrich
3. Dave Macomber
4. Steve Torres
5. Joey Shiflett

Open/Musical
1. Hoyoung Pak
2. Chris Casamassa
3. Dan McFarland
4. Larry Lam
5. Jose Pacheco

Women's Hard Style
1. Elsa Cordero
2. Kathy Quan
3. Kathy Marlor
4. Susan Suinn
5. Toni Lee

Women's Soft Style
1. Yung Chu Kim
2. Ava Powell
3. Geri James
4. Trudy Briker
5. Karen Lopez

Senior Men
1. Steve Curran
2. Rocky DiRico
3. Dewey Earwood
4. Phil Morgan
5. Felix Vasquez
   Richard King

Hard-Style Co-Ed Weapons
1. Mike Bernardo
2. Dan McFarland
3. Charlie Lee
4. Kathy Quan
5. Dave Macombar

Soft-Style Co-Ed Weapons
1. Hoyoung Pak
2. Anthony Marquez
3. Richard Brandon
4. Gary Dezarn
5. Phillip Wong

Senior Weapons
1. Steve Curran
2. Rocky DiRico
3. Dewey Earwood
4. Phil Morgan
5. James Hobby

Self-Defense

1. Dale McCutcheon
2. Laurie McCutcheon
3. Don Moden
4. Felix Vasquez
5. Nancy Deeg

Youth Fighting

Male (15–17)

1. Robert Hendrick
2. Mike Saxon
3. Sean Green
4. Keith Scott
5. Gaffer Adam

Male (12–14)

1. Brian Ruth
2. Jon Valera
3. Phillip Pippin
4. Todd Finney
5. Mike Shurina

Female (15–17)

1. Tiffany Costello
2. Lori Temple
3. Christina Muccini
4. Shellie Blanks
5. Kelly Holt

Female (12–14)

1. Krista Shearer
2. Jennifer Yanoff
3. Shannon Ashby
4. Rashia Scott
5. Lana Moseley

Co-Ed (11 & Under)

1. Seneca Luther
2. Nick Gingras
3. Adam Keister
4. Seth Anapolsky
5. Jimmy Fritsch

Youth Forms

Co-Ed (15–17)

1. Mike Saxon
2. David Oakley
3. Gaffer Adam
4. Keith Scott
5. Dietra Spencer

Co-Ed (12–14)

1. Jon Valera
2. Jeff Sue

3. Mike Chaturantabut
4. Jennifer Yanoff
5. Brian Ruth

Co-Ed (11 & Under)

1. Seneca Luther
2. Eddie Landa
3. Bernadette Ambrosia
4. Adam Keister
5. Jarrett Weeks

Weapons

1. Jeff Sue
2. Mike Saxon
3. Jon Valera
4. Seneca Luther
5. Robery Hendricks

1988 NATIONAL RATINGS

NORTH AMERICAN SPORT KARATE ASSOCIATION (NASKA)

Fighting

Men

1. Anthony Holloway
2. Hakim Alston
3. Jerry Fontanez
4. Anthony Price
5. Marty Eubanks
6. Anthony Young
7. Jerry Prince
8. Marc Jones
9. Steve Anderson
10. Jessie Thornton

Women

1. Brenda Hund
2. Chavela Aaron
3. Linda Denley
4. Christine Bannon
5. Nicki Carlson
6. Elsa Cordero
7. Kierston Sims
8. Cheryl Nance
9. Kathy Marlor
10. Kellyrae Marrs

Seniors

1. Belvin Eaves
2. Steve Curran

3. Wali Islam
4. Carl Clary
5. Geoffrey Canada

Juniors (13–15)

1. Robert Hedricks
2. Keith Scott
3. John Marshall
4. Michael Saxon
5. Arley Tree

Forms

Men

1. Charlie Lee
2. Richard Brandon
3. Jean Frenette
4. Andre Sack
5. Hosung Pak
6. Mike Bernardo
7. Chris Casamassa
8. Dan McFarland
9. Hoyoung Pak
10. Michael Dietrich

Women

1. Christine Bannon
2. Regina Gonzales
3. Kathy Quan
4. Elsa Cordero
5. Julie Fredericks
6. Kathy Marlor
7. Cori Ertha
8. Kelee Anderson
9. Yungchi Kim
10. Carla Fortney

Seniors

1. Jerry Otto
2. Steve Curran
3. Brian Ricci
4. Rocky DiRico
5. Lou Ferrer

Co-Ed Weapons

1. Dan McFarland
2. Hosung Pak
3. Mike Bernardo
4. Kevin Thompson
5. Richard Brandon
6. Christine Bannon
7. Jean Frenette
8. Chris Casamassa
9. Hoyung Pak
10. Terry Creamer

Senior Weapons
1. Jerry Otto
2. Steve Curran
3. Brian Ricci
4. Rocky DiRico
5. Felix Vasquez

PROFESSIONAL KARATE LEAGUE (PKL)

Fighting

Men Overall
1. Anthony Holloway
2. Tony Young
3. Tony Price
4. Steve Anderson
5. Jeff Gears
6. Jerry Fontanez
7. Hakim Alston
8. Billy Blanks
9. Terry Creamer
10. Chip Wright

Women Overall
1. Chavela Aaron
2. Linda Denley
3. Christine Bannon
4. Brenda Hund
5. Cheryl Nance
6. Nicki Carlson
7. Kim-Du Trinh
8. Veronica DeSantos
9. Nicole Quist
10. Elsa Cordero

Seniors
1. Belvin Eaves
2. Carl Clary
3. Wali Islam
4. Steve Curran
5. Sabu Lewis
6. Geoffrey Canada
7. Billy Bryant
8. Clarence Reeves
9. Larry Isaac
10. Doug Peoples

Divisional Ratings
MEN'S LIGHTWEIGHT
1. Tony Young
2. Saha Alston
3. Ibrahim Abdalla
4. Pedro Xavier

5. Gery Eblan

MEN'S MIDDLEWEIGHT
1. Anthony Holloway
2. Jeff Gears
3. Kevin Thompson
4. Marc Jones
5. Tony Morrison

MEN'S LIGHTHEAVYWEIGHT
1. Jerry Fontanez
2. Hakim Alston
3. Billy Blanks
4. Chip Wright
5. Michael Smith

MEN'S HEAVYWEIGHT
1. Anthony Price
2. Steve Anderson
3. Terry Creamer
4. Richard Plowden
5. Andre Richardson

WOMEN'S LIGHTWEIGHT
1. Christine Bannon
2. Brenda Hund
3. Cheryl Nance
4. Kim-Du Trinh
5. Elsa Cordero

WOMEN'S HEAVYWEIGHT
1. Chavela Aaron
2. Linda Denley
3. Nicki Carlson
4. Veronica DeSantos
5. Nicole Quist

Triple Crown Winner
Kevin Thompson

Forms

Men Overall
1. Charlie Lee
2. Hosung Pak
3. Jean Frenette
4. Keith Hirabayashi
5. Kevin Thompson
6. Domingo Llanos
7. Richard Brandon
8. Mike Bernardo
9. Sonny Onowo
10. Hoyoung Pak

Women Overall
1. Christine Bannon
2. Alice Chang-Chung
3. Regina Gonzales
4. Elsa Cordero

5. Kim-Du Trinh
6. Kelee Anderson
7. Cheryl Nance
8. Kathy Marlor
9. Yung Chu Kim
10. Cori Ertha

Co-Ed Weapons Overall
1. Keith Hirabayashi
2. Kevin Thompson
3. Richard Brandon
4. Hosung Pak
5. Jean Frenette
6. Mike Bernardo
7. Alice Chang-Chung
8. Christine Bannon
9. Hoyoung Pak
10. Charlie Lee

Seniors
1. Jerry Otto
2. Brian Ricci
3. Steve Curran
4. Felix Vasquez
5. Vic Coffin
6. Skipper Ingham
7. Ronald Williams
8. Billy Bryant
9. Edwin Rhodes
10. Frank Perry

Senior Weapons
1. Jerry Otto
2. Brian Ricci
3. Felix Vasquez
4. Steve Curran
5. Rocky DiRico

Divisional Ratings
CHINESE
1. Hosung Pak
2. Keith Hirabayashi
3. Richard Brandon
4. Hoyoung Pak
5. Javonne Holmes

JAPANESE/OKINAWAN
1. Jean Frenette
2. Kevin Thompson
3. Domingo Llanos
4. Mike Bernardo
5. Sonny Onowo

KOREAN
1. Charlie Lee
2. Michael Dietrich

3. Jerry Fontanez
4. Young Bok Lee
5. Dave Macombar

OPEN
1. Charlie Lee
2. Jean Frenette
3. Keith Hirabayashi
4. Kevin Thompson
5. Richard Brandon

HARD-STYLE WEAPONS
1. Kevin Thompson
2. Jean Frenette
3. Mike Bernardo
4. Charlie Lee
5. Jerry Otto

SOFT-STYLE WEAPONS
1. Keith Hirabayashi
2. Richard Brandon
3. Hosung Pak
4. Alice Chang-Chung
5. Hoyoung Pak

WOMEN'S HARD STYLE
1. Regina Gonzales
2. Elsa Cordero
3. Kim-Du Trinh
4. Cheryl Nance
5. Kathy Marlor

WOMEN'S SOFT-STYLE
1. Christine Bannon
2. Alice Chang-Chung
3. Kelee Anderson
4. Yung Chu Kim
5. Cori Ertha

Triple Crown Winner

Christine Bannon

Note: Bannon is the only competitor nationally rated in fighting, forms and weapons.

1987 NATIONAL RATINGS

NORTH AMERICAN SPORT KARATE ASSOCIATION (NASKA)

Fighting

Men Overall
1. Steve Anderson

2. Anthony Holloway
3. Tony Young
4. Terry Creamer
5. Keith Bowers
6. Marty Eubanks
7. Anthony Price
8. Billy Blanks
9. Jerry Prince
10. Joey Shiflett

Women Overall
1. Linda Denley
2. Christine Bannon
3. Nicole Quist
4. Cheryl Nance
5. Kim-Du Trinh
6. Veronica DeSantos
7. Chavela Aaron
8. Nicki Carlson
9. Kathy Faust
10. Michonne Keeble

Senior Men Overall
1. Steve Curran
2. Belvin Eaves
3. Ken Eubanks
4. Harold Burrage
5. Sadu Lewis
6. Lou Hopkins
7. J.C. Copeland
8. Wali Islam
9. Terry Crook
10. Clarence Reeves

Forms

Men
1. Jean Frenette
2. Charlie Lee
3. Phillip Wong
4. Keith Hirabayashi
5. Domingo Llanos
6. Andre Sack
7. Hosung Pak
8. Dan McFarland
9. Kevin Thompson
10. Terry Creamer

Women
1. Christine Bannon
2. Kim-Du Trinh
3. Regina Gonzales
4. Kathy Quan
5. Julie Frederick

6. Kelee Anderson
7. Helen Chung Vasilliadis
8. Patricia Humphrey
9. Alice Chang
10. Cheryl Nance

Senior Men
1. Steve Curran
2. Chuck Merriman
3. Jerry Otto
4. Gale Holden
5. Brian Ricci
6. Humberto Medeiros
7. Derry Doyle
8. Jack Scott
9. Dale Kirby
10. Terry Leman

Co-Ed Weapons
1. Keith Hirabayashi
2. Dan McFarland
3. Kevin Thompson
4. Terry Creamer
5. Hosung Pak
6. Phillip Wong
7. Deno Cain
8. Javonne Holmes
9. Kathy Quan
10. Chris Casamassa

PROFESSIONAL KARATE LEAGUE (PKL)

In 1987, the PKL added the American Karate League (AKL), embracing divisions for those sixteen years old and under. At year's end, it began ranking these younger national champions in divisional top tens.

Fighting

Men
1. Steve Anderson
2. Billy Blanks
3. Terry Creamer
4. Tony Young
5. Keith Bowers
6. Jerry Prince
7. Kevin Thompson
8. Anthony Holloway
9. Anthony Price
10. Jesse Thornton

Women

1. Linda Denley
2. Nicole Quist
3. Christine Bannon
4. Kim-Du Trinh
5. Cheryl Nance
6. Michonne Keeble
7. Nicki Carlson
8. Veronica DeSantos
9. Rhonda Alexander
10. Chavela Aaron

Executive Men

1. Steve Curran
2. Belvin Eaves
3. Johnny Copeland
4. Harold Burrage
5. Ken Eubanks
6. Sabu Lewis
7. Wali Islam
8. Lou Hopkins
9. Dale Kirby
10. Terry Crook

Forms

Men

1. Keith Hirabayashi
2. Jean Frenette
3. Charlie Lee
4. Phillip Wong
5. Hosung Pak
6. Javonne Holmes
7. Terry Creamer
8. Jerry Prince
9. Domingo Llanos
10. Sonny Onowo

Women

1. Kim Du-Trinh
2. Alice Chang
3. Christine Bannon
4. Helen Chung Visilliadis
5. Kathy Quan
6. Regina Gonzales
7. Patricia Humphrey
8. Julie Fredericks
9. Yung Chu Kim
10. Kelee Anderson

Executive Men

1. Steve Curran
2. Chuck Merriman
3. Jerry Otto

4. Gail Holden
5. Humberto Medeiros
6. Brian Ricci
7. Tom Jakubczyk
8. Edwin Rhodes
9. Terry Crook
10. Gerald Lemon

Co-Ed Weapons

1. Keith Hirabayashi
2. Alice Chang
3. Terry Creamer
4. Kathy Quan
5. Javonne Holmes
6. Kevin Thompson
7. Deno Cain
8. Dan McFarland
9. Phillip Wong
10. Hosung Pak

Triple Crown Winner

Terry Creamer

Note: Creamer is the only competitor nationally rated in fighting, forms and weapons.

AMATEUR KARATE LEAGUE (AKL)

Fighting

Co-Ed Adults

1. Teisha Chaplin
2. Maureen Matsumoto
3. Kevin Jackson
4. Mark Reeves
5. Gene Shaw
6. Tom Ambrose
7. Mark DeClements
8. Michelle DelGiorno
9. Nargil Grigsby
10. Melanie Kramer

Juniors

1. Seneca Luther
2. Chad Smith
3. Jeff Sue
4. Peter Allende
5. Carlos Moreno
6. Peter Sedivy
7. Jarrett Weeks
8. Kelly Gallant

9. Nick Milks
10. Shawn Grundlock

Forms

Co-Ed Adults

1. Michelle DelGiorno
2. Brenda Hund
3. Justina Hall
4. Maureen Matsumoto
5. Melanie Kramer
6. Lissa Uhl
7. Gene Shaw
8. John Martin
9. Matthew Emery
10. Carlo Falco

Co-Ed Juniors

1. Jeff Sue
2. Chad Smith
3. Mike Sue
4. Chris Smith
5. Jennifer Yanoff
6. Todd Humes
7. Hector Cortes
8. Jeff Melander
9. Jim Middleton
10. Robert Hendricks

Adult Weapons

1. Matthew Emery
2. Lee King
3. Kevin Jackson
4. Justina Hall
5. Joseph Aiello
6. James Frost
7. Anthony Cobbs
8. Jamie Shoemaker
9. Maurice Tyler
10. Mary Stephens

Junior Weapons

1. Jeff Sue
2. Chris Schroeder
3. Mike Sue
4. Jeremy Martin
5. Billy Alsborrks
6. Kim Curran
7. Robert Hendricks
8. Jeff Melander
9. Chris Alibrandi
10. Ricardo Royal

1986 NATIONAL RATINGS

PROFESSIONAL KARATE LEAGUE (PKL)

Fighting

Men

1. Steve Anderson
2. Chip Wright
3. Harold Burrage
4. Terry Creamer
5. Jesse Thornton
6. Joey Shiflett
7. Charles Fears
8. Dennis Chin
9. Randall DeLoach
10. Marty Eubanks

Women

1. Arlene Limas
2. Linda Denley
3. Kim-Du Trinh
4. Cheryl Nance
5. Karen Cook
6. Veronica DeSantos
7. Christine Bannon
8. Nicole Quist
9. Helen Chung
10. Andrea Decant

Seniors

1. Steve Curran
2. Tom Jakubczyk
3. Billy Bryant
4. Gary Nichols
5. Ken Eubanks

Juniors

1. Sean Higgins
2. Wesley Allen
3. Shawn Leverette

Forms

Men

1. Jean Frenette
2. Keith Hirabayashi
3. Tony Orr
4. Cezar Borkowski
5. William Chung
6. Scott Dinger
7. Chun Siev

8. Sonny Onowo
9. Norman Lacaden
10. Andre Sack

Women

1. Alice Chang
2. Kim-Du Trinh
3. Christine Bannon
4. Patricia Humphrey
5. Diane Palmer
6. Kathy Quan
7. Rose Casamassa
8. Marlon Monzo
9. Helen Chung
10. Arlene Limas

Co-Ed Weapons

1. Cezar Borkowski
2. William Chung
3. John Dufresne
4. Keith Hirabayashi
5. Tony Orr
6. Dan McFarland
7. Terry Creamer
8. Alice Chang
9. Norman Lacaden
10. Deno Cain

Seniors

1. Steve Curran
2. Bobby Barongan
3. Edwin Rhodes
4. Gail Holden
5. Tom Jakubczyk
   Billy Bryant
   Chuck Merriman

Juniors

1. Wesley Allen
2. Shawn Leverette
3. Russell Blumenthal

1985 NATIONAL RATINGS

KARATE ILLUSTRATED MAGAZINE

Note: This marked the final year of *KI's* prestigious national ratings.

Fighting

Men

1. Steve Anderson
2. Harold Burrage
3. Larry Tankson
4. Tony Young
5. Terry Creamer
6. Richard Plowden
7. Anthony Gipson
8. Chip Wright
9. Billy Blanks
10. Johnny Gyro

Women

1. Arlene Limas
2. Linda Denley
3. Karen Cook
4. Veronica DeSantos
5. Diane McCaughey
6. Lori Lantrip
7. Cheryl Nance
8. Mitzi Tyler
9. Janice Franks
10. Stacey Duke

Seniors

1. Steve Curran
2. Dale Kirby
3. Tom Jakubczyk
4. Mike Cvjetkobich

Juniors

1. John Palmer
2. Jun Barbick
3. Steve McCoy
4. Mike Tabacco

Forms

Men

1. Charlie Lee
2. Keith Hirabayashi
3. Jean Frenette
4. Tony & Cory Orr
5. Mike McCoy
6. Scott Dinger
7. Brian Fung
8. Normann Lacaden
9. Chun Siev
10. Cezar Borkowski

Women

1. Cynthia Rothrock

2. Alice Chang
3. Lori Lantrip
4. Diane McCaughey
5. Kim Warner
6. Kim Du-Trinh
7. Helen Chung
8. Patricia Humphrey
9. Christine Bannon
10. Rose Marie Casamassa

Weapons (Co-Ed)

1. Keith Hirabayashi
2. Tony Orr
3. Cynthia Rothrock
4. Cezar Borkowski
5. Dale Kirby
6. John Dufrense
7. Javonne Holmes
8. Cary Orr
9. William Chung
10. Alice Chang

Seniors

1. Steve Curran
2. Rose Marie Casamassa
3. Chuck Merriman
4. Frank Cariaga

Juniors

1. Shawn Leverepte
2. Dave Eckstrom
3. Klinton Klaas
4. Steve McCoy

1984 NATIONAL RATINGS

KARATE ILLUSTRATED MAGAZINE

Fighting

Men

1. Steve Anderson
2. Harold Burrage
3. Billy Blanks
4. Joey Shiflett
5. Chip Wright
6. Larry Tankson
7. Tony Young
8. Jessie Thornton

9. Richard Plowden
10. Terry Creamer

Women

1. Linda Denley
2. Arlene Limas
3. Lori Lantrip
4. Stacey Duke
5. Diane McCaughey
6. Rhonda Alexander
7. Cheryl Nance
8. Cissy Baird
9. Mitzi Tyler
10. Rebecca Novak

Forms

Men

1. John Chung
2. Keith Hirabayashi
3. Charlie Lee
4. Stuart Quan
5. Jean Frenette
6. Brian Fung
7. Scott Dinger
8. Mike McCoy
9. Tony & Cory Orr
10. Ernie Reyes, Jr.

Women

1. Cynthia Rothrock
2. Lori Lantrip
3. Helen Chung
4. Josie Candolita
5. Mitzi Tyler
6. Kim Warner
7. Beverly Jo Vining
8. Diane McCaughey
9. Margie Betke
10. Shelly Chacon

Weapons (Co-Ed)

1. Keith Hirabayashi
2. Stuart Quan
3. Cynthia Rothrock
4. Dale Kirby
5. Tony Orr
6. John Dufresne
7. Cory Orr
8. Josie Candolita
9. Deno Cain
10. Kim Warner

1983 NATIONAL RATINGS

KARATE ILLUSTRATED MAGAZINE

Fighting

Men

1. Billy Blanks
2. Steve Anderson
3. Ray McCallum
4. Larry Tankson
5. Tony Young
6. Richard Plowden
7. Arnold White
8. Sam Montgomery
9. Alvin Prouder
10. Harold Burrage

Women

1. Linda Denley
2. Arlene Limas
3. Lori Lantrip
4. Stacy Duke
5. Rhonda Alexander
6. Cheryl Nance
7. Lynice Mills
8. Kim Taylor
9. Rebecca Novak
10. Mitzi Tyler

Forms

Men

1. George Chung
2. Keith Hirabayashi
3. Stuart Quan
4. Charlie Lee
5. Jean Frenette
6. Gary Michak
7. Ernie Reyes, Jr.
8. Dayton Pang
9. Brian Fung
10. Toyotaro Miyazaki

Women

1. Cynthia Rothrock
2. Sophia Kikuchi
3. Lori Lantrip
4. Margie Betke
5. Shelly Chacon
6. Julie Chacon
7. Josie Candolita

8. Kathy Hasegawa
9. Beverly Jo Vining
10. Kim Warner

Weapons (Co-Ed)

1. Stuart Quan
2. Keith Hirabayashi
3. Cynthia Rothrock
4. George Chung
5. Toyotaro Miyazaki
6. Dale Kirby
7. Gary Michak
8. Pat McCarthy
9. Cezar Borkowski
10. Tony Orr

1982 NATIONAL RATINGS

KARATE ILLUSTRATED MAGAZINE

Fighting

Men

1. Steve Anderson
2. Ray McCallum
3. Larry Kelley
4. Billy Blanks
5. John Longstreet
6. Harold Burrage
7. Joey Shiflett
8. Gary Michak
9. Chris Ost
10. Robert Harris

Women

1. Arlene Limas
2. Linda Denley
3. Lynice Mills
4. Stacey Duke
5. Rhonda Alexander
6. Lori Lantrip
7. Kathy Faust
8. Mary Starks-Owens
9. Mitzi Tyler
10. Donna Judge

Forms

Men

1. John Chung
2. George Chung

3. Toyotaro Miyazaki
4. Charlie Lee
5. Stuart Quan
6. Ernie Reyes, Jr.
7. Gary Michak
8. Brian Fung
9. Sonny Onowo
10. Dayton Pang

Women

1. Cynthia Rothrock
2. Helen Chung
3. Margie Betke
4. Lori Lantrip
5. Shelly Chacon
6. Sophia Kikuchi
7. Arlene Limas
8. Belinda Davis
9. Karen Sheperd
10. Josie Candolita

Co-Ed Weapons

1. Cynthia Rothrock
2. Dale Kirby
3. Toyotaro Miyazaki
4. George Chung
5. Anthony Chan
6. Peter Morales
7. Shelly Chacon
8. Gary Michak
9. Arthur Keith
10. Stuart Quan

Triple Crown Winner

Gary Michak

Note: Michak is the only competitor nationally rated in fighting, forms and weapons.

1981 NATIONAL RATINGS

KARATE ILLUSTRATED MAGAZINE

Fighting

Men

1. Steve Anderson
2. John Longstreet
3. Robert Harris
4. Sam Montgomery
5. Ray McCallum

6. Zip White
7. Freddie Letuli
8. David Deaton
9. Russ Mapes
10. Larry Kelley

Women

1. Linda Denley
2. Arlene Limas
3. Mitzi Tyler
4. Mary Stark-Owens
5. Rhonda Alexander
6. Joanna Needham
7. Becky Chapman
8. Kathleen Garrity
9. Tessa Marcano
10. Janesa Kruse

Forms

Men

1. John Chung
2. George Chung
3. Sonny Onowo
4. Dayton Pang
5. Gary Michak
6. Peter Morales
7. Christian Wulf
8. Roger Tung
9. Toyotaro Miyazaki
10. Ernie Reyes, Jr.

Women

1. Cynthia Rothrock
2. Karen Sheperd
3. Belinda Davis
4. Lori Clapper
5. Arlene Limas
6. Margie Betke
7. Helen Chung
8. Carrie Ogawa
9. Sophia Kikuchi
10. Mitzi Tyler

Co-Ed Weapons

1. Dale Kirby
2. Cynthia Rothrock
3. George Chung
4. Peter Morales
5. Arlene Limas
6. Christian Wulf
7. Jamie Hooper
8. Vic Coffin
9. Karen Sheperd
10. Arthur Keith

1980 NATIONAL RATINGS

KARATE ILLUSTRATED MAGAZINE

Fighting

Men

1. Steve Anderson
2. Keith Vitali
3. Ray McCallum
4. Robert Harris
5. Larry Kelley
6. Al Francis
7. Bobby Tucker
8. Tokey Hill
9. Jessie Thornton
10. Sam Montgomery

Women

1. Linda Denley
2. Joanna Needham
3. Becky Chapman
4. Julia Ledbetter
5. Mitzi Tyler
6. Mary Stark-Owens
7. Oretha Grant
8. Margaret Beasley
9. Joyce Brown
10. Nancy Toby

Forms

Men

1. George Chung
2. John Chung
3. Peter Morales
4. Anthony Chan
5. Sonny Onowo
6. Vic Coffin
7. Denning Davis
8. Tayari Casel
9. Lee Wedlake
10. Ernie Reyes, Jr.

Women

1. Karen Sheperd
2. Julia Ledbetter
3. Cynthia Rothrock
4. Lori Clapper
5. Belinda Davis
6. Mitzi Tyler
7. Sophia Kokuchi

8. Kelly Wencel
9. Betty Fernandez
10. Rhonda Forbach

1979 NATIONAL RATINGS

KARATE ILLUSTRATED MAGAZINE

This year, *KI* excluded from its Top Ten ratings women's forms competition and ranked only eight male forms and four weapons champions.

Fighting

Men

1. Keith Vitali
2. Ray McCallum
3. Jimmy Tabares
4. Robert Harris
5. Steve Fisher
6. John Longstreet
7. Eddie Newman
8. Tony Palmore
9. Dan Anderson
10. Mike Genova

Women

1. Linda Denley
2. Becky Chapman
3. Julia Ledbetter
4. Lori Clapper
5. Ernestine Morgan
6. Judy Kolesar
7. Jennifer Hampton
8. Kim Hyde
9. Denise Coulter
10. Renee Smith

Forms

Men

1. George Chung
2. John Chung
3. Peter Morales
4. Ernie Reyes
5. Tayari Casel
6. Steve Fisher
7. Hidy Ochiai
8. William Pickells

Weapons

1. Peter Morales
2. Glenn Wilson
3. Dennis Brown
4. Dale Kirby

1978 NATIONAL RATINGS

KARATE ILLUSTRATED MAGAZINE

This year, before the magazine established its national ratings system, *KI* offered a published opinion on the top thirty-six male fighters. Women and forms competitors were excluded.

Men's Fighting

1. Keith Vitali
2. Ray McCallum
3. John Longstreet
4. Dan Anderson
5. Steve Fisher
6. Glenn McMorris
7. Gerald Robbins
8. Herb Johnson
9. Sam Shockley
10. James Cook

1977 NATIONAL RATINGS

BLACK BELT MAGAZINE

Karate: America

Men's Fighting (Alphabetical order)

Dan Anderson
James Cook
Steve Fisher
Steve Mackey
Ray McCallum
Sam Shockley
Ernie Smith
Ray Sua
Bobby Tucker
Keith Vitali

Women's Fighting

Mary Barnette
Elizabeth Bryant
Tammy Chrisawn
Linda Denley
Leona Schauble
Lana Hyde
Julia Ledbetter
Joanna Needham
Mary Powell
Wendi Weinshel

Karate: Europe

Journalist Zarko Modric was forced to mix seven traditional fighters with three full-contact fighters since *Black Belt* permitted only one set of ratings.

Men's Fighting

1. Dominique Valera (France)
2. Eugene Codrington (GRB)
3. Ticky Donovan (GRB)
4. William Higgins (GRB)
5. Patrice Belhriti (France)
6. Brian Fitkin (GRB)
7. Jorg Schmiedt (FRG)
8. Pierre Blot (France)
9. Francois Petitdemange (France)
10. John Roel Reeberg (Holland)

Karate: Japan

1. Junichi Hamaguchi
2. Kihei Sakamoto
3. Yoshiharu Osaka
4. Hisao Murase
5. Akio Takahashi
6. Toshikazu Sato
7. Yoichi Fukuda
8. Koji Matsuo
9. Norimasu Hayakawa
10. Joko Ninomiya

Judo: America

Men

1. Allen Coage
2. Teimoc Jonston Ono
3. Irwin Cohen
4. Leo White
5. Steve Cohen
6. Keith Nakasone
7. Tommy Riggs

8. Doug Davis
9. Jimmy Wooley
10. Mike Vincenti

Women

1. Linda Richardson
2. Lynne Lewis
3. Diane Pierce
4. Maureen Braziel
5. Amy Kublin
6. Christine Penich
7. Bonnie Korte
8. Pam Adams
9. Margaret Castro
10. Tammy Hostetler

Judo: Europe

1. Vladimir Nevzorov (USSR)
2. Sergei Novikov (USSR)
3. Valeri Dvoynikov (USSR)
4. Jean-Luc Rouge (France)
5. Shota Chochoshvili (USSR)
6. Ramaz Harshiladze (USSR)
7. Dietmar Lorenz (East Germany)
8. Keith Remfry (GRB)
9. Yves Delvingt (France)
10. Patrick Vial (France)

Judo: Japan

1. Yasuhiro Yamashita
2. Sumio Endo
3. Kazuhiro Ninomiya
4. Chonosuke Takagi
5. Haruki Uemura
6. Takafumi Ueguchi
7. Shozo Fujii
8. Yoshinari Shigematsu
9. Isamu Sonoda
10. Takeshi Yoshioka

1976 NATIONAL RATINGS

BLACK BELT MAGAZINE

Karate: America

Note: Because of "voting fragment-ation," *BB* featured one outstanding candidate for each of

the following "Fighter of the Year" classifications.

Heavyweight:
Ross Scott

Light Heavyweight:
Jeff Smith

Middleweight:
Bill Wallace

Lightweight:
Benny Urquidez

Noncontact:
Flem Evans

Female:
Marion Bermudez

Karate: Europe

1. Eugene Codrington (England)
2. Roger Paschy (France)
3. William Higgins (England)
4. Brian Fitkin (England)
5. Patrice Belhriti (France)
6. Ticky Donovan (England)
7. William Millerson (Holland)
8. Jean Luc Mami (France)
9. Robin McFarlane (Scotland)
10. John Roel Reeberg (Holland)

Karate: Japan

1. Masahiko Tanaka
2. Kunio Murakami
3. Takeshi Oishi
4. Kihei Sakamoto
5. Toshiro Mori
6. Takemichi Hirano
7. Yukio Tottori
8. Katsuaki Sato
9. Osamu Kamikado
10. Hatsuo Royama

Judo: American Men

1. Patrick Burris
2. Jimmy Wooley
3. Irwin Cohen
4. Teimoc Jonston-Ono
5. Dean Sedgwick
6. Steve Cohen
7. Chuck Wilson
8. Bernie Lepkofker

9. George Cozzi
10. Tommy Riggs

Judo: American Women
1. Amy Kublin
2. Maureen Braziel
3. Lynn Lewis
4. Bonnie Korte
5. Diane Pierce
6. Linda Richardson
7. Delores Brodie
8. Beckie Tushek
9. Francis Watkins
10. Devie Nelson

Judo: Europe
1. Vladimir Nevzorov (USSR)
2. Sergei Novikov (USSR)
3. Shota Chochoshvili (USSR)
4. Jean Luc Rouge (France)
5. Jean Paul Coche (France)
6. Ramaz Kharshiladze (USSR)
7. Dietmar Lorenz (E. Germany)
8. Valeri Dvoynikov (USSR)
9. Torsten Reissmann (E. Germany)
10. Antoni Reiter (Poland)

Judo: Japan
1. Sumio Endo
2. Haruki Uemura
3. Takafumi Ueguchi
4. Chonosuke Takagi
5. Kazuhiro Ninomiya
6. Shozo Fujii
7. Yasuhiro Yamashita
8. Tsuyoshi Yoshioka
9. Isamu Sonoda
10. Katsuhiko Iwata

1975 NATIONAL RATINGS

BLACK BELT MAGAZINE

Karate: America

Men's Fighting

Note: This year *BB* rated a mixture of full- and semi-contact fighters in the same top ten.
1. Jeff Smith
2. Bill Wallace

3. Everett Eddy
4. Joe Lewis
5. Mike Warren
6. Benny Urquidez
7. Flem Evans
8. Roy Kurban
9. Ron Shaw
10. Pat Worley

Women's (Alphabetical order)

Marion Bermudez
Debbie Bone
Barbara Bones
Malia Dacascos
Bernice Downs
Phyllis Evetts
Cheryl Mainenti
Jenice Miller
Mikie Rowe
Pauline Short

Karate: Europe
1. Dominique Valera (France)
2. Brian Fitkin (England)
3. William Higgins (England)
4. Eugene Codrington (England)
5. Roger Paschy (France)
6. William Millerson (Netherlands)
7. Robin McFarlane (Scotland)
8. Geert Lemmens (Belgium)
9. Willy Voss (W. Germany)
10. Jacques Abdurraman (France)

Karate: Japan
1. Toshiro Mori
2. Norimasa Hayakawa
3. Tetsuo Tabata
4. Katuaki Sato
5. Minoru Kawada
6. Hitoshi Shinjyo
7. Zenichi Ono
8. Toshinobi Omoto
9. Yasuo Kawamura
10. Hiroshi Kanehara

Judo: America
9. Tommy Riggs
10. Ramon Rivera

Judo: Europe
1. Vladimir Nevzorov (USSR)
2. Givi Onashvili (USSR)
3. Sergei Novikov (USSR)
4. Dzibilo Nizheradze (USSR)
5. Jean Paul Coche (France)
6. Dietmar Lorenz (E. Germany)
7. Shota Chochoshvili (USSR)
8. Jean Luc Rouge (France)
9. Antoni Reiter (Poland)
10. Brian Jacks (England)

Judo: Japan
1. Haruki Uemura
2. Chonosuke Takagi
3. Kazuhiro Ninomiya
4. Yasuhiro Yamashita
5. Nobuyuki Sato
6. Masatoshi Shinomaki
7. Yoshinari Shigematsu
8. Shozo Fujii
9. Takao Kawaguchi
10. Sumio Endo

PROFESSIONAL KARATE MAGAZINE, SPRING 1975

Forms

Co-Ed
1. Hidy Ochiai
2. Eric Lee
3. Tayari Casel
4. Malia Dacascos
5. Minobu Miki
6. Chong Lee
7. Alex Kwok
8. Bob Bowles
9. Lawrence Kuss
10. Albert Leong

PROFESSIONAL KARATE MAGAZINE, FALL 1975

Forms

Co-Ed
1. Alex Kwok
2. Hidy Ochiai
3. Lawrence Kuss
4. Ron Shaw

5. Tayari Casel
   Walt Bone
6. Glenn Premru
7. Malia Dacascos
8. Bob Bowles
9. Hiro Hamada
10. Bill Odom

1974 NATIONAL RATINGS

BLACK BELT MAGAZINE

Karate: America

Men's Fighting

1. Howard Jackson
2. Jeff Smith
3. Bill Wallace
4. Darnell Garcia
5. Everett Eddy
6. John Natividad
7. Fred Wren
8. Mike Warren
9. Flem Evans
10. Wayne Van Buren

Karate: Europe

1. Jan Kallenbach (Netherlands)
2. William Higgins (England)
3. Robin McFarlane (Scotland)
4. Geert Lemmens (Belgium)
5. Francoise Petitdemange (France)
6. Richard Scherer (W. Germany)
7. Francis Didier (France)
8. Roger Paschy (France)
9. Brian Fitkin (England)
10. Jean Luc Mami (France)

Karate: Japan

1. Kunio Murakami
2. Takeshi Oishi
3. Akihito Isaka
4. Masahiko Tanaka
5. Shinobu Tsuchiya
6. Tetsushi Ura
7. Shuichi Tsuboyama
8. Takemichi Hirano
9. Ichiro Takei
10. Osamu Kamikado

Judo: America

1. Irwin Cohen
2. Steve Cohen
3. Jimmy Wooley
4. Pat Burris
5. Tommy Martin
6. Jimmy Martin
7. Jack Anderson
8. Ramon Rivera
9. Roy Sakimoto
10. Rene Zeelenberg

Judo: Europe

1. Sergei Novikov (USSR)
2. Jean Paul Coche (France)
3. Givi Onashvili (USSR)
4. David Starbrook (England)
5. Dietmar Hotger (E. Germany)
6. Shota Chochoshvili (USSR)
7. Brian Jacks (England)
8. Sergei Melnichenko (USSR)
9. Jean Luc Rouge (France)
10. Goran Zuvela (Yugoslavia)

Judo: Japan

1. Nobuyuki Sato
2. Kazuhiro Ninomiya
3. Shozo Fujii
4. Sumio Endo
5. Chonosuke Takagi
6. Toyokazu Nomura
7. Yoshinari Shigematsu
8. Haruki Uemura
9. Mitsuyoshi Moroi
10. Takao Kawaguchi

PROFESSIONAL KARATE MAGAZINE, SPRING 1974

Men's Fighting

1. Jeff Smith
2. Howard Jackson
3. Fred Wren
4. Bill Wallace
5. John Natividad
6. Darnell Garcia
7. Everett Eddy
8. Steve Kijewski
9. Pat Worley
10. Jim Butin

PROFESSIONAL KARATE MAGAZINE, SUMMER 1974

Men's Fighting

1. Howard Jackson
2. Jeff Smith
3. Bill Wallace
4. Fred Wren
5. Darnell Garcia
6. John Natividad
7. Everett Eddy
8. Pat Worley
9. Jim Butin
10. Steve Kijewski

Women's Fighting

1. Malia Dacascos
2. Phyllis Evetts
3. Marlene Schumann
4. Jenice Miller
5. Joy Turberville
6. Marion Bermudez
7. Bernice Downs
8. Cindi Peterson
9. Mike Rowe
10. Pam Watson

PROFESSIONAL KARATE MAGAZINE, WINTER 1974–75

Note: With the publication of this issue, *Professional Karate* Magazine inappropriately combined full-contact and semi-contact fighters in its world ratings, much like mixing apples and oranges. From this point, *PK* favored kickboxing over karate point-fighting and thus ended its promotion of tournament karate.

Forms

Co-Ed

1. Hidy Ochiai
2. Eric Lee
3. Tayari Casel
4. Malia Dacascos
5. Minobu Miki
6. Chong Lee
7. Bob Bowles
8. Lawrence Kuss
9. Albert Leong
10. Alex Sternberg

1973 NATIONAL RATINGS

BLACK BELT MAGAZINE

Karate: America

Men's Fighting

1. Bill Wallace
2. Jeff Smith
3. John Natividad
4. Mike Warren
5. Roy Kurban
6. Fred Wren
7. Byong Yu
8. Howard Jackson
9. Jerry Piddington
10. Al Cheeks

Karate: Europe

1. Jan Kallenbach (Netherlands)
2. Dominique Valera (France)
3. Francis Didier (France)
4. William Higgins (England)
5. Francois Petitdemange (France)
6. William Millerson (Holland)
7. Hamish Adams (Scotland)
8. Luis Hubert Meyer (Holland)
9. Giorgio Schiappagasse (Italy)

Karate: Japan

1. Takeshi Oishi
2. Miyuki Miura
3. Shigeru Takada
4. Akihito Isaka
5. Koji Wada
6. Goshi Yamaguchi
7. Tadashi Misawa
8. Hiromasa Toyokura
9. Takashi Kaneko
10. Takumi Higashidani

Judo: America

1. Roy Sukimoto
2. James Wooley
3. Lee Person
4. Dean Sedgwick
5. Patrick Burris
6. Bill Sanford
7. David Pruzansky
8. Danny Kikuchi
9. Tommy Martin
10. Eugene Dee

Judo: Europe

1. Vitaly Kuznetsow (USSR)
2. Klaus Glahn (W. Germany)
3. Shota Chochoshvili (USSR)
4. David Starbrook (England)
5. Givi Onashvili (USSR)
6. Angelo Parisi (England)
7. Jean Jacques Mounier (France)
8. Antoni Zaykowsky (Poland)
9. Dietmar Hotger (E. Germany)
10. Jean Paul Coche (France)

Judo: Japan

1. Chonosuke Takagi
2. Haruki Uemura
3. Kazuhiro Ninomiya
4. Shozo Fujii
5. Nobuyuki Sato
6. Masatoshi Shinomaki
7. Masaki Nishimura
8. Mitsuyoshi Moroi
9. Toyokazu Nomura
10. Takafumi Uwaguchi

PROFESSIONAL KARATE MAGAZINE, SUMMER 1973

Note: PK magazine made its debut with this quarterly issue and ceased publishing in 1975. Throughout its tenure, it revolutionized sport karate and full-contact ratings.

Men's Fighting

1. Bill Wallace
2. Fred Wren
3. Byong Yu
4. Roy Kurban
5. Jeff Smith
6. Demetrius Havanas
7. Darnell Garcia
8. Mike Warren
9. John Natividad
10. Glenn Keeney

OFFICIAL KARATE MAGAZINE

Journalist and this book's author John Corcoran compiled the first set of top ten ratings for American martial arts forms competition for *Official Karate*'s inaugural yearbook. The champions appear in alphabetical order.

Men's Kata

Al Dacascos
George Dillman
Eric Lee
Chuck Merriman
Toyotaro Miyazaki
Glenn Premru
James Roberts, Jr.
Alex Sternberg
Mike Stone
Byong Yu

PROFESSIONAL KARATE MAGAZINE, FALL 1973

Men's Fighting

1. Fred Wren
2. Jeff Smith
3. Bill Wallace
4. John Natividad
5. Darnell Garcia
6. Pat Worley
7. Howard Jackson
8. Byong Yu
9. Al Dacascos
10. Steve Kijewski

1972 NATIONAL RATINGS

BLACK BELT MAGAZINE

Karate: America

Men's Fighting

1. Bill Wallace
2. Skipper Mullins
3. Ron Marchini
4. Glenn Kenney
5. Fred Wren
6. Byong Yu
7. John Natividad
8. Demetrius Havanis
9. Bob Dunek
10. Al Dacascos

Karate: Europe

1. Dominique Valera (France)
2. Jan Kallenbach (Netherlands)
3. Gilbert Gruss (France)
4. William Higgins (GRB)
5. Guy Sauvin (France)
6. Luciano Parisi (Italy)
7. Graham Mitchell (GRB)
8. Luis Hubert Meyer (Netherlands)
9. Harold LaRose (Netherlands)
10. Geert Lemmens (Belgium)

Karate: Japan

1. Takishi Oishi
2. Norihiko Iida
3. Koji Wada
4. Katsuaki Sato
5. Shigeru Takada
6. Masahiko Tanaka
7. Shunsuke Yanagida
8. Yasuhiko Oyama
9. Akio Takahashi
10. Shigeo Yoshinari

Judo: America

1. Doug Graham
2. Patrick Burris
3. Doug Nelson
4. Johnny Watts
5. Irwin Cohen
6. Brian Yakata
7. Richard Walters
8. James Wooley
9. Thomas Masterson
10. Teimoc Jonston Ono

Judo: Europe

1. Willem Russka (Netherlands)
2. Vitaly Kuznetsow (USSR)
3. Klaus Glahn (FRG)
4. Guy Auffray (France)
5. Dietmar Hotger (E. Germany)
6. Sergei Suslin (USSR)
7. David Starbrook (GRB)
8. Helmut Howiller (E. Germany)
9. Antony Zaykowsky (Poland)
10. Keith Remfry (GRB)

Judo: Japan

1. Shinobu Sekine
2. Masatoshi Shinomaki
3. Nobuyuki Sato

4. Hisakazu Iwata
5. Masaki Nishimura
6. Shozo Fujii
7. Hisashi Tsuzawa
8. Kazuhiro Ninomiya
9. Masayoshi Murai
10. Sumio Endo

1971 NATIONAL RATINGS

BLACK BELT MAGAZINE

Karate: America

Men's Fighting
1. Bill Wallace
2. Joe Hayes
3. Ron Marchini
4. Fred Wren
5. Mitchell Bobrow
6. Pat Worley
7. Byong Yu
8. Bill Watson
9. Louis Delgado
10. Joe Corley

Karate: Europe

1. Dominique Valera (France)
2. Gilbert Gruss (France)
3. Ennio Falsoni (Italy)
4. Richard Scherer (FRG)
5. Francis Didier (France)
6. Geert Lemmens (Belgium)
7. Ilija Jorga (Yugoslavia)
8. Harold La Rose (Netherlands)
9. Radoslav Cemovic (Yugoslavia)
10. Hubert Meyer (Netherlands)

Karate: Japan

1. Takeshi Oishi
2. Koji Wada
3. Norihiko Iida
4. Shigeru Takada
5. Kazuyuki Hasegawa
6. Shunsuke Yanagida
7. Masahiko Tanaka
8. Terutomo Yamazaki
9. Kazuake Hino
10. Masayuki Yamashita

Judo: America

1. Doug Nelson

2. Irwin Cohen
3. Arthur Canario
4. Roy Sukimoto
5. Patrick Burris
6. Rod Parr
7. Allen Coage
8. Paul Maruyama
9. David Long
10. Gene Garren

Judo: Europe

1. Willem Ruska (Netherlands)
2. Guy Auffray (France)
3. Vladimir Pokatayev (USSR)
4. Rudolf Hendel (E. Germany)
5. Jean Jacques Mounier (France)
6. Helmut Howiller (E. Germany)
7. Klaus Glahn (FRG)
8. Vitali Kuznetsow (USSR)
9. Givi Onashwily (USSR)
10. Guram Gogolauri (USSR)

Judo: Japan

1. Kaneo Iwatsuri
2. Masatoshi Shinomaki
3. Nobuyuki Sato
4. Kazuhiro Ninomiya
5. Masayoshi Murai
6. Isamu Sonoda
7. Masaki Nishimura
8. Yukio Maeda
9. Shuji Suma
10. Masayuki Yamashita

1970 NATIONAL RATINGS

BLACK BELT MAGAZINE

Karate: America

Men's Fighting

Note: Conspicuous by his absence is Joe Lewis, whose contemporaries considered him the sport's top fighter at the time.

1. Ron Marchini
2. Joe Hayes
3. Bill Wallace
4. Mitchell Bobrow
5. Fred Wren
6. Louis Delgado

7. Toyotaro Miyazaki
8. Artis Simmons
9. Dwight Frazier
10. Ken Knudson

Karate: Europe

1. Dominique Valera (France)
2. Gilbert Gruss (France)
3. Richard Scherer (FRG)
4. Guy Sauvin (France)
5. Luciano Parisi (Italy)
6. William Higgins (GRB)
7. Stanley Knighton (GRB)
8. Richard Kubisch (FRG)
9. Patrick Baroux (France)
10. Geert Lemmens (Belgium)

Karate: Japan

1. Takeshi Oishi
2. Yoshito Ito
3. Norihiko Iida
4. Terutomo Yamazaki
5. Shigeo Yamada
6. Akio Takahashi
7. Hideo Tanabe
8. Hideki Takahashi
9. Norimasa Takahashi
10. Makoto Toshima

Judo: America

1. Allen Coage
2. Hayward Nishioka
3. Paul Maruyama
4. Rodney Haas
5. Larry Fukuhara
6. Tosh Seino
7. Dale Lehman
8. Roy Sukimoto
9. Irwin Cohen
10. Larry Fryar

Judo: Europe

1. Klaus Glahn (FRG)
2. Vladimir Pokatayev (USSR)
3. Brian Jacks (GRB)
4. Willem Ruska (Neth)
5. Martin Poglajen (Neth)
6. David Rudman (USSR)
7. Sergei Suslin (USSR)
8. Klaus Hennig (East Germany)
9. Givi Onashvily (USSR)
10. Serge Feist (France)

Judo: Japan

1. Masatoshi Shinomaki
2. Masaki Nishimura
3. Nobuyuki Sato
4. Tsukio Kawahara
5. Isamu Sonoda
6. Yasuto Anzai
7. Shuji Suma
8. Kazuhiro Ninomiya
9. Kenichi Horiguchi
10. Koji Sato

1969 NATIONAL RATINGS

BLACK BELT MAGAZINE

Karate: America

Men's Fighting

1. Ron Marchini
2. Chuck Norris
3. Joe Lewis
4. Joe Hayes
5. Artis Simmons
6. Bill Wallace
7. Mitchell Bobrow
8. Louis Delgado
9. Skipper Mullins
10. Frank Smith

Karate: Europe

1. Dominique Valera (France)
2. Ilija Jorga (Yugoslavia)
3. Abdelhafid Saidane (France)
4. Gilbert Gruss (France)
5. Terry O'Neil (Great Britain)
6. Richard Scherer (West Germany)
7. Peter Duffy (Great Britain)
8. Guy Desnoes (France)
9. Richard Kozakiewicz (Belgium)
10. Gianfranco Cantagalli (Italy)

Karate: Japan

1. Takeshi Oishi
2. Mitsuhiro Ota
3. Masayoshi Yamagami
4. Manabu Taniguchi
5. Yoshito Ito
6. Yoshinobu Ishitobi
7. Hideo Ochi

8. Shinichi Chiba
9. Masaaki Ueki
10. Makoto Toshima

Judo: America

1. Allen Coage
2. Richard Walters
3. Paul Maruyama
4. Tosh Seino
5. Larry Fukuhara
6. Clyde Worthan
7. Isao Mura
8. Rod Haas
9. William McCauley
10. Irwin Cohen

Judo: Europe

1. Willem Ruska (Netherlands)
2. Petrus Snijders (Netherlands)
3. David Rudman (USSR)
4. Anatolij Bondarenko ((USSR)
5. Peter Herrmann (West Germany)
6. Sergei Susline (USSR)
7. Klaus Glahn (West Germany)
8. Wolfgang Hoffman (West Germany)
9. Vladimir Pokatayev (USSR)
10. Otto Smirat (USSR)

Judo: Japan

1. Isao Okano
2. Masatoshi Shinomaki
3. Yukio Maeda
4. Masayoshi Murai
5. Masaki Nishimura
6. Nobuyuki Sato
7. Isamu Sonoda
8. Takeshi Matsuzaka
9. Eiji Maruki
10. Koji Sato

1968 NATIONAL RATINGS

BLACK BELT MAGAZINE

Note: The top ten karate fighters for Japan were not rated by *Black Belt* this year.

Karate: America

Men's Fighting

1. Chuck Norris
2. Joe Lewis
3. Ron Marchini
4. Mitchell Bobrow
5. Frank Smith
6. Tom LaPuppet
7. Louis Delgado
8. Tonny Tulleners
9. N. Tanaka
10. John Gehlsen

Karate: Europe

1. Dominique Valera (France)
2. Guy Sauvin (France)
3. Patrick Baroux (France)
4. Richard Kozakiewicz (Belgium)
5. Abdelhafid Saidane (France)
6. Guy Desnoes (France)
7. Jean Dehaes (Belgium)
8. Gerard Grossetete (Switzerland)
9. Albert Boutboul (France)
10. Henri Jordan (Switzerland)

Judo: America

1. Larry Fukuhara
2. Tosh Seino
3. Paul Maruyama
4. Doug Graham
5. Richard Walters
6. Bill Paul
7. Hayward Nishioka

8. Allen Coage
9. Don Matsuda
10. James Westbrook

Judo: Europe (By weight class)

Heavy:

1. Klaus Glahn (FRG)
2. Anzor Kiknadze (USSR)

Light Heavy:

1. Peter Herrmann (FRG)
2. Helmut Howiller (E. Germany)

Middle:

1. Wolfgang Hoffmann (FRG)
2. Patrick Clement (France)

Light Middle:

1. Roini Magaltadze (USSR)
2. Otari Nataleshvili (USSR)

Light:

1. Sergei Susline (USSR)
2. Pirus Martkoplishvili (USSR)

Judo: Japan

1. Koji Sato
2. Nobuyuki Sato
3. Mitsuo Matsunaga
4. Isao Okano
5. Takeshi Matsuzaka
6. Masaharu Kato
7. Masayoshi Murai
8. Fumio Sasahara

9. Hiroshi Nakamura
10. Yukio Maeda

1967 NATIONAL RATINGS

BLACK BELT MAGAZINE

Note: Black Belt's national ratings were launched by then tournament karate king Joe Lewis, who named America's top ten karate fighters in the April 1967 issue. It marked the first set of fighter ratings for martial arts competition of any type.

These ratings, for undisclosed reasons, were divided into two "teams" of five fighters in random order. The names were listed alphabetically.

First Team

1. Joe Lewis
2. Steve Loring
3. Skipper Mullins
4. Chuck Norris
5. Allen Steen

Second Team

1. Carlos Bunda
2. Thomas LaPuppet
3. Julio LaSalle
4. Frank Smith
5. Tonny Tulleners

MARTIAL ARTS FILM AND VIDEO GUIDE

This is the only comprehensive film and video guide ever compiled for the martial arts movie genre. Every conceivable effort was made to list every martial arts movie of consequence and, in fact, some of no particular consequence except to avid buffs. To assure thoroughness in the compilation of this work, I scoured both published and private sources and consulted experts and aficionados.

This guide picks up Asian cinema in 1951 with famed Japanese director Akira Kurosawa's *Rashomon*. A unique feature is a subcategory in Chapter 16 featuring "classic scenes" from mainstream movies starting as early as 1942 (*Across the Pacific*, starring Humphrey Bogart), when the Asian martial arts first began appearing in Hollywood movies. The majority of entries deal with Eastern martial arts and their cinematic uses; there are but a few selected titles, mostly modern, featuring Western boxing—like *Rocky* and *Raging Bull*.

Excluded from this guide are movies that focus on wrestling, those among the so-called sword-and-sandal epics (except *Red Sonja*, featuring terrific martial artist Ernie Reyes, Jr.), the kind cranked out voluminously by Italian filmmakers, as well as English medieval films. Admittedly, there are many, many fine films in these genres: consider, for example, the Oscar-winning *Excalibur*, the sumptuous retelling of the King Arthur legend, or *All the Marbles*, the aesthetic wrestling film flamboyantly directed by John Avildsen (*Rocky*; *The Karate Kid*).

So prolific are the sword-and-sandal films that they could command a guide of their own. In this reviewer's opinion, however, for the most part these other, Westernized genres use a far different and less stylized type of screen fighting than do the films depicting Eastern martial arts. As a martial artist myself, I'd take a samurai film or a Chinese weapons picture over a medieval one any day. And I'd certainly opt for a kung-fu flick over a film about wrestling.

CHAPTER 15

PURE MARTIAL ARTS FILMS

This section contains 218 entries and is the most extensive list of films ever compiled and rated in this genre. Each entry, ideally, will include the movie's title(s), release date, country of origin, stars, plot synopsis, commentary, subtitles or dubbing, rating, running time, and availability on video. Other extraneous facts, such as a martial arts distinction or awards won, appear as necessary.

CRITICAL RATINGS

To observe an established industry standard, I've adopted the movie rating system used by *TV Guide*. Four stars (★★★★) means excellent, three (★★★) is good, two (★★) is fair, and one (★) is poor. A total bomb is noted by the Japanese word for self-destruction, *hara-kiri*. The ratings are strictly my own and should be viewed with caution; everyone has an opinion and despite my twenty-five years in the martial arts business, mine is perhaps no better than anyone else's.

I have personally seen the majority of these movies. For those I have not seen, before assigning a rating I've relied on the educated opinions of experts and veteran aficionados, such as martial arts film star Gary Daniels and film producer Paul Maslak, both of Los Angeles, among others. The only time a rating does not appear is when too few facts about a particular film are known. This is true of literally hundreds of Hong Kong martial arts films, which have never been globally distributed or were in limited release at some point as a drive-in quickie.

FILMOGRAPHIES

To help the reader or researcher find the titles of his or her favorite major martial arts stars, select filmographies appear in the following chapter. Consulting these filmographies first will save you considerable time by allowing you to go directly to the titles you seek in this section instead of wading through the entire list of films.

CATEGORIES

All the films in which the martial arts are employed or merely appear are divided into six categories: 1) Pure Martial Arts Films; 2) Martial Artists as Lead Characters; 3) Martial Arts as Story Line; 4) Classic Scenes; 5) Documentaries; and 6) Television. Each category is clearly explained in an introduction when necessary. These divisions should help separate the heavyweights from the lightweights in this genre.

ORDER OF APPEARANCE

In each category, film titles are listed in strict letter-by-letter spelling sequence. Separation of words and punctuation are ignored.

YEAR OF RELEASE

The year a film is first shown theatrically is the general standard. Foreign films are listed by year of release in the country of origin, which may vary greatly from their U.S. debut.

TITLE CHANGES

Chinese films in particular, as well as films that fail at the box office, are frequently retitled. And on the home video market, retitling is getting more and more commonplace each year. Where possible, the changes have been tracked and listed in cross-references to the main title by which the movie is known. Tracking all the multi-titled Hong Kong films, however, is impossible.

VIDEO AVAILABILITY

Every film available on home video is indicated with this symbol at the end of a review: [VIDEO]. Be aware that videos become in and out of "print" irregularly and without warning. The titles that are listed as available were so at the time of the printing of this book.

COUNTRY OF ORIGIN

In every case the country or countries in which the film was originally made is listed. If no country appears after the year of release, then it is a U.S. production.

RUNNING TIME

A number of films are artificially time-compressed for video. That means a film that ran over 90 minutes might be shaved to 90 minutes because the producers can save money by fitting it into a 90-minute cassette instead of a two-hour one. *Enter the Dragon*, for example, ran 98 minutes in theaters, but its running time is 90 minutes in video release. To accomplish this, in most cases *entire* scenes—as opposed to bits and pieces of several scenes—are cut from the original movie.

Length also necessitates that some films run on two video cassettes. This is true of two unusually long pictures, *Seven Samurai* and *Kagemusha*. Understandably, then, the rental or sales price is higher.

HONG KONG KUNG-FU FILMS

Starting in the spring of 1973, Hong Kong imports began flooding the American market, some of them low-budget even by Hong Kong standards and an inordinate number of them exploiting Bruce Lee's name. Just from the spring of 1973 to the end of 1974, for example—when the first wave of the so-called "chop-sockies" bombarded the United States—a total of sixty-four martial arts films were distributed here! Among them were such unforgivable titles as *King Kong Fu*, *The Big Zapper*, *Kung-Fu Mama*, and *Supermanchu*! (Of historic note: six of those sixty-four flicks were distributed by Cannon Films, which would later crank out a whole series of ninja and martial arts films and officially launch the

careers of Sho Kosugi and Jean-Claude Van Damme.)

In Hong Kong today, over one thousand Chinese-language pictures are available on videocassette, with a large proportion of them available in English versions. How many of these awful releases are worth seeing depends on one's tolerance for sustained torture. Also, consumers must beware of the quality, or lack of it, of Hong Kong's videotapes. Some videocassettes contain badly translated, illegible English subtitles. And naturally, all of the English-language Hong Kong output is subjected to unintentionally hilarious dubbing that has become the butt of jokes by stand-up comedians.

Quality is impaired when a PAL standard master tape is transferred to the NTSC standard used in the U.S. Hong Kong filmmakers do this because it's cheaper. The more expensive tape-to-tape transfer from the same NTSC standard eliminates annoying problems like blinking and the barely readable subtitles. Too, some of the new pictures are filmed in wide-screen Panavision, and 50 percent or more of the frame may be chopped off in the transfer to video.

So many of the spastic offerings, especially the "junk-fu" of the mid- and late 1970s, are nothing more than Hong Kong Xerox material lacking one iota of originality to recommend them. The majority of this constant-product output is sheer derivative action featuring campy, ridiculous leaps and the campier prolonged fight scenes that defy credulity. In most, the hero routinely employs armed and unarmed martial arts to remove extraneous characters from the script, *if* they used one. Prominent film critics Gene Siskel and Roger Ebert would hate them so much they'd probably cut off their thumbs.

In good conscience, too, I can't rationally contribute to the blatant ripoff of our greatest film star, the incomparable Bruce Lee. I therefore refuse to recognize here those despicable Bruce Lee exploitation films by such "graverobbers" as Bruce Le, Bruce Li, et al. As a long-time acquaintance of Linda Lee, Bruce's widow, I would demonstrate a terrible lack of respect for her should I mention these people and projects with anything other than the genuine disdain I have for them. If these imitators had anything useful to offer audiences other than a slight resemblance to Bruce, then where are they now? Their descent into oblivion says it all. Likewise, I have not tolerated similar ripoffs of other Hong Kong film stars like Jackie Chan, Cynthia Rothrock and Michelle Khan.

In conclusion, a lot of the Hong Kong kung-foolishness is just wasted celluloid, perhaps of interest only to the most hardcore fan. I have therefore tried to be very selective of those titles included in this guide.

On the positive side, some of these Hong Kong martial arts stars are simply incredible and absolutely must be seen by any martial artist with an ounce of genuine interest in cinema. When they're at their best, nobody does it better. This goes for the inimitable Jackie Chan and Samo Hung, to name just two of Hong Kong's enormously talented performers. As well, the Hong Kong genre is noted for colorful cinematography and settings, particularly with its exotic Shaolin Temple locations.

I have tried whenever possible to list the known films of recognized, legitimate Asian martial arts stars, but I admit to not being an expert on this subgenre. This includes the work of Hong Kong's Jackie Chan, Samo Hung, Mie (a.k.a. Lam Sum Mei), Angela Mao, Jet Lee, Johnny Liu, Jimmy Wang Yu, Chen Kuan-tai, Carter Wong, Chen Hui-min, Tam Tao-liang, Chen Sing and Don Wong-tao. I am confident, however, that there's enough here to satisfy average tastes for this type of picture.

JAPANESE SAMURAI FILMS

Japan's samurai films (what the Japanese call *chambara* or *chanbara*, meaning "sword-swinging") are the Eastern counterpart of our Westerns. They fall under the general heading of period film or *jidai-geki*, a term used to designate pictures set in the Tokugawa period that ended in 1868. (After that, the samurai were prohibited from wearing swords.) The *chambara* are renowned for their striking cinematography and swift, swashbuckling action—mind-blowing sword fights choreographed so tightly the frame squeaks. It is a genre that drew a sizable Western cult following, thanks to the brilliant early work of director Akira Kurosawa, long before the invasion of Hong Kong's so-called "chop-sockies."

Kurosawa's work has inspired many important films and filmmakers. First and commercially foremost is George Lucas's acknowledgment that his megahit *Star Wars* was chiefly based on Kurosawa's *The Hidden Fortress*. Then there is, of course, the obvious American remake of his *Seven Samurai* into *The Magnificent Seven* and its sequels. *Yojimbo* and *Sanjuro* were remade, respectively, as Sergio Leone's "spaghetti Westerns" *A Fistful of Dollars* and *For a Few Dollars More*, which made Clint Eastwood a star. (Eastwood also reportedly once negotiated with Katsu Productions to convert the *Baby Cart from Hell* concept to the Old West.) *Rashomon* was remade as *The Outrage*, starring Paul Newman. Tom Laughlin filmed *The Master Gunfighter*, based on *Goyokin*, and director Sam Peckinpah's *The Wild Bunch* owes its use of slow motion and long lenses to depict violent action to Kurosawa's influence.

One word of warning, however. Some of the samurai films are extremely graphic in portraying violence. There are realistic sequences of extended carnage, complete with severed limbs and cut arteries spurting blood, sometimes into a symbolically tranquil setting—sort of a yin–yang scenario of war and peace. The more graphic *chambara* are not for the squeamish. Also be careful of the "Roman porno" or "porno-samurai" elements introduced around 1970, which, taken as a whole, are no more than sexy erotica coupled with the martial arts. If you are offended by nudity, however, you will want to choose your titles with caution.

Those of you who have been introduced to the ninja through American-made pictures owe it to yourselves to see the original screen versions in Japanese films. These guys were leaping tall temples in a single bound before the word ninja was exported to the West and they make the Western counterparts look like white belts. Years ago, the ninja were portrayed as protagonists but sometime in the 1970s made the transition to villains whom the anti-hero samurai have been hired to destroy—or vice versa.

I have tried to find and include here all the eminent *chambara* and/or martial arts work by stars such as Toshiro Mifune, Shintaro Katsu, Tomisaburo Wakayama, Tetsuro Tamba, Sonny Chiba, Yoko Matsuyama and Junko Fuji.

The *chambara* genre unfortunately subsided during the 1980s as other trends, like the *yakuza-eiga* (gambler films), took hold with Japanese audiences. Consequently, most of the samurai flicks available stem from the genre's twenty-five-year zenith from the mid-1950s to the late 1970s. Don't worry. These classics age well.

⌐ •• ⌐

AMERICAN KICKBOXER (1991) ★ John Barrett, Keith Vitali. A blood feud between kickboxers. Same old exploitation angle. (R; 1:33) [VIDEO]

AMERICAN NINJA (1985) Hara-kiri. Michael Dudikoff, Steve James. Stationed in the Philippines, a GI takes on ninja warriors to wipe out a corrupt weapons dealer. Bad acting and mediocre martial arts in a 95-minute yawner. (R; 1:35) [VIDEO]

AMERICAN NINJA II: THE CONFRONTATION (1987) ★ Michael Dudikoff and Steve James as army rangers who come to the aid of the marines and wipe out an army of heroine dealers. A half-step above the original. (R; 1:36) [VIDEO]

AMERICAN NINJA III: BLOOD HUNT (1989) Hara-kiri. David Bradley, Steve James. Two martial artists discover that the Caribbean-based karate tournament they have entered is a front for chemical warfare experiments! The fight scenes look like they were done by the numbers. A waste of celluloid and James's talent. (R; 1:29) [VIDEO]

AMERICAN NINJA IV: THE ANNIHILATION (1991) Hara-kiri. Michael Dudikoff, David Bradley. Dudikoff, a retired agent, is dispatched to a fictional African nation to

David Bradley in *American Samurai*. Courtesy of Cannon Films

rescue a Delta Force team captured by a dippy Saddam Hussein clone in oil-sheik disguise. Perhaps the worst entry in the series, with nothing to recommend it except moments of unintended humor. (R; 1:39) [VIDEO]

AMERICAN NINJA V (1993) ★ David Bradley, Pat Morita, James Lew. The *American Ninja* concept ran out of creative juice after the very first film and has, as one English reviewer put it, "eked out an existence on thin plots and wooden actors ever since." This series entry, however, is supposed to be a spoof, despite occasional moments of manufactured tension, and it does work the laugh meter in places. Pat Morita makes only a brief appearance, and James Lew, as the caped villain named "Viper," is, as always, interesting to watch. (R; 1:35) [VIDEO]

AMERICAN SAMURAI (1992) David Bradley, Mark Dacascos. A story of two samurai-trained brothers in mortal conflict; essentially, "*Bloodsport* with blades," and notable for the impressive film debut of martial arts sensation Mark Dacascos. Some gratuitous gore. Cowritten by John Corcoran, this book's author, and therefore critically unrated. (R; 1:29) [VIDEO]

ANGEL TOWN (1989) ★ Olivier Gruner, Theresa Saldana. A foreign exchange student and champion kickboxer is forced to fight Los Angeles street gangs. An ill attempt to find another Jean-Claude Van Damme in European Gruner. (R; 1:30) [VIDEO]

ARMOUR OF GOD; ARMOUR OF THE GODS (1988; Chinese) ★★★★ Jackie Chan plays "Asian Hawk," an Indiana Jones–style character who finds pieces of ancient armor known as the "Armor of God," which he sells at an auction. But when his ex-girlfriend has been kidnapped by a religious cult, Chan has to ask for the armor back to use as ransom. Full of fantastic stunts and remarkable fight scenes, this is the movie where a dangerous stunt backfired and nearly killed Chan. The accident that occurred appears in the end credits. Chinese with English subtitles. (?; ?) [VIDEO]

ARMOUR OF GOD II: OPERATION CONDOR (1990; Chinese) ★★★★ Jackie Chan, Do Do Cheng, Eva Cobo, Shogo Ikeda. Chan, reprising his "Asian Hawk" role, is hired in post–World War II by the United Nations to find gold reputedly stolen and hidden by Nazis. Joining him is an archaeologist (Cheng, Hong Kong's top actress) and the daughter of one of the dead Nazis (Cobo). Their quest is impeded by mercenaries and Palestinians. This was Chan's biggest film to date, costing 80 million Hong Kong dollars and taking one full year to shoot in four countries. It has exceptional production values, plenty of action, humor and one of the greatest car chases on film. The finale is a battle across huge see-sawing slabs of clockwork machinery. Chinese with English subtitles. (?; ?) [VIDEO]

AVENGING FORCE (1986) ★★ Michael Dudikoff, Steve James, Bill Wallace. An ex–Secret Service agent (Dudikoff) comes to the aid of his former partner, a black man running for office (James), who's on a terrorist hit list. The best of the Dudikoff ZZzzz films. (R; 1:44) [VIDEO]

A.W.O.L.: SEE **LIONHEART**

BABY CART FROM HELL (series) (dates unknown; Japanese) ★★★★ One of Japan's all-time hit film series. Tomisaburo Wakayama as the former shogunate decapitator, Itto Ogami, who hires himself out as a mercenary. A threat to clan power, his life is constantly jeopardized by the ninja group hired to assassinate him. Accompanying him is his young charge in a wooden baby cart filled with an arsenal of inventive, imaginatively concealed weapons that transforms Ogami into a one-man army. Another title is *Lone Wolf on the River Styx*. [VIDEO]

BERRY GORDY'S THE LAST DRAGON: see **THE LAST DRAGON**

BEST OF THE BEST (1989) ★★★ Eric Roberts, James Earl Jones, Phillip Rhee, Sally Kirkland. Members of the U.S. karate team train for a match against the South Korean world champions. Surprise: a martial arts film with real actors in a real story-oriented script—a breakthrough for the genre. Watch actor–coproducer Phillip Rhee, whose star is rising in Hollywood starting with this picture. (PG-13; 1:40) [VIDEO]

BEST OF THE BEST II (1993) ★★★ Phillip Rhee, Eric Roberts, Wayne Newton, Chris Penn. A loose sequel in which members of the former U.S. karate team participate in underground death matches in Las Vegas. Very slick fight choreography by Simon Rhee, Phillip's brother, and first-rate warrior performance by star–coproducer Phillip. Sonny Landham is memorable as a hard-drinking mentor. (R; ?) [VIDEO]

BIG BOSS, THE: see **FIST OF FURY**

BIG BRAWL, THE (1980; Chinese—U.S.) ★★ Martial arts mish-mash applied to a 1930s gangster movie set in Chicago. Extremely disappointing American film debut of Jackie Chan, through no fault of his own. Chan had no control over his own destiny in this important transition, but should have. Indifferent script, restrictive choreography and typical mediocre Robert Clouse–Fred Weintraub (director–producer) treatment all work to castrate Chan's normal charisma and kung-fu craftsmanship. Not worth seeing; his Hong Kong films are far better. (R; 1:35) [VIDEO]

BIG PEONY GAMBLER, THE (197?; Japanese) Japan's most successful and best-produced female martial arts series, known there as *Hibotan Bakuto*. Gorgeous Junko Fuji stars as Oryu, the "Red Peony," who accepts the life of an early twentieth-century itinerant gambler in order to avenge the death of her *yakuza* father. Oryu defends herself with the capability of a man, using jujutsu, the sword, the dagger, the pistol or even a hairpin, which she throws with the skill of a ninja. This enormously successful series, which still comprises some of the best

Eric Roberts (left) and Phillip Rhee in *Best of the Best*. Courtesy of Phillip Rhee

Phillip Rhee in *Best of the Best II*. Courtesy of Phillip Rhee

of the *yakuza* genre, ended after six films because Fuji married and retired from showbiz. (?; ?)

BIG TROUBLE IN LITTLE CHINA (1986) ★★ An adventurous trucker (Kurt Russell) finds himself knee-deep in Chinatown intrigue when a friend's fiancée is kidnapped right before his eyes. He plunges beneath the streets of San Francisco's Chinatown to battle an army of spirits. High-tech Indiana Jones–style adventure from director John Carpenter (*The Thing*; *Starman*) has heavy tongue-in-cheek attitude and marvelous FX, but the martial arts are hokey. Look for all kinds of familiar Asian martial artists in the fight scenes; Carpenter hired just about everyone in Hollywood. (PG-13; 1:39) [VIDEO]

BLACK BELT (1992) ★ Don "The Dragon" Wilson, Matthias Hues, Deirdre Imershein, "Bad" Brad Hefton. Ex-cop-turned-detective (Wilson) falls for a beautiful rock star (Imershein) while protecting her from the mobsters and the invincible psychopath who stalk her. Good story ruined by weak direction and mediocre fights. (R; 1:20) [VIDEO]

BLACK BELT JONES (1974) ★ Jim Kelly follows up his *Enter the Dragon* role in this weak black-oriented martial arts film where he fights the Mafia to save his karate school. Offers a few funny moments, but ho-hum for the most part. With this mediocre film, the first of many to follow, the director–producer team of Robert Clouse and Fred Weintraub already show that it was Bruce Lee who singlehandedly made *Enter the Dragon* a classic. (PG; 1:27) [VIDEO]

BLACK DRAGON (1974) Hara-kiri. A young farm boy moves to the city and teams up with an undercover narcotics agent (Ron Van Clief) to infiltrate and destroy an underworld syndicate. Puh-*leese!* stop it. (R; 1:33) [VIDEO]

BLACK DRAGON'S REVENGE (1975) Hara-kiri. The "Black Dragon" arrives in Hong Kong to investigate the death of a great kung-fu master. Oh, no, not again! (R; 1:30) [VIDEO]

BLACK EAGLE (1988) ★★★ Sho Kosugi, Jean-Claude Van Damme. Well-made pre-*glasnost* martial arts flick about a CIA agent (Kosugi) sent to recover a top-secret laser-tracking device from a U.S. fighter downed in the Mediterranean. The KGB has also sent an agent (Van Damme), and the two spies do battle. Interesting physical exchanges between two visually exciting fighting stars; sumptuously photographed Malta locations. (R; 1:33) [VIDEO]

BLIND FURY (1990) ★★★ Rutger Hauer, Randall "Tex" Cobb, Terry O'Quinn, Sho Kosugi. A blind Vietnam vet (Hauer) battles the Las Vegas underworld in an anglicized version of Japan's "Zatoichi," the charismatic blind swordsman. A neat little martial arts drama made workable by Hauer's acting and martial arts skills. (R; 1:26) [VIDEO]

BLIND RAGE (1978) ★ Fred Williamson, Leo Fong, D'Urville Martin. When the U.S. government transports $15 million to the Philippines, five blind kung-fu masters want a piece of the action. Interesting concept, boring, low-budget execution. (R; 1:21) [VIDEO]

BLACK SAMURAI (1977) ★ When his girlfriend is held hostage, a martial arts warrior (Jim Kelly) stops at nothing to destroy the organization that abducted her. Signals the premature end of Kelly's movie career. (R; 1:24) [VIDEO]

BLIND SWORDSMAN (series) (early 1960s to date; Japanese) ★★★★ At last count, there were twenty-four films (only the first two were black and white) starring the swashbuckling adventures of Zatoichi, the famed blind swordsman. This iaido master, played masterfully by Shintaro Katsu, treads the back roads of feudal Japan eking out an existence as an itinerant masseur—a profession then reserved for the blind—but making his actual living by gambling. His keen hearing tells him which way the gambler's dice fall and whenever they are loaded. He has been known to expose loaded dice by tossing them into the air, drawing his sword and slicing

the suspect pair before they hit the ground. Japanese language. [VIDEO]

BLIND SWORDSWOMAN (series) (19??; Japanese) Known in Japan as *Mekura No Oichi*. Oichi, the title character, is played by Yoko Matsuyama, who carries a sword cane and, like Zatoichi, relies on her supersensitive hearing. Japanese language. [VIDEO]

BLONDE FURY, THE (1988; Chinese) ★★ Cynthia Rothrock stars as a San Francisco cop who goes undercover in Hong Kong as a newspaper reporter to break up a counterfeiting ring. A very basic story, but very good Hong Kong–style stunts and fight sequences. The lead villain is played by Ronnie Yu, who directed Brandon Lee in *Legacy of Rage*. Also entitled *Lady Reporter*. (?; ?) [VIDEO]

BLOODFIST (1989) ★ Don "The Dragon" Wilson, Rob Kamen, Billy Blanks. An amateur boxer-turned-kickboxer infiltrates Manila's prizefighting underworld in search of his brother's murderer. Wilson makes his screen debut in this low-budget entry produced by Roger Corman, "King of the B Movies." Wilson did what he could to improve his first shot by adding name fighters Billy Blanks and Rob Kamen, but the film is still a thinly veiled imitation of Van Damme's *Bloodsport*. (R; 1:26) [VIDEO]

BLOODFIST II (1990) ★ Don "The Dragon" Wilson, Maurice Smith, Richard Hill, James Warring. A retired kickboxing champion is abducted to a private island by a criminal millionaire and is forced to participate in gladiatorial fights to the death. Weak story, weak direction, many so-so fights. Wilson does, however, establish his pattern of using the talents of renowned world martial arts champions. (R; 1:25) [VIDEO]

BLOODFIST III: FORCED TO FIGHT (1992) ★★★ Don "The Dragon" Wilson, Richard Roundtree, Stan Longinidis. A wrongfully convicted martial arts expert (Wilson), along with his spiritual mentor (Roundtree), become marked for murder amidst racial tensions inside a corrupt penitentiary. Nominated for four of Joe Bob Briggs's "Drive-In Academy Awards," including Best Picture of the Year. Excellent story, good performances, so-so fights. (R; 1:30) [VIDEO]

BLOODFIST IV: DIE TRYING (1992) ★★ Don "The Dragon" Wilson, Amanda Wyss, James Tolkan, Gary Daniels. When his office workers are mercilessly machine-gunned, an unsuspecting repo man must take on the CIA, the FBI and an international arms cartel to recover his kidnapped daughter. Complex story, good direction, some good fights. (R; 1:26) [VIDEO]

BLOODFIST V: BLACKOUT (1993) ★★ Don "The Dragon" Wilson, Steve James, Denise Duff, Yuji Okumoto. An amnesia victim teams up with an attractive prostitute to uncover his true identity while on the run from unknown foreign assailants. Complex story and good fights sometimes burdened by uneven editing. (R; 1:26) [VIDEO]

BLOODMATCH (1991) ★ Thom Mathews, Benny Urquidez, Dale Jacoby, Pete Cunningham, Michel Qissi. A kickboxer (Mathews) seeks vengeance against his brother's killer by kidnapping all the suspects and kickboxing each to death until someone confesses. A poorly made thriller. (R; 1:30) [VIDEO]

BLOODSPORT (1988) ★★★ Jean-Claude Van Damme's breakthrough film. He portrays the first Westerner to win the "Kumite," an international freestyle competition staged in Hong Kong. Allegedly based on the true but unsubstantiated story of one Frank Dux, a Los Angeles martial artist. Nor can any of Dux's claims credited on screen be verified. But Dux aside, Van Damme makes a very impressive physical statement, enough to have made this low-budget film a solid box-office hit that eventually grossed some $20 million worldwide and put his motion-picture career in gear. (R; 1:32) [VIDEO]

BLOODY BUSHIDO BLADE, THE: see **THE BUSHIDO BLADE**

BODYGUARD, THE (1976) ★ Sonny Chiba, Aaron Banks, William Louie. The Yakuza versus New York mafiosa, featuring some name New York martial artists. Do miss it. (R; 1:29) [VIDEO]

BREAKER, BREAKER (1977) ★ Chuck Norris's first starring role as a trucker searching for his kid brother in a corrupt speed-trap town. Low-budget production values and bland, if not dismal, locations overwhelm

Jean-Claude Van Damme (kicking) versus Bolo Yeung in *Bloodsport*. Courtesy of Cannon Films

and undermine Chuck's debut as a blond-haired, blue-eyed Bruce Lee. (PG; 1:26) [VIDEO]

BRONSON LEE, CHAMPION (1978; Japan) ★ Notable only as the first starring role for martial arts sensation Tadashi Yamashita, and the first minor role for American forms champ Karen Sheperd. (PG; 1:21) [VIDEO]

BRONX EXECUTIONER, THE (1986) ★ Android, robot and human interests clash martial arts style in futuristic Manhattan. Pic is introduced by actor Michael Dudikoff. (R; 1:28) [VIDEO]

BUSHIDO BLADE, THE (1979; Japanese) ★★ Richard Boone, James Earl Jones, Toshiro Mifune, Mako, Sonny Chiba. Commander Matthew Perry (Boone) leads a group of his men in the recovery of a treasured sword in nineteenth-century Japan. Boone's last role; Mifune plays the Shogun, as he did in the later TV miniseries. Also entitled *The Bloody Bushido Blade*, it's worth watching. (Unrated; 1:44) [VIDEO]

CATCH THE HEAT (1987) ★ Tiana Alexandra (wife of former Bruce Lee student and Oscar-winning screenwriter Stirling Silliphant) stars as an undercover narcotics agent sent to infiltrate Rod Steiger's South American drug operation. No heat involved. (R; 1:30) [VIDEO]

CHALLENGE, THE (1982) ★★ Scott Glenn, Toshiro Mifune, Donna Kei Benz, Atsuo Nakamura. An American boxer–drifter (Glenn) gets caught in a conflict between two Japanese brothers—one a corrupt businessman, the other an honorable traditionalist—over a pair of ancient family swords. Given its talent, here's a picture that should have been a classic, but doesn't live up to expectations. It was directed by John Frankenheimer (*The Manchurian Candidate*, among many others) and coscripted by John Sayles (*Return of the Secaucus 7*), a rarity in that martial arts films typically do not acquire a big-name director and screenwriter. Moreover, Mifune, the ultimate feudal-era samurai, seems sadly out of place in this contemporary setting. (R; 1:52) [VIDEO]

CHASE FOR THE GOLDEN NEEDLES, THE: see **GOLDEN NEEDLES**

CHINA O'BRIEN (1988) Hara-Kiri. Cynthia Rothrock, Keith Hirabayashi, Richard Norton. A gorgeous martial arts–trained policewoman returns home for some R & R, but ends up fighting for justice. This flick is laden with superb martial artists, but through indifferent and inept treatment was turned into another Clouse–Weintraub (director and producer) disaster. Preposterously, the fight scenes were shot at abnormal speed to accelerate the action, a technique used in cheap Chinese chopsockies. The result makes the actors move like the old Keystone Cops of the silent film era. Once again, the Clouse–Weintraub team had a chance to build a star—this time out of Rothrock, a marvelous talent—but failed

Jackie Chan (left) and Gary Daniels in *City Hunter*. Courtesy of Gary Daniels

dismally, just like they did with Jackie Chan and Joe Lewis. (R; 1:30) [VIDEO]

CHINA O'BRIEN II (1989) ★ Filmed back-to-back with its predecessor, this sequel features the same cast and the same characters in a different story. This time sheriff Rothrock tracks an escaped convict. The only improvement is that its fight scenes unfold at normal speed. (R; 1:25) [VIDEO]

CHINESE CONNECTION, THE (1973; Chinese) ★★★★ Bruce Lee's second full-fledged film places him in Shanghai in the early 1900s, where he seeks vengeance on the murderers of his teacher. Graceful, powerful, humorous and charismatic, the king of kung-fu cinema at his best despite the awful dubbing. Asian history fuels its scenes. English dubbed. (R; 1:47) [VIDEO]

CIRCLE OF IRON (1978) ★★ David Carradine, Jeff Cooper and cameos by Christopher Lee, Roddy McDowall and Eli Wallach. Carradine portrays four characters in this offbeat blend of mysticism and martial arts action filmed in Israel. Cooper must pass trials posed by Carradine to find the secret book of knowledge. The Carradine role was originally cowritten by and for Bruce Lee by him and Oscar-winning screenwriter Stirling Silliphant and actor James Coburn. Cooper, Carradine's friend, was chosen over karate legend Joe Lewis to play the role originally created for Coburn. Martial arts sequences were a disaster. Lewis had to double for Cooper in insert scenes shot back in Hollywood. Worth seeing for its historical and novelty value. (R; 2:00) [VIDEO]

CITY HUNTER (1992) ★★★★ Jackie Chan, Joey Wong, Kumiko Goto, Richard Norton, Gary Daniels. Based on the popular Japanese manga cartoon character. Chan plays Ryu Saeba, a womanizing detective, hired by a Japanese newspaper mogul to find his runaway daughter (Goto). He follows her onto a cruise liner. Meanwhile, his secretary (Wong), who's madly in love with Saeba, is also aboard ship on holiday. Unknown to all is a band of terrorists on board, led by McDonald (Norton) and Kim (Daniels), who plan to hijack the ship. The entire movie is shot very brightly and colorfully in cartoon style. An extraordinary highlight has Chan and Daniels playing surrealistic rival characters from the popular "Streetfighter 2" Nintendo video game. A fine example of Chan's wildly creative work pushing the entertainment envelope. Chinese with English subtitles. (?; ?) [VIDEO]

CLEOPATRA JONES (1973) ★★ Tamara Dobson, Bernie Casey, Shelley Winters, Brenda Sykes, Antonio Fargas. Black bubble-gum offering with long-legged Dobson as a karate-chopping government agent on the trail of drug kingpins. Lots of action, and fight choreography by Bong Soo Han of *Billy Jack* fame, but the film wastes the talents of a good cast. (PG; 1:29) [VIDEO]

CLEOPATRA JONES AND THE CASINO OF GOLD (1975) Wild, woolly, sexy and violent sequel to *Cleopatra Jones*. Leggy Tamara Dobson returns as a federal agent, this time in Hong Kong to take on a powerful drug lord. Stella Stevens steals the show as the sexy Dragon Lady. (R; 1:36) [VIDEO]

CYBORG (1989) ★ Jean-Claude Van Damme as a soldier of the postapocalyptic future seeking vengeance against the savage gang that killed his family. Along the way he is pressed into service to bring home a cyborg that can cure a gruesome plague. A poorly scripted, badly directed science-fiction romp and thus an odd choice of vehicle for Van Damme. That it is the second of his first three-picture deal with Cannon Films perhaps explains some of the low standards. (R; 1:30) [VIDEO]

DAWN OF JUDO: see **JUDO SAGA**

DEADLY BET (1992) Hara-kiri. Jeff Wincott, Steven Vincent Leigh, Charlene Tilton. A kickboxer (Wincott) loses his girlfriend (Tilton) in a bet. Tilton plunges a long way from her *Dallas* days. (R; 1:35) [VIDEO]

DEATH MACHINES (1976) Hara-kiri. Former number-one-ranked American karate champ Ron Marchini joined the martial arts movie trend of the mid-1970s in this ultra-low-budget piece about a lady mobster and cronies who kill for pay. (R; 1:30) [VIDEO]

DIVINE ENFORCER, THE (1991) ★★ Jan-Michael Vincent, Erik Estrada, Jim Brown, Judy Landers, Don Stroud. A mysterious priest (Vincent) cleans up a crime-ridden neighborhood using martial arts and guns. Nice concept, good cast; could have been a classic if a martial arts star were used in the lead role and the choreography was better. (R; 1:30) [VIDEO]

DOLEMITE (1975) Hara-kiri. Awful karate gangster spoof set in the milieu of black nightclubs where star Rudy Ray Moore, a stand-up comedian, performs. Lowest of low-budget blaxploitation films used some recognized black karate stars in action scenes, but they probably don't want their names mentioned. (R; 1:28) [VIDEO]

DOUBLE IMPACT (1991) ★ Jean-Claude Van Damme plays identical twins bent on avenging their parents' murders in Hong Kong. Despite the bigger budget and big film-studio connection, this is one of Van Damme's most disappointing outings. It's very uneven and the performances just don't mesh. (R; 1:50) [VIDEO]

DRAGON: THE BRUCE LEE STORY (1993) ★★★★ Jason Scott Lee, Lauren Holly, Robert Wagner. Big-budget action biography of the late, great, flamboyant martial arts film star. Magnetic Jason Scott Lee (no relation) captures Lee's charming charisma and energetic spirit spectacularly. Although the film contains many historical distortions, it is as slick and provocative as Bruce was. The romance with wife Linda (Holly) is sometimes syrupy, but overall a hugely entertaining biopic. All the fights are world class, though a number of them are in the prolonged, brutal Hong-Kong style. Son Brandon Lee died shortly before *Dragon's* release and the filmmakers dedicated it to him. (PG-13; 2:00) [VIDEO]

DRAGON FIST (1978; Chinese) ★★ Jackie Chan. Produced back-to-back with *Spiritual Kung-Fu* in Korea, this is a straight kung-fu film in which Chan plays a dishonored karate teacher. Although it lacks Chan's provocative comedy, *Dragon Fist* does feature Jackie's frenetic fight choreography and execution. In the climax, Chan and two allies form a three-legged, crutch-wielding front against the bad guys. (?; ?) [VIDEO]

DRAGON FLIES, THE: see **THE MAN FROM HONG KONG**

Jason Scott Lee in *Dragon: The Bruce Lee Story*. Courtesy of Universal Studios

DRAGONS FOREVER; THREE BROTHERS (1987; Chinese) ★★★ Creative casting puts Jackie Chan, Samo Hung, Yuen Biao and Benny Urquidez together. Chan plays a defense attorney hired to defend a factory owner accused of dumping toxic waste into fish ponds owned by a beautiful woman. Chan hires two friends (Hung and Biao) to investigate, but things go awry when Chan and Hung fall in love with the leading lady and her cousin. Boasts some of the best screen fights to come out of Hong Kong cinema, against memorable protagonists played by Yuen Wah, Dick Wei and Billy Chow. Besides some hilarious situation comedy, Chan and Urquidez pull out all the stops in a frenetic finale as satisfying as their showstopper in *Meals on Wheels*. Chinese with English subtitles; also English dubbed. (?; ?) [VIDEO]

DRUNKEN MASTER, THE; DRUNKEN MONKEY IN A TIGER'S EYE (1978; Chinese) ★★★★ Jackie Chan as Naughty Panther, rambunctious son of a staid master. Chan ends up training with an alcoholic uncle noted for brutality. After undergoing pain and humiliation he escapes, only to humbly return after being beaten by a professional assassin. In the training sessions, Chan, who had almost complete creative control, uses the long-range fighting strategies of the mythical "Eight Drunken Fairies." Seven of these eight lurching, off-center styles are beautifully demonstrated in the climactic scene, and Chan fake-fights the eighth style. The box-office success of this film was phenomenal: $8 million (Hong Kong) in its first run, and by 1979 it broke the box-office record set by Bruce Lee. With it, kung-fu comedy had arrived with Chan its Chaplinesque champion. English dubbed. (?; 2:00) [VIDEO]

DYNASTY (1977) ★★ A leader of the Ming dynasty is killed by an evil Imperial Court eunuch, and his son the monk (Bobby Ming) sets out to avenge him. Although the fights are nothing out of the ordinary, this pic gained an international audience due to its status as the first 3-D martial arts film. (Unrated; 1:34) [VIDEO]

EAGLE'S SHADOW: see **SNAKE IN THE EAGLE'S SHADOW**

EASTERN CONDORS (1986; Chinese) ★★★★ Samo Hung directed and stars in this martial arts masterpiece with Yuen Biao, Dr. Haing Ngor, Joyce Godenzi, Yuen Wah and Dick Wei. Set in 1976 after the Vietnam War, *Condors* is a kind of *Dirty Dozen*. When the U.S. pulled out of Vietnam they left behind a huge arsenal of top-secret weapons and explosives. U.S. troops could not be sent back into Vietnam so a group of criminals is offered pardons if they go behind enemy lines and blow up the ammunitions dump. The group, led by Hung, not only succeed but give a dazzling display of action that never lets up throughout the entire film. There are impressive cameo roles by Joyce Godenzi, Yusakai Kurata and Billy

Bruce Lee in *Enter the Dragon*. Courtesy of Warner Bros.

The often-imitated but never duplicated Bruce Lee in a scene from his unsurpassed martial arts masterpiece *Enter the Dragon*. Courtesy of Warner Bros.

Chow. The memorable part played by Yuen Wah made him one of the most interesting villains of the 1980s. Hung is cited as one of the "new wave" kingpins of Hong Kong cinema and *Eastern Condors* one of the best movies to come out of Hong Kong in the past decade. Don't miss it. Chinese with English subtitles. (?; ?) [VIDEO]

ENTER THE DRAGON (1973; Chinese–U.S.) ★★★★ Bruce Lee, John Saxon, Jim Kelly, Shih Kien, Bob Wall, Bolo Yeung. Lee, as a secret agent, infiltrates an exotic martial arts tournament on an island fortress to investigate a major drug kingpin. The quintessential martial arts masterpiece and one of the genre's all-time box-office champs, *Enter* has grossed over $150 million to date. This was Bruce Lee's last fully filmed role before his premature death. *Enter* is the *Citizen Kane* of martial arts films

and the movie that made Lee a global phenomenon. It was also the first collaboration between producer Fred Weintraub and director Robert Clouse, who, over the years, have cranked out a string of silly, meaningless martial arts trash yet often take credit for *Enter's* enormous success. One pair of insightful critics had this observation: "After seeing *Return of the Dragon*, made before *Enter the Dragon*, we have no doubt that Bruce Lee, not Robert Clouse, directed *Enter*. Lee was credited [in *Enter*] with staging the fight scenes, but our guess is that he was well aware of the film's possible impact and exercised control over the creative nonacting facets of the film whenever he could." Don't miss this masterpiece; it's worth viewing repeatedly. (R; Various running times: video version should be 1:37) [VIDEO]

ENTER THE FAT DRAGON (19??; Chinese) ★★★ New Wave actor–director Samo Hung parodies *and* pays tribute to the late, great Bruce Lee. (Unrated; ?) [VIDEO]

ENTER THE NINJA (1981) ★★ Franco Nero as a ninja master who takes on other ninjas. OK martial arts adventure with choreography by karate champ Mike Stone. Notable as the first of Cannon Films' numerous ninja flicks, and for Sho Kosugi's screen debut. (R; 1:34) [VIDEO]

EYE FOR AN EYE, AN (1981) ★★ Chuck Norris, Christopher Lee, Richard Roundtree, Mako. When his partner is murdered, undercover cop Norris seeks vengeance against Lee and his cronies. OK Norris fist-fest. (R; 1:46) [VIDEO]

FANTASY MISSION FORCE (1985; Chinese) ★ Jackie Chan, Wang Yu, Bridget Lin, Hsing Chia. A military expert (Yu) is hired to assemble a commando team to rescue four army generals who have been captured by the Japanese. The team consists of crooks, gamblers and con artists. One of Jackie Chan's most disappointing films. Although Chan gets top billing, most of the action centers on the female lead until the climax, when Chan saves the day. Usually, in Hong Kong movies, the action is the saving grace, but unfortunately that is not so here. Chinese with English subtitles. (Unrated; 1:30) [VIDEO]

FEARLESS HYENA, THE (1979; Chinese) ★★★★ Jackie Chan, who also directed, stars as a fighting clown/con artist paid to attract students to a bogus kung-fu school. His irresponsible actions result in his grandfather's death, and he is trained for vengeance by a long-lost clan uncle who teaches him "emotional kung-fu." As writer–choreographer–star, Chan can't miss with the kung-fu in this picture. The training and fighting sequences are truly astonishing; the film is crammed with scenes in which he fights for morsels of food with chopsticks, fights as a silent comedy mime, as a cross-eyed buffoon or disguised as a girl. The final fight is based on the esoteric "wire technique," a series of exercises accompanied by uttering cries that Jackie converts to fighting. He translates the cries into "four emotions" to confound the villain. *Fearless Hyena* emerged as the second highest grossing Hong Kong film in 1979, out-grossing *all* previous kung-fu flicks. Chinese with English subtitles; also English dubbed. (Unrated; 1:37) [VIDEO]

FIRECRACKER (1981) Hara-kiri. A female martial arts expert (Jillian Kesner) retaliates against the crooks who murdered her sister. Only scene worth watching is when gorgeous Kesner stages her best fight semi-clothed. (R; 1:23) [VIDEO]

FISTFUL OF CHOPSTICKS, A: see THEY CALL ME BRUCE?

FIST OF FEAR, TOUCH OF DEATH (1980) ★ Fred Williamson, Ron Van Clief, Aaron Banks, William Louie. Boring, awful film, actually more a documentary, chronicling events at Banks's Madison Square Garden martial arts "circus." Recommended only for the short clips of Bruce Lee. (Not rated; 1:30) [VIDEO]

FISTS OF FURY; THE BIG BOSS (1972; Chinese) ★★★ Bruce Lee's first Hong-Kong film (shot under preposterously bad conditions in rural Thailand) is corny, but effective enough to show his magnificent talent and charisma. Story line is unimportant, just watch the king in action; nobody does it better. English dubbed. (R; 1:43) [VIDEO]

FIVE FINGERS OF DEATH (1973; Chinese) Hara-kiri. This nothing-special, horrendously dubbed picture became the first Hong Kong chop-sockie released in the West, just before Bruce Lee's *The Big Boss*, and therefore shares in the distinction of having ushered in the martial arts movie boom of the 1970s. However, this breakthrough film is mostly memorable for the "plucked eyeballs" scene that branded the genre for gross, unnecessary violence. Also known as *King Boxer*. (R; 1:42)

FORCED VENGEANCE (1982) ★★ Chuck Norris takes on mobsters in Hong Kong. Average Norris actioner. (R; 1:43) [VIDEO]

FORCE: FIVE (1980) ★★ Joe Lewis, Benny "The Jet" Urquidez, Bong Soo Han, Sonny Barnes, Richard Norton, Bob Schott, Pam Huntington. Karate legend Lewis and four others rescue a young girl from clutches of Han, head of a Reverend Moon–like religious cult. Retread of producer–director Fred Weintraub–Robert Clouse formula that, given its cast and gimmick of team as collective hero, could have been outstanding but once again falls flat due to commonplace, even indifferent, treatment. Han is conspicuously an uneven rival to fight Lewis in the disappointing finale. Choreography by veteran black belt Pat Johnson; script by karate black belts George Goldsmith and Emil Farkas ruined by Clouse's incompetent rewrite. (R; 1:35) [VIDEO]

FORCE OF ONE, A (1979) ★★★ Chuck Norris as a kickboxing champion who uses his expertise to help a small California town combat drug trafficking. Marks the screen debut of legendary world kickboxing champion Bill "Superfoot" Wallace in a costarring role as the heavy; polished kickboxing contender Eric Laneuville plays Norris's adopted son (Laneuville later went on to costar in TV's *St. Elsewhere* series and is today a director of TV programs and TV movies). Decent fights choreographed by Chuck's brother, Aaron, but the Norris–Wallace finale is a let-down. (?; 1:30) [VIDEO]

FORTY-SEVEN RONIN, PART I (1942; Japanese) ★★★★ Also known as *The Loyal 47 Ronin*. Director Kenji Mizoguchi's expressionistic two-part masterpiece of one of Japan's most enduring samurai legends. A melding of noble samurai sentiments and discreet passions, the films tell the story of the forty-seven loyal samurai-retainers of Lord Asano who avenge their lord's honor in 1703 following his forced hara-kiri. Parts I and II were later blended into one long-form classic. Black and white. English subtitles. (Unrated; 1:51) [VIDEO]

FORTY-SEVEN RONIN, PART II (1942; Japanese) ★★★★ Second half of the film follows Lord Asano's samurai as they commit themselves to avenging their leader. Black and white. English subtitles. (Unrated; 1:48) [VIDEO]

FUGITIVE SAMURAI (1984; Japanese) ★★ A samurai (Kinnosuke Yorozuya), with his young son, flees a vengeful shogun and seeks the friends who betrayed him. (Unrated; 1:32) [VIDEO]

FURIOUS (1983) ★★ Simon Rhee, Howard Jackson. The sister (Arlene Montano) of a young martial arts apprentice is killed by the master. Mucho, not overly violent action suitable for viewing by youngsters. (PG; 1:25) [VIDEO]

FUTUREKICK (1991) ★ Don "The Dragon" Wilson, Meg Foster, Chris Penn. A widow (Foster) hires a futuristic bounty hunter (Wilson) to track down the cyberhuman serial killers who butchered her husband. Good sci-fi story ruined by weak direction and barely passable fights. (R; 1:36) [VIDEO]

GAMBLING SAMURAI, THE (1960; Japanese) ★★★★ Toshiro Mifune as a feudal-era Robin Hood and his vengeful quest to restore justice to the village where he was born. Mifune plays Chuji, the gambling swordsman, who returns to his village to find it destitute and becomes a samurai to correct the wrongs done to his people. Also entitled *Kunisada Chuji*. Black and white. Japanese with English subtitles. (Unrated; 1:33) [VIDEO]

GAME OF DEATH (1979; Chinese) ★★ (The genuine Bruce Lee scenes are ★★★★) Gig Young, Hugh O'Brian, Colleen Camp, Dean Jagger, Kareem Abdul-Jabbar, Bob

Wall, Dan Inosanto, Chuck Norris. Lee died after shooting several fight scenes with his students Jabbar and Inosanto. Six years later, producer Fred Weintraub and director Robert Clouse assembled a cast and four different Bruce Lee doubles to complete the film. Except for Bob Wall's inventive fight (★★★) in the locker room, it's pretty standard stuff until the climactic scenes when the real Lee enters the picture, cocky and confident, and blows everyone away with sheer presence and incredible skill. Norris appears only in the opening sequence, a replay of his fight with Lee in the Roman Coliseum from *Return of the Dragon*. By then a star on his own, he tried to stop producers from exploiting him by using the sequence. Don't miss it for Bruce's sake—and your own. (Unrated; 1:42) [VIDEO]

GHOST WARRIOR (1984) ★★ Hiroshi Fujioka, Janet Julian. Awakened from suspended animation, a four-hundred-year-old samurai pits his skills against the violence of modern Los Angeles. Low budget doesn't mar decent offbeat science fiction; enough emotional range to feel sympathy for the transplanted warrior. (Unrated; 2:00) [VIDEO]

GOKUAKU BOZU (THE WICKED PRIEST SERIES) (19??; Japanese) ★★ Tomisaburo Wakayama (star of the famed *Baby Cart from Hell* series) portrays Shinkai, the renegade priest, who uses all manner of martial arts in his fights: bojutsu, iaido, judo and karate. (?; ?) [VIDEO]

GOLDEN NEEDLES; THE CHASE FOR THE GOLDEN NEEDLES (1974) ★ Joe Don Baker, Elizabeth Ashley, Jim Kelly. Clouse–Weintraub ho-hum karate action punctuates this melodrama about the pursuit, from Los Angeles to Hong Kong, of a statue concealing a coveted youth-restoring acupuncture secret. (?; 1:32) [VIDEO]

GOOD GUYS WEAR BLACK (1979) ★ Chuck Norris, Anne Archer, James Franciscus. A Vietnam veteran (Norris) launches his own investigation into the mysterious deaths of other soldiers from his military unit. Noted for Norris's slo-mo jumping side kick through a car windshield (it was actually performed by a double, Chuck's brother, Aaron Norris). Despite its mediocrity and annoying long-winded dialogue, this film, thanks to Chuck, singlehandedly restored Hollywood's interest in martial arts films after grossing something like $25 million. (PG; 1:36) [VIDEO]

GUYVER, THE (1992) Hara-kiri. Mark Hamill, Vivian Wu, Jack Armstrong. A suit of armor transforms a martial arts student (Armstrong) into a comic-book superhero. Corny special effects and pitifully inept fight scenes draw unintentional humor. Very possibly the worst American martial arts film ever made, and an embarrassment to Hamill of *Star Wars* fame. (PG-13; 1:35) [VIDEO]

GYMKATA (1985) ★ Kurt Thomas, Richard Norton, Bob Schott. Champion gymnast Thomas stars in another silly Clouse–Weintraub direction–production shot in Yugoslavia and based on Dan Tyler Moore's novel *The Terrible Game*. Here Thomas, a one-time practicing karateka, attempts to use his own blend of martial arts and gymnastic skill to conquer his enemies. Again, this director–producer team that brought you *Enter the Dragon* shows how they waste precious talent with indifferent treatment. (R; 1:30) [VIDEO]

HALF A LOAF OF KUNG-FU (1978; Chinese) ★★★★ Jackie Chan's seventh film and his first kung-fu comedy. Essentially a slapstick send-up of martial arts movies. Chan plays a klutz who reads fighting-instruction books upside down and stumbles when surrounded by crazed killers. His character wins by accident and the martial arts action is almost pure parody. For example, pinned to a wall by the throwing stars of twenty pursuers, Chan hangs with his arms outstretched to the strains of "Jesus Christ, Superstar." Or, in need of quick energy to rescue a damsel in distress, he eats spinach while the soundtrack delivers the "Popeye the Sailor Man" theme. Chan's too innovative. His outrageous approach outraged the director and the picture was shelved and only distributed two years later, in June 1980, when Chan was an established star. It then grossed $1 million Hong Kong in its first two months. (Unrated; 1:38) [VIDEO]

HARD TARGET (1993) ★★★ Jean-Claude Van Damme, Lance Henriksen, Yancy Butler, Wilford Brimley, Kasi Lemmons. Sadistic hunters stalk and kill homeless military veterans in and around New Orleans' French Quarter. They find easy prey until they meet the ultimate "hard target" in Chance Boudreaux (Van Damme). A nonstop but extremely violent and stunt-laden suspense thriller, loosely based on 1932's *The Most Dangerous Game*, *Hard Target* marks the Hollywood directorial debut of Hong Kong's brilliant John Woo (*The Killer*). Woo wows us with the frenzied, stylized violence that built his inimitable reputation, but his films, including this one, are definitely not for kids. (R; ?) [VIDEO]

HIBOTAN BAKUTO: see **THE BIG PEONY GAMBLER**

HIDDEN FORTRESS, THE (1958; Japanese) ★★★★ Toshiro Mifune stars in this crackling comedy–adventure directed by Akira Kurosawa. Story follows the adventures of a strong-willed feudal-era princess (Misa Uehara) and her wise, sword-wielding general (Mifune), who escorts her on a dangerous journey to their new homeland with royal fortune in tow: gold encased in wooden sticks. They're accompanied by two bumbling, greedy misfits hoping to steal part of the fortune who provide comic relief as they help and hinder Mifune's efforts. Mifune's in top form as a dedicated samurai; he's formidable in

Joe Lewis (standing) with legendary director John Huston in *Jaguar Lives*. Courtesy of American International Pictures

horseback battle and a yari (spear) duel against an opposing general. Perfectly cast misfits are hilarious throughout. One of Kurosawa's personal favorites and, admittedly, the chief inspiration for producer George Lucas's 1977 megahit *Star Wars*. Film won the International Critics prize and Best Director at the 1959 Berlin Film Festival. Black and white. English subtitles. (Unrated; 2:06. Some U.S. prints cut to 1:30; released in Japan at 2:19 and reissued in the U.S. in 1984 at that length.) [VIDEO]

HOT POTATO (1976) ★ Jim Kelly reprises his role as "Black Belt Jones" to rescue a senator's daughter from a megalomaniacal general. Kelly's fans, if there are any, might like it. (PG; 1:27) [VIDEO]

IN EAGLE SHADOW FIST: see **SNAKE IN THE EAGLE'S SHADOW**

INVINCIBLE KUNG-FU LEGS: see **LEG FIGHTERS**

INVINCIBLE SWORD, THE (197?; Chinese) ★★ Jimmy Wang Yu. A group of multi-talented entertainers attempt to rescue an imprisoned member of their community. OK actioner. (Not rated; 1:33) [VIDEO]

JACKIE CHAN'S POLICE FORCE; JACKIE CHAN'S POLICE STORY: see **POLICE STORY**

JAGUAR LIVES! (1979) ★ Joe Lewis, Barbara Bach, Christopher Lee, Donald Pleasence, Capucine, Joseph Wiseman, Woody Strode, John Huston. Karate legend Joe

Lewis's first starring role, surrounded by big-name stars chiefly from the James Bond films. He plays a secret agent sent to dispatch narcotics villains in various world capitals. Top cameo cast was brought to bear because original story was a spy thriller. During production flick was turned into a martial arts film and travelogue, through no fault of Lewis's. Working together led to a brief romantic relationship between Lewis and Bach before she married Beatle Ringo Starr. (R; 1:30) [VIDEO]

JUDO SAGA (1943, 1952, 1955, 1963; Japanese) ★★★★ Akira Kurosawa's first directorial effort, considered a martial arts classic; first released as *Sanshiro Sugata*. The hero, Sanshiro Sugata, advocates the newer art of judo against established traditional jujutsu masters. Before proving himself, Sanshiro undergoes the long ordeal of learning judo in a strikingly visual film extraordinary also for its explosive martial arts choreography. Highlights are Sanshiro's bout with a jujutsu sensei to decide which art is to be taught at the police academy and his final grudge match with the Higaki brothers, both irrational karate experts, in the snows of Mount Yakushi. *Judo Saga* was first filmed during World War II and was used by the Imperial government as an internal propaganda vehicle. The negative was apparently partially destroyed after its confiscation by the American Occupation authorities. It was subsequently reconstructed and prints were released in 1952. Remade in 1955 by Shigeo Tanaka and in 1965, as *Judo Saga*, it was produced by none other than Kurosawa and directed by his former assistant, Seiichiro Uchikawa. This last version starred Toshiro Mifune, by then Japan's biggest international star, as the judo founder Jigoro Kano character named Shogoro Yano, and pop singer–matinee idol Yuzo Kayama as the student Sanshiro. Given all this rich history, could you pass it up? Also entitled *Dawn of Judo*. English subtitles. (Unrated; 1:20) [VIDEO]

KARATE KIBA (1973; Japanese) ★★★ Sonny Chiba (a.k.a. Shin'ichi Chiba) as Kiba, a master of an obscure karate system who singlehandedly foils an airline hijacking. His deed makes him an instant celebrity and, when interviewed on television, he offers his services as a bodyguard. This premise established the series, which featured many tightly choreographed fight scenes. (Unrated; ?)

KARATE KID, THE (1984) ★★★★ Ralph Macchio, Pat Morita, Martin Kove. Teenager (Macchio) is beset by bullies until an unlikely mentor (Morita), the Japanese handyman in his apartment complex, teaches him about karate—and life. Old-fashioned manipulative movie that pushes all the right buttons, thanks to perfect direction by John Avildsen (*Rocky*). Winning performances by Macchio and Morita (who was Oscar-nominated for best supporting actor), poignant choreography by Pat John-

Ralph Macchio (left) and Pat Morita in *The Karate Kid*. Courtesy of Columbia Pictures

son and terrific script by veteran black belt Robert Kamen. The first martial arts film since *Enter the Dragon* to gross over $100 million. (PG; 2:06) [VIDEO]

KARATE KID II, THE (1986) ★★★ Ralph Macchio and Pat Morita return as the philosophic sensei and his student, each of whom clashes with rivals in Okinawa. Corny sequel was shot in Hawaii and is saved only by marvelous performances by Macchio and Morita. Has touches of the original magic, but can't tie an obi on the original. Still, it made a magic $100+ million. (PG; 1:35) [VIDEO]

KARATE KID III, THE (1989) ★★ Ralph Macchio, Pat Morita, Martin Kove, Thomas Ian Griffith, Robyn Lively. The Kid (Macchio at twenty-seven years old!) is set up for slaughter by nemesis Kove. When Morita refuses to train him, Macchio turns instead to Griffith, a sadistic millionaire Vietnam vet. Kid spirals until sensei steps in to save him. Worst entry of the series due to Macchio's inadequate martial arts skills. Rumors were he didn't train for the film and it showed. Consequently, box-office grosses dropped to about half of the earlier films, proving you can't fake it in this day and age. (PG; 1:45) [VIDEO]

KENTUCKY FRIED MOVIE (1977) ★★★ Numerous skits tie together this first film by the twisted creators of *Airplane* and *The Naked Gun*. In the segment called "A Fistful of Yen," considered the pic's highlight, Evan Kim parodies Bruce Lee in a lengthy takeoff of *Enter the Dragon*. The evil Mr. Han is played by hapkido master Bong Soo Han. (R; 1:18) [VIDEO]

KICKBOXER (1989) ★★★★ *The Karate Kid* meets *Rocky*—

call it a "Suki-Aki Rocky"—with Jean-Claude Van Damme and world heavyweight kickboxing champion Dennis Alexio as brothers brought up apart in America and Europe. Van Damme plays a charming Jackie Chan-esque bumpkin who studies Muay Thai with a mystical mentor named Xian (Dennis Chan) in order to battle the notorious Tong Po (Michelle Qissi, at the time Van Damme's manager), Thailand's Thai-boxing champ responsible for paralyzing Van Damme's older brother (Alexio). Superlative visual fight feast makes stunning use of editing jump cuts for both fight scenes as well as the training sequences. Ring fights might be too brutal for some discerning tastes. Film also brings back the Oriental mysticism that seems to infatuate Western audiences. (R;1:45) [VIDEO]

KICKBOXER 2: THE ROAD BACK (1991) ★ A fighter (Sasha Mitchell) challenges his brothers' killer (Michel Qissi). The producers should have been paging Jean-Claude to redeem this pitiful Van Damme–less sequel. (R; 1:30) [VIDEO]

KILL OR BE KILLED (1980) Hara-kiri. Pseudo-martial artist James Ryan plays a modern karate champ taking part in a tournament in which an ex-Nazi coach seeks revenge against the Japanese counterpart who bested him in a tournament in World War II. As dumb as it sounds. (PG; 1:40) [VIDEO]

KILL THE GOLDEN GOOSE (1979) ★★ Witnesses scheduled to testify before a U.S. Senate subcommittee are slain one by one; only the "Golden Goose" is spared. Bong Soo Han and Ed Parker in a grade-C production with gratuitous violence that never succeeded in acquiring theatrical release. Best-selling author and veteran martial artist Joe Hyams appears in a brief scene. Rarity makes it a genuine collector's item. (R; 1:31) [VIDEO]

KILL AND KILL AGAIN (1981) ★★ Pseudo-martial artist James Ryan plays a champion who attempts to rescue a kidnapped Nobel Prize–winning chemist who has developed a high-yield synthetic fuel. Fun, tongue-in-cheek romp. (PG; 1:40) [VIDEO]

KILLER METEOR (1977; Chinese) ★★ Jackie Chan's fourth film and the first and only one in which he plays a villain. No comedy in this period piece, but some impressive swordplay. (Unrated; ?) [VIDEO]

KING BOXER: see **FIVE FINGERS OF DEATH**

KING KUNG FU (1987) ★★ An outlandish and sometimes screamingly funny genre bender. A karate master raises a gorilla and sends it from Asia to the U.S. There, two out-of-work reporters decide to release it from captivity and then recapture it so they can get the story and some needed recognition. What they don't know, however, is that its master taught it kung-fu! A must-see for all martial arts film buffs. (G; 1:30) [VIDEO]

KOJIRO (1967; Japanese) ★★★★ Kikunosuke Onoe, Tatsuya Nakadai. Director Hiroshi Inagaki's epic, first-rate semi-sequel to *The Samurai Trilogy* casts Nakadai as fabled master swordsman Miyamoto Musashi, whose exploits made up the three previous films. Here, however, the focus is on Kojiro (Onoe), whose goal is to follow in Musashi's footsteps and become Japan's greatest swordsman. English subtitles. (Not rated; 2:32) [VIDEO]

KOWLOON ASSIGNMENT (1977) ★★ An assassin assigned to terminate Hong Kong's underworld kingpin must face a relentless policeman (Sonny Chiba) intent on stopping him at any cost. (Not rated; 1:33) [VIDEO]

KUNISADA CHUJI: see **THE GAMBLING SAMURAI**

LADY OKATSU (series) (19??; Japanese) ★★ Junko Miyazono plays the Tokugawa-era aristocrat of the title role who mastered kenjutsu to avenge the politically motivated deaths of her parents. Her cover is that of an itinerant singer and her sword is disguised as part of the shamisen with which she accompanies herself. Japanese language. (Unrated) [VIDEO]

LADY REPORTER: see **THE BLONDE FURY**

LADY SNOW BLOOD (series) (19??; Japanese) ★★ Meiko Kaji as Yuki, a turn-of-the-century lady gambler who learned swordplay to avenge the imprisonment and subsequent death of her mother. She carries a straight-edged sword disguised as the handle of her parasol, and regularly rights the wrongs of evildoers until overwhelmed by the police, who chastise her for her shenanigans. Japanese language. (Unrated) [VIDEO]

LAST DRAGON, THE (1985) ★★★ Taimak, Vanity, Ernie Reyes, Jr. Largely black cast in a teenage film about a would-be martial arts master (Taimak) who gets involved with glamorous veejay (Vanity) and some energetic gangsters. Released theatrically as *Berry Gordy's The Last Dragon* as a tribute to the founder of Motown. Mostly campy kid stuff, but pure good fun for all ages. Ernie Reyes, Jr. in action is a thrill to watch and so is the gorgeous Vanity, who's *always* worth the price of admission. Notably, of all the genuinely black-produced films of the 1980s, *The Last Dragon* was the fifth most profitable at $25.7 million in North American box-office grosses. (PG-13; 1:49) [VIDEO]

LEGACY OF RAGE (1988; Chinese) ★ Brandon Lee's only Hong Kong kung-fu film unfortunately does not stand above the crowd. (?; ?)

LEGEND OF THE EIGHT SAMURAI (1984; Japanese) ★★ Hiroku Yokoshimaru, Sonny Chiba. Disappointing de-

rivative fantasy about a princess who leads her warriors into battle against a giant centipede, ghosts and a nearly immortal witch. English dubbed. (Not rated; 2:10) [VIDEO]

LEGEND OF THE SEVEN GOLDEN VAMPIRES: see **SEVEN BROTHERS MEET DRACULA**

LEG FIGHTERS (198?; Chinese) ★★★ Tan Tao-Liang, Shiah Guang Lih. Tan plays the master of the Tan kick school who, after defeating the second master of the ground kick school, is hired to teach Phoenix (Lih), the spoiled, mischievous daughter of a wealthy man. At first, she despises Tan for his disciplined teaching methods, but after he rescues her from being assaulted she learns to respect him and accepts his teachings. Film displays some unique exercises for improving kicks, which should thrill all aspiring martial artists. The climactic fight predictably sees Tan and Phoenix do battle with the master of the ground kicks in an amazing footfest. The dubbing is sometimes very annoying, but *Leg Fighters* is a must-see since Tan has to be considered one of the best kickers in martial arts movie history. Alternate title is *Invincible Kung-Fu Legs*. English subtitles; also English dubbed. (?; ?) [VIDEO]

LIGHTNING SWORDS OF DEATH (1974; Japanese). ★★★★ Superior entry in the *Baby Cart from Hell* series (and the *Sword of Vengeance* subseries) finds the discredited samurai (Tomisaburo Wakayama) roaming medieval Japan with his son and a baby cart packed with concealed weapons in tow. Nonstop action and grand but bloody finale. Followed by *Shogun Assassin*. In English. (R; 1:23)

LIONHEART (1990) ★★★ Jean-Claude Van Damme, Harrison Page, Lisa Pelikan. Van Damme stars as a Foreign Legionnaire who deserts his African post when he learns of his brother's violent death in Los Angeles, and eventually becomes involved in an underground stateside bare-knuckle fighting circuit. An imaginative justification for both Van Damme's European persona and engagement in combat; and one of Jean-Claude's personal favorites among his own films. Competent fights and direction by Sheldon Lettich, who also directed *Double Impact* and *Only the Strong*. Also called *A.W.O.L.* and *The Wrong Bet*. (R; 1:05) [VIDEO]

LITTLE TIGER FROM CANTON (1971; Chinese) ★ Jackie Chan's movie debut. The problem is twofold: 1) it's a straight (noncomedy) martial arts flick in which Chan must avenge the murder of his parents; 2) to coincide with the popular fighting style of action films at the time, Chan uses more karate than kung-fu. (Unrated; ?)

MACHIBUSE (19??; Japanese) ★★★★ Toshiro Mifune reprises his *Yojimbo* character in this all-star production featuring Shintaro Katsu (of *Blind Swordsman* fame),

Kinnosuke Nakamura (*Musashi*) and Yujiro Ishihara (*Shadow Hunter*) with direction by Hiroshi Inagaki (*Samurai I–VI*). How could it miss? (?; ?)

MAGIC CRYSTAL, THE (1987; Chinese) ★ Fuses the fisticuffs of Cynthia Rothrock and Australian Richard Norton with a silly space rock. English dubbed. (Unrated; ?)

MAGNIFICENT BODYGUARD (1978; Chinese) ★★ Jackie Chan's eighth movie; an experimental film done in 3-D in which encounters with snakes and other dangers exploit the potential of three-dimensional effects. The martial arts action in this period costume drama is similarly played for shock realism and speed, especially the sword fights. Seeing it on the big screen in 3-D was its chief asset; otherwise, you're not missing much. (?; ?) [VIDEO]

MAGNIFICENT WARRIORS (198?; Chinese) ★★★ Michelle Khan, Richard Ng. Frenetic, nonstop actioner starring Michelle Khan (a.k.a. Michelle Yeoh), the ex-Miss Malaysia and one of Hong Kong's leading-lady fighters of the 1980s. Khan plays a freelance spy for the Chinese government who's sent to a small town occupied by the Japanese. Her mission is to locate a Chinese undercover spy and obtain essential information about the Japanese plans to build a poisonous chemical plant there. Of course, all doesn't go as planned, giving plenty of excuses for Ms. Khan to mesmerize us with her considerable martial arts grace and agility. Chinese with English subtitles. (?; ?) [VIDEO]

MANCHURIAN AVENGER, THE (1984) ★ Bobby Kim, Bill "Superfoot" Wallace. An Asian man who possesses "the fastest feet in the West" returns home to his adopted parents to find gangs have taken over his Colorado hometown. Only problem with this cockeyed low-budget offering is that Wallace, not the Asian man, has the fastest feet in the West, if not in the world, and Wallace's presence is the only reason to see the movie. (R; 1:27) [VIDEO]

MAN FROM HONG KONG, THE (1975; Australian–Chinese) ★★ Jimmy Wang Yu, George Lazenby. Stunt-laden saga of a Hong Kong emissary and kung-fu expert brought to Sydney, Australia, to help nail a drug lord. Originally titled *The Dragon Flies*, this star-filled coproduction was prompted by the global martial arts movie boom. Nothing special, but surprisingly triggered a hit song, "Sky High." (R; 1:43)

MARTIAL LAW (1990) ★ Chad McQueen, David Carradine, Cynthia Rothrock. A cop (McQueen, the late Steve McQueen's son) seeks vengeance on his brother's murderer (Carradine). Despite an impressive martial arts cast, this pic is annoyingly bad. (R; 1:30) [VIDEO]

MARTIAL LAW 2: UNDERCOVER (1991) ★ Jeff Wincott, Cynthia Rothrock. Cops weed out drug lords in Los Angeles. Leaves little to the imagination. (R; 1:35) [VIDEO]

MASTER KILLER (1978; Chinese) ★★★ Liu Chia Hui. Despite the terrible Americanized title, this engrossing film is a don't-miss favorite of Asian cinema buffs. It traces the monastery and martial arts training of the reluctant revolutionary Liu Yu Te, who was to become the famous real-life Shaolin monk San-Te. The protracted set of training sequences takes up most of the film and is first-rate. One sequence shows how San-Te invents the sophisticated three-sectional staff. If you've ever wondered what it took to become a Shaolin monk, this film shows you a good part of it. Also entitled *The Thirty-Sixth Chamber*. Chinese with English subtitles. (R; 1:46) [VIDEO]

MASTER OF THE FLYING GUILLOTINE, THE (1975; Chinese) ★★★ Corny but imaginative cult classic featuring the baddest weapon this side of Kathmandu. Jimmy Wang Yu, the biggest name in Hong Kong kung-fus until the arrival of Bruce Lee, gives an entertaining performance as a one-armed fighter. Contains sensational tournament with rogues' gallery of awesome competitors. Has to be seen to be believed. English dubbed.

MAXIMUM FORCE (1992) ★ Sam Jones, Sherrie Rose. Two Los Angeles cops go undercover to nail a crime lord. So-so. (R; 1:30) [VIDEO]

MEALS ON WHEELS (1983; Chinese) ★★★★ Jackie Chan, Samo Hung, Benny Urquidez, Keith Vitali, Yuen Biao, Lola Forner. Story follows the fortunes of two Chinese youths living in Spain. Thomas (Chan) and David (Biao) make a living selling fast food from their high-tech Mitsubishi van. Hung plays an apprentice private detective and the three principals become separately involved with the lovely Sylvia (Forner) who, unknown to all, is really an heiress whose uncle plots to keep her from her rightful inheritance. Using their martial arts skills, Thomas and David demolish all comers but finally meet their match in Urquidez and Vitali (in real life, two famous American martial arts champions). Chan's climactic fight against Urquidez is what one critic called "the best onscreen fight in either's careers." Also called *Spartan X*. English dubbed. (?; ?) [VIDEO]

MEKURA NO OICHI: see **BLIND SWORDSWOMAN**

MILLIONAIRE'S EXPRESS: see **SHANGHAI EXPRESS**

MIRACLE: see **MR. CANTON AND LADY ROSE**

MR. CANTON AND LADY ROSE (1989; Chinese) ★★★ A derivative tale, based on the Hollywood classic *Pocketful of Miracles*, where Jackie Chan plays a naive country boy who comes to the big city and, after buying a rose from an old lady, unwittingly gets involved in a gangland shoot-out between two mob bosses. As one of the bosses dies, with his last breath he names Jackie as his successor. Jackie accepts and, after proving himself worthy, leads the gang to much prosperity while swaying them away from crime and into more charitable pursuits. In this film, Chan focused more on story content than action. Therefore it is not packed with as much bone-crunching action as his other films. There are two outstanding fight scenes, one in a restaurant and an amazing confrontation in a rope factory that words can hardly describe appropriately. Also entitled *Miracle*. Chinese with English subtitles. (?; ?) [VIDEO]

MUSASHI I–VI (1960–67; Japanese) ★★★★ Six features based on swordsman–hero Miyamoto Musashi's life, starring Kinnosuke Nakamura and directed by Tomu Uchida. The sixth stanza of the series pinpoints the time when Musashi, facing a chain-and-sickle master, devised his renowned *nito-ryu* (two-sword) school of swordsmanship. See also *The Samurai Trilogy*.

MY LUCKY STARS (1984; Chinese) ★★★★ Another masterpiece of action–comedy; in fact, the textbook example of how to add humor to combat as demonstrated by the masters of the genre: Jackie Chan, Samo Hung, Yuen Biao and Michiko Nishiwaki. Chan and Biao are partners who chase the villains into a Japanese theme park, where they are unexpectedly ambushed by ninjas. Biao is captured. Jackie cannot return to rescue him because he'll be recognized, so his boss recruits Chan's old orphanage buddies, led by Hung, who has to be paroled from jail. The rest of the group is made up of veteran Hong Kong comedians, including Richard Ng. From here the movie focuses on their comedic talents until they reach Japan, where the action resumes full blast. Back in the theme park, Chan has to penetrate a haunted house featuring different "theme" rooms, each of which presents a challenge of its own. Japanese actress/bodybuilder Nishiwaki makes an impressive film debut as a Yakuza hitwoman. American Benny Urquidez, in a cameo role, fights Chan again. A genre classic. Released on European video as *Tokyo Powerman*. Chinese with English subtitles. (Unrated; 1:30) [VIDEO]

NEW FIST OF FURY (1976; Chinese) ★★ Jackie Chan's second film is a straight kung-fu picture set during World War II and directed by Lo Wei, who helmed Bruce Lee in *Fist of Fury*. Wei brought Chan back to Hong Kong from a lengthy visit to his parents in Australia. The fighting bears a slight resemblance to Lee's, but with Chan's acrobatics. Chan's sensational with the three-sectional staff. (Unrated; 2:00) [VIDEO]

NIGHT OF THE WARRIOR (1991) ★ An exotic dance-club owner (Lorenzo Lamas) pays his disco bills by fighting in illegal underground blood matches. Lamas stars with real-life wife Kathleen Kinmont and mother Arlene Dahl. (R; 1:36) [VIDEO]

NINE DEATHS OF THE NINJA (1985) ★ Even Sho Kosugi's earnest attempts can't save this low-budget ho-hummer about a ninja sent to rescue a congressman kidnapped by terrorists. Junk-fu. (R; 1:34) [VIDEO]

NINJA MOVIES

While compiling this guide, more than fifty imported ninja films were available in video release, many of them Chinese, not Japanese (the country where they originated), productions. I did not review these films since even their titles were imitative and derivative in nature. There are, however, several Chinese actors who portray ninja characters in more than one film and, depending on quality, consequently could become cult stars.

NINJA DRAGONS (1993) ★★★ Ted Jan Roberts, Stephen Furst, Don Wilson (cameo). Furst stars as Uncle Bob, a second-rate, alcoholic, gambling talent agent in Los Angeles whose bad habits catch up with him at the same time his niece and nephew (Roberts) pay him a visit. The kids' goal is to meet their respective idols. Ultimately, through Roberts's influence, Uncle Bob straightens up his act, and Roberts gets to meet his idol, Don "The Dragon" Wilson (playing himself), on a movie set. A seriocomic little film and thoroughly enjoyable romp that touches on some real wholesome human values. Roberts, a sound teenage actor, exhibits enormous star potential. (PG-13; 1:30) [VIDEO]

NINJA III: THE DOMINATION (1984) ★ Lucinda Dickey, Sho Kosugi, David Chung. *The Exorcist* meets *Enter the*

T.J. Roberts (center) in *Ninja Dragons*. Courtesy of Bob Gilmore and T.J. Roberts

Ninja. An evil contemporary ninja killed by the police forces his spirit on an innocent woman with ESP and an interest in ancient Japanese culture. She becomes possessed by his spirit when she inherits his magic sword, and only Kosugi can bring her bloody rampage to an end. Dickey, a dancer, doesn't cut it in a martial arts role. The opening sequence, a confrontation between the ninja antagonist and the police, is terribly bloody and violent. (R; 1:35) [VIDEO]

NINJA TURF (1986) ★★ Jun Chong, Bill "Superfoot" Wallace, James Lew, Phillip Rhee. A high school gang leader working as a security guard for a drug dealer steals a large sum of cash from his boss and later has to fend off a hired killer. Good cast. (R; 1:23) [VIDEO]

NINJA WARS (1984; Japanese) ★ Sonny Chiba. The title says it all. (R; 1:35) [VIDEO]

NO RETREAT, NO SURRENDER (1985; Chinese–U.S.) ★ Jean-Claude Van Damme stands out in this small vehicle marking his screen debut. In it, a teenager who continually gets beat up by bullies finds an instructor who's supposedly the ghost of Bruce Lee. Sounds dumb, and is for the most part. Some reviewers call it one of the ten worst martial arts films ever made, saved only by Van Damme's presence. Most embarrassing moment is when Lee, a Chinese, is referred to as "Sensei," the *Japanese* title for "teacher." (R; 1:25) [VIDEO]

NO RETREAT, NO SURRENDER II (1986; Chinese) Harakiri. Cynthia Rothrock and Loren Avedon star in a film that is not a sequel and, in fact, has nothing to do with the picture of the original title. It was retitled to dupe audiences into thinking Jean-Claude Van Damme, whose star was rising in Hollywood, was repeating his role. Story has a man accompanied by two martial arts experts searching the Vietnam jungles for his kidnapped fiancée. Rothrock, in her English-language debut film, is the only one worth watching. Also called *Raging Thunder.* (R; 1:32) [VIDEO]

OCTAGON, THE (1980) ★★★ Chuck Norris, Lee Van Cleef, Karen Carlson, Carol Bagdasarian, Tadashi Yamashita, Richard Norton. Norris is lured out of retirement to protect lovely lady (Carlson) from ninja assassins, the leader (Yamashita) of whom is Chuck's Asian half-brother. One of Norris's better karate films and a modern spin-off of the old retired-gunfighter theme; rich production values. Title refers to architectural shape of ninja headquarters. Only two complaints: parts of nocturnal fight scenes between Norris and ninja gang are too dark to see, and his climactic battle with weapons-whiz Yamashita could have been a scorcher but is practically nonexistent. Good choreography by Chuck's brother, Aaron. (R; 1:43) [VIDEO]

ONCE UPON A TIME IN CHINA (1991; Chinese) ★★★ Jet Lee, Yuen Biao, Rosamund Kwan. Lee plays the legendary Hung Kune master, Wong Fei Hung, who leads a local gang against foreign influence and fights with rival gangs. Film marks the return of traditional kung-fu movies to Hong Kong. Lee is in real life a five-time wushu champion and Hong Kong cinema's latest sensation. He supplies superb action for fans of the genre. Chinese with English subtitles. (?; ?) [VIDEO]

ONCE UPON A TIME IN CHINA II (1992; Chinese) ★★★★ Jet Lee, Rosamund Kwan, Donnie Yen. Lee reprises his role in this sequel to take on the evil White Lotus Society, whose members have taken a blood oath to rid China of all foreigners. A rare sequel that far surpasses the original. Some say the final twenty minutes contain some of the most exciting and entertaining fight footage ever shot. Chinese with English subtitles. (?; ?) [VIDEO]

ONE-EYED SWORDSMAN (1963; Japanese) ★★★ Tetsuro Tanba, Haruko Wanibuchi. A mysterious one-eyed, one-armed samurai (Tanba) fights for the underdogs in 1730 Japan. Interesting but derivative character based on a combination of the One-Armed Swordsman (made famous by Jimmy Wang Yu) and the Blind Swordsman (made famous by Shintaro Katsu). Still, great swordplay for fans of the genre. English subtitles. (Unrated; 1:35) [VIDEO]

OUT FOR BLOOD (1993) ★★ Don "The Dragon" Wilson, Shari Shattuck. A karate-trained defense attorney unwittingly falls in love with a mobster's mistress while secretly taking revenge against the crime ring that murdered his family. Low-budget *Batman* in a karate gi. Good story, performances and fights; some chaotic action sequences. (R; 1:30) [VIDEO]

PAINTED FACES (198?; Chinese) ★★★ Samo Hung, Lam Ching Ying, Cheng Pei Pei. A docudrama that follows the highly disciplined training and progress of the Peking Opera Troupe called the "7 Little Fortunes." Hung plays the venerable and strong-armed instructor Master Yu, who puts the students through their paces. We follow the students' trials and tribulations all the way to the closing of the school, when they get their first taste of movie work as underpaid stuntmen. This is a classic look at the traditional institution that produced Hung, Jackie Chan and Yuen Biao, three of the hottest action stars in Hong Kong cinema today. Chinese with English subtitles. (?; ?) [VIDEO]

PERFECT WEAPON, THE (1991) ★★ Jeff Speakman, Mako, James Hong. A karate expert (Speakman) is out to avenge his mentor's murder. Speakman's acting career was launched in this moderately budgeted kenpo–karate fest choreographed by the late kenpo grandmaster Ed Parker and released by Paramount. It offers some slick scenes, but nothing special emanates from its star. (R; 1:25) [VIDEO]

PICASSO TRIGGER (1988) Hara-kiri. James Bond–like ripoff with stagey action sequences, plentiful doses of T and A from *Playboy*-type models and another low-budget drug plot. Film debut for world heavyweight kickboxing champ Dennis Alexio; weapons sensation Keith Hirabayashi also has a bit part. The director didn't even remotely know how to shoot a fight scene and the choreography stinks. (R; 1:40) [VIDEO]

POLICE FORCE: see **POLICE STORY**

POLICE STORY; POLICE FORCE; JACKIE CHAN'S POLICE FORCE; JACKIE CHAN'S POLICE STORY (1985; Chinese) ★★★ Another incredibly stunt-filled feast starring and directed by the magnificent Jackie Chan, who, as usual, does all his own stunts. He plays a bumbling cop assigned to protect a star witness in a drug case. He's framed for murder and ends up on the run from his own comrades. Jaw-dropping opening grabber was duplicated almost shot for shot in Sly Stallone's 1990 *Tango and Cash*. Chan's climactic stunts in a shopping mall defy the imagination: you wonder how he's still living, or stays in one bodily piece. (PG-13; 1:41) [VIDEO]

POLICEWOMEN (1974) ★★ No-name cast in violent actioner salvaged only by talented Sondra Currie as a karate expert/cop. (R; 1:39)

PRAY FOR DEATH (1985) ★★★ Very violent Sho Kosugi vehicle in which he avenges the brutal murder of his family. (R; 1:33) [VIDEO]

PROJECT A (1987; Chinese) ★★★ Jackie Chan, Samo Hung, Yuen Biao. Chan plays an early twentieth-century Coast Guard sergeant. Due to budgetary problems and the fact that they have failed to nab some mean pirates, the Coast Guard is closed down and all its members are forced to join the police force. Chan quits the force and teams up with an old friend (Hung) who is now a professional thief. After Chan uncovers a corrupt police official, he gets the Coast Guard reinstated and puts "Project A" into operation to catch the pirates. A Chan classic with lots of Chaplin-style gags, great fights and plenty of the kinds of stunts that have made Jackie and his stunt team world famous. Chinese with English subtitles; also English dubbed. (?; ?) [VIDEO]

PROJECT A, PART II (1988; Chinese) ★★★ Jackie Chan, Maggie Cheung, Rosamund Kwan. Chan recreates his role as Sergeant Dragon Ma of the Hong Kong Coast Guard in this sequel that picks up where the original left off. Chan is assigned to help out an overworked police officer who is running a corrupt department. After using a fantastic demonstration of martial arts expertise to arrest a major gangster, Chan earns the respect of the department but the envy of Inspector Chun. This sequel is definitely slower than its predecessor, but Chan's action scenes make up for any awkward pacing. Some film critics feel this movie is the peak Jackie Chan experience.

Chinese with English subtitles; also English dubbed. (?; ?) [VIDEO]

RAGE OF HONOR (1987) ★ After the brutal murder of his partner, a Phoenix-based narcotics officer (Sho Kosugi) heads to Buenos Aires with vengeance on his mind. By this film, Sho's fight choreography is beginning to wear thin. There's also a pair of ninja midgets on hand! For die-hard Kosugi fans. (R; 1:31) [VIDEO]

RAGING THUNDER: see **NO RETREAT, NO SURRENDER II**

RAW FORCE (1982) Hara-kiri. Martial artists from the Burbank Karate Club versus the living dead in the Philippines!!! One of the worst martial arts films ever, but not bad *enough* to be good camp. Nevertheless, Jillian Kesner (*Firecracker*) is great to look at. (R; 1:26) [VIDEO]

REMO WILLIAMS: THE ADVENTURE BEGINS (1985) ★★★ Fred Ward, Joel Grey, Wilford Brimley. Juvenile action–adventure story based on the *Destroyer* novels and directed by James Bond–helmer Guy Hamilton. A New York City cop (Ward) is recruited by a secret society out to avenge society's wrongs and is trained by an inscrutable "Korean Sinanju" master (Grey). Almost works, but Ward isn't thoroughly likable as hero and numerous scenes misfire. Grey, who won an Oscar for *Cabaret*, is terrific (★★★★) as the mystic Oriental mentor; don't miss the scene where he dodges bullets. (PG-13; 2:01) [VIDEO]

RETURN OF THE CHINESE BOXER (1974; Chinese) ★★ Jimmy Wang Yu as a Chinese warrior who discovers a plot by the Japanese to invade his homeland by first dispatching advance spies. English dubbed. (Unrated; 1:33) [VIDEO]

RETURN OF THE DRAGON; WAY OF THE DRAGON (1974; Chinese) ★★★★ In his third film, Bruce Lee plays a country bumpkin visiting relatives who run a Chinese restau-

Bruce Lee (right) versus Chuck Norris in *Return of the Dragon*. Courtesy of Golden Harvest Studios

rant in Italy and fight off gangsters trying to take it over. Contains riveting, brilliant moments and shows Bruce's genuine flair for comedy and for filmmaking in general. He wrote the script, directed, produced and starred in *Return*. *Return of the Dragon* was made before *Enter the Dragon*, and it shows Lee's considerable directorial talent. Hard-hitting fight with Bob Wall. Finale is the now-legendary battle with Chuck Norris set in the Roman Coliseum. English dubbed. (*Way of the Dragon*, in Chinese with English subtitles, has loads of extra scenes not in the dubbed version.) (R; 1:31) [VIDEO]

RETURN OF THE STREET FIGHTER (1975; Japanese) ★ Sonny Chiba is back battling many formidable foes. (R; 1:17) [VIDEO]

REVENGE OF THE NINJA (1983) ★★ Sho Kosugi, Keith Vitali, Arthur Roberts. Cannon Films' follow-up to *Enter the Ninja*, in which three-time national karate champ Keith Vitali made his screen debut. In it, a good ninja (Kosugi) takes on an evil ninja (Roberts). A cut above the average chop-sockie. (R; 1:28) [VIDEO]

RIGHTING WRONGS (1986; Chinese) ★★★ Cynthia Rothrock, Yuen Biao, Melvin Wong and introducing Karen Shepard. Biao plays an attorney who prosecutes criminals during the day, but at night, when they are released because of technicalities, he acts as judge, jury and executioner. Rothrock plays a CID inspector assigned to investigate the murder of a Triad boss, who, unbeknownst to Rothrock, was killed by Biao. Before long she is hot on the attorney's trail until she catches him at the scene of a crime he didn't commit. In a long climax, Rothrock is grotesquely killed and Biao saves the day. One of Cyndi's best pieces of work. (Both Cyndi and Karen Sheperd were American forms and weapons champions on the national tournament circuit before making a transition to entertainment.) Chinese with English subtitles; also English dubbed. (?; ?) [VIDEO]

RING OF FIRE (1991) ★★ Don "The Dragon" Wilson, Maria Ford, Steven Leigh, Eric Lee, Dale Jacoby, Gary Daniels. A pacifist medical doctor (Wilson) discovers that his new romantic interest (Ford) has put him at odds with gang violence. Nice little film, good story, good fights. (PG-13 & R; 1:36) [VIDEO]

RING OF FIRE II: BLOOD AND STEEL (1993) ★★ Don "The Dragon" Wilson, Maria Ford, Sy Richardson, Ian Jacklin, Eric Lee. Wilson reprises his role as the pacifist medical doctor who now must rescue his kidnapped fiancée from a ruthless gang leader in this veiled tribute to Bruce Lee's *Enter the Dragon*. Weak story, fancy fights. (PG-13; 1:34) [VIDEO]

ROAD HOUSE (1989) ★★★ Patrick Swayze, Kelly Lynch, Sam Elliott, Ben Gazzara. *Dirty Dancing* meets *The Street-fighter*. Hot on the heels of his *Dirty Dancing* megahit,

Swayze plays a bar bouncer and New York University philosophy major who cleans out a Missouri saloon and tangles with local township kingpin Gazzara. A pure male action film crammed with rough-and-tumble fights—some of which are *very* violent—a high body count and a disappointing level of sexist humor. Fights were choreographed by world kickboxing champ Benny "The Jet" Urquidez, with whom Swayze, a veteran martial artist, was training at the time. (R; 1:48) [VIDEO]

SAGA OF THE VAGABONDS (1959; Japanese) ★★★ Toshiro Mifune is the protagonist, a Robin Hood–like bandit chieftain who leads a band of men, dressed in red armor, to distribute their plunder to needy peasants suffering oppression under greedy warlords. English subtitles. (Unrated; 1:55) [VIDEO]

SAMURAI SAGA (1959; Japanese) ★★★ Toshiro Mifune, again, as a gallant hero in a romantic love triangle set in 1599, as the Tokugawa Clan challenges the might of the Toyotomi Clan. Lovely princess falls in love with the handsome Toyotomi samurai (Mifune). Black and white. English subtitles. (Unrated; 1:52) [VIDEO]

SAMURAI TRILOGY, THE; SAMURAI I–III (1954; Japanese) ★★★★ *The* samurai films for the uninitiated. Epic three-picture series starring Toshiro Mifune as the legendary swordsman–hero Miyamoto Musashi. This brilliant and cinematically beautiful set of films by director Hiroshi Inagaki traces the development of the real swordsman's character from his wild youth through spiritual discovery under the influence of the priest, Takuan, to the final battle with his nemesis, Kojiro Sasaki (Koji Tsuruta). Essentially, the series shows how Musashi grew from a crude peasant to a great samurai. In *Part I*, Musashi is named Takezo, a competent but brash fighter who's also a fugitive. He's captured without a fight by the priest, Takuan, who begins teaching the rough-edged youth the Code of Bushido. He takes the samurai name Miyamoto Musashi and sets out on a solo journey to challenge other schools and improve his craft. This masterpiece won a 1955 Oscar as Best Foreign Film. *Samurai 2: Duel at Ichijoji Temple* opens with a very suspenseful duel at which Musashi faces and defeats a chain-and-sickle master, follows his romantic relationship and is climaxed by a tense mass battle pitting Musashi against *all* the students of a particular school of swordsmanship. In *Samurai 3: Duel at Ganryu Island*, Musashi settles his romantic affairs, saves a village from marauding desperadoes and engages in a final, thrilling duel with his nemesis Sasaki. In the end he finds spiritual awakening. As usual, Mifune is impeccable as a samurai. Black and white. English subtitles. A so-called semi-sequel is *Kojiro*. (Not rated; 5:05) [VIDEO]

SANJURO (1962; Japanese) ★★★★ Toshiro Mifune, Tatsuya Nakadai. Top-notch sequel to *Yojimbo*. Director–writer Akira Kurosawa teams again with Toshiro Mif-

Toshiro Mifune (slinging sword) in *The Seven Samurai.* Courtesy of Landmark Films

une as Tsubaki Sanjuro, essentially the same character as in the previous film, a wandering *ronin* (masterless samurai) recruited by nine bumbling younger warriors as their teacher and leader in exposing corruption among the elders of their clan. It pokes more fun at the genre's cliches and the laws of *bushido* ("way of the warrior"). Fastest finale in film history. Black and white. (Not rated; 1:36) [VIDEO]

SANSHIRO SUGATA: see **JUDO SAGA**

SEVEN BLOWS OF THE DRAGON (1973; Chinese) ★ David Chiang. Skilled outlaws team up with oppressed villagers to avenge a martial arts expert's death. English subtitles and English-language versions. (Unrated; 1:30) [VIDEO]

SEVEN BROTHERS MEET DRACULA (1974; British–Chinese) ★★ Peter Cushing, David Chiang, Julie Ege, Shih Szu. Hammer Films' last Dracula movie was a coproduction with Hong Kong's kung-fu tycoons, the Shaw Brothers, which accounts for this exotic mixture of the martial arts and horror–fantasy genres. In it, famed vampire hunter Professor Van Helsing (Cushing) is in China in the late nineteenth century to vanquish Dracula with the help of local martial artists. Stimulating mix of horror and high kicks reportedly worked better in the original 89-minute version. Also known as *The Legend of the Seven Golden Vampires.* (R; 1:55) [VIDEO]

SEVEN SAMURAI, THE (1954; Japanese) ★★★★ Toshiro Mifune, Takashi Shimura, Yoshio Inaba, Ko Kimura, Seiji Miyaguchi, Mioru Chiaki. Director Akira Kurosawa's classic about sixteenth-century Japanese villagers who hire a professional band of seven warriors to fend off an annual attack by marauding bandits. This scruffy bunch of misfit *ronin* (masterless samurai) risk their lives not for a noble cause but for a daily bowl of rice and a new adventure. Kurosawa's "Eastern Western" has served as a basis for many American films, the best known of which is *The Magnificent Seven.* Remarkable performance by Toshiro Mifune. Powerful action sequences; probably one of the ten best "pure" (non-special effects) action–adventure movies ever made. Black and white. English subtitles. (Not rated; 2:21 and a complete 3:28 long version that appears on two videotapes; 3:17 on some other tapes) [VIDEO]

SHANGHAI EXPRESS (1985; Chinese) ★★★ Cynthia Rothrock, Richard Norton, Lam Sum Mei, Yuen Biao, Dick Wei. Samo Hung directs this comedy with an all-star cast aboard a train called the Shanghai Express. The basic premise is that the train is besieged by bandits on its maiden voyage from Shanghai to Chendu. There are so many substories that there's plenty of opportunity for the typically zany Hong Kong humor and fast-paced action. This movie helped establish Rothrock as a new force in Hong Kong actioners; look for her brief but outstanding fight scene with Hung. Also entitled *Millionaire's Express.* Chinese with English subtitles. (?; ?) [VIDEO]

SHAOLIN TEMPLE, THE (1982; Chinese) ★★★★ What one critic called "the best kung-fu film since *Enter the Dragon,*" this period piece, set in seventh-century China, traces the history of the famed Shaolin Temple, a central birthplace of the martial arts. A martial arts classic starring the country's top wushu stylists; mixes action with characterization and plot. English subtitles. (Unrated; 1:51) [VIDEO]

SHAOLIN TEMPLE II, THE (19??; Chinese) ★★★ More Jet Lee exploits for his followers. English subtitles. (Unrated; ?) [VIDEO]

SHAOLIN WOODEN MAN; SHAOLIN WOODEN MEN (1976; Chinese) ★★★ Jackie Chan's third film, another straight kung-fu revenge-oriented piece. A renegade Shaolin monk trains Jackie to take on the awesome wooden fighters, 108 huge, activated warrior dummies, at the Shaolin Temple. In an ironic twist ending, Chan also avenges his father's death. Director Chen Chi Hwa and the choreographer gave Chan some creative freedom and he has the opportunity to express his real talent for the first time, which drew a few compliments, but had no effect on the box office. (Unrated; ?) [VIDEO]

SHOGUN ASSASSIN (1980; Japanese–U.S.) ★★★★ Tomisaburo Wakayama. Another superlative entry in the *Baby Cart from Hell* series brilliantly edited out of two different features in the *Sword of Vengeance* subseries, rescripted, rescored (by Mark Lindsay) and dubbed in English. It finds the discredited samurai (Tomisaburo Wakayama), as usual, wandering the countryside pushing his young son in a baby cart laden with concealed lethal weapons. Constantly pursued by ninjas and other assassins, he stops, or is stopped, only to engage in all manner of combat and aesthetically choreographed violence. As critic Leonard Maltin put it, an "absolutely stunning visual ballet of violence and bloodletting." This version was made strictly for Western audiences and is narrated by the child in the cart; it's sort of a sequel to *Lightning Swords of Death* in that it was edited from its sequel. (R; 1:29) [VIDEO]

SHOOTFIGHTER: FIGHT TO THE DEATH (1992) ★★★ Bolo Yeung, James Pax, Billy Zabka, Michael Bernardo, Bob Schott, Miryam D'Abo. A tale of two martial arts masters (Yeung and Pax), opponents since their youth, who twenty years later engage in a deadly battle in the shootfighting ring. A surprisingly good story and low-budget film. (R; 1:35) [VIDEO]

SIDEKICKS (1993) ★★★ Jonathan Brandis, Chuck Norris, Mako, Joe Piscopo, Richard Moll. Wholesome teen-kid fantasy about a super–Chuck Norris fan who meets his idol (Norris, playing himself) and gets his life straightened out. Basically a spin-off of *The Karate Kid* with Mako fine in the Pat Morita role. Brandis is superb as the kid with daydreaming problems. Good-hearted story and mild martial arts action. (PG; 1:40) [VIDEO]

SILENT ASSASSINS (1987) ★★★ Sam Jones, Jun Chong, Phillip Rhee, Mako, Linda Blair. Nicely executed buddy-actioner in which real-life instructor (Chong) and student, a commando (Jones), team up as a cop and his martial arts mentor to prevent ninja bad guys from getting a germ-warfare formula from kidnapped scientist. Tae kwon do master Chong, who also choreographed fight sequences, shows impressive kicks and he and Jones have close, humorous chemistry that comes across on film. Nice combo of real actors and real martial artists. There should be a sequel. (R; 1:35) [VIDEO]

SILENT FLUTE, THE: see **CIRCLE OF IRON**

SILENT RAGE (1982) ★★ *Breaker, Breaker* meets *Night of the Living Dead*. Small-town Texas sheriff Chuck Norris versus a genetically engineered, Frankenstein-like psychotic killer who is virtually indestructible. Offbeat, intriguing concept that might have worked better under different circumstances, but a mix of too many genres: karate–horror–thriller–Western! (R; 1:45) [VIDEO]

SLAUGHTER IN SAN FRANCISCO (1981; Chinese) Harakiri. Second run of 1974's *The Yellow-Faced Tiger* re-released to exploit Chuck Norris's stardom. Norris plays a supporting-role cardboard character as cigar-chomping mafioso and appears only briefly. Veteran karateman Dan Ivan also appears in this abysmal mess that will disappoint even hardcore chop-sockie fans. (R; 1:27) [VIDEO]

SNAKE AND CRANE ARTS OF SHAOLIN (1978; Chinese) ★★★ Jackie Chan's fifth film; another serious kung-fu and the first that drew serious attention to Jackie from Hong Kong filmmakers. The storyline is simple: Eight masters create a powerful style called "the eight steps of snake and crane" and place these secrets into a book; then they and the book mysteriously disappear. Chan turns up with the book and fights off a multitude of opposing clans who try to take it away from him. As martial arts director, Chan shot for the sky. He took two days to film the main title credits, a series of fifty-eight actions performed in one continuous take, the moves of which are timed and positioned to point up the opening credits as they appear. In the film itself, Jackie offers some swashbuckling single-sword work against multiple opponents. English dubbed. (Not rated; 1:35) [VIDEO]

SNAKE FIST FIGHTER: see **SNAKE IN THE EAGLE'S SHADOW**

SNAKE IN THE EAGLE'S SHADOW; SNAKE FIST FIGHTER; EAGLE'S SHADOW (1978; Chinese) ★★★★ Jackie Chan's ninth—and breakthrough—film. This genre trendsetter is considered the first of the "kung-fu comedies" despite the earlier *Half a Loaf of Kung-Fu*, which remained unreleased until 1980. Chan plays a brawny menial at a kung-fu school where he is abused by sadistic, pompous masters and students. He befriends a wily old vagabond who, in reality, is a master of the Snake-Fist style. He teaches Chan to escape from attacks, but avoids showing him the repressed Snake-Fist style until an encounter with two Eagle-Claw stylists almost costs him his life. Chan learns Snake-Fist and dukes it out with the Eagle-Claw villains to save his and his master's life. Chan is brilliant during his comically difficult solo and duo

Jackie Chan in *Snake in the Eagle's Shadow*. Courtesy of George Foon

training sequences. Terrific platform for introducing Chan's impish humor and theatrical flair. The pic's mixture of humor and martial excitement made Chan a star and a growing Asian box-office force. English dubbed. (Not rated; 1:30) [VIDEO]

SPARTAN X: SEE MEALS ON WHEELS

SPIRITUAL KUNG-FU (1978; Chinese) ★★★ Jackie Chan meets *Poltergeist*! In a mostly straight role, Chan is a happy-go-lucky bumpkin who must learn the lost secrets of the five traditional animal styles if he is to overcome his adversary. In a burned-out scripture hall rumored to be haunted by the spirits of the masters of the five styles, he finds their secret book, which has supposedly been destroyed. When he falls asleep, tiny ghosts of the Dragon, Snake, Tiger, Crane and Leopard styles emerge from hiding to make fun of him. He turns the tables and blackmails the ghosts into attaining human size and teaching him the lost fighting arts. Innovation of superimposing camera produces special FX wherein Chan, who also choreographed the fights, can engage in combat with the ghosts. (Unrated; 1:35) [VIDEO]

STING OF THE DRAGON MASTERS, THE (1974; Korean) ★ A film from the early martial arts boom era noted only for its status as one of only two movies starring Grandmaster Jhoon Rhee, the "father of American tae kwon do." (R; 1:36) [VIDEO]

STRANGER AND THE GUNFIGHTER, THE (1976; Italian–Chinese) ★★ Lee Van Cleef, Lo Lieh. *The Good, the Bad, and the Ugly* meets *Red Sun* as hard-drinking cowboy (Van Cleef) joins forces with kung-fu expert (Lieh) to recover a missing fortune, with portions of the map tattooed on the posteriors of assorted lovelies. Amusing low-budget mix of spaghetti Western and chop-sockie. (R; 1:47) [VIDEO]

STRANGER FROM SHAOLIN, THE (197?; Chinese) ★★ The story of Lim Wing Chun, founder of the wing chun style. Of interest to kung-fu history buffs. English subtitles. (Unrated; ?)

STREETFIGHTER, THE (1975; Japanese) ★★ Sonny Chiba. Ultraviolent fare gave this pic a dubious slice of cinema history: It was the first film the Motion Picture Association of America rated X for violence. Consequently, a butchered R-rated version, in which the film's guts have been removed, was released on home video. English dubbed. (R; 1:17) [VIDEO]

STREET FIGHTER'S LAST REVENGE, THE (1979; Japanese) A martial arts expert (Sonny Chiba) is hired to stop the underworld from stealing a landmark pharmaceutical formula. Like its predecessor, ultraviolent. English dubbed. (R; 1:20) [VIDEO]

STREET KNIGHT (1993) ★ White street vigilantes murder African-American and Hispanic gangs, making each think the other group is to blame. Ex-cop Jeff Speakman steps in to settle things with savage violence. A career slide for Speakman, who made his debut in the bigger and better *Perfect Weapon*. (R; ?) [VIDEO]

SUPERCOPS: SEE **YES, MADAM**

SURF NINJAS (1993) ★★ Ernie Reyes, Jr., Ernie Reyes, Sr., Leslie Nielsen, Rob Schneider, Tone Loc. Innocuous kid stuff in which two teenage brothers living in America embark on big adventure after discovering they are long-lost princes of an island in the South China Sea. There, they must use their martial arts skills to overthrow the island's dictator (Nielsen) so they can return to California, finish school and continue surfing. Plenty of *dude*-itude (PG; 1:30) [VIDEO]

SWORD OF DOOM, THE (1967; Japanese) ★★★ Stars Tatsuya Nakadai as a brutal samurai, trained by Toshiro Mifune, in a rousing samurai epic. Nakadai and Mifune are excellent as the blood-lusting warrior and his elder master. Fascinating action–adventure interweaves several stories, two of which, however, are left unresolved. Still, great for fans of samurai flicks. Black and white. English subtitles. (Not rated; 2:02) [VIDEO]

SWORD OF FURY I AND II (1973; Japanese) ★★★ A distinctively cold-blooded version of the story of master swordsman Miyamoto Musashi, one of Japan's legendary samurai, this one played by Hideki Takahashi and directed by Tai Kato. English subtitles. (Unrated; 1:17 and 1:16) [VIDEO]

SWORD OF JUSTICE, THE (197?; Japanese) ★★★ Series starring and produced by Shintaro Katsu (of *Blind Swordsman* fame) that incorporates both the erotic and martial arts genres that became popular with Japanese audiences around 1970. Katsu portrays a Tokugawa-era constable who, in one scene, might engage in a sai-versus-sword fight and in another interrogate a female suspect by subjecting her to the exquisite torture of sexual excesses! Despite the nudity and sexual content, the series is held together by a satirical thread and doesn't take itself too seriously. Great fun if you're open-minded, but not for kids. (Unrated) [VIDEO]

SWORDS OF DEATH (1971; Japanese) ★★★ Miyamoto Musashi (Konnosuke Nakamura), Japan's greatest swordsman, faces his chain-and-sickle-wielding antagonist, Shishio Baikan (Rentaro Mikune), in an exciting, stylistic duel to the death. In this pseudo-sequel to the Musashi *Samurai Trilogy*, Musashi develops his famous two-sword technique. English subtitles. (Unrated; 1:16) [VIDEO]

TALE OF FORTY-SEVEN LOYAL RETAINERS OF THE GEN-ROKU ERA, A: see **FORTY-SEVEN RONIN**

TEENAGE MUTANT NINJA TURTLES, THE MOVIE (1990) ★★★ Cowabunga, dude! They're lean, green and on the big screen! It's those four wacky comic-book cult heroes from the highest-rated cartoon in TV syndication, starring in a live-action, *un*animated romp. *TMNT, the Movie* set the all-time spring release box-office record with an opening release gross of $25.4 million, becoming the third most profitable debut in history just behind topper *Batman* and *Ghostbusters II*! It eventually grossed over $100 million. Ernie Reyes, Jr. and three Hong Kong stuntmen–martial artists, along with the magic of Jim Henson's animatronic muppetry, breathe life into the turtles' mucho fight scenes in this sometimes wildly funny film. A first-rate novelty for kids. (PG; 1:33) [VIDEO]

TEENAGE MUTANT NINJA TURTLES II: THE SECRET OF THE OOZE (1991) ★★ The reptiles confront the vengeful villain Shredder. Not as good as the original. (PG; 1:30) [VIDEO]

TEENAGE MUTANT NINJA TURTLES III (1993) ★★ Traces the bodacious adventures of the four whimsical, renaissance reptiles as they travel four hundred years back in time to ancient Japan to save their TV reporter friend from a ruthless Japanese warlord who thinks she's a witch, and a vicious pirate captain who thinks she's an enemy spy. Like, wow, most excellent for kids. (PG; ?) [VIDEO]

THEY CALL ME BRUCE? (1982) ★★ Johnny Yune, Margaux Hemingway, Ralph Mauro, Pam Huntington. Hollywood's first real attempt at comedy kung-fu; Jackie Chan has nothing to worry about. Korean comedian Yune plays an Asian immigrant who, because of a resemblance to Bruce Lee and an accidental exhibition of craziness misinterpreted as martial arts expertise, gets a reputation as a mean dude. Only occasionally funny parody. Could have been an imaginative concept, but many of the gags are based on TV commercials. Mauro, playing "Bruce's" chauffeur, steals the show. Also known as *A Fistful of Chopsticks*; sequel is *They Still Call Me Bruce*. (PG; 1:28) [VIDEO]

THEY STILL CALL ME BRUCE (1987) Hara-kiri. Johnny Yune, David Mendenhall, Pat Paulsen, Robert Guillaume, Joey Travolta. Comedian Yune returns in and codirects this useless, name-only sequel to *They Call Me Bruce?* He plays a Korean searching for the American GI who saved him years before and he winds up instead playing a big-brother figure to orphan Mendenhall. (PG; 1:31) [VIDEO]

THIRTY-SIXTH CHAMBER, THE: see **MASTER KILLER**

THREE BROTHERS: see **DRAGONS FOREVER**

Teenage Mutant Ninja Turtles 3. Photo by Robert Isenberg; courtesy of New Line Cinema

3 NINJAS (1992) ★★ Surprisingly good kid stuff when three junior martial artists (Michael Treanor, Max Elliott Slade and Chad Power) try to foil a smuggling scheme. Victor Wong, as the crazed ninja grandpa, is a scream and chief scene-stealer. (PG; 1:25) [VIDEO]

TIGER CLAWS (1991) ★ Jalal Merhi, Bolo Yeung, Cynthia Rothrock. A serial killer targets martial arts experts and a martial arts–trained cop (Rothrock) investigates. (R; 1:35) [VIDEO]

TO KILL WITH INTRIGUE (1978; Chinese) ★ Jackie Chan's sixth film, a Shaw Bros. imitation costumer notable only for some dazzling sword scenes. (Unrated; 1:47) [VIDEO]

TOKYO POWERMAN: see **MY LUCKY STARS**

TOP SQUAD: see **INSPECTOR WEARS SKIRTS**

TWINKLE, TWINKLE, LUCKY STARS (1987; Chinese) ★★★ Jackie Chan, Samo Hung, Yuen Biao, Richard Norton. Wonderful cast in wacky film featuring two humungous fights that allow viewers to compare Chan and Biao styles side-by-side. Director–actor Hung steals the show in hilarious sequence where he wages history's first clash of sai-versus-tennis racket! (Unrated; ?) [VIDEO]

ULTRA FORCE: see **YES, MADAM**

WARRIORS II (1978; Chinese) ★★★ Samo Hung, Casanova Wong, Lam Ching Ying. In this period piece, directed by Samo Hung, Wong, an exponent of Hung kung-fu, overhears a plot to kill the local mayor by the henchmen of local banker Mo. While seeking help he is discovered by one of Mo's men and subsequently beaten up. While escaping he encounters Samo Hung, who takes him to a Dr. Tsan. Meanwhile, to draw him out of hiding, the mayor and Casanova's mother are slain. Hung suggests that Casanova should learn Dr. Tsan's style, but the doctor refuses to teach it on the grounds that revenge is the wrong motive from which to learn, but the doctor finally acquiesces. Teaching and training sequences are a traditional staple of Hong Kong kung-fu cinema, but these in *Warriors II* are absolutely stunning, and make this flick a must for serious kung-fu genre fans. Chinese with English subtitles; also English dubbed. (?; ?) [VIDEO]

WATCH OUT, CRIMSON BAT (1969; Japanese) ★★★ A blind lady samurai (Yoko Matsuyama) must deliver a sack containing a valuable secret that can win a war. The female counterpart of the *Blind Swordsman*. (Unrated; 1:27) [VIDEO]

WAY OF THE DRAGON: see **RETURN OF THE DRAGON**

WHEN TAEKWONDO STRIKES (1983) ★ Grandmaster Jhoon Rhee plays a tae kwon do master who leads the Korean freedom fighters against the occupying Japanese army in World World II. For Mr. Rhee's fans. (R; 1:35) [VIDEO]

WICKED PRIEST, THE: SEE **GOKUAKU BOZU**

WRONG BET, THE: see **LIONHEART**

YELLOW-FACED TIGER, THE: see **SLAUGHTER IN SAN FRANCISCO**

YES, MADAM (1985; Chinese) ★★★★ Cynthia Rothrock, Michelle Khan, Dick Wei. American Cyndi Rothrock's debut film and still considered her best work. She and Michelle Khan tag-team against the Yakuza led by James Tien and his chief henchmen (Wei). Intriguing visual

Toshiro Mifune in *Yojimbo*.

style and considered one of the all-time best female fight films to come out of Hong Kong. Solid cameos by ex-Hong Kong kickboxing champ Eddie Mayer and famous Hong Kong director–producer Tsui Hark. Also entitled *Supercops*, and retitled *Ultra Force* for European video release. English dubbed. (?; ?) [VIDEO]

YOJIMBO ("THE BODYGUARD") (1961; Japanese) ★★★★ Director–cowriter Akira Kurosawa's powerful "Oriental Western" and first full-fledged comedy about an unemployed samurai (Toshiro Mifune) hired by two warring factions that are destroying a town. He teaches both sides a well-deserved lesson, but not before realizing he's become an anachronism in a nineteenth-century world of change. Much sword flashing and slashing. Mifune creates the role of the dirty, scratching *ronin* ("masterless samurai") later comically immortalized by *Saturday Night Live's* John Belushi in a parody of a parody. Superlative tongue-in-cheek samurai film and the inspiration for the 1964 "spaghetti Western" *A Fistful of Dollars*, which made an international star of Clint Eastwood. Sequel is *Sanjuro*. Black and white. English subtitles; also a version dubbed into English. (Not rated; 1:50) [VIDEO]

YOUNG MASTER, THE (1980; Chinese) ★★★★ A raucous Jackie Chan entry in which he's mistaken as the mysterious new brigand known only as "White Fan," whose skills are repeatedly tested during his efforts to bring his wayward friend back to the side of justice. He has several frenetic encounters with a letter-of-the-law sheriff and the sheriff's sawhorse-fighter son and "skirt-foot" fighter daughter, and wraps with perhaps the longest climactic fight ever staged. Jackie's main-title sequence, a Lion Dance fight over, under and around obstacles, is a must-see. So is his brilliant use of props in a fan-fight (for

A studio shot of Cynthia Rothrock, star of *Yes, Madam*. Courtesy of Cynthia Rothrock

which one of the actions reportedly required 328 takes!), and the sawhorse and skirt-foot fights. Then Chan, as a female impersonator (sporting a rugged-looking beard!), engages in some hilarious skirt-foot fighting himself. *Young Master* broke all previous box-office records in Hong Kong at the time of its release. Fans maintain this is Chan's last full martial arts film. After this, he combined a more realistic style of fighting with death-defying stunts. English dubbed. (Unrated; ?) [VIDEO]

YOUNG TIGER, THE (1980; Chinese) ★★ A 90-minute forgettable movie is followed by a 12-minute documentary on the inimitable Jackie Chan. A novelty. (R; 1:42) [VIDEO]

ZATOICHI, THE BLIND SAMURAI (196?) ★★★★ The legendary Blind Swordsman (Shintaro Katsu) of feudal Japan employs spectacular swordplay to defeat his enemies. See also: *Blind Swordsman* (series). (Unrated; 1:30) [VIDEO]

ZATOICHI MEETS HIS EQUAL (19??; Japanese) ★★★★ Engrossing series entry in which the Blind Swordsman crosses paths with the itinerant one-armed Chinese swordsman of Hong Kong movie fame played by star Jimmy Wang Yu. Predictably, there are spectacular sequences pitting Chinese and Japanese swordplay. In one, the unarmed Wang Yu uses kung-fu against multiple samurai. Japanese with English subtitles. (Unrated; ?) [VIDEO]

ZATOICHI MEETS YOJIMBO (1970; Japanese) ★★★★ Shintaro Katsu and Toshiro Mifune, two superstars of the Japanese samurai genre, square off in this comic entry in the long-running *Blind Swordsman* series. Katsu plays Zatoichi, the almost superhuman hero, in a story that's a send-up of Akira Kurosawa's *Yojimbo*, with Mifune doing a humorous turn on his most famous character, the grubby, scratching *ronin* (masterless samurai). Zatoichi returns to a once-peaceful village to find it overrun by gangsters who have hired the infamous mercenary Yojimbo to protect them and a stolen horde of the government's gold. A wonderful battle of wits and swords follows as Zatoichi takes on the gangsters, hired assassins and government spies before finally facing Yojimbo. Fans shouldn't miss it. See also: *Blind Swordsman* (series). English subtitles. (Not rated; 1:56) [VIDEO]

CHAPTER 16

FILMS WITH MARTIAL ARTS

Appearing here are 140 listings featuring films, documentaries and television shows of relevance to the martial arts. There are five categories, each preceded by a separate introduction:

Martial Artists as Lead Characters
Martial Arts as Story Line
Classic Scenes
Documentaries
Television

MARTIAL ARTISTS AS LEAD CHARACTERS

A subgenre, starting with Akira Kurosawa's samurai films and later restructured by several Chuck Norris films, came into its own in the 1980s: non-martial arts movies starring a martial artist. When Norris made the career-sensible transition from martial arts to the far more lucrative action–adventure genre—where he began earning almost $2 million per film—it opened the gate for others to follow ... and they did. Within this subgenre appear Dolph Lundgren, the giant Swede, aikido ace Steven Seagal and Jean-Claude Van Damme. Others will undoubtedly follow.

~ •• ~

ABOVE THE LAW (1988) ★★★★ Slam-bang screen debut of martial marvel Steven Seagal, the first martial artist to use "combat" aikido on film. Seagal combines Clint Eastwood's charisma with a wholly unique fight-scene savvy in a right-wing saga of a Chicago cop uncovering CIA-backed drug runners. Dazzling choreography of violent one-on-ones in which Seagal pulls no punches. Andrew Davis, who helmed Chuck Norris in *Code of Silence*, directs. Seagal coproduced and cowrote the story. (R; 1:37) [VIDEO]

Ray Harryhausen's brilliant stop-action special effects pits Jason of *Jason and the Argonauts* against an army of sword-slinging skeletons.

Steven Seagal (right) in *Above the Law*. Courtesy of Warner Bros.

ANGEL TOWN (1989) ★★ Olivier Gruner, Teresa Saldana. Kickboxer Olivier Gruner makes a comfortable starring debut in this action–drama as a foreign exchange student and kickboxer forced into combat with East Los Angeles street gangs. Directed by Eric Karson, who helmed Chuck Norris in *The Octagon*. (R; 1:30)

BATMAN (1989) ★★★★ Michael Keaton, Jack Nicholson, Kim Basinger. The blockbuster fantasy epic that brought the Caped Crusader (Keaton) to the big screen to face the infamous super-criminal Joker (Nicholson). Keaton's Batman employs all manner of martial arts in the pursuit of dark justice and the fight scenes are terrific. (PG-13; 1:26) [VIDEO]

BATMAN RETURNS (1992) ★★★★ Batman (Michael Keaton) reprises his dark role in another blockbuster epic, this time combatting the Penguin (Danny DeVito) and Catwoman (Michelle Pfeiffer). Slick fights. (PG-13; 2:10) [VIDEO]

BRADDOCK: MISSING IN ACTION III (1988) ★★ Colonel James Braddock (Chuck Norris) returns to Vietnam with heavy artillery to claim his Vietnamese wife, Amerasian son and an orphanage full of offspring of American soldiers. Brief but nicely executed Bangkok bar fight capped by slick gun disarmament. Aaron Norris, Chuck's brother, made his directorial debut. Mostly for Braddock fans. (R; 1:45) [VIDEO]

BUFFY THE VAMPIRE SLAYER (1992) ★★★ Kristy Swanson, Luke Perry, Donald Sutherland, Pee-wee Herman. Swanson plays a California teen whose destiny it is to slay vampires. Besides possessing uncanny natural gifts to carry out her duties, she is trained in martial arts and other skills by a mysterious mentor (Sutherland). Entertaining mix of comedy and action. (PG-13; 1:30) [VIDEO]

CODE OF SILENCE (1985) ★★★ Chuck Norris plays a Chicago police force loner who fights gang violence and remains untainted by cop corruption covered up by their own "code of silence." Norris's breakthrough to stardom and possibly his best work on film to date. As one critic called it, "Dirty Chuckie." Thrilling mass fight scene in barroom before which Norris utters one of the outstanding cinematic lines of the 1980s: "If I want your opinion, I'll beat it out of you." (R; 1:41) [VIDEO]

CYBORG COP (1993) ★ David Bradley, Todd Jensen, John Rys-Davies. Sibling DEA agents take on a drug lord, who transforms one brother (Jensen) into a robot. Could have been good, but isn't; low budget and bad acting kills a good concept. Even the fight scenes fail. (Not rated; 1:35) [VIDEO]

DEATH WARRANT (1990) ★★★ Jean-Claude Van Damme, Robert Guillaume, Cynthia Gibb. Van Damme plays a Royal Canadian Mountie who goes undercover in prison where inmates are perishing under mysterious circumstances. He's on the brink of solving the mystery when an inmate transferee threatens his cover. Contains less martial arts "Van Damage" than usual and was the first film to move Muscles from Brussels closer to the action–adventure genre. (R; 1:29) [VIDEO]

DELTA FORCE, THE (1986) ★★ A name cast surrounds Chuck Norris and Lee Marvin as they come to the rescue of plane passengers hijacked by terrorists in the Middle East. Very loosely based on the real-life TWA episode. Strictly action–adventure with no martial arts. (R; 2:09) [VIDEO]

DELTA FORCE 2: OPERATION STRANGLEHOLD (1990) ★★ Chuck Norris returns in a sequel he cowrote. He travels to South America to rescue DEA agents taken captive by a drug kingpin. Chuck's brother, Aaron Norris, directed. Production suffered notoriety when helicopter crash during filming in the Philippines killed cast members; it was the second such incident in an Aaron Norris–directed film. (R; 1:50) [VIDEO]

FAST GETAWAY (1990) ★ Corey Haim, Leo Rossi, Cynthia Rothrock. A teen (Haim) and his dad (Rossi) mastermind bank robberies and are chased by a determined female martial arts expert (Rothrock). (PG-13; 1:35) [VIDEO]

FIREWALKER (1986) Hara-kiri. Chuck Norris's first attempt at humor and, critically, his worst work on film. He and Lou Gossett, Jr. play two soldiers of fortune searching for hidden treasure. (PG; 1:36) [VIDEO]

HARD TO KILL (1990) ★★★ Steven Seagal plays a cop left for dead who reawakens after seven years in a coma to get revenge for the murder of his family, with the help of nurse (his real-life wife) Kelly LeBrock. Action not as consistently good as in Seagal's first film, *Above the Law*, but his fights work on every level. He's just terrific to watch. (R; 1:35) [VIDEO]

HERO AND THE TERROR (1988) ★★ Chuck Norris, Steve James, Ron O'Neal, Billy Drago. Norris is a cop stalked by a gigantic serial killer (former football player Jack O'Halloran) he once put away. As one critic put it, "Chuck put in Grade-A work—perhaps his best acting ever—but the movie is Grade B." (R; 1:36) [VIDEO]

HITMAN, THE (1991) ★ Chuck Norris leads a no-name cast, playing a cop undercover as a syndicate hitman. He triggers a three-way mob bloodbath between the Mafia, French-Canadian hoods and Iranian fanatics. A step backward for Chuck. (R; 1:35) [VIDEO]

HOUSE WHERE EVIL DWELLS, THE (1982) ★ Routine horror entry in which an American family (Edward Albert, Susan George) move into a stylish house in Kyoto haunted by ghosts of a doomed nineteenth-century love triangle involving two samurai. Some violent scenes, including the opening. (R; 1:31) [VIDEO]

INVASION U.S.A. (1985) ★ Chuck Norris, Richard Lynch, Billy Drago. A retired CIA agent (Norris) returns to active duty when Russian terrorists invade Florida and try to take over America by causing panic and turmoil. Enormous body count. For Norris fans only. (R; 1:30) [VIDEO]

LONE WOLF MCQUADE (1983) ★★★ Chuck Norris, David Carradine, Barbara Carrera. Norris's breakthrough to mainstream audiences. Chuck plays a maverick Texas Ranger out to nab gun-runners. Antagonist Carradine, a kung-fu practitioner, is no match for world karate champ Norris in the one-sided finale. Film does contain Chuck's best acting scenes with a woman, sexy Carrera. (PG; 1:47) [VIDEO]

MARKED FOR DEATH (1990) ★★★ Steven Seagal, Joanna Pacula, Basil Wallace. Vice cop Seagal retires from duty and returns to his hometown to find it overrun with violent Jamaican drug dealers led by a frightening mystery man (Wallace) who keeps his underlings and his enemies in line with voodoo. Fights are first-class violence as usual, but it's almost impossible to understand one word the heavily accented Jamaican actors spout. (R; 1:33) [VIDEO]

MISSING IN ACTION (1984) ★★ Chuck Norris as Colonel James Braddock, an embittered vet who becomes a one-man rescue party for POWs being held in Vietnam. Film was responsible for helping to launch the Vietnam movie trend of the 1980s, and was the biggest box-office hit of the year for an independent studio. Norris shows some neat stuff, but easily overwhelms less-capable Soon Teck-Oh in climactic fight scene. (R; 1:41) [VIDEO]

MISSING IN ACTION II: THE BEGINNING (1985) ★ Chuck Norris, Soon Teck-Oh. Prequel to the original, in which Norris escapes from the POW camp in Vietnam. Mainly for Norris lovers. (R; 1:36) [VIDEO]

NEMESIS (1992) ★★ Sleek, provocative hard-action thriller set in the future with Olivier Gruner as an L.A. cop trying to save humanity from being annihilated by cyborgs. This *Invasion of the Body Snatchers* for the '90s ponders whether we are worth his efforts. Some F/X fight scenes are unusual. (R; 1:35) [VIDEO]

NOWHERE TO RUN (1993) ★★ Jean-Claude Van Damme, Rosanna Arquette, Ted Levine. Van Damme plays a convict who escapes from prison and hides out on the farm of a pert young widow (Arquette), whose land is being eyed by an evil real-estate company. The con defends the widow while developing a paternal bond with her son. A tolerable update of the Western

Chuck Norris in *Invasion U.S.A.* Courtesy of the Showtime Channel

classic *Shane*, this was Van Damme's attempt to break into mainstream cinema with toned-down action. (?; ?) [VIDEO]

ONLY THE STRONG (1993) ★★★ A young army discharge (Mark Dacascos) returns to his Miami high school to turn the lives of twelve tough students around as he teaches them Capoeira, the acrobatic Brazilian martial art. Fine acting by the charismatic Dacascos, who exhibits an irresistible charm, and nice Capoeira choreography. Directed by Sheldon Lettich, who helmed two Van Damme films and knows what he's doing. (R; ?) [VIDEO]

OUT FOR JUSTICE (1991) ★★ Steven Seagal, William Forsythe, Jerry Orbach. A psychotic Brooklyn hood (Forsythe) launches a murder spree and lone-wolf cop Seagal races against other police and the mob to nail him. Great barroom-brawl scene shows Seagal at his brutal best. Very, very violent film overall. (R; 1:31) [VIDEO]

PASSENGER 57 (1992) ★★★ An airline security expert (Wesley Snipes) happens to be on a plane when an ace hijacker (Bruce Payne) grabs control and starts killing passengers. Slick, tense thriller in which Snipes, a veteran black belt, uses karate and the Brazilian art of Copeira to put the bad guys in their place. Some implausibility, but it's balanced by high energy and fast action. (R; 1:25) [VIDEO]

PROTECTOR, THE (1985; Chinese) ★★ Jackie Chan as an undercover New York cop traveling to Hong Kong to break up a major heroin ring that's shipping its goods to

Jackie Chan (kicking) in *The Protector*. Courtesy of Warner Bros. and Golden Communications

Studio shot of Dolph Lundgren, star of *The Punisher*. Courtesy of George Foon

New York City. More nicely filmed action sequences than kung-fu, but Chan's sense of humor is evident. Still, this could arguably be Jackie's worst film. Jackie Chan's second unsuccessful stab at mainstream American audiences. When will filmmakers realize Jackie's humor is universal, and package him for the global market appropriately—with the right concept, script, supporting stars and director? (R; 1:34) [VIDEO]

PUNISHER, THE (1990) ★ Dolph Lundgren as an ex-cop on a vendetta against New York's underworld. Same old plot, just a different face using some martial arts. (R; 1:35) [VIDEO]

RASHOMON (1951; Japanese) ★★★★ Toshiro Mifune, Machiko Kyo. By way of flashbacks, four people in twelfth-century Japan relate differing accounts of a rape–murder from the three people involved in the crime and the single witness. A superb study of truth and human nature. Excellent performances from the entire cast, particularly Mifune as a samurai bandit. Director Akira Kurosawa's dramatic masterpiece won a Best Foreign Film Oscar and established both him and Japanese cinema as major artistic forces. The film won many other critical awards, including the *New York Times* Ten Best list for 1951. Black and white. (Not rated; 1:55) [VIDEO]

RED SCORPION (1988) ★ Dolph Lundgren plays the ultimate Rambo-like Soviet fighting machine in this pre-*perestroika* film. Sent to assassinate a rebel leader in a fictitious African country, he switches sides to the pro-Western rebels. Now that Eastern Europe has gone Western, films like this are decidedly dated; plus, it's a thinly veiled reworking of *Rambo III*. Best promo points for this

film are Lundgren's awesome physique and more awesome haircut. (R; 1:40) [VIDEO]

RED SONJA (1985) Hara-kiri. Dino DeLaurentiis's silly sword-and-sorcery attempt to spin off his success with *Conan*. Unathletic Brigitte Nielsen plays a female Arnold Schwarzenegger after villainess Sandahl Bergman. Even Arnold's cameo as Conan and Ernie Reyes, Jr.'s costarring role as a spoiled child prince can't salvage Nielsen's—and concept's—damage. (PG; 1:29) [VIDEO]

RISING SUN (1993) ★★★ Sean Connery, Wesley Snipes, Mako. A first-class thriller about an American investigation into a Japanese corporate crime, based on Michael Crichton's best-selling novel. Snipes, a real-life veteran black belt, is first rate in his fight scenes, which take place against some of the world's most eminent karate masters (Fumio Demura, Tak Kubota and Tadashi Yamashita). (R; 2:10) [VIDEO]

SEARCH AND DESTROY (1981) ★ Perry King, Don Stroud, George Kennedy, Park Jong Soo. Four Vietnam veterans are stalked in New York by a Vietnamese official (Soo) they abandoned in the jungle. Filmed in 1978, it's notable only for the screen debut of Soo, the father of Canadian tae kwon do. (Not rated; 1:33) [VIDEO]

STEELE JUSTICE (1987) ★ A Vietnam vet (Martin Kove) seeks revenge when his best friend is murdered by a South Vietnamese general who has since become a California drug kingpin. Kove should stick to his supporting role in the *Karate Kid* films; he lacks star quality. (R; 1:35) [VIDEO]

STUDENT TEACHERS, THE (1970) Hara-kiri. Chuck Norris's second motion picture appearance; he plays a karate instructor in a brief scene teaching a class in a public park. He took the part without knowing it was a sexploitation film! (R; 1:19) [VIDEO]

THAT MAN BOLT (1973) Hara-kiri. Fred Williamson as international courier of syndicate money finds excuses for some routine martial arts fights while in Hong Kong, Las Vegas and Los Angeles. (R; 1:45)

THREE THE HARD WAY (1974) ★★★ Jim Brown, Fred Williamson, Jim Kelly. Top black action cast in nonstop thriller about a white fascist organization plotting to exterminate blacks by planting a deadly serum in the country's water supply. Kelly has some good kenpo–karate moves and moments, perhaps the best of the many yawners he's starred in. And here's a first: a black action film from the early 1970s rated PG! Sequel is *One Down, Two to Go*. (PG; 1:33) [VIDEO]

THRONE OF BLOOD (1957; Japanese) ★★★★ Director Akira Kurosawa's graphic, potent retelling of *Macbeth* in an atmospheric samurai setting may be the best adaptation of Shakespeare ever made, according to some critics. Toshiro Mifune gives a gripping performance as the Macbeth character. Heavy on plot and dialogue and probably too highbrow for most avid martial arts action fans. Black and white. English subtitles. (Unrated; 1:45) [VIDEO]

UGETSU; UGETSU MONOGATARI (1953; Japanese) ★★★★ Machiko Kyo, Masayuki Mori. Eerie ghost story set in feudal Japan mixes action and comedy in telling the saga of two peasants who leave their families to seek their fortunes in the world. One seeks wealth in the city and the other hopes to become a samurai, but their quest for

Sean Connery (left) with Master Fumio Demura behind the scenes of *Rising Sun*. Courtesy of Master Fumio Demura

Randall "Tex" Cobb (left) versus Patrick Swayze in *Uncommon Valor*. Courtesy of Paramount Pictures

greed and ambition brings disaster upon their families. Directed by Kenji Mizoguchi (*Forty-Seven Ronin*). Venice Film Festival prize winner and in 1972 was rated "#10 of the Best Films of All Time" by *Sight & Sound Survey*. (Not rated; 1:36) [VIDEO]

UNCOMMON VALOR (1983) ★★★ Great cast and performances in saga of a retired army officer (Gene Hackman) who gathers motley crew of Vietnam vets to invade Laos in search of his missing-in-action son. Part of motley crew is standout Randall "Tex" Cobb as a martial arts madman and a young Patrick Swayze. One of the first hit films to bring the Vietnam picture into vogue. (R; 1:45) [VIDEO]

UNDER SIEGE (1992) ★★★★ Steven Seagal, Tommy Lee Jones, Gary Busey, Patrick O'Neal, Nick Mancuso, Erika Eleniak. *Die Hard* on a ship. Terrorists, led by Jones, take over a U.S. battleship and terrorize its crew, and it's left to a cook and former Navy SEAL (Seagal) to repel the

Steven Seagal (left) versus Tommy Lee Jones in *Under Siege*. Courtesy of Warner Bros.

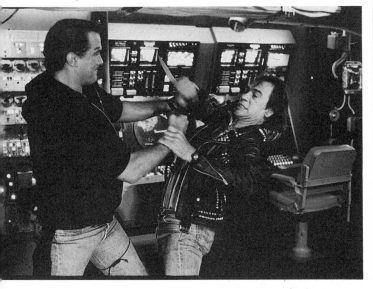

onslaught. The plot is to steal the ship's nuclear arsenal and deliver it to Iranians stationed nearby in a submarine. Busey plays a turncoat officer and Eleniak is the entertaining Miss July 1989, who starts out as a "boy toy" and ends up making toys of the boys. A superlative big-budget thriller marking Seagal's graduation with honors into the mainstream action–adventure genre. And there's sufficient Seagal-style martial arts to appease aficionados. Superbly directed by Andrew Davis (*Above the Law; Code of silence*). (R; 2:00) [VIDEO]

MARTIAL ARTS AS STORY LINE

In this category fall pictures where the plot or the lead characters, or their actions, are in some large way influenced by the martial arts or the warrior's philosophy.

❧

BILLY JACK (1971) ★★★ Tom Laughlin's second outing as the Robin-Hoodish half-breed karate expert and Vietnam vet became a box-office phenomenon and martial arts landmark film. In it, Billy Jack stands up for the rights of a "free school" and its teacher and students who are imperiled by prejudiced townspeople. Often ridiculed because its message of peace is punctuated by overt violence. Hapkido master Bong Soo Han choreographed fight scenes and doubled for Laughlin. First film to make martial arts an important part of the story line and the film that actually launched the martial arts boom of the early 1970s. Followed by *The Trial of Billy Jack* and *Billy Jack Goes to Washington*. (PG; 1:54) [VIDEO]

BILLY JACK GOES TO WASHINGTON (1977) Hara-kiri. Writer–director–star Tom Laughlin fights big-time cor-

ruption in the Senate. Long-winded update of the Oscar-winning *Mr. Smith Goes to Washington*, but Laughlin's no Jimmy Stewart. By now, his success has gone to his head and it shows in every aspect of his work. (PG; 2:35)

EMPIRE STRIKES BACK, THE (1980) ★★★★ Mark Hamill, Harrison Ford, Carrie Fisher, Billy Dee Williams. Spectacular sequel to *Star Wars* with Oscar-winning FX and nonstop excitement. Part of the story centers around the cosmic education of Luke Skywalker by the mystical Yoda, the quintessential sensei and wandering warrior. The training focuses on manifesting the "Force," that mysterious internal power known to martial artists as "ki" or "chi," which Skywalker then employs visually in unique laser-sword fights, as he did in the original. Whether planned or coincidental, a masterful integration of human and technical martial arts values, and a brilliant platform for cinematic wizardry. Winner of two Academy Awards. Superior on all counts. Followed by the last entry in the *Star Wars* trilogy, *Return of the Jedi*. (PG; 2:04) [VIDEO]

GATE OF HELL (1953) ★★★★ Atmospheric, Academy Award–winning tale of a samurai who becomes a monk to atone for his crime of driving a married woman to suicide. Winner of 1954 Oscar for Best Foreign Film. English subtitles. (Not rated; 1:26) [VIDEO]

IRON & SILK (1991) ★★★★ Mark Salzman, Pan Qingfu, Jeanette Lin Tsui, Vivian Wu. Gorgeous photography and moving performances drive the story of a young American (Salzman) searching for himself while he teaches English and learns martial arts in mainland China. His studies of martial arts and Chinese culture provide a model for his own students in their study of American language and culture. Film is based on the

In *The Empire Strikes Back*, part of the *Star Wars* trilogy, the mystical Yoda trains Luke Skywalker how to manifest the "force," which the hero later employs against the evil Darth

Vador in a laser-sword duel (144). Courtesy of Twentieth Century-Fox

Mark Salzman in *Iron & Silk*. Courtesy of Miramax Films

Richard Gere (left) versus Louis Gossett, Jr. in *An Officer and a Gentleman*.

critically acclaimed story of Salzman's own travels. This sensitive masterpiece is a sociological jewel in a genre that typically exhibits more violence than good sense. A must-see film for every sincere martial artist. (PG; 1:34) [VIDEO]

KAGEMUSHA: THE SHADOW WARRIOR (1980; Japanese) ★★★★ A sixteenth-century thief is spared execution if he will pose as a secretly deceased warlord whose throne is coveted by others. Epic combination of character and spectacle from legendary director Akira Kurosawa. Tatsuya Nakadai is superb in the dual role of warlord and thief. Winner of the grand prize at the Cannes Film Festival. Eminent film critic Gene Siskel placed *Kagemusha* tenth on his list of top-ten films of the 1980s. English subtitles. (PG; length necessitates that it appears on two videotapes: U.S. version 2:39, non-U.S. version 2:59).[VIDEO]

KILLER ELITE, THE (1975) Hara-kiri. James Caan, Robert Duvall, Bo Hopkins, Mako, Burt Young, Gig Young. Director Sam Peckinpah's martial arts disaster. Mercenary Duvall double-crosses partner Caan, leading to typical but lesser Peckinpah bloodbath. Huge cast of behind-the-scenes martial arts talent completely wasted. Reported running amok by all, with everyone a chief and no Indians until veteran Gene LeBell took charge of the choreography. By then it was too late: not one fight scene stands out. Script by martial arts booster Stirling Silliphant was all for naught. (PG; 2:02) [VIDEO]

KWAIDAN (1964; Japanese) ★★★★ Four eerie tales of the supernatural, based on works by Lafcadio Hearn, an American writer who lived in Japan in the late nine-

teenth century. An Oscar nominee, anthology focuses on samurai (Tatsuya Nakadai), balladeers, monks and spirits. Atmospheric, with visually stunning use of color. Too strong for children. English subtitles. (Not rated; 2:44) [VIDEO]

MASTER GUNFIGHTER, THE (1975) ★ *Billy Jack's* creator–star Tom Laughlin plays an intense gunfighter who carries a samurai sword and hates to kill but does it just the same. More dialogue than action in this remake of *Goyokin*. (PG; 2:01)

OFFICER AND A GENTLEMAN, AN (1982) ★★★★ Two misfits (Richard Gere and Debra Winger) seek direction in their dead-end lives—he by enrolling in Naval Officer Candidate school, she by trying to snag him as a husband. He's shown the way to personal best by drill instructor Louis Gossett, Jr., but not before the two heatedly clash physically and psychologically. The textbook example of poignant integration of martial artists and martial arts into a dramatic plot, and marked by terrific performances. Wonderfully romantic ending. Nominated for four Academy Awards; Oscars went to Gossett as Best Supporting Actor and for the hit pop song, "Up Where We Belong" by Joe Cocker. (R; 2:05) [VIDEO]

PAPER TIGER (1976; British) Hara-kiri. Snore-prone story of the kidnapped son of a Japanese ambassador (Toshiro Mifune) and his English tutor (David Niven), who sees the chance to act out his many fantasies about heroism that have impressed the youngster. Too cute, even with the few fight scenes that attempt to exploit the martial arts movie trend. One of Mifune's worst films. (PG; 1:39) [VIDEO]

Sylvester Stallone versus Dolph Lundgren in *Rocky IV*. Courtesy of United Artists

Robert De Niro in *Raging Bull*.

RAGING BULL (1980) ★★★★ Robert De Niro's compelling, Oscar-winning portrayal of former world boxing champ Jake LaMotta traces his life in and out of the ring, from champion to chump. This was the film for which De Niro gained fifty pounds to play the aging LaMotta. An intense picture of amazing character range; also shows how best to integrate combat with genuine character development. Shot purposely in atmospheric black and white by director Martin Scorsese. Brilliant, innovative fight choreography by Jimmy Nickerson (*Rocky I*), enhanced by slow-motion shots. Roger Ebert and Gene Siskel, perhaps America's best-known film critics, both voted *Raging Bull* their number-one picture for the 1980s. (R; 1:42) [VIDEO]

RAN (1985; Japanese–French) ★★★★ Epic Akira Kurasawa decade-in-the-making blockbuster based on Shakespeare's *King Lear* and samurai legends that traces a sixteenth-century warlord's (Tatsuya Nakadai) time of tragedy. He turns over his domain to his eldest son, launching a power struggle with his two younger sons. A brilliant example of using the martial arts as part of an epic viewpoint. Mixes humor and violence in unequal doses. Two superlative battles. Eminent film critic Roger Ebert voted *Ran* fifth on his list of top-ten films of the 1980s. English subtitles. (R; 2:40) [VIDEO]

RED SUN (1972; Italian–French–Spanish) ★★★ Big international cast in this offbeat story of a samurai (Toshiro Mifune) pursuing a valuable Japanese sword stolen from a train crossing the Old West. Sword is being transported as gift to a U.S. president. To increase his success, the warrior keeps in tow a train robber (Charles Bronson, at the height of his career) whose accomplices have deserted him and run off with the train's booty—and the sword. Intriguing elements and wonderful mix of East and West culture and humor. Catch Bronson showing Mifune how to make a fist ... then getting beat up! Directed by Terence Young, who directed three early James Bond films. (PG; 1:52) [VIDEO]

ROAD WARRIOR; MAD MAX II (1981) ★★★★ Mel Gibson stars as a postapocalyptic Robin Hood in this riveting sequel to *Mad Max*, and reputed remake of 1953's *Shane*. Genuinely inspired by Japanese samurai films, this Australian-made thriller's combat is chiefly motor vehicle versus motor vehicle (some of the best car stunts ever filmed) and Gibson's lone-wolf character is more closely akin to Toshiro Mifune's *Yojimbo* transplanted to the future than it is to Alan Ladd's *Shane*. Visually stunning range of colorful costumes and characters. Incredibly, *Road Warrior* has only fourteen lines of dialogue; action carries the entire movie. Never a dull moment. (R; 1:34) [VIDEO]

ROCKY I–V (SERIES) (1976–90) ★★★★ Moviegoers' most beloved boxing character; Sylvester Stallone's portrayal of underdog Rocky Balboa, the two-bit fighter who gets his million-to-one shot at fame, fortune and a heavyweight championship, but more importantly at self-respect. Sequels follow his ups and downs in and out of the ring as he fights one awesome opponent after another. The first film, which won Oscars for Best Picture, Director, and Editing, launched Stallone's career. The landmark ring fight scenes in the original were credited to Stallone, but were reportedly choreographed by Jimmy Nickerson (*Raging Bull*), who was instead given credit for "stunts" even though there were none in the picture. Nickerson's type of breakthrough choreography would continue throughout the series. Of interest to Asian martial arts fans is *Rocky IV*. Balboa trains in Russia for a match against a Soviet boxer whose high-tech conditioning has made him seemingly invincible. Kyokushinkai karate champ Dolph Lundgren of Sweden plays the deadly Russian, Ivan Drago. As it did for Rocky's opponents before him—Mr. T and Carl Weathers—the antagonist's role launched Lundgren's movie career (he had an earlier bit part in the James Bond film *A View to a Kill*). Compelling editing cuts from Stallone's primitive-type training to Lundgren's high-tech, equipment-aided workouts. Bloody, brutal ring fight somehow lacks the high drama present in the earlier *Rocky* films. Karate champ Billy Blanks won a role as a boxing contender in *Rocky V*. (Rated PG throughout) [VIDEO]

STAR WARS (1977) ★★★★ Spectacular tale of a callow youth (Mark Hamill) who becomes an interplanetary hero with the help of some human and robot friends. He is coached by a mystic warrior named Obi-Kinobi who teaches him how to manifest and apply the "Force," known to martial artists as "ki" or "chi." Introduces laser swords used in unique fight scenes where sword is only as strong as user's "Force." One of the most popular films of all time, it won seven Oscars for various technical achievements and a rousing score. Based chiefly on Akira Kurosawa's *The Hidden Fortress*. Winner of seven Academy Awards. Placed on the National Film Registry's list of twenty-five landmark films. The *Star Wars* trilogy is completed with sequels *The Empire Strikes Back* and *Return of the Jedi*. (PG; 2:01) [VIDEO]

STEELE JUSTICE (1987) Hara-kiri. Martin Kove, Bernie Casey, Soon Teck-Oh. Kove, best known as Pat Morita's protagonist in the *Karate Kid* films, squares off against the Vietnamese mafia in an abysmal stab at portraying a Chuck Norris–type character. (R; 1:34) [VIDEO]

TRIAL OF BILLY JACK (1974) ★ Long-winded sequel to hit *Billy Jack* wears thin as star Tom Laughlin begins taking himself too seriously. The final battle, pitting the title character and sidekick Bong Soo Han, the hapkido master, against a whole town, is a massacre that contradicts the film's message of nonviolence. (R; 2:55) [VIDEO]

YAKUZA, THE; BROTHERHOOD OF THE YAKUZA (1975) ★★★ Robert Mitchum attempts to rescue a friend's kidnapped daughter by returning to Japan after several years, and encounters the perpetrators in the Yakuza, the Japanese Mafia. Suspenseful action pic won high acclaim, but it's talky and boring much of the time. Major-league names involved: producer–director Sydney Pollack (*The Way We Were*) and scriptwriters Paul Schrader (*Taxi Driver*) and Oscar winner Robert Towne (*Chinatown*). (R; 1:52) [VIDEO]

CLASSIC SCENES

From the early 1940s to about 1972—the era prior to the explosive global distribution of pure martial arts films—the arts were used chiefly as a dramatic confrontational device or, conversely, a comedy gimmick. Each extreme is perhaps best exemplified in two long-running, mega-hit film series that began in the 1960s: James Bond (action and suspense) and the Pink Panther (comedy).

The films that follow carry many classic scenes that are simply a must-see for avid martial arts film buffs and historians. In examples too numerous to count, to be brutally frank, the end result of a big-budget picture with limited martial arts has a bigger audience impact than do many of the low-budget films devoted entirely to the subject. Call it high quality.

To get the full impact of a classic scene, it is recommended that the viewer watch the whole movie, not just scene-jump to the fight(s).

ACROSS THE PACIFIC (1942) ★★★ Humphrey Bogart, Mary Astor, Sydney Greenstreet. John Huston directed a reteaming of three *Maltese Falcon* leads in this breezy tour de force of intrigue on a Japanese freighter. Contains a quick mass-judo training segment on shipdeck, perhaps the first judo scene ever to appear on film. Look for a young Keye Luke, who in the 1970s plays the blind Master Po in TV's *Kung Fu* series. Black and white; also shown in computer colorization. (Not rated; 1:37)

ADVENTURES OF ROBIN HOOD, THE (1939) ★★★★ Errol Flynn, Olivia de Havilland, Basil Rathbone, Claude Rains, Alan Hale. Brilliant, imaginative, Oscar-winning version of the bandit of Sherwood Forest and his band of merry men. Flynn is the definitive swashbuckler, engaging in a memorable duel with wicked Rathbone and good-natured stick fight with Hale as Little John. (Not rated; 1:45) [VIDEO]

AIRPLANE! (1980) ★★★★ The king of airport disaster spoofs. Ever been bugged at the airport by those annoying Hare Krishna beggars? If so, you must see Robert

Stack, a pilot with short patience, deliver justice for all with his hands and feet. (PG; 1:28) [VIDEO]

BAD DAY AT BLACK ROCK (1954) ★★★★ Spencer Tracy, Robert Ryan, Anne Francis, Dean Jagger, Ernest Borgnine, Lee Marvin. Powerhouse cast in an exciting yarn about a one-armed man (Tracy) versus the sinister populace of a desert hamlet while looking for his Japanese-American farmer friend who has disappeared. The restaurant scene where the handicapped Tracy finally takes on his tormentors can match any of Clint Eastwood's comeuppance moments. Nominated for three Oscars. Black and white. (Not rated; 1:21) [VIDEO]

BEHIND THE RISING SUN (1943) ★★ Robert Ryan, J. Carrol Naish, Tom Neal. During World War II, a Cornell-educated Japanese switches his loyalties from the U.S. to Japan. Features the first karate-versus-Western-boxing fight on film. Given its crude choreography and ignorance of camera angles, the fight is still effective, down-and-dirty stuff. Black and white. (Not rated; 1:29) [VIDEO]

BLOOD ON THE SUN (1945) ★★★ In Japan during the 1930s, James Cagney sees trouble on the rising-sun horizon and attempts to combat it. Cagney, in real life a judo black belt, engages in a frenzied rough-and-tumble judo fight finale, the first such judo battle on screen. Black and white, and a computer-colorized version. (Not rated; 1:38) [VIDEO]

BORN LOSERS (1967) ★★ Tom Laughlin debuts as Billy Jack, the native American martial arts expert, in this biker exploitation film. Raw fight scenes; Laughlin was yet to meet hapkido master Bong Soo Han, who later doubled for the star and choreographed the slickly polished fights for the subsequent Billy Jack films. (Not rated; 1:52) [VIDEO]

CRIMSON KIMONO, THE (1959) ★★ Glenn Corbett, James Shigeta. Two L.A. detectives investigate a stripper's murder in and around Chinatown in this offbeat little film by postwar cult filmmaker Samuel Fuller. Poolroom brawl contains early karate scene. Black and white. (Not rated; 1:22)

CURSE OF THE PINK PANTHER (1983) ★★ (Martial arts scenes are ★★★★) Writer–director Blake Edwards's attempt to keep the *Pink Panther* series alive after Peter Sellers's death by surrounding unsuccessful Inspector Clouseau successor Ted Wass with major costars of earlier *Panther* films. In it, Clouseau is missing and an equally inept cop (Wass) is charged with finding him. Karate scenes by Ed Parker, Edwards's real-life original karate instructor, are an uproar. (PG; 1:49) [VIDEO]

DR. NO (1962; British) ★★★ The first James Bond film

Spencer Tracy flips Ernest Borgnine in *Bad Day at Black Rock*.

introduces charismatic Sean Connery investigating strange occurrences in Jamaica executed by master criminal Dr. No (Joseph Wiseman). When Connery, a one-time dabbler in boxing, rips through his first opponent with brutal efficiency, ending a confrontation by slamming the guy's head against a car hood, viewers immediately knew they could come to expect great fight scenes out of this quintessential Bond. Connery's fights are typically so good they look real; among professional actors (non-martial artists), he and Charles Bronson throw the best screen punches. (Not rated; 1:51) [VIDEO]

EXPOSURE (1991; Brazilian) ★★★ An American photographer (Peter Coyote) searches for his model's killer in Rio. Riveting set-up sequence where Coyote is taught scientific knife fighting and the payoff comes when he uses it to win the climactic fight scene. (R; 1:45) [VIDEO]

FIRST BLOOD (1982) ★★★ The movie that introduced ex–Green Beret John Rambo (Sylvester Stallone) as a Vietnam veteran falsely arrested by smalltown cops, after which he escapes and takes on cops and weekend warrior National Guards in the "jungles" of the Pacific Northwest. Excellent, effective fight scene when Stallone escapes from police station. The first film to bring the Vietnam picture into vogue. (R; 1:37) [VIDEO]

FIVE AGAINST THE HOUSE (1955) ★★★ Guy Madison, Kim Novak, Brian Keith, William Conrad, Kerwin Matthews. Engrossing crime caper scripted by martial arts pioneer Stirling Silliphant has five friends set out to rob a Reno casino. Keith plays a Korean War veteran who's a karate expert. Black and white. (Not rated; 1:24)

FROM RUSSIA WITH LOVE (1963; British) ★★★★ Second James Bond film, and one of the best, has Connery lured into a deathtrap by a beautiful Russian agent with the bait a secret decoding device. One of the most electrifying close-quarter fight scenes ever staged when Connery and assassin Robert Shaw square off for a slam-bang slugfest in a train compartment. Network rerun version is preposterously cut. See the original on video. Incidentally, this one's considered the most "cerebral" of the Bond films, yet makes use of exotic gimmicks. (Not rated; 1:58) [VIDEO]

F/X (1986) ★★★ Suspense thriller in which a movie special effects expert is duped into assassinating a mob figure turned state's witness. Neat fight scene pits protagonist against killer with hands tied behind his back. (R; 1:50) [VIDEO]

GOLDFINGER (1964; British) ★★★★ In this third James Bond adventure, Sean Connery seeks to stop Goldfinger from "robbing" Fort Knox of its gold. The king of the B guys in the king of the B movies; Connery at his most charismatic. Spectacular villains in Goldfinger (Gert Frobe) and Oddjob (pro wrestler and karateka Harold Sakata), who wields a razor-edged bowler. Great cat-and-mouse judo-flirting scene between Connery and Pussy Galore, played by real-life black belt Honor Blackman. Electrifying climax has Bond beat Oddjob by using brains over brawn. Probably one of the ten best adventure films ever made. The enormous success of the Bond movies by 1964 spawned a cottage industry of espionage-oriented films as well as numerous TV series like *The Wild, Wild West, The Avengers, Secret Agent Man, I Spy*, and *The Man from U.N.C.L.E.* In each the heroes routinely employed martial arts to dispatch villains, just like Bond. (PG; 1:48) [VIDEO]

HOT SHOTS! PART DEUX (1993) ★★★ Charlie Sheen stars in this inspired sequel that has nothing to do with the original *Hot Shots*. This one's a send-up of the *Rambo*-type movies where the pompous machismo connected to the one-man-army concept is expertly skewered. The hilarious opening martial arts fight, pitting Sheen against actor–martial arts expert James Lew, is a spin-off of Stallone's *Rambo III* grabber. (PG-13; ?) [VIDEO]

HOUSE WHERE EVIL DWELLS, THE (1982) ★★ American family moves into stylish old house in Kyoto that's haunted by nineteenth-century ghosts of doomed love triangle. Gory samurai fights, none of them classic. (R; 1:31) [VIDEO]

I'M GONNA GIT YOU SUCKA! (1989) ★★★★ Keenen Ivory Wayans, Bernie Casey, Jim Brown, Isaac Hayes, Steve James. Brilliant, hilarious parody of the early 1970s blaxploitation genre featuring numerous actors who starred in them. Frenetic pace and raucous gags in the mode of *Airplane* display comic genius of director–writer–star Wayans, who soon after launched TV's hit comedy *In Living Color*. Numerous uproarious martial arts skits, most of which are supplied by the late actor–black belt James. (R; 1:28) [VIDEO]

JACK'S BACK (1987) ★★★ James Spader, Cynthia Gibb. When a lunatic is killing Los Angeles prostitutes Jack-the-Ripper style, twin brothers (Spader in a dual role) mistakenly get involved. One of the brothers is accused of the murders and it is up to the other to either clear his name or provide the final evidence of guilt. A provocative, well-scripted story full of Hitchcockian twists and turns, with Spader using competent martial arts in the film's fight scenes. (R; 1:37) [VIDEO]

JASON AND THE ARGONAUTS (1963) ★★★ Jason (Toss Armstrong), son of the King of Thessaly, sails to Argo with his crew to find the magical Golden Fleece. Riveting family adventure with marvelous Ray Harryhausen special effects that bring to life, among other exotic crea-

Sean Connery (left), as James Bond, versus Oddjob (Harold Sakata) in *Goldfinger*. Courtesy of United Artists

Charlie Sheen (left, kicking) versus James Lew in *Hot Shots! Part Deux*. Courtesy of James Lew

tures, an army of sword-wielding skeletons. (Not rated; 1:44) [VIDEO]

LETHAL WEAPON (1987) ★★★★ Box-office blockbuster starring Mel Gibson as a burnt-out, suicidal cop who goes for broke in every scene, coupled with a clean-cut family man (Danny Glover). They prove a formidable team while pursuing a sleazy drug lord. Very rough-and-tumble fights choreographed by and fought against professional martial artists. Former nationally ranked forms champion Al Leong is the long-haired Oriental cat who gives Mel an electrifying experience. Climactic fight has Gibson versus Gary Busey in prolonged, rugged, rain-soaked altercation. (R; 1:50) [VIDEO]

MANCHURIAN CANDIDATE, THE (1962) ★★★★ Frank Sinatra, Laurence Harvey, Janet Leigh, Angela Lansbury, Khigh Deigh. Director John Frankenheimer's highly acclaimed adaptation of Richard Condon's story of cold-war political paranoia. Sinatra is a Korean War vet who believes a heroic former squad member has been brainwashed. Contains one of the most memorable of the early karate fight scenes. Black and white. (Not rated; 2:06) [VIDEO]

MAN WITH THE GOLDEN GUN, THE (1974; British) ★★★ Roger Moore, Christopher Lee, Britt Ekland, Herve Villechaize. Soon-Teck Oh as Bond sidekick. Moore's second film as Bond, in pursuit of the world's foremost assassin (Lee). Great car stunts and locales. The most poorly constructed of all the Bond films, it tapped into the kung-fu craze of the mid-1970s. Has terrific pentjak silat double-sword fight. Worth the price of admission to see *the* car stunt of the decade and how Bond beats a cocky black belt in a kumite match. (PG; 2:05) [VIDEO]

MARLOWE (1969) ★★ James Garner as Raymond Chandler's jaded detective Phillip Marlowe on a missing-persons case. Funny, memorable Bruce Lee cameo highlighted by his furniture-breaking office rampage; fans will groan over the way he's killed off, though. Slick script by Stirling Silliphant, a student of Lee's. (R; 1:35) [VIDEO]

MECHANIC, THE (1972) ★★ Charles Bronson is one of the world's leading professional assassins whose protégé (Jan-Michael Vincent) aspires to take his mentor's place. Karate scene featuring prominent master Takayuki Kubota. (R; 1:10) [VIDEO]

MELINDA (1972) ★ Jim Kelly made his screen debut in this ultraviolent melodrama about a black disc jockey out to get his girlfriend's killers. The type of film that helped kill the blaxploitation genre. (R; 1:49) [VIDEO]

NEVER SAY NEVER AGAIN (1983) ★★★ Sean Connery reprises his James Bond role after an eleven-year absence in this tongue-in-cheek remake of *Thunderball.*

Connery plays an aging yet ever-clever Bond to the hilt and shows how to inject humor into a fight scene when he squares off against a bearlike assassin in a clinic. Sexy Barbara Carrera won raves as primary Bond girl; chief antagonist Klaus Maria Brandauer was nominated for a Best Supporting Actor Oscar. (PG; 2:17) [VIDEO]

ON HER MAJESTY'S SECRET SERVICE (1969; British) ★★★ George Lazenby as the second James Bond is no Sean Connery, but he throws a screen punch better than athletically crippled Roger Moore, his successor. (PG; 2:20) [VIDEO]

OUR MAN FLINT (1966) ★★ One of the infinite James Bond spoofs, this one memorable for James Coburn's zestful portrayal as the man from Z.O.W.I.E. Not-bad fights for the period, thanks to Coburn's energetic style; choreography by karate pioneer Bruce Tegner, who was training Coburn in karate at the time. Coburn later studied under and befriended Bruce Lee. Followed by the sequel *In Like Flint.* (Unrated; 1:47)

PINK PANTHER, THE (series) (1964–76) ★★★★ Director Blake Edwards's delightful series of hit comedy capers starring Peter Sellers as the bumbling Inspector Jacques Clouseau began with *The Pink Panther* in 1964. The "Pink Panther" is actually a renowned cat burglar, but the entire series evolved around the Clouseau character, whom Sellers would portray intermittently until 1978, two years before his death. Edwards was a martial arts student of American karate pioneer Ed Parker and his interest in the arts is reflected throughout this film series: Clouseau is, unbelievably, a black belt karate expert who, in order to be constantly prepared for combat, has his faithful Asian servant Kato (Burt Kwouk) attack him unannounced at any time. These skits pay off big throughout the series, particularly when another piece of business is going on, like a real killer trying to do in Clouseau, and Kato's attack foils the attempt. Series gave much visibility to the martial arts, especially early on when the public was typically unfamiliar with them. A highlight of the series is 1978's *Revenge of the Pink Panther*, Sellers's final portrayal of the French detective. He's mistaken for dead, allowing him to find his killer incognito. Hilarious fight set-up has Clouseau sparring with Kato, as usual, but this time he's actually being stalked by an assassin played by Ed Parker. The clumsy inspector, through a marvel of ineptitude, dispatches both partner and assassin at the same time. Other series entries include *A Shot in the Dark* (1964); *The Return of the Pink Panther* (1975); *The Pink Panther Strikes Again* (1976); and *Trail of the Pink Panther.* See also *Curse of the Pink Panther.* (PG ratings throughout) [VIDEO]

POLICE ACADEMY 3: BACK IN TRAINING (1986) ★★★ Third installment for those police academy misfits. A highlight is human sound-FX-machine Michael Winslow, who performs the best Bruce Lee fight parody yet, complete with fantastic gymnastics and deliberately bad lip-sync dubbing. Karate pioneer Bill Ryusake, one of world kickboxing champion Benny Urquidez's instructors, plays one of Winslow's opponents. A police training scene also features world forms champion Jean Frenette of Canada (who, incidentally, also has a bit part in *Police Academy IV*). (PG; 1:27) [VIDEO]

PRESIDIO, THE (1988) ★★★ Sean Connery, Mark Harmon, Meg Ryan. A military murder mystery and must-see for Connery's brutal but sensational "I'll beat you with one finger" fight scene. Choreography by hapkido master Bong Soo Han. (R; 1:37) [VIDEO]

RAMBO III (1988) ★★ Whisks former Green Beret John Rambo to Afghanistan to rescue his mentor, who's been captured by the Soviets while smuggling Stinger missiles to the Afghan rebels. Check this out: The movie is rumored to have cost $60 million, the highest in history and a sizable percentage of the gross national product of the country where the picture purportedly takes place. When it was finished, Stallone realized there wasn't enough character development for Rambo so he resurrected a prologue, shot in Thailand, in which Rambo engaged in a violent stick fight against kickboxer Harold Diamond (a.k.a. Harold Roth) and retreated to a Buddhist monastery where he lived seeking inner peace. Stallone tried to mount a spectacular grabber in that opening sequence, but it fell flat due to ineffectual choreography. (R; 1:41) [VIDEO]

RETURN OF THE PINK PANTHER: see **THE PINK PANTHER**

REVENGE OF THE PINK PANTHER: see **THE PINK PANTHER**

ROOFTOPS (1989) ★★ Urban musical a la 1961's *West Side Story* about a teenage white male and his forbidden Hispanic girlfriend and a form of "combat dancing" employing martial arts footwork. Mixes music and melodrama as homeless teens battle crack dealers. Visually arresting integration of dance and the Brazilian martial art of capoeira shows how the arts can be provocatively applied as an artform. Directed by Robert Wise, who won an Oscar for his similar work in *West Side Story*. (R; 1:35) [VIDEO]

SEVEN (1979) ★★ Hired by U.S. intelligence to destroy a Hawaiian crime syndicate, muscular William Smith takes a team of seven specialists in with him. Another spin-off of Kurosawa's *Seven Samurai*. Mediocre film is rich with martial arts points of interest: 1) It contains the "shooting the swordsman" gag later immortalized in *Raiders of the Lost Ark*, which is actually a reversal of the outcome of Bruce Lee's classic nunchaku scene in *Enter the Dragon*; 2) look for Martin Kove in a pre–*Karate Kid* role; 3) sexy costar Barbara Leigh is the former wife of karate legend Joe Lewis; and 4) director Andy Sidaris, a

former sports director, directed the 1974 World Professional Karate Championship that launched the sport of kickboxing in the U.S. (R; 1:40) [VIDEO]

SHARKY'S MACHINE (1981) ★★ Violent Burt Reynolds vehicle about a vice cop's vendetta against a crime lord that intensifies after he falls for one of his high-priced call girls (Rachel Ward). Bruce Lee's protégé, Dan Inosanto, appears in action scenes as nunchaku- and balisong-wielding martial arts assassin. (R; 1:59) [VIDEO]

SHORT CIRCUIT (1986) ★★★★ Steve Guttenberg, Ally Sheedy, Fisher Stevens. A sophisticated robot, created as the ultimate war weapon, is zapped by lightning and comes alive. It escapes and accidentally lands at the home of an animal lover with its programmer and military brass in hot pursuit. Very funny fight scene in which robot, after digesting miscellaneous television fare, uses lasers accompanied by Bruce Lee battle cries to "dress down" a bad guy. (PG; 1:40) [VIDEO]

SHOT IN THE DARK, A: see **THE PINK PANTHER**

SPY WHO LOVED ME, THE (1977; British) ★★★★ Roger Moore finally hit his stride in this lavish production that's probably the greatest Bond adventure since *Goldfinger*. Moore throws his best—though still feeble—kicks and punches here and also is at his best doing battle with the steel-toothed "Jaws," played by 7-foot-2-inch Richard Kiel. Jaw-dropping opening skydiving sequence, and one of the best Bond girls ever, Barbara Bach. (PG; 2:05) [VIDEO]

THUNDERBALL (1965; British) ★★★ Oscar-winning FX distinguished this fourth 007 film that has Sean Connery once again saving the world from destruction. Scorcher

Roger Moore (kicking), as James Bond, in *The Spy Who Loved Me*. Courtesy of United Artists

of a fight—with an added twist—in opening sequence. It's so violently real that, even today, more than *twenty-five years* later, the network television version, rerun a zillion times, is edited to death; the original still can't pass network censorship standards. See the original on video. (Not rated; 2:09) [VIDEO]

TRAIL OF THE PINK PANTHER: see **THE PINK PANTHER**

WHITE NIGHTS (1985) ★★★ A famous ballet star and Russian defector (Mikhail Baryshnikov) ends up back in the Soviet Union after a forced plane landing. He's captured and placed with an American expatriate tap dancer (Gregory Hines) used as bait to wear down his resistance about fleeing the country again, but both decide to escape. Hines is in real life a karate black belt and former tournament competitor. In the film, to prepare for the escape, Hines secretly practices karate by integrating the techniques with dancing movements. If you appreciate beautiful form, you'll love the spectacular dance sequences. (PG-13; 2:15) [VIDEO]

WRECKING CREW, THE (1968) ★★ Dean Martin plays secret agent Matt Helm after a crime ring that's hijacked a train carrying a fortune in gold. First screen appearances for Chuck Norris, who has one line, and Joe Lewis. If you look close you can also see Ed Parker. Mike Stone doubled in fight scenes for star Dean Martin. All were hired by Bruce Lee, who choreographed the fight sequences for this spy spoof based on the books. (Unrated; 1:45)

YOU ONLY LIVE TWICE (1967; British) ★★★★ Lavish, lightning-paced James Bond production set in Japan. Sean Connery overcomes SPECTRE's plot to cause major powers to declare war on each other. Mixed critical reviews; people either love or hate this series entry. Connery has memorable, very rugged battle with muscular Japanese wrestler. First Western cinematic use of ninja and ninjutsu, plus training scenes depicting authentic Japanese martial arts masters. One dramatic sword master steals the show. (Not rated; 1:56) [VIDEO]

DOCUMENTARIES

BRUCE LEE: THE LEGEND (1984) ★★ Sockumentary tribute to Lee featuring rare footage and interviews with a number of the star's closest friends, including Steve McQueen and James Coburn. (Not rated; 1:28) [VIDEO]

BUDO (197?; Japanese) ★★★★ Critically acclaimed as the finest martial arts documentary yet made. Gritty and realistic, it follows the grueling training regimen of several martial artists, with an emphasis on karate and kendo.

CHINA'S LIVING TREASURES (1989) ★★★ Eight-volume documentary series filmed in mainland China with rare demonstrations by renowned kung-fu masters and Shaolin Temple monks. Lots of armed and unarmed sets performed from a wide variety of systems. Great for traditional martial arts viewers; gets boring, however, if you're not heavily into forms. (Total series running time is 6:56). [VIDEO]

DEADLIEST ART, THE: THE BEST OF THE MARTIAL ARTS FILMS (1990) ★★★ Fascinating genre overview narrated by *Enter the Dragon's* John Saxon. Features Bruce Lee, Jackie Chan, Samo Hung, Cynthia Rothrock, Kareem Abdul-Jabbar, Sho Kosugi and Yuen Biao. Narrated by Sandra Weintraub, daughter of martial arts film producer Fred Weintraub. (Unrated; ?) [VIDEO]

FIGHTING BLACK KINGS, THE (1976; Japanese) ★★ Japanese-language view of the late Mas Oyama and his kyokushin karate style. Competitors preparing to participate in Mas Oyama's 1st World Open Karate Tournament is the focal point. Some of the training regimens and tournament bouts are remarkable, but a lot of the fights are rough-and-tumble or just plain clumsy. Japanese without subtitles. (Not rated; 1:30) [VIDEO]

KARATE BEAR FIGHTER (197?; Japanese) ★★★ Sonny Chiba plays young Mas Oyama, who sought inner truth by training in complete isolation for several years. Oyama subsequently became one of the most famous karate masters in the world. Chiba shows why when he grapples with a grizzly bear barehanded. Interesting, though somewhat fictionalized story. English subtitles. (Unrated; ?) [VIDEO]

KYOKUSHIN WAY (1960?; Japanese) ★★★ Japanese-language study of Mas Oyama's style along with rare Oyama footage. (?; ?) [VIDEO]

MAKING OF ZATOICHI, THE (197?; Japanese) ★★★ Engrossing behind-the-scenes study of this famous samurai film series. Japanese without subtitles. [VIDEO]

MARTIAL ARTS: THE CHINESE MASTERS (198?) ★★ Features a rare look at Chinese martial arts masters conducting feats of board, brick and slab breaking. (Unrated; :53) [VIDEO]

MASTER CLASS (1985) ★★ A behind-the-scenes look at martial arts fight choreography hosted by Sho Kosugi, one of the genre's stars. (Unrated; 1:00) [VIDEO]

SPORTS IN ACTION, "CHOP CHOP" (1967) Paramount Studios' short documentary. Segment features jujutsu expert Michael DePasquale, Sr.

STRONGEST KARATE, THE (197?; Japanese) ★★ Study of Mas Oyama's rugged kyokushin style of karate; sequel to *Fighting Black Kings*. Japanese without subtitles. (?; ?) [VIDEO]

THIS IS ELVIS (1981) ★★★ Unusual but engrossing approach to filmmaking combines news clips, dramatizations and home movies to tell Presley's life story, from his early rise to stardom to his tragic death. Contains about half a minute of the martial arts pioneer actually performing karate, the only such footage in existence. (PG; 1:45) [VIDEO]

THIS IS KUNG FU (198?; Chinese) ★★★ Documentary featuring actor/wushu sensation Jet Lee. Chinese without subtitles. [VIDEO]

WARRIOR WITHIN, THE (1980) ★★★ Superior award-winning study of select contemporary martial artists shot with class and imagination. Cast includes Bruce Lee, Chuck Norris, Dan Inosanto, Fumio Demura and Mike Stone, among lesser known artists. Use of slow motion and special effects adds impact to certain sequences. (Unrated; 1:25) [VIDEO]

WORLD OF JACKIE CHAN, THE (198?; Chinese) ★★★★ British comedian Jonathan Ross hosts this incisive study of Hong Kong's biggest box-office star and king of kung-fu comedy. Jackie discusses every aspect of his spectacular career, from his rugged training as a youth in the Peking Opera, to his methods of setting up stunts, to his near-fatal accident performing a stunt on *Armour of God*. He candidly addresses his minor successes and major failures in American films. The interviews are interwoven with plenty of film clips from Chan's pictures, including outtakes of behind-the-scenes accidents and injuries he sustained during filming. This is definitely the most informative and entertaining study of Chan on the market. In English. (1:00) [VIDEO]

TELEVISION

Fans of the genre must remember that fight scenes on broadcast television programs are sanitized. Censorship of what is considered too much violence prohibits fancy and prolonged combative engagements. Even martial arts films that appear on TV are further edited to water down the amount of contact made between combatants.

This is especially true of broadcast (not cable) television, such as what you see aired on the big networks. That's why even a thirty-year-old fight scene like the classic between Sean Connery and Robert Shaw in *From Russia with Love* is still not shown in its entirety when it appears in network reruns. So don't expect too much of this medium.

Van Williams (left) and Bruce Lee, as Kato, in *The Green Hornet*.

AMAZING SPIDER-MAN, THE (1977) ★★ The Marvel Comics character is brought to life when a grad student (Nicholas Hammond) is bitten by a radioactive spider and transformed into a superhero who thwarts extortion plot. Spider-Man was also a martial arts expert in this pilot for the sporadic series; fights choreographed by Emil Farkas. (1:34) [VIDEO]

AVENGERS, THE (series) (1965–69) ★★★★ Patrick Macnee stars in arguably the finest British spy series (some say *The Protector* was) as agent John Steed with gorgeous Diana Rigg as the leather-garbed, kung-fu-trained Emma Peel. Charming, witty and ageless, this program is also distinguished for Peel's use of martial arts in every episode at a time when no other actresses were doing it. (Not rated; 52 minutes each) [VIDEO]

GREEN HORNET, THE (1967–68) ★★★ Where it all started. Bruce Lee made his acting debut as Kato, the Green Hornet's kung-fu-trained chauffeur, in this short-lived TV series based on the comic-book character. Lee's lightning-quick martial arts performances enticed viewers to sign up for lessons, launching the first martial arts boom in the United States. Variously packaged episodes are sporadically available on video and in underground bootleg editions of questionable quality that are traded openly on the market. Some legit tapes have as many as three episodes; most are 90-minute packages. "The Praying Mantis" episode, one of the best, pits Lee against Japanese actor Mako. No excuse for collectors not owning copies.

HERE COME THE BRIDES (late 1960s) The rare single

episode in which Bruce Lee costars circulates among collectors.

I LOVE LUCY (late 1950s) Kenpo karate pioneer Ed Parker appears in an episode teaching Lucy (Lucille Ball) self-defense.

JUDGE DEE AND THE MONASTERY MURDER (1974) ★ Khigh Dhiegh, Mako, Soon-Tech Oh, Miiko Taka, Irene Tsu, James Hong, Keye Luke. Murder mystery with a twist: the detective (Dhiegh) is a seventh-century Chinese sleuth. Based on Robert Van Gulick's Judge Dee mysteries and scripted by Nicholas Meyer (*The Seven Percent Solution*), this lavishly made TV pilot never made it to a series. Despite its colorful settings, martial artists will find it boring. (1:40)

KUNG FU (1971) ★★★★ David Carradine, Keye Luke, Phillip Ahn, Mako, Keith Carradine, Barry Sullivan. Stylish TV pilot that launched the highly popular, critically acclaimed series. Carradine plays Caine, the half-American, half-Chinese Shaolin monk who flees mainland China after he's accused of murder and wanders the Old West as a fugitive fighting injustice. Wonderful mix of action, philosophy, period costumes and atmosphere. This pilot and subsequent series, coupled with Bruce Lee's films, jointly established the martial arts craze of the early 1970s. Although Carradine has an awkward fighting style, his considerable acting talents give the character depth and the concept believability. He reprised the role twice, in 1986 and 1993, as his own grandson. A must-see. (1:05) [VIDEO]

KUNG FU: THE MOVIE (1986) ★★ David Carradine, Brandon Lee, Keye Luke, Mako, Benson Fong, Martin Landau. Carradine reprised his by-then cult role of Kwai Chang Caine from the original *Kung Fu* series, here being stalked by evil warlord Mako, who's mixed up in California's opium trade in the late 1880s. Bruce Lee's son Brandon makes his acting debut as a young Manchu assassin who clashes with Carradine, and, in flashbacks, Luke repeats his original role as Master Po, Caine's blind monk–mentor. Lacks the uniqueness and atmosphere of the original. Ironic to use Brandon to exploit Bruce's fame after Warner Bros., the producers, shot down his late, great father in favor of Carradine as star of the original series. (1:40)

KUNG FU: THE LEGEND CONTINUES (1992) ★★★ Pilot and series continuation in which David Carradine stars as Kwai Chang Caine, grandson of the character he created in the original series. This one's set in a contemporary metropolitan city, where Caine is reunited with his police-detective son, Peter (Chris Potter), whom he had given up for dead. A modern-day kung-fu master, Caine aids his tough-minded son as Peter fights crime for the city's metro force. The substory has it that fifteen years earlier, Caine, a widower, was raising young Peter alone at a Shaolin Temple he founded in northern California. That relationship was shattered, however, when a renegade priest, Caine's sworn enemy, burned the temple to the ground. Lots of superlative scripts (for television) and fascinating characters; produced by Michael Sloan,

Keye Luke (left) and David Carradine in *Kung Fu*. Courtesy of Warner Bros. Television

Brandon Lee (below left) versus David Carradine in *Kung Fu: The Movie*. Courtesy of Warner Bros. Television

who years ago produced TV's short-lived martial arts series *The Master*.

LAST NINJA, THE (1983) ★★ Michael Beck, Nancy Kwan, Mako, John Larroquette. An American art dealer who also practices ninjutsu is recruited to free a group of scientists from international terrorists. Its producers aimed at a contemporary *Kung Fu* series, but failed. (1:40)

LONGSTREET (1970) ★★★★ Bruce Lee, James Franciscus. *Not* the series pilot, but the superlative one-hour season opener entitled "The Way of the Intercepting Fist," written by Lee student and Oscar-winner Stirling Silliphant and overseen by another Lee student, Universal Studios executive Tom Tannenbaum. Franciscus, in real life another student of Bruce's, plays a New Orleans–based, blind insurance investigator who must confront a bully to save face and is trained for the confrontation by Lee. This is some of Bruce's best work on film because he explains the philosophical side of martial arts and viewers get to see some of the innovative training methods and approaches for which he was legendary. Chillingly effective final fight between Franciscus and bully with Bruce's voice-over instruction recalled by Franciscus to turn the tide of the fight. Some collectors have this superb show on video. After filming *The Big Boss* in the Orient, Lee returned for two more segments in which he was little more than a stage prop.

MASTER, THE; MASTER NINJA, THE, I–V (1984) ★★ A series of five videotapes, each containing two episodes, from the short-lived TV series starring Lee Van Cleef and Sho Kosugi. Concept follows the duo's adventures across the U.S. as they search for the Master's (Van Cleef's) long-lost daughter. Action in general and fighting in particular are restricted on television broadcasts by network censors and just about cripple any truly action-oriented martial arts concept. This one's no different. [VIDEO]

MEN OF THE DRAGON (1974) Hara-kiri. Robert Ito, Joseph Wiseman, Lee Tit War, David Chow. A team of kung-fu experts thwart a gang of modern white slavers, a concept that, given network restrictions on violence, could never make it on TV. (1:18)

SAMURAI (1979) Hara-kiri. TV movie about an eager-beaver San Francisco prosecutor (Joe Penny) who moonlights as a samurai swordsman to uphold justice! He's Caucasian, no less. The concept alone commits hara-kiri. (1:18)

SHOGUN (full-length version) (1980) ★★★★ Richard Chamberlain, Toshiro Mifune, Yoko Shimada, narrated by Orson Welles. The ten-hour original Emmy-winning

Studio shot of Bryan Genesee, costar of *Street Justice*. Courtesy of Shelley Jeffrey

blockbuster based on James Clavell's sweeping novel. It aired in five parts on NBC-TV and grabbed the second-highest rating of any program in television history to that time. Chamberlain began his reign as king of the miniseries with his portrayal of Blackthorne, the English sailor shipwrecked in feudal Japan and taken under the wing of a powerful warlord (Mifune) to become the first Western samurai. Its epic scope works magnificently. Perhaps the finest introduction of bushido to American audiences. (Not rated; 10:00) [VIDEO]

SHOGUN (1980) ★★★ Two-hour version of the epic TV miniseries. The flavor of the blockbuster from which this version was taken remains somewhat intact, but the subsequent pacing makes it run like a movie trailer. Too, this one has nudity and graphic violence added. (R; 2:00) [VIDEO]

STREET JUSTICE (1991–93) ★★ Carl Weathers, Bryan Genesee. A one-hour syndicated action–adventure series that's basically a "buddy" concept, with Weathers a cop and Genesee his friend, who just happens to be a martial arts expert. Genesee, a real-life black belt, invested authentic expertise in the show's better-than-average fight scenes.

TENSPEED AND BROWN SHOE (1980) ★★ Ben Vereen and Jeff Goldblum are mismatched gumshoes caught between American Nazis and the underworld in this pilot for the short-lived TV series. Goldblum, a fine actor, gives uniquely comic "I'm a karate expert" warning to foes.

CHAPTER 17

FILMOGRAPHIES

Readers can cross-reference this useful filmography with Chapters 15 and 16, the film and video guide, to find specific movies starring their favorite martial artists. Not all films appearing in these filmographies, however, are reviewed in the film/video guide. Some are obscure; some were Hong Kong productions obtainable on video only in Hong Kong; others are mainstream films and not categorically martial arts movies.

The filmographies appear in two styles. A three-column style is used for stars whose work spans more than one genre and sometimes more than one medium (like television and films). The shorter style, a single column listing the movie title and year of release, is used for those who've worked exclusively in martial arts films. In the case of Bruce Lee, Lee's various functions in his entire body of work have been elaborated.

The headings appear in alphabetical order by the artist's last name, and each artist's filmography then appears in chronological order by year of release.

JACKIE CHAN*

Year	Title	Type of Film
Motion Pictures		
1971	Little Tiger from Canton (a.k.a. Master with Cracked Fingers)	Martial Arts
1973	Not Scared to Die	Martial Arts
1973	Heroine	Martial Arts
1973	All in the Family	Martial Arts
1973	In the Eagle's Shadow Fist	Martial Arts
1976	Count Down in Kung-Fu	Martial Arts
1976	New Fist of Fury	Martial Arts
1976	Shaolin Wooden Man	Martial Arts
1977	Spiritual Kung-Fu	Martial Arts
1977	Killer Meteor	Martial Arts
1977–78	Snake and Crane Arts of Shaolin	Martial Arts
1978	To Kill with Intrigue	Martial Arts
1978	Half a Loaf of Kung-Fu	Martial Arts
1978	The Magnificent Bodyguard	Martial Arts

* Excludes child roles.

Jackie Chan, king of Asian cinema.

Year	Title	Type of Film
1978	Snake in the Eagle's Shadow	Comedy Kung-Fu
1978	Spiritual Kung-Fu	Comedy Kung-Fu
1978	Dragon Fist	Comedy Kung-Fu
1978	The Drunken Master (a.k.a. Drunken Monkey in a Tiger's Eye)	Comedy Kung-Fu
1979	The Fearless Hyena	Comedy Kung-Fu
1980	The Dragon Fist	Comedy Kung-Fu
1980	The Big Brawl	Comedy Kung-Fu
1981	The Young Master	Comedy Kung-Fu
1981	The Cannonball Run	Action Comedy
1981	Dragon Lord	Comedy Kung-Fu
1982	First Mission (a.k.a. Heart of the Dragon)	Action Comedy
1983	Meals on Wheels (a.k.a. Spartan X)	Action Comedy
1983	Winners and Sinners	Action Comedy
1984	My Lucky Stars	Action Comedy
1984	The Protector	Action
1985	Fantasy Mission Force	Action
1985	Police Story	Action
1986	Dragons Forever	Action Comedy
1986	Police Story II	Action
1987	Project A	Action Comedy
1987	Dragons Forever	Action Comedy
1988	Armour of God	Action Comedy
1988	Project A II	Action Comedy
1989	Painted Faces	Guest Role
1989	Mr. Canton and Lady Rose (a.k.a. Miracle)	Action Comedy
1990	Armour of God II: Operation Condor (a.k.a. Operation Eagle)	Action Comedy
1992	City Hunter	Martial Arts

SHO KOSUGI

Year	Title	Type of Film
Motion Pictures		
1974	Six Killer (Korea)	Martial Arts
1975	Stranger (Taiwan)	Martial Arts
1977	The Bad News Bears in Japan	Comedy

Year	Title	Type of Film
1981	Enter the Ninja	Martial Arts
1982	Revenge of the Ninja	Martial Arts
1983	Ninja III: The Domination	Martial Arts
1984	Nine Deaths of the Ninja	Martial Arts
1984	Hanauma Bay	Guest Star, Drama
1985	Pray for Death	Martial Arts
1986	Rage of Honor	Martial Arts
1987	Black Eagle	Martial Arts
1988	Aloha Summer	Drama
1989	Blind Fury	Martial Arts
1991	Journey of Honor (a.k.a.) Shogun Mayeda (Japan)	Adventure
Television		
1984-85	The Master (series)	Martial Arts
Documentaries		
1985	Master Class	Host

BRANDON LEE

Year	Title	Type of Film
Television		
1986	Kung Fu: The Movie	Martial Arts
Motion Pictures		
1988	Legacy of Rage	Martial Arts
1990	Laser Mission	Spy Thriller
1991	Showdown in Little Tokyo	Martial Arts
1992	Rapid Fire	Martial Arts
1993	The Crow	Horror–Thriller

BRUCE LEE*

Year	Title	Type of Role
Television		
1966-67	The Green Hornet	Costar as Kato
1966	Batman	Two guest roles as Kato
196?	Blondie	Obscure bit part
1969	Ironsides	Guest role
1970	Here Come the Brides	Guest role
1971	Longstreet	Costar

* Does not include Lee's early film work in Hong Kong as a youth.

Year	Title	Type of Film

Motion Pictures

Year	Title	Type of Film
1968	The Wrecking Crew	Fight Coordinator
1969	A Walk in the Spring Rain	Fight Coordinator
1969	Marlowe	Costar
1970	The Silent Flute	Coscreenwriter; (unreleased)
1972	Fists of Fury (a.k.a. The Big Boss)	Starring role
1972	The Chinese Connection	Starring role
1972	Return of the Dragon (a.k.a. Way of the Dragon)	Starring role
1973	Enter the Dragon	Starring role
1979	Circle of Iron	Adaptation from *The Silent Flute*; costory credit
1979	Game of Death	Partial footage of Lee shot in 1972; doubles/lookalikes used to complete film

DOLPH LUNDGREN

Year	Title	Type of Film
1985	A View to a Kill	Action
1986	Rocky IV	Action
1988	Masters of the Universe	Action–Fantasy
1989	Red Scorpion	Action
1990	The Punisher	Action
1990	I Come in Peace	Sci-Fi
1990	Cover Up	Action
1991	Showdown in Little Tokyo	Martial Arts
1992	Universal Soldier	Sci-Fi

TOSHIRO MIFUNE*

Rashomon (1951)
The Seven Samurai (1954)
Samurai I: Musashi Myamoto (1955)

* Includes only samurai/martial arts roles.

Samurai II: Duel at Ichijoji Temple (1955)
Samurai III: Duel at Ganryu Island (1956)
Throne of Blood (1957)
The Hidden Fortress (1958)
Samurai Saga (1959)
Saga of the Vagabonds (1959)
Gambling Samurai (1960)
Machibuse (196?)
Yojimbo (1961)
Sanjuro (1962)
Judo Saga (1963)
The Sword of Doom (1967)
Zatoichi Meets Yojimbo (1970)
Red Sun (1971)
The Bushido Blade (1979)
The Challenge (1982)

CHUCK NORRIS

Year	Title	Type of Film

Motion Pictures

Year	Title	Type of Film
1968	The Wrecking Crew	Bit Part
1973	The Student Teachers	Bit Part
1974	Return of the Dragon (shot in 1972)	Martial Arts
1977	Breaker! Breaker!	Martial Arts
1978	Good Guys Wear Black	Martial Arts
1979	A Force of One	Martial Arts
1979	Game of Death	Unauthorized replay of his fight with Bruce Lee from Return of the Dragon
1980	The Octagon	Martial Arts
1981	An Eye for an Eye	Martial Arts
1981	The Yellow-Faced Tiger (a.k.a. Slaughter in San Francisco; shot in '74)	Martial Arts
1982	Silent Rage	Martial Arts
1982	Forced Vengeance	Martial Arts
1983	Lone Wolf McQuade	Action
1984	Missing in Action	Action
1985	Missing in Action II: The Beginning	Action
1985	Code of Silence	Action
1985	Invasion U.S.A.	Action
1986	The Delta Force	Action

Year	Title	Type of Film
Motion Pictures (*continued*)		
1987	Firewalker	Action Comedy
1987	Braddock: Missing in Action III	Action
1988	Hero and the Terror	Action
1990	The Delta Force II: Operation Stranglehold	Action
1991	The Hitman	Action
1993	Sidekicks	Martial Arts
Television		
1990	The Ultimate Stuntman: A Tribute to Dar Robinson	Host
1993	Wind in the Wire	Guest Appearance
Documentaries		
1980	Warrior Within	Guest Appearance
1993	The Curse of Bruce Lee	Guest Appearance

ERNIE REYES, JR.

Year	Title	Type of Film
Motion Pictures		
1984	The Last Dragon	Martial Arts
1985	Red Sonja	Fantasy Adventure
1990	Teenage Mutant Ninja Turtles	Stunt double for Donatello; Action Fantasy
1991	Teenage Mutant Ninja Turtles II	Action Fantasy
1993	Surf Ninjas	Martial Arts
Television		
1986	The Last Electric Knight (Two-Hour Feature)	Martial Arts
1986-87	Sidekicks (series)	Martial Arts
1987	Highway to Heaven	Guest Role
1987	Circus of the Stars	Performer
1988	Circus of the Stars	Performer
1988	MacGyver	Guest Role
1991	Secret Bodyguard (Two-Hour feature)	Martial Arts

CYNTHIA ROTHROCK

Yes, Madam; Supercops (1985)
Shanghai Express; also Millionaire's Express (1985)
Righting Wrongs (1986)
No Retreat, No Surrender Part II (1986)
Above the Law (1986)
Magic Crystal (1987)
Inspectors Wear Skirts (1987)
The Blonde Fury; Lady Reporter (1988)
China O'Brien I (1988)
China O'Brien II (1989)
City Cop (1989)
Sun of the Sun (1989)
Fast Getaway (1990)
Martial Law (1990)
Triple Cross (1990)
Martial Law II: Undercover (1991)
Tiger Claws (1991)
Lady Dragon (1991)
Rage and Honor (1991)
Honor and Glory (1991)

Ernie Reyes, Sr. (left) and Ernie Reyes, Jr. in *Sidekicks*. Courtesy of Capital Cities/ABC, Inc.

Rage and Honor II (1992)
24 Hours to Midnight (1992)
Angel of Fury (1992)
Fatal Desire (1992)

STEVEN SEAGAL*

Above the Law (1988)
Hard to Kill (1989)
Marked for Death (1990)
Out for Justice (1991)
Under Siege (1992)
On Deadly Ground (1994)

* Seagal's films have all been primarily action–adventures in which he uses martial arts, but are not strictly martial arts films.

JEAN-CLAUDE VAN DAMME

Year	Title	Type of Film
1980	Rue Barbar	Drama
1985	No Retreat, No Surrender	Martial Arts
1986	Black Eagle	Spy / Martial Arts
1987	Bloodsport	Martial Arts
1988	Cyborg	Sci-Fi / Martial Arts
1989	Kickboxer	Martial Arts

Year	Title	Type of Film
1990	Death Warrant	Martial Arts
1991	Lionheart	Martial Arts
1991	Double Impact	Martial Arts
1992	Universal Soldier	Sci-Fi
1993	Nowhere to Run	Action
1993	The Last Action Hero	Cameo (as himself)
1993	Hard Target	Action

DON WILSON

Year	Title	Type of Film
1989	Bloodfist	Martial Arts
1990	Bloodfist II	Martial Arts
1991	Futurekick	Sci-Fi
1991	Ring of Fire	Martial Arts
1992	Bloodfist III: Forced to Fight	Drama
1992	Black Belt	Martial Arts
1993	Out for Blood	Martial Arts
1993	Bloodfist IV: Die Trying	Thriller
1993	Ring of Fire II: Blood and Steel	Martial Arts
1993	Bloodfist V: Blackout	Martial Arts

CHAPTER 18

ALL-TIME BOX-OFFICE CHAMPIONS (1967–93)

~•·•~

YOUR FAVORITE MARTIAL ARTS FILMS RATED BY PROFIT

The following compilation of all-time film rental champions is published annually by *Daily Variety*, a leading Hollywood trade magazine. It is essentially a listing of the most successful films in terms of film rentals generated at theaters only in "domestic" release (U.S. and Canada).

Variety's annual compilation is the only list of its type in the motion picture business. It is studied by readers, film historians and buffs and is quoted in overseas periodicals and reference books.

Variety's figures are based on domestic "rentals"— that is, money paid to each film's distributors—and *not* box-office grosses, which are substantially higher. *Variety* used to lump all films together, but in the 1990s changed its policy. Because of inflation, varying release patterns and the advantage to older films of periodic reissues, results of pictures from different eras cannot be compared accurately. *Variety's* latest lists include films with rentals of at least $3 million if they were released before 1981. The minimum is $10 million for releases since 1981.

Because of this new policy, for this chapter I chose to use *Variety's* latest 1993 list as well as earlier ones using the old system so that the rentals for more martial arts genre films could be added here. Here are its former policies for inclusion:

A film must have paid $4 million or more in domestic rentals to the distributors.

Worldwide film rentals, as well as worldwide box-office gross figures, are not used in tabulating the list of rental champions because these figures are not available on a comprehensive basis covering all films. Collection of worldwide data is particularly difficult since major distributors usually only report it for hit films, not relative flops, and increasingly a top film is distributed territorially by dozens of distributors, due to the growth of the independent producer and presale financing.

A sizable contingent of past releases has been round-figure estimated at $4 million, or close enough thereto, though more exact figures continue to be substituted when they become available.

Hence, readers should be aware that certain films now have rentals substantially different from those previously listed, due to distributors' efforts (or others) in updating their histories.

FORMAT

Each film is listed by financial rank, title, year of original release and total rentals received to date. Only pure martial arts films—that is, those that fall clearly and cleanly into the genre—and those whose stars are clearly martial artists, like, say, Steven Seagal and Chuck Norris, are listed.

Rank Title	(Year)	Total Rental*
1. *Teenage Mutant Ninja Turtles*	(1990)	$67,650,000
2. *The Karate Kid II*	(1986)	$58,310,000
3. *The Karate Kid*	(1984)	$43,120,000
4. *Teenage Mutant Ninja Turtles II*	(1991)	$41,900,000
5. *Under Siege*	(1992)	$40,000,000
6. *Billy Jack*	(1971)	$32,500,000
7. *The Trial of Billy Jack*	(1974)	$31,100,000

* These 1993 figures were published before the 1993 box-office figures were in for *Dragon: The Bruce Lee Story* and two Jean-Claude Van Damme films, *Nowhere to Run* and *Hard Target.*

8. *Hard to Kill*	(1990)	$30,000,000
9. *Passenger 57*	(1992)	$21,700,000
10. *Marked for Death*	(1990)	$20,000,000
11. *The Karate Kid III*	(1989)	$19,030,000
12. *Out for Justice*	(1991)	$18,500,000
13. *Universal Soldier*	(1992)	$16,000,000
14. *Born Losers*	(1967)	$14,750,000
15. *Road House*	(1989)	$12,616,000
16. *Double Impact*	(1991)	$12,050,000
17. *Teenage Mutant Ninja Turtles III*	(1993)	$12,000,000
18. *3 Ninjas*	(1992)	$11,861,000
19. *Enter the Dragon*	(1973)	$11,500,000
20. *The Last Dragon*	(1985)	$11,500,000
21. *Lionheart*	(1991)	$10,550,000
22. *Missing in Action*	(1984)	$10,000,000
23. *A Force of One*	(1979)	$9,980,000
24. *Good Guys Wear Black*	(1978)	$8,300,000
25. *Code of Silence*	(1985)	$8,277,723
26. *Above the Law*	(1988)	$8,200,000
27. *Lone Wolf McQuade*	(1983)	$7,000,000
28. *The Delta Force*	(1986)	$7,000,000
29. *Invasion U.S.A.*	(1985)	$6,923,802
30. *Kill or Be Killed*	(1980)	$6,800,000
31. *They Call Me Bruce?*	(1982)	$6,757,871
32. *An Eye for an Eye*	(1981)	$6,750,774
33. *Kickboxer*	(1989)	$6,500,000
34. *Big Trouble in Little China*	(1986)	$6,000,000
35. *Remo Williams: The Adventure Begins*	(1985)	$5,600,000
36. *The Octagon*	(1980)	$5,500,000
37. *9 Deaths of the Ninja*	(1985)	$5,500,000
38. *Return of the Dragon*	(1974)	$5,200,000
39. *Game of Death*	(1979)	$4,947,000
40. *Bloodsport*	(1988)	$4,661,000
41. *Five Fingers of Death*	(1973)	$4,600,000
42. *Firewalker*	(1986)	$4,500,000
43. *Kill and Kill Again*	(1981)	$4,300,000
44. *Missing in Action II*	(1985)	$4,217,312
45. *Force: Five*	(1981)	$4,200,000
46. *The Killer Elite*	(1975)	$4,129,734
47. *Cyborg*	(1989)	$4,100,000
48. *Cleopatra Jones*	(1973)	$4,100,000
49. *The Chinese Connection*	(1972)	$3,800,000
50. *Fists of Fury*	(1973)	$3,100,000
51. *The Big Brawl*	(1980)	$3,000,000

CHAPTER 19

CELEBRITY CONTACTS

Where to send fan mail to certain celebrities is one of the most frequently asked questions by the martial arts masses. Here are the current addresses for perhaps the most popular current martial arts film and television stars.

A number of the addresses are in care of current managers or public relations firms, but it must be understood that entertainment industry relationships have a rich tradition of changing rapidly and frequently. So contact through some of the following addresses cannot be guaranteed.

Fans should also understand that it's impossible for anyone to answer long, tedious letters filled with detailed questions. Celebrities typically do not answer such questionnaires, so keep your correspondence short and to the point. And be aware that, unfortunately, some celebrities do not answer fan mail at all.

David Carradine
c/o Warner Bros. Television
300 Television Plaza
Burbank, CA 91505

Jackie Chan
The JC Group
G/F, Unit B
Casapino
145 Waterloo Rd.
Kowloon, Hong Kong

Mark Dacascos
c/o James & Co.
11684 Ventura Blvd., #476
Studio City, CA 91604

Gary Daniels
c/o Beymark International
39 Laxey Rd.
Edgbaston, Birmingham B16 0JQ
England

Bryan Genesse
c/o Agency for the Performing
    Arts
9000 Sunset Blvd.

Suite 1200
Los Angeles, CA 90069

James Lew
c/o James & Co.
11684 Ventura Blvd., #476
Studio City, CA 91604

Dolph Lundgren
c/o David Schiff
United Talent Agency
9560 Wilshire Blvd., #500
Beverly Hills, CA 90212

Chuck Norris
Topkick Productions
17300 17th St., #J-251
Tustin, CA 92680

Michel Qissi
10153½ Riverside Dr.
P.O. Box 231
Toluca Lake, CA 91602

Ernie Reyes, Jr.
c/o West Coast Tae Kwon Do
810 W. Hamilton Ave.
Campbell, CA 95008

Phillip Rhee
C.F.C. Entertainment
200 N. Robertson Blvd., #343
Beverly Hills, CA 90211

T.J. Roberts
8306 Wilshire Blvd., #789
Beverly Hills, CA 90211

Cynthia Rothrock
c/o *Inside Kung Fu* Magazine
4201 Vanowen Pl.
Burbank, CA 91505

Steven Seagal
c/o Rogers and Cowan
10000 Santa Monica Blvd., #400
Los Angeles, CA 90067

Karen Sheperd
c/o James & Co.
11684 Ventura Blvd., #476
Studio City, CA 91604

Jeff Speakman
c/o Rogers & Cowan
10000 Santa Monica Blvd., #400
Los Angeles, CA 90067

Jean-Claude Van Damme
P.O. Box 4149
Chatsworth, CA 91313

Don "The Dragon" Wilson
c/o Green Tiger Entertainment
1741 N. Ivar Ave., #107
Hollywood, CA 90028

Bolo Yeung
P.O. Box 1880
Studio City, CA 91604

THE MARTIAL ARTS BUSINESS DIRECTORY

This part of the book represents the most extensive directory of global martial arts organizations and supply companies ever to appear in print.

Listed here are 1,008 associations, federations, organizations, confederations, societies and unions of all martial arts and styles from 80 countries. For the first time also, contact names, usually an officer, and phone and fax numbers are included for many of the listings.

This is also the first comprehensive directory in print of martial arts suppliers from around the world, comprising a total of 1,112 companies selling every imaginable product a martial artist will ever need. Phone and fax numbers are standardly listed here when available, as well as 800 numbers for credit card orders.

Chapter 21 of this section lists 451 suppliers from 20 countries and 40 of the United States. All of these companies feature a very comprehensive product inventory. These firms routinely sell all manner of martial arts supplies, equipment, apparel, videotapes and books, with the possible exception of trophies and mats.

Chapter 22, divided into 20 categories, lists 661 specialty shops and suppliers of exclusive lines and types of products in 28 countries. This should help the reader more readily match his or her specific needs. Some major companies have multiple listings, particularly for higher-priced items like, for example, stretching machines and trophies.

CHAPTER 20

WORLD DIRECTORY OF MARTIAL ARTS ASSOCIATIONS

This extensive global list—the largest and most comprehensive mailing list of organizations ever in print—includes 1,008 associations, federations, organizations, confederations, societies and unions of all martial arts and styles from 80 countries. Quite literally, it takes you from here to Kathmandu. For the first time also, contact names, usually an officer, and phone and fax numbers are included for many of the listings.

Every reasonable attempt was made to obtain full addresses with phone numbers. When possible, an officer such as the president or chief instructor was added, as was a fax number. Given all this information, then, this directory of world associations picks up where simple mailing lists leave off.

Understandably, affiliates are subject to change. This is particularly true of martial sports organizations. Some associations change officers on an annual basis. Hence, it

The current Shaolin Temple in the People's Republic of China. Courtesy of Gary Forbach

is impossible for *any* book to stay up to date given such organizational rotation. Typically, however, the central headquarters remains consistent. So readers and researchers seeking information on a given organization should contact its central headquarters whenever possible.

Readers and researchers, take note that in those countries where the martial arts are not government regulated, as in the United States, anyone can name an organization anything he or she wishes. Because of this problem, there exist many small organizations bearing titles that make them sound much larger.

The term "world" is perhaps the most abused. In these cases, a so-called "world" association could be a local fifty-member group run by one individual out of some small, obscure city. In Europe, where martial arts organizations are for the most part government regulated, the organizations tend to remain stable and consistent.

According to the Hong Kong Trade Development Council in Miami, Florida, almost all of the kung-fu associations centered in Hong Kong are actually schools with a limited student body. Despite its immediate access to reference and resource materials, the council had no record of, and could find no record of, any large international martial arts organizations.

The only alternative is to write to the president of the Hong Kong Ching Woo Athletic Association (see listing under Hong Kong). This association, founded in 1922, claims to be apolitical, according to Canadian instructor Jon Funk, who trained there, and offers classes twice a week in thirteen different styles. Whether any correspondence would be answered is anyone's guess, but if you intend to travel to and train in Hong Kong, this is the place to contact.

The Guardian Angels, although not a purely martial arts association per se, requires its members to have fundamental martial arts training in order to handle self-defense situations that may develop during its citizen's street patrols.

How can this chapter be used? Want to join a new or old organization? Want to establish foreign contacts in an art or style? Looking to affiliate with a big or small organization? Need to know foreign members of your organization? Hoping to work out with someone special while on vacation? Need information about certain arts or styles? Looking for an information exchange among numerous stylists? Want to check someone's credentials for legitimacy?

FORMAT

In addition to the listings for world association and affiliates, and a continental category for Europe, all listings are in alphabetical order first by country, then by spelling of the organization. Whenever possible, a contact name, phone and fax numbers are included. If you're searching for a large organization affiliated with a global one, check both the world association listing as well as the country under which it would normally appear. For convenience, such organizations are listed twice.

Organizations come in all sizes. In almost all cases, the larger and more established ones will have a street address and a phone number. Smaller ones, or those of apparently less stability, use post office boxes and did not have a phone number listed in the sources used to compile this chapter.

Preceding the organizations are addresses for renowned martial arts institutions, like the Kukkiwan and the Kodokan, the meccas for tae kwon do and judo, respectively.

For the sake of convenience, some words that appear regularly throughout the lists have been abbreviated: Inter. = International; Assn. = Association; Fed. = Federation; and Org. = Organization.

FAMOUS MARTIAL ARTS INSTITUTIONS

CHINA

For information on all available institutions in the People's Republic of China, contact:

International Wushu Fed.
3 Anding Rd.
Chaoyang District
Beijing 100101
People's Republic of China
(86) 1-491-3262
(86) 1-491-2151 (Fax)

Songshan Shaolin Monastery
Dengfeng County
Henen Province
People's Republic of China

GREAT BRITAIN

Budokwai
4 Gilston Rd.
London SW10
England

JAPAN

Japan Karate Assn.
Rose Center, 2nd Floor
1-6-1, Ebisu-Nishi Ebisu
Shibuya-ku, Tokyo
Japan
(03) 462-1415

Kodokan
1-16-30, Kasuga
Bunkyo-ku, Tokyo
Japan
(03) 811-7151

Museum of Sumo
Kokugikan Sumo Hall
1-3-28, Yokoami
Sumida-ku, Tokyo
Japan
(03) 622-0366

Nippon Budokan
2-3-3, Kitanomaru-koen
Chiyoda-ku, Tokyo
Japan
(03) 216-0781

KOREA

Korea Sports Science University
Kwan Duk Ko, President
CPO Box 4584
Seoul, Korea
477-2111

Kukkiwan
635, Yuksam-dong
Kangnam-ku
Seoul, Korea 135
2-566-2505
2-553-4728 (Fax)

WORLD ASSOCIATIONS AND AFFILIATES

Choi Kwang-do
Martial Art Inter.
Kwang Jo Choi, President
5643-B Bells Ferry Rd.
Acworth, GA 30101
(404) 924-1166

AFFILIATES

Australia
Lam Sal Thow
1st Floor, 41 Great Eastern Hwy.
Rivervale 6103
Western Australia
(09) 361-2855

England
Rodger Koo
Pil Sung Mornington Rd.
Ashford, Middlesex TW15 N.W.
England
0784-250567

New Zealand
Willie Lim
52 Malcohm St.
Hamilton, New Zealand
394-671

Chang Seng Chee
15 Lawson St., Sydenham
P.O. Box 7440
Christ Church, New Zealand
(3) 660-791

Goju-ryu Karate-do Gojukan
1-16-23, Zempukuji
Suginami-ku, Tokyo
Japan
(03) 395-2311; (03) 390-2929

Inter. Amateur Karate Fed. (IAKF)
Hidetaka Nishiyama, President
1930 Wilshire Blvd.
Los Angeles, CA 90057
(213) 483-8262

AFFILIATES

European Amateur Karate Fed.
(EAKF)
Postfach 571
D-3110 Uelzen 1
Germany

EAKF EXECUTIVE BOARD

Vasko Kostojcinovski, President
Rue Salvador Alijende 34
Skopje
Yugoslavia
091-239837

Dr. Carlenrico Bonizzoni, First
Vice-President
Via Civerchi, 38
26013 Crema
Italy
0373-83392

Ted Hedlund, Technical Director
Urmakaregatan 12
S-21465 Malmo
Sweden
040-89218

Percy Avery, Treasurer
Bend Edor, Woodchurch
Kent TN26 3RD
England
044-233-86339

Fritz Wendland, Secretary-
General
Postfach 571
3110 Uelzen 1
Germany
(0581) 78764

EAKF AFFILIATES

Osterreichischer Karatebund
Karl Neveceral, President
Pazmanitengasse 17
A-1020 Wien
Austria
(0222) 246-7213

Belgian Amateur Karate Fed.
Jacques van Lerberghe,
President
Rue de Merinos, 39
B-1030 Bruxelles
Belgium
02-242-2805

Dansk Karate Forbund
Vermlandsgade 75
2300 S. Kobenhavn
Denmark
577040

Karate Union of Great Britain
Keinosuke Enoeda, President
125 Hullbridge Rd.
South Woodham Ferrers
Essex, CM3 5LL
England

Deutscher Karateverband e.V.
Wolfgang Hagedorn, President
Grabenstrasse 37
4390 Gladbeck
Germany
(02043) 24007

Suomen Amatoori
Willie Ortiz
Karate-do Liitto
Kissanmaankatu 26K
33530 Tampere 53
Finland
931-611318

Greek Karate Corporation
George Saniotis, Secretary-
General
Argolidos Strasse 3-5
TT-605 Athens
Greece
691-7609

Irish Karate Control Board
Desmond Tracy, Secretary-
General
83 Lr. Camden St.
Dublin 2
Ireland
373899

Federazione Italiana Karate
Taekwondo e Discipline Affini
Piazzale delle Belle Arti, 3
I-00196 Roma
Italy
360-1555

Karate-do Bond Netherland
Ino Alberga, Secretary-General
Havikshorst 21
2317 AL Leiden
Netherlands

Norges Shotokan Forbund
W. Hagen, President
Kappelvn. 161
Oslo 4
Norway
222-8843

Centro Portugues de Karate
Romulu Machado, President
R. dos Bacalhoeiros, 139-2-Dto
1100 Lisbon
Portugal
872413

Hungarian Karate Section
Dr. Istvan Gortvay
Dozsa Gyorgy-ut 1-3
1143 Budapest
Hungary
640-233

Polish Karate Fed.
Kazimierz Krukowski, Vice-
President
ul. 1. Maja 23/18
71-627 Szczecin
Poland

Karate Union of Great Britain
Scottish Region
Paul Allan
Komorebi, Drumblade
Huntly AB 56 EJ
Scotland
(0466) 84203

Associacion Espanola Karate
Amateur
Jose Baeza Lopez
Midico Pascual
Perez, 17, 3B
Alicante—1
Spain
206778

Swedish Shotokan Assn.
Leif Almo, President
Camillavagen 32
21363 Malmo
Sweden
040-219695

Schweizerischer Karate-Verband
Hans Peter Wechsler, President
Schribersmatt
6074 Giswil-Grossteil
Switzerland
041-681046

Turkiye Judo ve Karate Fed.
Cihat Uskan, President
Bagdat Cad.
Selahattin Pinar Sok
Murat Apt. No. 8/12
Kiziltoprak, Istanbul
Turkey
382375

American Amateur Karate Fed.
Hidetaka Nishiyama, President
1930 Wilshire Blvd.
Los Angeles, CA 90057
(213) 483-8262

Karate Union of Great Britain
Welsh Region
Wilson Fallows, Regional Officer
Glan Elwy Cottages
Llangernyw, Near Abergele
Clwyd., North Wales
(0745) 76339

Karate Savez Jugoslavije
Dr. Vladimir Jorga, President
Strahinjica Bana 73/a
11000 Beograd
Yugoslavia
011-629821

REGIONAL IAKF ORGANIZATIONS & CONFEDERATIONS

African Amateur Karate Fed.
c/o Egyptian Karate Fed.
Major General Abdel Karim
Nafia, President
33 Sharif St.
Cairo, Egypt

Arabian Karate Fed.
Mohammad Fayez Al Kulaish,
President
P.O. Box 6042
11442 Riyadh
Saudi Arabia

Asia Oceania Amateur Karate Fed.
Shintaro Minema, President
No. 1-6-1 Chome, Ebisu-Nishi
Shibuya-ku, Tokyo 150
Japan

Bolivariana Karate Confed.
c/o Federacion Peruana de
Karate
Col. Hugo Diaz Velarde,
President
Estadio Nacional-Puerta 23-A
Lima, Peru

Central America/Carribbean
Karate Fed.
c/o Federacion Mexicana de
Karate

Dr. Manuel Mondragon K.,
President
Monterey 147 48 Piso
Mexico 7, D.F.
Mexico

Pan-American Karate Union
Jose Maria Carcia Maanon,
President
c/o Confederacion Argentina
Deportes
Juncal 1662-1062 Capital Federal
Buenos Aires
Argentina

Inter. Chinese Martial Arts Assn.;
Inter. Wing Tsun Martial Art
Assn.
Ting Leung, President
438 Nathan Rd., 1-F
Kowloon, Hong Kong
3-857115

AFFILIATES

United States

American Wing Tsun Org.
Robert Jacquet, General
Manager
15227 N. 23rd Place
Phoenix, AZ 85022
(602) 867-1525

International Judo Fed.
c/o Garcia de la Fluente
Hortaleza, 108, Madrid 4
Spain

Inter. Kajukenbo Assn.
Bill Owens, Director
P.O. Box 4674
7415 MacArthur Blvd.
Oakland, CA 94605
(510) 638-9990
(510) 635-3838 (Fax)

Inter. Kendo Fed.
2-3-4 Nishi, Shinagawa
Shinagawa-ku, Tokyo
Japan

Inter. Kenpo Karate Assn. (IKKA)
Leilani Parker, Director

Mike Sawyer, co-chairman of the International Sport Karate Association. Courtesy of Mike Sawyer

1705 E. Walnut St.
Pasadena, CA 91106
(213) 682-2456

Inter. Martial Arts Fed.
(Kokusai Budoin; Kokusai
   Budorenmei)
Shizuya Sato, World Director
3-24-1, Shinbori
Higashi-Yamato-Shi
Tokyo, Japan 189
0425-65-9146

AFFILIATES

United States

Dan Ivan and Brett Mayfield,
   Directors
6933 South Shore Dr. South
St. Petersburg, FL 33707
(813) 345-3109

Inter. Okinawan Goju-ryu Karate-
   do Fed.
Morio Higaonna, Chairman
1551 W. Mission Rd., Wuite A
San Marcos, CA 92069
(619) 744-6633
(619) 744-0371 (Fax)

Inter. Okinawan Martial Arts
   Union
Rod Sacharnoski, Director
P.O Box 31127
Dallas, TX 75231
(214) 361-0664

Inter. Shotokan Karate Fed.
Teruyuki Okazaki, President
222 S. 45th St.
Philadelphia, PA 19104
(215) 222-9382

Inter. Sport Karate Assn. (ISKA)
(World Council Western
   Headquarters)
Mike Sawyer, Co-Chairman
P.O. Box 90147
Gainesville, FL 32607
(904) 375-8144
(904) 371-2179 (Fax)

(World Council Eastern
   Headquarters)
Olivier Muller, Co-Chairman
58 Avenue Wendt
CH-1203 Geneva
Switzerland
(022) 734-9524
(022) 735-4751 (Fax)

(World Council Executive Director)
Robert Heale
100 N.W. 82 Ave.
Plantation, FL 33324
(305) 474-4811
(305) 584-6125 (Fax)

International Coordinator
Dwight Brown
1239 Iberville Blvd., Suite 403
Repentigny, Quebec, Canada J5Y
   3H7
(514) 585-8424 (Tel. & Fax)

REGIONAL OFFICES

ISKA Africa
Joe Viljoen, Director
Box 1154
Carletonville 2500, South Africa
(27 14) 91-46-39 (Tel. & Fax)

ISKA Australia
Dr. Peter Lewis, Director

1216 High St.
3143 Armadale, Australia
(61 3) 509-8937
(61 3) 822-7951 (Fax)

ISKA Canada
Paul Renaud, Director
700 Hurtubise
Gatineau, Quebec, Canada J8V
   4G7
(819) 643-1012
(613) 995-4519 (Fax)

ISKA Europe
Will Raven, Director
Landsteinerstrasse #5
Geleen, Netherlands 616 4XD
(31 46) 74-74-35
(31 46) 75-55-52 (Fax)

ISKA Russia
Igor Oransky, Director
5th Magistralnaya
Moscow 8, Russia
(7 095) 297-5692
(7 095) 940-2804 (Fax)

ISKA Scandanavia
Lars Martensson, Director
Langgatan 11
27432 Skurup, Sweden
(46 41) 14-08-02 (Tel. & Fax)

ISKA United Kingdom
John Day, Director
3 Fenn Farm Cott.
Hollow Lane, Washbrook
Ipswich, Suffolk, England IP8
   3HE
(44 473) 866-71 (Tel. & Fax)

Inter. Taekwon-do Fed. (ITF)
Gerasdoferstrasse 153
Haus-Nr. 23 A
1210 Vienna
Austria
(0222) 39-84-67
(0222) 39-55-09 (Fax)

Inter. Wushu Fed.
Li Menghua, President
3 Anding Rd.
Chaoyang, Beijing 100101
People's Republic of China
(86) 1-491-3262
(86) 1-491-2151 (Fax)

CONTINENTAL BRANCHES

European Wushu Fed.
Raymond W. Smith, President
11 Lucas Close
Yateley
Camberley GU17-7JD
England
(44) 252-878-641
(44) 1-456-6537 (Fax)

United States of America Wushu
    Kungfu Fed. (WKF)
Anthony Goh, Chairman
6315 Harford Rd.
Baltimore, MD 21214
(410) 444-6666
(410) 426-5524 (Fax)

Inter. Yoshinkai Aikido Fed.
Gozo Shioda, Chief Instructor
Kami Ochiai 2-28-8
Shinjuku-ku, Tokyo 161
Japan
(03) 368-5556

Isshin-ryu World Karate Assn.
Kichiro Shimabuku, President
829 Kyan
Gushikawa, Okinawa
Japan
(0989) 72-4185

Japan Karate Assn.
Rose Center, 2nd Floor
1-6-1, Ebisu-Nishi Ebisu
Shibuya-ku, Tokyo
Japan
(03) 462-1415

Japan Karate Fed.
Fumio Demura, President
1429 N. Bristol St.
Santa Ana, CA 92703
(714) 543-5550

Karate Inter. Council of Kickboxing
    (KICK)
Frank Babcock, President
P.O. Box 8931
St. Louis, MO 63102
(314) 225-7980

Kyokushinkai Kan
Mas Oyama, President

3-3-9, Nishi-Ikebukuro
Toshima-ku, Tokyo
Japan
(03) 984-7421

AFFILIATES

Austria
N. Jarets
Landstr. Hauptstr. 173-175/7
4A-1030 Wien
Austria

Belgium
J. Claes
Jan van Renesselaan 25
2150 Malle
Belgium

J. Corhay
86, Rue de la Brasserie
1050 Brussels
Belgium

Bulgaria
K. Bojilov
Gen Stoletov 15B
9002 Varna
Bulgaria

Denmark
Bryggervangen 19, 1.
2100 Copenhagen
Denmark

England
S. Arneil
145 Cambridge Rd.
West Wimbledon
London, SW 20 OPH
England

Germany
I. Freier
Hermanstrasse 256-258
1000 Berlin 44
Germany

France
G. Rosello
3, rue Cassini
06 Nice
France

P. Rouxel
15, rue Pierre Texier
Montgermont
35760 St. Gregoire
France

Greece
N. Varelopoulos
Papadakou 60
Nea Pagase, Volos
Greece

Hungary
I. Adamy
12 Ker Gyori VT4
Budapest 1123
Hungary

Ireland
L. Keaveney
58 Highfield Rd.
Chelmsford, Essex CM1 2NQ
England

Italy
T. Nicoletti
c/o Dr. G. Ferrari
S.S. 459 Gallipilo-Casarano
73052 Parabita (Lecce)
Italy

T. Wakiuchi
c/o Tommaso Cannizzaro
No. 262 98100 Messina
Sicilia, Italy

Liechtenstein
Z. Marxer
Postfach 94
9485 Nendlen
Liechtenstein

Netherlands
L. Netherlandser
P.O. Box 2673
Rotterdam
Netherlands

Norway
I. Rivenas
Hatleveien 3

5000 Bergen
Norway

Poland

A. Drewniak
ul. 31-130 Krakow
Kremerowska 3
Poland

Romania

I. Ilie
P.O. Box 6
Giurgiu 8315
Romania

Spain

A. Pinero
San Antonio Maria Claret 36-38
Zaragoza
Spain

Sweden

A. Meszaros
Box 12090
S-402 41 Goteborg
Sweden

Switzerland

P. von Rotz
Halde 14
6102 Malters
Switzerland

Turkey

I. Yatkin
Yildirin Mah Uzay Sok.
No. 7 Bayrampasa
Istanbul
Turkey

Okinawa Shorin-ryu Karate-do
　Shorinkan Assn.
Shugoro Nakazato, President
218 Aja
Naha, Okinawa
Japan
(0988) 61-2502

Sankudo Inter. Karate Org.
1189, rue du Boucherville
Quebec, Canada
(514) 641-2775
(514) 641-9136 (Fax)

Seishinkai Martial Arts
Shogo Kuniba, President
5913 Churchland Blvd.
Portsmouth, VA 23703
(804) 483-0195

Shotokan Karate Inter.
Hirokazu Kanazawa, Chief
　Instructor
Suzuden Bldg., Basement Floor
1-10 Yotsuya
Shinjuku-ku, Tokyo
Japan
(03) 359-6614

Sin Moo Hapkido
Grandmaster Han Jae Ji, President
1138 Forest Ave.
Pacific Grove, CA 93950

Uechi-ryu Karate-do Assn.
Kanyei Uechi, President
166 Futenma
Ginowan, Okinawa
Japan
(0988) 92-2409

United Fighting Arts Fed. (UFAF)
(Chuck Norris, President)
Danny Lane, Director
P.O. Box 5681
Huntington, WV 25703
(304) 525-5650

Viet Tai Chi World Fed.
2500 rue O'Neil
Ville de Sherbrooke, Quebec,
　Canada J1J 1M6
(819) 563-0531

World Assn. of Kickboxing
　Organizations (WAKO)
Ennio Falsoni, World President
34 Via Paganini
20052 Monza, Italy
22-85-6994
22-89-0827 (Fax)

AFFILIATES

WAKO Austria
Peter Kruckenhauser, Director
Winkl 24
A-6300 Worgl
Austria
(05332) 77739 (Phone & Fax)

WAKO Belgium
J. Goos, President
Kuypenevijer 8
B-3988 Laakdal, Belgium

WAKO Bermuda
Skipper Ingham, President
54 Court St.
Hamilton, Bermuda HM 12
(809) 292-2157

WAKO Canada
Jean Frenette, President
1189 Du Perche
Boucherville, Quebec, Canada
　J4B 6V3

WAKO Finland
Auvo Niiniketo, President
Radiokatu 12
SF-00240 Helsinki, Finland

WAKO France
George Boissin, President
Fed. National Boxe Americaine
1921 Rue de Dantzing
F-75015 Paris, France

WAKO Germany
Friedrich Meis, President
Am Kalbskopf 1
6078 Neu-Isenburg
Germany
(0 61 02) 3-33-70

WAKO Great Britain
Joe Johal, President
32 Palmeston Rd.
Forest Gate
GB London E7, 8BH
England

WAKO Greece
Simon Zahopoulos, President
Dagli 23
Kavala, Greece
22-84-86

WAKO Hungary
Richard Leyrer, President
Rajk Laszlo U. 114 V / 29
H-1138 Budapest, Hungary

WAKO Ireland
Eddie Ince, President
Waterstown Ave., Palmerstown
Dublin 20, Ireland

WAKO Isle Maurice
Madhookar Ramnarain,
    President
3, Avenue des Mouettes
Morc Sodnac
Q Bornes, Isle Maurice

WAKO Italy
See WAKO World Headquarters

WAKO Liechtenstein
Roman Oehri, President
Furstlich Liechtensteinischer
Sportverband
F.L. 9494 Schaan
Postfach 407, Liechtenstein

WAKO North Ireland
Frank Murney, President
76 Drumgullion Ave.
Newry, Co. Down, North
    Ireland

WAKO Norway
Erling Havna, President
4800 Arendal
Norway

WAKO Poland
Marek Frysz, President
Pl. Jednoschi Robotniczej 1
Room No. 142
00-661 Warsaw, Poland
322-882

WAKO Spain
Mariano Anton Hurtado,
    President
Gimnasio Esus
C./Maria Auxiliadora S/N
    Majadahonda
28220 Madrid, Spain

WAKO Sweden
Benny Hedlund, President
Husargatan 3
S-21128 Malmo, Sweden

WAKO Switzerland
Felix Hartmann, President
Nubrigweg, 4
4402 Frenkendorf, Switzerland

WAKO Turkey
Harabi Derin, President

Walter Flexstrasse 92
60 90 Russelsheim, Turkey

WAKO U.S.A.
Jim Lantrip, President
55 E. Center St.
Madisonville, KY 42431
(502) 825-5000
(502) 821-6774 (Fax)

WAKO Yugoslavia
Zarko Modric, President
P.P. 16, Novi Zagreb
YU-41020 Zagreb, Yugoslavia

PROVISIONAL MEMBERS

WAKO Algeria
Ahmed Guenad
7 Rue Racine
95140 Garges Les Gonesse,
    France

WAKO Argentina
Claudio Adolfo Ledwab
Monroe 4838 10 A
1431 Buenos Aires, Argentina

WAKO Australia
Les Anyos
P.O. Box 182
Maffra 3860
Victoria, Australia

WAKO Brazil
Jorge Octavio M. De Souza
Av. Rio Branco 245—31 Andar
Rio de Janeiro, Brazil

WAKO Colombia
Jose Luis Martinez
Apartado Aereo 49747
Bogota, D.E. Colombia

WAKO Ivory Coast
Dably Laurent
c/o Mondet Justin Pecaud
B.P. 103 Abidjan Cote d'Ivoir
Ivory Coast

WAKO Netherlands
Alex Copini
Zwenkgras 39
8935 HB Leeuwarden,
Netherlands

WAKO Portugal
Carlos Manuel Ramjanali
Rua D. Jose 1
Bloco H—1 Dt.
3080 Figuiera da Foz, Portugal

WAKO U.S.S.R.
Andrei Chistov
Zkinvse, Velmag
Electromash
Bolschija Okruzhanaja
Kiev, Ukraine

World Council of Jiu-Jitsu
    Organizations
Tony Maynard, Chairman
324 Barrington Park Lane
Kernersville, NC 27284
(919) 993-5488

World Ju-Jutsu Fed. (WJJF)
Robert Clark, President
Barlows Lane, Fazakerley
Liverpool 9
England
(051) 523-9611

AFFILIATES

Deutscher Ju-Jutsu Fed.
Kohlesrain 101
7950 Biberach 1
Germany

British Ju-Jutsu Fed.
(See World Headquarters)

World Ju Jitsu Fed. (WJJF)
Via Natale Battaglia 27
20127 Milano
Italy

World Karate Assn. (WKA)
Paul Ingram, President
Unit 8M
Castle Vale Industrial Estate
Maybrook Rd.
Minworth, Sutton Coldfield B76
    8AL
England
(021) 313-0040
(021) 313-0020 (Fax)

Dr. Un-Yong Kim, president of the World Taekwon-do Federation. Courtesy of the World Taekwon-do Federation

World Ki-Do Fed.
In Sun Seo, Chairman
3413 Atwater Ct.
Fremont, CA 94536
(510) 796-4115

World Muay Thai Assn.
Thom Harinck, President
van Hallstraat 52
1051 HH Amsterdam
Netherlands
20-867944

World Shorin-ryu Karate-do Fed.
Shoshin Nagamine, President
3-14-3 Kumoji
Naha, Okinawa
Japan
(0988) 33-3413

World Taekwon-do Fed. (WTF)
Dr. Un Yong Kim, President
635, Yuksam-dong
Kangnam-ku
Seoul, Korea 135
2-566-2505; 2-557-5446
82-02-553-4728 (Fax)

AFFILIATES

Fed. Andorrana de Taekwondo
Antoni Vidal Rabetllat,
    President
P.O. Box 82
Andorra la Vella
Principality of Andorra

Austrian Taekwondo Fed.
Dr. Georg Matuszek, President
Kornerstrasse 18
A-6020 Innsbruck
Austria

Barbados Taekwondo Assn.
Anthony Williams, President
P.O. Box 565
Bridgetown, Barbados

Fed. Boliviana de Taekwondo
Carlos Enrique Wiltersmann S.,
    Pres.
Gimnasio-Sede Calacoto Kwan
Avenida Arequipa No. 1130,
    casilla 20172
La Paz, Bolivia

Brazilian Taekwondo Assn.
Yong-Min Kim, President
Rua Voluntarios de Patria, 245-
    sobrado
CEP-22.270 Botafogo
Rio de Janeiro, Brazil

WTF Taekwondo Assn. of
    Canada
Chu Sam Park, Chairman
3078 Winston Churchill Blvd.
Mississagua, Ontario, Canada
    S7L 6H4

Chinese Taipei Amateur
    Taekwondo Assn.
No. 454, 5F, Chung-Shan N. Rd.
Sec. 6, Taipei, Taiwan Republic
    of China

Fed. Colombiana de Taekwondo
Calle 16 #9-64, Piso 4
Bogota, D.E., Colombia

Curaçao Taekwondo Assn.
Ashwin Feliz, President
Incastraat 10, POB 315
Curaçao, Netherlands Antilles

Fed. Ecuatoriana de Taekwondo
Ignacio Duenas, President
c/o Comite Olimpico
    Ecuatoriano
P.O. Box 4567
Guayaquil, Ecuador

Fed. Salvadorena de Taekwondo
Manuel Antonoi Gasca,
    President
Pasaje Los Pinos 4-129
Colonia Escalon, San Salvador
El Salvador, Central America

Finish Taekwondo Fed.
Jarmo Soila, President
Radiokatu 12
SF-00240 Helsinki
Finland

British Taekwondo Control
    Board
John Ingram, Chairman
53 Geary Rd.
Gladstone Park, London NW10
    1HJ
England

Greek Taekwondo Assn.
El. Missaelidis, President
c/o Hellenic Amateur Athletic
    Assn.
137, Syngrou Ave.
Athens 404, Greece

Hong Kong Taekwondo Assn.
Ma Ching Kwan, President
Room 1807, Wong On House
71 Des Voeux Rd.
Central, Hong Kong

Taekwondo Fed. of India
Lokpati Tripathi, President
33/26 B.N. Ghai Lane
Laibagh Lucknow-226001
Uttarpradesh, India

Iraqi Taekwondo Committee
Falah Hasan Jadou, President
P.O. Box 729
Baghdad, Iraq

Israel Taekwondo Fed.
Michel Madar, Chairman
32 Benjamin Meloudela St.
Jerusalem 92306
Israel

Fed. Ivorienne de Taekwondo
Edmond Bouazo Zegbehi,
    President
Ol B.P. 5451
Abidjan, Ol
Ivory Coast

Kuwait Taekwondo Fed.
Sheikh Khalifa Abdullah Al-
    Jaber Al-Sabha, Pres.
P.O. Box 795
Safat, Kuwait

Lebanese Fed. of Judo, Karate &
    Taekwondo
Jean Dfouny, President
P.O. Box 8189
Beirut, Lebanon

Malaysian Taekwondo Assn.
Y. Bhg. Datuk Setia Raja, Pres.
21-E, Jalan Tong Shin
50200 Kuala Lumpur
Malaysia

Nepal Martial Arts Assn.
Dashrath Rangashala
Tipureswor, Post Box 2090
Katmandu, Nepal

Netherlands Taekwondo Assn.
J. Janssen, President
Bondsbureau T.B.N.
    Wintersoord 7
6511 RP Jijmegen
Netherlands

Pakistan Taekwondo Assn.
Chowdhry Pervez Elahi
59 Britto Rd.
Karachi G.P.O. Box 1222
Karachi, Pakistan

Fed. Paraguayan de Taekwondo
Carlos Maria Moreno, President
Casilla Correos
No. 2215, Asuncion
Paraguay

Polisk Zwiazek Karate
Section Taekwondo
Marek Budzynski, Chairman
Stadion X-Lecia UL
Zieleniecka 1 PL-03-727
Warszawa, Poland

Panama Taekwondo
    Commission
Dr. Varo David Barragan Bech,
    Pres.
6-3352 El Dorado, Panama
Republic of Panama

Fed. de Taekwondo de Puerto
    Rico
Rafael Serranno, President
P.O. Box 1709 Ponce
P.R. 00731, Puerto Rico

Singapore Taekwondo Fed.
Ernest Koh, President
c/o Block 3, Queens Rd.
    #04-167
Singapore 1026
Singapore

Fed. Espanola de Taekwondo
Manuel Marco Saila, President
Calle Provenza, 238, 3, 4a
08008 Barcelona, Spain

Swaziland National Judo,
    Karate, Taekwondo Assn.
Sipho Zwane, President
P.O. Box 95
Manzing, Swaziland

United States Taekwon-do
    Union (USTU)
Robert Fujimura, President
1750 E. Boulder St.
Colorado Springs, CO 80909
(719) 578-4632

Fed. Venezolana de Taekwondo
Chong Koo Lee, President
Av. Bolivar 130-87 Mezanina
Valencia-EDO, Carabobo
Venezuela

Viet Tai Chi World Fed.
2500 rue O'Neil
Ville de Sherbrooke, Quebec,
    Canada J1J 1M6
(819) 563-0531

World Tang Soo Do Assn.
Jae C. Shin, President
709 Oregon Ave.
Philadelphia, PA 19148
(215) 468-2121
(215) 336-2121 (Fax)

AFFILIATES

CA; WA; OR; AK; HI
Gerry Stine
(503) 672-6190

CO; NM; AZ; UT; NV
Darryl Khalid
(602) 848-8773

ND; SD; NE; IA; MN; MT; ID; WY
Robert Willis
(218) 226-4182

MO; KS; OK; AR; TX
Andy Stewart

MI; WI; IL; IN; OH
Michael Romines
(313) 326-7661

FL; GA; AL; MS; LA; PR
Michael Hicks
(205) 281-5528

VA; WV; NC; SC; TN; KY
Robert Weichel
(803) 568-4255

NY; PA; NJ; MD; DE; DC
Jae C. Shin
(215) 468-2121

ME; NH; RI; MA; CT; VT
Marc Sattler
(203) 238-7369

Europe
Klaus Trogemann
49-8142-13773

South America
Larry Dercole
(619) 429-9122

World Union of Karate-do
    Organizations (WUKO)
Senpaku Shinko Bldg., 4th Floor
1-15-16 Toranomon

Minato-ku, Tokyo 105
Japan
(03) 503-6637

AFFILIATES

European Karate Union (EKU)
Jacques Delcourt, President
15 Av. de Chodsy
75013 Paris
France

Deutscher Karateverband e.V.
    (DKV)
Wolfgang Hagedorn, President
Grabenstrasse 37
4390 Gladbeck
Germany
(02043) 24007

USA Karate Fed.
George Anderson, President
1300 Kenmore Blvd.
Akron, OH 44314
(216) 753-6888
(216) 753-3114

Worldwide Nambudo
22 rue de Sablons
Paris 16, France
709-8411

NATIONAL AND CONTINENTAL ASSOCIATIONS

AFRICA

African Amateur Karate Fed.
c/o Egyptian Karate Fed.
Major General Abdel Karim Nafia,
    President
33 Sharif St.
Cairo, Egypt

Inter. Sport Karate Assn.
Joe Viljoen, Director
Box 1154
Carletonville 2500, South Africa
(27 14) 91-46-39 (Tel. & Fax)

ALGERIA

WAKO Algeria (provisional)
Ahmed Guenad
7 Rue Racine
95140 Garges Les Gonesse, France

ANDORRA

Fed. Andorrana de Taekwondo
Antoni Vidal Rabetllat, President
P.O. Box 82
Andorra la Vella
Principality of Andorra

ARGENTINA

Asociacion Inter. Wai Kung Pai
German Arancibia, Director
Cerrito 460
Buenos Aires, Argentina
35-7661

Fed. Sudamericana de Arte Marcial
    Chino
Lin Ching Sung, President
Av. Corrientes 4668 1 piso
Capital Federal
Buenos Aires, Argentina
88-6498

Pan-American Karate Union
Jose Maria Carcia Maanon,
    President
c/o Confederacion Argentina
    Deportes
Juncal 1662-1062 Capital Federal
Buenos Aires, Argentina

WAKO Argentina (provisional)
Claudio Adolfo Ledwab
Monroe 4838 10 A
1431 Buenos Aires, Argentina

AUSTRALIA

Aishin-Kai Karate Assn.
Karl Longley, President
Mt. French Rd.
Boonah 4310, Queensland
Australia
075-63-2991

All Okinawan Karate Goju-ryu
    Meibukan
Johanes Wong, Chief Instructor
(02) 636-4608

Australasian Traditional Martial
    Arts Assn.
Ross Mathers, Secretary
19 Hefferan St.
Fairfield, Queensland 4103
Australia

Australian Bujinkan Society
Andrew MacDonald
15 Alamein Ave.
Carlingford 2118, New South Wales
Australia
(02) 693-676

Australian Fed. of Wu Style Tai Chi
North Melbourne Community
    Centre
Buncle St.
North Melbourne 3051, Victoria
Australia
(03) 460-4746; (03) 336-2180

Australian Ju Jitsu Assn.
4th Floor, YMCA
489 Elizabeth St.
Melbourne 3000, Victoria
Australia
(03) 369-2712

Australian Kickboxing Fed. (AKF)
H.J. Hoffman, Honorary President
RMB 1535
Lima East, Victoria
(057) 68-2468

Australian Martial Arts Assn. of
    Queensland
P.O. Box 145
Sandgate 4017, Queensland
Australia

Australian Shito-Ryu Karate-do
    Assn.
K.W. Loh, Chief Instructor
13 Mitchell St.
Blackburn North, Victoria
(03) 878-7019

Australian Shukokai Karate Assn.
Alan Murdoch, Chief Instructor
145 Foster St.
Dandenong 3175, Victoria
Australia
(03) 794-6005; (03) 794-9859

Australian Society of Ju Jitsuans
(Clubs throughout the continent)
Vince McCann
(02) 771-6680

Australian Taekwon-do Assn.
Ke Hyung No, President
173 Bayswater Rd.
Croydon 3136, Victoria
Australia
(03) 723-4640

Australian Tae Kwon Do Moo Duk
   Kwan Assn.
Alan Williams, Chief Instructor
32 Penhurst St.
Penhurst, New South Wales
57-2433; 371-9110

Australian Tang Soo Do Assn.
C.H. Tnay, Chief Instructor
(Melbourne, Victoria)
(03) 841-9213

Budokan Inter. Martial Arts—
   Australia
Jack Harris, Chief Instructor
59 Greenhill Rd.
Bayswater North 3153, Victoria
Australia
(03) 729-0323

Budokan Karate of Australia
GPO Box 1304
Sydney, New South Wales 2001
Australia

Choi Kwang Do Inter.
Sai Thow Lam, Chief Instructor
P.O. Box 3032
Rivervale 6103
Western Australia
(09) 361-2855
(09) 470-3214 (Fax)

Choy Lee Fut Fed.
Chen Yong-Fa, Executive Director

213-215 Thomas St.
Sydney 2000, New South Wales
Australia

Fed. of Australian Tae Kwon Do
   Orgs.
Tiger Kim, President
P.O. Box H174
Harris Park, New South Wales 2174
Australia

Goju-Kensha Australia
Manuel Carydis
22 Fore St.
Canterbury 2193, New South Wales
Australia
(02) 78-6590

Goshin-ryu Karate Assn.
Richard Bradford, Chief Instructor
161 Adderton Rd.
Carlingford 2118, New South Wales
Australia
(02) 871-7014; (02) 630-4112

Iaido Assn. of Victoria
Andrew Pirog
4 Ballandry Crescent
Greensborough 3088, Victoria
Australia
(03) 435-0027

Iaido Assn. of Western Australia
P.O. Box 682
Cannington 6107
Western Australia
(09) 451-3909

Iaido Fed. of Australia
P.O. Box 980
Norwood 5067
South Australia
(08) 231-0767; (08) 271-8686

Inter. Karate-do Shobukai
(08) 297-1719

Inter. Kyokushin Karate—
   Australia
Eddie Emin, Director
130-132 Tennyson St.
Elwood 3184, Victoria
Australia
(03) 531-3853; (03) 531-9645

Inter. Okinawan Goju-ryu Karate-
   do Fed.
T.J. Bradford, Chief Instructor
15 Schmitt St.
Whittington 3219, Geelong
Australia
(052) 48-1439

Inter. Sport Karate Assn.
Dr. Peter Lewis, Director
1216 High St.
3143 Armadale, Australia
(61 3) 509-8937
(61 3) 822-7951 (Fax)

Inter. Taekwon-do Fed.
P.O. Box 170
Scone 2337, New South Wales
Australia
(065) 45-2878

Ki Society Inter.
100 Bowen St.
Spring Hill 4000, Queensland
Australia
369-9710; 82-1203

Kokusai Karate-do Kyo Kai-Kubota
Wamoana Terupe, Chief Instructor
P.O. Box 702
Woodridge 4114, Queensland
Australia
(07) 208-8568

Karate-do Shotokai Soyo Juku
   Assn.
Graham Slater, Chief Instructor
Melbourne, Australia
(03) 763-0595; (03) 762-6072

Kokusai Ju Jitsu Ryu Australia
John Bear, Chief Instructor
c/o 27 Shannon Circuit
Kaleen 2617, ACT
(062) 41-4659

Kokusai Karate-do Kyo Kai
Ron Goninan, Chief Instructor
C/-34 Short St.
Wellington 2820, New South Wales
Australia

National East Coast Karate League
161 Adderton Rd.

Carlingford 2118, New South Wales
Australia
(02) 871-7014

National Martial Arts League
Glenn Rushton, President
116 Calam Rd.
Sunnybank Hills 4109, Queensland
Australia
(07) 273-5954
(07) 808-2325 (Fax)

NMAL New South Wales
(02) 521-6483

NMAL Victoria
(03) 763-7949

Szlagowski Karate Assn.
c/o 118 The Crescent
Helenburgh 2508, New South
   Wales
Australia

Shorin-ryu Martial Arts Fed.
Norm Small, Chief Instructor
39 Plunkett Rd.
Dandenong 3175, Victoria
Australia
(03) 793-5177

Shotokan Karate Inter.—Australia
P.O. Box H244
Australia Square 2000
Sydney, New South Wales
Australia
(02) 887-2226

Sikaran-Arnis Inter.
Jesse Diestro, President
Campsie Fitness Centre, 43 North
   Pde.
Campsie, New South Wales
Australia
(02) 750-4136; (02) 789-1208

Tang Soo Tao Physical Culture &
   Oriental Studies Society
Glen Kriton, Chief Instructor
G.P.O. Box 73
Canberra 2601, ACT
(062) 58-8302

Traditional Okinawan Goju-ryu
   Karate-do Assn.
Graham Ravey, Chief Instructor
Lot 4, Scrubby Creek Rd.
Woodford 4514, Queensland
Australia
(07) 197-1731

United Martial Arts Assn.
Graeme Bingham, Director
34 Short St.
Wellington 2820, New South Wales
Australia
(068) 452-318

WAKO Australia
Les Anyos, President
P.O. Box 182
Maffra 3860
Victoria, Australia
(051) 486-257

Women's Martial Arts Fed.
P.O. Box 882
Darlinghurst 2010, New South
   Wales
Australia

World Budo Martial Arts (Ju-Jitsu
   Australia)
Peter McAnalen, Chairman
c/o Brisbane Sports School
1188-92 Stanley St. East
East Coorparoo 4151, Queensland
Australia

Yun Inter. Taekwon-do Fed.
Young Ku Yun, President
12 Tutoko Court
Aspley Heights 4034, Queensland
Australia
(07) 263-5926
(07) 263-5926 (Fax)

Bugeido Karate Assn.
Geoff Reddish, Chief Instructor
P.O. Braxholm 7254
Tasmania, Australia
(003) 54-6271

Tasmanian Tae Kwon Do Fed.
29 Chris St.
Launceston, TAS 7250
Tasmania, Australia

AUSTRIA

Austrian Taekwondo Fed.
Dr. Georg Matuszek, President
Kornerstrasse 18
A-6020 Innsbruck
Austria

Inter. Amateur Kickboxing Sport
   Karate Assn. (IAKSA)
Peter Land, Director
Pluddemanngasse 93 A/16
A-8010 Graz
Austria
(0316) 465701
(0316) 473539 (Fax)

Inter. Taekwon-do Fed. (ITF)
Stollgasse 8/2
A-1070 Wien
Austria
(0222) 963035

Jiu Jitsu Verband Osterreich (JJVO)
Prager Strasse 20
A-1210 Wien
Austria
(0222) 455-2695

Kyokushinkai Kan
N. Jarets
Landstr. Hauptstr. 173-175/7
4A-1030 Wien
Austria

Osterreichischer Bundes
   Fachverband for Kickboxen
   (OBFK)
Louis Kofler
Freundsbergstrasse 6
6020 Innsbruck/Tirol
Austria

Osterreichischer Karatebund
Karl Neveceral, President
Pazmanitengasse 17
A-1020 Wien
Austria
(0222) 246-7213

Osterreichischer Shotokan Karate
   Dachverband (OSKV)
c/o Stolberggasse 21
A-1050 Wien
Austria

Ta Sheng Yuan Taoist Society
Richard Dean
P.O. Box 110
A-3300 Amstetten
Austria
(07472) 39065

WAKO Austria
Peter Kruckenhauser, Director
Winkl 24
A-6300 Worgl
Austria
(05332) 77739 (Phone & Fax)

World Kick-Boxing Assn.
Ronald Hitz, Director
Mariahilferstrasse 111
A-1060 Wien
Austria
(0222) 568113
(0222) 5969735 (Fax)

BARBADOS

Barbados Taekwondo Assn.
Anthony Williams, President
P.O. Box 565
Bridgetown, Barbados

BELGIUM

Belgian Amateur Karate Fed.
Jacques van Lerberghe, President
Rue de Merinos, 39
B-1030 Bruxelles
Belgium
02-242-2805

European Kendo Fed.
c/o Alan Ducarme
4 rue du Busard
1170 Brussels
Belgium

Kyokushinkai Kan
J. Claes
Jan van Renesselaan 25
2150 Malle
Belgium

WAKO Belgium
J. Goos, President
Kuypenevijer 8
B-3988 Laakdal, Belgium

BERMUDA

WAKO Bermuda
Skipper Ingham, President
54 Court St.
Hamilton, Bermuda HM 12
(809) 292-2157

BOLIVIA

Fed. Boliviana de Taekwondo
Carlos Enrique Wiltersmann S.,
    Pres.
Gimnasio-Sede Calacoto Kwan
Avenida Arequipa No. 1130, casilla
    20172
La Paz, Bolivia

BRAZIL

Assn. Budokan de Ribeirao Preto
Roberto Chaves Sant'Anna, Pres.
Avenida Francesco Junqueira
    2291-S
CEP 14090, Ribeirao Preto SP
Brazil

Assn. Cultural de Artes Marciais
Yassuo Kobayashi, Director
Av. Eng. Armando Arruda Pereira,
    1692
1 andar
Jabaquara, São Paulo, SP
Brazil
(011) 578-2803

Assn. Faixas-Pretas de Karate do
    Ceara
Luiz Carlos, President
Rua Pedro Rufino, 40
Varjeta, Forteleza, Ceara
CEP 50175-000
Brazil

Assn. Fei Hok Phai Kung-Fu Wu-
    Shu
Rua Santo Andre, 662
Santo Andre, São Paulo, SP
Brazil
(011) 444-4829
(011) 449-1780 (Fax)

Assn. de Karate Butoku-kai
Tomeji Ito, Director

Rua Domingos de Moraes, 928
Vila Mariana/SP
Brazil

Assn. Karate-do Wado-kai
Andre Luiz Branco, Director
Rua Alexandre Dumas, 1129
Chacara, Santo Antonio/SP
Brazil
(011) 521-8300

Assn. de Karate-do Ipiranga
Edgar Ferraz, Director
Rua Bom Pastor, 1056
Ipiranga, São Paulo/SP
Brazil
(011) 273-9840

Assn. Kyokushinkai de Karate
Seiji Isobe, Director
Av. Liberdade, 1086
Liberdade, São Paulo/SP, CEP
    01502-001
Brazil
(011) 279-7234; (011)279-1392

Assn. Lung de Kung-Fu
Alberto Gomes, President
Rua Julio Davi, 36
Ribeira, Salvador BA, CEP
    40420-230
Brazil
(011) 248-3274

Assn. Moy Yat de Ving Tsun Kung-
    Fu
Leo Imamura, President
Av. Cursino, 2327, Salas 1 e 2
São Paulo/SP, 04133-200
Brazil
(011) 275-8028
(011) 275-2650 (Fax)

Assn. Shaolin de Kung-Fu
Prof. Amaral, Director
Rua da Consolacao, 2267
São Paulo/SP, CEP 01301-000
Brazil
(011) 259-9245
(011) 256-3404 (Fax)

Assn. Shoku-kan de Karate-do Vial
    Maria
Nilton Kuriyama, Director
Av. Conceicao, 3294

Vila Maria Alta, São Paulo/SP
Brazil
(011) 201-2199

Assn. de Taekwon-do do Brazil
Yun Sik Kim, President
Rua da Graca, 89-4 andar
Bom Retiro, São Paulo/SP
Brazil
(011) 223-0486

Assn. Yuubu-kan de Karate-do
Ozias Araujo, Director
Av. Cel Sezefredo Fagundez, 1807
s/7 Jd.
Tremembe, São Paulo/SP
Brazil
(011) 204-0149

Brazilian Taekwondo Assn.
Yong-Min Kim, President
Rua Voluntarios de Patria, 245-
    sobrado
CEP-22.270 Botafogo
Rio de Janeiro, Brazil

Fed. Paulista de Aikido
Paulo Nakamura, President
Rua M.M.D.C., 205
Butanta/SP, CEP 05510
Brazil
(011) 813-7536; 578-2803

Inter. Union Shorin-ryu Karate-do
    Fed.
Yoshihide Shinzato, President
Av. Senador Feijo, 219, 2 andar
Santos/SP, CEP 11015
Brazil

Union Karate-do Goju-ryu do
    Brazil
Joao Matos, President
Av. Eng. Heitor Antonio Eiras
    Garcia, 1393
s/3 Pq.
Sao Domingos, Butanta/SP
Brazil
(011) 268-1309; (011) 869-4126

Wado-ryu Karate-do Renmei
Koji Takamatsu, President
Av. Pompeia, 1466
São Paulo
Brazil
(011) 263-0161

WAKO Brazil (provisional)
Jorge Octavio M. De Souza
Av. Rio Branco 245—31 Andar
Rio de Janeiro, Brazil

BULGARIA

Kyokushinkai Kan
K. Bojilov
Gen Stoletov 15B
9002 Varna
Bulgaria

CANADA

Canadian Chinese Martial Arts
    Fed.
Wah Dunn, President
1077 Gerrard St. E.
Toronto, Ontario, Canada
(416) 463-5669

Canadian Inter. Jiu-Jitsu Fed.
John Therien, President
259 Ste. Anne St.
Vanier, Ontario, Canada K1L 7C3
(613) 746-5402

Cloud Forest World Chinese
    Martial Arts Assn.
P.O. Box 4008, Station A
Victoria, B.C., Canada V8X 3X4

Guardian Angels
Dennis Watson, Coordinator
10215 150th St., #326
Surrey, B.C., Canada V3R 4A8
(604) 585-4139

International All-Style Martial Arts
    League (IMAL)
John Williams, President
Box 2335, Station "A"
Moncton, N.B., Canada E1C 8J3
(506) 857-0434

Inter. Sport Karate Assn. (Canada)
Paul Renaud, Director
700 Hurtubise
Gatineau, Quebec, Canada J8V 4G7
(819) 643-1012
(613) 995-4519 (Fax)

Sankudo Inter. Karate Org.
1189, rue du Boucherville
Quebec, Canada
(514) 641-2775
(514) 641-9136 (Fax)

Thai Boxing Assn. of Canada
P.O. Box 4165, Station E
Ottawa, Ontario, Canada K15 5B2
United Taekwon-Do Inter.
21 Kootenay Dr.
Saskatoon, Sask., Canada S7K 1J2
(306) 934-5900
(306) 934-5907 (Fax)

United Taekwon-do of North
    America
4707 48 St., 2nd Floor
Camrose, Alberta, Canada T4V 1L2
(403) 672-3500

Universal Kung-Soo-Do Assn.
Andrew Paton, President
Box 237
Novar, Ontario, Canada P0A 1R0
(705) 789-2550

Viet Tai Chi World Fed.
2500 rue O'Neil
Ville de Sherbrooke, Quebec,
    Canada J1J 1M6
(819) 563-0531

WAKO Canada
Jean Frenette, President
1189 Du Perche
Boucherville, Quebec, Canada J4B
    6V3

Western Sikaran Arnis Assn.
Henry Bio, President
P.O. Box 637
Rosthern, Saskatchewan
Canada S0K 3R0
(306) 232-4713

WTF Taekwondo Assn. of Canada
Tae Eun Lee, President
3078 Winston Churchill Blvd.
Mississagua, Ontario, Canada S7L
    6H4

CEYLON: SEE
SRI LANKA

CHINA

All China Sports Fed.
9, Tiyuguan Rd.
Beijing
People's Republic of China

China Fuzhou Wushu Assn.
c/o Li Yi Duan
#1 Qunzhong Rd.
Fuzhou 350005
People's Republic of China

Inter. Wushu Fed.
Li Menghua, President
3 Anding Rd.
Chaoyang, Beijing 100101
People's Republic of China
(86) 1-491-3262
(86) 1-491-2151 (Fax)

CHINESE TAIPEI

Chinese Kuoshu Worldwide
 Promotion Assn.
4th Floor, No. 33 Roosevelt Rd.
Section II, Taipei, Taiwan
Republic of China
(02) 392-0305; (02) 392-5676

Chinese Taipei Amateur
 Taekwondo Assn.
No. 454, 5F, Chung-Shan N. Rd.
Section 6, Taipei, Taiwan
Republic of China

COLOMBIA

Fed. Colombiana de Taekwondo
Calle 16 #9-64, Piso 4
Bogota, D.E., Colombia
WAKO Colombia (provisional)
Jose Luis Martinez
Apartado Aereo 49747
Bogota, D.E. Colombia

CUBA

Fed. Cubana de Karate
Comite Olimpico Cubano
Calle 13 C y D
Vedado, Ciudad Havana
Cuba

CURAÇAO

Curaçao Taekwondo Assn.
Ashwin Feliz, President
Incastraat 10, POB 315
Curaçao, Netherlands Antilles

DENMARK

Dansk Karate Forbund
Vermlandsgade 75
2300 S. Kobenhavn
Denmark
577040

Kyokushinkai Kan
Bryggervangen 19, 1.
2100 Copenhagen
Denmark

ECUADOR

Fed. Ecuatoriana de Taekwondo
Ignacio Duenas, President
c/o Comite Olimpico Ecuatoriano
P.O. Box 4567
Guayaquil, Ecuador

EGYPT

Egyptian Taekwon-do Fed.
P.O. Box 91
Abbasia, Cairo
Egypt

EL SALVADOR

Fed. Salvadorena de Taekwondo
Manuel Antonoi Gasca, President
Pasaje Los Pinos 4-129
Colonia Escalon, San Salvador
El Salvador, Central America

ENGLAND

All British Karate Org.
8 Clockhouse
Ashford, Kent TN23 2B
England
(0233) 39063

Amateur Martial Assn. (AMA);
Amateur Karate Assn. (AKA);
Amateur Ju-Jitsu Assn. (AJJA);
Amateur Kung-Fu Assn. (AKFA);
Amateur Taekwondo Assn.
 (ATKDA);
Amateur Nunchaku Assn. (ANA);
Amateur Bu-Jitsu Assn. (ABJA)

All of the above can be contacted at:

AMA
Tom Hibbert, Secretary
120 Cromer St.
London WC1H 8BS
England
(071) 837-4406
(071) 278-7738 (Fax)

Bak Shaolin Ji Eagle Claw
Wu-Shu Assn.
Leung Fu, Chief Instructor
The Irish Centre
96-104 Chatham St.
Reading, Berks RG1 7RD
England
(0734) 393096

British Aikido Fed.
Minoru Kanetsuka, Technical
 Director
Yew Tree Cottage
Toot Baldon, Oxford OX9 9NE
England
(086) 738-500

British All Styles Martial Arts
 Assn.
Greg Wallace, Chief Instructor
629B High Rd.
Seven Kings, Ilford, Essex IG3 8RB
England
(081) 598-1855

British Combat Assn.
3 Fairfield Court
618/620 Harrogate Rd.
Leeds LS17
England
(0831) 576509;
(0203) 361-1741

British Fed. of All Styles Karate
  Orgs.
P.O. Box 112
Feltham TW14 8LA
England
(0932) 253382

British Institute of Black Belts
47 Prospect Square
Westbury, Wilts. BA13 3ET
England

British Ju-Jutsu Fed.
See: World Ju-Jutsu Fed.

British Karate Assn.
18 Swan St.
Manchester M4 5JN
England
(061) 832-8204

British Karate Kyokushinkai
Steve Arneil, Chief Instructor
145 Cambridge Rd.
West Wimbledon
London, SW 20 OPH
England

British Kempo Ju-Jitsu Fed.
Centaur House
8/10 Lily Rd.
Litherland, Merseyside L21 6NX
England
(051) 922-7698 (Fax)

British Kendo Assn.
10 Broad Oaks
Wickford, Essex SS12 9BQ
England

British Kickboxing Fed.
(0734) 663263; (0628) 34812

British Kickboxing Union
282 Staines Rd.
Twickenham, Middlesex TW8 5AS
England

British Kuoshu Promotion Assn.
Raymond Goh
8 Popes Lane
Ealing, London W5 4NA
England
(0908) 322450

British Nanbudo Assn.
(0555) 4014

British Muay Thai Assn.
(081) 461-0230

British Okinawan Karate Bugeikai
Rick Woodhams, Chief Instructor
Greenways, Mill Lane
Titchfield, Hampshire PO15 5DU
England
0329-42240

British Sankukai Karate Assn.
Butch White, Chief Instructor
8 Perrin Ave.
Kiddermonster, Worchester DY11
  6LL
England
(0562) 68171

British Shorinji Kempo Assn.
Terry Goodman, Secretary
(071) 281-8907

British Shotokan Karate Assn.
Charles Mack, Chief Instructor
The London Karate Club
28 Ashburnham Mansions
Chelsea, London SW10 0PA
England
(071) 352-7716

British Sombo Fed.
Sittingbourne Sports Centre, East
  St.
Sittingbourne, Kent ME10 2BL
England

British Taekwondo Control Board
John Ingram, Chairman
53 Geary Rd.
Gladstone Park, London NW10 1HJ
England

British Taekwondo Fed.
(0253) 41918

British Takeuchi Ryu Jujitsu Assn.
Charles Mack, Chief Instructor
28 Ashburnham Mansions
Chelsea, London SW10 0PA
England
(071) 352-7716

British Taijiquan & Shaolin Wushu
  Assn.
28 Linden Farm Dr.
Countesthorpe, Leicester LE8 3SX
England

British Thai Boxing Council
19 Walsden St.
Clayton, Manchester M11 4NJ
England

British United Karate Org.
Flat 1, 116 Eastern Rd.
Brighton, E. Sussex BN2 2AJ
England
(0273) 606762

Combat Sports Assn.
Box No. FM 299
Derbyshire
England

English Budo Karate Assn.;
English Budo Kung-Fu Assn.
30 Sussex Ave.
Margate, Kent CT9 1TN
England
(0843) 295091

English Contact Karate Assn.
(021) 557-1976

English Goju-Ryu Karate-do Assn.
George Andrews
31 Matson House
Southwark Park Rd.
London SE16
England
(01) 237-2029

English Shukokai Karate Assn.
Sylvester Walsh, Chief Instructor
258 Middlewich St.
Crewe, Cheshire CW1 4DP
(0270) 581050

European Aikido Assn.
(0268) 490392

European Martial Arts Assn.
4 Fraser Dr.
Sheffield S8 OJG
England
(0742) 747825

Freestyle Sport Karate Assn.
Alfie Lewis, Chief Instructor
(061) 969-0399

Global Taekwondo Inter.
Tony Sewell
(0332) 270863

Goshin Inter.
M. Upham, Chief Instructor
142 Sandy Rd.
Seaford, Liverpool L21 1AW
England
(051) 920-9734

Goshin Kai Inter.
Hawthorne Health & Fitness
   Centre
237 Hawthorne Rd.
Bootle L20 4AW
England
(051) 922-4766

Independent Korean Karate Assn.
No. 4 Irwin Court
470 London Rd.
Ashford, Middlesex TW15 3AD
England
(0784) 251110

Inter. Budo Fed.
Sittingbourne Sports Centre, East
   St.
Sittingbourne, Kent ME10 2BL
England

Inter. Fighting Arts Fed.
c/o General Secretary
Flat 1, 116 Eastern Rd.
Brighton, East Sussex BN2 2AJ
England
(0273) 606762 (Phone & Fax)

Inter. Register of Martial Artists
98 Arlington
Ashford, Kent TN23 2W
England
(0233) 39063

Inter. Sport Karate Assn.
John Day, Director
3 Fenn Farm Cott.
Hollow Lane, Washbrook
Ipswich, Suffolk, England IP8 3HE
(44 473) 866-71 (Tel. & Fax)

Karate Union of Great Britain
Keinosuke Enoeda, President
125 Hullbridge Rd.
South Woodham Ferrers
Essex, CM3 5LL
England

Kempo JuJitsu Budo Assn. of Great
   Britain
Wanstead Leisure Centre
Redbridge Lane West
Wanstead, London E11
England
(081) 471-3204

Martial Arts Commission
(The governing body of Great
   Britain's martial arts)
51 Palmers Rd.
London N11 1RJ
England
or: Martial Arts Commission
Brian Eustace, Vice-Chairman
1st Floor, Broadway House
15/16 Deptford Broadway
London SE8 4PE
England
(01) 691-3433

Mid-West Tae-Kwon-Do Assn.
S. Taylor
30 Waveney Rise
Oadby, Leicester
England
(0533) 714504

National Assn. of Karate and
   Martial Arts Schools
21 Queen St.
Ashford, Kent TN23 1RF
England
(0233) 647003
(0233) 647002 (Fax)

Nippon Dai Budo Kai Inter.
R. Hayabuchi, President
Barlows Lane, Fazakerley
Liverpool 9
England
(051) 523-9611

Nippon Jujutsu & Kobudo Inter.
231 Downham Way
Bromley, Kent BR1 5GL
England
(081) 461-0627

Oriental Martial Arts Society
Chris Davies, Director
(0875) 340900

Pak Mei Kung-Fu Assn.
Cho Tak Tang, Chief Instructor
(0322) 60971

Shotokan Karate Union Great
   Britain (SKUGB)
25 Quebec Rd.
Orford, Warrington, Cheshire WA2
   7SB
England

Spirit Combat Inter.
The Thickets
51 The Ridings
Woodham, Woking GU 21
England
(0483) 720054

Sport Kickboxing Org.
42 Fern Hurst Dr.
Brierley Hill
West Midlands DY5 4PU
England
(0384) 483628 (Phone & Fax)

Toyakwai Karate Assn.
17 Holmbury View
Upper Clapton, London E5 9EG
England
(071) 249-6155

United Budo Assn.
I.J. Thorogood, Secretary
66 Chestnut Ave.
Hornchurch, Essex RM12 4JH
England
(0402) 475700

United Kingdom Aikikai
(0952) 812755

United Kingdom All Styles Karate
   Org.
9 The Meade
Chorltonville, Manchester M21 2FA
England
(061) 873-7771

United Kingdom All Styles Kung-
   Fu Assn.
356 Chester Rd.

Cornbrook, Manchester M16 9EA
England
(061) 860-5255

United Kingdom Choi Kwang-Do
    Fed.
Roger Koo, Chief Instructor
21 Mornington Rd.
Asford, Middlesex TW15 INP
England
(0784) 250567
(0784) 240166 (Fax)

United Kingdom Ju-Jitsu Fed.
G. Salders, Chief Instructor
220 Merrevale Rd.
Bearwood, Warley, West Midlands
    B66
England
(021) 420-1677

United Kingdom Sulkido Assn.
472 Caledonia Rd.
London N7 8TB
England
(01) 607-9517

United Kingdom Tae Kwon Do
    Fed.
Roger Koo, Chief Instructor
21 Mornington Rd.
Asford, Middlesex TW15 INP
England
(0784) 250567

United Kingdom Wing Chun
    Kung-Fu Assn.
19 Golding Crescent
Stanford-le-Hope, Essex SS17 7AZ
England
(0375) 640579

United Taekwondo Assn.
T. W. Shin, Chief Instructor
557 Chester Rd.
Old Trafford, Manchester M16 0GN
England
(061) 848-7426
(061) 848-0436 (Fax)

WAKO Great Britain
Joe Johal, President
32 Palmeston Rd.
Forest Gate
GB London E7, 8BH
England

World Combat Assn.
51 The Riding
Woodham, Woking, Surrey GU21
    5TD
England

World Ju-Jutsu Fed. (WJJF);
British Ju-Jutsu Fed.
Robert Clark, President
Barlows Lane, Fazakerley
Liverpool 9
England
(051) 523-9611

World Karate Assn.
Paul Ingram, President
Unit 8M
Castle Vale Industrial Estate
Maybrook Rd.
Minworth, Sutton Coldfield B76
    8AL
England
(021) 313-0040
(021) 313-0020 (Fax.)

Wu Kung Fed.
91 Tilsworth Rd.
Stanbridge, Beds LU7 9Y
England

EUROPE

European Amateur Karate Fed.
    (EAKF)
Postfach 571
D-3110 Uelzen 1
Germany

European Judo Union (EJU)
c/o Dardenne
43 Rue des Plantes
Paris 16
France

European Karate Union (EKU)
15 Av. de Chodsy
75013 Paris
France

AFFILIATES

Deutscher Karateverband e.V.
    (DKV)
Wolfgang Hagedorn, President

Grabenstrasse 37
4390 Gladbeck
Germany
(02043) 24007

European Kendo Fed.
c/o Alan Ducarme
4 rue du Busard
1170 Brussels
Belgium

European Moo Duk Kwan Tang
    Soo Do Fed.
Willebrordusstraat 142
3037 TX Rotterdam
Netherlands
010-467-1279

European Ninjutsu Org.
Wolfgang Ettig
Saalburgstrasse 151
6380 Bad Homburg v.d.H.
Germany
(06172) 39626

European Taekwondo Union
c/o Heinz
Maximillian Slats, 12
8000 Munich 2
Germany

European Wing Tsun Org.
Keith Kernspecht, Chief Instuctor
6901 Schloss
Langenzell
Germany
06223 / 47250
06223 / 48250 (Fax)

European Wushu Fed.
Raymond W. Smith, President
11 Lucas Close
Yateley, Camberley GU17-7JD
England
(44) 252-878-641
(44) 1-456-6537 (Fax)

Inter. Judo Fed.
c/o Garcia de La Fluente
Hortaleza, 108
Madrid 4
Spain

Inter. Sport Karate Assn. Europe
Will Raven, Director
Landsteinerstrasse #5
Geleen, Netherlands 616 4XD
(31 46) 74-74-35
(31 46) 75-55-52 (Fax)

Shorei-Kan Europe
La Barre de l'Ange
45380 La Chapelle-Saint-Mesmin
France
(16) 38.72.54.98

FINLAND

Finnish Taekwondo Fed.
Jarmo Soila, President
Radiokatu 12
SF-00240 Helsinki
Finland

Suomen Amatoori
Willie Ortiz
Karate-do Liitto
Kissanmaankatu 26K
33530 Tampere 53
Finland
931-611318

WAKO Finland
Auvo Niiniketo, President
Radiokatu 12
SF-00240 Helsinki, Finland

FRANCE

Assn. Franco-Japonaise de Tenri
9, rue Victor Considerant
75014 Paris
France
(1) 43.35.11.86

Fed. Francaise d'Aikibudo
5, rue Victor
91350 Grigny
France
(1) 69.06.46.56

Fed. Francaise Aikido, Aiki-budo
    et Affinitaires
72, rue des Grands Champs
75020 Paris
France
43.48.22.22

Assoc. de Baton de Combat et de
    Self-Defense
15, av. du Marechal Foche
31400 Toulouse
France
(16) 61.52.56.15

Fed. Francaise d' Aikido
11 Rues Jules Valles
75011 Paris
France
(1) 4348.22.22

Fed. Francaise de Boxe Francaise
    Savate (FFBFS)
25, Blvd. des Italiens
75002 Paris
France
(1) 47.42.82.27

Fed. Francaise de Boxe
    Thailandaise
90, rue de la Jonquiere
75017 Paris
France
46.27.07.25

Fed. Francaise Bujinkan Ninjutsu
24, rue des Chataigniers
68680 Kembs-Loechle
France
(16) 89.48.42.60

Fed. Francaise des Ecoles d'Arts
    Martiaux (FFST)
Traditional and Modern Arts
68, rue Castagnary
75015 Paris
France
(1) 45.31.41.29

Traditional Arts
83, rue Michel Ange
75016 Paris
France
(1) 47.02.49.01

Fed. Francaise Escrime
45, rue de Liege
75008 Paris
France
42.94.91.38

Fed. Francaise de Goshindo
28-30, rue Voltaire

08000 Charlesvilles-Mezieres
France
(16) 24.37.50.95
(16) 24.59.27.69

Fed. Francaise de Hakko-ryu Ju
    Jitsu
43, rue des Plantes
75014 Paris
France
45.42.80.90

Assn. Francaise de Hapkido
    Traditionnel
11, rue Armagis
78100 St. Germain-en-Laye
France
45.31.56.72

Fed. Francaise de Ju Jitsu
    Butokukai et Disciplines
    Associes
19, rue des Fosses-St. Jacques
75005 Paris
France
49.60.76.77
43.29.37.49

Fed. Francaise de Karate
    Commission Nationale Tai-Jitsu
122, rue de la Tombe d'Issoire
75014 Paris
France
43.95.42.00

Assn. Francaise de Karate-do
Goju-ryu d'Okinawa (AFKGO)
46, rue du Moulin Vert
29000 Quimper
France
98.55.89.30
98.55.89.31 (Fax)

Fed. Francaise de Karate,
    Taekwondo et Arts Martiaux
    Affinitaires
122, rue de la Tombe-Issoire
75014 Paris
France
45.40.65.53

Fed. Francaise Karate, Taekwondo
    et Judo (FFKTJ)
B.P. 90
91350 Grigny
France

Fed. Francaise de Kendo Iai-Do
62, avenue Parmentier
75011 Paris
France
(1) 43.57.22.45

Fed. Francaise de Kobudo
   Traditionnel Japonais
BP 90
91350 Grigny
(1) 69.06.46.56

Fed. Francaise de Kung Fu Contact
Secretariat-General
183, Bd de la Madeleine
06000 Nice
France

AFFILIATES

Bretagne–Normandie–Nord–Pas-de-Calais
9, impasse des Abeilles
14630 Cagny
France

Paris–Ile-de-France
Joel Goncalves
32, rue D'aillon
77310 Orgenoy
France

Auvergne–Rhone–Alpes–Dauphine-Savoie
Jean-Louis Blancard
295, route de Genas
69100 Villeurbanne
France

Aquitaine–Provence–Cote D'Azur–Corse
Serge Lvoff
59, avenue de la Lanterne
06200 Nice
France

Fed. Francaise de Kung Fu Wu Shu
   (FFKW)
46, rue Blanche
75009 Paris
France
(1) 48.74.83.45

Fed. Francaise de Nunchaku
   Sportif (FFNS)
29, rue Traverse de Pia
66000 Perpignan
France
68.52.00.54

Fed. Francaise des Tai Chi Chuan
   Traditionnels (FFTCCT)
78, rue de Rennes
75006 Paris
France
45.43.03.96

Fed. Francaise de Tai Chi et de
   Kung Fu
Tran Kinh, President
Gymnase de l'Eglise Americaine
65, quai d'Orsay
75007 Paris
France
45.77.44.71

Fed. Francaise de Wa-Jutsu
1, bis Chemin de Puech-Long
34430 St.-Jean de Vedas
France
67.47.38.19

Fed. Sportive des Sourdes de
   France
84, rue Turenne
75003 Paris
France

FFLAB (Aikikai de France)

REGIONAL COMMITTEES

Alsace
Rene Fantini, President
12, rue des Schnug
67100 Strasbourg-Neuhof
France
88.39.36.13

Aquitaine
Michel Cadiou, President
61, cours de Verdun
33210 Langdon
France
56.63.17.14

Atlantique
M.J.P. Audiau, President
4, impasse des Orangers

44800 St. Herblain
France
40.46.57.24

Auvergne
J.C. Champagneux, President
7, av. de la Republique
03000 Montlucon, France
70.05.27.09

Bourgogne
Francois Colinot, President
57, route de Corcelles
Marzy 58000 Nevers
France
86.57.37.07

Bretagne
Jean Tardif, President
4, rue Thiers
35600 Redon
France

Centre
Michel Benart, President
7, rue Nicolas-Poussin
45100 Orleans
France
38.63.50.77

Champagne
Pierre Sevin, President
9, rue Paul Percheron
52220 Moutiers-en-Der
France
25.04.66.99

Charentes-Poitou
M.A. Guillon, President
Boite Postale 116
17004 La Rochelle Cedex
France
46.41.68.96

Cote D'Azur
Pierre Grimaldi, President
Rue de l'Officier Principal
Mecanicien Challier
83430 St. Mandrier S/Mer
France
94.63.66.81

Dauphine Savoie
Jean-Marc Vernier, President
6, rue des Ecureuils
73100 Aix-les-Bains
France
79.35.54.35

Flandres-Artois
Gaby Bizien, President
6, rue du Pont du Lion d'Or
59800 Lille, France

Franche Comte
Dr. Andre Petrequin, President
18, rue du Reservoir
25400 Audincourt
France
81.30.60.25

Ile-de-France
Gerard Gras, President
101-103, av. de la Republique
93170 Bagnolet
France
45.22.41.38

Languedoc-Roussillon
Guy Carriere, President
B.P. 111
34002 Montpellier Cedex
France
67.92.68.86

La Reunion
Alain Courtois, President
63, allee des Pailles-en-Queue
Cap Champagne
97434 St.-Gilles-les-Bains
Reunion, France

Limousin
Jean-Claude Beaudufe,
    President
13, impasse J.-J. Rousseau
87170 Isle
France
55.50.24.67

Lorraine
Paul Freidrich, President
10, rue Gabriel-Faure
54500 Vandoeuvre
France
83.32.97.67

Lyonnais
Michel Gillet, President
25, rue Juliette-Recamier
01000 Bourg-en-Bresse
France
74.22.50.25

Midi Pyrenees
Anne Simon, President
13, bis rue de la Providence
31500 Toulouse
France
61.54.16.81

Normandie
Yvette Corbineau, President
1, rue du Pre Clair
14000 Caen
France
31.94.81.12

Nouvelle-Caledonie
Christian Pauleau, President
B.P. 572 Noumea
France
19.687.25.44.36

Picardie
Jean-Pierre Horrie, President
5, rue des Francs-Juges
Residence Berlioz
80000 Amiens
France
22.92.34.61; 22.43.41.97

Provence
Michel Pouplier, President
11, rue Revoil
84140 Montfavet
France
90.32.01.73

France Shoto Karate Assn.
68, rue de Castagnary
75015 Paris
France
(1) 45.31.41.29

Inter. Tai Chi Chuan Assn.
11, rue Florain
30100 Ales
France
66.30.45.85; 66.52.27.23

Kyokushinkai Kan
G. Rosello
3, rue Cassini
06 Nice
France

Mutuelle Nationale des Sports
45, rue de Clichy
75442 Paris
France
42.85.05.01

Raimeikan
62, avenue Parmentier
75011 Paris
France
43.57.32.40

Sankudo France
c/o Robert Bouchet
Villa l'Arleri
135, Chemin de Lauvert
06160 Juan-les Pins
France
93.61.25.83 (Phone & Fax)

Sanshin Kan France
9, square de la Metairie
50300 Avranches
France
33.68.26.61

Shorin-Ryu Karate Inter.
Richard Lee, President
1, rue du Chateau d'Eau
75010 Paris
France

Societe Francaise de Judo et Arts
    Martiaux (SFJAM)
97, rue Nationale
95000 Cergy-Village
France
(1) 30.30.17.22; (1) 30.31.18.13

Union Nationale des Associations
    & Amicales de Karate
83, rue Michel Ange
75016 Paris
France
46.30.05.99

WAKO France;
Fed. Nationale Boxe Americaine
George Boissin, President
1921 Rue de Dantzing
F-75015 Paris, France

World Union of Qwan Ki Do
Pham Xuan Tong, President
352 Avenue Marcel Castie
83100 Toulon
France

Worldwide Nambudo
22 rue de Sablons
Paris 16, France
709-8411

GERMANY

Aikikai Deutschland—
    Fachverband for Aikido e.V.
Karl-Friedrich Leisinger
Berghamsweg 72
4470 Meppen
Germany
(05931) 16523

Bushido Union Deutschland Org.
    e.V.
Bushido Sportclub
Melkbrink 13
26121 Oldenburg
Germany
(0441) 85726
(0441) 884198 (Fax)

Deutsch-Asiatische Kampfkunst
    Org. (DAKO)
Im Osttal 21
D-7833 Endingen
Germany

Deutsche Budo Org. e.V. (DBO)
(WKA affiliate)
J. Lutz
Bannwaldallee 46
7500 Karlsruhe 21
Germany
(0721) 86640

Deutsche Hwarang-Do and Sulsa
    Org.
Herbert Grudzenski
Lulfstrasse 47
D-4350 Ricklinghausen
Germany
(02361) 8486; (02305) 32571

Deutsche Kickbox Union e.V.
    (DKBU)
Friedrich, Meis, President
Am Kalbskopf 1
6078 Neu-Isenburg
Germany
(06102) 3-33-70

AFFILIATES

Baden-Wurrtemberg Kickbox
    Verband
Information: Gerda Mack
Eschkopfstrasse 8
6800 Mannheim 1
Germany
(0621) 82-50-54

Bayerische Amateur Kickbox
    Union
Information: Heinz Klupp
Munchenerstrasse 112
8058 Erding
Germany
(08122) 2-08-02

Berliner Kickbox Union
Information: Lutz Wiesner
c/o Sportschule Blankenburg
Ollenhauerstrasse 4-5
1000 Berlin 51
Germany
(030) 4-95-40-65
(030) 4-96-90-72 (Fax)

Hamburger Kickbox Verband
Information: Hella Arenz
Anklamer Ring
2000 Hamburg 73
Germany
(040) 6-47-16-92

Hessischer Kickbox Verband
Information: Walter Renner
Friedbergerstrasse 23
6382 Friedrichsdorf
Germany
(06175) 18-29
(06175) 74-51 (Fax)

Niedersachsischer Kickbox
    Verband
Geschaftsstelle: Antonio Spatola
Postfach 10 06 42
3180 Wolfsburg
Germany
(05361) 7-49-86

Nordrhein-Westfalischer
    Kickbox Verband
Geschaftsstelle: Kornelia
    Sommerhoff
Haupstrasse 12
5232 Ziegenhain
Germany
(02685) 75-53

Rheinland-Pfalzischer Kickbox
    Verband
Geschaftsstelle: Bernd Mannerz
Schutzenstrasse 31
6700 Ludwigshafen
Germany
(0621) 58-46-16
(0621) 5-29-61-66

Schleswig-Holsteinischer
    Kickbox Verband
Geschaftsstelle: Heinz Prietsche
Eutiner Strasse 94
2409 Pansdorf
Germany
(04504) 48-13

Deutscher Amateur Kick-Box
    Verband (DAKV)
Schmuckenberg 5
4933 Blomberg
Germany

Deutscher Arnis Verband e.V.
Wolfgang Schnur
Dr.-H-Gremmels Strasse 15
3308 Konigslutter
Germany
(05353) 8328

Deutscher Asien Kampfsport
    Verband (DAV)
Erich Brandl
Bertholdstrasse 33
8535 Emskirchen
Germany
(09104) 1337

Deutscher Dan-Trager and Budo-
    Lehrer-Verband e.V.
Lothar Sieber
Eichenstrasse 1
8028 Taufkirchen
Germany
(089) 403970; 612-2478

Deutscher Jiu-Jitsu Bund e.V.
Herrn Jansen
Hoherweg 27
4000 Dusseldorf 1
Germany
(0211) 733-4532

Deutscher Ju-Jutsu Fed.
Kohlesrain 101
7950 Biberach 1
Germany

Deutscher Jiu Jitsu Ring
Erich Rahn e.V.
Dietmar Gdanietz
Ortrudstrasse 5
1000 Berlin 41
Germany

Deutscher Jiu Jitsu Union
Bachstrasse 19
5802 Wetter 2
Germany
(02335) 66206

Deutscher Judo-Bund (DJB)
Lessingstrasse 12
6500 Mainz 1
Germany

SECTIONS

Aikido
Rainer Brauhardt
Fludersbach 104
5900 Siegen
Germany
(0271) 51710

Ju-Jitsu
Siegmund Sobolewski
A, Salteich 366
2057 Reinbek
Germany
(040) 722-7150; (040) 2880-1538

Karate
Ottmar Luxon
Hochstrasse 28
5473 Kruft
Germany
(02652) 7181

Kyudo
Lessingstrasse 12
Postfach 1749
6500 Mainz 1
Germany
(06131) 672031

Deutscher Karateverband e.V.
(DKV)
Wolfgang Hagedorn, President
Grabenstrasse 37
4390 Gladbeck
Germany
(02043) 24007

Deutscher Kick-Box
Verband e.V. (DKBV)
Gabi Laube
Post Thurnau
8656 Alladorf
Germany
(09271) 1247

Deutscher Taekwondo Bund (DTB)
Manuela Austen and Horst Brandt
Oberer Buschweg 14
5000 Koln 50
Germany
(02236) 63984; (02236) 62734

Deutscher Wun Hop Kuen Do-
Kung Fu-Verband e.V.
Michael Timmermann
Speckmoorstrasse 6
2400 Lubeck 16 (Schlutup)
Germany
(0451) 690510

Deutsche Sportkarate Union e.V.
(DSU)
Heinz Holitschke
Thiestrasse 3
3451 Hunzen
Germany
(05533) 5236

Deutsche Taekwondo Union e.V.
Heinz Marx
Maximillianplatz 12
8000 Menchen 2
Germany
(089) 222710

Deutsche Union der Kick-Box-
Verbande (DUKV)
Frau Montenero-Roth
Ernst-Reuter-Strasse 13
4048 Grevenbroich
Germany
(02181) 68634

Deutsche Wushu Fed. (DWF)
Elpenroder Strasse 4
6315 Mucke 2
Germany
(06400) 7359

EIKO Germany e.V.
Berliner Strasse 238
6050 Offenbach
Germany
(069) 800-1962

European Taekwondo Union
c/o Heinz
Maximillian Slats, 12
8000 Munich 2
Germany

European Wing Tsun Org.;
Inter. Wing Tsun Org.
Keith Kernspecht, Chief Instuctor
6901 Schloss
Langenzell
Germany
(06223) 47250
(06223) 48250 (Fax)

German Kun-Tai-Ko Budo Assn.
e.V.
Norbert Punzet, Director
Maiwandstrasse 3
8204 Brannenburg
Germany
(080) 34-3330
(080) 34-7362 (Fax)

Goju-ryu Karate-Bund
Deutschland e.V.
Fritz Nopel
Ostkamp 64
4708 Kamen
Germany
(02307) 72388

Hakushinkai Reinbek e.V. [Iaido]
Karl-Heinz Lubcke
Prahlsdorfer Weg 29b
2057 Reinbek
Germany
(040) 722-9030

Inter. All-Style Assn.
Sakir Yavuz, Director
Meesenring 15
2400 Lubeck
(0451) 625333
(0451) 624273 (Fax)

Inter. Amateur Kickboxing Sport
    Karate Assn. (IAKSA)
Geert Lemmens, Director
Schulstrasse 2
2243 Bunsoh
Germany
(04835) 699
(04835) 311 (Fax)

Inter. Amateur Sport Karate Assn.
    (IASKA)
Karl-Heinz Frank, Director
In der Fuldaaue 3
3513 Staufenberg
Germany
(05543) 3549
(05543) 3251 (Fax)

Inter. Budo Fed.—Deutschland
    (IBF)
Raingarten 14
7172 Westgarten
Germany
(0791) 55388

Inter. Budo-Total Fed. (IBTF)
J. Gottschling
Bohlweg 66a
Postfach 2441
D-3300 Braunschweig
Germany

Inter. Kampfkunst Org. (IKO)
Peter Albert
Schonaustrasse 19
D-7850 Lorrach 2
Germany
(07621) 49082

Inter. Ninjutsu Assn.—Germany
John Frohlich
Philipp-Reis-Strasse 13a
D-6057 Dietzenbach
Germany
(06074) 28954

Inter. Phetjan Thaiboxing Assn.
    (IPTA)
Wolfgang Gier, Director
Palmerstrasse 9
2000 Hamburg
Germany
(040) 258872
(040) 2509420 (Fax)

Inter. Taekwon-do Fed.
    Deutschland e.V. (ITF)
Doncheweg 8
3500 Kassel
Germany
(0561) 15622; (0561) 35969

Inter. Tai Chi Chuan Assn.
    (ITCCA)
Frieder Anders
Am Weingarten 12-14
6000 Frankfurt 90
Germany
(069) 779076

Inter. Tscheng-Tao Assn. e.V.
    (ITTA)
Postfach 1210
D-2202 Barmstedt
Germany
(04123) 6536

Inter. Turk Kick-Box Fed. (ITKF)
Harabi Derin, Director
Hans Sachs Strasse 85
6090 Russelsheim
Germany
(06142) 8-24-86
(06134) 5-63-42 (Fax)

K.I.C.K. Assn.
Bergheimerstrasse 5
4048 Grevenbroich
Germany

Kobudo-Kwai e.V.
Leinritt 2
8756 Kahl/Main
Germany

Kobudo Inter.
Jamal Measara
Blutenstrasse 11
8429 Ihrlerstein
Germany
(09441) 9826

Kyokushinkai Kan
I. Freier
Hermanstrasse 256-258
1000 Berlin 44
Germany

Muay-Thai-Bund Deutschland e.V.
    (MTBD)
Bergheimer Strasse 5
4048 Grevenbroich
Germany
(02181) 63238
(02181) 64427 (Fax)

Nederlandse Kick-Boxing Bond
    (NKBB)
Lex Kristel, Secretary
Mercuriusstraat 11

NL-1561 PM Krommenie
(075) 217666 (Phone & Fax)

Nordrhein-Westfalischer Taekwon-
    do Bund e.V.
Postfach 1808
5880 Ludenscheid
Germany

Principal's Worldwide Society of
    Martial Arts
M. Fritsche
Postfach 420221
1000 Berlin 42
Germany

Sankudo Germany
c/o Andreas Lindemann
An der Birkenkaute 4
6350 Bad Nauheim
Germany
(06032) 8-22-86

Shorin-ryu Seibukan Karate
    Union—Deutschland
Werner Bachhuber
Landshuter Allee 69/318
8000 Munchen 19
Germany
(089) 167-5226

Shotokan Karate Inter.—
    Deutschland e.V. (SKID)
Bernd Geupel
Postfach 24
7401 Pliezhausen
Germany
(07127) 18667

Shuriken Verband Inter. (SVI)
Bertholdstrasse 33
8535 Emskirchen
Germany

Tai Chi Chuan Inter.
Handelstrasse 6
5000 Koln
Germany
(0221) 238217

United Black Belt Centers of Kwon
    Taekwon-do e.V.
Jae-Hwa Kwon, President
Postfach 3502
8520 Erlangen
Germany
(06121) 45727

World Ju Jitsu Fed. (WJJF)
Kohlesrain 101
7950 Biberach 1
Germany

World Kick-Boxing Assn.
Egon Haag, Director
Kronauerstrasse 2a
6833 Waghausel 1
Germany
(07254) 73040

GREECE

Greek Karate Corporation
George Saniotis, Secretary-General
Argolidos Strasse 3-5
TT-605 Athens
Greece
691-7609

Greek Taekwondo Assn.
El. Missaelidis, President
c/o Hellenic Amateur Athletic
    Assn.
137, Syngrou Ave.
Athens 404, Greece

Kyokushinkai Kan
N. Varelopoulos
Papadakou 60
Nea Pagase, Volos
Greece

WAKO Greece
Simon Zahopoulos, President
Dagli 23
Kavala, Greece
22-84-86

GUAM

Guardian Angels
Daniel Sabuan, Coordinator
P.O. Box 275
Agana, Guam 96910
(671) 734-2026

HONG KONG

Hong Kong Ching Woo Athletic
    Assn.
Liu Kwok Chuen, President
Hunghom Commercial Centre
Room 905, 9th Floor, Tower A
37-39 Ma Tau Wei Rd.
Kowloon, Hong Kong

Hong Kong Taekwondo Assn.
Ma Ching Kwan, President
Room 1807, Wong On House
71 Des Voeux Rd.
Central, Hong Kong

Inter. Chinese Martial Art Assn.;
Inter. Wing Tsun Martial Art Assn.
Ting Leung, President
440/442 Nathan Rd.
8A/Fl, Hong Kong
3-857115

Ving Tsun Athletic Assn.
2C Nullah Rd., 2nd Floor
Kowloon, Hong Kong

HUNGARY

Hungarian Karate Section
Dr. Istvan Gortvay
Dozsa Gyorgy-ut 1-3
1143 Budapest
Hungary
640-233

Hungarian Kickboxing-Karate
    Assn.
Richard Leyrer, President
Rajk Laszlo U. 114 V/29
H-1138 Budapest
Hungary

Kyokushinkai Kan
I. Adamy
12 Ker Gyori VT4
Budapest 1123
Hungary

WAKO Hungary
Richard Leyrer, President
Rajk Laszlo U. 114 V/29
H-1138 Budapest, Hungary

INDIA

All India Korean Karate Assn.
Sumanta Sadhukhan, Director
12, Protap Chatterjee Lane
Calcutta, 700012
West Bengal, India

Taekwondo Fed. of India
Lokpati Tripathi, President
33/26 B.N. Ghai Lane
Laibagh Lucknow-226001
Uttarpradesh, India

IRAN

Karate-do Fed. of Iran
Hadji Habibolah Nazarian,
Chairman
Azadi Stadium, Karag
Iran

IRAQ

Iraqi Taekwondo Committee
Falah Hasan Jadou, President
P.O. Box 729
Baghdad, Iraq

IRELAND

European Bujinkan Ninjutsu
Society
B.M. McCarthy, Chief Instructor
90 Verbena Ave.
Sutton, Dublin 13
Ireland
(032) 12-5182

Irish Karate Control Board
Desmond Tracy, Secretary-General
83 Lr. Camden St.
Dublin 2, Ireland
373899

Irish Kenpo Karate Union
Ambrose Moloney, Chief Instructor
(01) 376861

Kyokushinkai Kan (Ireland)
L. Keaveney
58 Highfield Rd.
Chelmsford, Essex CM1 2NQ
England

WAKO Ireland
Eddie Ince, President
Waterstown Ave., Palmerstown
Dublin 20, Ireland

IRELAND (NORTHERN)

United Kingdom All Styles Karate
Org.
166 Drumachose Park
Limavady, Co. Derry

N. Ireland BT49 OSJ
(0504) 765440

WAKO North Ireland
Frank Murney, President
76 Drumgullion Ave.
Newry, Co. Down, N. Ireland

ISLE MAURICE

WAKO Isle Maurice
Madhookar Ramnarain, President
3, Avenue des Mouettes
Morc Sodnac
Q Bornes, Isle Maurice

ISRAEL

Israel Taekwondo Fed.
Michel Madar, Chairman
32 Benjamin Meloudela St.
Jerusalem 92306
Israel

ITALY

International Karate League
Ennio Falsoni, World President
34 Via Paganini
20052 Monza, Italy
22-85-6994
22-89-0827 (Fax)

Federazione Italiana Karate
Taekwondo e Discipline
Affinitaires
Piazzale delle Belle Arti, 3
I-00196 Rome
Italy
360-1555

Kyokushinkai Kan
T. Nicoletti
c/o Dr. G. Ferrari
S.S. 459 Gallipilo-Casarano
73052 Parabita (Lecce)
Italy

World Assn. of Kickboxing
Organizations (WAKO)
Ennio Falsoni, World President
34 Via Paganini

20052 Monza, Italy
22-85-6994
22-89-0827 (Fax)

World Ju Jitsu Fed. (WJJF)
Via Natale Battaglia 27
20127 Milano
Italy

IVORY COAST

Fed. Ivorienne de Taekwondo
Edmond Bouazo Zegbehi,
President
Ol B.P. 5451
Abidjan, Ol
Ivory Coast

WAKO Ivory Coast (provisional)
Dably Laurent
c/o Mondet Justin Pecaud
B.P. 103 Abidjan Cote d'Ivoir
Ivory Coast

JAPAN

All Japan Judo Fed.
c/o Kodokan
1-16-30, Kasuga
Bunkyo-ku, Tokyo
Japan
(03) 811-7151

All Japan Jukendo Assn.
Akio Kinjo, President
804 Shimozato
Hirara City, Miyako, Okinawa
Japan

All Okinawa Kobudo Fed.
Shinpo Matayoshi, President
34-342 Sobe
Naha, Okinawa
Japan
(0988) 34-7866

All Okinawa Shorinji-ryu Karate-
do Assn.
Joen Nakazato, President
589 Chinen
Chinen Ward, Okinawa
Japan
(0989) 47-2253

Amateur Archery [Kyudo] Fed. of
  Japan
Kishi Memorial Hall, 4th Floor
1-1-1, Jinnan
Shibuya-ku, Tokyo
Japan
(03) 481-2387

Asia Oceania Amateur Karate Fed.
Shintaro Minema, President
No. 1-6-1 Chome, Ebisu-Nishi
Shibuya-ku, Tokyo 150
Japan

Chubu Shorin-ryu Karate-do Assn.
Zenpo Shimabuku, President
1003 Yoshihara
Chatan Ward, Okinawa
Japan
(0989) 38-0997

Fed. of All Japan Karate-do
  Organizations (FAJKO)
Senpaku Shinko Bldg. 4F
1-15-16 Toranomon
Minato-ku, Tokyo 105
Japan
(03) 502-2371, Ext. 326

AFFILIATES

All Japan High School Students
  Fed.
All Japan Collegiate Fed.
All Japan Worker's Fed.
Gojukai
JKA
Kyokushinkai
Renbukai
Rengokai
Shitokai
Wadokai

Goju-ryu Karate-do Gojukan
1-16-23, Zempukuji
Suginami-ku, Tokyo
Japan
(03) 395-2311; (03) 390-2929

Hayashi-Ha Shito-ryu Kai
549-I Nagata Higashi
Osaka City, Osaka
Japan

Honshin-ryu Karate and Kobudo
  Preservation Society
Masakazu Miyagi, President
3-21 Toguchi
Motobu, Okinawa
Japan
(0980) 47-2984

Inter. Aikido Fed.
17-18, Wakamatsucho
Shinjuku-ku, Tokyo
(03) 203-9236

Inter. Karate and Kobudo Fed.
Choboku Takamine, President
174 Yosemiya
Naha, Okinawa
Japan

Inter. Kendo Fed. (IKF)
2-3-4 Nishi, Shinagawa
Shinagawa-ku, Tokyo
Japan

Inter. Martial Arts Fed.
(Kokusai Budoin; Kokusai
  Budorenmei)
Shizuya Sato, World Director
3-24-1, Shinbori
Higashi-Yamato-Shi
Tokyo, Japan 189
0425-65-9146

Inter. Meibukan Goju-ryu Karate-
  do Assn.
Grandmaster Meitoku Yagi,
  Chairman
2-20-21 Kume
Naha, Okinawa
Japan

Inter. Ryukyu Karate Research
  Society
Patrick McCarthy, Director
101-1585-2 Kugenuma
Fujisawa City, Japan 251

Inter. Yoshinkai Aikido Fed.
Gozo Shioda, Chief Instructor
Kami Ochiai 2-28-8
Shinjuku-Ku, Tokyo 161
Japan
(03) 368-5556

Ishimine-ryu Karate-do
  Preservation Society
Shinyei Kaneshima, President
1-16 Samukawa Cho
Shuri, Naha, Okinawa
Japan
(0988) 34-1705

Isshin-ryu World Karate Assn.
Kichiro Shimabuku, President
829 Kyan
Gushikawa, Okinawa
Japan
(0989) 72-4185

Itokazu-kei Goju-ryu Research
  Assn.
Yoshio Itokazu, President
967 Funakoshi
Tamaki Ward, Okinawa
Japan

Japan Amateur Sumo Fed.
c/o Kishi Memorial Hall
1-1-1, Jinnan
Shibuya-ku, Tokyo
Japan
(03) 481-2377

Japan Karate Assn.
Rose Center, 2nd Floor
1-6-1, Ebisu-Nishi Ebisu
Shibuya-ku, Tokyo
Japan
(03) 462-1415

Grandmaster Meitoku Yagi, chairman of
the Meibukan Goju-ryu Karate-do Association. Courtesy of Karate Master Anthony Mirakian

Japan Karate-do College
(Yamaguchi Goju-ryu)
6-2, 1 Chome
Zempukiji, Suginamiku, Tokyo
Japan

Japan Kendo Fed.
c/o Nippon Budokan
2-3, Kitanomaru-koen
Chiyoda-ky, Tokyo
Japan
(03) 211-5804/5

Ki Society Inter.
Koichi Tohei, President
Tochigi Ken, Hagagun
Ichiba-memura, Akabane
Japan

Kushin-ryu Karate-do Research
Society
Shintaro Yoshizato, President
101-2 Ojana
Ginowan, Okinawa
Japan
(0988) 97-3340

Kyokushinkai Kan
Mas Oyama, President
3-3-9, Nishi-Ikebukuro
Toshima-ku, Tokyo
Japan
(03) 984-7421

Kyudokan Shorin-ryu Promotion
Society
Yuchoku Higa, President
60 Tsuboya
Naha, Okinawa
Japan
(0988) 32-4307

Martial Arts Assn.
Seitoku Higa, President
43-1-2 Chome, Gibo
Shuri, Naha, Okinawa
Japan
(0988) 32-8620

Matsumura Shorin-ryu Karate-do
Assn.
Seiki Arakaki, President
662 Kiyuna
Ginowan, Okinawa
Japan
(0988) 34-1705

Motobu-ryu Kobu-jutsu Assn.
Seikichi Uehara, President
419-1 Ojana
Ginowan, Okinawa
Japan
(0988) 97-2651

Nihon Sumo Kyokai
c/o Kokugikan Sumo Hall
1-3-28, Yokoami
Sumida-ku, Tokyo
Japan
(03) 623-5111

Okinawa Kenpo Fed.
Taketo Nakamura, President
481 Nago
Nago, Okinawa
Japan

Okinawa Kenpo Karate-Kobudo
Fed.
Seikichi Odo, Director
272 Agena
Gushikawa, Okinawa
Japan

Okinawa Shorin-ryu Karate-do
Assn.
Katsuya Miyahira, President
210-1 Tsuboya
Naha, Okinawa
Japan
(0988) 32-2413

Okinawa Shorin-ryu Karate-do
Shorinkan Assn.
Shugoro Nakazato, President
218 Aja
Naha, Okinawa
Japan
(0988) 61-2502

Okinawan Goju-kai
4-30-2, Sendagaya
Shibuya-ku, Tokyo
Japan
(03) 402-0123

Okinawan Goju-ryu Karate-do
Assn.
Eiichi Miyazato, President
433 Asato
Naha, Okinawa
Japan
(0988) 32-0011

Ryuei-ryu Karate Kobudo
Preservation Society
Kenko Nakaima, President
166 Miyazato
Nago, Okinawa
Japan
(0980) 53-2468

Ryukyu Shorin-ryu Karate-do
Assn.
Seijin Inamine, President
261 Yoshihara
Chatan Ward, Okinawa
Japan
(0989) 38-3249

Seibukan Dojo
60, Izumigawacho
Shimogamo, Sakyo-ku, Kyoto
Japan
(075) 701-3121

Shinpan Shiroma Kei Shito-ryu
Karate Preservation Society
Horoku Ishikawa, President
4-105 Torihori
Shuri, Naha, Okinawa
Japan
(0988) 34-2741

Shito-ryu Kenpo Karate-do Assn.
1333-3 Banchi
Minami-ku, Itoman, Okinawa
Japan
(0988) 92-3850

Shotokan Karate Inter.
Hirokazu Kanazawa, Chief
Instructor
Suzuden Bldg., Basement Floor
1-10 Yotsuya
Shinjuku-ku, Tokyo
Japan
(03) 359-6614

Society for the Promotion and
Preservation of Ryukyuan
Kobudo
Eisuke Akamine, President
677 Nesabu
Tomishiro Ward, Okinawa
Japan
(0988) 57-3160

Uechi-ryu Karate-do Assn.
Kanyei Uechi, President
166 Futenma
Ginowan, Okinawa
Japan
(0988) 92-2409

World Shorin-ryu Karate-do Fed.
Shoshin Nagamine, President
3-14-3 Kumoji
Naha, Okinawa
Japan

Wado-ryu Honbu
Master Arakaki, Director
Tokyo Physical Center, 3-13
Daikan-Yama, Shinbuya-ku, Tokyo
Japan

World Union of Karate-do
   Organizations (WUKO)
Senpaku Shinko Bldg., 4th Floor
1-15-16 Toranomon
Minato-ku, Tokyo 105
Japan
(03) 503-6637

KOREA

Korea KiDo Assn.
122-2 Nam Yang Building 300
Non Hyun Dong, Kang Nam Gu
Seoul, Korea
(02) 540-2156-7

Korea Taekwon-do Assn. (KTA)
635, Yuksam-dong
Kangnam-ku
Seoul, Korea 135
2-566-2505
2-553-4728 (Fax)

Korean Yudo Assn.
Kwan Duk Ko, President
CPO Box 4584
Seoul, Korea

World Taekwon-do Fed. (WTF)
Dr. Un Yong Kim, President
635, Yuksam-dong
Kangnam-ku
Seoul, Korea 135
2-566-2505
2-553-4728 (Fax)

KUWAIT

Kuwait Taekwondo Fed.
Sheikh Khalifa Abdullah Al-Jaber
   Al-Sabha, Pres.
P.O. Box 795
Safat, Kuwait

LEBANON

Lebanese Fed. of Judo, Karate &
   Taekwondo
Jean Dfouny, President
P.O. Box 8189
Beirut, Lebanon

LIECHTENSTEIN

Kyokushinkai Kan
Z. Marxer
Postfach 94
9485 Nendlen
Liechtenstein

WAKO Liechtenstein
Roman Oehri, President
Furstlich Liechtensteinischer
Sportverband
F.L. 9494 Schaan
Postfach 407, Liechtenstein

MALAYSIA

Malaysia Karate-do Fed.
26 Jalan SS 14 / 8C
Subang Jaya, Selangor
Kuala Lumpur
Malaysia

Malaysian Taekwondo Assn.
Y. Bhg. Datuk Setia Raja, Pres.
21-E, Jalan Tong Shin
50200 Kuala Lumpur
Malaysia

MEXICO

Central America / Carribbean
   Karate Fed.
c/o Federacion Mexicana de
   Karate

Dr. Manuel Mondragon K.,
   President
Monterey 147 48 Piso
Mexico 7, D.F.
Mexico

MOROCCO

Fed. Royale Morocaine Taekwondo
Belle Vue Agdal Rabat
Morocco
729-67

NEPAL

Nepal Martial Arts Assn.
Dashrath Rangashala
Tipureswor, Post Box 2090
Katmandu, Nepal

NETHERLANDS

Bujinkan Dojo Ninjutsu Society
J. Hesselman, Advisor
Postbus 5050
3502 JB Utrecht
Netherlands

Karate-do Bond Netherland
Ino Alberga, Secretary-General
Havikshorst 21
2317 AL Leiden
Netherlands

Kyokushinkai Kan
L. Netherlandser
P.O. Box 2673
Rotterdam
Netherlands

NederlandsKickboxing Bund
Postbus 6276
1005 EG Amsterdam
Netherlands

Netherlands Taekwondo Assn.
J. Janssen, President
Bondsbureau T.B.N. Wintersoord 7
6511 RP Jijmegen
Netherlands

NetherlandseTang Soo Do Moo
    Duk Kwan Bond
Willebrordusstraat 142
3037 TX Rotterdam
Netherlands
010-467-1279

WAKO Netherlands (provisional)
Alex Copini
Zwenkgras 39
8935 HB Leeuwarden, Netherlands

World Muay Thai Assn.
Thom Harinck, President
van Hallstraat 52
1051 HH Amsterdam
Netherlands
20-867944

NEW ZEALAND

Australasian Toyakwai Karate
    Assn.
Miles Smith, Chief Instructor
P.O. Box 88-031
Clendon Town, South Auckland
New Zealand

Iaido Assn. of New Zealand
(03) 79-5079; (03) 49-6221

Kokusai Karate-do Kyo Kai-Kubota
Dave Toko, Chief Instructor
1033 Colombo St.
Edgeware S. Island, Christchurch
New Zealand
(03) 5-6720

Kokusai Karate-do Kyo Kai-Kubota
Mike Tuhiwai, Chief Instructor
2/30 Trinity Crescent
Napier N. Island
New Zealand
(070) 43-7175

Korean Martial Arts Assn.
Julian Lim
2/8 Freeland Ave.
Mt. Roskill, Auckland 4
New Zealand

NORWAY

Kyokushinkai Kan
I. Rivenas
Hatleveien 3
5000 Bergen
Norway

Norges Shotokan Forbund
W. Hagen, President
Kappelvn. 161
Oslo 4
Norway
222-8843

WAKO Norway
Erling Havna, President
4800 Arendal
Norway

OKINAWA: SEE JAPAN

PAKISTAN

Pakistan Taekwondo Assn.
Chowdhry Pervez Elahi
59 Britto Rd.
Karachi G.P.O. Box 1222
Karachi, Pakistan

PANAMA

Panama Taekwondo Commission
Dr. Varo David Barragan Bech,
    Pres.
6-3352 El Dorado, Panama
Republic of Panama

PARAGUAY

Fed. Paraguayan de Taekwondo
Carlos Maria Moreno, President
Casilla Correos
No. 2215, Asuncion
Paraguay

PEOPLE'S REPUBLIC
OF CHINA: SEE CHINA

PERU

Bolivariana Karate Confed.
c/o Federacion Peruana de Karate
Col. Hugo Diaz Velarde, President
Estadio Nacional-Puerta 23-A
Lima, Peru

POLAND

Kyokushinkai Kan
A. Drewniak
ul. 31-130 Krakow
Kremerowska 3
Poland

Polish Fed. of Far Eastern Martial
    Arts
Ryszard Musat, President
ul. Lindleya 14a/18
02-013 Warszawa
Poland
21-26-09

Polish Karate Fed.
Kazimierz Krukowski, Vice-
    President
ul. 1. Maja 23/18
71-627 Szczecin
Poland

Polisk Zwiazek Karate
Section Taekwondo
Marek Budzynski, Chairman
Stadion X-Lecia UL
Zieleniecka 1 PL-03-727
Warszawa, Poland

WAKO Poland
Marek Frysz, President
Pl. Jednoschi Robotniczej 1
Room No. 142
00-661 Warsaw, Poland
322-882

PORTUGAL

Centro Portugues de Karate
Romulu Machado, President
R. dos Bacalhoeiros, 139-2-Dto
1100 Lisbon
Portugal
872413

WAKO Portugal (provisional)
Carlos Manuel Ramjanali
Rua D. Jose 1
Bloco H—1 Dt.
3080 Figuiera da Foz, Portugal

PUERTO RICO

Fed. de Taekwondo de Puerto Rico
Rafael Serranno, President
P.O. Box 1709 Ponce
Puerto Rico 00731

Inter. Shotokan Karate Fed. of
    Puerto Rico
Andres Escobar, Chief Instructor
P.O. Box 1109
Sabana Grande
Puerto Rico 00637

Puerto Rico Karate Assn.
Andy Escobar, Director
Ave. De Diego 910 2DO
Piso, Reparto Metropolitano
Rio Piedras
Puerto Rico 00921

ROMANIA

Kyokushinkai Kan
I. Ilie
P.O. Box 6
Giurgiu 8315
Romania

RUSSIA

Inter. Sport Karate Assn.
Igor Oransky, Director
5th Magistralnaya
Moscow 8, Russia
(7 095) 297-5692
(7 095) 940-2804 (Fax)

SAMOA

Kokusai Karate-do Kyo Kai-Kubota
Tautai Sinila, Chief Instructor
P.O. Box 6322
Afega Apia
Western Samoa

SAUDI ARABIA

Arabian Karate Fed.
Mohammad Fayez Al Kulaish,
    President
P.O. Box 6042
11442 Riyadh
Saudi Arabia

SCOTLAND

British Nanbudo Assn.
(Scottish Regional Secretary)
(0875) 813-431

Karate Union of Great Britain
Scottish Region
Paul Allan
Komorebi, Drumblade
Huntly AB 56 EJ
Scotland
(0466) 84203

Mid-West Tae-Kwon-Do Assn.
B. Coswaite
(0592) 265261

Scottish Kickboxing Board of
    Control
(0224) 488508

United Kingdom All Styles Karate
    Org.
97 Portman St.
Glasgow G41 1EJ
Scotland
(041) 429-1021

United Kingdom Taekwon-do Fed.
0506-52099

SINGAPORE

Singapore Taekwondo Fed.
Ernest Koh, President
c/o Block 3, Queens Rd. #04-167
Singapore 1026
Singapore

SOUTH AFRICA

Inter. Kung-Fu Fed.
James Van Blerk, Director
P.O. Box 494
Edenvale, 1610 Tvl
South Africa

SOVIET UNION (COMMONWEALTH OF INDEPENDENT STATES)

Inter. Sport Karate Assn.
Igor Oransky, Director
5th Magistralnaya
Moscow 8, Russia
(7 095) 297-5692
(7 095) 940-2804 (Fax)

Soviet Assn. of Martial Arts
    (SAMA)
Ilya Gouliev, President
109172 Malye Kamenchiki, 14
Moscow, Russia
011-7-095-272-4931
011-7-095-230-2200 (Fax)

WAKO Russia
All-Union Kickboxing Assn.
Andray Chistov, Chairman
Laesha Gavra St., 5 kv. 94
252211 Kiev
Ukraine
484-1280
484-1282 (Fax)

SPAIN

Asociacion Espanola de Kung-Fu
Apartado 11.188
46080 Valencia
Spain
(96) 373-76-75

Asociacion Espanola Karate
    Amateur
Jose Baeza Lopez
Midico Pascual
Perez, 17, 3B
Alicante—1
Spain
206778

Fed. Espanola de Taekwondo
Manuel Marco Saila, President
Calle Provenza, 238, 3, 4a
08008 Barcelona, Spain

Fed. Nacional de Karate
    Profesional Y S. L.
Apartado de Correos 6061
48080 Bilbao
Spain
(94) 421-4986

International Judo Fed.
c/o Garcia de la Fluente
Hortaleza, 108, Madrid 4
Spain

Kyokushinkai Kan
A. Pinero
San Antonio Maria Claret 36-38
Zaragoza
Spain

WAKO Spain
Mariano Anton Hurtado, President
Gimnasio Esus
C./Maria Auxiliadora S/N
    Majadahonda
28220 Madrid, Spain

SRI LANKA

Ceylon Karate Assn.
No. 5 David Ave.
Colombo 10
Sri Lanka

SURINAME

Suriname Taekwon-do Union
P.O. Box 787
Paramaribo, Suriname

SWAZILAND

Swaziland National Judo, Karate,
    Taekwondo Assn.
Sipho Zwane, President
P.O. Box 95
Manzing, Swaziland

SWEDEN

Kyokushinkai Kan
A. Meszaros
Box 12090
S-402 41 Goteborg
Sweden

Ostsvenska Wado-kai
Ray Young, Chief Instructor
Vallentuna, Sweden
(0762) 51087

Svenska Wing Tsun Assn.
Jan Svensson
(031) 194662

Swedish All-Style Fighting Assn.
    (SAFA)
Benny Hedlund, President
Husaqrgatan 3
21128 Malmo
Sweden
040-111606

Swedish Shotokan Assn.
Leif Almo, President
Camillavagen 32
21363 Malmo
Sweden
040-219695

Tai-Nui & Modern Arnis Assn.
P.O. Box 11058
72411 Vasteras, Sweden
021-137863; 021-358049

WAKO Sweden;
Svenska Kickboxing Forbundet
Benny Hedlund, President
Husargatan 3
S-21128 Malmo, Sweden

SWITZERLAND

Inter. Sport Karate Assn.
(World Council Eastern
    Headquarters)
Olivier Muller, Co-Chairman
58 Avenue Wendt
CH-1203 Geneva
Switzerland
(022) 734-9524
(022) 735-4751 (Fax)

Kyokushinkai Kan
P. von Rotz
Halde 14
6102 Malters
Switzerland

Sankudo Suisse
Maurizio Cannizzaro, Director
Honergut 2
8754 Netsal
Switzerland
058-61-75-25 (Phone & Fax)

Schweizerischer Karate-Verband
    (SKV)
Hans Peter Wechsler, President
Schribersmatt
6074 Giswil-Grossteil
Switzerland
041-681046

Swiss Union of Qwan-Ki-Do
Haus Ginseng
Pras. W. Eisenhofer
Ch-7265 Davos Laret
Switzerland
083 / 44140

WAKO Switzerland
Felix Hartmann, President
Nubrigweg, 4
4402 Frenkendorf, Switzerland

World Ju Jitsu Fed. (WJJF)
Postfach 208
CH-9100 Herisau
Switzerland

TASMANIA: SEE
AUSTRALIA

TURKEY

Kyokushinkai Kan
I. Yatkin
Yildirin Mah Uzay Sok.
No. 7 Bayrampasa
Istanbul
Turkey

Turkiye Judo ve Karate Fed.
Cihat Uskan, President

Bagdat Cad.
Selahattin Pinar Sok
Murat Apt. No. 8/12
Kiziltoprak, Istanbul
Turkey
382375

WAKO Turkey
Harabi Derin, President
Walter Flexstrasse 92
60 90 Russelsheim, Turkey

UNITED STATES

Aikido Assn. of America
Fumio Toyoda, Chief Instructor
1016 W. Belmont
Chicago, IL 60657
(312) 525-3141

Aikido Assn. of North America
  (AANA)
Yukio Utada, President
5836 Henry Ave.
Philadelphia, PA 19128
(215) 483-3000

Alabama Karate Assn. (AKA)
Yuki Koda, President
P.O. Box 3271
Montgomery, AL 36109

All American Taekwon-do Fed.
Suh Chong Kang, President
P.O. Box 9430
Wilmington, DE 19809

Allegheny Shotokan Karate Assn.
4 Penn Ave.
North Irwin, PA 15642

All Japan Soryu Karate-do Fed.
(U.S. Headquarters)
James Caldwell, Chief Instructor
2432 Cornhusker Rd.
Omaha, NE 68123
(402) 291-0267

All Kenukan Kenpo Karate-do
Inter. Rengokai
Bob Boggs, Chief Instructor
220 West Cedar
Olathe, KS 66061

All Style Inter. and American
  Martial Arts Assn.
175 S. Capitol Ave., Ste F
San Jose, CA 95127

Amateur Athletic Union (AAU)
3400 W. 86th St.
Indianapolis, IN
(317) 972-2900

Amateur Athletic Union National
Chinese Martial Arts Division
Phillip Starr, Chairman
6056 Maple St.
Omaha, NE 68104

Amateur Org. of Karate (AOK)
Ishmael Robles, President
6123 Avenue R
Galveston, TX 77551
(409) 740-2467
(409) 740-1344 (Fax)

American Aiki-Jujitsu Fed. (AAJF)
G. Lewis, Director
6652 S. Broadway
Hicksville, NY 11801
(516) 938-8079

American Amateur Taekwondo
  Union
S.R. Moreland, President
2205-A Decker Blvd.
Columbia, SC 29206
(803) 738-1788

American Bando Assn.
Maung Gyi, President
P.O. Box 2763
Atlanta, GA 30310

American Black Belt Fed.
1910 Brady St.
Davenport, IA 52803
(319) 322-3547

American Amateur Karate Fed.
Hidetaka Nishiyama, President
1930 Wilshire Blvd.
Los Angeles, CA 90057
(213) 483-8262

American Bujinkan Dojo Assn.
Box 724
Lodi, CA 95421

American Chung Do Kwan Tae
  Kwon Do Assn.
Ike Stafford, Director
1255 E. Republic Rd.
Springfield, MO 65807
(417) 883-7327

American Collegiate Taekwon-do
  Assn.
Ken Min, President
103 Harmon Gym
University of California
Berkeley, CA 94720
(415) 642-7100

American Fed. of Jujitsu & Arnis
720 Broadway
Milton, PA 17847

American Fed. of Muay Thai
  Boxing
Gerard Finot, President
22740 Shore Center Dr.
Euclid, OH 44123
(216) 731-3006

American Hap Ki Do Assn.
Mike Wollmersauser, Advisor
157 Cambridge St.
Feeding Hills, MA 01030
(413) 786-8290

American Independent Karate
  Instructors Assn. (AIKIA)
Dr. Jerry Beasley, President
P.O. Box 402
Christiansburg, VA 24073
(703) 382-9260

American JKA Karate Associations
Randall Hassell, President
P.O. Box 15853
St. Louis, MO 63114
(314) 426-7011

American Ju-Jitsu Assn.
George Kirby, President
P.O. Box 1357
Burbank, CA 91507
(818) 760-1475

Grandmaster Haeng Ung Lee (center), president of the American Taekwon-do Association, supervises a board-breaking feat by then–Arkansas Governor Bill Clinton. Courtesy of the World Taekwon-do Federation

American Karate Assn. (AKA)
John Sharkey, President
P.O. Box 214
Momence, IL 60954
(815) 472-4259

American Karate Fed.
250 New Litchfield St.
Torrington, CT 06790
(203) 756-4381

American Kenpo Karate Assn.
Bart Vale, President
6469 S.W. 8th St.
Miami, FL 33144
(305) 266-1601

American Korean Tae Kwon Do
   Assn.
Choon Lee, President
11453 W. 64th St.
Shawnee Mission, KS 66203
(913) 631-1414

American Koshiki Karate Org.
Kiyoshi Arakaki, President
153 E. 4370 So.
Murray, UT 84107
(801) 262-1785

American Moo Duk Kwan Tang
   Soo Do Assn.
Jae Joon Kim, President

428 W. Brandon Blvd.
Brandon, FL 33511
(813) 684-2284

American-Okinawan Karate Assn.
Lou Lizotte, President
6 Somerset Lane
Somers, CT 06071
(203) 749-2517

American Shotokan Karate Fed.
Jerry Larson, President
(612) 269-5425

American Taekwon-do Assn.
Haeng Ung Lee, President
6210 Baseline Rd.
Little Rock, AR 72209
(800) 872-2821

American Taekwon-do Fed.
Y.K. Kim, President
1630 E. Colonial Dr.
Orlando, FL 32803
(407) 898-2084

American Taekwondo Foundation
Yun Sung Chung, President
465 North Eastern Blvd.
Montgomery, AL 36117
(205) 277-2627

American Taekwon-do Union
Young Ho Jun, President

1303 W. Busch Blvd.
Tampa, FL 33612
(813) 935-8888

Arkansas Karate Circuit (AKC)
Keith Kirk, President
(501) 661-0715

American Wing Tsun Org.
Robert Jacquet, General Manager
15227 N. 23rd Place
Phoenix, AZ 85022
(602) 867-1525

Black Belts of the Faith Inter.
412 N. Canal St.
Carlsbad, NM 88220
(505) 887-1383

Bujinkan Fellowship Inter.
7290 Lakeshore Blvd.
Mentor, OH 44060
(216) 946-2836

Bushido-kai Kenkyukai
Tony Annesi, Director
21 Blandin Ave.
Framingham, MA 01701

Central Illinois Shotokan Karate
   Assn.
Rick Brewer, Director
7681 Aspen Lane
Delevan, IL 61734

Chinese Kara-Ho Kenpo Assn.
Sam Kuoha, Director
13320 Camino Canada, #6
El Cajon, CA 92021

Chinese Kung-Fu Wu-Su Assn.
Alan Lee, President
28 West 27th St.
New York, NY 10001
(212) 725-0535

Chinese Martial Arts Assn.
5156 Hollywood Blvd.
Los Angeles, CA 90027

Chinese Martial Arts Assn.
4356 N. Milwaukee Ave.
Chicago, IL 60641
(312) 202-9254

Chosin Do Society
Michael Atamian, Founder
P.O. Box 1156
Coventry, RI 02816

Christian Martial Arts Foundation
P.O. Box 202087
San Diego, CA 92120

Colorado Karate Assn.
Dan Swenson, President
(303) 442-4311

Doce Pares USA
(Filipino Eskrima Assn.)
236 Webster St.
Jersey City, NJ 07306

East Coast Seido-Kai
Don Kennedy, President
267 S. York St.
Pottstown, PA 19464
(215) 327-1567

Fed. of Practicing Jujutsuans
Mike DePasquale Sr., President
450 Livingston St.
Norwood, NJ 07648
(201) 768-2199

Filipino Eskrima Assn.
236 Webster Ave.
Jersey City, NJ 03707
(201) 792-5792

Florida Affiliation of Martial Arts
    Events (FAME)
Dianne McCaughey, President
2195 S.E. Ocean Blvd.
Stuart, FL 34996
(407) 288-2010

Florida Black Belt Assn. (FBBA)
Manny Reyes, President
555 E. 25th St., Suite 216
Hialeah, FL 33013
(305) 696-0099

Global Martial Arts Fed.
Lum Chi Ping, Chairman
P.O. Box 1330
Venice, FL 34285
(813) 488-4196 (Phone & Fax)

Goju-kai Karate-do U.S.A.
Gosei Yamaguchi, President
97 Collingwood St.
San Francisco, CA 94114
(415) 861-9987

Guardian Angels
(Inter. Headquarters)
Curtis Sliwa, President
982 E. 89th St.
New York, NY 11236
(212) 397-7822

AFFILIATE

Region 1 (Northeast)
Dennis Hanks; Charley
    Melinger, Coordinators
P.O. Box 593
Boston, MA 02108
(617) 357-5579

Region 2 (Mid-Atlantic)
(See Inter. Headquarters)

Region 3 (Southeast)
Thomas Hunt, Coordinator
11 Haynes St.
Atlanta, GA 30313
(404) 659-1636

Region 4 (Florida)
Sean Kelly, Coordinator
5309 Lakeworth Rd.
Lakeworth, FL 33461
(407) 641-0382

Region 5 (Midwest)
Mary Haney, Coordinator
403 E. Grand River
Lansing, MI 48906
(517) 485-3011

Region 5-B (Midwest)
Willie Brooks, Coordinator
8410 West Lynx
Milwaukee, WI 53225
(414) 353-7761

Region 6 (Mid-South)
Jason Lee, Coordinator
P.O. Box 1015
Chattanooga, TN 37401

Curtis Sliwa (right), president of the Guardian Angels, presents John Corcoran, this book's author, with a plaque in gratitude for the author's support. Photo by Mike Shuhmann; courtesy of the John Corcoran Archives

Region 7 (Plains–Mountains)
Chris Evers, Coordinator
P.O. Box 25143
Minneapolis, MN 55458
(612) 874-9732

Region 8 (Texas)
Kit Van Cleave, Coordinator
P.O. Box 66156
Houston, TX 77266
(713) 527-0606

Region 9 (Northwest)
Patti Whitehead, Coordinator
3434 S. 144th St., #205
Seattle, WA 98168
(206) 244-1459

Region 10 (No. Calif.)
Scott McKeown, Coordinator
1346 Martino Rd.
Lafayette, CA 94549
(415) 283-2615

Region 11 (So. Calif.)
Weston Conwell, Coordinator
P.O. Box 86968
Los Angeles, CA 90086
(213) 467-2052

Hakkoryu Martial Arts Fed.
Dennis Palumbo, President
12028-F E. Mississippi Ave.
Aurora, CO 80019
(303) 671-7267

Illinois State Karate Assn.
William Matthews, Chief Instructor
P.O. Box 1705
Evanston, IL 60204
(708) 491-1804

Inter. Amateur Karate Fed.
Hidetaka Nishiyama, Executive
    Director
1930 Wilshire Blvd.
Suite 1208
Los Angeles, CA 90057
(213) 483-8262

Inter. Assn. of Martial Arts
Gary Alexander, Director
P.O. Box 2204
Edison, NJ 08818
(201) 287-5755

Inter. Bak Fu Pai Assn.
Doo Wai, Director
250-2 South Orance, Suite 531
Escondido, CA 92025
(619) 480-4862

Inter. Boxing Fed. (IBF)
Robert Lee, President
134 Evergreen Place, 9th Floor
East Orange, NJ 07018
(201) 414-0300
(201) 414-0307 (Fax)

Inter. Cha Yon Ryu Martial Arts
    Assn.
Kim Soo, President
1740 Jacquelyn Dr.
Houston, TX 77055
(713) 681-9261
(713) 681-9262 (Fax)

Inter. Combat Hapkido Fed.
1859 N. Pine Island Rd., Suite 1181
Plantation, FL 33322

Inter. Fed. of Ju-Jutsuans
Michael DePasquale Jr., Director
P.O. Box 8585
Woodcliff Lake, NJ 07675

Inter. Fed. of Knife Fighting
P.O. Box 1828
Aiea, HI 96701

Inter. Kajukenbo Assn.
Bill Owens, Director
P.O. Box 4674
7415 MacArthur Blvd.
Oakland, CA 94605
(510) 638-9990
(510) 635-3838 (Fax)

Inter. Karate Assn.
Takayuki Kubota, President
1236 S. Glendale Ave.
Glendale, CA 91205
(213) 244-0800

Inter. Karate Assn. of New York
Grant Campbell, Chief Instructor
168-01 Jamaica Ave., 3rd Floor
Jamaica, NY 11432
(718) 658-0800

Grandmaster Kim Soo, president of the
International Cha Yon Ryu Association.
Courtesy of Grandmaster Kim Soo

Inter. Karate Org.
Joko Ninomiya, President
4730 E. Colfax Ave.
Denver, CO 80220
(303) 320-7632

Inter. Kajukenbo Assn.
Bill Owens, President
7515 MacArthur Blvd.
Oakland, CA 94605
(415) 638-9990

Inter. Karate-Kobudo Fed.
C. Bruce Heilman, Director, Chief
    Instructor
Rt. 61 & Cleveland Ave.
Reading, PA 19605
(215) 921-3601

Inter. Kenpo Karate Assn. (IKKA)
Leilani Parker, Administrator
1250 S. Los Robles
Pasadena, CA 91106

Inter. Kokondo Assn.
Paul Arel, Director
79 Good Hill Rd.
South Windsor, CT 06074
(203) 644-9634

Inter. Kung-Fu Fed.
Che Cheng Chiang, Director
987 N. Broadway
Los Angeles, CA 90012

Inter. Martial Arts Assn.
P.O. Box 15251
Lenexa, KS 66215

Inter. Martial Arts Fed.
Dan Ivan and Brett Mayfield,
    Directors
6933 South Shore Dr. South
St. Petersburg, FL 33707
(813) 345-3109

REGIONAL DIRECTORS

Ken Rosson
1214½ Main St., Suite 204
Delano, CA 93215

Norman Belsterling
2508 5th St.
Oliverhain, CA 92024

Michael Ganci
78 Cope Farms Rd.
Farmington, CT 06032

Karl Scott
201 North 4th Ave.
Ann Arbor, MI 48103

Arthur Carallo
8251 Kenwood
Romulus, MI 48174

Dan Hirsch
6306 N. 115 Court
Omaha, NE 68184

Terry Maccarrone
P.O. Box 933
Patchogue, NY 11772

Dale Kirby, Sr.
234 Louise Ave., #234
Nashville, TN 37203

Inter. Martial Arts League
P.O. Box 4231
Rockford, IL 61110

Inter. Ninja Society
P.O. Box 1221
Dublin, OH 43017

Inter. Okinawan Goju-ryu Karate-
do Fed.
Morio Higaonna, Chief Instructor
1551 W. Mission Rd., Suite A
San Marcos, CA 92069
(619) 744-6633
(619) 744-0371 (Fax)

Inter. Okinawan Martial Arts
Union
Rod Sacharnoski, Director
P.O. Box 31127
Dallas, TX 75231
(214) 361-0664

Inter. Ryukyu Kempo & Kobudo
Assn.
Seiyu Oyata, President
19105 E. 30th St.
Independence, MO 64057
(816) 795-8308

Inter. Shotokan Karate Fed.
Teruyuki Okazaki, President
222 S. 45th St.
Philadelphia, PA 19104
(215) 222-9382

Inter. Shuai Chiao Assn.
Gene Chicoine, Director
3808 Magadore Rd.
Magadore, OH 44260

Inter. Society of Traditional Judo
(ISTJ)
Rod Sacharnoski, President
P.O. Box 5704
Rockford, IL 61125

Inter. Sport Karate Assn. (ISKA)
(Western Headquarters)
Mike Sawyer, Co-Chairman
P.O. Box 90147
Gainesville, FL 32607
(904) 375-8144
(904) 371-2179 (Fax)

AFFILIATE

United States
Robert Heale, Executive Director
100 N.W. 82 Ave., #204
Plantation, FL 33324
(305) 474-4705
(305) 755-0604 (Fax)

Inter. Taekwon-do Assn.
James Benko, President
P.O. Box 281
Grand Blanc, MI 48439
(313) 232-6482

Inter. Wing Tsun Martial Art Assn.
Robert Jacquet, U.S. Director
15227 N. 23rd Pl.
Phoenix, AZ 85022

Inter. Yi Tsung Assn.
H.L. Mayle, Director
108 S. Main St.
Swanton, OH 43558
(419) 825-1691

Japanese Swordsmanship Society
P.O. Box 1116

Rockefeller Center Station
New York, NY 10185
(212) 873-0055

Japan Karate Assn.
1218 Fifth St.
Santa Monica, CA 90401

Japan Karate-do Assn.
3350 Sports Arena Blvd.
San Diego, CA 92110

Japan Karate-do Organization
Carl Hultin, Chief Instructor
6866 Village Parkway
Dublin, CA 94568

Japan Karate Fed.
Fumio Demura, President
1429 N. Bristol St.
Santa Ana, CA 92703
(714) 543-5550

Japan Karate Org.
6743 Dublin Blvd.
Dublin, CA 94566

Master Fumio Demura, president of the Japan Karate Federation. Courtesy of Master Fumio Demura

Jeet Kune Do Society
4051 Glencoe Ave., #12
Marina del Rey, CA 90292
(213) 822-7313

Jow Ga Assn.
Raymond Wong, Director
143 Florida Ave. N.W.
Washington, DC 20001

Jujitsu America
Prof. Wally Jay, President
2055 Eagle Ave.
Alameda, CA 94501
(415) 523-8949

Jukido Jiujitsu Inter.
Paul Arel, Director
79 Good Hill Rd.
South Windsor, CT 06074
(203) 644-9634

Juko-Kai Inter.
Rod Sacharnoski, President
P.O. Box 668
Murphy, NC 28906

AFFILIATE

George R. Parulski
P.O. Box 321
Webster, NY 14580

Karate Helps Kick Diabetes
Jeff Smith, President
1912 Valley Wood Rd.
McLean, VA 22101
(703) 534-0058

Karate Inter. Council of Kickboxing
(KICK)
Frank Babcock, President
P.O. Box 8931
St. Louis, MO 63102
(314) 225-7980

Karate Referees Assn. of New
England (KRANE)
Rich Baptista, President
24 Swan Rd.
E. Boston, MA 02128
(617) 567-4989

Master Anthony Mirakian, general manager of the Meibukan Karate-do Association in the United States.

Kempo Inter.
E. Orem, Director
P.O. Box 160
Fall River Mills, CA 96028

Kodenkan Danzan Ryu Jujitsu
Assn.
Sig Kufferath, Director
P.O. Box 29
Walnut Bottom, PA 17266

Korea Hapkido Assn.
Chong Min Lee, Director
P.O. Box 2701
Westfield, NJ 07091
(201) 233-0150

Korean Hap Ki Do Fed.
James Garrison, Director
12246 N.W. Kearney
Portland, OR 97229

Louisiana Karate Assn.
Takayuki Mikami, Director
2563 Metairie Ave.

New Orleans, LA 70009
(504) 835-6825

Lua Lima Hawaiian Karate Assn.
Soloman Kaihewalu, President
429 N. Sacramento St.
Orange, CA 92667

Martial Arts of China Historical
Society
P.O. Box 31578
San Francisco, CA 94131
(205) 974-7002

Maui Aikido Ki Society
P.O. Box 724
Maui, HI 96793
(808) 244-5165

Meibukan Goju-ryu Karate-do
Assn.
(U.S. Headquarters)
Anthony Mirakian, General
Manager
151 Mount Auburn St.
Watertown, MA 02172
(617) 923-2338

Michigan Arts Promotion Assn.
Shannon Roxborough, President
5139 S. Clarendon
Detroit, MI 48204

Michigan Karate Circuit (MKC)
Marcia Fuentes
9849 Quandt
Allen Park, MI 48101
(313) 383-2820

Midwest Tae Kwon Do Assn.
James Benko, President
P.O. Box 281
Grand Blanc, MI 48439
(313) 655-6434

National AAU Jujitsu Committee
Ken Regennitter, Chairman
7808 West 64th St.
Shawnee Mission, KS 66202
(913) 432-6015

National Arnis Assn.
5606 Yale
Houston, TX 77076

Larry Carnahan (far left), president of the North American Sport Karate Association, at the Battle of Atlanta with (left to right) Chuck Norris, Bill Wallace and Joe Corley. Courtesy of Joe Corley

National Assn. of Pentjak Silat
Chao Yuen, Director
P.O. Box 6185
Moreno Valley, CA 92554

National Black Belt League
Mark Reeves, Commissioner
P.O. Box 9899
Bowling Green, KY 42102
(502) 843-0958

National College of Martial Arts
David Box, Jr., Director
1713 S. Jackson
Joplin, MO 64804
(417) 781-4052

National Players Assn.
Dan McFarland, President
416-B 7th St., N.E.
Atlanta, GA 30308
(404) 892-1914

National Weapon Registry
P.O. Box 1063
New Hyde Park, NY 11040

National Women's Martial Arts
Fed.

Coleen Gragen, Director
5680 San Pablo Ave.
Oakland, CA 94608

New World Martial Arts Assn.
Daniel Stanton, President
R.R. #1 Box 580-2 Baldwin Rd.
Cayuga, NY 13034

Nick Cerio's Inter. Martial Arts
Assn.
Nick Cerio, Director
1904-6 Warwick Ave.
Warwick, RI 02889
(401) 738-9111
(401) 738-2850 (Fax)

North American Amateur Contact
Karate/Kickboxing Assn.
Jim Harrison, President
255 S.W. Higgins
Missoula, MT 59803
(406) 728-8187

North American Chinese Martial
Arts Fed.
Anthony Goh, Director
P.O. Box 10850
Baltimore, MD 21234

North American Hapkido Assn.
Dave Weaterly, President
109 E. Main St.
Flushing, MI 48433
(313) 659-2519

North American Muay Thai Assn.
Gerard Finot, President
22740 Shore Center Dr.
Euclid, OH 44123
(216) 731-3006

North American Sport Karate
Assoc. (NASKA)
Larry Carnahan, President
433 South 7th St.
Suite 1917
Minneapolis, MN 55415
(612) 770-0490

North American Wing Chun Assn.
Philip Holder, President
P.O. Box 206
Maple Shade, NJ 08052
(609) 482-7427

North Central Karate Assn.
(NCKA)
Larry Carnahan
433 S. 7th St., Suite 1917
Minneapolis, MN 55415
(612) 770-0490

Northwest Tai Chi Chuan Assn.
P.O. Box 10071
San Bernadino, CA 92423
(714) 787-4105

Ohio Traditional Karate Assn.
Pat Hickey, Chief Instructor
1544 Ritchie Rd.
Stow, OH 44224
(216) 686-1628

Okinawan Goju-ryu Shobukan
(U.S. Headquarters)
John Porta, Director
268 Wanaque Ave.
Pompton Lakes, NJ 07442
(201) 835-5473
(201) 942-8405 (Fax)

Okinawan Shorin-Ryu Matsumura
Kenpo Karate Kobudo Assn.
George Alexander, Director

3372 Lake Worth Rd.
Lake Worth, FL 33461
(407) 968-3231

Okinawa-Te Org.
Gordon Doversola, President
3178 Glendale Blvd.
Los Angeles, CA 90039

Oklahoma State Taekwondo Assn.
D.W. Kang, President
6202 S. Sheridan
Tulsa, OK 74133
(918) 494-9691

Oregon Karate Assn.
Bruce Terrill, President
9212 S.E. Ramona St.
Portland, OR 97266
(503) 771-5114

Pan American Tae Kwon Do Fed.
6 E. Main St.
Ramsey, NJ 07446
(201) 327-7080

Park's Tae Kwon Do Fed.
Jung Soo Park, President

Master Kang Rhee (left), president of the Pasaryu Martial Arts Association, with his former student the late Elvis Presley. Courtesy of Master Kang Rhee

2310 E. Atlantic Blvd.
Pompano Beach, FL 33062
(305) 782-0789; (305) 978-6328

Pasaryu Martial Arts Assn.
Kang Rhee, President
1911 Poplar
Memphis, TN 38104
(901) 726-4100

Philippine Martial Arts Society
Rene Latosa, Chief Instructor
P.O. Box 214433
Sacramento, CA 95821
(916) 972-9958

Physicians Fed. on Martial Arts
Dr. L. Bruce Holbrook, President
P.O. Box 1848
St. Albans, WVA 15177
(304) 756-2070

Professional Karate Assn. (PKA)
Joe Corley, President
3290 Coachman's Way
Atlanta, GA 30075
(404) 998-4610
(404) 998-3680 (Fax)

Professional Karate Commission
    (PKC)
Dale McCutcheon
616 W. Maple St.
Hartville, OH 44632
(216) 877-9600

Professional Karate League
Glen Hart, President
P.O. Box 1269
Sandwich, MA 02563
(617) 477-2770

Pro-West Martial Arts Assn.
316 E. First St.
Newberg, OR 97132
(503) 538-9673

Pukulan Assn. of America
8439 Zephyr St.
Arvada, CO 80005
(303) 420-2094

Regional Sport Karate Circuit
    (RSKC)

Joe Corley, president of the Professional Karate Association. Courtesy of Joe Corley

Ken Eubanks, President
201 U.S. 31, W. By-Pass
Bowling Green, KY 42101
(502) 781-5555

Seishinkai Martial Arts
Shogo Kuniba, President
5913 Churchland Blvd.
Portsmouth, VA 23703
(804) 483-0195

Shadows of Iga [Ninja] Society
Stephen K. Hayes, President
P.O. Box 231
Germantown, OH 45327

Shotokan Karate Assn.
Osama Ozawa, Chief Instructor
P.O. Box 80478
Las Vegas, NV 89180
(702) 873-0891
(702) 795-4776 (Fax)

Shotokan Karate of America
Tsutomu Ohsima, President
4300 Melrose Ave.
Los Angeles, CA 90029

Sin Moo Hapkido
Grandmaster Han Jae Ji, President
1138 Forest Ave.
Pacific Grove, CA 93950

Society of Black Belts
U.S. Hwy. 206
Flanders, NJ 07836

South Carolina Karate Circuit
    (SCKC)
Marty Knight, President
(803) 226-5750

Southeastern Tae Kwon Do Assn.
Sang K. Pak, President
164 Gadsen St.
Cester, SC 29706
(803) 377-8509

Southern Louisiana Assn. Martial
    (Arts) (SLAM)
15082 Pinecrest
Gonzales, LA 70737
(504) 622-2076

Southwest Martial Arts Assn.
3403 E. Plaza Blvd.
National City, CA 92050

Southwest Tae Kwon Do Assn.
Keith Yates, President
1218 Cardigan St.
Garland, TX 75040
(214) 841-3553

Tai-Chi Chuan Assn. of Indiana
Laura Stone, Director
110 S. Indiana Ave.
P.O. Box 1834
Bloomington, IN 47402

Tennessee Karate-do Assn.
Adrian Ellis, Chief Instructor
114 Stuart Rd., Suite 327
Cleveland, TN 37312
(615) 479-7555

Texas Black Belt Commission
Keith Yates, Chairman
3402 Ridgemoor Dr.
Garland, TX 75042

Tompkins Karate Assn.
Dale Tompkins, President
2334 University Blvd.
East Adelphi, MD 20783

Tournament Promoters Assn.
    (TPA)
David Torres, President

9471 Telegraph Rd.
Pico Rivera, CA 90660
(213) 949-2737

Traditional Martial Arts Assn.
Richard Borrell, President
220 E. Main St.
Batavia, NY 14020
(716) 343-1321

Traditional Wushu Assn.
Dr. Bernard Jou, U.S. Director
3340 W. Ball Rd., #A
Anaheim, CA 92804

United Fighting Arts Fed. (UFAF)
(Chuck Norris, President)
Danny Lane, Director
P.O. Box 5681
Huntington, WV 25703
(304) 525-5650

United Kenpo Karate Assn.
    (UKKA)
Jay T. Will, Chairman
P.O. Box 2557
Springfield, OH 45501
(614) 654-6038

United Martial Artists Assn.
867 Lowell Ave.
Central Islip, NY 11722
(516) 232-3218

United Martial Arts Assn.
Chris Jensen
6807D W. 12th
Little Rock, AR 72204
(501) 664-6204

United Nations Martial Arts Fed.
Joe Ming Shih, Chairman
P.O. Box 1330
Venice, FL 34285
(813) 488-4196 (Phone & Fax)

United States Air Force Tae Kwon
    Do Assn.
Major Craig Lightfoot, Secretary
403-A Beard Ave. (HAFB)
Honolulu, HI 96818
(808) 449-6331

United States All-Style Karate
    Instructor's Assn.

P.O. Box 484
Sullivan, MO 63080

United States Chinese Kuoshu Fed.
Huang Chien-Liang, President
8801 Orchard Tree Lane
Towson, MD 21204
(410) 823-8818
(410) 823-8819 (Fax)

United States Chinese Martial Arts
    Council
Jeff Bolt, Director
0528 Meadow Glen
Houston, TX 77042

United States Combat Martial Art
    Assn. Inter.
Christopher Kemp, Director
P.O. Box 32091
Shawnee Mission, KS 66212

United States Combat Martial Arts
    Assn.
Box 336
Maryville, MO 64468

United States Judo Fed.
Phil Porter, President
19 North Union Blvd.
Colorado Springs, CO 80909
(303) 633-7750

United States Kali Assn. Inter.
P.O. Box 5876
Madison, TN 37116

United States Kali/Jeet Kune Do
    Alliance
Lamar Davis II, Director
267 West Valley Ave., #223
Birmingham, AL 35209

United States Karate Alliance
Jim Hawkes, President
P.O. Box 8643
Albuquerque, NM 87198
(505) 831-6202

United States Karate Assn. (USKA)
Roberta Trias-Kelly, President
P.O. Box 17135
Phoenix, AZ 85011
(602) 277-9505

United States Karate Org.
Joe Pagliuso, President
6706 Magnolia Ave.
Riverside, CA 92506
(714) 686-1505

United States Kum Do Assn.
1423 18th St.
Bettendorf, IA 52722
(319) 359-7000

United States Martial Arts Assn.
230 East Union St.
Pasadena, CA 91101
(818) 564-4206

United States Matsubayashi-Ryu
Karate-Do Fed.
1718 Queen City Ave.
Cincinnati, OH 45214
(513) 244-6976

United States Naginata Fed.
P.O. Box 32212
Aurora, CO 80041

United States Olympic Committee
1750 E. Boulder St.
Colorado Springs, CO 80909

United States Shuai-Chiao Assn.
Dr. Chi-Hsiu D. Weng, President
3033 Indianola Ave.
Columbus, OH 43202
(614) 263-4701

United States Taekwondo Assn.
Richard Chun, President
220 E. 86th St.
New York, NY 10028
(212) 772-8918
(212) 772-8919 (Fax)

United States Taekwon-do Fed.
Chuck Sereff, President
6801 W. 117th Ave., #E-5
Broomfield, CO 80020
(303) 466-4963

NEW ENGLAND REGION

Connecticut

Jon Palais, Director
(203) 236-7591

Massachusetts

Louis or John Reyes, Directors
(508) 388-6278

New Hampshire

J.D. Shellon, Director
(603) 868-2163

Vermont

Mark Plante, Director
(802) 748-3343

SOUTHEAST REGION

Florida

Mel Steiner, Director
(305) 595-8007

Georgia

Rickey Maske
(404) 942-0227

North Carolina

Alan Jacobs
(704) 536-2442

United States Taekwon-do Union
(USTU)
Robert Fujimura, President
1750 E. Boulder St.
Colorado Springs, CO 80909
(719) 578-4632

United States Tang Soo Do
Moo Duk Kwan Fed.
(800) 365-TSDI

United States Wrestling Assn.
405 Hall of Fame Ave.
Stillwater, OK 74075
(405) 377-5242

United States of America Wushu
Kungfu Fed. (WKF)
Anthony Goh, Chairman
6315 Harford Rd.
Baltimore, MD 21214
(410) 444-6666
(410) 426-5524 (Fax)

USA Karate Fed.
George Anderson, President

1300 Kenmore Blvd.
Akron, OH 44314
(216) 753-6888

U.S. Chung Do Kwan Assn.
Edward Sell, President
P.O. Box 1474
Lakeland, FL 33802

U.S. Korean Karate Assn.
Ray Walters, President
23021 / 2 10th Ave. South
Great Falls, MT 59405
(406) 452-7283

U.S. Moo Duk Kwan Fed.
Sun Hwan Chung, President
3501 Stadium Dr.
Kalamazoo, MI 49008
(616) 372-2171

U.S. Police Defensive Tactics Assn.
Ray Szuch, National Director
3419 West Blvd.
Cleveland, OH 44111
(216) 651-4337

U.S. Practical Junior Tae Kwon Do
Fed.
Y.D. Choi, President
16800 E. Mississippi Ave.
Aurora, CO 80017

U.S. Shito-Ryu Karate Assn.
Rudy Crosswell, Director
8839 E. Via Linda, Suite #201
Scottsdale, AZ 85258
(602) 661-0212

U.S. Shorin-Ryu Karate Assn.
Frank Hargrove, President
P.O. Box 75747
Hampton, VA 23666
(804) 827-0400

U.S. Taekwon-do Assn.
163 E. 86th St.
New York, NY 10028

U.S. Taekwon-do Fed. (USTF)
Chuck Sereff, President
6801 W. 117th Ave., Suite E-5
Broomfield, CO 80020
(303) 466-4963

U.S. Wado-kai Karate-do Fed.
Yoshiaki Ajari, Chairman
2728 Martin Luther King Jr. Way
Berkeley, CA 94703
(510) 841-7893

U.S. Yoseikan Budo Assn.
P.O. Box 1214
Tuscaloosa, AL 35403

Warrior Inter.
Robert Bussey, President
P.O. Box 601
Fremont, NE 68025
(402) 721-6465

Wing Chun Kung-Fu Council
Robert Heimberger, Director
P.O. Box 2158
Orem, UT 84059

World Assn. of Kickboxing
Organizations (WAKO)
(U.S. Headquarters)
Jim Lantrip, President
55 E. Center St.

Grandmaster Dr. Joo Bang Lee, president of the World Hwarang-do Association. Photo by Christopher Flicker; courtesy of John Huppuch

Madisonville, KY 42431
(502) 825-5000
(502) 821-6774 (Fax)

World Black Belt Bureau
706 Germantown Parkway, #70
Memphis, TN
(901) 757-5040

World Chang Moo Kwan Assn.
Grandmaster Nam Suk Lee,
    President
P.O. Box 1330-CMK
Venice, FL 34284
(813) 488-4196

World Council of Jiu-Jitsu
    Organizations
Tony Maynard, Chairman
324 Barrington Park Lane
Kernersville, NC 27284
(919) 993-5488

World Eagle Claw Assn.
Gini Lau, Director
768 Admiral Callaghan
Vallejo, CA 94591

World Hapkido Fed.
Kwang Sik Myung, President
1119 S. Maple Ave.
Los Angeles, CA 90015

World Hwarang-do Assn.
Joo Bang Lee, President
8200 Firestone Blvd.
Downey, CA 90241
(213) 861-0111
(213) 861-3762 (Fax)

World Kajukenbo Org.
Gary Forbach, Director
P.O. Box 474
San Clemente, CA 94086

World Kuk Sool Won Assn.
In Hyuk Suh, Director
907 El Dorado Blvd., #110
Houston, TX 77062

World Karate, Inc.
1137 Rachel Dr.
Louisville, KY 40219
(502) 968-2206

World Kickboxing Council
1081 Camino del Rio South, Suite
    121
San Diego, CA 92108
(619) 296-7000

World Ki-Do Fed.
In Sun Seo, Chairman
3413 Atwater Ct.
Fremont, CA 94536
(510) 796-4115

World Martial Arts Assn.
Sang Kyu Sim, President
17625 West 7 Mile Rd.
Detroit, MI 48235

World Martial Arts Congress for
    Education
Jhoon Rhee, President
4068 Rosamora Court
McLean, VA 22201
(703) 532-5901
(703) 532-1667 (Fax)

World Council of Jiu-Jitsu Orgs.
Tony Maynard, Chairman
324 Barrington Park Lake
Kernersville, NC 27284

World Council of Martial Arts
S. Henry Cho, Director
46 West 56th St., 3rd Floor
New York, NY 10019
(212) 245-4499

In Sun Seo (right), chairman of the Korean KiDo Federation, with Tae Woo Roh, the president of Korea. Courtesy of James Dussault

Grandmaster Jhoon Rhee (left), president of the World Martial Arts Congress for Education, with then–United States President George Bush. Courtesy of Grandmaster Jhoon Rhee

World Karate
1137 Rachel Dr.
Louisville, KY 40219
(502) 968-2206

World Kickboxing Council
Tim Deans, Commissioner
1001 Camino del Rio South
Suite 121
San Diego, CA 92108
(619) 296-7000

World Ki-Do Fed.
In Sun Seo, Chairman
3413 Atwater Ct.
Fremont, CA 94536
(510) 796-4115

World Kuk Sool Won Assn.
In Hyuk Suh, Director
541 Valencia St.
San Francisco, CA 94110
(415) 553-8141

World Practical Tae Kwon Do Assn.
Bok Kim, President
3200 W. 72nd Ave.
Westminster, CO 80030
(303) 794-8088

World Seido Karate Org.
Tadashi Nakamura, Chairman
61 W. 23rd St.
New York, NY 10010

World Shorin-ryu Karate-do Assn.
Eihachi Ota, Chief Instructor
4003 West Olympic Blvd.
Los Angeles, CA 90019
(213) 936-9663

World Tae Kwon Do Assn.
4320 Roswell Rd.
Atlanta, GA 30342
(404) 252-8947

World Tai Chi Fed.
1331 Touhy
Chicago, IL 60626
(312) 973-4312

World Tang Soo Do Assn.
Jae Chul Shin, President
1709 Oregon Ave.
Philadelphia, PA 19148
(215) 468-2121
(215) 336-2121 (Fax)

World Traditional Hapkido Fed.
Jung Hwan Park, President
1955 East Bay Dr.
Largo, FL 33541
(813) 584-7525

World White Dragon Kung-Fu Society
Tony Galiano, Director
9231 Washington St.
Thornton, CO 80229

World Wing Chun Kung-Fu Assn.
236 S. Rainbow Blvd., Suite 101
Las Vegas, NV 89128
(702) 873-9488; (702) 646-4781

Wu Hsin Tao Kung-Fu Assn.
1012 De La Vina St.
Santa Barbara, CA 93101

Wu Mei Kung-Fu Assn.
Ken Lo, Director
626 Broadway
New York, NY 10012

Yoseikan Hombu Dojo
(Chito-ryu Karate U.S. Headquarters)
William Dometrich, Chief Instructor
22 Martin St.
Covington, KY 31011

Yoshukai Inter.
Mike Foster, President
P.O. Box 4382
South Daytona, FL 32127

UNITED SOVIET SOCIALIST REPUBLIC (USSR): SEE SOVIET UNION

VENEZUELA

Fed. Venezolana de Taekwondo
Chong Koo Lee, President
Av. Bolivar 130-87 Mezanina
Valencia-EDO, Carabobo
Venezuela

VIRGIN ISLANDS

Virgin Islands Tae Kwon Do Assn.
P.O. Box 1383
Roy Washington, St. Thomas
Virgin Islands 00801
(809) 775-6336

WALES

British Nanbudo Assn.
(Welsh Regional Secretary)
(06333) 64297

Karate Union of Great Britain
Welsh Region
Wilson Fallows, Regional Officer
Glan Elwy Cottages
Llangernyw, Near Abergele
Clwyd., North Wales
(0745) 76339

United Kingdom All Styles Karate
  Org.
17 Derwen Close
Ystrad-Mynach, Hengoed
Mid Glamorgan CF8 7DE
Wales
(0443) 815891

Welsh Karate Assn.
71 Brooklyn Gardens
Baglan Moors
Port Talbot, West Glam. SA12 7PD
Wales
(0639) 820975

YUGOSLAVIA

Karate Savez Jugoslavije
Dr. Vladimir Jorga, President
Strahinjica Bana 73 / a
11000 Beograd
Yugoslavia
011-629821

WAKO Yugoslavia
Zarko Modric, President
P.P. 16, Novi Zagreb
YU-41020 Zagreb, Yugoslavia

CHAPTER 21

WORLD DIRECTORY OF MARTIAL ARTS SUPPLY COMPANIES

This is the first comprehensive directory in print of martial arts suppliers from around the world, comprising 1,112 companies selling every imaginable product a martial artist will ever need. This chapter features 451 major suppliers from 20 countries.

Like martial arts organizations, supply companies and manufacturers of martial arts equipment come in all sizes, and, likewise, can suffer business setbacks. They could be here today, as I write this book, but gone tomorrow.

Invariably, the larger and more established firms will use a street address and a phone number. A number of smaller firms typically used post office boxes and did not list a phone number in the research sources used to compile this chapter. Consequently, the author or publisher cannot be responsible for changes of address or phone numbers, nor for outfits that have gone out of business by the time this book is published.

Be aware also that certain martial arts weapons and self-defense training equipment is prohibited by law in some states and is also typically not sold to minors. The author and publisher disclaim all liability from the sale and use of products in this book.

Phone and fax numbers are standardly listed here when available. Readers should be aware that if an 800 phone number is included for U.S. companies, it is usually reserved for credit card orders and *not* for customer service or information about products. Note that phone numbers in France employ periods between numbers instead of dashes.

Most of the companies listed handle mail order as well as on-site sales. However, there are some that transact only mail-order business.

When you have questions about a company's product line, call or write for a catalog. The larger martial arts supply houses may or may not charge customers for a catalog. Some may deduct the cost of the catalog, usually a few dollars, from your first order.

FORMAT

All listings appear in alphabetical order, first by country, then by state and, finally, by city. Some foreign countries, like Australia, appear by province, and then by city.

COMPLETE PRODUCT LINES

AUSTRALIA

A.C.T.

Wizard Martial Arts Supplies
28 Townshend St.
Phillip A.C.T. 2606
Australia
(06) 282-2983

QUEENSLAND

Combined Martial Arts Supplies
1 / 171 Nerang St.
Southport, Queensland 4215
Australia
(07) 531-2877

Jols
820 Stanley St.
Wooloongabba, Queensland 4120
Australia
(07) 891-5388

NEW SOUTH WALES

Martial Arts World
265H Victoria Rd.
Gladesville, New South Wales 2111
Australia
(02) 816-4970

Genesis Trading Co.
P.O. Box 208
Glebe, New South Wales 2037
Australia
(02) 808-1342

Jai Martial Arts
442 Bunnerong Rd.
Matraville, New South Wales
Australia
(02) 311-3175

Zoe's Martial Arts Centre
Shop 25, Civic Centre
48 George St.
Paramatta 2150, New South Wales
Australia
(02) 891-4737

Bodybuilder's World & Combat
   Supply
Shop 3, 767-773 Punchbowl Rd.
Punchbowl, New South Wales 2186
Australia
(02) 709-2450

Myriam's Martial Arts Centre
Fairfield Showground, No. 415,
   Smithfield Rd.
Smithfield, New South Wales
Australia
(02) 610-5770

Martial Arts & Sports
Shope 308, Chinatown Centre
25-29 Dixon St.
Haymarket, Sydney 2000
Australia
281-1014

Sensei's Martial Arts Store
Shop 4, Barker St.
Rooty Hill
Australia
(02) 832-1389

Tan's Martial Arts & Fitness
   Equipment
30 Dale St., Fairfield
Sydney 2165, New South Wales
Australia
(02) 72-9908

Zen Imports
P.O. Box 201, Rozelle
Sydney 2039, New South Wales
Australia

Zoe's Martial Arts Centre
815 Princes Highway
Tempe 2044, New South Wales

Australia
(02) 558-8518

The Master's Den
P.O. Box 1591
407 Crown St.
Wollongong 2500, N.S.W.
Australia
(04) 228-5588

VICTORIA

Eastern Suburbs Martial Arts
   Supplies
Shop 1, 211 Scoresby Rd.
Boronia 3155, Victoria
Australia
(03) 762-9636

Samurai Martial Arts Imports
81A Foster St.
Dandenong, Victoria
Australia
(03) 792-1664

Peninsula Martial Arts Supplies
Shop 12, Peninsula Centre
425 Nepean Hwy.
Frankston 3199
Australia
783-6317

Jols
148A Moorabool St.
Geelong, Victoria
Australia
(05) 223-2492

Martial Arts Supply
10 / 37 Morgan Ct.
Glenroy 3046, Melbourne
Australia
306-0899

Chinatown Martial Arts Supplies
26A Corrs Lane, 1st Floor
Melbourne 3000, Victoria
Australia
(03) 662-3652

Tan's Martial Arts & Fitness
   Equipment
9 Murray Place, Ringwood
Melbourne 3134, Victoria

Australia
(03) 870-0813
(03) 873-3637 (Fax)

Jols
296 High St.
Northcote 3070
Australia
(03) 489-2333

Bushido Martial Arts Supplies
Shop 3, Terrylands St.
Burnie 7320, Tasmania
Australia
(004) 315-200

Samurai Martial Arts Imports
52 Atherton Rd.
Oakleigh, Victoria
Australia
(03) 568-2096

Samurai Martial Arts Imports
666 Centerbury Rd.,
Surry Hills, Victoria 3127
Australia
(03) 890-0720

WESTERN AUSTRALIA

Ronin Martial Arts Equipment
163 Scarborough Beach Rd.
Mount Hawthorn 6016
Western Australia
(09) 443-1917

Ray Hana's Martial Arts Supplies
158 William St.
Perth 6000
Western Australia
(09) 321-3021
(09) 481-2674 (Fax)

BELGIUM

Asahi Sports Gent
Fred. Burvenichstraat 38
Gent, Belgium
091-317598

Budo House
132 Henri Jasper
1060 Brussels, Belgium

BERMUDA

Sahaba Co. Industries
31 Court St.
Hamilton 5-25, Bermuda

BRAZIL

Loja Campos
Rua Eng. Silva Lima, no. 38
Salvador, Bahia, CEP 40040
Brazil
(071) 321-4322; (071) 243-6808

Combat Sport Comercio Material
    Esportivo Ltda.
Ave. Ipiranga, 818—6 andar
São Paulo/SP, 01040-000
Brazil
(011) 220-0674; (011) 233-6745

Pro-Sport
rua Americo de Campos, no. 46
Liberdade, São Paulo/SP, CEP
    01506-010
Brazil
(011) 278-5731
(011) 279-5337 (Fax)

S. Craft Industria e Comercio Ltda.
Av. Irai, 516
Indianopolis, São Paulo/SP, CEP
    04082
Brazil
(011) 543-5400

SA Sports
Alameda dos Aicas, 1397
Moema, São Paulo/SP
Brazil
(011) 61-7267

CANADA

BRITISH COLUMBIA

Al Cheng's Martial Arts Supplies
156 E. 7th Ave.
Vancouver, B.C., Canada V5T 1M6

Mikado Enterprises
701 E. Hastings
Vancouver, B.C., Canada V6A 1R3

Japan Martial Arts Supplies
23 W. Burnside Rd.
Victoria, B.C., Canada V9A 6Z7

ONTARIO

Black Belt Martial Arts Supply
1109 Main St. East
Hamilton, Ont., Canada L8M 1N9

Zen Martial Arts
19 John St. North
Hamilton, Ont., Canada L8B 1H1

Black Belt Martial Arts Supply
120 Dundas St.
London, Ont., Canada

Dojo Supply
212 Horton St.
London, Ont., Canada

Jukado
540 E. Henri-Bourassa
Montreal, Ont., Canada H3L 1C6

Pals Enterprises
80 Nashdene Rd. #67-68
Scarborough, Ont., Canada M1V
    5E4
(416) 299-8168

Champion Enterprises
1077 Gerrard St. East
Toronto, Ont., Canada M4M 1Z9
(416) 463-5669

Warrior's Fighting Arts Supply Co.
647 Yonge St.
Toronto, Ont., Canada M4Y 1Z9

Tigron Canada
885 Erie St. E.
Windsor, Ont., Canada N9A 3Y7
(519) 254-9555

QUEBEC

Genesport Industries
150 King St.
Montreal, Quebec, Canada H3C
    2P3

ENGLAND

Kik Sports
Traders Shopping Centre
16-18 Station Rd.
Reading, Berkshire
England
(0860) 308201; (0628) 72432

Cimac Martial Arts Wear
606 Stratford Rd.
Birmingham B11 4AP
England
(021) 778-2000; (021) 778-5981/2
(021) 777-9988 (Fax)

Giko
681/683 Stratford Rd.
Sparkhill, Birmingham B11 4DX
England
(021) 777-7666

Hornet Martial Arts
25 Hurst St.
Birmingham B5 4BB
England
(021) 622-3631

Martial Arts Merchandising
P.O. Box 1310
Selly Oak, Birmingham B29 7JT
England
(021) 472-2043

Martec
8 Armstrong St.
Horwich, Bolton BL6 5PW
England
(0204) 696574

Shogun Gifts
(The Ninja Centre)
30 Churchill Square
Brighton
England
(0273) 203868

Express Martial Arts
Maggs House
78 Queens Rd.
Clifton, Bristol 8
England

Hayashi
58 West St.
Old Market, Bristol BS2 OBL
England
(0272) 555560; (0272) 552002
(0272) 559385 (Fax)

Hero Martial Arts
29 Broadweir
Bristol BS1 3AY
England
(0272) 291971

British Warrior Martial Arts
    Supplies
Unit 9, Greys Court
Kingsland Grange
Woolston, Warrington, Cheshire
    WA1 4SH
England
(0925) 818045

British Warrior Martial Arts
    Supplies
1st Floor, Evans House
Orford Lane
Warrington, Cheshire
England
(0925) 445293

Freestyle Martial Arts
45 Winwick St.
Warrington, Cheshire
England
(0925) 413517

Kamae
Ewart St.
Saltney Ferry, Chester C4 OBL
England
(0244) 677534

Far East Martial Arts Sportswear
108 Spon End
West Midlands, Coventry CV1 3HF
England
(0203) 26595; (0203) 714746

Sharma Textiles Manufacturing
35 Vecqueray St.
Coventry CV1 2HP
England
(0203) 520631

Croydon Martial Arts
Shops Centre, Unit 42
68-74 Church St.
Croydon CR0 1RB
England
(01) 667-0806

Chikara
Brittania Mills
Markeaton St.
Derby DE3 3AW
England
(0332) 40074; (0332) 380369
(0332) 292443 (Fax)

Sensei Martial Arts
27 Indoor Market
High Street
Epsom KT19 5BY
England
(03727) 40258

NKA Sports & Leisure
Unit 21, Bond Industrial Estate
Wickhamford, Nr. Evesham
Worcs. WR11 6RT
England
(0386) 831016
(0386) 831538 (Fax)

D & S Sports
(Contact Sports)
130 Barton St.
Gloucester, England
(0452) 410974

Forbidden Shadows
Unit 24, Peerglow Trading Estate
Olds Approach
Rickmansworth, Herts.
England

Bukonkai Combat Sports
Shirethorn Centre
Prospects St.
Hull HU2 8AY
England
(0482) 228848

Kato Fighting Art Supplies
46 High St.
Chatham, Kent ME4 3DS
England
(0634) 409024

Japan Martial Arts
112 Bellgrove Rd.
Welling, Kent DA16 3QD
England
(081) 303-2276; (081) 303-4336
(081) 303-8850 (Fax)

Leigh Martial Arts
86 Railway Rd.
Leigh, Lancaster WN7 4AN
England
(0942) 677994

Bukonkai Combat Sports
10 Boar Lane
Leeds
England
(0532) 453958

Lemas Martial Arts
48 Silver Arcade
Silver Street
Leicester
England
(0533) 402195

Shaolin World
8 Berry St.
Liverpool L1 4JF
England
(051) 709-1008

Cobra 2000
115B Malden Rd.
London NW5 4HK
England
(071) 267-7894

Dragon Martial Arts
128 Myddleton Rd.
London N22 4NO
England
(01) 889-0965

London Martial Arts
1104 Harrow Rd.
London NW10 5NL
England
(081) 960-7099
(071) 624-6289 (Fax)

Atoz
11 Kenway Rd.
London SW5 0RP
England
(071) 370-0236

D.H. Martial Arts Centre
46 Carnaby St.
London W1
England
(01) 734-9461

Fox Martial Arts
158 Queensway
London W2 6LY
England
(01) 229-9008

Karate & Oriental Arts
102 Felsdram Rd.
London SW 15 1DQ
England

Meijin Martial Arts Supplies
141 Goldhawk Rd.
Shepherd Bush
London W12 8EN
England
(01) 749-9070; (01) 749-9506

Musashi
The Japan Centre
66-68 Brewer St.
London W1
England
(01) 439-8035

Orient Sports Mart
Northington House
59 Gray's Inn Rd.
Holborn, London WC1
England

Shaolin Way
10 Little Newport St.
London WC2
England
(01) 734-6391

Chung Yee Martial Arts
106 Portland St.
Manchester M1 4JR
England
(061) 236-0966; (061) 236-7033
(061) 236-0865 (Fax)

J. Milom
Springfield Mills, Sherborne St.
Manchester M3 1ND
England
(061) 832-6155

Oriental World
14-18 Swan St.
Manchester M4 5JN
England
(061) 832-8204

Pedalers Martial Arts
388 Northolt Rd.
South Harrow, Middlesex HA2
    8EX
England
(01) 422-5807; (01) 422-4590

Sakura Trading Co.
10 Thornbury Rd.
Isleworth, Middlesex TW7 44G
England

Dudley Martial Arts Centre
Gladstone Bldg., New St.
Dudley, West Midlands
England
212408

Chojin Martial Arts
10-12 Low Friar St., 3rd Floor
Newcastle-upon-Tyne NE1 5UE
England
(091) 261-9859

Marks Martial Arts
110 Sovereign Way
Anglia Square, Norwich NR3 1ER
England
(0603) 630485

Arnold Sports
57 Front St.
Arnold, Nottingham
England
(0602) 201508

Dee Sports
Reading
576865

Sabre Martial Arts
132 The Wicker
Sheffield, England S3 8JD
(0742) 750940

Budo Arts Limited
P.O. Box 10
Ministerley, Shrewsbury SY5 0ZZ
England
(058) 861610

British Contact Sports
79 Cannock Rd., Heath Hayes
Cannock, Staffs.
England
(0543) 71989; (05435) 71851

O.S.S. Martial Art Shop
1D Lynton Rd.
Burnham-on-Sea, Somerset TA8
    1PW
England
(0278) 789894

Lucky Crane
Southampton
England
222529

Kenjo Martial Arts Supplies
86 Church Rd.
Stockton, England

MB Sports
39 Bond St.
Ipswich, Suffolk IP4 1JD
England
(0473) 213056

Eagle Martial Arts
P.O. Box 148
Weybridge, Surrey KT13 8NA
England
(0932) 859695

Sakura Publications
P.O. Box 18
Ashtead, Surrey KT 21 JD
England

Battle Orders Shogun UK
71 Eastbourne L. Willingdon
Eastbourne, East Sussex BN20 9NR
England
(032) 12 5182 / 3

Jade Martial Arts
10 Castle St.
Hastings, East Sussex
England
(0424) 433298

Shodan U.K.
54 George St.
Brighton, East Sussex BN2 2LJ
England
(0273) 698809
(0273) 207965 (Fax)

SIAM Martial Arts
28 Blondell Dr.
Aldwick
Bognor Regis
West Sussex PO21 4BN
England
(0243) 263956
(0243) 868612 (Fax)

Martial World
114 School St.
Wolverhampton WV3 0NR
England
(0902) 28404

Zanshin Martial Arts
37 Peel Palace
Barnsley, S. Yorkshire
England
(0226) 730537

Shinbuko Martial Arts
164 Westgate
Bradford 1, W. Yorkshire
England
(0274) 306641

FRANCE

SEDIREP
44, rue de la Belle-Feuille
92105 Boulogne
France
(1) 46.03.12.46

Shodan Sports
Route de Carnon
34970 Lattes
France
67.64.66.07

Judogi
82, rue Tete-d'Or
69006 Lyon
France
78.52.45.42

Mialot Sports
Boite Postale 3212
03100 Monlucon
France
(1) 70.03.94.46
(1) 70.28.51.60 (Fax)

SFJAM Noris Sports
(Headquarters for a network of
    nationwide outlets)
11, rue de la Pompe
Cergy St. Christophe R.N. 14
95801 Cergy-Pontoise Cedex
France
(1) 30.30.17.22
(1) 30.30.23.27 (Fax)

Judogi
107, bd Beaumarchais
75003 Paris
France
(1) 42.72.95.59

Budokai
4, rue Henry Monnier
75009 Paris
France
(1) 40.16.02.19

Budostore
34, rue de la Montagne
Ste. Genevieve, BP 225,
75227 Paris
France
43.26.19.46

Ichiban
220, rue St. Jacques
75005 Paris
France
(1) 46.33.86.76

Judo International
34 rue de la Montagne
Ste. Genevieve, 75005 Paris
France

Club European d'Arts Martiaux
56, rue de la Rochefoucauld
Metro Pigalle, 75009 Paris
France
48.74.12.43

C.I.G. Arts Martiaux
30, rue Sant-Yves
75014 Paris
France
(1) 42.79.80.03

Disportex
18, rue Victor Masse

75009 Paris
France
(1) 42.80.18.97

P.P.A.M.
13, avenue de la Porte Montmartre
75018 Paris
France
42.62.51.10
42.58.13.81 (Fax)

Sport 7
8, rue de la Bidassoa
75020 Paris 8
France
46.36.06.01

Versport
36-38m rue Victor Masse
75009 Paris
France
16 / 1 / 42.81.06.06

S.L.S. Equipment
51, Bd A. Briand
17208 Royan Cedex
France
46.05.29.55

Budo Plus
3, Allee Helene Boucher
93270 Sevran
France
43.83.55.29

GERMANY

Budo Artikel Velte
Postfach 2464
Saalburgstrasse 151
D-6380 Bad Homburg v.d.H.
Germany
06172 / 3 60 39
06172 / 3 58 38 (Fax)

Budoland
Gewerbepark 3
8206 Bruckmuhl
Germany
(08062) 2072
(08062) 6528 (Fax)

Verlag Weinmann
Beckerstrasse 7
1000 Berlin 41
Germany
(030) 855-4895

Waffen Pietzke
Bismarckstrasse 52
Dusseldorf-Mitte
Germany
(0211) 320999

Budoartikel Versand
Plitterdorferstrasse 198
D-5300 Bonn 2
Germany
(0228) 356302

Sportimex
J.F. Baer gmbH
Am Deich 42
Postfach 101364
D-2800 Bremen 1
Germany
(0421) 50 08 81/82

Kwon
Rudolf Diesel Strasse 8
8060 Dachau
Germany
08131/1631(33)

Asahi Sports
Postfach 26
7242 Dornhan
Germany
07455/553

Sport Rhode
Postfach 10 22 20
Frankfurter Strasse 121
6072 Dreieich
Germany
06103/3 40 75

Matzuro
Kaiserstrasse 310-400
Duisburg 18
Germany

Asia Sport
Eggstrasse 21
9100 Herisau
Germany
071-523455

Asia Sport
1/61 Gneisenaustrasse 8
U-Bahn Mehringdamm
Germany
691-9538

K. Import Export Co.
Harzstrasse 30a
8400 Regensburg
Germany
09 41/66849

Budo Shop
Heidemarie Lisse
Hogenellweg 3a
2948 Schortens
Germany
(04461) 3966

Karate-Budo Journal
Abonnenten Service
Postfach 810640
D-7000 Stuttgart 80
Germany

US Sports
Munsterstrasse 55
4712 Werne
Germany
02389/52552

GREECE

Sport Centre
(Chr. Pavlou)
90 Embedocleous St.
Pangrati, Athens
Greece

HONG KONG

Kung Fu Supplies Co.
188 Johnson Rd., &C
Wanchai, Hong Kong

HOLLAND: SEE NETHERLANDS

INDIA

Sumanta Sadhukhan
12, Protap Chatterjee Lane
Calcutta, 700012
West Bengal, India

ITALY

Bruce Lee Kung-Fu
Via G. Donizetti
10/6 CAP, 16154 Sestn. P
Genova, Italy

JAPAN

Tokyo Budo Shokai
Oki Bldg.
Chuou-ku Tanimachi 5-6-3
557 Osaka
Japan
(06) 764-4678

Asahi World Co.
Dogenzaka 2-20-26
Shibuya-ku,150 Tokyo
Japan
(03) 477-0770
(03) 476-1826 (Fax)

Isami Co.
Tomigaya 2-41-10
Shibuya-ku,151 Tokyo
Japan
(03) 467-8242

Shureido
6-1-1 Chome Tomari
Naha-shi, Okinawa
Japan
81-0988-61-5621

Tokyo Shureido Co.
Yanagibashi 1-10-9
Daito-ku, 111 Tokyo
Japan
(03) 866-9409
(03) 864-9646 (Fax)

KOREA

WTF Taekwondo
World Taekwon-do Fed.
635, Yuksamdong, Kangnamku
Seoul, Korea 135
82-02-566-2505; 82-02-567-1058
82-02-553-4728

MALAYSIA

Flo Enterprises
42-3 Jalan SS 21/58
Damansara Ultama, Selangor
Malaysia

NETHERLANDS

Aiki Budosport
Burg. V Leeuwenlaan 59
1064 KL Amsterdam
Netherlands
020-136764

Antraco Postorder
Hoekslootstraat 9
1069 EJ Amsterdam
Netherlands
020-105830

Asahi Sports Netherlands
Overtoom 360
hoek J.P. Heijestraat
Amsterdam, Netherlands
020-127373

The Fox-Thaismai
Roelantstraat 6
1055 LP Amsterdam
Netherlands
020-828217

Matzuro
Assendelstraat 6a
Amsterdam, Netherlands

Windy
Roelanstraat 6
1055 LP Amsterdam
Netherlands
020-828217

Windy
Middelveldstraat 53
1069 GJ Amsterdam-Osdorp
Netherlands
020-190169

Hercules Sportorders
Postbus 451
2501 CL Den Haag
Netherlands

Todos International BV
Postbus 451
2501 CL Den Haag
Netherlands

H. De Vries
27 Oude Gracht
2000 Ag Haarlem
Netherlands

Nikko Toshogu
Geldropseweg 9a
5611 SB Eindhoven
Netherlands
040-111222

Budo 2000
Padangstraat 82
Enschede, Netherlands
053-339293

Asahi Sports Rotterdam
Middellandplein 16
Rotterdam, Netherlands
010-477-3883

Asahi Sports Tilburg
Molenstraat 136
Tilburg, Netherlands
013-365120

Body Promotion
Min Talmanstraat 22
3555 GH Utrect-Zwilen
Netherlands

NEW ZEALAND

Auckland Martial Arts Supplies
476 Queen St.
Auckland, New Zealand
09-377-1891

Martial Arts Supplies NZ Ltd.
68 Dixon St.
P.O. Box 6495 Te Aro
Wellington, New Zealand
04-384-7832

OKINAWA: SEE JAPAN

SCOTLAND

M.A. Sports
Kings Court Shopping Centre
Guild Hall St.
Dumfermline, Fife
Scotland
(0383) 730637

Do-Su
41 Barklay Place
Edinburgh EH1 4HW
Scotland

Kickback Martial Arts Supplies
121 St. Georges Rd.
Glasgow G3
Scotland
041-332-1455

Replicas
Glasgow
Scotland
3320386

M.A. Sports
36 The Arcade, Kings St.
Stirling, Stirlingshire
Scotland
(0786) 65109

SPAIN

Fuji Sport
Fernando, 44
8002 Barcelona
Spain
(93) 318-60-85

Ninja Distribution
c/. Nicaragua, 136-138, 1-1
09029 Barcelona
Spain
230-32-08 / 230-32-09

Pedidos A Fuji Madrid
C/Andres Mellado, 42
28015 Madrid
Spain
549-9837
544-6324 (Fax)

SWEDEN

Budo-Centum Ab
Box 53 208
S-400 16 Gotenborg
Sweden

Budo-Nord AB
Sveavagen 90
11359 Stockholm
Sweden
08-30-42-02

Svarspost
Kundnummer 53559001
54600 Karlsborg
Sweden
0505-30422

TASMANIA: SEE AUSTRALIA

UNITED STATES

ALABAMA

Chung's International Fitness
1433 E. Montgomery Hwy.
Birmingham, AL 35216

Yoon's Academy
4122 Government Blvd., Hwy. 90
Mobile, AL 36609

Stewart's Tae Kwon Do
Box 664
601 S. Alabama Ave.
Monroeville, AL 36461

ALASKA

Genesis Martial Arts Supplies
P.O. Box 74118
Fairbanks, AK 99707

ARIZONA

Butokukai
P.O. Box 430
Cornville, AZ 86325
(800) 747-6280
(602) 634-6280
(602) 634-1203 (Fax)

Classical Kung Fu Equipment
15227 N. 23rd Pl.
Phoenix, AZ 85022
(602) 867-1625

Karate Mart Supply Centres
1411 W. Indian School Rd.
Phoenix, AZ 85013
(602) 265-6858

Golden Dragon Martial Arts
   Supply
10425 N. Scottsdale Rd.
Scottsdale, AZ 85254

Lancer's Militaria
P.O. Box 100
Sims, AZ 71967

Karate Mart Supply Centres
831 S. Rural Rd.
Tempe, AZ 85281
(602) 894-6778

Karate Mart Supply Centres
2501 N. Campbell
Tucson, AZ 85719
(602) 326-9379

North American Martial Arts
   Supply
1913 E. Broadway
Tucson, AZ 85719

Takagi Imports
817 N. 1st St.
Phoenix, AZ 85004

ARKANSAS

Lancer Militaria
P.O. Box 100
Sims, AR 71967

CALIFORNIA

California S & P
1129 Solano Ave.
Albany, CA 94706

KUMA Design
P.O. Box 7216
Alhambra, CA 91802
(213) 732-7810

Dynasty Martial Arts Supply
2500 W. Lincoln Ave.
Anaheim, CA 92801

Martial Art Supply Co.
2060 W. Lincoln Ave.
Anaheim, CA 92801

Dancing Dragon Designs
5670 West End Rd., Suite 4
Arcata, CA 95521

Artesia Sporting Goods
18622 Pioneer Blvd.
Artesia, CA 90701

Sang Moo Sa
16631 Bellflower Blvd.
Bellflower, CA 90706
(213) 866-5378
(800) 346-3116

Larry Reed Martial Arts Supply
7453 Fair Oaks Blvd.
Carmichael, CA 95608

Arete Press
1420 N. Claremont Blvd.
Suite 111-B
Claremont, CA 91711
(909) 624-7770
(909) 398-1840 (Fax)

Zinja Corp.
1214 1/2 Main St., Suite 204
Delano, CA 93215
(805) 725-0100
(800) 527-8879

Japan Karate Organization
6743 Dublin Blvd.
Dublin, CA 94566

California S & P
10545-B San Pablo Ave.
El Cerrito, CA 94530
(510) 527-6032

Twin Dragons Martial Arts Supply
9067 Elk Grove Blvd.
Elk Grove, CA 95624

Bugei Trading Company
3790 Manchester Ave.

Encinitas, CA 92024
(619) 942-8675
(800) 437-0125

Kim Pacific Trading Corp.
4141 Business Center Dr.
Fremont, CA 94538
(510) 490-0300
(800) 227-0500
(510) 490-5553 (Fax)

I & I Sports Supply Co.
1524 W. 178th St.
Gardena, CA 90248
(213) 715-6800
(213) 715-6822 (Fax)

Kim Pacific Trading Corp.
24475 Mission Blvd.
Hayward, CA 94110

Formosa Martial Art Supply
6100 Watt Ave. N.
Highlands, CA 95660

Oriental Traders
470 S. Coast Hwy.
Laguna Beach, CA 92651

Sun Kim Martial Arts
1331 N. Hacienda Blvd.
La Puente, CA 91744

Far East Supplies & Mfg.
12913 S. Broadway
Los Angeles, CA 90061
(213) 515-7290

Hawkins Supply Co.
10853 Venice Blvd.
Los Angeles, CA 90034

Know Now
P.O. Box 3449
Los Angeles, CA 90078

Mantis Supply Co.
P.O. Box 3749
Los Angeles, CA 90028

Martial Arts Supplies Co.
10711 Venice Blvd.
Los Angeles, CA 90034
(310) 870-9866

Nozawa Trading Co.
735 S. LaBrea Ave.
Los Angeles, CA 90036
(213) 938-7161
(800) 552-5249

Ryukyu Enterprises
3627 W. Pico Blvd.
Los Angeles, CA 90019
(213) 731-3016

Shudokan Martial Art Supply
2004 McHenry Ave., Ste. B
Modesto, CA 95350

Black Dragon Martial Arts
   Supplies
884 Abrego St.
Monterey, CA 93940
(408) 372-5484

Eagle Trading Co.
1243 Highland Ave.
National City, CA 92050

Formosa Martial Arts Supply
6100 Watt Ave.
North Highlands, CA 95660
(916) 348-3118

K. Roonngsang
P.O. Box 17136
North Hollywood, CA 91605
(818) 591-0526

Valley Martial Arts Supply
5638 Lankershim Blvd.
North Hollywood, CA 91601
(818) 769-0436
(800) 458-6438

Young's Trading
5705 Telegraph Ave.
Oakland, CA 94609
(415) 547-0121

House of Armand
508 Mission Ave.
Oceanside, CA 92054

Oceanside Martial Arts Supply
205 N. Hill St.
Oceanside, CA 92054
(619) 722-3637

Martial Arts Supplies
1732 N. Tustin
Orange, CA 92665
(714) 538-8277

R & R Supply Co.
634 Chapman Ave.
Placentia, CA 92670
(714) 524-6364

Butterfly Martial Arts
152 W. Holt Ave.
Pomona, CA 91768

A/S Martial Arts Supplies Co.
3390 S. Market St.
Redding, CA 90061

U.S. Martial Arts Supply Co.
178 W. Highland Ave.
San Bernadino, CA 92405

Pioneer Interstate
1541 Industry Rd.
San Carlos, CA 94070
(415) 595-3456
(800) 821-5090

Dragon Fist Martial Arts Supply
4094 Fairmont Ave.
San Diego, CA 92105
(619) 281-5396
(800) 227-8730

Hawk Karate Supplies
3223 Fairmount Ave.
San Diego, CA 92105

Hong-Bo Oriental Imports
950 5th Avenue at Broadway
San Diego, CA 92101

Nippon To
5019 Santa Monica Blvd.
San Diego, CA 92107

California S & P
360 Swift Ave., #26
San Francisco, CA 94080

Co-Mart International
P.O. Box 16194
San Francisco, CA 94116
(415) 759-8640
(415) 665-4657 (Fax)

Kaplan's Sporting Goods
1055 Market St.
San Francisco, CA 94103

Kim Pacific Trading Corp.
2567 Mission St.
San Francisco, CA 94110

Brendan Lai's Supply Co.
2075 Mission St.
San Francisco, CA 94110
(415) 626-8850
(800) 362-8850
(415) 626-3410 (Fax)

Mutual Supply Co.
1090 Sansome St.
San Francisco, CA 94111

Pacific Rim Products
P.O. Box 31578
San Francisco, CA 94131
(415) 992-1007
(800) 824-2433

White Crane Supply Co.
47 Golden Gate Ave.
San Francisco, CA 94102
(415) 861-6363

Nichi Bei Bussan
140 Jackson St.
San Jose, CA 95112

Young's Trading Co.
86 N. Market St.
San Jose, CA 95113

Kim Pacific Trading Co.
1451 Doolittle Dr.
San Leandro, CA 94577

Musashi Martial Arts
1842 S. Grand Ave.
Santa Ana, CA 92705

Golden Glove
3447-B El Camino Real
Santa Clara, CA 95055

Eastern Trades
1515 Mission St.
Santa Cruz, CA 95060

DLW Supply Co.
16149 Roscoe Blvd.
Sepulveda, CA 91343

Musashi Martial Arts
12463 Beach Blvd.
Stanton, CA 90680
(714) 894-4021

Tibon's Martial Arts Supplies
923 N. Yosemite
Stockton, CA 95203
(209) 465-0943

Martial Art Supplies Co.
18918 Ventura Blvd.
Tarzana, CA 91335

Rancho California Martial Arts
42111-B Avenida Alvarado
Temecula, CA 92390

American Liquidators
4009 Pacific Coast Hwy.
Torrance, CA 90505

Tai Mantis Supplies
2081 Torrance Blvd.
Torrance, CA 90501

R & R Supply Co.
382 East "C" St.
Upland, CA 91786
(909) 985-9897
(800) 422-3699

David German Sports Equip.
781 Pinefalls Ave.
Walnut, CA 91789

K. Inoda & Co.
10913 W. Pico Blvd.
West Los Angeles, CA
(310) 475-4691

I & I Sports
2979 S. Sepulveda Blvd.
West Los Angeles, CA 90064
(310) 444-9988
(310) 715-6822 (Fax)

Phil Hall Martial Art Supply
6431 Westminster Ave.
Westminster, CA 92683
(714) 898-4545

Tai Mantis Supplies
6341 Westminster Ave.
Westminster, CA 92683

Medinas Martial Arts Supply
8002 S. Broadway
Whittier, CA 90606

COLORADO

Buda Ya
12028-F E. Mississippi Ave.
Aurora, CO 80021

Bu-Jin Design
640 Dewey Ave.
Boulder, CO 80304
(303) 444-7663

Phoenix Associates
P.O. Box 693
Boulder, CO 80306

Fighting Arts Supply Co.
2306-C Platte Ave.
Colorado Springs, CO 80909

Dragon Lady Martial Arts Supply
516 S. Broadway
Denver, CO 80209
(303) 778-0590

Sabaki
4730 E. Colfax Ave.
Denver, CO 80220
(303) 320-5618

Tigron Colorado
2037 S. Federal
Denver, CO 80219
(303) 937-7771

Tiger Mountain
P.O. Box 1712
Wheat Ridge, CO 80033
(303) 431-0573

FLORIDA

East Coast Martial Arts Supply
106 Longwood Ave.
Altamonte Springs, FL 32701

Beaver Products
P.O. Box 1700
Anna Maria, FL 33501

Brown's Trophies
2114 Drew St.
Clearwater, FL 34625
(813) 441-1120

Midas Karate
P.O. Box 935
Dundee, FL 33838
(813) 439-5722

Merten's Martial Market
1505 N.E. 26th St.
Ft. Lauderdale, FL 33305

Hialeah Martial Arts Supply
1234 W. 68th St.
Hialeah, FL 33014

Black Tiger Enterprises
621 Ridgewood Ave.
Holly Hill, FL 32017

The Immortal Dragon
6212 Johnson St.
Hollywood, FL 33024
(305) 987-7626

USA Martial Arts Supply
6135 Powers Ave.
Jacksonville, FL 32217
(800) 848-5425
(904) 737-5559
(904) 731-3395 (Fax)

Pathman's Sport Center
7134 Collins Ave.
Miami Beach, FL 33141

East Coast Martial Art Supplies
1809 E. Colonial Dr.
Orlando, FL 32803
(407) 896-2487

Y.K. Kim Taekwon-do Center
1630 E. Colonial Dr.
Orlando, FL 32803
(305) 898-2084

Bushido Academy
5201 Park Blvd.
Pinellas Park, FL 34665
(813) 541-3340

Jim Graden's Florida Karate
9112 Seminole Blvd.
Seminole, FL 34642
(813) 392-3198

Oh's Taekwon-do Center
7520 Seminole Blvd.
Seminole, FL 34642
(813) 393-4567

Adam's Kung Fu
6512 4th St. N.
St. Petersburg, FL 33702
(813) 521-3765

John Graden's USA Karate
1000 58th St. N.
St. Petersburg, FL 33710
(813) 323-0830

Brown's Trophies
3180 Central Ave.
St. Petersburg, FL 33712
(813) 323-2811

Tigron South
6122 S.E. Federal Hwy.
Stuart, FL 33497
(800) 330-3344
(800) 223-8208

Rosalyn Martial Art Supplies
6450 Hillsborough Ave. W.
Tampa, FL 33634
(813) 884-3066

GEORGIA

Defense Arts
Pine Tree Plaza
5269-5 Buford Hwy.
Doraville, GA 30340

Defense Arts
1345 Morrow Ind. Blvd.
Morrow, GA 30360

Defense Arts
Belmont Village
1026-4 Cherokee Rd.
Smyrna, GA 30080

HAWAII

Lee Supply Shop
851 Leilani St.
Hilo, HI 96720
(808) 935-0914

Golden Fist Enterprises
1007 Dillingham Blvd., Rm. 201
Honolulu, HI 96817

Hawaii Martial Arts Supply
102 N. King St.
Honolulu, HI 96817

IDAHO

Jon's Karate Studio
2212 Main St.
Boise, ID 83501

ILLINOIS

Casey's Sport Co.
7601 S. Cicero Ave.
Chicago, IL 60652

Choi Brothers
4149 W. Montrose
Chicago, IL 60641
(312) 282-9797

East West Markets Exchange
5533 North Broadway
Chicago, IL 60640
(312) 878-7711

KC Sports Co.
433 E. 47th St.
Chicago, IL 60653

Lee's Martial Arts Supplies
3505 N. Elston Ave.
Chicago, IL 60618

Lions Oriental Martial Arts Supply
3505 North Elston Ave.
Chicago, IL 60618
(800) 582-5466

Soo Kim Martial Arts Supply
1207 W. Main St.
Peoria, IL 61606

INDIANA

Sampan Oriental Imports
202 Ash St.
Utica, IN 47130
(800) 284-8499

IOWA

TKD Enterprises
P.O. Box 217
Davenport, IA 52805
(319) 355-5452
(800) 388-5966

Kim's Martial Arts Supplies
3407 Glenn Ave.
Sioux City, IA 51106
(712) 174-7135

KANSAS

Ringside Products
P.O. Box 14171
Lenexa, KS 66215
(800) 527-2831

C & S Co.
10816-A W. 105th St.
Overland Park, KS 66214

Kansas City Fire Dragon
7711 W. 81st St.
Overland Park, KS 66204

Martial Arts Unlimited
628A So. Kansas
Topeka, KS 66603

KENTUCKY

Dragon Enterprises
1533 Eastland Parkway, #9
Lexington, KY 40505

A-1 Martial Arts Supplies
7406 Preston Hwy.
Louisville, KY 70219
(502) 968-3373

LOUISIANA

J. Ehara International
4735 Sanford St.
Metairie, LA 70002

Pak's Karate & Supplies
1936 Gause Blvd.
Slidell, LA 70461
(504) 641-1365

MARYLAND

Tompkins Karate Association
2334 University Blvd.
East Adelphi, MD 20783

The Kiyota Co.
2326 N. Charles St.
Baltimore, MD 21218
(410) 366-8275
(800) 783-2232
(410) 366-3540 (Fax)

Crofton Martial Arts
1713 Aberdeen Court
Crofton, MD 21114

TKA Gladiator Sports
15904 LuAnne Dr.
Gaithersburg, MD 20877

The Ninja Store
10051 N. 2nd St.
Laurel, MD 20707
(301) 953-3845

Flying Dragon Imports
11226 Georgia Ave.
Wheaton, MA 20902
(301) 946-0462

MASSACHUSETTS

Chinese-American Co.
81-83 Harrison Ave.
Boston, MA 02111

Bak Lee Tat
Central Square
566 Massachusetts Ave.
Cambridge, MA 02139

Martial Arts Supply of Everett
940 Broadway
Everett, MA 02149

Martial Arts Supply
470 Main St.
Woburn, MA 01801

MICHIGAN

Kim's Sports-Martial Arts Supplies
406 E. Liberty St.
Ann Arbor, MI 48104
(313) 996-2414

Tigron Martial Arts Supplies
22618 Gratoit Ave.
East Detroit, MI 48021
(800) 451-9382

Kwon
P.O. Box 888313
Grand Rapids, MI 49588
(616) 940-8889
(800) 968-5944
(616) 940-3004 (Fax)

Golden Pagoda Martial Arts
2712 N. Franklin Ave.
Flint, MI 48506

Warrior Martial Arts Supply
16231 Woodward
Highland Park, MI 48203

Bushido Martial Arts Supplies
2415 N. Michigan
Saginaw, MI 48602

Lots of Nichols
34904 Michigan Ave.
Wayne, MI 48184
(313) 728-1313

MINNESOTA

Iai Supply
2050 Marshall Ave.
St. Paul, MN 55104
(612) 647-6987

The Karate Chop
779 7th St.
St. Paul, MN 55106

MISSOURI

Chin's Imports
3240 S. Grand Blvd.
St. Louis, MO 63118

Gateway Oriental Supply
8503 Natural Bridge
St. Louis, MO 63121

C & S Co.
6821-B Wildwood Dr.
Raytown, MO 64133

Sung Chae Kim
1437 S. Glenstone
Springfield, MO 60804

Yong Cho Martial Arts
202 E. Manchester Rd.
Winchester, MO 63011

MONTANA

Jade Dragon Martial Arts Supplies
23031/2 10th Ave. S.
Great Falls, MT 59405
(406) 452-7283

NEBRASKA

Japan Karate & Oriental Weapons
7350 Maple St.
Omaha, NE 68134

Omaha Martial Arts Supply
909 South 27th St.
Omaha, NE 68105
(402) 346-7952

Shogun Martial Arts Supply
2040 N. 72nd St.
Omaha, NE 68144

NEVADA

All Martial Arts Supplies
1814 E. Charleston
Las Vegas, NV 89104

All Martial Arts Supplies
5217 W. Charleston
Las Vegas, NV 89104

Dragon Spring
1707 S. Wells Ave.
Reno, NV 89502

NEW JERSEY

New Orient Supplies
511 Main St.
Avon, NJ 07717

Four Dragons Martial Arts
Supplies
1819 Woodbridge Ave.
Edison, NJ 08817
(201) 819-8396

KAM Industries
11 Ackerman Ave.
Emerson, NJ 07630
(201) 265-4847

Seven & Seven Trading Co.
P.O. Box 1748
Englewood Cliffs, NJ 07632
(201) 944-1450

Dolan's Sports
26 Highway 547
P.O. Box 26
No. 26 Squankumn Hwy.
Farmingdale, NJ 07727
(201) 938-6656

Martial Arts Supplies
405 Black Horse Pike
Haddon Heights, NJ 08035
(609) 547-5445
(609) 931-8467 (Fax)

Champion Martial Arts Supplies
2824 Kennedy Blvd.
Jersey City, NJ 07306
(201) 659-8291

Eagles Proud Products
614 Bergen Blvd.
Ridgefield, NJ 07657
(201) 943-2121
(201) 943-5445 (Fax)

Ninja World
516 Landis Ave.
Vineland, NJ 08360
(609) 691-2544; (609) 692-1143

Wing Chun Supplies
P.O. Box 410
Wrightstown, NJ 08562
(609) 724-9484

NEW MEXICO

Chinese Cultural Center
3015 Central N.E.
Albuquerque, NM 87106

Shorin-Ryu Karate
533 Louisiana Ave.
Albuquerque, NM 87108

NEW YORK

Kinji San Martial Arts Supplies
3010 Avenue M
Brooklyn, NY 11210
(718) 338-0529

G. Pacillo Co.
P.O. Box 1643
1390 Hertel Ave.
Buffalo, NY 14216
(716) 873-4333

S & P of New York Budo
6049 Transit Rd.
P.O. Box 2
Depew, NY 14043
(716) 681-7911

S & J Martial Arts Supplies
2590 Hempstead Turnpike
East Meadow, NY 11554
(516) 579-2270

S & J Martial Art Supplies
135-02 Roosevelt Ave.
Flushing, NY 11355

East Coast Martial Arts Supply
432 Commerce St.
Hawthorne, NY 10532
(914) 769-7804

Dragon-Tiger Kung-Fu Center
1265 W. Broadway
Hewlett, NY 11557

BLT Supplies
35-01 Queens Blvd.
Long Island City, NY 11101
(718) 392-5671
(718) 392-5705 (Fax)

Martial Arts Warehouse
120 Lake Ave. S., Suite 15
Nesconset, NY 11767
(516) 265-1555

Ba La Far
89-57B 165th St.
New York, NY 11432

Bok Lei Tat
213 Canal St.
New York, NY 10013
(212) 226-1703

Butokukai
53 W. 72nd St.
New York, NY 10023

Chinatown Trading Co.
28 Pell St.
New York, NY 10013

Eastern Karate Center
1487 First Ave.
New York, NY 10021

Honda Associates
61 West 23rd St.
New York, NY 10010
(212) 620-4050
(800) 872-6969
(800) 989-7929 (Fax)

Master, Inc.
1250 Broadway, Suite 3000
New York, NY 10001
(212) 868-1919
(212) 629-0975 (Fax)

Shaolin Mountain
1 Penn Plaza, Ste. 100
New York, NY 10119
(212) 868-1121, Ext. 103
(800) 348-0500

Shorei-Kan USA Hdqtrs.
87 5th Ave.
New York, NY 10003

Contact Sports
167 S. Service Rd.
Plainview, NY 11803

Hokkaido Karate
12 Tom Miller Rd.
Plattsburg, NY 12901

Emporium World of Martial Arts
856 Portion Rd.
Ronkonkoma, NY 11779
(516) 471-4437

Three Dragons
G.P.O. Box 948
Staten Island, NY 10314

S & J Martial Arts Supplies
219-10 S. Conduit Ave.
Springfield Gardens, NY 11413
(718) 978-9797

NORTH CAROLINA

Karate Korner
P.O. Box 30156
Charlotte, NC 28230
(704) 399-4400
(800) 843-5236

J & M Martial Arts Supplies
417 S. Bragg Blvd.
Spring Lake, NC 28390
(919) 497-3942

OHIO

Ahn's Martial Arts Supply
7606 Reading Rd.
Cincinnati, OH 45237

Wolverine Brand Judo-Karate
4179 Pearl Rd.
Cleveland, OH 44109

Monkey's Retreat
2400 N. High St.
Columbus, OH 43202

Hess's Martial Arts
3011/2 W. State
Fremont, OH 44035

North Coast Martial Arts Supply
7667 Mentor Ave.
Lowe Level
Mentor, OH 44060
(216) 951-0463

High Kick Martial Arts Supplies
877 Walnut St.
Milville, OH 45013

Hess's Martial Arts
634½ Hancock St.
Sandusky, OH 44870

OKLAHOMA

Century Martial Arts Supply
1705 National Blvd.
Midwest City, OK 73110

(405) 732-2226
(800) 626-2787
(800) 633-3996 (Canada)
(405) 737-8954 (Fax)

OREGON

The Karate Chop
2495 Williamette St.
Eugene, OR 97405

Gala Enterprises
P.O. Box 1022
McMinnville, OR 97128

PENNSYLVANIA

Amkor Martial Arts Supplies
255 Concord Rd.
Aston, PA 19014

WKI Martial Arts
529 S. Clewell St.
Bethlehem, PA 18015

Royal Martial Arts Supplies
2605 Peach St.
Erie, PA 16508
(814) 454-2774

Asian World of Martial Arts
917-21 Arch St.
Philadelphia, PA 19107
(215) 925-1161
(800) 345-2962

Universal Trading
265 Atwood St.
Pittsburgh, PA 15213

Tram Martial Arts Supplies
1502 Westchester Pike
Westchester, PA 19382

Brodart
500 Arch St.
Williamsport, PA 17701

RHODE ISLAND

New England Tae Kwon Do Ctr.
350 Dyer Ave.
Cranston, RI 02920
(401) 943-9136

Ninja World
6964-A Post Rd.
North Kensington, RI 02852
(401) 884-2992

Hong's Tae Kwon Do
180 Mathewson St.
Providence, RI 02903
(401) 273-6190

Ninja World
16 High St.
Westerly, RI 02891
(401) 596-8870

Ninja World
1703 Warwick Ave.
Warwick, RI 02888
(401) 732-3777

TENNESSEE

Samurai Shop
119 38th Ave. N.
Ashville, TN 37209

Dach Oriental Imports
3011 Austin Peay Hwy.
Memphis, TN 38128
(901) 377-3770

TEXAS

Riding's Martial Arts Co.
205 N. Velasco
Angleton, TX 77515

Lang Son Traders
1815 E. Park Row
Arlington, TX 76010

Chinese Martial Arts
80 Flag Lake Rd.
Clute, TX 77531

Texas Martial Arts & Supplies
5435 E. Grand Ave.
Dallas, TX 75223

American Karate Club
2309 Holly Dr.
Dickinson, TX 77539

Tejas Sports
702 W. Wheatland
Duncanville, TX 75116
(214) 296-2228

S.W. Martial Arts Equipment
7930 W. Hwy. 80
Fort Worth, TX 76116

Beijing Imports
9111 Jackwood St.
Houston, TX 77036
(713) 771-8828

Harmon's Survival & Combat
   Supplies
7655 Park Pl.
Houston, TX 77087

Victor Sports
1731 Blalock
Houston, TX 77080

Victor Sports
2023 S. Shepherd
Houston, TX 77019

Wang's Martial Art & Supplies
7211 FM 1960, #270
Humble, TX 77338
(713) 446-4456

Neal's Martial Arts
2707 Strawberry
Pasadena, TX 77502

World Martial Arts Supplies
1974 Nantucket
Richardson, TX 75080
(214) 783-1437

UTAH

O.K. Martial Arts Supply
153 E. 4370 So.
Murray, UT 84107
(801) 262-1785

Utah Valley Martial Arts
24 N. University Ave.
Provo, UT 84601

Accel Martial Arts Supply
171 E. 300 South
Salt Lake City, UT 84111

Asian Martial Arts Supplies
544 S. State St.
Salt Lake City, UT 84101

Martial Arts Supply Co.
423 South at 235 West
Salt Lake City, UT 84101

VIRGINIA

ASAP Martial Art Supply
3019 N. Claredon Blvd.
Arlington, VA 22001
(703) 841-1977

Dragon Supply House
P.O. Box 7115
Charlottesville, VA 22906
(804) 973-7858

Flying Dragon Imports
3853-A Pickett Rd.
Fairfax, VA 22031
(703) 764-0770

Chinatown Import Co.
428 Granby St.
Norfolk, VA 23510

Dong's Tae Kwon Do
8109 W. Broad St.
Richmond, VA 23229
(804) 747-6166

Bushido Martial Arts
556 Garrisonville Rd., Unit 2A
Stafford, VA 22554
(703) 720-3412

WASHINGTON

All Martial Arts Supplies
29007 Pacific Hwy. So.
Federal Way, WA 98003

New World Martial Arts Supplies
5622 Pacific Ave.
Lacey, WA 98503

CSI Productions
16212 Bothell-Everett Hwy., #F307
Mill Creek, WA 98012
(800) 755-8862

Seattle Martial Arts Equipment
688 S. King St.
Seattle, WA 98104

Yun's Martial Arts
4341/2 University Way N.E.
Seattle, WA 98105
(206) 771-9557

Rice's Surplus & More
8606 A.E. Mill Plain Blvd.
Vancouver, WA 98664

WEST VIRGINIA

White Eagle
397 Netherlands Ave.

Westover, WV 26502
(304) 296-2966

WISCONSIN

Oriental Arts Supply
815 Stewart St.
Madison, WI 53713

Judo-Karate International
5812 Fond du Lac
Milwaukee, WI 53218

Kim Lee Imports
527 W. Wisconsin Ave.
Milwaukee, WI 53203

Duk Kwan Yun Tae Kwon Do
3947 S. 27th St.
Milwaukee, WI 53221

Hong's Tae Kwon Do
7701 W. Greensfield Ave.
West Allis, WI 53214

WALES

Balan Sports
132 Osbourne Rd.
Pontypool, Gwent NP4 6LT
Wales
(041) 332-0386

CHAPTER 22

SPECIALTY SUPPLIERS

Companies that specialize in just one product, like safety equipment, for instance, appear in this chapter. Divided into 20 categories, here you will find 661 specialty shops and suppliers of exclusive lines and types of products in 28 countries.

There are many one-shot book publishers and videotape producers that are *not* included in this directory. I have tried to include only those who have produced two or more books or videotapes. Some, it must be noted, market materials devoted to a specific martial art or style.

How to use this information: Looking for a local sup-

ply company, or the largest in a particular country? Shopping for an exotic product not carried at your local supplier? Interested in foreign products you can't get at home? Have a product you want to promote or distribute?

FORMAT

All listings appear in alphabetical order, first by country, then by state and, finally, by city. Some foreign countries, like Australia, appear by province, and then by city.

APPAREL/CLOTHING/ UNIFORMS

ARGENTINA

Koryo
Lavalle 2641, 6 Piso
Cap. Federal (1052)
Argentina
961-6356

AUSTRALIA

Taipan
12 Grove St.
Bondi, New South Wales 2026
Australia
(02) 389-5638

Taipan
c/o Fitness World
Shop 7, Westlane Arcade

Darwin, Northern Territory 5790
Australia
(08) 981-7331

Taipan
217 High St.
Northcote, Victoria 3070
Australia
(03) 486-2311
(03) 482-3104 (Fax)

Muscle Corporation Pty.
67 Hope St.
Brunswick, Victoria 3056
Australia

BRAZIL

Shizen
Rua Dona Primitiva Vianco, 351 e
343 A.
Osasco/SP, CEP 06010
Brazil
(011) 703-0501

Hachiman Industria e Comercio
Ltda.
Rua Cesar Guimaraes, 39
São Paulo/SP, CEP 01545
Brazil
(011) 63-6139; (011) 215-6404

Dojo
Rua Francisco Marinho, 232
Casa Verde, São Paulo/SP, CEP
02523
Brazil
(011) 858-6725; (011) 265-1552

Bonotto
Rua Gradau, 297
Vila Prudente, São Paulo, CEP
03201-010
Brazil
(011) 272-0657

Meikyo
Rua Gustavo da Silveira, 58
São Paulo/SP, CEP 04376-000
Brazil
(011) 563-6664

CANADA

DNS Inter.
P.O. Box 46065
6650 Roblin Blvd.
Winnipeg, Manitoba, Canada R3R
   3S3
(204) 895-2042 (Phone & Fax)

ENGLAND

Rema Leisure
180-182 Fazeley St.
Digbeth, Birmingham B55 SE
England
(021) 766-8299

Leeds Martial Arts
60 North St.

Leeds LS2 7PN
England
(0532) 426346

Meijin
141 Goldhawk Rd.
Shepherd's Bush
London W12 8EN
England
(081) 749-9506; (081) 749-9070

Corriebest
Bradley House, 33 Dale St.
Manchester M1 2A
England
(061) 236-1919

Makoto
77, The Dale

Widley
Portsmouth, Hants PO7 5DD
England

TL Productions
2 Wisbech Rd., Outwell
Nr. Wisbech, W. Norfolk PE14 8PA
England
(0945) 772490

FRANCE

Body Trading
B.P. 13
66700 Argeles-Sur-Mer
France
68.82.02.85

S.E.K.
94851 Ivry Cedex
France
(1) 46.72.59.59
(1) 46.58.63.18 (Fax)

GERMANY

Imex Sport-Artikel
Theordor-Fontane-Strasse 49
7410 Reutlingen
Germany
07121 / 34162

SPAIN

Flash Sport
Ruben Dario, 8 bjos.
La Morera, Badalona
Spain
(93) 383-56-39
(93) 383-56-66 (Fax)

SWEDEN

Talets Kampsportsklader
Krukmakargatan 3
11651 Stockholm
Sweden
(08) 720-6890
(08) 720-6960

UNITED STATES

Dragonmaster
1832 S. Marengo Ave., #41
Alhambra, CA 91803
(213) 265-0201

Trading cards, one of the most unusual products, from Martial Arts Masters, Ltd.

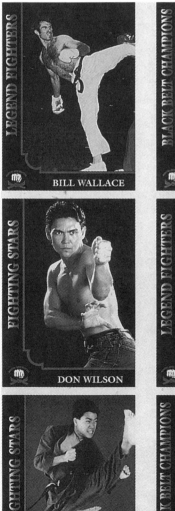

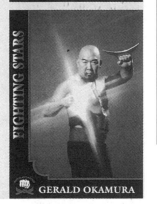

Kamikaze USA
227 N. Fenimore Ave.
Azusa, CA 91702
(818) 334-7009
(818) 915-4715 (Fax)

MG Sportswear
3435 East Home
Fresno, CA 93703
(209) 237-4417

Taekwondo Tees
P.O. Box 270545
San Diego, CA 92128

Excel International Co.
5746 Geary Blvd.
San Francisco, CA 94121
(415) 751-8890
(800) 825-5266

David Wagner
P.O. Box 123
San Leandro, CA 94577

Otomix
1548 18th St.
Santa Monica, CA 90404
(310) 449-1802
(800) 597-5425
(310) 277-0970 (Fax)

Platinum Everywear
1754 Lincoln Blvd.
Santa Monica, CA 90404
(800) 669-0991
(310) 396-5135 (Fax)

Jet Connection
The Jet Center
14540 Friar St.
Van Nuys, CA 91401
(813) 780-6774

CHI
11626 N. Kendall Dr.
Miami, FL 33176
(305) 595-8007

2001 Sales
P.O. Box 1310
Miami, FL 33265
(305) 221-8866

AB & B T-Shirts
P.O. Box 8661
Port St. Lucie, FL 34985

Chi Design
482 Fairfield Way
Evans, GA 30809

Southeastern Martial Arts
7058 Hodgson Memorial Dr.
Savannah, GA 31406
(912) 354-8686

Coastal Graphlex
60 Ocean Blvd.
St. Simons Island, GA 31522

Karate Casuals
245 N. Bridge
St. Anthony, ID 83445
(208) 624-3115

Andover Martial Arts
P.O. Box 549
Andover, KS 67002
(316) 733-5146

Kamikaze USA
7700 Read Blvd., #3
New Orleans, LA 70127
(504) 243-2802
(504) 243-2803 (Fax)

Stance
71 Lewiston St.
Brockton, MA 02402

Watson Enterprises
P.O. Box 642
Marshfield, MA 02050

American Martial Arts
19 Sixth Rd.
Woburn, MA 01801
(617) 933-8789
(800) 888-1121

Jhoon Rhee Sports
9000 Mendenhall Ct.
Columbia, MD 21045
(202) 872-1000
(800) 247-2467

AMK Distributors
P.O. Box 554
Hibbing, MN 55746

Ninjaman Activewear
P.O. Box 20383
Minneapolis, MN 55420

A.T. Patch Co.
P.O. Box 682, Rm. 141
Littleton, NH 03561
(603) 444-3423

Keri Enterprises
P.O. Box 150
Pompton Plains, NJ 07444

Philoso-Tees
P.O. Box 28P
Toms River, NJ 08754
(908) 929-0588

Yanagi Martial Arts
425 Conklin St.
Farmingdale, NY 11735

Yan Wah Co.
71-05 60th Lane
Ridgewood, Queens, NY 11385
(718) 456-8850

Team USA
7319-A Six Forks Rd.
Raleigh, NC 27615

Patterns, Inc.
8501 E. Reno, #6
Midwest City, OK 73110

Flying Side Sportswear
9 Highland Ave.
Wakefield, RI 02879
(401) 789-4290

Magic Martial Arts
140 N. Stevens, Ste. 300
El Paso, TX 79905
(915) 532-2289

Kamikaze USA
8318 Edgemoore
Houston, TX 77036
(713) 265-3035

Sport It
7 Woodall Dr.
Hampton, VA 23666
(804) 766-1082

Dragon International
12310 Hwy. 99 S., Unit 106
Everett, WA 98204
(206) 745-5176
(800) 535-7573
(206) 514-0197 (Fax)

Karate Graphics
P.O. Box 13604
Wauwatosa, WI 53213

ARTISTIC RENDERINGS

UNITED STATES

Action Portrait Studios
13931 Fox Hollow Dr.
Novelty, OH 44072
(216) 338-3409

BELTS (CHAMPIONSHIP KICKBOXING)

Milk and Gym
18, rue du dr. Roux
91160 Longjumeau
France
(1) 60.47.15.65 (Phone & Fax)

BOOK DEALERS

ARGENTINA

Sensei Book Club
Pasteur 133 1oD (1028) BS.
AS. Argentina
51-0746

AUSTRALIA

Blitz Book & Video Vault
G.P.O. Box 2064S
Melbourne, Victoria 3001
Australia

Book & Film Services
P.O. Box 226
Artarmon 2064, New South Wales
Australia
(02) 439-6155

CANADA

ALBERTA

Apple Books
Westbrook Mall
1200 37th S.W.
Calgary, Alberta, Canada T3C 1S2

Audrey Books
10702 Jasper Ave.
Edmonton, Alberta, Canada

BRITISH COLUMBIA

Griffin Books
587 Johnson St.
Victoria, B.C., Canada V8W 1M2

Sophia Bookstore
725 Nelson St.
Vancouver, B.C., Canada

MANITOBA

Candlewood Books
Brandon Shoppers Mall
Brandon, Manitoba, Canada R7A 5C5

CHINESE TAIPEI

Cave's Books
103 Chung Shan N. Rd.
Sec. 2, Taipei

DENMARK

CHR Steinbach
Claus Storm Pallesen
Vesterbrogad 19
1620 Copenhagen V
Denmark

ENGLAND

Another World
23 Silver St.
Leicester, England

Atoz Book Centre
3 Macclesfield St.
London W1V 7LB
England

Fighting Arts International Book
    Club
P.O. Box 26
Birkenhead, Merseyside L43 4YQ
England
(051) 652-3998

Hand Picked Books
40 Voltaire Rd.
London SW4 6DH
England

Sakura Publications
P.O. Box 18
Ashtead, Souttey, London
England

Fantasy World
10 Market Square Arcade
Hanley, Stoke-on-Trent, Staffs
England
(0782) 279294

Shodan U.K.
54 George St.
Brighton, East Sussex BN2 2LJ
England
(0273) 698809
(0273) 207965 (Fax)

FRANCE

Chiron
40, rue de Seine
75006 Paris
France
43.26.47.56

GERMANY

Wu Shu Verlag
Kantstrasse 6
2448 Burg/Fehmarn
(04371) 4581

GREECE

G.C. Eleftheroudakis
SA 4 Nikis St.
Athens, Greece

HOLLAND: SEE NETHERLANDS

HONG KONG

Hong Kong Book Centre
25 Des Voeux Rd. C.
Hong Kong

Swindon Books
13-15 Lock Rd.
Tsimshatsui, Kowloon
Hong Kong

INDIA

Wilco Publishing
33 Ropewalk Lane
Fort Bombay 400 023
India

ITALY

American Bookstore
Via Camperino 16
Milano 20123
Italy

Sport Promotion
Via Natale Battaglia 27
Milano
Italy
02/285-6994

Ulrico Hoepoli Booksellers
Via Lurico Hoepoli
Milano, Italy

JAPAN

West Book & Trading
5-14 Mizutani 3-Chome
Higashiku, Fukuoka
Japan

Sanseido Book Store
1-1 Jimbocho, Kanda
Chiyoda-ku, Tokyo 101
Japan

MALAYSIA

Popular Book Co.
SDN BHD No. 34 Jalan Hang
   Lekur
5000 Kuala Lumpur
Malaysia

University Book Store
34 Jalan Lumut
Kuala Lumpur, Malaysia

NETHERLANDS

Wodan Books
Hembrugstraat 13
1013 WV Amsterdam
Netherlands

Zendokan Book Service
Antwoordnummer 277
2000 VB Haarlem
Netherlands

Lankamp and Brinkman B.V.
Spiegelgracht 19
Netherlands

NORWAY

Chi Mobech
Younstorget 3
Oslo 1, Norway

PHILIPPINES

Alex Squadron Shoppe
28 Chinatown
Greenhis, San Juan
Philippines

SINGAPORE

Popular Book Co.
47-67A Bras
Basah Complex 0718
Singapore

Graham Brash
36-C Prinsep St. 0718
Singapore

UNITED STATES

ALASKA

Lin's International Gifts
Country Village Mall
Benson & Sewart
Anchorage, AK 99503

Lin's Oriental Imports
University Center
3801 Old Seward Hwy.
Anchorage, AK 99503

ARIZONA

Royal Book Store
2340 N. 32nd St.
Phoenix, AZ 85008

E & E Bookmark
4765 E. Speedway
Tucson, AZ 85712

CALIFORNIA

Hyun Kimm
34177 Fremont Blvd.
Fremont, CA 94555
(510) 795-1007

Fresno Bookland
4225 E. Shields
Fresno, CA 93746

Amerasia Book Store
338 E. 2nd St.
Los Angeles, CA 90012

Bodhi Tree Bookstore
8585 Melrose Ave.
Los Angeles, CA 90069

Books Nippon
532 W. 6th St.
Los Angeles, CA 90014

Chew Yuen Co.
459 Ginling Way
Los Angeles, CA 90012

King's Gift Shop
504 Chung King Ct.
Los Angeles, CA 90012

Kinokuniya
110 S. Los Angeles St., Ste. 12
Los Angeles, CA 90012

Li Min Books
969 Hill St.
Los Angeles, CA 90012

Kwang Sik Myung
P.O. Box 15523
Los Angeles, CA 90015

Tower Books #28
630 San Antonio
Mountain View, CA 94040

Books As You Like It
1553-C Novato Blvd.
Novato, CA 94947

Oriental Bookstore
630 E. Colorado Blvd.
Pasadena, CA 91101

Silky Way
1226 Hilltop Mall Rd.
Richmond, CA 94806

Beers Book Center
1406 "J" St.
Sacramento, CA 95814

Tower Books
2538 Watt Ave.
Sacramento, CA 95821

Tower Books #12
1600 Broadway
Sacramento, CA 95818

Clairmont Books
4711 Clairemont Square
San Diego, CA 92117

Harcourt, Brace, Jovanovich Books
555 "A" St.
San Diego, CA 92107

Brothers Trading Co.
1848 29th Ave.
San Francisco, CA 94122
(415) 665-9642

China Books & Periodicals
125 5th Ave.
San Francisco, CA 94110
(415) 282-2994

Eastwind Books & Arts
1435-A Stockton St.
San Francisco, CA 94133

Everybody's Bookstore
17 Brenham Pl.
San Francisco, CA 94108

Kinokuniya
Japan Center (West Bldg.)
1581 Webster St.
San Francisco, CA 94115

Logos Books & Records
1117 Pacific Ave.
Santa Cruz, CA 95060

Heritage Books
52 S. Washington St.
Sonora, CA 95370

Avenue Books
2341 Pacific Ave.
Stockton, CA 95204

Harding Way News
113 W. Harding Way
Stockton, CA 95204

Dragon Books
P.O. Box 6039
Thousand Oaks, CA 91359
(818) 889-3856
(818) 889-3890 (Fax)

Book Mark
1388 N. Moorpark Rd.
Thousand Oaks, CA 91360

Asia Book Store
2100 W. Redondo Beach Blvd.
Torrance, CA 90504

Dragon Publishing Corp.
3718 River Farm Dr.
Westlake Village, CA 91361

COLORADO

Pearl of the Orient
3245 Dillon Dr.
Pueblo, CO 81008

CONNECTICUT

Key Book Service
425 Asylum St.
Bridgeport, CT 06610

DELAWARE

Bookland
6 Bran Mar Plaza
Wilmington, DE 19810

DISTRICT OF COLUMBIA

Da Hsin Co.
811 7th St., N.W.
Washington, DC 20001

Hong Kong Co.
620 H St., N.W.
Washington, DC 20001

Nam Shan Co.
1119 H St., N.W.
Washington, DC 20005

Jhoon Rhee Sports
2000 L St., N.W.
Washington, DC 20036

FLORIDA

Bookworks
6935 Red Rd.
Coral Gables, FL 33143

Hong Kong Gallery
72 Miracle Mile
Coral Gables, FL 33134

Exotica Imports
5315 Firestone Rd.
Jacksonville, FL 32244

Haslam's Book Store
2025 Central Ave.
St. Petersburg, FL 33713
(813) 822-8616

Hin Tsong Books
5907 54th Ave. N.
St. Petersburg, FL 33709

GEORGIA

Tapes 'N Things
4376 Victory
Columbus, GA 31903

HAWAII

K.C. Co.
98-027 Hekaha St.
Bldg. #3, Unit #6
Aiea, HI 96701

Hakubundo Book Co.
100 N. Beretania St.
Honolulu, HI 96817

King Fort Magazine Shop
1122 Fort St. Mall
Honolulu, HI 96813

IDAHO

Book Shop
98 Main St.
Boise, ID 83702

Book & Game Co.
1804 E. 19th
Lewiston, ID 83501

ILLINOIS

China Books & Periodicals
174 W. Randolph St.
Chicago, IL 60601

Redig's Randolph Books
5 W. Randolph St.
Chicago, IL 60601

Van Boskirk's
7334 S. Halsted St.
Chicago, IL 60621

Peking Book House
1520 Sherman Ave.
Evanston, IL 60201

Books, Etc.
403 Main St.
Marion, IL 62959

Andich Bros. News Co.
2115 4th Ave.
Rock Island, IL 61201

Scholarly Book Center
3828 Hawthorn Court
Waukegan, IL 60087

INDIANA

Book Corner
100 N. Walnut
Indianapolis, IN 47401

Denco of Indy
731 E. Troy Ave.
Indianapolis, IN 46203

Ho Tai Oriental
4 N. Pennsylvania St.
Indianapolis, IN 46204

Oriental Gifts
Washington Square, #646
Indianapolis, IN 46229

Oriental World
710 Promenade
Richmond, IN 47374

IOWA

Oriental Gifts & Imports
1914 Brady St.
Davenport, IA 52803

KANSAS

Crossroads
304 N. Main
Hutchinson, KS 67501

The Book Barn
410 Delaware
Leavenworth, KS 66048

Ryukyu Imports
Box 535
Olathe, KS 66061
(913) 384-3345

Budo Books & Videos
P.O. Box 4727
Overland Park, KS 66204

MAINE

Bookland
Auburn Mall
Auburn, ME 04210

Bookland
Bath Shopping Center
Bath, ME 04011

Bookland
5 Point Shopping Center
Biddeford, ME 04005

Bookland
Cook's Corner Shop. Ctr.
Brunswick, ME 04011

Bookland
Promenade Mall
Lewiston, ME 04240

Bookland
Windham Mall
N. Windham, ME 04062

Bookland Downtown
102 Maine Savings Pl.
Portland, ME 04101

Bookland
Saco Valley Shopping Ctr.
Saco, ME 04072

Bookland
Mall Plaza
S. Portland, ME 04106

MARYLAND

Aquarian Age Bookstore
813 N. Charles St.
Baltimore, MD 21201

Gladiator Sports & Awards
15904 Luanne Dr.
Gaithersburg, MD 20877

MASSACHUSETTS

Book Emporium
452 Great Rd.
Acton, MA 01720

Chinese American Co.
81-83 Harrison Ave.
Boston, MA 02111

Zuber & Co.
1556 Commonwealth Ave.
Boston, MA 02135

Bushido-Kai Budoya
21 Blandin Ave.
Framingham, MA 01701

Bayberry Books
368 Main St.
Hyannis, MA 02601

Larry's Sales & Service
270 Philips Ave.
New Bedford, MA 02746

A Book Haven
1552 Hancock St.
Quincy, MA 02169

Derby Square Book Store
215 Essex St.
Salem, MA 01970

Ephraim's Book Store
80 Franklin St.
Worcester, MA 01140

MICHIGAN

Book Nook
18690 Ecorse Rd.
Allen Park, MI 48101

Kim Embroidery
307 S. 5th Ave.
Ann Arbor, MI 48104

Middlearth Book Store
761 N. Saginaw St.
Flint, MI 48503

Book Nook
42 S. Monroe St.
Monroe, MI 48161

MINNESOTA

Granada News
15 W. Superior St.
Duluth, MN 55802

People's Books & Crafts
1808 Farwell Ave.
Minneapolis, MN 55403

Shinder's Readmore Bookstore
628 Hennepin Ave.
Minneapolis, MN 55403

Bubbling Well
3728 Avenue North
St. Cloud, MN 56301

Hungry Mind
1648 Grand Ave.
St. Paul, MN 55105

MISSOURI

Metro News Book Store
415 Broadway
Cape Girardeau, MO 63701

Orient
Village Square
59 Old Towne
Hazelwood, MO 63043

Time to Read News
7 W. 12th St.
Kansas City, MO 64105

C & S Co.
6821 Wildwood Dr.
Raytown, MO 64133

MONTANA

Reader's World #2
Holiday Shopping Ctr.
Havre, MT 59501

NEVADA

Sierra Nevada Book Store
P.O. Box 4269
Incline Village, NV 89450

NEW JERSEY

Sadye & Sam's Card Shop
712 Broadway
Bayonne, NJ 07002

Whemen Bros.
Morris County Mall
Ridgedale Ave.
Cedar Knolls, NJ 07927

Autumn Booksellers
1043 Springfield Ave.
Irvington, NJ 07111

Book Beat
122 Main St.
Woodbridge, NJ 07095

World Imports
Woodbridge Center
Woodbridge, NJ 07095

NEW MEXICO

Classic News Agency
129 E. 3rd
Roswell, NM 88201

NEW YORK

Adco International
80-00 Cooper Ave., Bldg. 3
Glendale, NY 11385

Ba-La-Far
89-57B 165th St.
Jamaica, NY 11432

Barnes & Noble Bookstore
206 E. 18th St.
New York, NY 10003

Book Dynamics
836 Broadway
New York, NY 10003

Central News Agency
One World Trade Center, No. 2167
New York, NY 10048

China Books & Periodicals
125 5th Ave.
New York, NY 10013

Coliseum Books
250 W. 57th St., Ste. 715
New York, NY 10019

Japantopia Books
69 W. 10th St.
New York, NY 10011

Kinokuniya Bookstore
10 W. 49th St.
New York, NY 10020

Number One Jewelry & Gift
1545 Broadway
New York, NY 10036

Orienthouse Enterprises
424-426 Broadway
New York, NY 10013

Samuel Weiser
740 Broadway
New York, NY 10003

S.L.T. Corp.
265 W. 42nd St.
New York, NY 10036

Continental Sports
667 Monroe Ave.
Rochester, NY 14604

Yonkers Bookstore
Cross Country
Yonkers, NY 10794

NORTH CAROLINA

East West Gifts
1105 Walnut St.
120 Cary Village Mall
Cary, NC 27511

Carolina News
245 Tillinghast St.
Fayetteville, NC 28302

Tyler's News & Camera Shop
819 Elm St.
Eutaw S/C, Fayetteville, NC 28301

Coins & Stuff
825 N. Main St.
High Point, NC 27260

Cutters Edge
Rt. 2, Box 266 D
Leicaster, NC 28748

Half Price Bookstore
3805 Arendell St.
Moorehead City, NC 28557

Horizon Books
Carmel Commons Shop. Ctr.
7715 Pineville-Matthews Rd.
Pineville, NC 28134

OHIO

Aquarius Bookshop
831 Main St.
Cincinnati, OH 45203

Asia House
313 Prospect Ave.
Cleveland, OH 44115

Eastern Genuines
43 Colonial Arcade
Cleveland, OH 44094

Kay's Books & Magazines
620 Prospect Ave.
Cleveland, OH 44115

Practical Publications
P.O. Box 08591-A
Cleveland, OH 44108

Jammer Books
147 Southland Mall
Columbus, OH 43207

Sidney Newsstand Bookstore
108 N. Main St.
Sidney, OH 45365

Fine Print Books
112 Xenia Towne Square
Xenia, OH 45385

OKLAHOMA

K & S Arms Books
801 Randall Rd.
Edmond, OK 73034

Peace of Mind Bookstore
1401 E. 15th St.
Tulsa, OK 74120

OREGON

Anzen Importers
736 N.E. Union
Portland, OR 97232

Powell's Bookstore
1005 W. Burnside
Portland, OR 97207

PENNSYLVANIA

Valor Sports
800 Streets Run Rd.
Baldwin Borough, PA 15236

Marlo Book Store
2339 Cottman Ave.
Philadelphia, PA 15213

Meridian Book Store
340 South St.
Philadelphia, PA 19147

Robin's Book Store
6 N. 13th St.
Philadelphia, PA 19107

RHODE ISLAND

Kim Lee Oriental Imports
208 Union St.
Providence, RI 02903

TENNESSEE

Gateway Bookstore No. 1
6305 Baum Dr.
Knoxville, TN 37901

TEXAS

ABC Newsstand
331 S. Bowen Rd.
Arlington, TX 76013

The Book People
4006 S. Lamar, Ste. 250
Austin, TX 78704

Grok Books
503B W. 17th
Austin, TX 78701

Chan's Imports
5430 Padre Staples Mall
Corpus Christi, TX 78411

Commerce St. Newsstand
1513 Commerce
Dallas, TX 75201

Royal East
2031 Red Bird Mall
Dallas, TX 73237

Arcade News
201 E. Avenue D
Killeen, TX 76541

Laredo Office World
813 Grant St.
Laredo, TX 78040

The Book Barrel
1819 Troup Hwy.
Tyler, TX 75701

VIRGINIA

Smith Books
5266 Fairfield S/C
Virginia Beach, VA 23464

WASHINGTON

Imprint Bookstore
925 Water St.
Port Townsend, WA 98368

Magus Bookstore
1408 N.E. 42nd
Seattle, WA 98105

WISCONSIN

Book World
30 S. Main St.
Janesville, WI 53545

Pic-a-Book
815 Stewart St.
Madison, WI 53713

WYOMING

Marv's Place
223 W. 16th St.
Cheyenne, WY 82001

WALES

Mona Books
55 Bridge St.
Llangefni, Anglesey, Gwynedd.
Wales
LL77 7PN
(0248) 723-486

BOOK PUBLISHERS

ENGLAND

Asian Publishing
P.O. Box 1142
Slough, Berkshire SL1 3NR
England
(0753) 36465

Ronin Publishing
P.O. Box 26
Birkenhead, Merseyside L43 4YQ
England
(051) 652-3998

Snetter's Book Promotions
("Martial Arts Directory of Clubs")
P.O. Box 125 Snettisham
King's Lynn, Norfolk PE31 7RY
England

FRANCE

Amphora Editions S.A.
14, rue de l'Odeon
75006 Paris
France
(1) 43.26.10.87
(1) 40.46.85.76 (Fax)

C.I.G.
30, rue St. Yves
75014 Paris
France

SEDIREP
44, rue de la Belle-Feuille
92100 Boulogne
France
(1) 46.03.12.46

S.I.A.M.
1, rue du Chateau-d'Eau
75010 Paris
France

Societe Europeenne de Magazines
2, bis rue Mercoeur
75011 Paris
France
(1) 43.48.40.08
(1) 43.48.17.86 (Fax)

GERMANY

Budo Artikel Velte
Postfac 2464
Saalburgstrasse 141
D-6380 Bad Homburg v.d.H.
Germany
061 72/3 60 39
06172/3 58 38 (Fax)

Wu Shu-Verlag
Kantstrasse 6
2448 Burg/Fehmarn
Germany
(04371) 4581

Tao Hirper Verlag
Postfach 1205
7053 Kernen
Germany

ITALY

Advertising Master Publisher
Via Natale Battaglia, 27
20127 Milano
Italy
02/285-6994

JAPAN

Jobido Shuppan
Bunkyo-ku Suido 1-8-2
112 Tokyo
Japan
(03) 814-4351
(03) 814-4355 (Fax)

Kodansha International
2-2, Otowa 1-chome
Bunkyo-ku, Tokyo 112
Japan
(03) 944-6491

Charles H. Tuttle Co.
2-6 Suido 1-Chome
Bunkyo-ku, Tokyo
Japan

Weatherhill Publications
7-6-13 Roppongi
Minato-ku, Tokyo 106
Japan

UNITED STATES

Ohara Publications
24715 Rockefeller
P.O. Box 918
Santa Clarita, CA 91380
(805) 257-4066
(805) 257-3028 (Fax)

Unique Publications
4201 Vanowen Place
Burbank, CA 91505
(818) 845-2656
(800) 332-3330
(818) 845-7761 (Fax)

Hee Il Cho's Taekwondo Center
11304½ Pico Blvd.
Los Angeles, CA 90064
(310) 477-4067
(800) 527-4833
(310) 473-7555 (Fax)

Wayfarer Publications
P.O. Box 26156
Los Angeles, CA 90026
(800) 888-9119

Kuk Sool Won Production Co.
543 Valencia St.
San Francisco, CA 94110
(415) 553-8100; (415) 553-8141

Dragon Books
P.O. Box 6039
Thousand Oaks, CA 91359

USTF Headquarters
6801 W. 117th Ave., #E-5
Broomfield, CO 80020
(303) 466-4963

Paladin Press
P.O. Box 1307
Boulder, CO 80306
(303) 443-7250
(800) 872-4993
(303) 442-8741 (Fax)

Y.K. Kim
1630 E. Colonial Dr.
Orlando, FL 32803
(407) 898-2084

Reece Publications
P.O. Box 1073
Des Moines, IA 50311

Heritage Total Concept Martial
   Arts
148 Marquette St.
La Salle, IL 61301
(Call Waco, Texas, headquarters:)
(817) 776-7929

Universal Taekwondo Association
1207 W. Main
Peoria, IL 61606
(309) 673-2000

Dr. He-Young Kimm
P.O. Box 14891
Andrew Jackson College
Baton Rouge, LA 70808

Chinese Wushu Research Institute
246 Harrison Ave.
Boston, MA 02111
(617) 426-0958

Yang's Martial Arts Association
38 Hyde Park Ave.
Jamaica Plain, MA 02130
(617) 524-8892

Bubbling Well Press
Box 961
St. Cloud, MN 56302

Dragon Door Publications
P.O. Box 4381
St. Paul, MN 55104
(612) 645-0517
(800) 247-6553

Richard Chun Tae Kwon Do
   Center
163 E. 86th St.
New York, NY 10028
(212) 722-2200

Condor Books
351 W. 54th St.
New York, NY 10019
(212) 586-4432

W.H. Smith
112 Madison Ave.
New York, NY 10016
(212) 532-6600

Sports Training Institute
6252 Dark Hollow Rd.
Medford, OR 97501
(503) 535-3188

Tai Pan Martial Arts Publishing Co.
1150-D Richardine
Austin, TX 78721
(512) 422-6959

BUSINESS/ MARKETING SERVICES AND INSTRUCTION

AUSTRALIA

Rod Edwards & Co
(School Insurance)
313 Albert St.
Brunswick 3056, Victoria
Australia
(03) 696-2577

UNITED STATES

American Billing Co.
P.O. 6800
North Little Rock, AR 72116
(800) 622-6290
(501) 758-5469 (Fax)

International Martial Arts
  Management Systems
1619 S. Main St.
Milpitas, CA 95035
(408) 262-6403

KF Funds Company
(800) 875-6101

T.A. Corp.
San Diego, CA
(619) 942-8622;
(619) 530-0033

Words & Co.
243 N. Hwy. 101, Ste. 11
Solana Beach, CA 92075
(619) 259-0218

Amerinational Management
  Services
P.O. Box 149007
Orlando, FL 32814
(407) 895-1996
(800) 275-1600

Scott Smith
(407) 367-7594

Y.K. Kim
1630 E. Colonial Dr.
Orlando, FL 32803
(407) 898-2084

Black Belt Management
John Graden, President
1362 86th Terrace North
St. Petersburg, FL 33702
(813) 578-2012 (Phone & Fax)

Tracy's Business Systems
Al Tracy
P.O. Box 24228
Lexington, KY 40524
(606) 271-5987

Comprehensive Credit
  Management

P.O. Box 10870
Baltimore, MD 21234
(800) 433-5425

Educational Funding Co.
Nick Cokinos, President
5110 Ridgefield Rd., Suite 410
Bethesda, MD 20816
(301) 654-8677
(301) 654-7750 (Fax)

Enrollment Success
5939 John R Rd.
Troy, MI 48098

John Worley
P.O. Box 394
Excelsior, MN 55331
(612) 474-3192

Salt Spring Distributors
P.O. Box 14111
Albuquerque, NM 87191

Teacher's Edge
2 Birchwood Lane
Newburgh, NY 12550

Markel Rhulen Underwriters
  (insurance)
4600 Cox Rd.
Glen Allen, VA 23060
(800) 431-1270, Ext. 526

Athletic Funding of America
P.O. Box 802311
Houston, TX 77280
(800) 444-0807

Jeff Smith
4421 Jon Marr Dr.
Annandale, VA 22003
(703) 750-3999

Jhoon Rhee
World Martial Arts Congress for
  Education
4068 Rosamora Ct.
Arlington, VA 22207
(703) 532-5901

Professional Karate Marketing
645 Oakley Ave.
Lynchburg, VA 24501
(804) 845-2467

International Instructor's Dynamic
  Marketing Management
Byung Kon Cho, President
2960 Allied Dr.
Green Bay, WI
(414) 336-0551

COMPUTER SOFTWARE

UNITED STATES

Dojo Master
14125 Phillips Rd.
Matthews, NC 28105

EMBROIDERY/ EMBLEMS/PATCHES

ENGLAND

Pan Martial Arts
P.O. Box 44
Stevenage, Hertfordshire SG1 4SJ
England
(0438) 315002

J & S Business Services
Hanover Cottage, Hanover St.
Herne Bay, Kent CT6 5RW
England

UNITED STATES

California Hat Pins & Emblems
P.O. Box 292009
Sacramento, CA 95829
(916) 383-4643
(916) 383-2054 (Fax)

HSU
P.O. Box 710187
San Jose, CA 95171
(408) 996-8989
(408) 252-0162 (Fax)

National Designs
P.O. Box 693944E
Miami, FL 33269
(305) 653-9434

Graphic Communication Centre
1810 State St., Suite 3
Bettendorf, IA 52722

Sport Karate Emblems
1929 E. 52nd St.
Indianapolis, IN 46205
(317) 257-1424
(800) 942-5454
(317) 257-1425 (Fax)

Branded Emblem Co.
7920 Foster
Overland Park, KS 66204
(913) 648-7920

Gold Medal
P.O. Box 5523
Hopkins, MN 55343

A.T. Patch Company
Box 305
Littleton, NH 03561
(603) 444-3423

Eosin-Panther
1237 Main Ave.
Clifton, NJ 07011
(201) 546-1066

Medallion Custom Emblems
1406 10th St.
North Bergen, NJ 07047

Stadri
61 James St.
New York, NY 10014
(212) 929-2293

The Martial Art Company
6714 Kingston Pike
Knoxville, TN 37919
(615) 588-0281
(615) 588-3099 (Fax)

WALES

Merit Badges, Inc.
1 Brighton Rd.
Rhyl, Clwyd
Wales
(0745) 343875

EQUIPMENT (SPEED AND POWER MEASUREMENT)

UNITED STATES

Impulse Sports Training Systems
30612 Salem Dr.
Bay Village, OH 44140
(216) 835-5410

Century Martial Arts Supply
1705 National Blvd.
Midwest City, OK 73110
(405) 732-2226
(800) 626-2787
(800) 633-3996 (Canada)
(405) 737-8954 (Fax)

JEWELRY

ENGLAND

A.M. Designer Jewelers
10, Hatton Garden
London E.C.I., England
(01) 405-6031; (01) 441-3835

FRANCE

C.I.G. Arts Martiaux
30, rue Sant-Yves
75014 Paris
France
(1) 42.79.80.03

Societe Europeenne de Magazines
2, bis rue Mercoeur
75011 Paris
France
(1) 43.48.40.08
(1) 43.48.17.86 (Fax)

UNITED STATES

Ancient Circles
P.O. Box 787
Laytonville, CA 95454
(707) 984-8033

Krasner Manufacturing Jewelers
861 Sixth Ave., Suite 711
San Diego, CA 92101
(619) 234-0531

Martial Innovations
1433 Santa Monica Blvd., Suite 336
Santa Monica, CA 90404

Rich M. Creations
P.O. Box 1934
New Port Richey, FL 34656

Artistic Engraving
P.O. Box 998
Southwick, MA 01077
(413) 569-5204

T.R. Hawkinson
P.O. Box 6553
St. Paul, MN 55106

Aikido of Charlotte
9415 Peckham Rye Rd.
Charlotte, NC 28227
(704) 545-8584

Yanagi Martial Arts
425 Conklin St.
Farmingdale, NY 11735
(516) 249-6050
(800) 678-8449

Ronnie Smith Jewelers
37 W. 47th St., #19
New York, NY 10036
(212) 944-2647

C.E. Enterprises
735-A Chestnut St.
Philadelphia, PA 19106
(800) 392-2728

Custom Gold Design
733 Sansom St.
Philadelphia, PA 19106
(215) 925-5636

Song Tae Hong
3230 S. 57th St.
Milwaukee, WI 53219

Park's Martial Art Jewelry
P.O. Box 1973
Waukesha, WI 53187
(414) 549-9300

KICKBOXING EQUIPMENT

FRANCE

Cobop
35, rue du Maine
78500 Sartrouville
France
39.15.16.74
30.86.94.75 (Fax)

MAGAZINES

ARGENTINA

Sensei
(Spanish language)
Pasteur 133 1oD (1028) BS.
AS., Argentina
51-0746

AUSTRALIA

Australasian Fighting Arts
P.O. Box 673
Manley, Sydney, New South Wales
    2095
Australia
(02) 943361

Australasian Taekwondo
P.O. Box 895
Bayswater, Victoria 3153
(03) 720-7488

*Australasian Traditional Martial Arts
    Association*
19 Hefferan St.
Fairfield, Queensland 4103
Australia

Blitz
8/22 Station St.
Bayswater, Victoria 3153
Australia
(03) 720-7488

BRAZIL

Budo (Spanish language)
Rua Serra de Botucatu, 39
Tatuape, São Paulo/SP, CEP 03317
Brazil
(011) 295-6030

Combat Sport (Spanish language)
Ave. Ipiranga, 818, 6 andar
São Paulo/SP, 01040-000
Brazil
(011) 220-0674

Kiai (Spanish language)
Rua Pelotas, 426
São Paulo/SP, CEP 04012
Brazil
(011) 572-4838; (011) 575-3018

Ninja (Spanish language)
Caixa Postal 15613
Tatuape, São Paulo/SP, CEP 03398
Brazil
(011) 294-4074

CHINA

China Sports (English language)
8 Tiyuguan Rd.
Beijing, China
Order through:
China Inter. Book Trading Corp.
(Guoji Shudian)
P.O. Box 399
Beijing, China

ENGLAND

Combat
99 John Bright St.
Birmingham B1 1BE
England

Fighters
Peterson House, Northbank
Berry hill Industrial Estate
Droitwich, Worcs WR9 9BL
England
(0905) 795564
(0905) 795905

Fighting Arts International
P.O. Box 26
Birkenhead, Merseyside L43 4YQ
England
(051) 652-3998

Martial Arts Illustrated
8A, Revenue Chambers
St. Peter's St.
Huddersfield HD1 1DL
England
(048) 443-5011

FRANCE

BF Savate (French language)
25, Bd. des Italiens
75002 Paris
France
(1) 47.42.82.27

Bushido (French language)
25, av. Poincare
75016 Paris
France
47.27.09.22

Karate-Bushido (French language)
2, rue Gobert
75011 Paris
France
(1) 43.48.40.08
(1) 43.48.17.86 (Fax)

Kung Fu Wu Shu (French language)
14, rue Leon Bertrand "Les Iris"
06200 Nice
France
93.72.54.18

Le Magazine def Rings
(French language; 50% kickboxing
    content)
110 bis rue des Moines
75017 Paris
France

GERMANY

*Karate-Budo Journal; Budo
    International*
(German language)
Bergstrasse 18, Postfach 12 08
D-4152 Kempen 3
Germany
0 28 45/8 02 54
0 28 45/8 03 92 (Fax)

Kicksider (German language)
Postfach 1248
6140 Bensheim 1
Germany
(0 62 57) 6 23 33 (Tele. & Fax)

ITALY

*Banzai International; Samurai/
    Bushido*
(Italian language)
Via Natale Battaglia, 27
20127 Milano, Italy
011-392-285-6994
011-392-289-0827

JAPAN

Budo Karate (Japanese language)
Jobido Shuppan Publishing Co.
Bunkyo-ku Suido 1-8-2
112 Tokyo
Japan
(03) 814-4351
(03) 814-4355 (Fax)

KOREA

WTF Taekwondo (English language)
World Taekwon-do Fed.
635, Yuksamdong, Kangnamku
Seoul, Korea 135
82-02-566-2505; 82-02-567-1058
82-02-553-4728 (Fax)

NETHERLANDS

Zendokan (Dutch language)
Postbus 9126
1006 AC Amsterdam
Netherlands
020-195308

POLAND

Czarny Pas (Polish language)
Polish Fed. of Far Eastern Martial
    Arts
ul. Lindleya 14a/18
02-013 Warszawa

Poland
21-26-09

SPAIN

Cinturon Negro (Spanish language)
C/Andres Mellado, 42
28015 Madrid
Spain
543-7543
544-6324 (Fax)

El Budoka (Spanish language)
c/Valencia, 234
08007 Barcelona
Spain
(93) 253-75-06

Dojo
Ferraz, 11
28008 Madrid
Spain
(91) 241-34-00

SWEDEN

The Swedish Fighter International
(Swedish language)
Box 4416
20315 Malmo
Sweden
46-40-23-15-00

THAILAND

The Fighter (Thai language)
Bangkok, Thailand
282-0649

Muay Thai (English language)
Artasia Press Co. Ltd.
G.P.O. Box 1996
Bangkok, Thailand
(662) 234-5360
(662) 235-9328
(662) 236-7242 (Fax)

UNITED STATES

CALIFORNIA

*Inside Karate Magazine;
Inside Kung Fu Magazine;
Inside Tae Kwon Do;
Masters Series*
(Plus special editions)
4201 Van Owen Place
Burbank, CA 91505
(818) 845-2656
(818) 845-7761 (Fax)

Aikido Today
1420 N. Claremont Blvd.
Suite 111-B
Claremont, CA 91711
(909) 624-7770
(909) 398-1840 (Fax)

Judo Journal
P.O. Box 18485
Irvine, CA 92713
(714) 645-1674

T'ai Chi
2601 Silver Ridge Ave.
Los Angeles, CA 90039
(213) 665-7773
(213) 665-1627 (Fax)

Master
P.O. Box 31578
San Francisco, CA 94131

*Black Belt;
Karate/Kung-Fu Illustrated;
Martial Arts Training*
24715 Rockefeller
P.O. Box 918
Santa Clarita, CA 91380
(805) 257-4066
(805) 257-3028 (Fax)

Dragon Times (newspaper)
P.O. Box 6039
Thousand Oaks, CA 91359
(818) 889-3856
(818) 889-3890 (Fax)

FLORIDA

Sport Karate News
P.O. Box 1628
Goldenrod, FL 32733
(407) 671-6878

IOWA

Tae Kwon Do Times
1423 18th St.
Bettendorf, IA 52722
(319) 359-7202
(319) 355-7299 (Fax)

NEW JERSEY

Karate International
P.O. Box 8538
Woodcliff Lakes, NJ 07675
(201) 573-8028

NEW YORK

Sport Karate International
(Formerly *S.M.A.S.H.*; a tabloid)
343 East Fairmount Ave.
Lakewood, NY 14750
(716) 763-1111

OHIO

Karate Profiles
P.O. Box 1187
West Chester, OH 45071
(513) 874-8678

TENNESSEE

Taekwondo World
P.O. Box 898
Yankton, SD 57078
(605) 665-9909

TEXAS

Internal Arts
P.O. Box 1777
Arlington, TX 76004
(800) 223-6984

MATS

AUSTRALIA

Aussie Jigsaw Mats
10 Webster St.
Burwood, Victoria 3125
Australia
(03) 836-1242
(03) 428-2779 (Fax)

ENGLAND

Hit-Man Martial Arts Supplies
Unit 4, Chasewood Park Business
 Centre
Hednesford Rd.
Heath Hayes WS12 5HL
England
(0543) 271109 (Phone & Fax)

Tatami Mat Company
(0298) 71264

GERMANY

Sport Rhode
Postfach 10 22 20
Frankfurter Strasse 121
6072 Dreieich
Germany
06103 / 3 40 75

UNITED STATES

Linkamat System
The Chestnut Group
Box 256L
Newton, MA 02164

Gleie Distributors
881 Colonial Rd.
Franklin Lakes, NJ 07417

Honda Associates
61 W. 23rd St.
New York, NY 10010
(212) 620-4050
(800) 872-6969
(800) 989-7929 (Fax)

Pro-Mat Sales
P.O. Box 12
Greensburg, PA 15601

PROTECTIVE EQUIPMENT

ARGENTINA

Gran-Marc
25 De Mayo 786
5 Piso BS. AS.
Argentina
311-5677 / 5713

BRAZIL

Importacao e Exportacao Ltda.
Rua Peixoto, 175
Aclimacao, São Paulo/SP, CEP
 01543-000
Brazil
(011) 277-1972
(011) 277-1283 (Fax)

ENGLAND

Rema Leisure
180-182 Fazeley St.
Digbeth, Birmingham B55 SE
England
(021) 766-8299

Bellamer Sport
Supersport House
Landsdowne Industrial Estate
Gloucester Rd., Cheltenham
England
(0242) 573851

Giko
681 / 683 Stratford Rd.
Sparkhill, Birmingham B11 4DX
England
(021) 777-7666

Hayashi
58 West St.
Old Market, Bristol BS2 OBL
England
(0272) 555560; (0272) 552002
(0272) 559385 (Fax)

FRANCE

RPS
76, rue du Panorama
77500 Chelles
France
(1) 60.20.56.86
(1) 60.08.48.64 (Fax)

S.L.S. Equipment
51, Bd A. Briand
17208 Royan Cedex
France
46.05.29.55

GERMANY

Top Ten Sportartikel
Hohenzollerndamm 177
D-1000 Berlin 31
Germany
030-860216

Kwon
Rudolf Diesel Strasse 8
8060 Dachau
Germany
08131/1631(33)

Sportimex
J.F. Baer gmbH
Am Deich 42
Postfach 101364
D-2800 Bremen 1
Germany
(0421) 50 08 81/82

Sport Rhode
Postfach 10 22 20
Frankfurter Strasse 121
6072 Dreieich
Germany
06103/3 40 75

ITALY

Vis
16040 S. Salvatore Dei Fieschi
Genova, Italy
270630

JAPAN

Tokyo Budo Shokai
Oki Bldg.
Chuou-ku Tanimachi 5-6-3
557 Osaka
Japan
(06) 764-4678

Asahi World Co.
Dogenzaka 2-20-26
Shibuya-ku, 150 Tokyo
Japan
(03) 477-0770
(03) 476-1826 (Fax)

UNITED STATES

Masterline Co.
26951 Ruether Ave., Unit #E
Canyon Country, CA 91351
(805) 298-2299
(800) 333-1170

Masterline Co.
1200 S. Brand Blvd., #3
Glendale, CA
(818) 547-4522

Tiger Claw
1541 Industry Rd.
San Carlos, CA 94070
(415) 595-3456
(800) 821-5090

K.P. Sporting Goods
1451 Doolittle Dr.
San Leandro, CA 94577
(415) 430-0101
(800) 227-0500

Shihan Imports
27 Tanglewood Dr.
Norwich, CT 06360
(203) 822-1012
(800) 877-2647
(203) 822-1108 (Fax)

Macho Products
2550 Kirby Ave. N.E.
Palm Bay, FL 32905
(407) 729-6137
(800) 327-6812
(407) 768-2598 (Fax)

East West Markets Exchange
5533 North Broadway
Chicago, IL 60640
(312) 878-7711

Sampan Oriental Imports
1402 Eastern Blvd.
Clarksville, IN 47130
(800) 284-8499

S.S.I.
P.O. Box 404
Annapolis, MD 21404
(410) 268-9609

Jhoon Rhee Sports
9000 Mendenhall Ct.
Columbia, MD 21045
(202) 872-1000
(800) 247-2467

Protect Manufacturing
1251 Ferguson Ave.
St. Louis, MO 63133
(800) 325-1652

Masterline Co.
c/o AA Action
3025 Desert Inn Rd., #7
Las Vegas, NV
(702) 733-7788

Impact Martial Arts
336 W. Lacey Rd., Suite 123
Forked River, NJ 08731
(800) 851-0045

Medi-Fight
3982 E. Blackhorse Pike
Mays Landing, NJ 08330
(609) 625-7633

Fist Training Equipment
25 Jay St.
Brooklyn, NY 11201
(800) 252-3478

Century Martial Arts Supply
1705 National Blvd.
Midwest City, OK 73110
(405) 732-2226
(800) 626-2787
(800) 633-3996 (Canada)
(405) 737-8954 (Fax)

SCROLLS

ENGLAND

Kobuko Company
32, Peel Close
Heslington, York YO1 5EN
England

STRETCHING MACHINES

ENGLAND

Martial Arts Merchandising
P.O. Box 1310
Selly Oak, Birmingham B29 7JT
England
(021) 472-2043

Lazer Stretchosizers
Barn Field, Main St.
Brandon, Coventry CV8 3W
England
(0203) 543354

Marks Martial Arts
110 Sovereign Way
Anglia Square, Norwich NR3 1ER
England
(0603) 630485

Shodan U.K.
54 George St.
Brighton, East Sussex BN2 2LJ
England
(0273) 698809
(0273) 207965 (Fax)

SIAM Martial Arts
28 Blondell Dr.
Aldwick
Bognor Regis, West Sussex PO21
  4BN
England
(0243) 263956
(0243) 868612 (Fax)

GERMANY

Imex Sport-Artikel
Theordor-Fontane-Strasse 49
7410 Reutlingen
Germany
07121 / 34162

UNITED STATES

Carson Hurley Enterprises
2945 Orange Ave., N.E.
P.O. Box 12783
Roanoke, VA 24028
(703) 342-7550

Century Martial Arts Supply
1705 National Blvd.
Midwest City, OK 73110
(405) 732-2226
(800) 626-2787
(800) 633-3996 (Canada)
(405) 737-8954 (Fax)

Flexport
P.O. Box 468238
Atlanta, GA 30346
(404) 723-9087

Kinetic Performance
(800) 647-5853

Super-Stretch
6829 Stonykirk
San Antonio, TX 78240

Treco Products
11846 Tug Boat Lane
Newport News, VA 23606
(804) 873-1177
(800) 624-9000

Ultrastretch
P.O. Box 10556
Portland, OR 97210
(503) 224-8326

TRADING CARDS

UNITED STATES

Martial Arts Masters, Ltd.
1548 18th St.

Santa Monica, CA 90404
(310) 449-1404
(310) 449-1805 (Fax)

TROPHIES

CANADA

Trophies International
756 St. Clair Ave. W.
Toronto, Ontario, Canada M6C 1B5
(416) 651-6000

ENGLAND

Sabre Trophies
132 The Wicker
Sheffield S3 8JD
England
(0742) 750940

Jack Hesketh
The Firs
6 Pitt Rd.
Epsom, Surrey KT17 4ET
England
(0372) 725566

UNITED STATES

WASHINGTON, DC

Everhart's Trophy and Awards
530 7th St. S.E.
Washington, DC 20003
(202) 543-3400
(800) 528-3478
(202) 399-5291 (Fax)

FLORIDA

Lane 4 Awards
P.O. Box 451591E
Miami, FL 33345
(305) 742-8609

Brown's Trophies
3180 Central Ave.
St. Petersburg, FL 33712
(813) 323-2811

ILLINOIS

Doris Bros. Trophies
217 Main St.
Clay City, IL 62824
(800) 582-8595 (trophies)
(800) 723-7261 (equipment)
(618) 676-1881

KENTUCKY

A-1 Martial Arts Supplies
7406 Preston Hwy.
Louisville, KY 70219
(502) 968-3373

MICHIGAN

Lots of Nichols
34904 Michigan Ave.
Wayne, MI 48184
(313) 728-1313

MISSISSIPPI

Tri State Trophy
7047 302 Industrial Dr.
Southaven, MS 38671
(601) 349-3774

NEW JERSEY

KAM Industries
11 Ackerman Ave.
Emerson, NJ 07630
(201) 265-4847

NEW YORK

Klein's All Sports
216 Oriskany Blvd.
Utica, NY 13502
(315) 724-4126

Crown Trophy
1 Odell Plaza
Yonkers, NY 10701
(914) 963-0005
(800) 227-1557

OKLAHOMA

Century Martial Arts Supply
1705 National Blvd.
Midwest City, OK 73110
(405) 732-2226
(800) 626-2787
(800) 633-3996 (Canada)
(405) 737-8954 (Fax)

PENNSYLVANIA

Jacobs Wholesale Trophies &
   Awards
4th and 9th
New Kensington, PA 15068
(412) 337-4641

VIDEOCASSETTE SUPPLIERS (INSTRUCTIONAL; MOVIES; DOCUMENTARIES)

Here's a range of major to minor videotapes comprising companies that manufacture and/or distribute just about every tape in the business. Keep in mind that a company can continually add new tapes to its product line. For best results, call and inquire about the current titles or request a catalog.

AUSTRALIA

Blitz Book & Video Vault
G.P.O. Box 2064S
Melbourne, Victoria 3001, Australia

MTG Video
P.O. Box 792
Murwillumbah
NSW 2484, Australia
(01) 61-66-797145
(01) 61-66-797028 (Fax)

Bushido Video
2 Broadlea Crescent, Viewbank
3084 Victoria, Australia
(03) 457-5283

Cine News Productions
1 Antigua Grove
West Lake South 5021
Australia

AUSTRIA

Taodo Hou Chuan Society
P.O. Box 110
A-3300 Amstetten
Austria

BERMUDA

Zenji Productions
P.O. Box HM 2140
Hamilton HM JX
Bermuda
(809) 292-2157

CANADA

United Taekwon-do of North
   America
4707 48 St., 2nd Floor
Camrose, Alberta, Canada T4V 1L2
(403) 672-3500

Impact Par Data
(Video exchange only)
Box 8056 Substation #141
London, Ontario, Canada N6G 2B0

ENGLAND

Asian Publishing
60 Kendal Dr.
Slough, Berkshire SL2 5JA
England
(0753) 536465

M.A.M. Video Club
P.O. Box 1310
Selly Oak, Birmingham B29 7JT
England
(021) 472-2043

Thaismai U.K.
19 Rayden Crescent
Westhoughton, Bolton BL5 2ES
England
(0942) 811685

VMA International
White House Studios
40 New St.
Wigton, Cumbria CA7 9AL
England
06973-43886

Take Five Productions
15 Raglan Rd.
Frinton, Essex
England

TVC (Video Search Service)
152 Shawclough Way
Rochdale, Lancaster OL12 6EE
England

Budokwai
4 Gilston Rd.
London SW10
England

Chow Gar Praying Mantis
27 Romford Rd.
Stratford, London E15 4LJ
England

Centred-Mind Films
22 Clacton Rd.
London E17 8AR
England
520-0827

Video Magic
35 Prioress Rd.
West Norwood, London SE 27
England
(01) 766-6034

Chojin Martial Arts
10-12 Low Friar St., 3rd Floor
Newcastle-upon-Tyne NE1 5UE
England
(091) 261-9859

Budo-Arts Ltd.
P.O. Box 10
Minsterley, Shrewsbury, Shropshire
  SY5 0ZZ
England
(058) 861-610

Eastman Educational
96-98 Cannock Rd.
The Scotlands, Wolverhampton
  WV10 0AE
England
0902-731685

FRANCE

Societe Europeenne de Magazines
2, bis rue Mercoeur
75011 Paris
France
(1) 43.48.40.08
(1) 43.48.17.86 (Fax)

Chardin Distribution
30 ter, rue Gassendi
75014 Paris
France
43.22.28.52

Panda Films
8, rue Pradier
75019 Paris
France
42.08.45.66

Budostore
34, rue de la Montagne
Ste. Genevieve, BP 225, 75227 Paris
France
43.26.19.46

GERMANY

Satori Verlag
Postfach 1208
4152 Kempen 3
Germany

Tao Hirper Verlag
Postfach 1205
7053 Kernen
Germany

VPG Videoproduktions
Klingenstrasse 22
7401 Pliezhausen
Germany
(07127) 18667

JAPAN

Aiki News
Demeure Saito Annex 201
Daikyo-cho 3, Shinjuku
Tokyo 160, Japan
(03) 359-6265

Champ Co.
Suginami Ku
Koenji Minami 4-6-8
166 Tokyo To
Japan
(03) 315-3190
(03) 314-5868 (Fax)

Keijutsukai
Shimbashi Shinwa Bldg., 4th Floor
5-15, 4-Chome, Shimbashi

Minato-ku, Tokyo 105
Japan

Media Eito
Mitsutomo Bldg. 3F
Ningyo Cho 2-28-2
Chu O Ku Nihonbashi
103 Tokyo
Japan
(03) 639-4588

Nippon Sport Eizo
Bunkyo-ku Shiroyama 2-2-6
112 Tokyo
Japan
(03) 817-0931

KOREA

WTF TAEKWONDO
World Taekwon-do Fed.
635, Yuksamdong, Kangnamku
Seoul, Korea 135
82-02-566-2505; 82-02-567-1058
82-02-553-4728

NETHERLANDS

Multi-Trade (Thai Boxing videos)
02158-6260

SWEDEN

Feneco AB (Thai Boxing videos)
Speldosegatan 6
42146 V. Frolunda
Sweden

UNITED STATES

ALABAMA

Martial Arts of China Library
P.O. Box 105
Moulton, AL 35650
(205) 974-7002
(800) 628-6552

ARIZONA

WINN Enterprises
P.O. Box 17898
Fountain Hills, AZ 85268
(602) 837-0315

Smart Moves Productions
P.O. Box 80587
Phoenix, AZ 85060

Martial Arts Video Productions
8839 E. Via Linda, Suite #201
Scottsdale, AZ 85258
(602) 661-0212

Phoenix & Dragon Society
P.O. Box 12514
Tucson, AZ 85732

CALIFORNIA

Association of Wing Chun
5889 Kanan Rd., Suite 188
Agoura, CA 91301
(818) 707-9464

Professor Wally Jay
2055 Eagle Ave.
Alameda, CA 94501
(415) 523-8949

San Soo
9059 Alondra Blvd.
Bellflower, CA 90706

CNS Productions
8306 Wilshire Blvd., Suite 7034
Beverly Hills, CA 90211

Samurai Productions
Box 527
Beverly Hills, CA 90213

Firelight Pictures
139 N. Florence
Burbank, CA 91505
(818) 567-2773

Unique Publications Video
4201 Vanowen Place
Burbank, CA 91505
(818) 845-2656
(800) 332-3330
(818) 845-7761 (Fax)

Rod Mindlin TV Productions
1974 Manchester Ave.
Cardiff, CA 92007
(800) 457-1757

Dr. Weng's Kung-Fu School
P.O. Box 1221
Cupertino, CA 95015

Chuan Tao Association
P.O. Box 160
Fall River Mills, CA 96028

Hyun Kimm
34177 Fremont Blvd.
Fremont, CA 94555
(510) 795-1007

British Shotokan Videos
P.O. Box 5726
Huntington Beach, CA 92615

Karl-Lorimar Home Video
17942 Cowan
Irvine, CA 92714
(800) 624-2694

Young C. Choi
P.O. Box 2686
Lancaster, CA 93539

Quantum FX
P.O. Box 15611
Long Beach, CA 90815
(800) 756-5489

Buck Sam Kong
1818 N. Alexandria Ave.
Los Angeles, CA 90027

Hee Il Cho's Taekwondo Center
11304½ Pico Blvd.
Los Angeles, CA 90064
(213) 477-4067

Interarts
1283 S. La Brea Ave., Ste. 162
Los Angeles, CA 90019

IM Arts
4391 Sunset Blvd., #433
Los Angeles, CA 90029

Kwang Sik Myung
P.O. Box 15523
Los Angeles, CA 90015

Wayfarer Publications
P.O. Box 26156

Los Angeles, CA 90026
(213) 665-7773
(213) 665-1627

Vision Press Films
P.O. Box 641278
Los Angeles, CA 90060

Pencak Silat Mande Muda
2554 Lincoln Blvd., Suite 673
Marina Del Rey, CA 90291
(213) 470-8918

Action Videos
107 Minnis Circle
Milpitas, CA 95035
(800) 722-5441 (Calif.)
(800) 255-5441 (Outside Calif.)

International Martial Arts
  Federation
23725 Via Fabricante, #E
Mission Viejo, CA 92691

Closed Door Systems
P.O. Box 6185
Moreno Valley, CA 92313
(714) 242-1679

Central Coast Educational
  Productions
2760 Main St.
Morro Bay, CA 93442
(805) 772-4844

Syber Vision
Fountain Square
6066 Civic Terrace Ave.
Newark, CA 94560
(800) 227-0600

Gong Productions
3525 Dimond Ave., Suite #309
Oakland, CA 94602
(415) 482-2164

Nine Little Heaven
P.O. Box 3007
Orange, CA 92665

Ching Lung Martial Arts
  Association
P.O. Box 52144
Pacific Grove, CA 93950

MBB Productions
6105 Reseda Blvd.
Reseda, CA 91335

U.S.K.O.
6706 Magnolia Ave.
Riverside, CA 92506
(714) 686-1505

Kenpo Karate
P.O. Box 60422
Sacramento, CA 95860

Panther Productions
1010 Calle Negocio
San Clemente, CA 92672
(714) 498-7765
(800) 332-4442
(714) 492-7533 (Fax)

Kuk Sool Won Production Co.
543 Valencia St.
San Francisco, CA 94110
(415) 553-8100; (415) 553-8141

One Hand Video
P.O. Box 15-584
San Francisco, CA 94115

Sifu Gene Chen
1470 21 Ave.
San Francisco, CA 94122

Black Belt Magazine Videos
24715 Rockefeller
P.O. Box 918
Santa Clarita, CA 91380
(805) 257-4066
(805) 257-3028 (Fax)

Karate Connection
P.O. Box 4067
Seal Beach, CA 90740

Simi Valley Tai Chi Club
Box 3812
Simi Valley, CA 93063

Ross Hunt Productions
12438 Moorpark St.
Studio City, CA 91604
(818) 763-6045

Gracie Videos
1951-B West Carson St.

Torrance, CA 90501
(800) 237-8400, Ext. 312

Burton Productions
Box 6875
Westlake, CA 91359

Shaw's Tai Chi Productions
Box 7700
Woodland Hills, CA 91367

COLORADO

CEP
Box 869
Boulder, CO 80306

Sul Sa I
1121 South Pearl
Denver, CO 80210

Action Communications
7315 E. Peakview
Englewood, CO 80111

Denver Chen Style Society
312 Crawford St.
Golden, CO 80401
(303) 278-9894

CONNECTICUT

S.K. Productions
401 Silas Deane Hwy.
P.O. Box 290206
Wethersfield, CT 06129
(203) 529-7770

DISTRICT OF COLUMBIA

Aikido Shobukan Dojo
421 Butternut St. N.W.
Washington, DC 20012

FLORIDA

Explorer Video
P.O. Box 454
Fruitland Park, FL 34731
(800) 874-5374

Aiki Productions
6120-10 Powers Ave, #159
Jacksonville, FL 32217

Taekwondo Video
Box 1474
Lakeland, FL 33802
(813) 687-8145

Yamazato Productions
3372 Lake Worth Rd.
Lake Worth, FL 33461
(407) 968-3231

J. Park World Center
1955 East Bay Dr.
Largo, FL 33541
(813) 584-7525

Marc McFann
9212 Quail Roost
Navarre, FL 32566
(904) 939-5678

Inter. Combat Hapkido Fed.
1859 N. Pine Island Rd., Suite 1181
Plantation, FL 33322

Bob Robare
3803 Pine Ave.
Sanford, FL 32773

RW Productions
7154 N. University Dr.
Suite 183
Tamarac, FL 33321
(800) 752-4671

GEORGIA

Ohki Trading
Box 49487
Atlanta, GA 30359

World Tae Kwon Do Association
4320 Roswell Rd.
Atlanta, GA 30342
(404) 252-8947

Okinawan Karate Tapes
3175 Buford Hwy.
Duluth, GA 30136

Defensefax
1853 Guardian Way
Lawrenceville, GA 30243
(404) 621-5715

Professional Karate Association
3290 Coachman's Way
Roswell, GA 30075
(404) 998-4610

IOWA

U.S. Kum-Do Assn.
1423 18th St.
Bettendorf, IA 52722
(319) 359-7000

TKD Enterprises
P.O. Box 217
Davenport, IA 52805
(319) 355-5452
(800) 388-5966

ILLINOIS

Palm Tree Productions
P.O. Box 135
Berwyn, IL 60402

AAA Video
1016 W. Belmont
Chicago, IL 60657
(312) 525-3141

Universal Taekwondo Association
1207 W. Main
Peoria, IL 61606
(309) 673-2000
(309) 673-0212 (Fax)

KANSAS

YBK Martial Arts
2101 Zeandale Rd.
Manhattan, KS 66502

KENTUCKY

Tracy's Kenpo
P.O. Box 24228
Lexington, KY 40524
(606) 271-5987

MASSACHUSETTS

Modern Arnis
30 Mason St.
Beverly, MA 01915
(617) 927-8722

Chinese Wushu Research Institute
246 Harrison Ave.
Boston, MA 02111
(617) 426-0958

Bushido-Kai Budoya
21 Blandin Ave.
Framingham, MA 01701
(508) 520-0115

Yang's Martial Arts Association
38 Hyde Park Ave.
Jamaica Plain, MA 02130
(617) 524-8892

American Hap Ki Do Association
403 Page Blvd.
Springfield, MA 01104
(413) 732-4403

MICHIGAN

Panda Productions
P.O. Box 2426
Petoskey, MI 49770
(616) 347-5469

MINNESOTA

Bubbling Well Press
Box 961
St. Cloud, MN 56302

Educational Video Associates
P.O. Box 1192-B
St. Paul, MN 55101
(800) 338-2843

Ert/Bendickson Productions
762 E. 7th St.
St. Paul, MN 55106
(800) 772-7912

Gin Foon Mark
P.O. Box 75308
St. Paul, MN 55175

Mountaintop Publishing
P.O. Box 50655
Minneapolis, MN 55405

MISSOURI

Oyata Productions
19105 E. 30th St.

Independence, MO 64057
(816) 795-8308

Universal Capoeira
2734 La Fayette
St. Louis, MO 63104

NEVADA

Buksan International
P.O. Box 3363
Carson City, NV 89702

Academy of Kenpo
3025 D.I. Rd., #7
Las Vegas, NV 89121

NEW JERSEY

Wing Chun Video
P.O. Box 123
Bridgeton, NJ 08302
(609) 453-9072

Master D.J. Kim
P.O. Box 341
Carlstadt, NJ 07072
(201) 939-3934

Kamekan
P.O. Box 419
Dumont, NJ 07628
(201) 385-7335

Chong Min Lee
469 South Ave.
P.O. Box 2701
Westfield, NJ 07091
(908) 233-0150
(908) 233-2840 (Fax)

Michael DePasquale Jr. Enterprises
P.O. Box 8538
Woodcliff Lake, NJ 07675
(201) 573-8028

NEW YORK

Dragon Claw Institute
2819 Fulton St.
Brooklyn, NY 11207
(718) 235-3192

Toguchi Productions
2 Reynolds Lane
Buchanan, NY 10511